THE LONGMAN ANTHOLOGY OF DETECTIVE FICTION

Deane Mansfield-Kelley
University of Texas at El Paso

Lois A. Marchino
University of Texas at El Paso

PEARSON
Longman

New York   San Francisco   Boston
London   Toronto   Sydney   Tokyo   Singapore   Madrid
Mexico City   Munich   Paris   Cape Town   Hong Kong   Montreal

Vice President and Editor-in-Chief: Joseph A. Terry
Managing Editor: Erika Berg
Senior Marketing Manager: Melanie Craig
Production Manager: Charles Annis
Development Editor: Barbara Santoro
Senior Supplements Editor: Donna Campion
Project Coordination and Electronic Page Makeup: Electronic Publishing Services
    Inc., NYC
Senior Cover Designer/Manager: Nancy Danahy
Cover Photo: © Bill Fredericks Studio
Manufacturing Buyer: Roy Pickering

For permission to use copyrighted material, grateful acknowledgment is made to the
copyright holders on pp. 479–480, which are hereby made part of this copyright page.

Library of Congress Cataloging-in-Publication Data
The Longman anthology of detective fiction / [edited] by Deane Mansfield-Kelley,
Lois A. Marchino.
    p. cm.
  Includes index.
  ISBN 0-321-19501-9
  1. Detective and mystery stories, American. 2. Detective and mystery stories, American—History and criticism. 3. Detective and mystery stories, English. 4. Detective and
mystery stories, English—History and criticism. 5. Popular literature—English-speaking
countries—History and criticism. I. Mansfield-Kelley, Deane. II. Marchino, Lois A.
PS648.D4L66 2005
813'.087208—dc22
                              2004009462

Please visit our website at www.ablongman.com

ISBN 0-321-19501-9

We dedicate this book in memory of our mothers,

Mary Nell Edwards Mansfield

and Dorothy McCormick Marchino,

who bought us our first mysteries.

W. H. AUDEN
'DETECTIVE STORY'

Who is ever quite without his landscape,
The straggling village street, the house in trees,
All near the church? Or else, the gloomy town-house,
The one with the Corinthian pillars, or
The tiny workmanlike flat, in any case
A home, a centre where the three or four things
That happen to a man do happen?
Who cannot draw the map of his life, shade in
The country station where he meets his loves
And says goodbye continually, mark the spot
Where the body of his happiness was first discovered?

An unknown tramp? A magnate? An enigma always,
With a well-buried past: and when the truth,
The truth about our happiness comes out,
How much it owed to blackmail and philandering.

What follows is habitual. All goes to plan:
The feud between the local common sense
And intuition, that exasperating amateur
Who's always on the spot by chance before us;
All goes to plan, both lying and confession,
Down to the thrilling final chase, the kill.
Yet, on the last page, a lingering doubt:
The verdict, was it just? The judge's nerves,
That clue, that protestation from the gallows,
And our own smile . . . why, yes . . .
But time is always guilty. Someone must pay for
Our loss of happiness, our happiness itself.

CONTENTS

II. THE PRIVATE INVESTIGATOR 205

III. THE POLICE 337

APPENDIX A

APPENDIX B

PREFACE

The Longman Anthology of Detective Fiction is intended for the lover and would-be lover of detective fiction. It includes works by many of the greatest mystery writers and provides a wide range of diverse and highly teachable stories. In addition, it offers valuable critical commentary on detective fiction and discussion of the lives and contributions of the authors.

This anthology is designed for an introduction to detective fiction course or any course with a mystery or detective fiction emphasis. It can also be used to supplement general introduction to fiction courses, providing students the opportunity to read and study in depth the popular genre of detective fiction. These stories appeal to students of all levels, therefore helping to develop and encourage an interest in fiction. This anthology is also useful for creative writing courses that concentrate on fiction writing, since the selected stories serve as models for good writing and show a wide range of examples of character development, plot construction, and point of view, as well as introduce students to some of the best writing in the mystery field.

Organization and Approach

This book is organized to make the material as accessible as possible for teacher, student, and general reader. A general Introduction provides an explanation of the genre of detective fiction and its history and popularity. A critical essay by one of the major writers on the genre adds to this overview of detective fiction and its importance in literary history.

The book is then divided into the three basic classifications of detective fiction: the amateur detective, the private investigator, and the police. Within these categories, the stories are arranged in chronological order to illustrate changes and developments in the literary tradition of mystery writing and to show how the past influences the present. Each of the three sections contains an Introduction with a definition and a chronological overview of that classification of works, two well-respected critical essays on that particular classification, plus carefully selected short stories by leading writers.

Each story in the anthology is headlined with biographical information about the author as well as a discussion of that author's contributions to the literature of detective fiction. Every selection contains suggestions for further works by that author as well as references to other authors with similar approaches. This gives both teachers and students information for further reading and additional authors to research and explore. An appendix that explains the notable awards for mystery and detective fiction is also included.

Selection of Stories and Commentaries

The short stories selected for the anthology range chronologically from Edgar Allan Poe's "The Murders in the Rue Morgue" (1841) to S.J. Rozan's "Going Home" (2002). All of the stories have appeared in critically acclaimed detective fiction collections. Many stories included here have received the most prestigious awards in detective short fiction. For example, Peter Robinson's "Missing in Action" received the Edgar Award for Best Short Story of 2000. They are among the best examples of detection fiction writing and lend themselves readily to classroom discussion and analysis.

The commentaries and critical essays in the anthology were chosen to provide both a general working knowledge about detective fiction and to present valuable, in-depth analysis of works in the three classifications of the genre. For example, in Raymond Chandler's famous essay, "The Simple Art of Murder," he writes the definitive analysis of the private investigator and his world. In "The Puzzle-Game," Patricia Maida and Nicholas Spornick examine the complex structure of the "puzzle" novels of Agatha Christie. These essays and others like them were carefully selected for their approachability and their significant insights into the literary world of detective fiction. They also serve as models and as reference points for students to write their own critical essays on a particular story or group of stories.

Beneficial Features

The Longman Anthology of Detective Fiction contains the following useful features:

- A **general Introduction** discusses the development of the genre and places the various authors in their historical context, to benefit examination and discussion of individual works and their interrelationships with other stories.
- Specific **section Introductions** on the three basic classifications of detective fiction include the characteristics of each category to help the reader consider the general themes and contexts in which to evaluate and appreciate individual stories.
- **A varied selection of short stories** from different time periods, and with different approaches to plot and theme, provide diverse choices of material and an overview of the mystery field.

- Well-respected and accessible **critical essays and commentaries** on detective fiction enhance the depth of understanding about the genre and provide information about approaches to studying the works.
- **Informative headnotes** introduce the authors, briefly discuss their contributions to the literature of detective fiction, and provide a context for the story that follows. These headnotes also help readers see the historical development of the genre and know more about the people who write mysteries.
- **Recommended other works** by each author, and recommended additional authors for further study and enjoyment, aid students in research and writing projects.
- An **appendix on the notable awards** for mystery and detective fiction explains the awards often mentioned in the biographies and makes note of the important organizations associated with detective fiction.

Acknowledgements

As authors we would like to thank our editors at Longman Publishers: Erika Berg, Michelle Cronin, and Barbara Santoro, for their valuable advice and encouragement, and also David Glenn at Longman for supporting the concept of this book. We would like to thank the students in our detective fiction courses at the University of Texas at El Paso for inspiring us to write this book. We would like to express our gratitude to the following reviewers of the book who gave us important suggestions: Katherine Ackley, formerly of the University of Wisconsin, Stevens Point; Robert Aguirre, Wayne State University; Mary Crouch, California State University , Fullerton; April Flowers, Foothill College; Rhonda Frederick, Boston College; Gary Goshgarian, Northeastern University; George Grella, University of Rochester; Susan Howard, DuQuesne University; Albert Hutter, University of California, Los Angeles; Patricia Medeiras, Scottsdale Community College; Bonnie Plummer, Eastern Kentucky University; Marilyn Rye, Farleigh Dickinson University; Gregory Sarceno, Broome Community College; Marcia Songer, East Tennessee State University; and Lawrence Wharton, University of Alabama.

Additional thanks go to Dean James and the staff of *Murder by the Book* in Houston, Texas, for their help. We also thank Dr. Mary Beth Harris, who has been supportive throughout the process of preparing this anthology. And we especially thank Harold L. Kelley, without whose technical expertise and constant encouragement we would have been much longer in completing this book.

INTRODUCTION

Detective fiction is an immensely popular and influential literary genre. It is not unusual for at least three or four of the ten novels on the *New York Times* best-seller list to be detective fiction. Because it is an important aspect of both popular culture and of literature, it is also the subject of considerable attention from literary scholars. The stories collected here offer the opportunity to consider the richness and variety of short mystery fiction, and the critical essays provide access to a sampling of some of the outstanding discerning commentary on the genre.

Organization of this Anthology

Detective fiction is a literary genre, either in novel or short story form, dealing with a crime or crimes, usually murder, in which a detective or detectives seek justice for the victim and on behalf of society. Detective fiction writers and literary critics traditionally divide the genre into three major categories based on the type of detective at the center of the story: the amateur detective, the private investigator, and the police. The genre itself was historically developed in that chronological order, starting with the unofficial "amateur" sleuth, followed by the introduction of the detective as an occupation—the "P.I.," and then stories about police officers in criminal investigation. Once created, works in each of these three styles have continued to be written in all subsequent eras. All three categories are abundant in contemporary detective novels and short stories. That the categories occasionally blur or overlap is a testimony to the rich variety of short stories and novels that have been published since 1841 when Edgar Allan Poe wrote the first fully acknowledged detective story, "The Murders in the Rue Morgue."

This anthology is thus divided into "Amateur," "P.I.," and "Police" sections to reflect the natural or obvious categories according to the type of protagonist

1

in the story. Critical commentary in the introductory section provides an overview of the entire genre. Other critical essays and commentaries appear at the beginning of each of the three sections. These essays introduce the category and provide information and theories about the specific type of stories included in the section. The essays are from varied time periods and further illustrate the kinds of critical attention mystery fiction has received, past and present.

The stories in each of the three sections are arranged in chronological order to give a sense of historical perspective and to trace developments and changes in the genre as well as to compare approaches to writing by authors of different eras. Detective fiction is always a commentary on the social attitudes of its writers and their times, whether reaffirming shared values or helping to implement a new social vision.

All the selected stories are by well-known and highly respected writers, popular with both the reading public and literary critics in the area of mystery fiction. The awards given annually for outstanding mystery works started with the Edgar Awards in 1946, and all of the writers included here whose works were published after that time are award winners either for their short stories or their novels or for both. A list of the major awards and how the winners are selected is provided in Appendix A.

Each story is introduced with biographical information about the author, a commentary on his or her works, and a notation of the author's original contributions to detective fiction. Recommendations for further readings of works by the author are provided. "Other recommended authors" gives a brief list of three other mystery writers whose works would be of interest because of similar themes, settings, characters, or styles of writing.

Why Read Detective Fiction?

Detective fiction, or mystery fiction, a term often used interchangeably with detective fiction, is possibly the most widely read of any kind of literature. Detective fiction writer and critic Julian Symons, in his history of the mystery genre, *Bloody Murder* (3rd edition, 1992), estimates that of all books published in the United States as well as those published in the United Kingdom and several other countries, at least 25 percent are in the mystery category, and that this percentage has been relatively stable for the past century. He assumes that the percentage may be much higher in the past few decades with the enormous popularity of paperback reprint editions, for which no accurate figures are available (Symons 6).

Without question, there are, and long have been, countless millions of mystery readers. Of these, few people read merely one or two works; many are avid fans who read a wide variety of mysteries and continue to do so over the course of many years. Numerous reviewers and critics have addressed the question, "Why do we read mysteries?" The fact that this is a persistent question is itself an indication of the popularity of such works. It is also an intriguing commentary on the genre, because it is not a question typically asked of any other literary category. No one seems to say, "Why do we read biographies?" or entertain endless speculations about why we read poetry or Westerns or historical novels.

The theories about why we read mystery fiction start with "we read for pleasure" and continue to the observation that mysteries obviously supply some unspecified element of satisfaction for the reader. In between are numerous psychological analyses of reader needs, historical patterns of the reading public, interpretations based on economic influences, deconstructionist theories of texts, psychoanalytical views of the human psyche, and commentaries about the detective as the modern version of the valiant knight, Romantic hero, or loner cowboy hero in the stories of the American West.

Recognition of the varieties in types and subgenres of detective fiction also influences the way a particular story is read and what satisfactions the reader gets from it. The reader may guess at or solve a puzzle, thrill to the suspense, like the characters, enjoy the details of the settings, learn about forensic methodology and scientific developments, explore the relationship between the individual and society, ponder motives and impulses to murder, find infinite reflections on life and death, or even read mysteries to learn to write them. As with any type of literature, one satisfaction is that the reader is allowed to play the roles of any or all of the characters. With detective fiction, the reader can identify with the sleuth, the victim, and the villain, whether at a conscious or a subliminal level.

No matter why we read them, mysteries themselves have certain literary requirements. The detective story, unlike other forms of literature, must have a clear and definite plot. The writers must, as mystery writer Gladys Mitchell comments, "tidy up the loose ends; must supply a logical solution to the problem they have posed, combine the primitive lust and energy of the hunter with the cold logic of the scholarly mind" (Mitchell 15). Carolyn Heilbrun, whose academic mysteries appear under the pen name Amanda Cross, states it succinctly: "Murder stories must have an orderly ending. It may be the only order we've got left" (Budd 19).

Three other important reasons for reading detective fiction are linked to the nature of the style itself, suggested by definite plot and orderly ending. The most essential one is that detective stories keep alive a sense of justice. In life, justice is often random, inadequate, or altogether missing. Detective stories repeatedly show that it is possible to care about those who are victimized and to identify and to stop those who committed the crime, a crime not just against an individual but also against society. The second reason is that detective fiction, in telling an enthralling story, also keeps alive a sense of the importance of stories themselves in the constant re-creation of what it means to be a human being and what kind of societies we need to create. The third reason is that detective fiction emphasizes the art of character creation. A single detective with his or her surrounding "family" of characters can sustain a thirty book series. Character often becomes as important or more important than the crime in reader appeal.

A History of Detective Fiction

In a general sense, mystery stories have existed for as long as language and stories themselves, as the storytellers or writers try to make sense of their tragic events and of the very existence and condition of human life. Certainly the earliest literature included elements of mystery and detection. The Bible, for example, is rich in this type of story, starting with Adam and Eve's son Cain killing his brother Abel—the first murder, with God as the all-knowing but interrogating detective. *Oedipus Rex*, Sophocles's famous play from ancient Greece, circa 441 B.C.E., describes the most unusual circumstance of a man vowing to search out who killed the previous king, only to discover that he himself is the murderer. In more modern literary works prior to Poe in 1841, there are stories and novels that revolve around crime and the need to identify the perpetrators. Many critics have pointed out antecedents to what is now called detective fiction, such as English writer William Godwin's novel *Caleb Williams* (1794), in which a young man's curiosity leads him to pry into a murder from the past. The *Memoirs* of François Vidocq (the first of three volumes appearing in 1838, all probably written by ghostwriters rather than Vidocq) is sometimes cited as an early detective fiction work, since it features highly exaggerated accounts of Vidocq's life, first as a criminal and then as chief of detectives with the Paris police before being dismissed from the force for falsifying records. (Edgar Allan Poe's amateur detective in "The Murders of the Rue Morgue" mentions Vidocq dismissively, as someone who saw details but lost sight of the larger matters.) It was Edgar Allan Poe who earned the distinction of being "the father of detective fiction," when he created a character who specifically sets out to solve a killing, one he has read about in a newspaper. Like endless sleuths to follow, Poe's protagonist declares, "My ultimate object is only the truth" (Poe 50).

Poe set the pattern for much of the detective fiction that followed. His three mystery stories that feature Chevalier C. Auguste Dupin introduce the eccentric and brilliant individual sleuth whose forte is logic combined with keen observation of details, whether or not this observation comes from actual scene-of-the-crime experience. Dupin is superior to the officers of the law in the stories at solving cases, as would be countless sleuths that followed. The stories are narrated by Dupin's less capable sidekick, who marvels at Dupin's deductive and inductive genius. The narrator functions in the role of the reader, one who is endlessly baffled and impressed by the achievements of the brilliant sleuth. This device borrowed from Poe was made forever famous with Arthur Conan Doyle's narrator Dr. Watson, always in awe of his friend Sherlock Holmes.

In addition, each of Poe's three Dupin stories, which he called "tales of ratiocination," of logic and reasoning, introduces basic conventions into detective fiction that subsequent writers have continued to use today. "The Murders of the Rue Morgue" set the precedent of a catchy title that emphasized "murder," that fundamental life/death theme and ultimate crime against another, plus the follow-up street named "Morgue," resonating as a place where bodies are kept prior to identification and disposal (the term comes from the name of a building in Paris used for this purpose). The story was also the first of the "locked room" or "impossible crime" mysteries, in which it appears that no one could have committed the murder because the room is locked from the inside, the key still in the lock. Versions of the puzzling "locked room" were used by Wilkie Collins in "A Terribly Strange Bed" (1852), Arthur Conan Doyle in "The Adventures of the Speckled Band" (1892), Jacques Futrelle in "The Problem of Cell 13" (1905), and numerous others, such as G. K. Chesterton, S. S. Van Dine, Ellery Queen, and, perhaps most notably, John Dickson Carr.

With "The Mystery of Marie Rogêt" (1842–43), once subtitled "A Sequel to 'The Murders in the Rue Morgue,'" Poe created the detective series, a staple device used by later writers. Indeed, the most famous mystery writers are those whose protagonist sleuth appears in several short stories and/or novels. Readers want to continue their experience with the character, often almost regardless of the plot of the story.

"The Mystery of Marie Rogêt" emphasized the "armchair detective," the sleuth who can solve a case solely on information provided by others. Sherlock Holmes's older brother Mycroft Holmes is a prime example of this type of sleuth. The term comes from Sherlock saying, "If the art of the detective began and ended in reasoning from an armchair, my brother would be the greatest criminal agent that ever lived," in Arthur Conan Doyle's 1893 short story, "The Greek Interpreter" (Doyle 597).

Other writers who use this convention of the sedentary sleuth include Baroness Emmuska Orczy's "Old Man in the Corner" series; the unnamed old man receives his information from newspapers and by other details supplied by a young reporter. Agatha Christie, in *The Thirteen Problems* (1932) (also published as *The Tuesday Club Murders*), has Miss Jane Marple and others sit around a dinner table as each person presents a mystery to which only he or she knows the answer; Miss Marple is always the one to deduce the correct solution. Josephine Tey, in *The Daughter of Time* (1951), shows Inspector Alan Grant of Scotland Yard confined to bed after an injury, and he entertains himself by focusing on the historical mystery of Richard III and the deaths of the two princes. Among others who use the armchair detective technique, the most notable is Rex Stout, whose ever-popular Nero Wolfe chooses not to leave his house on West 35th Street unless there are dire circumstances; instead, Wolfe relies for information on his "legman," Archie Goodwin, who is also the narrator of the stories.

"The Purloined Letter" (1844), the third Poe story featuring Auguste Dupin, introduces the method of psychological deduction, the ability of the sleuth to think like the criminal and thus predict what that person has done or might do. The specific example in the story is the device of hiding something in the most obvious place, with only Dupin able to understand the reasoning of the thief "hiding" the letter where the police would not bother to look.

Subsequent fictional sleuths have often understood the point Poe makes in "The Purloined Letter" about the necessity of understanding how other people think. The use of psychology to explore the criminal mind is used by many, for example by Arthur Conan Doyle's Sherlock Holmes, Agatha Christie's Hercule Poirot, and S. S. Van Dine's Philo Vance. Currently, police departments both in fiction and in reality use such psychology in criminal profiling. Robert B. Parker's private investigator Spenser is aided in his cases by his psychologist companion, Susan Silverman, who provides insights on both the criminals and the victims. Likewise, Patricia Cornwell creates a major character, Benton Wesley, a Federal Bureau of Investigation (F.B.I.) psychological profiler, in her popular Kay Scarpetta series. The use of psychological deduction in detective fiction easily extends from Poe to the present.

What happened with the development of detective fiction after Poe is the subject of many books, and the genre continues to develop. Anna Katherine Green (1846–1935) is frequently designated "the mother of the detective novel" based on her landmark novel *The Leavenworth Case* (1878), a best-seller for decades, and the series that followed. She also created the "spinster sleuth," Miss Amelia Butterworth, in *That Affair Next Door* (1897). Agatha Christie specifically credits Green's influence in her own creation of the amazing Miss Jane Marple.

The end of the nineteenth century saw the creation of the first "Great Detective," meaning an immensely popular mystery fiction hero, when Arthur Conan Doyle first introduced Sherlock Holmes in *A Study in Scarlet* (1887). Doyle published 56 short stories and four novels about Holmes, known to worldwide Sherlockians as "the Canon." Sherlock Holmes remains the most recognized name among fictional sleuths.

"The Golden Age of Mystery" refers to the period roughly between World War I and World War II, especially in Britain. Scores of new great detectives appeared in novels that often emphasized puzzles and classical complicated plots. The two great writers of the period are Agatha Christie (who created memorable characters such as Hercule Poirot, Miss Marple, and Tommy and Tuppence) and Dorothy L. Sayers (Lord Peter Wimsey, Harriet Vane). Christie continues to be one of the top selling authors of all time.

Starting in the 1920s, almost concurrent with the popularity of the more socially "genteel" Golden Age mysteries, American writers created the "hard-boiled detective," typically a loner facing the violence and nihilism of the post-World War I world. Although Carroll John Daly is arguably the first hard-boiled writer, authors Dashiell Hammett (whose major detectives are the Continental Op and Sam Spade) and Raymond Chandler (P. I. Philip Marlowe), followed by John D. MacDonald (Travis McGee), and Ross Macdonald (Lew Archer), had the most influence on this type of detective fiction. They firmly established the portrait of the tough P.I. that remains the dominant image many people throughout the world have of American detective fiction.

In the 1950s and 1960s, although detective fiction continued in all three major categories (amateur, P.I., and police), the trend was toward spy, thriller, and suspense stories. Suspense novels often blended with romance or adventure elements. It was a boom time for crime fiction thrillers, often in the form of "pulp" paperbacks with lurid cover illustrations. In this post-World War II "Cold War" era, spy novels with the emphasis on international intrigue were particularly popular, as exemplified by English writers Ian Fleming and John le Carré. Fleming's twelve James Bond novels, starting with *Casino Royale* (1953), created a contemporary fantasy hero in the elegant Agent 007. The role of James Bond, set against the background of global danger, was too popular with readers and filmmakers to end with Fleming's death in 1964; since then three other writers have produced over 30 James Bond novels. John le Carré portrayed a more realistic and grim world of spies in a long list of best-selling books, most notably *The Spy Who Came in from the Cold* (1963).

In 1972 P. D. James in England published *An Unsuitable Job for a Woman*, introducing the modern female detective, and the woman P.I. in detective fiction became famous in the United States during a time of serious and widespread feminist activism, mainly through the works of Marcia Muller, whose Sharon McCone first appeared in *Edwin of the Iron Shoes* (1977); Sue Grafton, who created Kinsey Millhone in *"A" is for Alibi* (1982); and Sara Paretsky, who introduced tough and socially conscious V. I. Warshawski in *Indemnity Only* (1982). Each of these three authors has established a long and continuing series, popular with both critics and readers, and numerous other writers have joined them in creating women sleuths of many different types.

The 1980s onward has seen an explosion of detective fiction of all types written increasingly by more women, more writers of varied ethnic backgrounds, and more writers outside the United States and Great Britain. It is a time of unparalleled diversity, expansion, and cultural influence in a genre that has already been popular for more than a century and a half.

Developing an Audience for Detective Fiction

The audience for detective fiction obviously begins at an early age. Countless mystery books are written for children as well as for adults: everything from picture books or read-aloud stories for preschoolers to books designed for adolescents and young adults. The trend was apparent as early as the first decade of the 1900s, when the highly successful syndicate founded by Edward Stratemeyer began hiring writers to collaboratively mass-produce dozens of mystery series for children, such as Tom Swift, the Dana Girls, the Bobbsey Twins, and the Hardy Boys. The most popular and long-lasting legacy of the syndicate is Nancy Drew, stories about whom are now produced in a variety of series specifically designed for different age groups.

Nancy Drew, the most famous of all the "girl sleuths," first appeared in *The Secret of the Old Clock* in 1930. The idea for Nancy came from Stratemeyer, who died shortly before the first volume was published. Carolyn Keene, listed as the author, is a pseudonym for literally dozens of women and men hired to write for the syndicate. The most distinguished of the early Nancy Drew authors was Mildred Wirt Bensen, who wrote 23 of the first 30 novels and established Nancy as an independent, daring, and likeable heroine. From the beginning, however, plot outlines were often created by one writer and the manuscript written by another. By the 1950s, most of the early books were revised and shortened for a new generation of readers, some rewritten by Harriet S. Adams, daughter of Edward Stratemeyer. Sometimes language, plots, and characters were altered drastically. Currently the Nancy Drew books are produced by Megabooks, a "book packager" that, as before, hires writers for a flat fee to complete books based on simple outlines and titles. Nancy Drew as a character continues through endless permutations by different writers and film and television scriptwriters. She remains one of the most recognized names in children's literature, and she is perhaps the most cited fictional character in late-twentieth century and early twenty-first century detective fiction by women, where the context is often someone asking the protagonist, "Who do you think you are, Nancy Drew?"

Just as the audience for detective fiction is not limited by age, it is not limited to books. Detective fiction was for many years a staple of radio programs, was well established in the film industry by the 1930s, and was immediately popular with the advent of widespread television viewing in the early 1950s. It is the subject of comic books, comic strips, and computer games. It appears in other formats as well, from jigsaw puzzles to act-out mystery games, in which those present take on character roles and must solve the "crime," using prepackaged instructions and scripts. The detective fiction "genres" are stronger than ever, drawing writers, critics, and readers into their ever-expanding worlds.

Critiques of Detective Fiction

Critiques of detective fiction started early and have become a thriving enterprise by both writers of mystery fiction themselves and by scholars and literary critics in general. The proliferation of such criticism in the latter part of the twentieth century and early twenty-first century attests to the burgeoning popularity of the mystery genre and to its respectability in the academy. Detective fiction is now studied in many college and university courses, and resources for exploring the works of individual writers and the literary genre are abundant, including extensive reference materials online.

The task of the critic, as in the discussion of any literary work, is to analyze the work and present information or an interpretation that can help the reader better understand and appreciate the story. The critique may involve a close textual analysis that focuses on style and such matters as imagery and symbolism. It may provide interpretations of theme or themes, character analysis, the relevance of the setting in the story or novel, or the importance of the narrative point of view. It may be as seemingly simple as discussing the connection of the title to the story itself or evaluating the reviews and critical reception of the story when it was first published. It may be as far ranging as relating the story to other stories and writers or placing the story in its historical context, in terms of what was happening in the time period and culture and what other writers of the time were publishing.

The critique may use one of various types of literary criticism: psychological, psychoanalytical, desconstructionist, feminist, reader-response theory, or any other established practice, or it may combine approaches. The ways to critique a given work are endless. The ultimate goal is to make the reader of the critique think more fully about the literary work itself, indeed, to make the reader want to read or re-read the work being analyzed.

"The Murders in the Rue Morgue," with its famous label as the first true detective story, continues to interest critics and thus highlights some of the numerous critical approaches to writing about mystery fiction. Two very different approaches among the many more literary ones can serve as examples. A favorite critique with readers is to spot possible mistakes in the story that undermines it as a story of rational deduction. Julian Symons in *Bloody Murder* cites a critique of "The Murders in the Rue Morgue" by Laura Riding, in which Riding points out in detail the fact that no one could have entered the window and landed on the head of the bed as Poe has it, especially since the bed itself obstructed part of the window. Poe refers to the "lower sash"; if only the lower sash moved, the upper half of the window would have restricted landing on the head of the bed. If the upper sash moved too, the intruder, on climbing out and shutting the window behind him as the story says, could not have fastened this upper sash by the secret catch, and the window would have remained open. Poe made some changes in later versions of the story, increasing the length of the broken nail in the frame of the window and shortening the distance between house and shutter, but these do not affect Riding's observation (Symons 36).

A second example of a critical approach is that of Ronald R. Thomas, in his *Detective Fiction and the Rise of Forensic Science* (1999). Thomas points out that Poe began writing his detective stories at the same time he became interested in photography and cryptology. Louis Jacques Daguerre and Henry Fox Talbot separately announced the process that would be called photography in 1839.

In the slightly more than a year between these announcements and the publication of his first mystery story, Poe wrote three articles about this revolutionary new technology, two of which appeared in the same magazine in which he published "The Murders in the Rue Morgue."

During the period that Poe wrote his three Dupin mysteries and others such as "The Gold Bug" and "Thou Art the Man," Samuel F. B. Morse was developing the cryptographic "Morse code" necessary in his invention of the telegraph. Poe published nonfiction on that topic also, just three months after he published "The Murders in the Rue Morgue," and he used cryptography as a major element in "The Gold Bug," published in 1843 (Thomas 111). Thomas neatly ties Poe's simultaneous interest in scientific developments to his interest in criminal detection. Poe may have also understood that the reading public would be interested in detective fiction as a means of learning how science could be used in criminal investigation. The inventions Poe knew about, as well as later technology, led to such developments as the mug shot, fingerprinting, the lie detector (polygraph), computerized police files, and DNA testing, many of which became best known to the public through the reading of detective stories.

Conclusion

Detective fiction is part of the rich treasure that is literature. The classic tradition of literature as *dulce et utile*, as the Roman poet Horace put it, sweetness and usefulness, refers to the long-held belief in the informative and aesthetic power of literature. It is often paraphrased as meaning that the purpose of literature is to entertain and to instruct. We hope that each reader will find the satisfactions of both aspects of literature in these selections of notable mystery short stories and critical essays.

Works Cited

Budd, Elaine. *13 Mistresses of Murder*. New York: Unger, 1986.

Doyle, Arthur Conan. "The Greek Interpreter." *Sherlock Holmes: The Complete Novels and Stories, Volume I*. New York, Toronto, London, Sydney, and Auckland: Penguin Books, 1986. 525–612.

Mitchell, Gladys. "Why Do People Read Detective Stories?" *Murder Ink: The Mystery Reader's Companion*. Ed. Dilys Winn. New York: Workman Publishing, 1977. 12–15.

Poe, Edgar Allan. "The Murders in the Rue Morgue." *Thirty-Two Stories*. Ed. Stuart Levine and Susan F. Levine. Indianapolis and Cambridge: Hackett Publishing, Inc., 2000. 138–158.

Symons, Julian. *Bloody Murder: From the Detective Story to the Crime Novel*, 3rd Revised Edition. New York and London: Mysterious Press, 1992.

Thomas, Ronald R. *Detective Fiction and the Rise of Forensic Science*. Cambridge, UK: Cambridge University Press, 1999.

CRITICAL ESSAY

JOHN BALL

Murder at Large

It may well be that when the historians of literature come to discourse upon the fiction produced by the English-speaking peoples in the first half of the twentieth century, they will pass somewhat lightly over the compositions of the "serious" novelists and turn their attention to the immense and varied achievement of the detective writers.

W. Somerset Maugham

On 30 September 1840 a gentleman who is remembered only as S. Maupin wrote a letter which is today preserved in the Boston Public Library. In that letter, which was addressed to Edgar Allan Poe, the terms were set down under which C. Auguste Dubouchet could be engaged to teach French in the city of Richmond, Virginia. That particular letter would have passed very quickly into limbo except for one interesting fact: In the April 1841 issue of the Philadelphia publication *Graham's Magazine*, Poe published "The Murders in the Rue Morgue" featuring a private detective known as C. Auguste Dupin, and thereby fired a literary shot heard 'round the world.

That Dupin story, and two others that followed, founded a form of literature that was to grow and develop during the next century and a third into overwhelming worldwide popularity. There had been previous writings approaching the same vein, just as Americans had played various sorts of stick-and-ball games before Abner Doubleday, but it was unquestionably Poe who first defined the form and breathed into it both life and a strong measure of immortality.

He did it so well that the subsequent passage of more than thirteen decades has only added to his popularity and the stature of the work he produced. Over the years millions of readers have experienced vicariously the thrill of finding buried treasure as they stalked through the pages of "The Gold Bug," and there are certainly few readers of American literature who have not had their blood chilled by the fascinating, frightening tales of horror that flowed from Poe's pen.

Possibly conscious of the fact that he was venturing into unexplored literary territory, Poe began "The Murders in the Rue Morgue" with a considerable windup before he pitched. But in spite of the flowery language common in his day, and the need to display learning by providing quotations in the original Greek (as in "The Man of the Crowd"), he could, when he chose, get down to business in a hurry. His immortal story "The Cask of Amontillado" begins with one of the greatest opening sentences in the English language: "The thousand injuries of Fortunato I had borne as I best could, but when he ventured upon insult, I vowed revenge." In twenty-one words Poe set the stage, introduced the two principal characters, supplied a powerful motive, and began the action. Such is genius.

The way having been pointed, detectives in literature began to be fruitful and to multiply, but they had not yet found their Eden. The creation took place in the British publication *Beeton's Christmas Annual* for 1887, which was made available to the public at one shilling per copy. Those who invested a little less than a quarter for some entertaining reading discovered a story that had been rejected several times before it had landed on the desk of Professor G. T. Bettany, the chief editor of Ward, Lock and Co. Although he had not been able to see any way to use it for at least a year, he had offered twenty-five pounds for all rights to the short novel.

The author had not been pleased, either with the amount of the offer or the long delay before publication, but he had had very little choice—a situation with which authors are all too familiar to this day. He finally accepted both. That was in 1886. Something over a year later the story, in the words of Dorothy L. Sayers, was "flung like a bombshell into the field of detective fiction." Unfortunately, the brilliant Miss Sayers was not available to publish her opinion, her age being minus six at the time, and the public was not yet aware that a titan had been born. Or, to be more accurate, two of them. The story, called *A Study in Scarlet*, was by a young physician whose medical skills were under-appreciated by potential patients who, in invisible droves, failed to consult him. He therefore spent his otherwise unoccupied time in writing. The hand that held the pen was that of (Sir) Arthur Conan Doyle, but the words that flowed on paper were the words of Dr. John H. Watson, M. D. By this means Dr. Watson, physician and man of letters, gave to the world the greatest detective of all time, his friend and companion Mr. Sherlock Holmes.

The immediate impact was limited. Prior to Dr. Watson, the mystery story had yet to attain respectability; it had already been typecast as something weighed in the balances and found unimportant. The Sherlockian scholar, Dr. Julian Wolff of New York, has exhumed a review which appeared in *The Graphic* (London) for 1 September 1888, and which stated in part: "There is no trace of vulgarity or slovenliness so often characteristic of detective stories." The reviewer did concede that "he (Doyle) has actually succeeded in inventing a brand new detective."

Indeed he had, and long before the days of Lord Peter Wimsey, Dr. Gideon Fell, Nero Wolfe, Sam Spade, Philip Marlowe, Hildegarde Withers, Miss

Marple, Gideon, Dr. Thorndyke, Hercule Poirot, Perry Mason, Father Brown, Maigret, and Inspector Napoleon Bonaparte, to cite only a few of those who have achieved world fame.

Before very long Sherlock Holmes and his physician friend rose to international acclaim and, well within Doyle's own lifetime, to immortality. A very good case could be made that Sherlock Holmes is the best-known and most read-about Englishman of all time, despite the formidable competition of William Shakespeare, Sir Winston Churchill, and several of the distinguished monarchs who have occupied the throne. Obviously no one would challenge the Olympian stature of *Macbeth* or dare to propose that Doyle, even at his sterling best, could approach such a literary level, but on the plane on which he wrote he too knew how to turn a majestic phrase.

> "He said that there were no traces upon the ground round the body. He did not observe any. But I did—some little distance off, but fresh and clear."
>
> "Footprints?"
>
> "Footprints."
>
> "A man's or a woman's?"
>
> Dr. Mortimer looked strangely at us for an instant and his voice sank almost to a whisper as he answered:
>
> "Mr. Holmes, *they were the footprints of a gigantic hound!*"

The paralyzing chills that that scene has created for uncounted millions of readers make it very nearly as memorable as Lady Macbeth's "*Out, damned spot.*"

Meanwhile, who were the authors whose detective stories were characterized, in one reviewer's opinion, by "vulgarity and slovenliness"? Some bad ones surely, but it is not so easy to dismiss Emile Gaboriau, Honoré de Balzac, Eugene Sue, Wilkie Collins, Victor Hugo, and Charles Dickens, not to mention Poe himself.

In this connection Dickens deserves a special word. In *Bleak House* he created the celebrated detective Inspector Bucket, about whom much has been written, and deservedly so. But *The Mystery of Edwin Drood* remains to this day one of the most remarkable of all crime stories, and one of the most discussed. It could hardly be otherwise. It is a gripping story full of the kinds of characters that put their creator among the immortals. Durdles, the drunken stonemason, is a good example. For twenty-three compelling chapters the mystery unfolds and then it ends—unfinished. Dickens had a fatal seizure and did not live to complete the story. Unfortunately for posterity, he had not told anyone who survived him what the outcome was to be. As a result, the mystery-without-a-solution has challenged some of the most formidable intellects of the literary world to try and resolve it. There are tantalizing clues in certain illustrations prepared for the book-to-be that depict scenes not in the text. Hints of disguises are present, as is a heroine with the remarkable name of Rosa Budd, an appellation that is topped only by Gilbert and Sullivan's Japanese ingenue Yum-Yum.

Many authors have attempted to finish *Edwin Drood* and to resolve the mystery. An outstanding event was the "trial" of John Jasper, one of the suspects in the story, which was staged in London in January 1914 with a sterling cast that included G. K. Chesterton as the judge and George Bernard Shaw as the foreman of the jury. Other distinguished writers and attorneys appeared during the "trial" as jurymen and characters in the story. The proceedings were as lively and arresting as might be expected, particularly when the presiding judge fined Shaw and the entire jury panel for contempt of court. It was Mr. Chesterton's private opinion that the mystery of Edwin Drood was insoluble without Dickens to tell where his supremely gifted imagination was to take him. The jury disagreed; its members returned a verdict that found Jasper guilty of murder.

Where did it all begin, the fascinating recounting of crime and detection? It would be easier to identify an alley cat's grandfather than to be definitive on that point. The Bible has been cited as containing crime stories and an early mention of spies. Régis Messac has made the suggestion that the account of Archimedes' discovery of the principle of liquid displacement, while investigating a possible crime, may properly be regarded as a detective story. It certainly qualifies insofar as a sensational ending is concerned, with one of the greatest intellects of the ancient world running naked through the streets shouting *Eureka!*

If a starting point must be chosen, then the story of the three princes and the missing camel is an important landmark. During their travels three Persian princes were asked if they had seen a camel that had wandered away and become lost.

They reported that they had not seen it, but by any chance was it the one that was blind in one eye, had a tooth missing, and was lame?

Despite their noble rank, the three princes were brought before the monarch and accused of stealing the animal that they had described so accurately. If they were innocent, His Majesty wanted to know, how had they acquired all that information?

The princes then explained. The camel had grazed on only one side of the road, despite the fact that the grass was better on the other. They had observed partially chewed clumps of grass that were just the size of a camel's tooth scattered along the way and marks in the dust that clearly showed that the animal had been dragging one foot.

The story has been told many times, but what is quite possibly the original version appears in *The Arabian Nights*.

During the forty-six years between "The Murders in the Rue Morgue" (what a title!) and *A Study in Scarlet* quite a bit occurred. In 1843–44 Sir James Graham, the British Home Secretary, added a new and pungent word to the English language. He selected a few of the most capable and intelligent officers of the London Police, formed them into a special unit, and called them *The Detective Police*. It is regrettable that the word "detective" had not been coined a little sooner, as Poe could have made good use of it.

A note must also be inserted concerning the first professional detective to enter the pages of history, the flamboyant Eugene François Vidocq, who was in full cry during this period. The career of M. Vidocq is probably unmatched in history, which is perhaps just as well. He was a dashing detective who produced one sensational exploit after another; he founded the *Sûreté* and served as its chief for two terms, a total of twenty-eight years. His sensational successes and natural flair for publicity made him a great celebrity. He was a master of disguises, had a phenomenal memory for faces and events, and an unerring sense of the dramatic. At the climactic moment of capture he was known to cry "I am Vidocq!", paralyzing his quarry into terrified submission. Which was not a bad performance for a several-times escaped convict and perhaps the only man known to have risen to such prominence following earlier employment as a galley slave.

M. Vidocq did not rest on his laurels. He became an author and published his *Memoires* which kept the bedroom candles of Paris burning far into the night. To call them exciting reading would be an under-statement. He became the subject of stage dramas and his career was the basis of the exploits of Balzac's famous Vautrin. There was even one memorable occasion when the great detective and the great author set out to solve a mysterious crime together. What an event *that* would have been to witness!

Obviously Balzac profited from the association in more ways than might be obvious. In his *Maître Cornélius* he scored a formidable first by introducing a resourceful detective who was none other than King Louis XI of France. In Balzac's account, His Majesty takes on a knotty problem and by means of an ingenious device successfully identifies a totally unsuspected criminal. Later on, in "The Adventure of the Golden Pince-Nez" the same technique was employed by Sherlock Holmes himself.

A major event occurred in 1862 when Victor Hugo wrote *Les Miserables*. The cordial Gallic hatred of the police, which had been well instilled for decades, was given additional spiritual nourishment. France was not yet prepared for Maigret, but its citizens cheered for Vidocq largely because the former convict headed a separate bureau that constantly embarrassed the police by beating them at their own game.

The first French novelist to risk presenting a police officer in a favorable light was Alexandre Dumas. The creator of *The Three Musketeers* and *The Count of Monte Cristo* published *Les Mohicans de Paris* in 1854–55, a book which introduced the police detective Monsieur Jackal. He is not a very important personage, but he did have his moment in history when he first uttered the immortal phrase *Cherchez la femme!* It unquestionably set a style, and femmes have been assiduously cherched ever since.

In England Wilkie Collins, lawyer, painter, and novelist, wrote a number of books which are today all but forgotten, except for two detective stories notable for their immensely complicated plots. *The Woman in White* introduced Count Fosco, who became the prototype for uncounted numbers of despicable villains yet to come. This 1860 work, which was based on an actual case in France, used the now familiar device of confining a perfectly sound person to an insane asylum simply to keep him or her out of the way. It was dramatized with great success, and may well have influenced Collins's very close and good friend, Charles Dickens, in his subsequent works.

Eight years later, suffering acutely from gout and frequently under the influence of the opium he used to kill the pain, Collins dictated *The Moonstone*, one of the best detective novels ever written and one of the longest. In it he introduced Sergeant Cuff, a detective whose place in history is secure. He was drawn from an actual individual, Inspector Whicher of Scotland Yard. The inspector, who was well-known at the time, enjoyed a unique distinction: He served as the model for two different detectives created by two internationally celebrated authors. Dickens also depicted the inspector under a thin alias as Sergeant Witchem in "Three Detective Anecdotes."

Then came Baker Street and the status, stature, and format of the detective story was altered for all time to come. Sherlock Holmes created an enthusiasm that rose like a tidal wave and has not abated to this day. The world's greatest detective's fame reached to even the most remote areas of the globe; his career was followed with intense interest over decades and no one since his retirement has ever ventured to challenge his preeminent position. The Canon left us by Dr. Watson includes a total of sixty works, fifty-six of which are short stories. The literature about Holmes and Watson, apart from the Canon itself, is astonishingly vast and continuously growing. It is, in itself, a miracle without parallel; were Sir Arthur here to view it, he would probably be overcome, particularly because he was himself one of the few great literary lights of the world who did not regard Sherlock Holmes as an incredible achievement. In fact, Sir Arthur once made an earnest effort to get rid of Holmes so that he could turn to "more serious work."

More serious work indeed! Despite the claims of the sponsors of Tarzan of the Apes, who might be said to represent a voice crying from the wilderness, Sherlock Holmes is undoubtedly the most world-celebrated personage ever to emerge from the pages of literature. He is also responsible for the Baker Street Irregulars.

Early in the career of the Baker Street sage we meet this band of street urchins who go forth in a pack to do their master's bidding for a payment of a shilling each per day. They were useful while Holmes was in active practice and they are even more so today. They publish *The Baker Street Journal*, a learned quarterly to which some of the most august by-lines in the world have contributed. They hold meetings, notably on the Master's birthday (January 6th), and read scholarly papers, some of which are astonishingly profound. Almost every aspect of the Canon has been explored in depth by the most distinguished living experts in various fields of specialization. As an example, in "The Musgrave Ritual" Holmes recovers the ancient crown of England that had been lost for generations. This raises the logical question: *Which* crown?

The Irregulars were fully equal to that one; in *The Baker Street Journal* for April 1953 (Vol. 3, No. 2 [New Series]) the distinguished Sherlockian, Nathan L. Bengis, identified the crown in question as the ancient one of St. Edward the Confessor. This essay was by no means the first on the subject; a number of other crowns had been proposed by various scholars and their findings were vigorously researched through every kind of available source material. However, Mr. Bengis firmly established that: "Not only does this crown fit all the requirements of the Canon, no other crown does." He then launched into some highly technical data concerning the various crowns of England which fully supported his conclusion.

That, however, is not the end of the story. Mr. Bengis, who is nothing if not thorough, wrote to the Keeper of Her Majesty's Jewel House, Major General H. D. W. Sitwell, C.B., M.C., and asked his opinion on the matter. General Sitwell responded from the Tower of London with a superbly written historical account entitled "Some Notes on St. Edward's Crown and the Musgrave Ritual," one of the most exciting pieces of reading that has ever graced the *Journal*. This astonishing revelation of British history is filled with fiery action and proves for all time that Sherlock Holmes did indeed recover for the Throne the priceless crown of St. Edwards, General Sitwell's magnificent contribution was later endorsed, according to reliable report, by Her Majesty the Queen Mother.

President Franklin D. Roosevelt was a member of the Baker Street Irregulars while in office and despite the enormous weight of his responsibilities, he too found time to write for the *Journal*. It was the President who designated the Secret Service areas at Shangri-La (Camp David) as Baker Street. The headquarters is, of course, 221B—a London address even more famous than 10 Downing Street.

Students of the Canon, the 660,382 authentic words concerning the life and career of Mr. Sherlock Holmes, are acutely aware of the fact that Dr. Watson set them some very tricky little problems. Dates are supplied that don't work out. Facts are given that appear directly to contradict one another. Key individuals are concealed behind pseudonyms. It is obvious that the Illustrious Client is King Edward VII but it is less easy to decipher the precise identification of a piece of deep blue eggshell pottery of the Ming period, loaned from His Majesty's own collection, particularly when Sir Eric MacLaglan, the director of the Victoria and Albert Museum, stated while addressing the Sherlock Holmes Society of London that there is *no* Ming eggshell pottery of anything like that color.

Mrs. Hudson, the immortal landlady at 221B Baker Street, once was replaced without warning by a lady of another name, but that difficulty is as nothing compared to the occasion when Mary Morstan Watson addressed her husband as "James" when the entire world knew that his name was John.

There are hundreds of these apparent inconsistencies, all of which the Irregulars have taken it upon themselves to explain. No problem in the Canon is more renowned than the matter of Dr. Watson's wound. It is absolutely definite that Dr. Watson was struck by a Jezail bullet during the Battle of Maiwand while serving as assistant surgeon with the Fifth Northumberland Fusiliers. In the doctor's own words:

"There I was struck on the shoulder by a Jezail bullet, which shattered the bone and grazed the subclavian artery. I should have fallen into the hands of the murderous Ghazis had it not been for the devotion and courage shown by Murray, my orderly, who threw me across a packhorse, and succeeded in bringing me safely to the British lines."

Praise and gratitude forever to the house of Murray!

However, in "The Sign of the Four" (sometimes rendered "The Sign of Four") Dr. Watson speaks of his wounded *leg*. "I had had a Jezail bullet through it some time before, and though it did not prevent me from walking it ached wearily at every change of the weather." Later, in the same account, Holmes asks if Watson's leg will prevent him following the trail of the criminals.

The plot thickens. Early in their acquaintanceship Holmes himself refers to the wound as being in the *arm*. Then, again in "The Sign of the Four" the wound is back in the leg. "What was I, an Army surgeon with a weak leg . . . . " We later learn, in Watson's words, that he is "a half-pay officer with a damaged tendo Achillis" (which is in the ankle). All this sounds very much like two wounds, but that absolutely cannot be, because in the famous episode in "The Resident Patient" where Holmes apparently reads Watson's thoughts (as Dupin did for his unnamed companion—presumably Poe) the Master said, "Your hand stole toward your own old wound."

Where, then, was Watson wounded?

The explanation: Out on the open battlefield, with complete disregard for his own safety, Dr. Watson was kneeling, bent over a fallen comrade and ministering to him, when he was shot in the left buttock. Any suggestion of cowardice in that he was not "facing the foe" is an unwarranted slander; he was ignoring the presence of the enemy. When he later wrote A *Study in Scarlet*, the excessive restraints of the Victorian era compelled him to bowdlerize the historical facts and he conveniently relocated his wound in his shoulder, both in referring to it himself and in reporting Holmes' observation of his condition.

For this yielding to expediency he was definitely upbraided by Holmes during the Master's criticism of A *Study in Scarlet*, quoted in "The Sign of the Four." Immediately thereafter Watson refers to his wounded leg, which is materially closer to the truth. Perhaps too close, hence the second evasion when he mentioned the tendon of Achilles. It is, of course, virtually impossible to imagine a bullet lodged semipermanently in that area.

How do we know this? Read again Dr. Watson's account of his rescue from the battlefield. Note that Murray threw him *across* the packhorse. A man wounded in either the shoulder or the ankle would most certainly have been *seated* on the horse, permitting him to retire to the hospital with some measure of dignity. If he had been wounded in the shoulder, a position across the horse would have been disastrous; the pain would have been multiplied many times over, the injury would certainly have been compounded, and the bleeding greatly intensified. Dr. Watson was thrown across his horse for the very good reason that he had been shot in the buttock, and therefore a normal seated position would have represented the acme of discomfort. With this single honorable, if undignified, wound he was removed from the arena of conflict and saved for his appointment with destiny.

Incidentally, it is known that the bullet was later surgically removed, because during the final pursuit in "The Hound of the Baskervilles" Dr. Watson is discovered to have recovered the full use of his limbs, enabling him to follow the climactic events of the tragedy on the dead run. In "The Adventure of Charles Augustus Milverton" Watson was in a physical condition that permitted him to scale a six-foot wall and then run for two miles without undue difficulty. (Ref: *Leaves From the Copper Beeches*, Livingston Publishing Co., Narberth, Pa., 1959, pages 121-126 inc.)

It should be added that the Irregulars have long agreed that the true author of the stories is Dr. Watson; the fact that the name of the good doctor's literary agent appears as author has also been explained (The Second Collaboration; *The Baker Street Journal*, April 1954, Vol. 4, No. 2 [New Series], page 69). In this exclusive company Sir Arthur is always referred to as the Agent: a higher tribute than any other author of so-called popular literature has ever been paid.

The makeup of the Baker Street Irregulars is notable: some of the most distinguished men and women of science, literature, business, the arts, and politics, make up the roster of this extraordinary fan club devoted to the careers of Sherlock Holmes, Dr. Watson, and the Agent. When considered sufficiently qualified by reason of service and achievement, a member may receive an investiture—at which time he is awarded the canonical recompense of one shilling. The Irregular Shilling has been treasured by some of the greatest names in America.

From their beginning, mystery stories have not lacked endorsement from high levels. In the words of Howard Haycraft: "Abraham Lincoln . . . was the first of the countless eminent men who have turned to the detective story for stimulation and solace." He is reported to have reread Poe's Dupin stories regularly every year. President Woodrow Wilson particularly enjoyed J. S. Fletcher's *The Middle Temple Murder* and praised it publicly. The success of the James Bond stories by Ian Fleming was substantially enhanced when President John F. Kennedy told how much he enjoyed reading the adventures of this larger-than-life superspy. President Franklin D. Roosevelt provided the plot for *The President's Mystery Story*. President Roosevelt was seldom topped, but in this instance he was by Baron Tweedsmuir, the governor general of Canada, who as John Buchan (his correct name) wrote one of the classic spy stories of all time, *The*

Thirty-Nine Steps. The work was also memorable because it represents one of the few instances where the motion-picture version (the original one with Robert Donat and Madeleine Carroll) is superior to the original. *Topkapi*, which was made from Eric Ambler's *The Light of Day*, is another.

During much of the Victorian era, and beyond, a novel was not considered to be of satisfactory length unless it ran to a full three volumes—the celebrated three-decker. This requirement caused many authors to indulge in a good deal of stretching, including providing detailed biographies of the characters in the story and explanations of how they got into the mess they were in when the story began. This exposition naturally slowed up the action and imposed a considerable strain on the detective-story writers who were required to maintain suspense and mystery for so long a time. Gradually this need for length lessened until, by 1920, it had passed from the scene. Sherlock Holmes continued to triumph in short stories and in a novel of lesser length, *The Valley of Fear.* Then, not abruptly but visibly, a considerable change took place.

A whole new generation of mystery writers appeared and began to produce work that once again revitalized their medium. The parade of mystery writing never stopped, but there was a period of relative doldrums around the turn of the century until the new wave of talent began to make itself felt. At that point the modern detective story, as it is currently known, came into its own and the position that it occupied has never been relinquished.

Earl Derr Biggers produced the Chinese-American detective of the Honolulu Police Department, Charlie Chan, who subsequently became the central character in numerous motion pictures. His Japanese counterpart, but an altogether different personality, appeared when Mr. Moto bowed into the picture. The variety of detectives, official and otherwise, multiplied, with sheer novelty sometimes the only discernable motive for their creation. Several were blind, the most notable being Max Carrados, who was introduced by Ernest Bramah (a pseudonym). One was more than a hundred years old. Many were women of various ages and occupations. Out of a near maelstrom of entries certain authors and their detectives emerged into permanent world fame.

A complete list of the great detectives and their creators is far beyond the scope of this chapter, but among them can be mentioned—after Sherlock Holmes, of course—such international figures as the late Hercule Poirot (Agatha Christie); Dr. Gideon Fell (John Dickson Carr); Father Brown (G. K. Chesterton); Ellery Queen (Ellery Queen); Jules Maigret (Georges Simenon); Inspector Schmidt (Aaron Marc Stein as George Bagby); Superintendent Gideon (John Creasey as J. J. Marric); Lord Peter Wimsey (Dorothy L. Sayers); Nero Wolfe (Rex Stout); Detective Inspector Napoleon Bonaparte (Arthur W. Upfield); Dr. John Thorndyke (Richard Austin Freeman); Miss Hildegarde Withers (Stuart Palmer); Sam Spade (Dashiell Hammett); Chief Fellows (Hillary Waugh); Perry Mason (Erle Stanley Gardner); Lew Archer (Ross Macdonald); Philip Marlowe (Raymond Chandler), and many more. All of the above have appeared in long series of stories, but there are others who have made virtuoso appearances that have been all too brief. This regrettable list is headed, obviously, by the Chevalier C. Auguste Dupin. But where there is life in the author there is hope, and we may yet hear more from some highly significant, relative newcomers who have appeared during the past several years.

By the time that the United States was girding up to celebrate its bicentennial, the detective story was firmly established as the most popular form of entertainment reading ever offered to the public. But it had achieved considerably more than that. Admittedly much that was published was of little consequence and quickly disappeared, but a great deal more attained the status of enduring literature. The Father Brown stories of Chesterton are celebrated because of their own merit, not because their author is a great name in English letters. If the novels and stories of Dashiell Hammett are currently receiving fresh attention, it is because they reveal within themselves far more than the cops-and-robbers type action which was their first excuse for being.

Some critics have contended that the mystery story is something that is worthless once read and the secret learned. They fall into the same category as those savants who predicted unfailingly that Robert Fulton's steamboat would not be able to move upstream. Not every mystery story deserves to be regarded as literature, but just as the Sherlock Holmes stories give a fascinating contemporary view of the Victorian age in London, so the Inspector Napoleon Bonaparte novels of Arthur Upfield provide a compelling overview of the Australian outback.

Much of the time the detective story tells of murder. This is a long established tradition that has Madame L'Espanaye and her daughter Camille as the first victims, a not unlikely consequence of their having taken up residence in the Rue Morgue. And let no purist complain that they were not murdered in the strict technical sense of the term; they were not only murdered, they were done in within a locked room and thus one of the great traditions of the genre was born. But murder within the pages of the detective story is not done so that the readers may fulfill their lust for gore; murder is done because it is an ultimate crime, one which cannot be reversed and for which restitution cannot be made. Even the traitor may in some way, perhaps, manage to undo the effects of his terrible crime, but when the murderer has struck the deed is done and there is no calling it back this side of the Day of Judgment.

It has been pointed out that while there is only one means of getting born, there are unlimited ways in which to die. Therefore the hidden criminal may strike in many different manners, such as the unique means employed in Dorothy Sayers's *The Nine Tailors*. And there are also innumerable places in which to expire against every imaginable background. Many authors of the murder mystery take pains to see that while their victims die, no blood is spilled. Very often, as in most of Hildegarde Withers' adventures, the deceased has already attained that status before he or she is introduced into the story. Only very rarely is the victim someone whom the reader has come to know well, to admire and to like, before demise sets in. This has sometimes happened in the Colonel Hugh North stories of F. Van Wyck Mason, but it is a rarity. Also, the reader for a considerable time was spared attending autopsies, funerals, or interments. More recently these events have been given greater attention and the TV watcher is often taken on trips to the morgue to view the remains.

The comment has frequently been made that the public has a definite taste for violence and enjoys seeing it depicted on the printed page and on the screen. Some movie producers are fond of pointing out that "everyone stops to look at a bad traffic accident." Unfortunately, both statements are probably true, but it does not follow that the fictional detective needs to litter his trail with an array of dismembered corpses in order to attract the reader's attention. One of the happier aspects of murder is that the victim cannot sit up after a suitable interval, assist his revival with a quick brandy, and then give evidence concerning who did him in, why, and how. Dead men (and women) can tell tales, but they must do so passively and therefore give the detective on the case something to challenge his powers.

Violence for its own sake has appeared in detective literature—Mickey Spillane is noted for this—but the detective story does not exist for the purpose of appeasing the reader's Dracula-like tendencies. The true detective story requires the reader to think, to match his wits with those of the investigator in the narrative, and to participate, as it were, in the events as they unfold. If the tale is simply one of smash-bang violence with none of the elements of the classic mystery story, it is likely to die a quick and deserved death. Nick Carter has been kept alive largely by continuous transfusions of printer's ink, but none of the almost countless stories about this well-known character stands out enough to be remembered by name.

The mystery story does have certain limitations, but they are not severe. The development of character, of background, and of human actions, offers unlimited scope. These are prime ingredients of story telling, no matter what format has been chosen or how distinguished the author. The restrictions imposed are those that enhance the mystery story itself and widen its appeal. The author must play fair with his reader; he cannot say, "At that moment Graspingham Featherkill bent over and picked up a small object that lay all but hidden on the rug; after studying it carefully for a moment, he slipped it covertly into his side pocket." If the detective saw the object, the reader must see it too and be given the same chance to apply it as a clue to the solution of the mystery.

The murderer may turn out to be a highly unlikely person, and frequently does, but it is *verboten*, for example, to disclose that the supposed victim in actuality committed suicide. These rules are fundamental although like all rules, they are occasionally broken.

Sometimes the reader may penetrate the mystery; if he does he usually feels quite happy about his achievement. If he is misled, the chances are he will enjoy it even more. There are generally two types of readers who have been through the pages of *The Agony Column* by Earl Derr Biggers: those who were completely fooled, and those who have disgraced themselves by peeking in the back—an unforgivable sin. Another book famous for its surprise ending is *The Murder of Roger Ackroyd* by Agatha Christie, and there is a notable bomb waiting for the reader as he nears the conclusion of *Murder Down Under* by Arthur Upfield. (This superb story was all but ruined by its British title, which virtually gives away the ending.)

Mystery stories of the classic kind are filled with memorable characters, and they constitute the most compelling ingredient. Sherlock Holmes' personality alone would have carried him to international fame. Another detective whose presence dominates every scene in which he appears is Nero Wolfe, who resides at a frequently revised address on West 35th Street in New York.

Probability is not an essential ingredient; some of John Dickson Carr's best locked-room puzzles depend on solutions that are somewhat beyond the edge of likelihood. One of them, at least, was literally done with mirrors, but the best of them display such ingenuity that the fact that it *could* have been done that way is enough. It is a little surprising that the chief of police in a small Connecticut community would have quite as many baffling cases spreading gore on his doorstep as does Chief Fellows of Stockford, but this in no way diminishes the enjoyment of Hillary Waugh's stories of this quietly competent policeman who draws inspiration from the display of fetching nudes that decorates one wall of his office.

Of what use is the mystery story, and how does it advance the world's work? Of what precise practical use is a nocturne by Chopin except as something to play or to listen to? What is the international significance of the all-star game? What is the point of spending extra money to go out on New Year's Eve? And why should a woman buy another dress when she already owns one that fits her reasonably well?

It is possible to fabricate a whole host of reasons why the mystery story is a significant contribution from an entirely practical standpoint, but such rationalizations are not needed. There is no requirement that literature be boring, or confined to reporting the sufferings of various segments of humanity as they endure their wretched lives. *Tom Sawyer* is literature; it is also immensely entertaining. Sufficient to say that the mystery story has more than come of age, and the public has so willed it by providing millions of readers, generation by generation, to be instructed, baffled, and entertained. The standards have steadily risen and the quality of the product continues to improve as men and women from every facet of life turn to it for relaxation, mental stimulation, and escape from endless pressures. They can find the same thing in the inspiration of great music, and they sometimes do both at the same time.

Living—except as a hermit—imposes so many strains and requirements that the human organism and intellect are forced to work under pressures they were not meant to endure. And in modern society the pressures grow worse, not better. We now have dental anesthetics, but we have also gained smog and the Internal Revenue Service. We have Social Security, but it is increasingly difficult to find a little patch of land on which to live.

There is much to be gained by feeling the texture of soil and learning from it that nature still does exist, no matter how distorted and suppressed. There is relief in a good dinner and dancing, in almost any activity that successfully shunts aside the bitter realities that force themselves upon almost everyone as the computers pour out their deluge of bills, regulations, requirements, credit ratings, and harassments of every description. Occasionally the distressed human may lie down to rest, hoping to find some peace within himself. Then how glorious it would be to be awakened by a hand on the shoulder, to look up into the eager, alert face of Sherlock Holmes revealed in the darkness, and hear the blood-pounding words:

"Come, Watson come; the game is afoot!"

PART I

THE AMATEUR DETECTIVE

The first and most popular classification of detective fiction features an amateur as the detective. This means the crime is solved by a person, either male or female, who has not been issued a license as a private investigator or is not designated as a member of an official police force. The amateur detective story is the oldest form of the genre, begun by Edgar Allan Poe in 1841 with "The Murders in the Rue Morgue," which introduced the first recognized amateur detective, C. Auguste Dupin. This tale of detection established for all time the five basic rules for amateur detective fiction:

1. There must be a crime, preferably murder, because it fascinates readers more than any other crime and there appears to be an unlimited number of ways in which people can die.

2. There must be a detective, someone with superior powers of inductive and deductive reasoning, who is capable of solving the crime that baffles the official police system.

3. Thirdly, the police must be seen as either incompetent or as incapable of solving a certain type of complex crime.

4. The reader must be given all the information or "clues" to be able to solve the crime if the "clues" are properly interpreted.

5. The detective must explain who the criminal is and the motive, means, and opportunity by the conclusion of the story.

The amateur detective story is based on the concept of "fair play" with the reader. The reader must pit his or her wits against those of both the detective and the criminal, and this is one of the basic reasons for the popularity of this category.

If "The Murders in the Rue Morgue" created the basic rules for the amateur detective form, it also helped illustrate what the characteristics of the amateur detective were to be. For example, amateur detectives can be anyone, in any profession, of any age, or any class. They do not necessarily have any special training in criminal investigation. They often blunder into situations that are unforeseen or unexpected. Their interest is generated in the crime because of a friend, a relative, someone associated with the crime, or because of sheer curiosity or the need for intellectual stimulation. In certain cases they may even be asked for help by the police because of special knowledge in a related area. They are often eccentric, but each possesses his or her own particular type of intelligence. These detectives receive no pay for what they do other than their own personal satisfaction of outwitting the murderer. What motivates the amateur detective is well stated by Margery Allingham in her Albert Campion novel, *Death of a Ghost* (1934):

> There is an optimistic belief widespread among the generous-hearted that the average human being has only to become sufficiently acquainted with another's trouble or danger to transfer it to his own shoulders not merely unhesitatingly but gladly. The fact remains, of course, that the people who say to themselves, "There is real danger here, and I think it had better confront me rather than this helpless soul before me" are roughly divided into three groups.
>
> There are the relatives, and it is extraordinary how the oft-derided blood tie decides the issue, who, moved by that cross between affection and duty, perform incredible feats of self-sacrifice.
>
> Then there are those misguided folk, half hero, half busybody, who leap into danger as if it were the elixir of life.
>
> And finally there is a small group of mortals who are moved partly by pity and partly by a passionate horror of seeing tragedy slowly unfolded before their eyes, and who act principally through a desire to bring things to a head and get the play over, at whatever the cost. (175–176)

They may be amateurs, but they triumph over the professionals and discover the criminal. They pursue the truth with courage and tenacity, often at the risk of their own lives. In these detectives can be found the best of human qualities: a genuine concern for others and the belief that justice must prevail.

The detectives themselves divide into two categories: the "amateur-amateur" and the "professional-amateur." The first group is aptly represented by Agatha Christie's Miss Marple, the elderly, busybody sleuth from Saint Mary's Mead, or Dorothy Sayer's Lord Peter Wimsey, the elegant aristocrat who pursues crime as a hobby. The second group finds its amateur detectives among the professions: lawyer, doctor, forensic scientist, archeologist, university professor, chef, book publisher, priest or rabbi, sports agent, and numerous other categories. Some of these have work connected with legal issues and some do not. In this category the reader can discover Edmund Crispin's eccentric Oxford professor, Gervase Fen, or the lawyer turned judge, Deborah Knott, creation of Margaret Maron.

However, the argument still rages about where to place Arthur Conan Doyle's Sherlock Holmes, the most famous fictional detective in the world. Introduced in *A Study in Scarlet (1887)*, Holmes defines himself as "the world's first consulting detective" and is sometimes paid to solve crimes; yet he is not a private investigator in the Sam Spade or Philip Marlowe tradition, which seems to define the current concept of the private investigator. Holmes has educated himself in the history of crime, and has honed his faculties to observe that which others miss, so he is no rank amateur. However, like the professional-amateur, in many of his cases he acts as a consultant to the police for whom he has little respect, and his motivation to investigate the crime is the need for mental stimulation. He seems to have a foothold in both the amateur and private investigator worlds, which partially helps explain his popularity.

Following Holmes the amateur detective continued to dominate the mystery scene and other great writers offered their version of this type of detective. The 1920s, 1930s, and 1940s were considered the "Golden Age" of the detective novel. Agatha Christie, Dorothy Sayers, and Ellery Queen, to mention three, gave the reader the great "puzzle" mysteries filled with intricate plotting and ingenious murders. John Dickson Carr added the "locked room mysteries" with their impossible crimes and touch of humor. Edmund Crispin and Phoebe Atwood Taylor concentrated on introducing mysteries with a sense of "place," such as Gervase Fen at Oxford or Asey Mayo as the "Cape Cod Sherlock." The world of the amateur detective was ever expanding to new regions, new professions, and certainly to new methods of how to commit a murder.

Although the 1930s and 1940s created an interest in the private investigator, and the 1950s introduced the police as important figures in detective fiction, the amateur detective still remains the readers' favorite. In the amateur detectives readers can recognize themselves. A reader could be an English professor in an "academic" mystery or a chef in a "culinary" mystery or an innocent bystander in an outrageous, slapstick "laugh out loud" mystery. As the categories of amateur mysteries expand, so does the involvement of the reader.

Readers are attracted to the amateur detective story not only for the variety of types of detectives but also because it offers the best "puzzle" mysteries. The emphasis is on elaborate and challenging plots filled with false clues, a number of likely suspects, and a murderer who fools everyone but the talented amateur sleuth. Early critics of this classification were mainly interested in the ability of the writer to create an intellectual game for the reader and the various strategies involved in accomplishing this. Plot was the essential factor, and characters were not required to have either depth or complexity. Current critics find amateur detectives involved with multilayered "puzzles," social and cultural conflicts and intelligent and devious suspects with complex motives, but the amateur still finds the culprit.

In the early 2000s there are too many fine writers of amateur detective fiction to mention them all. A very select list of American and British writers should include the following: Susan Wittig Albert, Margot Arnold, Nancy Atherton, Stephanie Barron, Harlan Coben, Dorothy Cannell, Patricia Cornwell, Lucha Corpi, Amanda Cross, Diane Mott Davidson, Aaron Elkins, Linda Fairstein, Earlene Fowler, Dick Francis, Carolina Garcia-Aguilera, Pamela Thomas-Graham, Carolyn Hart, Julie Kaewert, Jane Langton, Margaret Maron, Allana Martin, Sharyn McCrumb, Elizabeth Peters, Nancy Pickard, Kathy Reichs, Virginia Rich, Sarah Shankman, Mary Willis Walker, and Minette Walters. These writers continue to create the amateur detectives that readers love. With their wits and inductive and deductive powers, plus imagination, determination, and a little luck, these amateurs find the clues, solve the puzzle, deduce the motive, provide the proof, and bring the guilty to justice.

CRITICAL ESSAYS AND COMMENTARIES

PATRICIA D. MAIDA AND NICHOLAS B. SPORNICK

From "The Puzzle-Game"

The heart of the classical detective story is the puzzle—that complex structure which offers the reader intrigue and intellectual stimulation. Agatha Christie, who was well versed in the puzzle tradition, distinguishes herself from other writers of the genre in her conception of the murder puzzle: "I don't like messy deaths. Anyway, I'm more interested in peaceful people who die in their own beds and no one knows why. I don't like violence."[1] Though her puzzles may be shrouded in mystery, the bloodstains are few; for Christie distances the reader from the garish effects of murder by focusing instead on "whodunit" and engaging the reader in the pursuit of the murderer. The reader then moves with the sleuth as an armchair detective in a detection process which is both an entertainment and a heady challenge—a puzzle-game.

Among the most enthralling of puzzle-games are those found in the detective story, for those puzzles operate on multiple levels with varying complexities devised by the ingenious author. The detection game offers, in fact, several different player combinations: the game played between the murderer and the sleuth, the game played between the reader and the murderer, the game played between the reader and the sleuth, and even the game played between the author and the reader. Traditionally, the puzzle-game has followed certain formulas; when Ronald Knox set up "Rules" for detective fiction in 1918, he was codifying those conventions which had already been accepted by most practitioners of the genre. Consequently, the reader approaches detective fiction with a particular set of expectations. The reader expects the mystery and the challenge of the careful plot; he expects to find a puzzle, but he does not expect to be tricked since the "fair" puzzle places the means of solving the enigma within a given range of difficulty. The fair play doctrine is an attempt to ensure validity of evidence, adequate presentation of facts (but not enough to spoil the mystery), and readiness to grant the reader an opportunity to "play the game."

Some authors of detective fiction, including Agatha Christie, increase the dimensions of their works by weaving "games within games."[2] One such amusement is the "recognition game" in which the author refers to real-life murderers to highlight similarities between reality and fiction. A favorite murder case often referred to by Christie is the "Brides in the Bath," as the image of Dr. Crippen is seen in counterpoint to one of her murderers. In *Mrs. McGinty's Dead*, for example, Christie employs clever allusions to newspaper accounts of famous murders and their crimes as an integral part of the clue-hunting and subsequent solution to the McGinty murder. But Christie's most celebrated "game within the game" is her parodying of detective sleuths and their creators in *Partners in Crime*, a collection of short stories featuring Tommy and Tuppence—a detective couple.[3] This husband and wife team assume the mind-set, the techniques, the language and total style of illustrious practitioners of detection. Their role playing becomes a guessing game for the reader who is asked to identify such luminaries as Sherlock Holmes, Dr. Thorndyke, Father Brown, Inspector French, Max Carrados and even Hercule Poirot (fair game). The tone of these sketches is light and humorous as Christie playfully pokes fun at the over-worked devices and rusty machinery of the genre.

Christie was not above self-parody, particularly in the case of her female sleuth, Ariadne Oliver. When she places Mrs. Oliver in charge of a murder game in *Dead Man's Folly*, Christie makes a series of double plays to involve the reader in a game within the puzzle-game. Ariadne Oliver is invited to set up and supervise a Murder Hunt—a game similar to a treasure hunt in which participants are challenged to solve a theoretical murder. As the players enter the game area, they are given cards containing the first clue which, if interpreted correctly, will lead then to the next clues. Players carry score cards to be filled in as the game progresses with the name of the murderer, the weapon, the motive and the cover-up. However, Mrs. Oliver's game soon turns into a *real* murder in a clever reversal engineered by a clever killer. The reader is then thrust into a puzzle-game that is heightened by the interplay between the two games.

Game plans and "gaming" devices abound in Christie's detective stories. Actual games, as in Ariadne Oliver's treasure hunt, often become the frames upon which the puzzle-game is played. In the *Halloween Party*, a young girl bobbing for apples is drowned in the tub by a mysterious assailant; in *Cards on the Table*, the host is stabbed in a covert attack during a bridge game. And in *A Murder is Announced*, bemused neighbors drop in at Little Paddocks to participate in what they assume will be a new parlor game—a staged murder-game. To their astonishment, real gunshots and death ensue. A gaming device that Christie uses to tease the reader and to provide additional clues is a nursery rhyme conundrum. *Ten Little Indians, One Two, Buckle My Shoe, A Pocket Full of Rye, Hickory Dickory Death*, and *Crooked House* are among the novels in which a nursery rhyme functions as an advantage for the reader who may be able to discover whodunit by interpreting the rhyme correctly. These variations upon the essential puzzle-game reveal Christie's gift for maintaining a delicate balance between levity and horror in what might be considered a serio-comic perspective.

At the heart of the detective story is the puzzle-game. Although its structure is among the more complex, it possesses components common to all games:

a goal (whodunit), a field or playing board (setting), players (murderer, suspects, sleuth), devices used to reach goal (clues), barriers and handicaps (cover-up schemes including red herrings), and rules for fair play (conventions of the genre). The individual author creates puzzles bearing his or her own imprint, for the uniqueness of the puzzle derives from the way in which the author perceives and then manipulates each of the components. Thus the game situation, which requires a playing area where the moves and countermoves are enacted, must be a thriving social environment. Christie's field may be a country estate, a transcontinental express train or a Nile River steamer—but it must be a commodious place with relatives, colleagues, fellow guests or travellers in active pursuit of their social routines. Though the victim may expire in the privacy of a bedroom, library or stateroom, just as often a murder occurs in a crowded drawing room. The targeting of the victim by the mysterious murderer in their midst serves to alert the rest of the group to danger and possible threats to their own lives. Since *bloody* murder is not the rule in a Christie puzzle, details of the crime are given as succinctly and clinically as possible; greater emphasis is then placed on the circumstances of the crime.

The game requires players engaged in a competitive struggle to achieve a goal. In the detective story, it is the murderer who makes the initial challenge which will subsequently plunge the victim, the other members of the community (who will become suspects) and the sleuth into a life-death struggle. Who is likely to be murdered? According to Christie, anyone—male, female, adult, child—anyone who in some way crosses the wrong person. The potential victim, Christie believes, is a person who *could* be killed—someone who is vulnerable. Given the closed society which Christie portrays, the victim is frequently a member of the inner circle who poses a threat to another person in the group. Although occasionally the innocent suffer, most often the victim is someone who has brought the event upon himself. . . .

No matter how well placed the victim is or no matter how sterling his character may be, Christie does not engage the sympathy of the reader; her focus is on the solution to the murder. By developing means of emotional distancing for the reader, she makes the puzzle solving all the more challenging. The focus then shifts from the victim to the murderer.

In order to discover the murderer, the sleuth must go through a process of elimination to reduce the number of suspects to *one*. Since anyone and everyone on the scene can be a suspect, the range and variety of suspects in a Christie puzzle is broad. Her typical method of building suspicion is through the gradual uncovering of information which incriminates the characters one by one, slowly expanding the circle of suspects. The circle widens until practically everyone is included; as likely suspects emerge from the group, possible motives and opportunities are established. As the reader begins to make judgments about certain suspects, Christie sets up reversals and complications. One of her favorite devices for surprising the reader is hidden identity; she develops the

Janus-faced character in graphic terms, displaying over and over again how easy it is for a person to pretend to be someone else and how readily the public will be taken in. Impersonation, hidden, and mistaken identity dominate Christie's portraits. In *A Murder Is Announced*, for example, four cases of hidden identity out of a group of twelve suspects provide continuous surprises.

Perhaps Christie's most renowned case of hidden identity is to be found in "Witness for the Prosecution." In this short story the reader participates by following the defense attorney's activities and sharing his impressions. Attorney Mayherne is attempting to win acquittal for his client, a young man accused of murdering an elderly woman. But the pivotal figure in the case is Romaine Heilger, the accused's common-law wife: instead of testifying for the defense, as Mayherne had hoped, she testifies for the prosecution—offering evidence as to her hatred for her one-time lover. Luck comes to the rescue, or so Mayherne believes, when an aged woman with a grudge against Heilger offers to sell him letters written by Heilger to an unknown lover in which she discloses her intentions of incriminating the accused. When Mayherne introduces these letters in court, Heilger's credibility as a witness is destroyed—the jury rejects her testimony and acquits the young man. Belatedly, Mayherne (and the reader) discovers that he has been tricked. By playing a series of double roles, Romaine Heilger outwits all the other "players." While presenting herself as the accused's wife, she is in reality not his wife. And by *impersonating* an old woman, she fools even an experienced attorney. She accomplishes her coup by playing "a lone hand," by misdirecting the perceptions of all the other players—even to the final twist when she reveals that she acted to save the accused because he was, in fact, *guilty*.

Suspects can, wittingly or unwittingly, provide a cover for the murderer. They complicate the puzzle-game by their very presence, for each one must be investigated in the methodical process of elimination. When one suspect finally emerges as the dominant figure, this character will become the most likely suspect. Although Christie follows the conventions on how and when to reveal the most likely suspect, she varies her puzzles so that the reader can never assume that a particular suspect is the murderer. Consider Christie's *Cards on the Table* in which she sets up a puzzle with *four* likely suspects. In the Foreword to this novel she warns the reader that although some detective stories are "rather like a big race—a number of starters—likely horses and jockeys, . . . *this is not that kind of book*."[4] In this case there are four starters—all capable of murder—matched by four able sleuths. This particular novel also provides a good introduction to the "gaming" aspects of Christie's puzzles. Obviously not all writers of detective fiction present their cases with the challenge and sportive tone usually found in Christie's work. *Cards on the Table* actually includes a series of games—a card game, a cat and mouse foray, and a detection game.

The game begins when the victim invites four people who have gotten away with murder to dine with four notable sleuths: Hercule Poirot, Inspector Battle, Colonel Race and Ariadne Oliver. The victim, Mr. Shaitana, arranges for the party for his own sadistic pleasure as he baits individuals, insinuating knowledge of their hidden crimes and threatening exposure. However, Shaitana loses control of the game. Assuming the position of overseer, he relaxes in a fireside chair while his guests play bridge. While his guard is down, one of the players makes a secret, yet deadly move. Shaitana is discovered dead—stabbed with a dagger from his own collection. No one but the eight players has entered the room; consequently, everyone realizes that one of them is the murderer. Although each has been involved in the bridge contest, one individual has obviously made a successful *double* play. . . .

In the puzzle-game, the murderer makes the initial moves to thwart the efforts of the puzzle-solvers. A Christie murderer is astute in shielding himself with that well-devised fabrication known as a cover-up. Within the multitudinous schemes to be found in her stories the following are the ones that Christie's murderers use most frequently:

1. *Hidden Identity or Impersonation:* This procedure allows the murderer to move freely within a familiar environment without arousing any suspicion. For example, in *Third Girl* part of the murder team lives a double life assisted by a wig and appropriate makeup. In other situations, the murderer impersonates another person for the purpose of casting suspicion on that person; often this is part of a process of incrimination set up to make an innocent party the scapegoat, such as in *Lord Edgware Dies.*

2. *The Frame-Up:* This elaborate scheme of directing guilt to another person is perhaps the best cover for the murderer. We see it used effectively in *The Mysterious Affair at Styles* as well as in *The ABC Murders,* where the scheme is so cunning that it even convinces the duped party of his guilt. (In most cases, however, the frame-up victim fights back, providing added conflict to the plot.)

3. *The Red Herring:* The false clue, deliberately left by the murderer, confuses the police and usually the sleuth. In *The Clocks,* for example, the killer arranges a roomful of clocks at the scene of the murder, all set at different times; the significance of the clocks sends the police in all directions—away from the murderer.

4. *The Cover-up Victim:* The person who threatens to reveal the killer's identity is likely to be murdered. Numerous blackmailers meet their fates this way as do innocent individuals who are unaware of what they know. Gladys, the scatter-brained maid in *A Pocket Full of Rye,* has no idea that the tryst she runs off to keep in the garden will end in murder. She, and other cover-up victims like her, are doomed by the special knowledge that they may have gained from eavesdroppings, snooping or just being an involuntary witness.

One of Christie's most renowned puzzle-games, *The ABC Murders*, contains her most clever cover-up. In this novel, the murderer invents a scheme to divert attention from himself by hiding a single murder within a series of murders, and then by setting up a scapegoat to pay for the crimes. The game plan is to make the killer seem to be a demented individual who chooses his victims by alphabetical order. An ABC railway guide is left at the scene of each murder, and the victim's surnames, ranging from A through D, correspond with a town of the same initial letter. The significant victim, Sir Carmichael Clarke from the town of Churston, thus appears to be chosen in the same fashion as the other three victims. Actually, Sir Clarke is the brother of the murderer who hopes to inherit the estate; the ancient Cain and Abel motif is developed with a new twist. . . .

In order to match wits with the murderer, the sleuth must sidestep the pitfalls of the cover-up and interpret the clues correctly. A fire burning in a hearth on a warm evening, an open window, a long-distance telephone call—the Christie puzzle includes commonplace clues like these, clues that the less astute observer might easily overlook. Of the two kinds of clues—genuine and false—the false clue or red herring is the major handicap because it not only obstructs the truth but also delays solving the puzzle. If the detective follows all leads until he has proven their authenticity, by a process of elimination the field narrows down to a select group of genuine clues.

The genuine clue is not complete until it is seen in relation to a combination of other genuine clues. For example, in *Sleeping Murder* a suitcase hastily packed with the *wrong* clothes becomes much more meaningful against a background of other clues which imply that the victim may not have left home of her own accord. The keystone of the puzzle, however, is that final clue—in a Christie puzzle, the one reserved until the eleventh hour. When it finally surfaces or is finally interpreted correctly (it may have been there from the beginning), the keystone of the puzzle fits the psychology of the crime and focuses on the killer and his method.

Although many Christie clues are physical objects or facts that can be used as evidence, other clues are found in people—in body language or personality quirks that reflect the individual's true character. These intangible clues often lead to the murderer. In some novels, for example, intangible clues in the form of body language lead to the correct solution to the murders. *A Caribbean Mystery* develops as Jane Marple assesses the expression on the face of Major Palgrave just as he is about to tell her about a wife-killer. And the look on the face of an actress as she greets a guest at a reception tells Miss Marple enough to help her solve the mystery of *The Mirror Crack'd*.

Devotees of Christie tend to expect certains kinds of clues, just as they look forward to favored settings and recognizable characters. In fact, part of the allure of the game is the element of expectation. As Cawelti points out in his study of the genre, the reader anticipates "highly predictable structures that guarantee the fulfillment of conventional expectations."[5] Authors have used variations of formulas since the inception of the detective story. For the reader, the formula has several positive functions: it sets up a series of conventions which the reader looks forward to encountering in subsequent stories; it permits the reader to relax, inviting a sense of *deja vu* and coaxing him into involvement with the story; and it encourages the analytical thinker to match wits with the other players in the puzzle-game. As we have seen thus far, Christie's puzzles are rendered in a basically traditional manner, yet with a uniqueness that reflects the author's personal and aesthetic values. To become attuned to Christie's style is not to be bored or to be able to predict the outcome of her puzzles, for her work cannot be reduced to a formula. Although the detective story is of necessity formulaic, Christie invents imaginative variations to the basic formula.

In using the Watson-narrator device, Christie was relying on a pattern developed by Poe and transmitted through Arthur Conan Doyle. This point of view appears in a large portion of her detective fiction, yet perhaps her most famous novel, *The Murder of Roger Ackroyd*, is a clever variation on this well-known device. In this novel, Christie effectively handicaps the reader who assumes that the first person narrator is providing an accurate and full account of the mystery. As Champigny observes in his study, Dr. Sheppard is not only the narrator, he is a diarist using a "tricky style."[6] And he is also a credible character—a physician who is respected in the community and an assistant to Poirot (substituting for the absent Captain Hastings).

The characterization of Dr. Sheppard is accomplished with subtle strokes. Christie purposely understates him to the point where the reader is lulled into false security and accepts him at face value as an ordinary, if not stereotypical, country doctor. Although the experienced reader *should* realize that no one is beyond suspicion, the reading public was taken by surprise at the outcome of this puzzle.

Did Christie play fair with the reader? In examining the fabric of the narrative, one discovers that the narrator's account is true in the sense that no false information is presented. Ingenuous as Sheppard may be, he does not lie. Instead, he omits certain details which then produces a false picture or, as Champigny says, "a fictional image of the basic narrative."[7] Commenting in her *Autobiography* on this technique, Christie points out that concealment and ambiguity with respect to "lapses of time" are the key factors in manipulating point of view.[8] The fictional image is conveyed by Dr. Sheppard's narrative from the point when he takes the reader to the scene of the crime and then through the process of discovery that follows. Only when Poirot readjusts the picture at the *dénouement* does the reader discover that Sheppard has killed Ackroyd and staged an almost perfect cover-up.

Solving this puzzle is made progressively difficult because Sheppard seems to recede into the background when a most likely suspect emerges. However, the master detective relies less on tangible clues and more on the psychology of the killer. The turning point occurs when Poirot senses that there is too much evidence, that a frame-up is likely. When viewed as a puzzle-game, we perceive that a deadly match is going on between Sheppard and Poirot. The reader assumes that the two players are on the same team, working together to solve the mystery of Ackroyd's murder. However, at the *dénouement* it becomes clear that Sheppard has played a reverse role, feigning support for Poirot while at the same time manipulating evidence to lead him astray. But Sheppard is no match for Poirot. We see this initially when Sheppard mistakenly identifies the renowned detective as a hairdresser, having jumped to that conclusion based on Poirot's fastidious grooming. Poirot, however, is a better judge of character, for he does not accept the doctor at face value. After investigating his background, Poirot makes the correct deductions.

Once Christie pulled off her coup in this novel, she did not use the same device again. The term "ackroydism" emerged subsequently as a generic label, but once the trick had been turned by Christie, other writers were not game to try an imitation—and neither was Christie. Nevertheless, Christie continued to experiment with point of view, achieving notable success in alternating points of view in two of her most famous novels, *The ABC Murders* and *Ten Little Indians*.

Another component of the traditional formula which Christie chose to modify is the basic triad of victim, murderer, sleuth. In two exceptionally fine puzzles, *Murder on the Orient Express* and *Ten Little Indians*, Christie complicates the riddling process by increasing the number of personae. In *Murder on the Orient Express*, complicity among twelve likely suspects produces red herrings and a proliferation of clues—none of which seems to point to the identity of the traditional murderer. The concept of a ritualistic murder, an execution carried out by twelve individuals, is so removed from the expectations of the reader that the mystification structure seems significantly different from the basic formula.[9] Actually though, only one element—the number of murderers—has been modified.

The puzzle-game which defies all conventions, however, is *Ten Little Indians*. In this novel, all the players change positions so that ten individuals play three distinct roles: victim, suspect and sleuth. One of the ten also plays a fourth role, that of murderer. Although there is not a conventional sleuth in the story, which is often billed as "a detective story without a detective," the characters participate in the detection process and so does the reader.

Ten people, including a housekeeper and caretaker, have been induced to go to a guest house on a remote island off the coast of Devon, where they discover themselves to be the only inhabitants. Although they seem to have nothing in common, it is soon revealed that each is secretly responsible for the death of another human being. An accusation of guilt blares forth from a recording naming the guilty parties and their victims, even to the date on which the deaths occurred. Though the accuser is anonymous, his tone is menacing. The ten claim that they are innocent of all charges, but when the first murder occurs that evening it becomes apparent that each of them is in danger. Unable to leave the island or to communicate with the mainland, they unite to unmask the killer. While each participates in the detection process, each is still a suspect (until he or she becomes a victim), since no outsider has been discovered on the island.

If one considers the story a puzzle-game, it becomes apparent that although there are ten players, one of those players is in complete control of all the moves. This person manipulates the others so that each will participate in a cat and mouse chase. Though one assumes that the profile of the murderer might be deduced by one or more of the potential victims, the game is complicated by the reality that each of the players has taken a life before. Thus the issue becomes not *who* is capable of murder but rather who is capable of this kind of murder scheme. (Not all the victims are murdered directly, but each death is brought about by the machinations of one person.)

The point of view provides the reader-participant with certain advantages. Though in public these individuals deny the charges brought against them, the omniscient narrator permits the reader to hear the truth when each character silently recalls the details of the crime. The shifting narrative focus from one group to the individual allows for moments when each of the guests is alone and privately acknowledges personal responsibility for his deeds. Nevertheless, the omniscient narrator does not reveal the murderer.

A riddle entitled "Ten Little Indians" is the only tangible clue. The riddle is found framed on the wall of each bedroom, and ten china figurines stand on the drawing room table. This riddle depicts the scheme which the murderer has devised: the ten guests suffer the fate ascribed to the appropriately numbered Indian. As each person is killed, a figurine mysteriously disappears from the table. At one point, Vera Clathorne—victim number ten—almost solves the riddle. The line, "A red herring swallowed one, then there were three," causes her to probe the demise of victim number seven. This leads her to the judge who is noted for his lack of mercy—and who is indeed a likely suspect. Clathorne comes very close to the truth, but fails. Still, the reader may possibly succeed at this point if the error in Clathorne's thinking is deduced.

As in most Christie puzzles, the pyschology of the murderer is the key to discovering the identity. The murderer is obviously obsessed with justice, assuming a judgmental position; the scheme is patently an execution plan. Judge Wargrave is the obvious suspect, yet he is reportedly shot and killed, victim number six; consequently one assumes that he cannot be the murderer. The problem then shifts from whodunit to *howdunit*. An account of how the judge carried out his plan is ultimately found in a bottle. Many purists feel that the use of this *deus ex machina* device is the single flaw in an otherwise brilliant puzzle. Obviously, Christie tried an unusual combination for this puzzle—an almost impossible design with ten people dead, including the perpetrator of the scheme. The novel can hardly be deemed formulaic.

As we have seen, Christie puzzle-games share common components, but they cannot be reduced to a simple formula. The puzzles we have examined reveal creative structures which depart from a single pattern. Although the seasoned reader can anticipate typical Christie devices and components, the variations upon typical designs render her better puzzles unique. (Granted Christie was not brilliant all the time, but she managed an amazing number of successes.) A Christie puzzle which may seem ordinary on the surface frequently develops into a full-blown mystery, revealing hidden dimensions, unusual variations, and surprising turns. Consequently, we challenge the assertion that anyone can "tune" in to Christie and figure out whodunit early on. While familiarity with her methods and ideas may dispose the reader to feel comfortable or to anticipate the use of certain devices, this disposition alone cannot solve the puzzle. In fact, familiarity often handicaps the reader whose assumptions may easily lead him astray.

Why then is Christie so successful at the puzzle-game? As we look at the components, we find that she operates in a seemingly traditional manner but that she is capable of unusual twists and turns. The Christie puzzle is methodical and often creative. Through various methods of distancing, Christie maintains a playful tone—sorrow, blood, sadism do not intrude upon the scene. From her predecessors in the genre, Christie learned the conventions of the genre, the formulas, the varieties of the puzzles; but out of her own genius, she invented new game plans. She judged correctly those elements which worked well for her, combining them into successful patterns that have earned for her fame and fortune.

Notes

1. Marcelle Bernstein, "Agatha Christie: 'Queen of Crime' is a Gentlewoman." The *Los Angeles Times*, 8 March 1970, p. 60.

2. For a discussion of detectival games, see Jane Gottschalk, "The Games of Detective Fiction," *Armchair Detective*, 10 (January 1977), 74.

3. *Partners in Crime* offers a treatment of such games.

4. *Cards on the Table* (New York: Dell Publishing Company, 1964), Foreword.

5. John D. Cawelti, *Adventure, Mystery, and Romance*. (Chicago: University of Chicago Press, 1976), p. 2.

6. Robert Champigny, *What Will Have Happened?* (Bloomington: Indiana University Press, 1977), p. 81.

7. Champigny, p. 81.

8. Agatha Cristie, *An Autobiography* (New York: Dodd, Mead & Company, 1977), p. 329.

9. For a discussion of mystification structure, see Cawelti, p. 110.

NANCY ELLEN TALBURT
AND JUANA R. YOUNG

The Many Guises of the
Contemporary Amateur Detective

A body shot through the head lies in a puddle of blood in the Asian history section of the public library; a corpse sits upright in the medieval stocks on the village green with its throat cut; the remains of a young woman are spread-eagled in the middle of a mystic circle; a man's body slumps from a newly opened mummy case in the Cairo Museum. Who will solve these murders? An amateur detective will. The first fictional detective was an amateur, Edgar Allan Poe's C. Auguste Dupin, in "The Murders in the Rue Morgue" (1841), and despite the later development of mysteries focused on police and private investigators (P.I.s), the amateur has remained the most popular sleuth in the genre. While it is not possible to define the amateur exactly, typically such detectives are not licensed, are not employed in the crime-fighting professions, and are not paid for investigating. Their popularity reflects readers' enjoyment of the amateurs' ability to outwit the professionals and their freedom to pursue investigations and achieve justice on their own terms.

The first amateur detectives were men. Some had time on their hands, and money and connections to the top levels of society. Others were professionals in law, medicine, religion, academia, or the arts. When female amateurs came on the scene, they tended to be spinster homemakers, also with discretionary time but possessing connections to village life and an eye for the vagaries of human nature. At the beginning of the twenty-first century, the amateur detective is very often a woman. Amateurs of both sexes follow professions and careers of every kind or enjoy retirement, and they exhibit a far greater diversity than previously seen in amateur detection. They continue to skirt or shatter the law, outwit the police, shield the innocent, save their own skins or sanity as well as those of others, and trip up or judge and execute the guilty in countless climes, professions, and contexts. Youth does not limit and age does not diminish their wit and sagacity. Some inhabit streets as mean as those of any private eye, and others work in conditions as crime-ridden and depressing as the veteran policeman or policewoman.

Works of mystery fiction in general appeal, succeed, and endure primarily because of character, interest and complexity of problem and solution, and narrative voice. For the amateur, another important element that supports success is the effective integration of interesting or esoteric information and insights, or lore. Many authors of amateur detective works write about their own experiences with people, places they live, how they grew up, and their careers, all of which contribute to the quality of their insights. Readers are attracted to the story or novel because of the opportunity to go behind the scenes in an occupation or profession, a new location, or a time in the past to see how things are done there. Amateur sleuths have more opportunities than their professional counterparts to embody as well as to interpret such lore for the reader.

Unfettered by police commissioners, the press, or imperious employers overseeing their detection, amateurs are freer in their approaches to solving mysteries. They more often exhibit exuberance in the form of a "joie de mystere" than the P.I. and police investigators, whose familiarity with the nature of crime and the insufficiency of the courts may lead to the angst typical of "noir" fiction, which focuses primarily on the dark and dangerous. Wit and humor are staples in amateur detective fiction, with slapstick and farce quite at home and downright silliness not unknown.

Amateurs move as insiders in circles other than those of the police and P.I.s. They are free to work on the mysteries that interest them rather than those they are assigned or hired to pursue, and they work out of their homes or the offices they use primarily for another purpose. Amateur detectives often have partners or friends who help with their investigations and some of these are police officers. Some of the partnerships turn into romance, leading to marriage after a few novels.

As amateur detectives number in the hundreds, this essay focuses on unlicensed investigators who appear in a series of at least three novels, one of which was published in 1990 or after. These limits necessarily leave on the sidelines some equally good writing in the form of earlier series, short stories, and non-series works by such authors as Robert Barnard, Caleb Carr, Mary Higgins Clark, Umberto Eco, Dick Francis, Carl Hiassen, P.D. James, Elmore Leonard, Ruth Rendell, Scott Turow, and Minette Walters. The series sleuth, unlike the detectives in non-series works, discovers an avocation in detecting and develops this talent over the course of more than one investigation. The last 20 years have seen the introduction of a bumper crop of amateur detectives with styles to meet readers' range of expectations.

Selected series detectives are showcased throughout this work, beginning with brief profiles of some who have a more singular profession, environment, or situation than is common—one that is somewhat outside the mainstream of more typical amateur detectives. Names of series sleuths are followed by the author's name in parenthesis.

Kate Shugak (Dana Stabenow) makes her debut in *A Cold Day for Murder* (1992), a novel awarded the Mystery Writers of America Edgar for best paperback original. Amateur detectives have often abandoned an earlier career in professional investigative work, and Kate is no exception, having had her throat cut while carrying out an assignment as an investigator for the D.A.'s office in Alaska, and having had to kill her assailant to save a child and escape. An Aleut homesteader, Kate frequently works with the police as a paid investigator, although she is not a licensed P.I. Her survival qualities of discipline and toughness aid in her investigative abilities. Undercover work and other special assignments call upon Kate's professional skills in a series of more than a dozen novels, and political issues and tribal concerns challenge her personally.

Anna Pigeon (Nevada Barr) makes a career change, becoming an employee in the National Park Service following the accidental death of her husband. She is a ranger with some training in law enforcement. Her confidante is her psychologist sister, Molly, to whom she maintains a telephone lifeline. Like so many detectives, Anna is a loner, and her love of her work and the natural habitats into which she goes on assignment in various national parks are her substitute for a more extensive society of her own. The first series novel, *The Track of the Cat* (1993), set in Texas in the Guadalupe Mountains National Park, where author Nevada Barr herself worked as a ranger, won Agatha and Anthony Awards as Best First Mystery Novel. Conditions in Anna's work are physical and dangerous, but she uses intelligence and observation as her primary means of solving mysteries. She is impeded by natural disasters, prejudice, and the limitations of her colleagues.

Stephanie Plum (Janet Evanovich) is a uniquely comic figure, set firmly in a blue-collar world. A female amateur detective as bounty hunter was bound to appear in time, but few would have expected it to be in Trenton, New Jersey. Enterprising and energetic, Stephanie is nevertheless an example of the comically inept investigator, combining characteristics of an updated Had-I-But-Known school of detection with a slightly submerged instinct for what she ought to be doing and what is going on. The result is a hilarious series of misadventures that leads to satisfactory results in each investigation with lots of laugh-out-loud comic moments and small personal triumphs and disasters along the way, beginning with *One for the Money* (1994). The series has garnered many awards and an enormous number of readers.

Jo Beth Sidden (Virginia Lanier) has the leading role in the series' slam-bang first novel, *Death in Bloodhound Red* (1995). The bloodhounds she breeds and trains are important characters in their own right as professionals, not pets. Jo Beth investigates both problems in her life and cases that arise when she leads her bloodhounds in searches to assist the police. She is no armchair detective, and being in harm's way trudging through the Okefenokee swamp seems her natural habitat as the novels continue.

Jenny Cain (Nancy Pickard) is the director of a charitable foundation, and her investigations grow out of professional and personal situations. In *Marriage is Murder* (1987), the fourth novel in the series, it appears that an epidemic of domestic violence has hit Port Frederick, Massachusetts, and Jennie's wedding plans are affected, as many of her acquaintances seem to be involved. *I.O.U.*

(1991) centers around Jennie's dysfunctional family and her investigation of her mother's past. Pickard received her second Agatha Best Novel award for this one, following one for *Bum Steer* (1990). *I.O.U.* also won the Macavity for Best Novel, as did *Marriage is Murder*.

In addition to these amateur detectives with more unusual lines of work, a larger number have relatively traditional professions. Amateur detectives of all kinds tend to possess a wider world as compared to that inhabited by police and the private eye. It is not so consistently dysfunctional. It is not so sordid, not so crime-ridden. In many series it is a world in which crime and violence are rare and clash to a greater extent with the rest of the milieu. There are more families, children, and pets. There is more of everyday society outside the work place, more social events of different kinds, often more food and drink. There may be more than one crime to a novel, but they are typically connected. Known, habitual criminals are less common. As the world is wider and brighter, so the detectives are less prone to broken lives and alcoholism, less prey to depression and fierce indignation at the failure of their world and its inhabitants and institutions to cope with the larger social problems. Titles are sometimes waggish and suggest the incongruity of slime and crime in the suburbs.

Examples of more traditionally occupied amateur detectives are noted by category in this section. Even within the same line of work, however, it can be seen that amateur detectives are remarkably varied, and that comedy and crime mix well.

Lawyer, barrister, and **solicitor** are long-familiar titles for amateur sleuths. Within these ranks, Rumpole of the Bailey (John Mortimer) works like Perry Mason (Erle Stanley Gardner's famous courtroom lawyer) to find the guilty party and free his client. Unlike Mason, he often uses technicalities to defend those known to be guilty. Rumpole has a cynical view of the legal system and of most of its participants including fellow barristers and judges, and he has a devastating wit and sharpness of repartee. In collections of stories beginning with *Rumpole of the Bailey* (1978), Rumpole defends such individuals as Jim Timson, the sixteen-year-old son in a large and industrious family of South London villains ("Rumpole and the Younger Generation"). Outside the courtroom he spends time sparring in his chambers with other lawyers such as Guthrie Featherstone, Q.C., and maintaining an uneasy truce with his wife, Hilda, She Who Must Be Obeyed.

An equally brilliant British legal mind is that of Hilary Tamar (Sarah Caudwell) who unites academic and legal perspectives to identify solutions to challenges facing London-based friends in legal practice. These friends share international adventures bordering on farce, and the literate and allusive novels create high comedy. The series started with *Thus Was Adonis Murdered* (1981), and the second novel, *The Sirens Sang of Murder* (1989), won the Anthony Award for Best Novel. The author does not use pronouns like "he" or "she" in reference to Hilary, and neither do any of the other characters in the novels. Consequently, the series poses a secondary mystery of its own for the reader. Is detective Hilary Tamar a man or a woman?

The much-honored series featuring lawyer-then-Judge Deborah Knott (Margaret Maron) begins with *Bootlegger's Daughter* (1992) and is effective in several dimensions. This includes analysis of the challenges of effecting justice within the constraints of the legal system and presenting contemporary Southern culture in its contradictory complexity through plots constructed around an active and reflective protagonist. Deborah is often at philosophical or practical odds with a large, multigenerational family and many of her neighbors. Her voice contributes to the appeal of the novels as does her use of topical issues in her plots.

Myron Bolitar (Harlan Coben) has a Harvard law degree but is a sports agent. Beginning with *Deal Breaker* (1995) he and his friend, Win Lockwood, sort out mysteries having to do with sporting events and sports figures who are Myron's clients. They tangle with opposing interests including organized crime and when caught in the middle are capable of serving as executioners as well as investigators. Myron's integrity and feelings play an important role in directing his actions, and there is an attractive naive quality to his character. The action is fast-paced, wisecracks are plentiful, and the novels are real page-turners. The first novel will remind the reader of Robert B. Parker's private eye, Spenser, with Win in the role of Hawk.

Other lawyers such as Stone Barrington (Stuart Woods) involve themselves directly in crime and solutions and deal with all kinds of institutional corruption and organized crime as well as the amateur criminal in such novels as *Dirt* (1996). The first novel in the Harry Devlin (Martin Edwards) series, *All the Lonely People* (1991), set in Liverpool, focuses on Harry, a solicitor whose estranged wife is killed with him as a suspect. The series reflects the city's character and past with novel titles taken from popular songs from the 1960s, such as *Suspicious Minds* (1992) and *The Devil in Disguise* (1998). Elsewhere in the U.K., Edinburgh solicitor Tam Buchanan (Joyce Holms) is propelled into amazing adventures for so staid a young man by his madcap associate, streetwise Fizz, in *Payment Deferred* (1996). Brady Coyne (William Tapply) serves the Boston elite whose problems interest him and takes every opportunity for other pursuits including fly-fishing. Lawyer Coyne moves through a variety of situations in a series beginning with *Death at Charity's Point* (1984) and continuing through many other novels such as *Past Tense* in 2001.

Journalists have an edge as amateur sleuths because their daily job involves researching facts and gathering information to establish an accurate picture of an event. They often have access to sources less available to ordinary citizens. In this category, an outstanding protagonist is Molly Cates, a fifty-something and thrice-divorced investigative reporter who deals with murder and other tragedies in the riveting and complex novels of Mary Willis Walker. She inhabits a world both recognizable and threatening. *Under the Beetle's Cellar* (1995) is a particularly disturbing novel. In it Molly is threatened both with death and the failure to solve the mystery in time to save the hostages. For those and other reasons, the series offers the reader the kind of experience that only great literary works can provide. In such novels, despite solution of the mystery and the death or neutralization of the killer, the community is both saddened and permanently diminished by the death of the heroic victims.

The glamorous Jemima Shore (Antonia Fraser), introduced in *Quiet as a Nun* (1977), is a London-based investigative television reporter whose active sleuthing often takes place in the glittering world of the celebrity. Britt Montero (Edna Buchanan) is a police-beat reporter whose investigations reflect the experience of the author in volatile Miami beginning with *Contents under Pressure* (1992). Across the Atlantic, Lindsay Gordon (Val McDermid) describes herself as a "cynical, socialist lesbian feminist journalist" in the first novel of the series, *Report for Murder* (1987). Gordon changes significantly over the course of the series, continuing to illuminate gay subculture and obstacles faced by lesbians while refining her investigative techniques and interacting with increasingly complex characters.

What's A Girl Gotta Do? (1994) is the hilariously funny debut of Robin Hudson (Sparkle Hayter), television journalist in Manhattan, who has planted her window box with poison ivy to dissuade burglars. Inventive incidents, usually of Robin's instigation, move the six novels through dizzying turns and very entertaining moments. Augustus Maltravers (Robert Richardson), English journalist and novelist, first appears in *The Latimer Mercy* (1985) set during a Cathedral festival. A celebrity actress who has taken part in a new play in the cathedral disappears, and bloody clues are left deliberately to challenge the police.

Chicago journalist Cat Marsala (Barbara D'Amato) embodies the energy and philosophy of the first generation of female hard-boiled detectives. The first series novel, *Hardball* (1992), begins with the person Cat intends to interview, the leader of an initiative to legalize drugs, being blown up while sitting alongside Cat at a cocktail party. Cat evades death three times in the first novel before she eliminates most suspects and then stumbles on the killer. Economically told, the Chicago-based novels continue to address larger issues and have an affinity with Sara Paretsky's V. I. Warshawski private eye novels. Tess Monaghan (Laura Lippman), a former journalist turned informal private eye, hits her stride in the third novel of the series, *Butchers Hill* (1998). Novels in the Baltimore-based series have received Edgar, Shamus, Agatha, Anthony, and Nero Wolfe Awards.

In a different vein, journalist Jim "Qwill" Qwilleran (Lilian Jackson Braun) has an unusual pair of sidekicks, the Siamese cats KoKo and Yum Yum. Qwilleran follows the tradition of the original amateurs in being sufficiently wealthy to pick interesting things to investigate. The series gained public attention beginning with *The Cat Who Saw Red* (1986) followed by many more including *The Cat Who Brought Down the House* (2003). These popular novels established the cat novel and remain favorites with readers of such works.

Doctors as amateur detectives have declined in number, but detectives whose focus is on humans or their remains continue to be popular series figures. It is the forensic pathologists and anthropologists (many of whom work in the criminal justice system) who are most common today, along with psychological profilers, doctors of philosophy in many cases.

Alex Delaware (Jonathan Kellerman) is a clinical psychologist who investigates by analysis of the interrelated relationships and motivations that provide the reasons for crime. His policeman colleague is a gay Los Angeles homicide detective, Milo Sturgis. These best-selling and award-winning novels, beginning with *When the Bough Breaks* (1985), are complex and compelling works of fiction that are designed to engage and challenge the reader. In Britain, Tony Hill (Val McDermid) is also a psychologist but his talent is for profiling. He appears in novels with detective chief inspector Carol Jordan, and they bring different approaches to the search for a serial killer in the award-winning first novel, *The Mermaids Singing* (1995). Hill has sufficient personal vulnerability to bring him into a direct confrontation with the killer and the skill as a psychologist to get himself out, barely alive. An ITV (U.K.) television series, with a second in production, is bringing the pair to wider audiences in Australia, the U.K., and the U.S.A. (BBC America).

The exceptionally popular Kay Scarpetta (Patricia Cornwell) is a professional pathologist and medical examiner for the state of Virginia. Still, like so many fellow professionals and amateurs, she goes beyond her professional responsibilities by moving outside the site of death and examinations of remains in her laboratory and goes into the field to pursue her own theories regarding her autopsy findings and her demons. Putting herself routinely in harm's way, working with or separate from the police, she becomes both a bold and a vulnerable figure. She increasingly reflects the angst of her time and profession from *Post Mortem* (1990), which won three major first novel awards, through the more recent novel, *Blow Fly* (2003).

Points of similarity exist between Scarpetta and "Tempe" (Temperance) Brennan (Kathy Reichs), a forensic anthropologist for the state of North Carolina whose first case is recorded in *Deja Dead* (1997). Brennan is seconded to Montreal for duty, and the culture of the city and province adds a significant dimension to these novels. Brennan has a daughter, while Scarpetta's most congenial relative is her niece, and Scarpetta's love life is decidedly more tragic.

Another forensic anthropologist, Gideon Oliver (Aaron Elkins), is in his second decade as an academic at the University of Washington. He earns the title of the "Skeleton Detective" from his analyses of remains both old and new. *Old Bones* (1987) won the Edgar Award for Best Novel. Oliver travels to conventions, reunions, and special assignments in England, France, Tahiti, and Mexico. Often with his wife, Julie, a park ranger whom he marries in an early adventure, he encounters mysteries, accidentally unearths bones, and discovers recent corpses. All of these doctor detectives focus on first unlocking the mysteries of the human body or the human brain in order to solve the classic mysteries of, why, how, and by whom murder was done.

Academic sleuths tend to exhibit the confidence and eccentricity associated traditionally with the Ivory Tower, but some see academic life as a kind of jungle. One more recent development is the numbers of women who are professors. Such characters as Professor Kate Fansler (Amanda Cross, pseudonym of Professor Carolyn Heilbrun) provide convincing feminist perspectives on crime and academia. *Death in a Tenured Position* (1981) represents an esteemed university as being guilty of egregious sexism, and Fansler's investigations of such academic matters as scholarship and sexual politics in the university are set against a background of pervasive institutional resistance to change, including equity for female faculty members.

Homer Kelly (Jane Langton) is a colorful academic figure, a former police detective and lawyer turned Harvard literature professor. From *The Transcendental Murder* (1964) through *The Deserter: Murder at Gettysburg* (2003), the novels are full and varied, including environmental issues, examination of the lives of literary figures, and lore on many topics. Similarly eccentric is Peter Shandy (Charlotte MacLeod), whose specialty is the rutabaga. *Rest You Merry* (1978), the first novel in the series, introduces the bucolic Balaclava Agricultural College and its assorted denizens and is one of the funniest of holiday mysteries.

Teacher Amanda Pepper (Gillian Roberts) picks up some of her savvy from her high school students' experiences with learning and emerging adulthood, and it is reflected in well-constructed plots, beginning with *I'd Rather Be in Philadelphia* (1988). Among many other notable series detectives in the academic world are Kate Ivory (Veronica Smallwood) as writer-in-residence in Oxford in *Oxford Mourning* (1995), Karen Pelletier (Joanne Dobson), English professor at a small prestigious Eastern college in *Cold and Pure and Very Dead* (2000), and Nick Hoffman (Lev Raphael), a Jewish and gay English professor at a university in Michigan in *Little Miss Evil* (2000).

There are also librarians and bookshop owners who connect to the academic world. In *Death on Demand* (1987), mystery bookshop owner Annie Darling (Carolyn G. Hart) becomes a suspect when a weekly gathering of famous authors ends with murder. Allusions to favorite books and authors season the mixture of romance and mystery in this series set in the fictional town of Broward's Rock, South Carolina. Claire Malloy (Joan Hess) is the divorced mother of an adolescent daughter, Caron, and operates a bookstore in Farberville, Arkansas, a university town. *A Diet to Die For* (1989) won the American Mystery Award. The important events and issues of adolescence and daily small-town life, conveyed with humor through Claire's voice, provide the material in these entertaining yet serious mysteries. Policeman Peter Rosen becomes a friend and rival or partner in investigations.

Religious detectives connect sin and crime, associate divine and human punishment, and bring a special eye for evil to their investigations. Father

Robert Koesler (William X. Kienzle), a Roman Catholic priest, solves crimes beginning with a somewhat different perspective, the shortcomings of his church. *The Rosary Murders* in 1979 is the first in a series of novels in which the priest not only provides the solution to the crime but identifies larger social issues and problems, including those directly related to the Catholic Church. Taking a more traditional approach, Sister Mary Helen (Carol Anne O'Marie) solves crimes in the context of changing convent life and the challenges of retirement starting with *A Novena for Murder* (1984) and continuing in several other novels. Rabbi David Small (Harry Kemelman) makes his first appearance in *Friday the Rabbi Slept Late* (1964). Through the last novel in 1996, *The Day the Rabbi Left Town*, he continues to apply the lessons of Jewish law and teachings to the solution of crime while the issues and politics of synagogue life provide an effective counterpoint. His colleague is the local chief of police.

Today, many religious sleuths, along with other types of amateur sleuths, appear in **period or historical novels**. An enduringly popular figure is the medieval Brother Cadfael (Ellis Peters) whose first novel, *A Morbid Taste for Bones* (1977) initiated a series both widely read and seen on television, with the last novel appearing in 1994. The Cadfael novels mix accurate history and religious perspective with romance and detection. The worldly yet cloistered Cadfael's approach to crime has created a great appetite among readers for period and historical mysteries. In this widening field, many eras are illuminated by investigators of assorted views and practices.

The energetic suffragette Nell Bray (Gillian Linscott), like Cadfael, has a calling, and it is reflected in pointed political satire in novels set in early twentieth-century England. Nell's spirited activism in pursuit first of the vote for women and then a seat in Parliament brings her into situations where she must solve mysteries to keep herself out of jail. *Absent Friends* (1999) received the Herodotus Award from the Historical Mystery Appreciation Society and the Crime Writers' Association Ellis Peters Historical Dagger Award.

Other series use actual historical figures as detectives, such as those featuring Jane Austen (Stephanie Barron), including *Jane and the Ghosts of Netley* (2003); Eleanor Roosevelt (Elliott Roosevelt) including *Murder in the Lincoln Bedroom* (2002); and Bertie, the Prince of Wales and future Edward VII (Peter Lovesey). Lovesey wrote three Bertie books, of which *Bertie and the Tinman* (1987) was the first. Bertie narrates the novels with a self-deprecating comic eye, reflecting his successes and weaknesses as prince and detective. The books appear true to the public image of the prince and touching in their depiction of his relationship with his mother, Queen Victoria.

Of special note among the period mysteries are the widely popular adventures of Amelia Peabody (Elizabeth Peters), British Victorian archaeologist. The series deliberately recalls the novels of H. Rider Haggard with significant updating of attitude and tone. Searching the sands for evidence of lost cultures, Amelia picks up a husband (fellow archaeologist Radcliffe Emerson) and bears a son, Ramses, while discovering hidden civilizations, solving ancient and present-day mysteries, and often narrowly escaping death. Amelia's combination of enthusiasm and common sense in response to one challenge after another keeps these novels moving at a fast and unpredictable pace as do the high spirited and witty exchanges among family members. *The Last Camel Died at Noon* (1991), *The Hippopotamus Pool* (1996), and *He Shall Thunder in the Sky* (2000) are representative novels in the series begun in 1975.

Other contemporary period or historical mysteries feature fictional characters from earlier eras as their protagonists. Arthur Conan Doyle's 1887 creation, Sherlock Holmes, for example, serves as the detective in many new mystery series. The best known is written by Laurie R. King, beginning with *The Beekeeper's Apprentice* (1994), which presents Holmes and his young American apprentice Mary Russell. Irene Adler, "the woman" from the original Holmes' story "A Scandal in Bohemia" (1891), has her own series, written by Carole Nelson Douglas, which examines the dark secrets of Victorian society beginning with *Good Night, Mr. Holmes* (1990).

Since the criminal is typically the adversary in detective fiction, when a lawbreaker becomes the detective, he or she is necessarily an amateur at detection. **Caper crime novels** focus on an anti-hero detective, a character who may break the law with impunity and stretch conventions of the form. In solving mysteries against the backdrop of their unsavory, criminal, or dramatically adventurous lives, the criminal detectives fit under the amateur umbrella and attract a special readership among those who do not agree with Arthur Conan Doyle that a criminal should never be the hero.

Among the characters in the caper novel, few are more appealing than Lovejoy (Jonathan Gash), who has achieved a wide and appreciative readership and television audience. Lovejoy's irreverent, self-deprecating, and confessional voice and his almost-religious enthusiasm for an antique bring the character colorfully and immediately to life. A "divvie" who knows an authentic antique on sight (bells ring), Lovejoy's sleuthing generally results from his pursuit of a treasure and his desire to thwart a scam directed at what he considers his spoils. Despite his ability to con and seduce, Lovejoy has a basic, indeed slovenly, lifestyle and lives for the challenge of adventure. Following *The Judas Pair* (1977), there are over 20 novels in the series.

Different in tone and style, but similarly irreverent are the "Fletch" (Irwin R. Fletcher) novels by Gregory McDonald, beginning with *Fletch* (1974). Undercover as a journalist and consorting with beach people, Fletch is commissioned for three million dollars to kill the man offering him the money. He manages to earn the three million without becoming a murderer and is brought back in a sequel. McDonald won back-to-back Edgar awards for his first and second Fletch novels and continued the series through *Fletch Reflected* (1994), one of two "son of Fletch" novels.

Fitzroy Maclean Angel (Mike Ripley) is a sometime professional musician who drives an unlicensed London cab and has a tendency to borrow what he needs from others without their permission. Such is the case in *Angels in Arms* (1991) when a friend, Werewolf, requires rescue from thugs holding him for ransom in Brittany. Going into battle with a monk, several hives of bees, and a six-foot-four musician (Lucinda), Angel and his band prevail in the struggle, with a few good moves by each participant.

Lovejoy, Fletch, and Angel exhibit unconventional behavior and commit the odd illegal act as the norm, but actor Philip Fletcher (Simon Shaw) takes criminality a step further. Completely amoral and very clever, he appears in a series of adventures and investigations characterized by dark and surreal humor and does not scruple to commit murders or solve a crime and then allow a murderer he has caught to go free in exchange for a step up in his career. The intrigues, jealousies, and rivalries of the theatre provide the perfect setting for these six novels, beginning in 1988 with *Murder Out of Tune* and concluding in 1997 with *Act of Darkness*. Simon Shaw and Mike Ripley have each won the British Crime Writers' Association Last Laugh Award twice.

Also on the lighter side of crime are the caper novels featuring professional thief John Dortmunder (Donald E. Westlake) whose ability to think crimes through accurately is exceeded only by his inability to carry them out successfully. Beginning in 1970 with *The Hot Rock*, Westlake continues to write the occasional novel about Dortmunder and his hapless associates all of which achieve a level of humor and entertainment that has resulted in several being made into films. Bernie Rhodenbarr (Lawrence Block) is a knowledgeable bookshop owner in Manhattan, but he is a professional burglar. The Burglar series began in 1977 with *Burglars Can't Be Choosers* and includes *The Burglar Who Dropped in on Elvis* (2000). These excellent comic tales reflect the style and craftsmanship of crime writer Lawrence Block, through the exploits of a gentlemanly criminal who solves mysteries to avoid his own being uncovered. Bernie is a romantic, too, as can be seen in *The Burglar Who Thought He Was Bogart* (1995).

Homemaker and home services detectives are growing in number despite a history of such novels, and their detectives, being taken lightly. Being overlooked can work to the detective's advantage when she is ignored as a source of danger by the criminal, but to her disadvantage when appealing to police to respect her conclusions. In a similar situation are the amateur detectives who are paid housekeepers or who provide services for which skills traditionally belonging to women are requisite. The domestic detective novel differs significantly from the P.I. and police novels. Jane Jeffry (Jill Churchill) is the widowed mother of three in a series of novels beginning with *Grime and Punishment* (1989), which won both Agatha and McCavity Awards for Best First Mystery Novel. Jane and her more organized neighbor, Shelley, stumble upon bodies and come up with clues and solutions in a very lighthearted and girlish approach to crime, with mild humor and little subtlety. However, in *A Quiche Before Dying* (1993) Jane puts the case for the importance of the homemaker to her date, Mel VanDyne (a detective): "Look here, Detective VanDyne, I know you're a big, macho cop. You think you've seen the real nitty gritty of life, and housewives are just dust-bunny-brains worrying about trivialities, but you've got it wrong. Any woman who's had to turn a baby upside down and smack it nearly senseless to dislodge a penny stuck in its throat knows as much of life and death as you do. . . . " (121).

Blanche White (Barbara Neely) made quite an impression in *Blanche on the Lam* (1992), which earned three Best First Mystery Novel awards. As an African-American domestic worker, Blanche occupies an even lower rung on the social ladder than the homemaker but has the advantage of being almost invisible to employers and their associates. Blanche is a strong and engaging character with a will of her own and excellent insight into what goes on around her in both her communities. Like so many amateur detectives, her impetus toward detection begins with self-preservation and continues because of her sense of injustice. Blanche appeals to the reader on the basis of her no-nonsense attitude and her strength of character combined with the inevitable vulnerability of her position.

Goldy Bear (Diane Mott Davidson), owner of Goldilocks Catering, works hard to make a living and support her son after an abusive marriage, eventually marrying policeman Tom Schulz. Her courage and energy are her greatest assets as she takes on the troubles of her friends in her investigations. Recipes of foods served in the novels are provided, and titles such as *The Last Suppers* (1994) and *The Main Corpse* (1996) suggest a typical humor. In a similar domestic series, Judith McMonigle (Mary Daheim) owns Hillside Manor Inn, a bed-and-breakfast house and also has one son and (eventually) a second husband who is a policeman. A typical but nontrivial domestic issue is remodeling the toolshed as a home for Judith's mother. Titles in this series include *Just Desserts* (1991), *Fowl Prey* (1991) and *Bantam of the Opera* (1993). In a different line of work, Abigail Timberlake (Tamar Myers) is divorced with two children, one in college and one who lives with his father and stepmother. Abby runs the Den of Antiquity store in Charlotte, North Carolina. In *Gilt by Association* (1996), a body is delivered inside an expensive French armoire, and Abby assists the police in an effort to get her shop reopened. Abby is a contrast to Jane Jeffry in her greater independence, humorous and satiric observations, and saltier language.

Senior sleuth John Putnam Thatcher (Emma Lathen) is Senior Vice President of the world's third largest bank. Consistent with the bank's movement into new ventures and geographic areas, Thatcher, a widower in his sixties, finds much to concern him in the operations of newly associated firms, and it is typically his assignment to remove problems. Colleagues at the bank serve Thatcher as a set of experts that would rival those of the police. In a sophisticated context, these novels are defined by the deadpan wit and droll humor consistent with Thatcher's accumulated experience and wise skepticism. The first novel in the long-running series was published in 1961. *Murder Against the Grain* (1967) won the Crime Writers' Association Gold Dagger for best novel, and the series ended with the publication of *A Shark Out of Water* in 1997.

Sheila Malory (Hazel Holt) is a middle-aged widow who usually investigates mysteries involving contemporary village life. However, she has a son at Oxford, and in *The Cruellest Month* (1991) she investigates crime at Oxford, her own past there, and a crime from the war years. Melita Pargeter (Simon Brett) is an active widow and her investigations reflect her curiosity and sense of justice. In her late sixties, she has energy, a talent for observation, a strong sense of logic, and a great appetite for life. Useful to her in her investigations are the special talents of the guardian-like employees of her late husband, a kingpin of crime beloved by colleagues. It is one of these men, in *Mrs. Pargeter's Package* (1990), who produces a new passport for her.

The Southern Sisters novels (Anne George) have much in common with the comic caper novel, despite the fact that sibling rivalry, rather than criminal intent, stimulates many of Mary Alice's actions and Patricia Anne's reactions. These very different sixty-something women, one a retired schoolteacher, the other wealthy and thrice-widowed, create non-stop action as they pry into, search out, and investigate strange happenings in their town. Their first outing in *Murder on a Girls' Night Out* (1996) won an Agatha award and was followed by seven other novels also set in the author's native Birmingham, Alabama. They include titles such as *Murder on a Bad Hair Day* (1996) and the final one in the series, *Murder Boogies With Elvis* (2001).

Another pair of opposites are Angela Benbow and Caledonia Wingate (Corinne Holt Sawyer) who live in Camden-sur Mer, near San Diego, an upscale retirement community where crime stalks the halls. In the first novel, *The J. Alfred Prufrock Murders* (1988), a fellow resident is found to be a blackmailer. By 1997, in *Murder Olé!*, the murder occurs on a trip to Mexico. Contrasting personalities allow the two women to explore different aspects of the crimes they encounter, and the novels maintain a light and humorous tone while treating the issues of life in a retirement home with sensitivity.

A retired professional, Henrietta O'Dwyer Collins (Carolyn G. Hart), was a journalist and Pulitzer Prize winner. She is repeatedly called upon by friends and by colleagues from her professional life as a journalist to help them unravel mysteries. She is an active and well-traveled investigator who lays traps for criminals and tricks them into revealing their guilt. From her first appearance in *Dead Man's Island* (1993) where she goes to the aid of a former colleague and lover, Henrie O addresses serious social issues as she solves crimes.

Clara Gamadge (Eleanor Boylan) is an active widow who investigates for friends by discerning the solution to the mystery and proving it by means of a counterplot against the villain as she does in Dublin in *Murder Machree* (1992). Clara first appears in a series of mysteries by Elizabeth Daly, Agatha Christie's favorite mystery writer, where, as the young wife of a noted amateur detective, Henry Gamadge, she is involved in many of his cases. After his death, she solves cases on her own in the series by Boylan. Clara has a significant other, Sadd, who is often present in the role of confidante and friend.

G. D. H. Pringle (Nancy Livingston), retired tax inspector, has an intrepid partner, Mavis Bignell, whom he met in her professional status as a nude model for an art class. She accompanies him in his travels and investigations. As the title of the sixth novel, *Mayhem in Parva* (1990), suggests, these novels do not take the classic crime novel with great seriousness. Active senior sleuths presage an expanded future for amateur detectives (and their readers), and the creation of active, self-sufficient, attractive, and effective senior sleuths of both sexes is a signal development in the tradition.

The amateur detective can be anyone from any place. In contemporary novels, readers can find pro-golfers, dog-sled racers, herb shop owners, horse trainers, hair-stylists, actors, book publishers, vampire-killers, and even vampires themselves serving as fighters against crime. Such detectives inhabit the small town and the big city, coming from professions of highest prominence to the most menial positions. For example, Jimmy Flannery (Robert Campbell) is a low-key blue-collar detective, a common man determined to do the right thing. *The Junkyard Dog* (1986) introduces him and his place in Chicago political life. Flannery is a sewer inspector, who takes his job seriously, and is good at it. He is a precinct captain for his party where he is equally hard working. He feels responsible for constituents and has a sense of humor and full awareness, in practical terms, of the ways of his world. The novel won Anthony and Edgar Awards for Best Paperback Original.

Books and stories featuring an amateur detective include and even merge disparate elements and conventions from the traditional and contrasting hard-boiled and "cozy" traditions. They draw on contemporary social movements and issues to broaden their scope and deepen the significance of their themes and plots. Tone, voice, and style vary as in other forms of fiction, but genre continues to dictate structure in broad terms. For the majority of works, the detective is a central figure, a complex and apparently insoluble problem is the focus, and a solution or resolution is achieved by the conclusion, at least for the reader. Apart from their vocations, amateur detectives are characterized or distinguished in terms of their philosophy and value systems, ethnicity, culture, race, class, life experiences, sex and sexual preference, or in terms of age. At their best, amateurs have a style, a manner, an M.O. (*modus operandi*), a milieu, or a voice or idiom that is distinctive and that firmly engages the reader. The greatest appeal of the amateur genre, perhaps, is that its readers would like to think that, given the right circumstances, they themselves could be amateur detectives.

Secondary Sources
Ashley, Mike, compiler. *The Mammoth Encyclopedia of Modern Crime Fiction*. London: Constable and Robinson Ltd., 2002.
Ball, John, ed. *The Mystery Story*. San Diego, California: University of California Extension, 1976.
Carr, John C. *The Craft of Crime: Conversations with Crime Writers*. Boston: Houghton Mifflin Company, 1983.

Duncan, Paul. *The Third Degree: Crime Writers in Conversation.* Harpenden, Hertfordshire, U.K.: No Exit Press, 1997.

Herbert, Rosemary, ed. *The Oxford Companion to Crime and Mystery Writing.* New York and London: Oxford University Press, 1999.

Husband, Janet G. and Jonathan F. *Sequels: An Annotated Guided to Novels in Series,* 3rd ed. Chicago and London: American Library Association, 1997.

Klein, Kathleen Gregory. *Great Women Mystery Writers: Classic to Contemporary.* Westport, Connecticut: Greenwood Press, 1994.

Pederson, Jay and Taryn Pfalzgraf, eds. *St. James Guide to Crime and Mystery Writers.* Detroit, Michigan: St. James Press, 1996.

Saricks, Joyce G. *The Readers' Advisory Guide to Genre Fiction.* Chicago and London: American Library Association, 2001.

STORIES

EDGAR ALLAN POE
1809–1849

The acknowledged "Father of the Detective Story," Edgar Allan Poe was born in Boston, Massachusetts. Orphaned at an early age, Poe was taken into the home of the wealthy merchant John Allan and his wife, and raised in Richmond, Virginia. He was educated in England in his early years, and later attended the University of Virginia and West Point. Poe is considered one of the most important figures in nineteenth century American literature and recognized as an outstanding poet, critic, editor, and author of incomparable psychological horror stories. His creation of the detective story or tale of "ratiocination," a term Poe devised, began with "The Murders in the Rue Morgue" (1841) and continued through three more tales: "The Mystery of Marie Rogêt," (1842–1843), "The Purloined Letter" (1844), and "Thou Art the Man" (1844). These four stories establish the basic principles of detective story technique still used today: the sensational thriller, the analytical and fictional treatment of real-life crime, the classic detective as secret agent, and a murder mystery solved by the narrator. To honor Poe as the inventor of the detective fiction genre, the Mystery Writers of America have created the Edgar, their most prestigious award, given for the best in mystery writing. Likewise, the lifetime achievement award for significant contributions to the mystery field is the Edgar Grand Master Award.

Poe's famous amateur detective is C. Auguste Dupin. Introduced in "The Murders in the Rue Morgue," Dupin is featured in three of Poe's four tales. He is eccentric, aristocratic, scholarly, and extremely cerebral. He dislikes the daylight, preferring to walk the streets of Paris at night seeking "mental excitement." He has little patience with humanity in general, and has a recognizable contempt for the methods of the police in particular. For Dupin, crime is an intellectual pursuit where he can demonstrate his superiority in inductive and deductive reasoning. His close friend, the anonymous narrator of the tales, is certainly Dupin's intellectual inferior and a great admirer of the detective's mental agility. Poe's "The Murders in the Rue Morgue" first appeared in the April 1841 issue of *Graham's Magazine*.

Recommended Poe works: "The Gold Bug," "The Mystery of Marie Rogêt," and "The Purloined Letter."

Other recommended authors: Wilkie Collins, Patricia Cornwell, Kathy Reichs.

The Murders in the Rue Morgue[1]

*What song the Syrens sang, or what name Achilles assumed
when he hid himself among women, although puzzling
questions, are not beyond all conjecture.*

Sir Thomas Browne.[2]

The mental features discoursed of as the analytical, are, in themselves, but lit-tle susceptible of analysis. We appreciate them only in their effects. We know of them, among other things, that they are always to their possessor, when inor-dinately possessed, a source of the liveliest enjoyment. As the strong man exults in his physical ability, delighting in such exercises as call his muscles into action, so glories the analyst in that moral activity which *disentangles*. He derives plea-sure from even the most trivial occupations bringing his talents into play. He is found of enigmas, of conundrums, of hieroglyphics; exhibiting in his solu-tions of each a degree of *acumen* which appears to the ordinary apprehension præternatural. His results, brought about by the very soul and essence of method, have, in truth, the whole air of intuition.

The faculty of re-solution is possibly much invigorated by mathematical study, and especially by that highest branch of it which, unjustly, and merely on account of its retrograde operations, has been called, as if *par excellence*, analy-sis. Yet to calculate is not in itself to analyze. A chess-player, for example, does the one without effort at the other. It follows that the game of chess, in its effects upon mental character, is greatly misunderstood. I am not now writing a treatise, but simply prefacing a somewhat peculiar narrative by observations very much at random; I will, therefore, take occasion to assert that the higher powers of the reflective intellect are more decidedly and more usefully tasked by the unostentatious game of draughts[3] than by all the elaborate frivolity of chess. In this latter, where the pieces have different and *bizarre* motions, with various and variable values, what is only complex is mistaken (a not unusual error) for what is profound. The *attention* is here called powerfully into play. If it flag for an instant, an oversight is committed, resulting in injury or defeat.

---

[1]The "Rue Morgue" doesn't seem to be a real place (Carlson 2). But for a discussion of the "Morque" (*Morgue*) of Paris and the *Quartier* in which it was located see "Posthumous Letters of Charles Edwards, Esq. No. IV" in *Blackwood's* (December 1824), pp. 669–70. To the best of anyone's knowledge, Poe had never been to France.

[2]Poe quotes *Hydriolaphia, or Urn-Burial*, a famous and beautifully written essay by Sir Thomas Browne (1605–82), English physician and essayist. Poe would have found many aspects of Browne's point of view sym-pathetic. The point of the quotation is that conjecture—in this story, inspired guesswork—can be helpful when pure logic fails. Browne's name was very much in the public mind when Poe's story was published, for in 1840 his coffin was opened and his skull stolen and sold. Poor Browne got his head back in 1922.

[3]Checkers.

The possible moves being not only manifold but involute, the chances of such oversights are multiplied; and in nine cases out of ten it is the more concentrative rather than the more acute player who conquers. In draughts, on the contrary, where the moves are *unique* and have but little variation, the probabilities of inadvertence are diminished, and the mere attention being left comparatively unemployed, what advantages are obtained by either party are obtained by superior *acumen*. To be less abstract—Let us suppose a game of draughts where the pieces are reduced to four kings, and where, of course, no oversight is to be expected. It is obvious that here the victory can be decided (the players being at all equal) only by some *recherché*[4] movement, the result of some strong exertion of the intellect. Deprived of ordinary resources, the analyst throws himself into the spirit of his opponent, identifies himself therewith, and not unfrequently sees thus, at a glance, the sole methods (sometimes indeed absurdly simple ones) by which he may seduce into error or hurry into miscalculation.

Whist has long been noted for its influence upon what is termed the calculating power; and men of the highest order of intellect have been known to take an apparently unaccountable delight in it, while eschewing chess as frivolous. Beyond doubt there is nothing of a similar nature so greatly tasking the faculty of analysis. The best chess-player in Christendom *may* be little more than the best player of chess; but proficiency in whist implies capacity for success in all these more important undertakings where mind struggles with mind. When I say proficiency, I mean that perfection in the game which includes a comprehension of *all* the sources whence legitimate advantage may be derived. These are not only manifold but multiform, and lie frequently among recesses of thought altogether inaccessible to the ordinary understanding. To observe attentively is to remember distinctly; and, so far, the concentrative chess-player will do very well at whist; while the rules of Hoyle[5] (themselves based upon the mere mechanism of the game) are sufficiently and generally comprehensible. Thus to have a retentive memory, and to proceed by "the book," are points commonly regarded as the sum total of good playing. But it is in matters beyond the limits of mere rule that the skill of the analyst is evinced. He makes, in silence, a host of observations and inferences. So, perhaps, do his companions; and the difference in the extent of the information obtained, lies not so much in the validity of the inference as in the quality of the observation. The necessary knowledge is that of *what* to observe. Our player confines himself not at all; nor, because the game is the object, does he reject deductions from things external to the game. He examines the countenance of his partner, comparing it carefully with that of each of his opponents. He considers the mode of assorting

---

[4]Rare, exquisite, choice.

[5]**whist:** A card game, an ancestor of the modern bridge. **Hoyle:** Sir Edmund Hoyle (1672–1769), who published in 1742 *Short Treatise on the Game of Whist* and later a number of books on other games.

the cards in each hand; often counting trump by trump, and honor by honor, through the glances bestowed by their holders upon each. He notes every variation of face as the play progresses, gathering a fund of thought from the differences in the expression of certainty, of surprise, of triumph, or chagrin. From the manner of gathering up a trick he judges whether the person taking it can make another in the suit. He recognizes what is played through feint, by the air with which it is thrown upon the table. A casual or inadvertent word; the accidental dropping or turning of a card, with the accompanying anxiety or carelessness in regard to its concealment; the counting of the tricks with the order of their arrangement; embarrassment, hesitation, eagerness or trepidation—all afford, to his apparently intuitive perception, indications of the true state of affairs. The first two or three rounds having been played, he is in full possession of the contents of each hand, and thenceforward puts down his cards with as absolute a precision of purpose as if the rest of the party had turned outward the faces of their own.

The analytical power should not be confounded with simple ingenuity; for while the analyst is necessarily ingenious, the ingenious man is often remarkably incapable of analysis. The constructive or combining power, by which ingenuity is usually manifested, and to which the phrenologists (I believe erroneously) have assigned a separate organ, supposing it a primitive faculty,[6] has been so frequently seen in those whose intellect bordered otherwise upon idiocy, as to have attracted general observation among writers on morals. Between ingenuity and the analytic ability there exists a difference far greater, indeed, than that between the fancy and the imagination, but of a character very strictly analogous. It will be found, in fact, that the ingenious are always fanciful, and the *truly* imaginative never otherwise than analytic.

The narrative which follows will appear to the reader somewhat in the light of a commentary upon the propositions just advanced.

Residing in Paris during the spring and part of the summer of 18—, I there became acquainted with a Monsieur C. Auguste Dupin.[7] This young gentleman was of an excellent—indeed of an illustrious family, but, by a variety of untoward events, had been reduced to such poverty that the energy of his character succumbed beneath it, and he ceased to bestir himself in the world, or to care

---

[6]It was not yet clear in Poe's day that phrenology, the science of studying personality through examination of the shape of the head, was a scientific dead end. Though the field rapidly fell into the hands of quacks, the pioneers in the area had been serious scientists. Phrenology, which adapted some of the concepts of "faculty psychology," assumed that each inherent power of the mind was located in a specific portion of one's head. It was hoped that once phrenologists were sure which "faculties" were basic, they could examine subjects' crania and produce what we would perhaps call personality or aptitude profiles. The concept is not in nature different from the assumptions of 20th-century work on the physiology of the brain.

[7]Poe seems to have borrowed the name Dupin from a character in some articles about the French Minister of Police, François Eugene Vidocq (1775–1857), which appeared in *Burton's Gentleman's Magazine* in 1838 (A. H. Quinn).

for the retrieval of his fortunes. By courtesy of his creditors, there still remained in his possession a small remnant of his patrimony; and, upon the income arising from this, he managed, by means of a rigorous economy, to procure the necessaries of life, without troubling himself about its superfluities. Books, indeed, were his sole luxuries, and in Paris these are easily obtained.

Our first meeting was at an obscure library in the Rue Montmartre, where the accident of our both being in search of the same very rare and very remarkable volume, brought us into closer communion. We saw each other again and again. I was deeply interested in the little family history which he detailed to me with all that candor which a Frenchman indulges whenever mere self is the theme. I was astonished, too, at the vast extent of his reading; and, above all, I felt my soul enkindled within me by the wild fervor, and the vivid freshness of his imagination. Seeking in Paris the objects I then sought, I felt that the society of such a man would be to me a treasure beyond price; and this feeling I frankly confided to him. It was at length arranged that we should live together during my stay in the city; and as my worldly circumstances were somewhat less embarrassed than his own, I was permitted to be at the expense of renting, and furnishing in a style which suited the rather fantastic gloom of our common temper, a time-eaten and grotesque mansion, long deserted through superstitions into which we did not inquire, and tottering to its fall in a retired and desolate portion of the Faubourg St. Germain.

Had the routine of our life at this place been known to the world, we should have been regarded as madmen—although, perhaps, as madmen of a harmless nature. Our seclusion was perfect. We admitted no visitors. Indeed the locality of our retirement had been carefully kept a secret from my own former associates; and it had been many years since Dupin had ceased to know or be known in Paris. We existed within ourselves alone.

It was a freak of fancy in my friend (for what else shall I call it?) to be enamored of the Night for her own sake; and into this *bizarrerie*, as into all his others, I quietly fell; giving myself up to his wild whims with a perfect *abandon*. The sable divinity would not herself dwell with us always; but we could counterfeit her presence. At the first dawn of the morning we closed all the massy shutters of our old building, lighting a couple of tapers which, strongly perfumed, threw out only the ghastliest and feeblest of rays. By the aid of these we then buried our souls in dreams—reading, writing, or conversing, until warned by the clock of the advent of the true Darkness. Then we sallied forth into the streets, arm in arm, continuing the topics of the day, or roaming far and wide until a late hour, seeking, amid the wild lights and shadows of the populous city, that infinity of mental excitement which quiet observation can afford.

At such times I could not help remarking and admiring (although from his rich ideality I had been prepared to expect it) a peculiar analytic ability in Dupin. He seemed, too, to take an eager delight in its exercise—if not exactly in its display—and did not hesitate to confess the pleasure thus derived. He boasted to me, with a low chuckling laugh, that most men, in respect to himself, wore windows in their bosoms, and was wont to follow up such assertions by direct and very startling proofs of his intimate knowledge of my own. His manner at these moments was frigid and abstract; his eyes were vacant in expression; while his voice, usually a rich tenor, rose into a treble which would have sounded petulantly but for the deliberateness and entire distinctness of the enunciation. Observing him in these moods, I often dwelt meditatively upon the old philosophy of the Bi-Part Soul, and amused myself with the fancy of a double Dupin—the creative and the resolvent.

Let it not be supposed, from what I have just said, that I am detailing any mystery, or penning any romance. What I have described in the Frenchman, was merely the result of an excited, or perhaps of a diseased intelligence.[8] But of the character of his remarks at the periods in question an example will best convey the idea.

We were strolling one night down a long dirty street, in the vicinity of the Palais Royal. Being both, apparently, occupied with thought, neither of us had spoken a syllable for fifteen minutes at least. All at once Dupin broke forth with these words:—

"He is a very little fellow, that's true, and would do better for the *Théâtre des Variétés*."

"There can be no doubt of that," I replied unwittingly, and not at first observing (so much had I been absorbed in reflection) the extraordinary manner in which the speaker had chimed in with my meditations. In an instant afterward I recollected myself, and my astonishment was profound.

"Dupin," said I, gravely, "this is beyond my comprehension. I do not hesitate to say that I am amazed, and can scarcely credit my senses. How was it possible you should know I was thinking of—?" Here I paused, to ascertain beyond a doubt whether he really knew of whom I thought.

—"of Chantilly," said he, "why do you pause? You were remarking to yourself that his diminutive figure unfitted him for tragedy."

This was precisely what had formed the subject of my reflections. Chantilly was a *quondam* cobbler of the Rue St. Denis, who, becoming stage-mad, had attempted the *rôle* of Xerxes, in Crébillon's tragedy so called, and been notoriously Pasquinaded for his pains.[9]

"Tell me, for Heaven's sake," I exclaimed, "the method—if method there is— by which you have been enabled to fathom my soul in this matter." In fact I was even more startled than I would have been willing to express.

---

[8]A hint that Dupin ultimately has more than analytical ability, that some "faculty" unnamed by the narrator (who, like Holmes's sidekick, Dr. Watson, never *really* understands his friend) is present.

[9]*quondam:* Former. **Crébillon:** Prosper Jolyot de Crébillon (1674–1762), French dramatist who wrote a number of plays on classical subjects. The narrator is amused by the thought of the cobbler playing a heroic character based on Xerxes the Great (c.519–c.465 B.C.E.), Persian king whom the Greeks defeated at Salamis in 480 B.C.E. **Pasquinaded:** Ridiculed or lampooned.

"It was the fruiterer," replied my friend, "who brought you to the conclu-sion that the mender of soles was not of sufficient height for Xerxes *et id genus omne.*"[10]

"The fruiterer!—you astonish me—I know no fruiterer whomsoever."

"The man who ran up against you as we entered the street—it may have been fifteen minutes ago."

I now remember that, in fact, a fruiterer, carrying upon his head a large bas-ket of apples, had nearly thrown me down, by accident, as we passed from the Rue C— into the thoroughfare where we stood; but what this had to do with Chantilly I could not possibly understand.

There was not a particle of *charlatanerie* about Dupin. "I will explain," he said, "and that you may comprehend all clearly, we will first retrace the course of your meditations, from the moment in which I spoke to you until that of the *rencontre* with the fruiterer in question. The larger links of the chain run thus—Chantilly, Orion, Dr. Nichol, Epicurus, Stereotomy, the street stones, the fruiterer."

There are few persons who have not, at some period of their lives, amused themselves in retracing the steps by which particular conclusions of their own minds have been attained. The occupation is often full of interest; and he who attempts it for the first time is astonished by the apparently illimitable distance and incoherence between the starting-point and the goal. What, then, must have been my amazement when I heard the Frenchman speak what he had just spoken, and when I could not help acknowledging that he had spoken the truth. He continued:

"We had been talking of horses, if I remember aright, just before leaving the Rue C—. This was the last subject we discussed. As we crossed into this street, a fruiterer, with a large basket upon his head, brushing quickly past us, thrust you upon a pile of paving-stones collected at a spot where the causeway is undergoing repair. You stepped upon one of the loose fragments, slipped, slightly strained your ankle, appeared vexed or sulky, muttered a few words, turned to look at the pile, and then proceeded in silence. I was not particularly attentive to what you did; but observation has become with me, of late, a species of necessity.

"You kept your eyes upon the ground—glancing, with a petulant expression, at the holes and ruts in the pavement, (so that I saw you were still thinking of the stones,) until we reached the little alley called Lamartine, which has been paved, by way of experiment, with the overlapping and riveted blocks. Here your countenance brightened up, and, perceiving your lips move, I could not doubt that you murmured the word 'stereotomy,' a term very affectedly applied to this species of pavement. I knew that you could not say to yourself 'stereotomy' with-out being brought to think of atomies, and thus the theories of Epicurus; and

---

[10]And all of that sort.

since, when we discussed this subject not very long ago, I mentioned to you how singularly, yet with how little notice, the vague guesses of that noble Greek had met with confirmation in the late nebular cosmogony, I felt that you could not avoid casting your eyes upward to the great *nebula* in Orion, and I certainly expected that you would do so. You did look up; and I was now assured that I had correctly followed your steps. But in that bitter *tirade* upon Chantilly, which appeared in yesterday's 'Musée,' the satirist, making some disgraceful allusions to the cobbler's change of name upon assuming the buskin, quoted a Latin line about which we have often conversed. I mean the line

Perdidit antiquum litera prima sonum.

I had told you that this was in reference to Orion, formerly written Urion; and, from certain pungencies connected with this explanation, I was aware that you could not have forgotten it. It was clear, therefore, that you would not fail to combine the two ideas of Orion and Chantilly.[11] That you did combine them I saw by the character of the smile which passed over your lips. You thought of the poor cobbler's immolation. So far, you had been stooping in your gait; but now I saw you draw yourself up to your full height. I was then sure that you reflected upon the diminutive figure of Chantilly. At this point I interrupted your meditations to remark that as, in fact, he *was* a very little fellow—that Chantilly—he would do better at the *Théâtre des Variétés*."

Not long after this, we were looking over an evening edition of the "Gazette des Tribunaux," when the following paragraphs arrested our attention.

"EXTRAORDINARY MURDERS.—This morning, about three o'clock, the inhabitants of the Quartier St. Roch were aroused from sleep by a succession of terrific shrieks, issuing, apparently, from the fourth story of a house in the Rue Morgue, known to be in the sole occupancy of one Madame L'Espanaye, and her daughter, Mademoiselle Camille L'Espanaye. After some delay, occasioned by a fruitless attempt to procure admission in the usual manner, the gateway was broken in with a crowbar, and eight or ten of the neighbors entered, accompanied by two *gendarmes*. By this time the cries had ceased; but, as the

---

[11]**stereotomy:** The art of cutting solids, especially stones, as in masonry or, here, paving. **Epicurus (341–270 B.C.E.):** Greek philosopher who did, in fact, follow Democritus in the matter of atomism. **nebular cosmogony:** Probably a reference to Charles de Laplace's 1796 postulation of "a cosmogony of the solar system with the planets developing from rings abandoned by a rotating, contracting nebula." Poe knew of Laplace's work; interestingly, American scientific writers in Poe's day often did not. His source is likely John P. Nichol, *Views of the Architecture of the Heavens in a Series of Letters to a Lady* (1837) which Mabbott (9, II) says Poe liked. Dupin mentions Nichol three paragraphs above; Poe does not repeat the reference here, but without it, a link is missing in Dupin's chain of associations. **buskin:** A type of boot associated with actors in tragedies. **Perdidit . . . sonum:** May be translated, "The first letter has lost its ancient sound." **Chantilly:** The cobbler's change of name on becoming an actor and the change in spelling suggest other changes and associations: cobbler—hobbler (bad actor); Orion, a giant and a great hunter in Greek mythology and the diminutive Chantilly; and, possibly, an association in Poe's mind between cobblestone and a cobbler which could be the origin of the whole business.

party rushed up the first flight of stairs, two or more rough voices, in angry contention, were distinguished, and seemed to proceed from the upper part of the house. As the second landing was reached, these sounds, also, had ceased, and everything remained perfectly quiet. The party spread themselves, and hurried from room to room. Upon arriving at a large back chamber in the fourth story, (the door of which, being found locked, with the key inside, was forced open,) a spectacle presented itself which struck every one present not less with horror than with astonishment.

"The apartment was in the wildest disorder—the furniture broken and thrown about in all directions. There was only one bedstead; and from this the bed had been removed, and thrown into the middle of the floor. On a chair lay a razor, besmeared with blood. On the hearth were two or three long and thick tresses of gray human hair, also dabbled in blood, and seeming to have been pulled out by the roots. Upon the floor were found four Napoleons, an ear-ring of topaz, three large silver spoons, three smaller of *métal d'Alger*,[12] and two bags, containing nearly four thousand francs in gold. The drawers of a *bureau*, which stood in one corner, were open, and had been, apparently, rifled, although many articles still remained in them. A small iron safe was discovered under the *bed* (not under the bedstead). It was open, with the key still in the door. It had no contents beyond a few old letters, and other papers of little consequence.

"Of Madame L'Espanaye no traces were here seen; but an unusual quantity of soot being observed in the fire-place, a search was made in the chimney, and (horrible to relate!) the corpse of the daughter, head downward, was dragged therefrom; it having been forced up the narrow aperture for a considerable distance. The body was quite warm. Upon examining it, many excoriations were perceived, no doubt occasioned by the violence with which it had been thrust up and disengaged. Upon the face were many severe scratches, and, upon the throat, dark bruises, and deep indentations of finger nails, as if the deceased had been throttled to death.

"After a thorough investigation of every portion of the house, without further discovery, the party made its way into a small paved yard in the rear of the building, where lay the corpse of the old lady, with her throat so entirely cut that, upon an attempt to raise her, the head fell off. The body, as well as the head, was fearfully mutilated—the former so much so as scarcely to retain any semblance of humanity.

"To this horrible mystery there is not as yet, we believe, the slightest clew."

The next day's paper had these additional particulars.

"*The Tragedy in the Rue Morgue.* Many individuals have been examined in relation to this most extraordinary and frightful affair." [The word '*affaire*' has not yet, in France, that levity of import which it conveys with us,] "but nothing

---

[12]*Métal d'Alger* or Metal of Algiers is a combination of pewter, lead, and antimony.

whatever has transpired to throw light upon it. We give below all the material testimony elicited.

"*Pauline Dubourg*, laundress, deposes that she has known both the deceased for three years, having washed for them during that period. The old lady and her daughter seemed on good terms—very affectionate towards each other. They were excellent pay. Could not speak in regard to their mode or means of living. Believed that Madame L. told fortunes for a living. Was reputed to have money put by. Never met any persons in the house when she called for the clothes or took them home. Was sure that they had no servant in employ. There appeared to be no furniture in any part of the building except in the fourth story.

"*Pierre Moreau*, tobacconist, deposes that he has been in the habit of selling small quantities of tobacco and snuff to Madame L'Espanaye for nearly four years. Was born in the neighborhood, and has always resided there. The deceased and her daughter had occupied the house in which the corpes were found, for more than six years. It was formerly occupied by a jeweller, who under-let the upper rooms to various persons. The house was the property of Madame L. She became dissatisfied with the abuse of the premises by her tenant, and moved into them herself, refusing to let any portion. The old lady was childish. Witness had seen the daughter some five or six times during the six years. The two lived an exceedingly retired life—were reputed to have money. Had heard it said among the neighbors that Madame L. told fortunes—did not believe it. Had never seen any person enter the door except the old lady and her daughter, a porter once or twice, and a physician some eight or ten times.

"Many other persons, neighbors, gave evidence to the same effect. No one was spoken of as frequenting the house. It was not known whether there were any living connexions of Madame L. and her daughter. The shutters of the front windows were seldom opened. Those in the rear were always closed, with the exception of the large back room, fourth story. The house was a good house—not very old.

"*Isidore Musét, gendarme*, deposes that he was called to the house about three o'clock in the morning, and found some twenty or thirty persons at the gateway, endeavoring to gain admittance. Forced it open, at length, with a bayonet—not with a crowbar. Had but little difficulty in getting it open, on account of its being a double or folding gate, and bolted neither at bottom nor top. The shrieks were continued until the gate was forced—and then suddenly ceased. They seemed to be screams of some person (or persons) in great agony—were loud and drawn out, not short and quick. Witness led the way up stairs. Upon reaching the first landing, heard two voices in loud and angry contention—the one a gruff voice, the other much shriller—a very strange voice. Could distinguish some words of the former, which was that of a Frenchman. Was positive that it was not a woman's voice. Could distinguish the words 'sacré' and 'diable.' The shrill voice was that of a foreigner. Could not be sure whether it was the voice of a man or of a woman. Could not make out what was said, but believed the language to be Spanish. The state of the room and of the bodies was described by this witness as we described them yesterday.

"*Henri Duval*, a neighbor, and by trade a silversmith, deposes that he was one of the party who first entered the house. Corroborates the testimony of Musèt in general. As soon as they forced an entrance, they reclosed the door, to keep out the crowd, which collected very fast, notwithstanding the lateness of the hour. The shrill voice, the witness thinks, was that of an Italian. Was certain it was not French. Could not be sure that it was a man's voice. It might have been a woman's. Was not acquainted with the Italian language. Could not distinguish the words, but was convinced by the intonation that the speaker was an Italian. Knew Madame L. and her daughter. Had conversed with both frequently. Was sure that the shrill voice was not that of either of the deceased.

"—*Odenheimer, restaurateur*. This witness volunteered his testimony. Not speaking French, was examined through an interpreter. Is a native of Amsterdam. Was passing the house at the time of the shrieks. They lasted for several minutes—probably ten. They were long and loud—very awful and distressing. Was one of those who entered the building. Corroborated the previous evidence in every respect but one. Was sure that the shrill voice was that of a man—of a Frenchman. Could not distinguish the words uttered. They were loud and quick—unequal—spoken apparently in fear as well as in anger. The voice was harsh—not so much shrill as harsh. Could not call it a shrill voice. The gruff voice said repeatedly '*sacré*,' '*diable*' and once '*mon Dieu*.'[13]

"*Jules Mignaud*, banker, of the firm of Mignaud et Fils, Rue Deloraine. Is the elder Mignaud. Madame L'Espanaye had some property. Had opened an account with his banking house in the spring of the year—(eight years previously). Made frequent deposits in small sums. Had checked for nothing until the third day before her death, when she took out in person the sum of 4000 francs. This sum was paid in gold, and a clerk sent home with the money.

"*Adolphe Le Bon*, clerk to Mignaud et Fils, deposes that on the day in question, about noon, he accompanied Madame L'Espanaye to her residence with the 4000 francs, put up in two bags. Upon the door being opened, Mademoiselle L. appeared and took from his hands one of the bags, while the old lady relieved him' of the other. He then bowed and departed. Did not see any person in the street at the time. It is a bye-street—very lonely.

"*William Bird*, tailor, deposes that he was one of the party who entered the house. Is an Englishman. Has lived in Paris two years. Was one of the first to ascend the stairs. Heard the voices in contention. The gruff voice was that of a Frenchman. Could make out several words, but cannot now remember all. Heard distinctly '*sacré*' and '*mon Dieu*.' There was a sound at the moment as if of several persons struggling—a scraping and scuffling sound. The shrill voice

---

[13]Literally, "holy," "devil," and "my God." Poe intends for the reader to understand that the witnesses heard fragments of French expletives.

was very loud—louder than the gruff one. Is sure that it was not the voice of an Englishman. Appeared to be that of a German. Might have been a woman's voice. Does not understand German.

"Four of the above-named witnesses, being recalled, deposed that the door of the chamber in which was found the body of Mademoiselle L. was locked on the inside when the party reached it. Every thing was perfectly silent—no groans or noises of any kind. Upon forcing the door no person was seen. The windows, both of the back and front room, were down and firmly fastened from within. A door between the two rooms was closed, but not locked. The door leading from the front room into the passage was locked, with the key on the inside. A small room in the front of the house, on the fourth story, at the head of the passage, was open, the door being ajar. This room was crowded with old beds, boxes, and so forth. These were carefully removed and searched. There was not an inch of any portion of the house which was not carefully searched. Sweeps were sent up and down the chimneys. The house was a four story one, with garrets (*mansardes*). A trap-door on the roof was nailed very securely—did not appear to have been opened for years. The time elapsing between the hearing of the voices in contention and the breaking open of the room door, was variously stated by the witnesses. Some made it as short as three minutes—some as long as five. The door was opened with difficulty.

"*Alfonzo Garcio*, undertaker, deposes that he resides in the Rue Morgue. Is a native of Spain. Was one of the party who entered the house. Did not proceed up stairs. Is nervous, and was apprehensive of the consequences of agitation. Heard the voices in contention. The gruff voice was that of a Frenchman. Could not distinguish what was said. The shrill voice was that of an Englishman—is sure of this. Does not understand the English language, but judges by the intonation.

"*Alberto Montani*, confectioner, deposes that he was among the first to ascend the stairs. Heard the voices in question. The gruff voice was that of a Frenchman. Distinguished several words. The speaker appeared to be expostulating. Could not make out the words of the shrill voice. Spoke quick and unevenly. Thinks it the voice of a Russian. Corroborates the general testimony. Is an Italian. Never conversed with a native of Russia.

"Several witnesses, recalled, here testified that the chimneys of all the rooms on the fourth story were too narrow to admit the passage of a human being. By 'sweeps' were meant cylindrical sweeping-brushes, such as are employed by those who clean chimneys. These brushes were passed up and down every flue in the house. There is no back passage by which any one could have descended while the party proceeded up stairs. The body of Mademoiselle L'Espanaye was so firmly wedged in the chimney that it could not be got down until four or five of the party united their strength.

"*Paul Dumas*, physician, deposes that he was called to view the bodies about day-break. They were both then lying on the sacking of the bedstead in the chamber where Mademoiselle L. was found. The corpse of the young lady was much bruised and excoriated. The fact that it had been thrust up the chimney would sufficiently account for these appearances. The throat was greatly chafed. There were several deep scratches just below the chin, together with a series of livid spots which were evidently the impression of fingers. The face was fearfully discolored, and the eye-balls protruded. The tongue had been partially bitten through. A large bruise was discovered upon the pit of the stomach, produced, apparently, by the pressure of a knee. In the opinion of M. Dumas, Mademoiselle L'Espanaye had been throttled to death by some person or persons unknown. The corpse of the mother was horribly mutilated. All the bones of the right leg and arm were more or less shattered. The left *tibia*[14] much splintered, as well as all the ribs of the left side. Whole body dreadfully bruised and discolored. It was not possible to say how the injuries had been inflicted. A heavy club of wood, or a broad bar of iron—a chair—any large, heavy, and obtuse weapon would have produced such results, if wielded by the hands of a very powerful man. No woman could have inflicted the blows with any weapon. The head of the deceased, when seen by the witness, was entirely separated from the body, and was also greatly shattered. The throat had evidently been cut with some very sharp instrument—probably with a razor.

"*Alexandre Etienne*, surgeon, was called with M. Dumas to view the bodies. Corroborated the testimony, and the opinion of M. Dumas.

"Nothing further of importance was elicited, although several other persons were examined. A murder so mysterious, and so perplexing in all its particulars, was never before committed in Paris—if indeed a murder has been committed at all. The police are entirely at fault—an unusual occurrence in affairs of this nature. There is not, however, the shadow of a clew apparent."

The evening edition of the paper stated that the greatest excitement still continued in the Quartier St. Roch—that the premises in question had been carefully re-searched, and fresh examinations of witnesses instituted, but all to no purpose. A postscript, however, mentioned that Adolphe Le Bon had been arrested and imprisoned—although nothing appeared to criminate him, beyond the facts already detailed.

Dupin seemed singularly interested in the progress of this affair—at least so I judged from his manner, for he made no comments. It was only after the announcement that Le Bon had been imprisoned, that he asked me my opinion respecting the murders.

I could merely agree with all Paris in considering them an insoluble mystery. I saw no means by which it would be possible to trace the murderer.

"We must not judge of the means," said Dupin, "by this shell of an examination. The Parisian police, so much extolled for *acumen*, are cunning, but no more. There is no method in their proceedings, beyond the method of the

---

[14]Shin bone.

moment. They make a vast parade of measures; but, not unfrequently, these are so ill adapted to the objects proposed, as to put us in the mind of Monsieur Jourdain's calling for his *robe-de-chambre—pour mieux entendre la musique*.[15] The results attained by them are not unfrequently surprising, but, for the most part, are brought about by simple diligence and activity. When these qualities are unavailing, their schemes fail. Vidocq, for example, was a good guesser, and a persevering man. But, without educated thought, he erred continually by the very intensity of his investigations. He impaired his vision by holding the object too close. He might see, perhaps, one or two points with unusual clearness, but in so doing he, necessarily, lost sight of the matter as a whole. Thus there is such a thing as being too profound. Truth is not always in a well.[16] In fact, as regards the more important knowledge, I do believe that she is invariably superficial. The truth lies not in the valleys where we seek her, but upon the mountain-tops where she is found. The modes and sources of this kind of error are well typified in the contemplation of the heavenly bodies. To look at a star by glances—to view it in a side-long way, by turning toward it the exterior portions of the *retina* (more susceptible of feeble impressions of light than the interior), is to behold the star distinctly—is to have the best appreciation of its lustre—a lustre which grows dim just in proportion as we turn our vision *fully* upon it. A greater number of rays actually fall upon the eye in the latter case, but, in the former, there is the more refined capacity for comprehension. By undue profundity we perplex and enfeeble thought; and it is possible to make even Venus herself vanish from the firmament by a scrutiny too sustained, too concentrated, or too direct.

"As for these murders, let us enter into some examinations for ourselves, before we make up an opinion respecting them. An inquiry will afford us amusement," [I thought this an odd term, so applied, but said nothing] "and, besides, Le Bon once rendered me a service for which I am not ungrateful. We will go and see the premises with our own eyes. I know G—, the Prefect of Police, and shall have no difficulty in obtaining the necessary permission."

The permission was obtained, and we proceeded at once to the Rue Morgue. This is one of those miserable thoroughfares which intervene between the Rue Richelieu and the Rue St. Roch. It was late in the afternoon when we reached it; as this quarter is at a great distance from that in which we resided. The house was readily found; for there were still many persons gazing up at the closed shutters, with an objectless curiosity, from the opposite side of the way. It was an ordinary Parisian house, with a gateway, on one side of which was a

---

[15]A "*robe-de-chambre*" is a dressing gown. The joke, however, turns on the word "*chambre*," chamber. In Molière's *Le Bourgeois Gentilhomme*, the nouveau riche M. Jourdain, in order to listen to chamber music better, wants his "chamber robe." He says to his servants, "*Donnez-moi ma robe pour mieux entendre. . . .*" Poe completed the sentence by adding the words "*la musique.*"

[16]**Vidocq:** See note 7. Contemporary accounts of Vidocq do not suggest that he was notable for the qualities Poe assigns to him.

glazed watch-box, with a sliding panel in the window, indicating a *loge de concierge*.[17] Before going in we walked up the street, turned down an alley, and then, again turning, passed in the rear of the building—Dupin, meanwhile, examining the whole neighborhood, as well as the house, with a minuteness of attention for which I could see no possible object.

Retracing our steps, we came again to the front of the dwelling, rang, and, having shown our credentials, were admitted by the agents in charge. We went up stairs—into the chamber where the body of Mademoiselle L'Espanaye had been found, and where both the deceased still lay. The disorders of the room had, as usual, been suffered to exist. I saw nothing beyond what had been stated in the "Gazette des Tribunaux." Dupin scrutinized every thing—not excepting the bodies of the victims. We then went into the other rooms, and into the yard; a *gendarme* accompanying us throughout. The examination occupied us until dark, when we took our departure. On our way home my companion stopped in for a moment at the office of one of the daily papers.

I have said that the whims of my friend were manifold, and that *Je les ménageais*.[18]—for this phrase there is no English equivalent. It was his humor, now, to decline all conversation on the subject of the murder, until about noon the next day. He then asked me, suddenly, if I had observed any thing *peculiar* at the scene of the atrocity.

There was something in his manner of emphasizing the word "peculiar," which caused me to shudder, without knowing why.

"No, nothing *peculiar*," I said; "nothing more, at least, than we both saw stated in the paper."

"The 'Gazette,'" he replied, "has not entered, I fear, into the unusual horror of the thing. But dismiss the idle opinions of this print. It appears to me that this mystery is considered insoluble, for the very reason which should cause it to be regarded as easy of solution—I mean for the *outré*[19] character of its features. The police are confounded by the seeming absence of motive—not for the murder itself—but for the atrocity of the murder. They are puzzled, too, by the seeming impossibility of reconciling the voices heard in contention, with the facts that no one was discovered up stairs but the assassinated Mademoiselle L'Espanaye, and that there were no means of egress without the notice of the party ascending. The wild disorder of the room; the corpse thrust, with the head downward, up the chimney; the frightful mutilation of the body of the old lady; these considerations, with those just mentioned, and others which I need not mention, have sufficed to paralyze the powers, by putting completely at fault the boasted *acumen*, of the government agents. They have fallen into the

---

[17]A doorkeeper's apartment.
[18]I handled them tactfully.
[19]Strange, odd.

gross but common error of confounding the unusual with the abstruse. But it is by these deviations from the plane of the ordinary, that reason feels its way, if at all, in its search for the true. In investigations such as we are now pursuing, it should not be so much asked 'what has occurred,' as 'what has occurred that has never occurred before.' In fact, the facility with which I shall arrive, or have arrived, at the solution of this mystery, is in the direct ratio of its apparent insolubility in the eyes of the police."

I stared at the speaker in mute astonishment.

"I am now awaiting," continued he, looking toward the door of our apartment—"I am now awaiting a person who, although perhaps not the perpetrator of these butcheries, must have been in some measure implicated in their perpetration. Of the worst portion of the crimes committed, it is probable that he is innocent. I hope that I am right in this supposition; for upon it I build my expectation of reading the entire riddle. I look for the man here—in this room—every moment. It is true that he may not arrive; but the probability is that he will. Should he come, it will be necessary to detain him. Here are pistols; and we both know how to use them when occasion demands their use."

I took the pistols, scarcely knowing what I did, or believing what I heard, while Dupin went on, very much as if in a soliloquy. I have already spoken of his abstract manner at such times. His discourse was addressed to myself; but his voice, although by no means loud, had that intonation which is commonly employed in speaking to some one at a great distance. His eyes, vacant in expression, regarded only the wall.

"That the voices heard in contention," he said, "by the party upon the stairs, were not the voices of the women themselves, was fully proved by the evidence. This relieves us of all doubt upon the question whether the old lady could have first destroyed the daughter, and afterward have committed suicide. I speak of this point chiefly for the sake of method; for the strength of Madame L'Espanaye would have been utterly unequal to the task of thrusting her daughter's corpse up the chimney as it was found; and the nature of the wounds upon her own person entirely preclude the idea of self-destruction. Murder, then, has been committed by some third party; and the voices of this third party were those heard in contention. Let me now advert—not to the whole testimony respecting these voices—but to what was *peculiar* in that testimony. Did you observe anything peculiar about it?"

I remarked that, while all witnesses agreed in supposing the gruff voice to be that of a Frenchman, there was much disagreement in regard to the shrill, or, as one individual termed it, the harsh voice.

"That was the evidence itself," said Dupin, "but it was not the peculiarity of the evidence. You have observed nothing distinctive. Yet there *was* something to be observed. The witnesses, as you remark, agreed about the gruff voice; they were here unanimous. But in regard to the shrill voice, the peculiarity is—not that they disagreed—but that, while an Italian, an Englishman, a Spaniard, a

Hollander, and a Frenchman attempted to describe it, each one spoke of it as that *of a foreigner*. Each is sure that it was not the voice of one of his own countrymen. Each likens it—not to the voice of an individual of any nation with whose language he is conversant—but the converse. The Frenchman supposes it the voice of a Spaniard, and 'might have distinguished some words *had he been acquainted with the Spanish.*' The Dutchman maintains it to have been that of a Frenchman; but we find it stated that '*not understanding French this witness was examined through an interpreter.*' The Englishman thinks it the voice of a German, and '*does not understand German.*' The Spaniard 'is sure' that it was that of an Englishman, but 'judges by the intonation' altogether, '*as he has no knowledge of the English.*' The Italian believes it the voice of a Russian, but '*has never conversed with a native of Russia.*' A second Frenchman differs, moreover, with the first, and is positive that the voice was that of an Italian; but, *not being cognizant of that tongue*, is, like the Spaniard, 'convinced by the intonation.' Now, how strangely unusual must that voice have really been, about which such testimony as this *could* have been elicited!—in whose *tones*, even, denizens of the five great divisions of Europe could recognise nothing familiar! You will say that it might have been the voice of an Asiatic—of an African. Neither Asiatics nor Africans abound in Paris; but, without denying the inference, I will now merely call your attention to three points. The voice is termed by one witness 'harsh rather than shrill.' It is represented by two others to have been 'quick and unequal.' No words—no sounds resembling words—were by any witness mentioned as distinguishable.

"I know not," continued Dupin, "what impression I may have made, so far, upon your own understanding; but I do not hesitate to say that legitimate deductions even from this portion of the testimony—the portion respecting the gruff and shrill voices—are in themselves sufficient to engender a suspicion which should give direction to all farther progress in the investigation of the mystery. I said 'legitimate deductions'; but my meaning is not thus fully expressed. I designed to imply that the deductions are the *sole* proper ones, and that the suspicion arises *inevitably* from them as the single result. What the suspicion is, however, I will not say just yet. I merely wish you to bear in mind that, with myself, it was sufficiently forcible to give a definite form—a certain tendency—to my inquiries in the chamber.

"Let us now transport ourselves, in fancy, to this chamber. What shall we first seek here? The means of egress employed by the murderers. It is not too much to say that neither of us believe in præternatural events. Madame and Mademoiselle L'Espanaye were not destroyed by spirits. The doers of the deed were material, and escaped materially. Then how? Fortunately, there is but one mode of reasoning upon the point, and that mode *must* lead us to a definite decision.—Let us examine, each by each, the possible means of egress. It is clear that the assassins were in the room where Mademoiselle L'Espanaye was found, or at least in the room adjoining, when the party ascended the stairs. It is then only from these two apartments that we have to seek issues. The police have laid bare the floors, the ceilings, and the masonry of the walls, in every direction. No *secret* issues could have escaped their vigilance. But, not trusting to *their* eyes, I examined with my own. There were, then, *no* secret issues. Both doors leading from the rooms into the passage were securely locked, with the keys inside. Let us turn to the chimneys. These, although of ordinary width for some eight or ten feet above the hearths, will not admit, throughout their extent, the body of a large cat. The impossibility of egress, by means already stated, being thus absolute, we are reduced to the windows. Through those of the front room no one could have escaped without notice from the crowd in the street. The murderers *must* have passed, then, through those of the back room. Now, brought to this conclusion in so unequivocal a manner as we are, it is not our part, as reasoners, to reject it on account of apparent impossibilities. It is only left for us to prove that these apparent 'impossibilities' are, in reality, not such.

"There are two windows in the chamber. One of them is unobstructed by furniture, and is wholly visible. The lower portion of the other is hidden from view by the head of the unwieldy bedstead which is thrust close up against it. The former was found securely fastened from within. It resisted the utmost force of those who endeavored to raise it. A large gimlet-hole had been pierced in its frame to the left, and a very stout nail was found fitted therein, nearly to the head. Upon examining the other window, a similar nail was seen similarly fitted in it; and a vigorous attempt to raise this sash failed also. The police were now entirely satisfied that egress had not been in these directions. And, *therefore*, it was thought a matter of supererogation to withdraw the nails and open the windows.

"My own examination was somewhat more particular, and was so for the reason I have just given—because here it was, I knew, that all apparent impossibilities *must* be proved to be not such in reality.

"I proceeded to think thus—*à posteriori.*[20] The murderers *did* escape from one of these windows. This being so, they could not have re-fastened the sashes from the inside, as they were found fastened;—the consideration which put a stop, through its obviousness, to the scrutiny of the police in this quarter. Yet the sashes *were* fastened. They *must*, then, have the power of fastening themselves. There was no escape from this conclusion. I stepped to the unobstructed casement, withdrew the nail with some difficulty, and attempted to raise the sash. It resisted all my efforts, as I had anticipated. A concealed spring must, I now knew, exist; and this corroboration of my idea convinced me that my premises, at least, were correct, however mysterious still appeared the circumstances attending the nails. A careful search soon brought to light the hidden spring. I pressed it, and, satisfied with the discovery, forebore to upraise the sash.

"I now replaced the nail and regarded it attentively. A person passing out through this window might have reclosed it, and the spring would have caught—

---

[20]"After the fact"—that is, beginning by assuming that I was correct.

but the nail could not have been replaced. The conclusion was plain, and again narrowed in the field of my investigations. The assassins *must* have escaped through the other window. Supposing, then, the springs upon each sash to be the same, as was probable, there *must* be found a difference between the nails, or at least between the modes of their fixture. Getting upon the sacking of the bedstead, I looked over the head-board minutely at the second casement. Passing my hand behind the board, I readily discovered and pressed the spring, which was, as I had supposed, identical in character with its neighbor. I now looked at the nail. It was as stout as the other, and apparently fitted in the same manner—driven in nearly up to the head.

"You will say that I was puzzled; but, if you think so, you must have misunderstood the nature of the inductions. To use a sporting phrase, I had not been once 'at fault.' The scent had never for an instant been lost. There was no flaw in any link of the chain. I had traced the secret to its ultimate result,—and that result was *the nail*. It had, I say, in every respect, the appearance of its fellow in the other window; but this fact was an absolute nullity (conclusive as it might seem to be) when compared with the consideration that here, at this point, terminated the clew. 'There *must* be something wrong,' I said, 'about the nail.' I touched it; and the head, with about a quarter of an inch of the shank, came off in my fingers. The rest of the shank was in the gimlet-hole, where it had been broken off. The fracture was an old one (for its edges were incrusted with rust), and had apparently been accomplished by the blow of a hammer, which had partially imbedded, in the top of the bottom sash, the head portion of the nail. I now carefully replaced this head portion in the indentation whence I had taken it, and the resemblance to a perfect nail was complete—the fissure was invisible. Pressing the spring, I gently raised the sash for a few inches; the head went up with it, remaining firm in its bed. I closed the window, and the semblance of the whole nail was again perfect.

"The riddle, so far, was now unriddled. The assassin had escaped through the window which looked upon the bed. Dropping of its own accord upon his exit (or perhaps purposely closed), it had become fastened by the spring; and it was the retention of this spring which had been mistaken by the police for that of the nail,—farther inquiry being thus considered unnecessary.

"The next question is that of the mode of descent. Upon this point I had been satisfied in my walk with you around the building. About five feet and a half from the casement in question there runs a lightning-rod. From this rod it would have been impossible for any one to reach the window itself, to say nothing of entering it. I observed, however, that the shutters of the fourth story were of the peculiar kind called by Parisian carpenters *ferrades*—a kind rarely employed at the present day, but frequently seen upon very old mansions at Lyons and Bordeaux. They are in the form of an ordinary door, (a single, not a folding door) except that the upper half is latticed or worked in open trellis—thus affording an excellent hold for the hands. In the present instance these shutters are fully three feet and a half broad. When we saw them from the rear of the house, they were both about half open—that is to say, they stood off at right angles from the wall. It is probable that the police, as well as myself, examined the back of the tenement; but, if so, in looking at these *ferrades* in the line of their breadth (as they must have done), they did not perceive this great breadth itself, or, at all events, failed to take it into due consideration. In fact, having once satisfied themselves that no egress could have been made in this quarter, they would naturally bestow here a very cursory examination. It was clear to me, however, that the shutter belonging to the window at the head of the bed, would, if swung fully back to the wall, reach to within two feet of the lightning-rod. It was also evident that, by exertion of a very unusual degree of activity and courage, an entrance into the window, from the rod, might have been thus effected.—By reaching to the distance of two feet and a half (we now suppose the shutter open to its whole extent) a robber might have taken a firm grasp upon the trellis-work. Letting go, then, his hold upon the rod, placing his feet securely against the wall, and springing boldly from it, he might have swung the shutter so as to close it, and, if we imagine the window open at the time, might even have swung himself into the room.

"I wish you to bear especially in mind that I have spoken of a *very* unusual degree of activity as requisite to success in so hazardous and so difficult a feat. It is my design to show you, first, that the thing might possibly have been accomplished:—but, secondly and *chiefly*, I wish to impress upon your understanding the *very extraordinary*—the almost præternatural character of that agility which could have accomplished it.

"You will say, no doubt, using the language of the law, that 'to make out my case' I should rather undervalue, than insist upon a full estimation of the activity required in this matter. This may be the practice in law, but it is not the usage of reason. My ultimate object is only the truth. My immediate purpose is to lead you to place in juxta-position that *very unusual* activity of which I have just spoken, with that *very peculiar* shrill (or harsh) and *unequal* voice, about whose nationality no two persons could be found to agree, and in whose utterance no syllabification could be detected."

At these words a vague and half-formed conception of the meaning of Dupin flitted over my mind. I seemed to be upon the verge of comprehension, without power to comprehend—as men, at times, find themselves upon the brink of remembrance, without being able, in the end, to remember. My friend went on with his discourse.

"You will see," he said, "that I have shifted the question from the mode of egress to that of ingress. It was my design to suggest that both were effected in the same manner, at the same point. Let us now revert to the interior of the room. Let us survey the appearances here. The drawers of the bureau, it is said, had been rifled, although many articles of apparel still remained within them. The conclusion here is absurd. It is a mere guess—a very silly one—and no more.

How are we to know that the articles found in the drawers were not all these drawers had originally contained? Madame L'Espanaye and her daughter lived an exceedingly retired life—saw no company—seldom went out—had little use for numerous changes of habiliment. Those found were at least of as good quality as any likely to be possessed by these ladies. If a thief had taken any, why did he not take the best—why did he not take all? In a word, why did he abandon four thousand francs in gold to encumber himself with a bundle of linen? The gold *was* abandoned. Nearly the whole sum mentioned by Monsieur Mignaud, the banker, was discovered, in bags, upon the floor. I wish you, therefore, to discard from your thoughts the blundering idea of *motive*, engendered in the brains of the police by that portion of the evidence which speaks of money delivered at the door of the house. Coincidences ten times as remarkable as this (the delivery of the money, and murder committed within three days upon the party receiving it), happen to all of us every hour of our lives, without attracting even momentary notice. Coincidences, in general, are great stumbling-blocks in the way of that class of thinkers who have been educated to know nothing of the theory of probabilities—that theory to which the most glorious objects of human research are indebted for the most glorious of illustration. In the present instance, had the gold been gone, the fact of its delivery three days before would have formed something more than a coincidence. It would have been corroborative of this idea of motive. But, under the real circumstances of the case, if we are to suppose gold the motive of this outrage, we must also imagine the perpetrator so vacillating an idiot as to have abandoned his gold and his motive together.

"Keeping now steadily in mind the points to which I have drawn your attention—that peculiar voice, that unusual agility, and that startling absence of motive in a murder so singularly atrocious as this—let us glance at the butchery itself. Here is a woman strangled to death by manual strength, and thrust up a chimney, head downward. Ordinary assassins employ no such modes of murder as this. Least of all, do they thus dispose of the murdered. In the manner of thrusting the corpse up the chimney, you will admit that there was something *excessively outré*—something altogether irreconcilable with our common notions of human action, even when we suppose the actors the most depraved of men. Think, too, how great must have been that strength which could have thrust the body *up* such an aperture so forcibly that the united vigor of several persons was found barely sufficient to drag it *down*!

"Turn, now, to other indications of the employment of a vigor most marvellous. On the hearth were thick tresses—very thick tresses—of gray human hair. These had been torn out by the roots. You are aware of the great force necessary in tearing thus from the head even twenty or thirty hairs together. You saw the locks in question as well as myself. Their roots (a hideous sight!) were clotted with fragments of the flesh of the scalp—sure token of the prodigious power which had been exerted in uprooting perhaps half a million of hairs at a time.

The throat of the old lady was not merely cut, but the head absolutely severed from the body: the instrument was a mere razor. I wish you also to look at the *brutal* ferocity of these deeds. Of the bruises upon the body of Madame L'Espanaye I do not speak. Monsieur Dumas, and his worthy coadjutor Monsieur Etienne, have pronounced that they were inflicted by some obtuse instrument; and so far these gentlemen are very correct. The obtuse instrument was clearly the stone pavement in the yard, upon which the victim had fallen from the window which looked in upon the bed. This idea, however simple it may now seem, escaped the police for the same reason that the breadth of the shutters escaped them—because, by the affair of the nails, their perceptions had been hermetically sealed against the possibility of the windows having ever been opened at all.

"If now, in addition to all these things, you have properly reflected upon the odd disorder of the chamber, we have gone so far as to combine the ideas of an agility astounding, a strength superhuman, a ferocity brutal, a butchery without motive, a *grotesquerie* in horror absolutely alien from humanity, and a voice foreign in tone to the ears of men of many nations, and devoid of all distinct or intelligible syllabification. What result, then, has ensued? What impression have I made upon your fancy?"

I felt a creeping of the flesh as Dupin asked me the question. "A madman," I said, "has done this deed—some raving maniac, escaped from a neighboring *Maison de Santé.*"[21]

"In some respects," he replied, "your idea is not irrelevant. But the voices of madmen, even in their wildest paroxysms, are never found to tally with that peculiar voice heard upon the stairs. Madmen are of some nation, and their language, however incoherent in its words, has always the coherence of syllabification. Besides, the hair of a madman is not such as I now hold in my hand. I disentangled this little tuft from the rigidly clutched fingers of Madam L'Espanaye. Tell me what you can make of it."

"Dupin!" I said, completely unnerved; "this hair is most unusual—this is no *human* hair."

"I have not asserted that it is," said he; "but, before we decide this point, I wish you to glance at the little sketch I have here traced upon this paper. It is a *facsimile* drawing of what has been described in one portion of the testimony as 'dark bruises, and deep indentations of finger nails,' upon the throat of Mademoiselle L'Espanaye, and in another, (by Messrs. Dumas and Etienne,) as a 'series of livid spots, evidently the impression of fingers.'

"You will perceive," continued my friend, spreading out the paper upon the table before us, "that this drawing gives the idea of a firm and fixed hold. There is no *slipping* apparent. Each finger has retained—possibly until the death of the victim—the fearful grasp by which it originally imbedded itself. Attempt,

---

[21]Insane asylum.

now, to place all your fingers, at the same time, in the respective impressions as you see them."

I made the attempt in vain.

"We are possibly not giving this matter a fair trial," he said. "The paper is spread out upon a plane surface; but the human throat is cylindrical. Here is a billet of wood, the circumference of which is about that of the throat. Wrap the drawing around it, and try the experiment again."

I did so; but the difficulty was even more obvious than before.

"This," I said, "is the mark of no human hand."

"Read now," replied Dupin, "this passage from Cuvier."[22]

It was a minute anatomical and generally descriptive account of the large fulvous Ourang-Outang of the East Indian Islands. The gigantic stature, the prodigious strength and activity, the wild ferocity, and the imitative propensities of these mammalia are sufficiently well known to all. I understood the full horrors of the murder at once.

"The description of the digits," said I, as I made an end of reading, "is in exact accordance with this drawing. I see that no animal but an Ourang-Outang, of the species here mentioned, could have impressed the identations as you have traced them. This tuft of tawny hair, too, is identical in character with that of the beast of Cuvier. But I cannot possibly comprehend the particulars of this frightful mystery. Besides, there were *two* voices heard in contention, and one of them was unquestionably the voice of a Frenchman."

"True; and you will remember an expression attributed almost unanimously, by the evidence, to this voice,—the expression, '*mon Dieu!*' This, under the circumstances, has been justly characterized by one of the witnesses (Montani, the confectioner,) as an expression of remonstrance or expostulation. Upon these two words, therefore, I have mainly built my hopes of a full solution of the riddle. A Frenchman was cognizant of the murder. It is possible—indeed it is far more than probable—that he was innocent of all participation in the bloody transactions which took place. The Ourang-Outang may have escaped from him. He may have traced it to the chamber; but, under the agitating circumstances which ensued, he could never have re-captured it. It is still at large. I will not pursue these guesses—for I have no right to call them more—since the shades of reflection upon which they are based are scarcely of sufficient depth to be appreciable by my own intellect, and since I could not pretend to make them intelligible to the understanding of another. We will call them guesses then, and speak of them as such. If the Frenchman in question is indeed, as I suppose, innocent of this atrocity, this advertisement, which I left last night, upon our return home, at the office of 'Le Monde,' (a paper

---

[22]Baron Georges Cuvier (1769–1832), great French naturalist whose classification of animals was one of the standard guides to the subject until Darwin.

devoted to the shipping interest, and much sought by sailors,) will bring him to our residence."

He handed me a paper, and I read thus:

CAUGHT—*In the Bois de Boulogne, early in the morning of the—inst., (the morning of the murder,) a very large, tawny Ourang-Outang of the Bornese species. The owner, (who is ascertained to be a sailor, belonging to a Maltese vessel,) may have the animal again, upon identifying it satisfactorily, and paying a few charges arising from its capture and keeping. Call at No.—, Rue—, Faubourg St. Germain—au troisième.*

"How was it possible," I asked, "that you should know the man to be a sailor, and belonging to a Maltese vessel?"

"I do *not* know it," said Dupin. "I am not *sure* of it. Here, however, is a small piece of ribbon, which from its form, and from its greasy appearance, has evidently been used in tying the hair in one of those long *queues* of which sailors are so fond. Moreover, this knot is one which few besides sailors can tie, and is peculiar to the Maltese. I picked the ribbon up at the foot of the lightning-rod. It could not have belonged to either of the deceased. Now if, after all, I am wrong in my induction from this ribbon, that the Frenchman was a sailor belonging to a Maltese vessel, still I can have done no harm in saying what I did in the advertisement. If I am in error, he will merely suppose that I have been misled by some circumstance into which he will not take the trouble to inquire. But if I am right, a great point is gained. Cognizant although innocent of the murder, the Frenchman will naturally hesitate about replying to the advertisement—about demanding the Ourang-Outang. He will reason thus:—'I am innocent; I am poor; my Ourang-Outang is of great value—to one in my circumstances a fortune of itself—why should I lose it through idle apprehensions of danger? Here it is, within my grasp. It was found in the Bois de Boulogne—at a vast distance from the scene of the butchery. How can it ever be suspected that a brute beast should have done the deed? The police are at fault—they have failed to procure the slightest clew. Should they even trace the animal, it would be impossible to prove me cognizant of the murder, or to implicate me in guilt on account of that cognizance. Above all, *I am known*. The advertiser designates me as the possessor of the beast. I am not sure to what limit his knowledge may extend. Should I avoid claiming a property of so great value, which it is known that I possess, I will render the animal, at least, liable to suspicion. It is not my policy to attract attention either to myself or to the beast. I will answer the advertisement, get the Ourang-Outang, and keep it close until this matter has blown over.'"

At this moment we heard a step upon the stairs.

"Be ready," said Dupin, "with your pistols, but neither use them nor show them until at a signal from myself."

The front of the house had been left open, and the visitor had entered, without ringing, and advanced several steps upon the staircase. Now, however, he seemed to hesitate. Presently we heard him descending. Dupin was moving quickly to the door, when we again heard him coming up. He did not turn back a second time, but stepped up with decision and rapped at the door of our chamber.

"Come in," said Dupin, in a cheerful and hearty tone.

A man entered. He was a sailor, evidently,—a tall, stout, and muscular-looking person, with a certain dare-devil expression of countenance, not altogether unprepossessing. His face, greatly sunburnt, was more than half hidden by whisker and *mustachio*. He had with him a huge oaken cudgel, but appeared to be otherwise unarmed. He bowed awkwardly, and bade us "good evening," in French accents, which although somewhat Neufchatel-ish,[23] were still sufficiently indicative of a Parisian origin.

"Sit down, my friend," said Dupin. "I suppose you have called about the Ourang-Outang. Upon my word, I almost envy you the possession of him; a remarkably fine, and no doubt a very valuable animal. How old do you suppose him to be?"

The sailor drew a long breath, with the air of a man relieved of some intolerable burden, and then replied, in an assured tone:

"I have no way of telling—but he can't be more than four or five years old. Have you got him here?"

"Oh no; we had no conveniences for keeping him here. He is at a livery stable in the Rue Dubourg, just by. You can get him in the morning. Of course you are prepared to identify the property?"

"To be sure I am, sir."

"I shall be sorry to part with him," said Dupin.

"I don't mean that you should be at all this trouble for nothing, sir," said the man. "Couldn't expect it. Am very willing to pay a reward for the finding of the animal—that is to say, any thing in reason."

"Well," replied my friend, "that is all very fair, to be sure. Let me think!—what should I have? Oh! I will tell you. My reward shall be this. You shall give me all the information in your power about these murders in the Rue Morgue."

Dupin said the last words in a very low tone, and very quietly. Just as quietly, too, he walked toward the door, locked it, and put the key in his pocket. He then drew a pistol from his bosom and placed it, without the least flurry, upon the table.

The sailor's face flushed up as if he were struggling with suffocation. He started to his feet and grasped his cudgel; but the next moment he fell back into his seat, trembling violently, and with the countenance of death itself. He spoke not a word. I pitied him from the bottom of my heart.

"My friend," said Dupin, in a kind tone, "you are alarming yourself unnecessarily—you are indeed. We mean you no harm whatever. I pledge you the honor

---

[23]Neufchâtel is a town in northern France. Mabbott (9, II) suggests that "Neufchâtel-ish" implies rustic.

of a gentleman, and of a Frenchman, that we intend you no injury. I perfectly well know that you are innocent of the atrocities in the Rue Morgue. It will not do, however, to deny that you are in some measure implicated in them. From what I have already said, you must know that I have had means of information about this matter—means of which you could never have dreamed. Now the thing stands thus. You have done nothing which you could have avoided—nothing, certainly, which renders you culpable. You were not even guilty of robbery, when you might have robbed with impunity. You have nothing to conceal. You have no reason for concealment. On the other hand, you are bound by every principle of honor to confess all you know. An innocent man is now imprisoned, charged with that crime of which you can point out the perpetrator."

The sailor had recovered his presence of mind, in a great measure, while Dupin uttered these words; but his original boldness of bearing was all gone.

"So help me God," said he, after a brief pause, "I *will* tell you all I know about this affair,—but I do not expect you to believe one half I say—I would be a fool indeed if I did. Still, I *am* innocent, and I will make a clean breast if I die for it."

What he stated was, in substance, this. He had lately made a voyage to the Indian Archipelago. A party, of which he formed one, landed at Borneo, and passed into the interior on an excursion of pleasure. Himself and a companion had captured the Ourang-Outang. This companion dying, the animal fell into his own exclusive possession. After great trouble, occasioned by the intractable ferocity of his captive during the home voyage, he at length succeeded in lodging it safely at his own residence in Paris, where, not to attract toward himself the unpleasant curiosity of his neighbors, he kept it carefully secluded, until such time as it should recover from a wound in the foot, received from a splinter on board ship. His ultimate design was to sell it.

Returning home from some sailors' frolic on the night, or rather in the morning of the murder, he found the beast occupying his own bed-room, into which it had broken from a closet adjoining, where it had been, as was thought, securely confined. Razor in hand, and fully lathered, it was sitting before a looking-glass, attempting the operation of shaving, in which it had no doubt previously watched its master through the key-hole of the closet. Terrified at the sight of so dangerous a weapon in the possession of an animal so ferocious, and so well able to use it, the man, for some moments, was at a loss what to do. He had been accustomed, however, to quiet the creature, even in its fiercest moods, by the use of a whip, and to this he now resorted. Upon sight of it, the Ourang-Outang sprang at once through the door of the chamber, down the stairs, and thence, through a window, unfortunately open, into the street.

The Frenchman followed in despair; the ape, razor still in hand, occasionally stopping to look back and gesticulate at its pursuer, until the latter had nearly come up with it. It then again made off. In this manner the chase continued for a long time. The streets were profoundly quiet, as it was nearly three o'clock in the morning. In passing down an alley in the rear of the Rue Morgue, the fugitive's attention was arrested by a light gleaming from the open window of Madame L'Espanaye's chamber, in the fourth story of her house. Rushing to the building, it perceived the lightning-rod, clambered up with inconceivable agility, grasped the shutter, which was thrown fully back against the wall, and, by its means, swung itself directly upon the headboard of the bed. The whole feat did not occupy a minute. The shutter was kicked open again by the Ourang-Outang as it entered the room.

The sailor, in the meantime, was both rejoiced and perplexed. He had strong hopes of now recapturing the brute, as it could scarcely escape from the trap into which it had ventured, except by the rod, where it might be intercepted as it came down. On the other hand, there was much cause for anxiety as to what it might do in the house. This latter reflection urged the man still to follow the fugitive. A lightning-rod is ascended without difficulty, especially by a sailor; but, when he had arrived as high as the window, which lay far to his left, his career was stopped; the most that he could accomplish was to reach over so as to obtain a glimpse of the interior of the room. At this glimpse he nearly fell from his hold through excess of horror. Now it was that those hideous shrieks arose upon the night, which had startled from slumber the inmates of the Rue Morgue. Madame L'Espanaye and her daughter, habited in their night clothes, had apparently been arranging some papers in the iron chest already mentioned, which had been wheeled into the middle of the room. It was open, and its contents lay beside it on the floor. The victims must have been sitting with their backs toward the window; and, from the time elapsing between the ingress of the beast and the screams, it seems probable that it was not immediately perceived. The flapping-to of the shutter would naturally have been attributed to the wind.

As the sailor looked in, the gigantic animal had seized Madam L'Espanaye by the hair, (which was loose, as she had been combing it,) and was flourishing the razor about her face, in imitation of the motions of a barber. The daughter lay prostrate and motionless; she had swooned. The screams and struggles of the old lady (during which the hair was torn from her head) had the effect of changing the probably pacific purposes of the Ourang-Outang into those of wrath. With one determined sweep of its muscular arm it nearly severed her head from her body. The sight of blood inflamed its anger into phrenzy. Gnashing its teeth, and flashing fire from its eyes, it flew upon the body of the girl, and imbedded its fearful talons in her throat, retaining its grasp until she expired. Its wandering and wild glances fell at this moment upon the head of the bed, over which the face of its master, rigid with horror, was just discernible. The fury of the beast, who no doubt bore still in mind the dreaded whip, was instantly converted into fear. Conscious of having deserved punishment, it seemed desirous of concealing its bloody deeds, and skipped about the chamber in an agony of nervous agitation; throwing down and breaking the furniture as it moved, and dragging the bed from the bedstead. In conclusion, it seized first the corpse of the daughter, and thrust it up the chimney, as it was found; then that of the old lady, which it immediately hurled through the window headlong.

As the ape approached the casement with its mutilated burden, the sailor shrank aghast to the rod, and, rather gliding than clambering down it, hurried at once home—dreading the consequences of the butchery, and gladly abandoning, in his terror, all solicitude about the fate of the Ourang-Outang. The words heard by the party upon the staircase were the Frenchman's exclamations of horror and affright, commingled with the fiendish jabberings of the brute.

I have scarcely anything to add. The Ourang-Outang must have escaped from the chamber, by the rod, just before the breaking of the door. It must have closed the window as it passed through it. It was subsequently caught by the owner himself, who obtained for it a very large sum at the *Jardin des Plantes*. Le Bon was instantly released, upon our narration of the circumstances (with some comments from Dupin) at the *bureau* of the Prefect of Police. This functionary, however well disposed to my friend, could not altogether conceal his chagrin at the turn which affairs had taken, and was fain to indulge in a sarcasm or two, about the propriety of every person minding his own business.

"Let them talk," said Dupin, who had not thought it necessary to reply. "Let him discourse; it will ease his conscience. I am satisfied with having defeated him in his own castle. Nevertheless, that he failed in the solution of this mystery, is by no means that matter for wonder which he supposes it; for, in truth, our friend the Prefect is somewhat too cunning to be profound. In his wisdom is no *stamen*. It is all head and no body, like the pictures of the Goddess Laverna—or, at best, all head and shoulders, like a codfish. But he is a good creature after all. I like him especially for one master stroke of cant, by which he has attained his reputation for ingenuity. I mean the way he has '*de nier ce qui est, et d'expliquer ce qui n'est pas.*' "[24]

SIR ARTHUR CONAN DOYLE
1859–1930

The creator of Sherlock Holmes, the best known detective in literature, Arthur Conan Doyle was born in Edinburgh, Scotland, to an aristocratic and artistic Irish family. He was educated at the Jesuit schools of Hodder and Stonyhurst; then he studied for a year at Feldkirch in Austria before

---

[24]**the Goddess Laverna:** The patroness of thieves in ancient Roman religion. *de nier . . . n'est pas: Rousseau, Nouvelle Héloise* [Poe's note]. Jean-Jacques Rousseau's *Julie ou La Nouvelle Héloise* (1760). The French may be translated, "Of denying that which is, and of explaining that which is not."

returning to the University of Edinburgh for a degree in medicine. In 1879 he sold his first story, "The Mystery of the Sasassa Valley," to *Chamber's Journal* to help pay for his educational expenses. Following his graduation, he spent some months at sea as a medical officer, and in 1882 he opened his own medical practice in Southsea, Portsmouth, England. With a very small clientele, Doyle began to write in his spare time. In 1884, inspired by Poe's detective, C. Auguste Dupin, Doyle wrote his first detective story, *A Study In Scarlet*, which introduced Sherlock Holmes and Dr. Watson. It was published in 1887, and in 1890 the second Holmes' mystery, *The Sign of Four*, was serialized in *Lippincott's Magazine*. At this time, Doyle gave up his medical career to write full-time. Writing historical fiction and adventure novels as well as detective fiction, Doyle was knighted in 1902 for his literary work. He was most noted, however, for his creation of the four short novels and 56 short stories that comprise the Sherlock Holmes canon.

With the entrance of Sherlock Holmes in *A Study In Scarlet*, the most popular detective of all time came on the literary scene. Tall, slender, hawk-nosed and with a piercing glance, Holmes personifies the eccentric cerebral detective. He plays the violin well; he smokes bad-smelling tobacco, does chemical experiments in his apartment, and takes cocaine to stimulate his mind when there is no difficult crime to solve. His knowledge of crime, science, and the law is extensive and sometimes overwhelming. He is an excellent boxer, fencer, and mountain climber. His abilities to observe, to analyze, to reconstruct, and to solve the crime surpass all other fictional detectives. Holmes distrusts most women except for Mrs. Hudson, his landlady. His best friend and confidant is Dr. John Watson, who chronicles the cases that Holmes undertakes. Beginning in 1903, Holmes became a main character in films too numerous to mention with the best series starring Basil Rathbone and Nigel Bruce. From 1930 on, Sherlock Holmes was featured in a series of radio programs and several plays were written based on the Doyle stories. Both BBC and A&E present Sherlock Holmes' adventures on television, and numerous authors continue to write stories and novels based on the Holmes' characters and tales. "Silver Blaze," an early Holmes story, was first published in *The Strand* magazine in December 1892, and later appeared in the *Memoirs of Sherlock Holmes* in 1894.

Recommended Doyle works: "A Scandal in Bohemia," "The Adventure of the Empty House," *The Hound of the Baskervilles*.

Other recommended authors: Carole Nelson Douglas, Laurie R. King, Edgar Allan Poe.

Silver Blaze

'I am afraid, Watson, that I shall have to go,' said Holmes, as we sat down together to our breakfast one morning.

'Go! Where to?'

'To Dartmoor—to King's Pyland.'

I was not surprised. Indeed, my only wonder was that he had not already been mixed up in this extraordinary case, which was the one topic of conversation through the length and breadth of England. For a whole day my companion had rambled about the room with his chin upon his chest and his brows knitted, charging and recharging his pipe with the strongest black tobacco, and absolutely deaf to any of my questions or remarks. Fresh editions of every paper had been sent up by our newsagent only to be glanced over and tossed down into a corner. Yet, silent as he was, I knew perfectly well what it was over which he was brooding. There was but one problem before the public which could challenge his powers of analysis, and that was the singular disappearance of the favourite for the Wessex Cup, and the tragic murder of its trainer. When, therefore, he suddenly announced his intention of setting out for the scene of the drama, it was only what I had both expected and hoped for.

'I should be most happy to go down with you if I should not be in the way,' said I.

'My dear Watson, you would confer a great favour upon me by coming. And I think that your time will not be misspent, for there are points about this case which promise to make it an absolutely unique one. We have, I think, just time to catch our train at Paddington, and I will go further into the matter upon our journey. You would oblige me by bringing with you your very excellent field-glass.'

And so it happened that an hour or so later I found myself in the corner of a first-class carriage, flying along, *en route* for Exeter, while Sherlock Holmes, with his sharp, eager face framed in his ear-flapped travelling-cap, dipped rapidly into the bundle of fresh papers which he had procured at Paddington. We had left Reading far behind us before he thrust the last of them under the seat, and offered me his cigar-case.

'We are going well,' said he, looking out of the window, and glancing at his watch. 'Our rate at present is fifty-three and a half miles an hour.'

'I have not observed the quarter-mile posts,' said I.

'Nor have I. But the telegraph posts upon this line are sixty yards apart, and the calculation is a simple one. I presume that you have already looked into this matter of the murder of John Straker and the disappearance of Silver Blaze?'

'I have seen what the *Telegraph* and the *Chronicle* have to say.'

'It is one of those cases where the art of the reasoner should be used rather for the sifting of details than for the acquiring of fresh evidence. The tragedy has been so uncommon, so complete, and of such personal importance to so many people that we are suffering from a plethora of surmise, conjecture, and hypothesis. The difficulty is to detach the framework of fact—of absolute, undeniable fact—from the embellishments of theorists and reporters. Then, having established ourselves upon this sound basis, it is our duty to see what inferences may be drawn, and which are the special points upon which the whole mystery turns. On Tuesday evening I received telegrams, both from Colonel Ross, the owner of the horse, and from Inspector Gregory, who is looking after the case, inviting my co-operation.'

'Tuesday evening!' I exclaimed. 'And this is Thursday morning. Why did you not go down yesterday?'

'Because I made a blunder, my dear Watson—which is, I am afraid, a more common occurrence than anyone would think who only knew me through your memoirs. The fact is that I could not believe it possible that the most remarkable horse in England could long remain concealed, especially in so sparsely inhabited a place as the north of Dartmoor. From hour to hour yesterday I expected to hear that he had been found, and that his abductor was the murderer of John Straker. When, however, another morning had come and I found that, beyond the arrest of young Fitzroy Simpson, nothing had been done, I felt that it was time for me to take action. Yet in some ways I feel that yesterday has not been wasted.'

'You have formed a theory then?'

'At least I have a grip of the essential facts of the case. I shall enumerate them to you, for nothing clears up a case so much as stating it to another person, and I can hardly expect your co-operation if I do not show you the position from which we start.'

I lay back against the cushions, puffing at my cigar, while Holmes, leaning forward, with his long thin forefinger checking off the points upon the palm of his left hand, gave me a sketch of the events which had led to our journey.

'Silver Blaze,' said he, 'is from the Isonomy stock, and holds as brilliant a record as his famous ancestor. He is now in his fifth year, and has brought in turn each of the prizes of the turf to Colonel Ross, his fortunate owner. Up to the time of the catastrophe he was first favourite for the Wessex Cup, the betting being three to one on. He has always, however, been a prime favourite with the racing public, and has never yet disappointed them, so that even at short odds enormous sums of money have been laid upon him. It is obvious, therefore, that there were many people who had the strongest interest in preventing Silver Blaze from being there at the fall of the flag next Tuesday.

'This fact was, of course, appreciated at King's Pyland, where the Colonel's training stable is situated. Every precaution was taken to guard the favourite. The trainer, John Straker, is a retired jockey, who rode in Colonel Ross's colours before he became too heavy for the weighing-chair. He has served the Colonel for five years as jockey, and for seven as trainer, and has always shown himself to be a zealous and honest servant. Under him were three lads, for the establishment was a small one, containing only four horses in all. One of these lads sat up each night in the stable, while the others slept in the loft. All three bore excellent characters. John Straker, who is a married man, lived in a small villa about two hundred yards from the stables. He has no children, keeps one maid-servant, and is comfortably off. The country round is very lonely, but about half a mile to the north there is a small cluster of villas which have been built by a Tavistock contractor for the use of invalids and others who may wish to enjoy the pure Dartmoor air. Tavistock itself lies two miles to the west, while across the moor, also about two miles distant, is the larger training establishment of Capleton, which belongs to Lord Backwater, and is managed by Silas Brown. In every other direction the moor is a complete wilderness, inhabited only by a few roaming gipsies. Such was the general situation last Monday night, when the catastrophe occurred.

'On that evening the horses had been exercised and watered as usual, and the stables were locked up at nine o'clock. Two of the lads walked up to the trainer's house, where they had supper in the kitchen, while the third, Ned Hunter, remained on guard. At a few minutes after nine the maid, Edith Baxter, carried down to the stables his supper, which consisted of a dish of curried mutton. She took no liquid, as there was a water-tap in the stables, and it was the rule that the lad on duty should drink nothing else. The maid carried a lantern with her, as it was very dark, and the path ran across the open moor.

'Edith Baxter was within thirty yards of the stables when a man appeared out of the darkness and called to her to stop. As he stepped into the circle of yellow light thrown by the lantern she saw that he was a person of gentlemanly bearing, dressed in a grey suit of tweed with a cloth cap. He wore gaiters, and carried a heavy stick with a knob to it. She was most impressed, however, by the extreme pallor of his face and by the nervousness of his manner. His age, she thought, would be rather over thirty than under it.

' "Can you tell me where I am?" he asked. "I had almost made up my mind to sleep on the moor when I saw the light of your lantern."

' "You are close to the King's Pyland training stables," she said.

' "Oh, indeed! What a stroke of luck!" he cried. "I understand that a stable boy sleeps there alone every night. Perhaps that is his supper which you are carrying to him. Now I am sure that you would not be too proud to earn the price of a new dress, would you?" He took a piece of white paper folded up out of his waistcoat pocket. "See that the boy has this tonight, and you shall have the prettiest frock that money can buy."

'She was frightened by the earnestness of his manner, and ran past him to the window through which she was accustomed to hand the meals. It was already open, and Hunter was seated at the small table inside. She had begun to tell him of what had happened, when the stranger came up again.

' "Good evening," said he, looking through the window, "I wanted to have a word with you." The girl has sworn that as he spoke she noticed the corner of the little paper packet protruding from his closed hand.

' "What business have you here?" asked the lad.

' "It's business that may put something into your pocket," said the other. "You've two horses in for the Wessex Cup—Silver Blaze and Bayard. Let me have the straight tip, and you won't be a loser. Is it a fact that at the weights Bayard could give the other a hundred yards in five furlongs, and that the stable have put their money on him?"

' "So you're one of those damned touts," cried the lad. "I'll show you how we serve them in King's Pyland." He sprang up and rushed across the stable to unloose the dog. The girl fled away to the house, but as she ran she looked back, and saw that the stranger was leaning through the window. A minute later, however, when Hunter rushed out with the hound he was gone, and though the lad ran all round the buildings he failed to find any trace of him.'

'One moment!' I asked. 'Did the stable boy, when he ran out with the dog, leave the door unlocked behind him?'

'Excellent, Watson; excellent!' murmured my companion. 'The importance of the point struck me so forcibly, that I sent a special wire to Dartmoor yesterday to clear the matter up. The boy locked the door before he left it. The window, I may add, was not large enough for a man to get through.

'Hunter waited until his fellow-grooms had returned, when he sent a message up to the trainer and told him what had occurred. Straker was excited at hearing the account, although he does not seem to have quite realized its true significance. It left him, however, vaguely uneasy, and Mrs Straker, waking at one in the morning, found that he was dressing. In reply to her inquiries, he said that he could not sleep on account of his anxiety about the horses, and that he intended to walk down to the stables to see that all was well. She begged him to remain at home, as she could hear the rain pattering against the windows, but in spite of her entreaties he pulled on his large mackintosh and left the house.

'Mrs Straker awoke at seven in the morning, to find that her husband had not yet returned. She dressed herself hastily, called the maid, and set off for the stables. The door was open; inside, huddled together upon a chair, Hunter was sunk in a state of absolute stupor, the favourite's stall was empty, and there were no signs of his trainer.

The two lads who slept in the chaff-cutting loft above the harnessroom were quickly roused. They had heard nothing during the night, for they are both sound sleepers. Hunter was obviously under the influence of some powerful drug; and, as no sense could be got out of him, he was left to sleep it off while the two lads and the two women ran out in search of the absentees. They still had hopes that the trainer had for some reason taken out the horse for early exercise, but on ascending the knoll near the house, from which all the neighbouring moors were visible, they not only could see no signs of the favourite, but they perceived something which warned them that they were in the presence of a tragedy.

'About a quarter of a mile from the stables, John Straker's overcoat was flapping from a furze bush. Immediately beyond there was a bowl-shaped depression in the moor, and at the bottom of this was found the dead body of the unfortunate trainer. His head had been shattered by a savage blow from some heavy weapon, and he was wounded in the thigh, where there was a long, clean cut, inflicted evidently by some very sharp instrument. It was clear, however, that Straker had defended himself vigorously against his assailants, for in his right hand he held a small knife, which was clotted with blood up to the handle, while in his left he grasped a red and black silk cravat, which was recognized by the maid as having been worn on the preceding evening by the stranger who had visited the stables.

'Hunter, on recovering from his stupor, was also quite positive as to the ownership of the cravat. He was equally certain that the same stranger had, while standing at the window, drugged his curried mutton, and so deprived the stables of their watchman.

'As to the missing horse, there were abundant proofs in the mud which lay at the bottom of the fatal hollow, that he had been there at the time of the struggle. But from that morning he has disappeared; and although a large reward has been offered, and all the gipsies of Dartmoor are on the alert, no news has come of him. Finally an analysis has shown that the remains of his supper, left by the stable lad, contain an appreciable quantity of powdered opium, while the people of the house partook of the same dish on the same night without any ill effect.

'Those are the main facts of the case stripped of all surmise and stated as baldly as possible. I shall now recapitulate what the police have done in the matter.

'Inspector Gregory, to whom the case has been committed, is an extremely competent officer. Were he but gifted with imagination he might rise to great heights in his profession. On his arrival he promptly found and arrested the man upon whom suspicion naturally rested. There was little difficulty in finding him, for he was thoroughly well known in the neighbourhood. His name, it appears, was Fitzroy Simpson. He was a man of excellent birth and education, who had squandered a fortune upon the turf, and who lived now by doing a little quiet and genteel bookmaking in the sporting clubs of London. An examination of his betting-book shows that bets to the amount of five thousand pounds had been registered by him against the favourite.

'On being arrested he volunteered the statement that he had come down to Dartmoor in the hope of getting some information about the King's Pyland horses, and also about Desborough, the second favourite, which was in charge of Silas Brown, at the Capleton stables. He did not attempt to deny that he had acted as described upon the evening before, but declared that he had no sinister designs, and had simply wished to obtain first-hand information. When confronted with the cravat he turned very pale, and was utterly unable to account for its presence in the hand of the murdered man. His wet clothing showed that he had been out in the storm of the night before, and his stick, which was a

Penang lawyer, weighted with lead, was just such a weapon as might, by repeated blows, have inflicted the terrible injuries to which the trainer had succumbed.

'On the other hand, there was no wound upon his person, while the state of Straker's knife would show that one, at least, of his assailants must bear his mark upon him. There you have it all in a nutshell, Watson, and if you can give me any light I shall be infinitely obliged to you.'

I had listened with the greatest interest to the statement which Holmes, with characteristic clearness, had laid before me. Though most of the facts were familiar to me, I had not sufficiently appreciated their relative importance, nor their connection with each other.

'Is it not possible,' I suggested, 'that the incised wound upon Straker may have been caused by his own knife in the convulsive struggles which follow any brain injury?'

'It is more than possible; it is probable,' said Holmes. 'In that case, one of the main points in favour of the accused disappears.'

'And yet,' said I, 'even now I fail to understand what the theory of the police can be.'

'I am afraid that whatever theory we state has very grave objections to it,' returned my companion. 'The police imagine, I take it, that this Fitzroy Simpson, having drugged the lad, and having in some way obtained a duplicate key, opened the stable door, and took out the horse, with the intention, apparently, of kidnapping him altogether. His bridle is missing, so that Simpson must have put it on. Then, having left the door open behind him, he was leading the horse away over the moor, when he was either met or overtaken by the trainer. A row naturally ensued, Simpson beat out the trainer's brains with his heavy stick without receiving any injury from the small knife which Straker used in self-defence, and then the thief either led the horse on to some secret hiding-place, or else it may have bolted during the struggle, and be now wandering out on the moors. That is the case as it appears to the police, and improbable as it is, all other explanations are more improbable still. However, I shall very quickly test the matter when I am once upon the spot, and until then I really cannot see how we can get much further than our present position.'

It was evening before we reached the little town of Tavistock, which lies, like the boss of a shield, in the middle of the huge circle of Dartmoor. Two gentlemen were awaiting us at the station; the one a tall fair man with lion-like hair and beard, and curiously penetrating light blue eyes, the other a small alert person, very neat and dapper, in a frock-coat and gaiters, with trim little side-whiskers and an eyeglass. The latter was Colonel Ross, the well-known sportsman, the other Inspector Gregory, a man who was rapidly making his name in the English detective service.

'I am delighted that you have come down, Mr Holmes,' said the Colonel. 'The Inspector here has done all that could possibly be suggested; but I wish to leave no stone unturned in trying to avenge poor Straker, and in recovering my horse.'

'Have there been any fresh developments?' asked Holmes.

'I am sorry to say that we have made very little progress,' said the Inspector. 'We have an open carriage outside, and as you would no doubt like to see the place before the light fails, we might talk it over as we drive.'

A minute later we were all seated in a comfortable landau and were rattling through the quaint old Devonshire town. Inspector Gregory was full of his case, and poured out a stream of remarks, while Holmes threw in an occasional question or interjection. Colonel Ross leaned back with his arms folded and his hat tilted over his eyes, while I listened with interest to the dialogue of the two detectives. Gregory was formulating his theory, which was almost exactly what Holmes had foretold in the train.

'The net is drawn pretty close round Fitzroy Simpson,' he remarked, 'and I believe myself that he is our man. At the same time, I recognize that the evidence is purely circumstantial, and that some new development may upset it.'

'How about Straker's knife?'

'We have quite come to the conclusion that he wounded himself in his fall.'

'My friend Dr Watson made that suggestion to me as we came down. If so, it would tell against this man Simpson.'

'Undoubtedly. He has neither a knife nor any sign of a wound. The evidence against him is certainly very strong. He had a great interest in the disappearance of the favourite, he lies under the suspicion of having poisoned the stable boy, he was undoubtedly out in the storm, he was armed with a heavy stick, and his cravat was found in the dead man's hand. I really think we have enough to go before a jury.'

Holmes shook his head. 'A clever counsel would tear it all to rags,' said he. 'Why should he take the horse out of the stable? If he wished to injure it, why could he not do it there? Has a duplicate key been found in his possession? What chemist sold him the powdered opium? Above all, where could he, a stranger to the district, hide a horse, and such a horse as this? What is his own explanation as to the paper which he wished the maid to give to the stable boy?'

'He says that it was a ten-pound note. One was found in his purse. But your other difficulties are not so formidable as they seem. He is not a stranger to the district. He has twice lodged at Tavistock in the summer. The opium was probably brought from London. The key, having served its purpose, would be hurled away. The horse may lie at the bottom of one of the pits or old mines upon the moor.'

'What does he say about the cravat?'

'He acknowledges that it is his, and declares that he had lost it. But a new element has been introduced into the case which may account for his leading the horse from the stable.'

Holmes pricked up his ears.

'We have found traces which show that a party of gipsies encamped on Monday night within a mile of the spot where the murder took place. On

Tuesday they were gone. Now, presuming that there was some understanding between Simpson and these gipsies, might he not have been leading the horse to them when he was overtaken, and may they not have him now?'

'It is certainly possible.'

'The moor is being scoured for these gipsies. I have also examined every stable and outhouse in Tavistock, and for a radius of ten miles.'

'There is another training stable quite close, I understand?'

'Yes, and that is a factor which we must certainly not neglect. As Desborough, their horse, was second in the betting, they had an interest in the disappearance of the favourite. Silas Brown, the trainer, is known to have had large bets upon the event, and he was no friend to poor Straker. We have, however, examined the stables, and there is nothing to connect him with the affair.'

'And nothing to connect this man Simpson with the interests of the Capleton stable?'

'Nothing at all.'

Holmes leaned back in the carriage and the conversation ceased. A few minutes later our driver pulled up at a neat little red-brick villa with overhanging eaves, which stood by the road. Some distance off, across a paddock, lay a long grey-tiled outbuilding. In every other direction the low curves of the moor, bronze-coloured from the fading ferns, stretched away to the skyline, broken only by the steeples of Tavistock, and by a cluster of houses away to the westward, which marked the Capleton stables. We all sprang out with the exception of Holmes, who continued to lean back with his eyes fixed upon the sky in front of him, entirely absorbed in his own thoughts. It was only when I touched his arm that he roused himself with a violent start and stepped out of the carriage.

'Excuse me,' said he, turning to Colonel Ross, who had looked at him in some surprise. 'I was day-dreaming.' There was a gleam in his eyes and a suppressed excitement in his manner which convinced me, used as I was to his ways, that his hand was upon a clue, though I could not imagine where he had found it.

'Perhaps you would prefer at once to go on to the scene of the crime, Mr Holmes?' said Gregory.

'I think that I should prefer to stay here a little and go into one or two questions of detail. Straker was brought back here, I presume?'

'Yes, he lies upstairs. The inquest is tomorrow.'

'He has been in your service some years, Colonel Ross?'

'I have always found him an excellent servant.'

'I presume that you made an inventory of what he had in his pockets at the time of his death, Inspector?'

'I have the things themselves in the sitting-room, if you would care to see them.'

'I should be very glad.'

We all filed into the front room, and sat round the central table, while the Inspector unlocked a square tin box and laid a small heap of things before us.

There was a box of vestas, two inches of tallow candle, an ADP briar-root pipe, a pouch of sealskin with half an ounce of long-cut cavendish, a silver watch with a gold chain, five sovereigns in gold, an aluminium pencil-case, a few papers, and an ivory-handled knife with a very delicate inflexible blade marked Weiss & Co., London.

'This is a very singular knife,' said Holmes, lifting it up and examining it minutely. 'I presume, as I see blood-stains upon it, that it is the one which was found in the dead man's grasp. Watson, this knife is surely in your line.'

'It is what we call a cataract knife,' said I.

'I thought so. A very delicate blade devised for very delicate work. A strange thing for a man to carry with him upon a rough expedition, especially as it would not shut in his pocket.'

'The tip was guarded by a disc of cork which we found beside his body,' said the Inspector. 'His wife tells us that the knife had lain for some days upon the dressing-table, and that he had picked it up as he left the room. It was a poor weapon, but perhaps the best that he could lay his hand on at the moment.'

'Very possible. How about these papers?'

'Three of them are receipted hay-dealers' accounts. One of them is a letter of instructions from Colonel Ross. This other is a milliner's account for thirty-seven pounds fifteen, made out by Madame Lesurier, of Bond Street, to William Darbyshire. Mrs Straker tells us that Darbyshire was a friend of her husband's, and that occasionally his letters were addressed here.'

'Madame Darbyshire had somewhat expensive tastes,' remarked Holmes, glancing down the account. 'Twenty-two guineas is rather heavy for a single costume. However, there appears to be nothing more to learn, and we may now go down to the scene of the crime.'

As we emerged from the sitting-room a woman who had been waiting in the passage took a step forward and laid her hand upon the Inspector's sleeve. Her face was haggard, and thin, and eager; stamped with the print of a recent horror.

'Have you got them? Have you found them?' she panted.

'No, Mrs Straker; but Mr Holmes, here, has come from London to help us, and we shall do all that is possible.'

'Surely I met you in Plymouth, at a garden party, some little time ago, Mrs Straker,' said Holmes.

'No, sir; you are mistaken.'

'Dear me; why, I could have sworn to it. You wore a costume of dove-coloured silk with ostrich feather trimming.'

'I never had such a dress, sir,' answered the lady.

'Ah; that quite settles it,' said Holmes; and, with an apology, he followed the Inspector outside. A short walk across the moor took us to the hollow in which the body had been found. At the brink of it was the furze bush upon which the coat had been hung.

'There was no wind that night, I understand,' said Holmes.

'None; but very heavy rain.'

'In that case the overcoat was not blown against the furze bushes, but placed there.'

'Yes, it was laid across the bush.'

'You fill me with interest. I perceive that the ground has been trampled up a good deal. No doubt many feet have been there since Monday night.'

'A piece of matting has been laid here at the side, and we have all stood upon that.'

'Excellent.'

'In this bag I have one of the boots which Straker wore, one of Fitzroy Simpson's shoes, and a cast horseshoe of Silver Blaze.'

'My dear Inspector, you surpass yourself!'

Holmes took the bag, and descending into the hollow he pushed the matting into a more central position. Then stretching himself upon his face and leaning his chin upon his hands he made a careful study of the trampled mud in front of him.

'Halloa!' said he, suddenly, 'what's this?'

It was a wax vesta, half burned, which was so coated with mud that it looked at first like a little chip of wood.

'I cannot think how I came to overlook it,' said the Inspector, with an expression of annoyance.

'It was invisible, buried in the mud. I only saw it because I was looking for it.'

'What! You expected to find it?'

'I thought it not unlikely.' He took the boots from the bag and compared the impressions of each of them with marks upon the ground. Then he clambered up to the rim of the hollow and crawled about among the ferns and bushes.

'I am afraid that there are no more tracks,' said the Inspector. 'I have examined the ground very carefully for a hundred yards in each direction.'

'Indeed!' said Holmes, rising, 'I should not have the impertinence to do it again after what you say. But I should like to take a little walk over the moors before it grows dark, that I may know my ground tomorrow, and I think that I shall put this horseshoe into my pocket for luck.'

Colonel Ross, who had shown some signs of impatience at my companion's quiet and systematic method of work, glanced at his watch.

'I wish you would come back with me, Inspector,' said he. 'There are several points on which I should like your advice,' and especially as to whether we do not owe it to the public to remove our horse's name from the entries for the Cup.'

'Certainly not,' cried Holmes, with decision; 'I should let the name stand.'

The Colonel bowed. 'I am very glad to have had your opinion, sir,' said he. 'You will find us at poor Straker's house when you have finished your walk, and we can drive together into Tavistock.'

He turned back with the Inspector, while Holmes and I walked slowly across the moor. The sun was beginning to sink behind the stables of Caple-ton, and the long sloping plain in front of us was tinged with gold, deepening into rich, ruddy brown where the faded ferns and brambles caught the evening light. But the glories of the landscape were all wasted upon my companion, who was sunk in the deepest thought.

'It's this way, Watson,' he said, at last. 'We may leave the question of who killed John Straker for the instant, and confine ourselves to finding out what has become of the horse. Now, supposing that he broke away during or after the tragedy, where could he have gone to? The horse is a very gregarious crea-ture. If left to himself, his instincts would have been either to return to King's Pyland or go over to Capleton. Why should he run wild upon the moor? He would surely have been seen by now. And why should gipsies kidnap him? These people always clear out when they hear of trouble, for they do not wish to be pestered by the police. They could not hope to sell such a horse. They would run a great risk and gain nothing by taking him. Surely that is clear.'

'Where is he, then?'

'I have already said that he must have gone to King's Pyland or to Caple-ton. He is not at King's Pyland, therefore he is at Capleton. Let us take that as a working hypothesis, and see what it leads us to. This part of the moor, as the Inspector remarked, is very hard and dry. But it falls away towards Capleton, and you can see from here that there is a long hollow over yonder, which must have been very wet on Monday night. If our supposition is correct, then the horse must have crossed that, and there is the point where we should look for his tracks.'

We had been walking briskly during this conversation, and a few more min-utes brought us to the hollow in question. At Holmes' request I walked down the bank to the right, and he to the left, but I had not taken fifty paces before I heard him give a shout, and saw him waving his hand to me. The track of a horse was plainly outlined in the soft earth in front of him, and the shoe which he took from his pocket exactly fitted the impression.

'See the value of imagination,' said Holmes. 'It is the one quality which Gregory lacks. We imagined what might have happened, acted upon the sup-position, and find ourselves justified. Let us proceed.'

We crossed the marshy bottom and passed over a quarter of a mile of dry, hard turf. Again the ground sloped and again we came on the tracks. Then we lost them for half a mile, but only to pick them up once more quite close to Capleton. It was Holmes who saw them first, and he stood pointing with a look of triumph upon his face. A man's track was visible beside the horse's.

'The horse was alone before,' I cried.

'Quite so. It was alone before. Halloa! what is this?'

The double track turned sharp off and took the direction of King's Pyland. Holmes whistled, and we both followed along after it. His eyes were on the trail, but I happened to look a little to one side, and saw to my surprise the same tracks coming back again in the opposite direction.

'One for you, Watson,' said Holmes, when I pointed it out, 'you have saved us a long walk which would have brought us back on our own traces. Let us follow the return track.'

We had not to go far. It ended at the paving of asphalt which led up to the gates of the Capleton stables. As we approached a groom ran out from them.

'We don't want any loiterers about here,' said he.

'I only wished to ask a question,' said Holmes, with his finger and thumb in his waistcoat pocket. 'Should I be too early to see your master, Mr Silas Brown, if I were to call at five o'clock tomorrow morning?'

'Bless you, sir, if anyone is about he will be, for he is always the first stirring. But here he is, sir, to answer your questions for himself. No, sir, no; it's as much as my place is worth to let him see me touch your money. Afterwards, if you like.'

As Sherlock Holmes replaced the half-crown which he had drawn from his pocket, a fierce-looking elderly man strode out from the gate with a hunting-crop swinging in his hand.

'What's this, Dawson?' he cried. 'No gossiping! Go about your business! And you—what the devil do you want here?'

'Ten minutes' talk with you, my good sir,' said Holmes, in the sweetest of voices.

'I've no time to talk to every gadabout. We want no strangers here. Be off, or you may find a dog at your heels.'

Holmes leaned forward and whispered something in the trainer's ear. He started violently and flushed to the temples.

'It's a lie!' he shouted. 'An infernal lie!'

'Very good! Shall we argue about it here in public, or talk it over in your parlour?'

'Oh, come in if you wish to.'

Holmes smiled. 'I shall not keep you more than a few minutes, Watson,' he said. 'Now, Mr Brown, I am quite at your disposal.'

It was quite twenty minutes, and the reds had all faded into greys before Holmes and the trainer reappeared. Never have I seen such a change as had been brought about in Silas Brown in that short time. His face was ashy pale, beads of perspiration shone upon his brow, and his hands shook until the hunting-crop wagged like a branch in the wind. His bullying, overbearing manner was all gone too, and he cringed along at my companion's side like a dog with its master.

'Your instructions will be done. It shall be done,' said he.

'There must be no mistake,' said Holmes, looking round at him. The other winced as he read the menace in his eyes.

'Oh, no, there shall be no mistake. It shall be there. Should I change it first or not?'

Holmes thought a little and then burst out laughing.

'No, don't,' said he. 'I shall write to you about it. No tricks now or—'

'Oh, you can trust me, you can trust me!'

'You must see to it on the day as if it were your own.'

'You can rely upon me.'

'Yes, I think I can. Well, you shall hear from me tomorrow.' He turned upon his heel, disregarding the trembling hand which the other held out to him, and we set off for King's Pyland.

'A more perfect compound of the bully, coward, and sneak than Master Silas Brown I have seldom met with,' remarked Holmes, as we trudged along together.

'He has the horse, then?'

'He tried to bluster out of it, but I described to him so exactly what his actions had been upon that morning, that he is convinced that I was watching him. Of course, you observed the peculiarly square toes in the impressions, and that his own boots exactly corresponded to them. Again, of course, no subordinate would have dared to have done such a thing. I described to him how when, according to his custom, he was the first down, he perceived a strange horse wandering over the moor; how he went out to it, and his astonishment at recognizing from the white forehead which has given the favourite its name that chance had put in his power the only horse which could beat the one upon which he had put his money. Then I described how his first impulse had been to lead him back to King's Pyland, and how the devil had shown him how he could hide the horse until the race was over, and how he had led it back and concealed it at Capleton. When I told him every detail he gave it up, and thought only of saving his own skin.'

'But his stables had been searched.'

'Oh, an old horse-faker like him has many a dodge.'

'But are you not afraid to leave the horse in his power now, since he has every interest in injuring it?'

'My dear fellow, he will guard it as the apple of his eye. He knows that his only hope of mercy is to produce it safe.'

'Colonel Ross did not impress me as a man who would be likely to show much mercy in any case.'

'The matter does not rest with Colonel Ross. I follow my own methods, and tell as much or as little as I choose. That is the advantage of being unofficial. I don't know whether you observed it, Watson, but the Colonel's manner has been just a trifle cavalier to me. I am inclined now to have a little amusement at his expense. Say nothing to him about the horse.'

'Certainly not, without your permission.'

'And, of course, this is all quite a minor case compared with the question of who killed John Straker.'

'And you will devote yourself to that?'

'On the contrary, we both go back to London by the night train.'

I was thunderstruck by my friend's words. We had only been a few hours in Devonshire, and that he should give up an investigation which he had begun so brilliantly was quite incomprehensible to me. Not a word more could I draw from him until we were back at the trainer's house. The Colonel and the Inspector were awaiting us in the parlour.

'My friend and I return to town by the midnight express,' said Holmes. 'We have had a charming little breath of your beautiful Dartmoor air.'

The Inspector opened his eyes, and the Colonel's lips curled in a sneer.

'So you despair of arresting the murderer of poor Straker,' said he.

Holmes shrugged his shoulders. 'There are certainly grave difficulties in the way,' said he. 'I have every hope, however, that your horse will start upon Tuesday, and I beg that you will have your jockey in readiness. Might I ask for a photograph of Mr John Straker?'

The Inspector took one from an envelope in his pocket and handed it to him.

'My dear Gregory, you anticipate all my wants. If I might ask you to wait here for an instant, I have a question which I should like to put to the maid.'

'I must say that I am rather disappointed in our London consultant,' said Colonel Ross, bluntly, as my friend left the room. 'I do not see that we are any further than when he came.'

'At least, you have his assurance that your horse will run,' said I.

'Yes, I have his assurance,' said the Colonel, with a shrug of his shoulders. 'I should prefer to have the horse.'

I was about to make some reply in defence of my friend, when he entered the room again.

'Now, gentlemen,' said he, 'I am quite ready for Tavistock.'

As we stepped into the carriage one of the stable lads held the door open for us. A sudden idea seemed to occur to Holmes, for he leaned forward and touched the lad upon the sleeve.

'You have a few sheep in the paddock,' he said. 'Who attends to them?'

'I do, sir.'

'Have you noticed anything amiss with them of late?'

'Well, sir, not of much account, but three of them have gone lame, sir.'

I could see that Holmes was extremely pleased, for he chuckled and rubbed his hands together.

'A long shot, Watson; a very long shot!' said he, pinching my arm. 'Gregory, let me recommend to your attention this singular epidemic among the sheep. Drive on, coachman!'

Colonel Ross still wore an expression which showed the poor opinion which he had formed of my companion's ability, but I saw by the Inspector's face that his attention had been keenly aroused.

'You consider that to be important?' he asked.

'Exceedingly so.'

'Is there any other point to which you would wish to draw my attention?'

'To the curious incident of the dog in the night-time.'

'The dog did nothing in the night-time.'

'That was the curious incident,' remarked Sherlock Holmes.

Four days later Holmes and I were again in the train bound for Winchester, to see the race for the Wessex Cup. Colonel Ross met us, by appointment, out-side the station, and we drove in his drag to the course beyond the town. His face was grave and his manner was cold in the extreme.

'I have seen nothing of my horse,' said he.

'I suppose that you would know him when you saw him?' asked Holmes.

The Colonel was very angry. 'I have been on the turf for twenty years, and never was asked such a question as that before,' said he. 'A child would know Silver Blaze with his white forehead and his mottled off foreleg.'

'How is the betting?'

'Well, that is the curious part of it. You could have got fifteen to one yes-terday, but the price has become shorter and shorter, until you can hardly get three to one now.'

'Hum!' said Holmes. 'Somebody knows something, that is clear!'

As the drag drew up in the enclosure near the grandstand, I glanced at the card to see the entries. It ran:

Wessex Plate. 50 sovs. each, h ft, with 1,000 sovs. added, for four- and five-year olds. Second £300. Third £200. New course (one mile and five furlongs).

1. Mr Heath Newton's The Negro (red cap, cinnamon jacket).
2. Colonel Wardlaw's Pugilist (pink cap, blue and black jacket).
3. Lord Backwater's Desborough (yellow cap and sleeves).
4. Colonel Ross's Silver Blaze (black cap, red jacket).
5. Duke of Balmoral's Iris (yellow and black stripes).
6. Lord Singleford's Rasper (purple cap, black sleeves).

'We scratched our other one and put all hopes on your word,' said the Colonel. 'Why, what is that? Silver Blaze favourite?'

'Five to four against Silver Blaze!' roared the ring. 'Five to four against Sil-ver Blaze! Fifteen to five against Desborough! Five to four on the field!'

'There are the numbers up,' I cried. 'They are all six there.'

'All six there! Then my horse is running,' cried the Colonel, in great agita-tion. 'But I don't see him. My colours have not passed.'

'Only five have passed. This must be he.'

As I spoke a powerful bay horse swept out from the weighing enclosure and cantered past us, bearing on its back the well-known black and red of the Colonel.

'That's not my horse,' cried the owner. 'That beast has not a white hair upon its body. What is this that you have done, Mr Holmes?'

'Well, well, let us see how he gets on,' said my friend, imperturbably. For a few minutes he gazed through my field-glass. 'Capital! An excellent start!' he cried suddenly. 'There they are, coming round the curve!'

From our drag we had a superb view as they came up the straight. The six horses were so close together that a carpet could have covered them, but half-way up the yellow of the Capleton stable showed to the front. Before they reached us, however, Desborough's bolt was shot, and the Colonel's horse, coming away with a rush, passed the post a good six lengths before its rival, the Duke of Balmoral's Iris making a bad third.

'It's my race anyhow,' gasped the Colonel, passing his hand over his eyes. 'I confess that I can make neither head nor tail of it. Don't you think that you have kept up your mystery long enough, Mr Holmes?'

'Certainly, Colonel. You shall know everything. Let us all go round and have a look at the horse together. Here he is,' he continued, as we made our way into the weighing enclosure where only owners and their friends find admittance. 'You have only to wash his face and his leg in spirits of wine and you will find that he is the same old Silver Blaze as ever.'

'You take my breath away!'

'I found him in the hands of a faker, and took the liberty of running him just as he was sent over.'

'My dear sir, you have done wonders. The horse looks very fit and well. It never went better in its life. I owe you a thousand apologies for having doubted your ability. You have done me a great service by recovering my horse. You would do me a greater still if you could lay your hands on the murderer of John Straker.'

'I have done so,' said Holmes, quietly.

The Colonel and I stared at him in amazement. 'You have got him! Where is he, then?'

'He is here.'

'Here! Where?'

'In my company at the present moment.'

The Colonel flushed angrily. 'I quite recognize that I am under obligations to you, Mr Holmes,' said he, 'but I must regard what you have just said as either a very bad joke or an insult.'

Sherlock Holmes laughed. 'I assure you that I have not associated you with the crime, Colonel,' said he, 'the real murderer is standing immediately behind you!'

He stepped past and laid his hand upon the glossy neck of the thorough-bred.

'The horse!' cried both the Colonel and myself.

'Yes, the horse. And it may lessen his guilt if I say that it was done in self-defence, and that John Straker was a man who was entirely unworthy of your confidence. But there goes the bell; and as I stand to win a little on this next race, I shall defer a more lengthy explanation until a more fitting time.'

We had the corner of a Pullman car to ourselves that evening as we whirled back to London, and I fancy that the journey was a short one to Colonel Ross as well as to myself, as we listened to our companion's narrative of the events which had occurred at the Dartmoor training stables upon the Monday night, and the means by which he had unravelled them.

'I confess,' said he, 'that any theories which I had formed from the newspaper reports were entirely erroneous. And yet there were indications there, had they not been overlaid by other details which concealed their true import. I went to Devonshire with the conviction that Fitzroy Simpson was the true culprit, although, of course, I saw that the evidence against him was by no means complete.

'It was while I was in the carriage, just as we reached the trainer's house, that the immense significance of the curried mutton occurred to me. You may remember that I was distrait, and remained sitting after you had all alighted. I was marvelling in my own mind how I could possibly have overlooked so obvious a clue.'

'I confess,' said the Colonel, 'that even now I cannot see how it helps us.'

'It was the first link in my chain of reasoning. Powdered opium is by no means tasteless. The flavour is not disagreeable, but it is perceptible. Were it mixed with any ordinary dish, the eater would undoubtedly detect it, and would probably eat no more. A curry was exactly the medium which would disguise this taste. By no possible supposition could this stranger, Fitzroy Simpson, have caused curry to be served in the trainer's family that night, and it is surely too monstrous a coincidence to suppose that he happened to come along with powdered opium upon the very night when a dish happened to be served which would disguise the flavour. That is unthinkable. Therefore Simpson becomes eliminated from the case, and our attention centres upon Straker and his wife, the only two people who could have chosen curried mutton for supper that night. The opium was added after the dish was set aside for the stable boy, for the others had the same for supper with no ill effects. Which of them, then, had access to that dish without the maid seeing them?

'Before deciding that question I had grasped the significance of the silence of the dog, for one true inference invariably suggests others. The Simpson incident had shown me that a dog was kept in the stables, and yet, though some-one had been in and had fetched out a horse, he had not barked enough to arouse the two lads in the loft. Obviously the midnight visitor was someone whom the dog knew well.

'I was already convinced, or almost convinced, that John Straker went down to the stables in the dead of the night and took out Silver Blaze. For what purpose? For a dishonest one, obviously, or why should he drug his own stable boy? And yet I was at a loss to know why. There have been cases before now where trainers have made sure of great sums of money by laying against their own horses, through agents, and then prevented them from winning by fraud. Sometimes it is a pulling jockey. Sometimes it is some surer and subtler means. What was it here? I hoped that the contents of his pockets might help me to form a conclusion.

'And they did so. You cannot have forgotten the singular knife which was found in the dead man's hand, a knife which certainly no sane man would choose for a weapon. It was, as Dr Watson told us, a form of knife which is used for the most delicate operations known in surgery. And it was to be used for a delicate operation that night. You must know, with your wide experience of turf matters, Colonel Ross, that it is possible to make a slight nick upon the tendons of a horse's ham, and to do it subcutaneously so as to leave absolutely no trace. A horse so treated would develop a slight lameness which would be put down to a strain in exercise or a touch of rheumatism, but never to foul play.'

'Villain! Scoundrel!' cried the Colonel.

'We have here the explanation of why John Straker wished to take the horse out on to the moor. So spirited a creature would have certainly roused the soundest of sleepers when it felt the prick of the knife. It was absolutely necessary to do it in the open air.'

'I have been blind!' cried the Colonel. 'Of course, that was why he needed the candle, and struck the match.'

'Undoubtedly. But in examining his belongings, I was fortunate enough to discover, not only the method of the crime, but even its motives. As a man of the world, Colonel, you know that men do not carry other people's bills about in their pockets. We have most of us quite enough to do to settle our own. I at once concluded that Straker was leading a double life, and keeping a second establishment. The nature of the bill showed that there was a lady in the case, and one who had expensive tastes. Liberal as you are with your servants, one hardly expects that they can buy twenty-guinea walking dresses for their women. I questioned Mrs Straker as to the dress without her knowing it, and having satisfied myself that it had never reached her, I made a note of the milliner's address, and felt that by calling there with Straker's photograph, I could easily dispose of the mythical Darbyshire.

'From that time on all was plain. Straker had led out the horse to a hollow where his light would be invisible. Simpson, in his flight, had dropped his cravat, and Straker had picked it up with some idea, perhaps, that he might use it in securing the horse's leg. Once in the hollow he had got behind the horse, and had struck a light, but the creature, frightened at the sudden glare, and with the strange instinct of animals feeling that some mischief was intended, had lashed out, and the steel shoe had struck Straker full on the forehead. He had already, in spite of the rain, taken off his overcoat in order to do his delicate task, and so, as he fell, his knife gashed his thigh. Do I make it clear?'

'Wonderful!' cried the Colonel. 'Wonderful! You might have been there.'

'My final shot was, I confess, a very long one. It struck me that so astute a man as Straker would not undertake this delicate tendon-nicking without a little practice. What could he practise on? My eyes fell upon the sheep, and I asked a question which, rather to my surprise, showed that my surmise was correct.'

'You have made it perfectly clear, Mr Holmes.'

'When I returned to London I called upon the milliner, who at once recognized Straker as an excellent customer, of the name of Darbyshire, who had a very dashing wife with a strong partiality for expensive dresses. I have no doubt that this woman had plunged him over head and ears in debt, and so led him into this miserable plot.'

'You have explained all but one thing,' cried the Colonel. 'Where was the horse?'

'Ah, it bolted and was cared for by one of your neighbours. We must have an amnesty in that direction, I think. This is Clapham Junction, if I am not mistaken, and we shall be in Victoria in less than ten minutes. If you care to smoke a cigar in our rooms, Colonel, I shall be happy to give you any other details which might interest you.'

AGATHA CHRISTIE

1890–1976

Unquestionably the most widely known female mystery writer in the world, Dame Agatha Mary Clarissa Miller Christie Mallowan was born in Torquay, on the south coast of Devon, England. She was educated first at home and then in Paris. In 1914 she married Archibald Christie, and during World War I she served as a volunteer nurse, which contributed to her knowledge of drugs and poisons often used in her mysteries. Her only child, Rosalind, was born in 1919. Agatha was divorced in 1928 and in 1930 married Max Mallowan, an archeologist, whom she accompanied on digs in the Middle East. This experience provided an interesting setting for some of her mysteries. In *An Autobiography* (1977), Christie says that she wrote her first novel, *The Mysterious Affair at Styles*, in response to a challenge from her sister Madge, and that she dashed off the manuscript in a scant two weeks in 1916. The first publisher she sent it to rejected it, as did several others, but when it was published in 1921, it was an instant success. In 1955 Christie was the first writer ever to be named Grand Master by the Mystery Writers of America. In 1971 she was awarded one of Britain's highest honors, Dame Commander, Order of the British Empire.

Christie is one of the best-selling authors in history, and her widely translated works continue to sell millions of copies. She created two of the all time best-loved series characters, Hercule Poirot and Miss Jane Marple. Poirot (introduced in Christie's first novel) is a retired Belgian police officer, now a meticulous amateur detective who uses his "little grey cells" to solve mysteries. Miss Marple (introduced in *Murder at the Vicarage* in 1930) is an elderly, inquisitive amateur detective from the village of St. Mary's Mead. Christie's murder mystery play *The Mousetrap* has been playing continuously in London since its opening in 1952, by far the longest run in theater history. Christie's great strength as a writer of classic mysteries centers around "puzzles," her ingenuity in plotting stories with sufficient misdirection to keep the reader wondering "whodunit." She epitomizes the Golden Age of mystery, yet was a rule-breaker who could make the narrator the murderer or have multiple people guilty of the same murder. "Witness for the Prosecution" was first published in 1933. Christie then developed the story as a play (first performed in 1954), and it was later adapted in two full-length films.

Recommended Christie works: *The Murder of Roger Ackroyd, Murder on the Orient Express, Miss Marple: The Complete Short Stories.*

Other recommended authors: Dorothy Gilman, Dorothy L. Sayers, Patricia Wentworth.

The Witness for the Prosecution

Mr Mayherne adjusted his pince-nez and cleared his throat with a little dry as dust cough that was wholly typical of him. Then he looked again at the man opposite him, the man charged with wilful murder.

Mr Mayherne was a small man, precise in manner, neatly, not to say foppishly dressed, with a pair of very shrewd and piercing grey eyes. By no means a fool. Indeed, as a solicitor, Mr Mayherne's reputation stood very high. His voice, when he spoke to his client, was dry but not unsympathetic.

'I must impress upon you again that you are in very grave danger, and that the utmost frankness is necessary.'

Leonard Vole, who had been staring in a dazed fashion at the blank wall in front of him, transferred his glance to the solicitor.

'I know,' he said hopelessly. 'You keep telling me so. But I can't seem to realize yet that I'm charged with murder—*murder*. And such a dastardly crime too.'

Mr Mayherne was practical, not emotional. He coughed again, took off his pince-nez, polished them carefully, and replaced them on his nose. Then he said:

'Yes, yes, yes. Now, my dear Mr Vole, we're going to make a determined effort to get you off—and we shall succeed—we shall succeed. But I must have all the facts. I must know just how damaging the case against you is likely to be. Then we can fix upon the best line of defence.'

Still the young man looked at him in the same dazed, hopeless fashion. To Mr Mayherne the case had seemed black enough, and the guilt of the prisoner assured. Now, for the first time, he felt a doubt.

'You think I'm guilty,' said Leonard Vole, in a low voice. 'But, by God, I swear I'm not! It looks pretty black against me, I know that. I'm like a man caught in a net—the meshes of it all round me, entangling me whichever way I turn. But I didn't do it, Mr Mayherne, I didn't do it.'

In such a position a man was bound to protest his innocence. Mr Mayherne knew that. Yet, in spite of himself, he was impressed. It might be, after all, that Leonard Vole was innocent.

'You are right, Mr Vole,' he said gravely. 'The case does look very black against you. Nevertheless, I accept your assurance. Now, let us get to facts. I want you to tell me in your own words exactly how you came to make the acquaintance of Miss Emily French.'

'It was one day in Oxford Street. I saw an elderly lady crossing the road. She was carrying a lot of parcels. In the middle of the street she dropped them, tried to recover them, found a 'bus was almost on top of her and just managed to reach the curb safely, dazed and bewildered by people having shouted at her. I recovered her parcels, wiped the mud off them as best I could, retied the string of one, and returned them to her.'

'There was no question of your having saved her life?'

'Oh! dear me, no. All I did was to perform a common act of courtesy. She was extremely grateful, thanked me warmly, and said something about my manners not being those of most of the younger generation—I can't remember the exact words. Then I lifted my hat and went on. I never expected to see her again. But life is full of coincidences. That very evening I came across her at a party at a friend's house. She recognized me at once and asked that I should be introduced to her. I then found out that she was a Miss Emily French and that she lived at Cricklewood. I talked to her for some time. She was, I imagined, an old lady who took sudden and violent fancies to people. She took one to me on the strength of a perfectly simple action which anyone might have performed. On leaving, she shook me warmly by the hand, and asked me to come and see her. I replied, of course, that I should be very pleased to do so, and she then urged me to name a day. I did not want particularly to go, but it would have seemed churlish to refuse, so I fixed on the following Saturday. After she had gone, I learned something about her from my friends. That she was rich, eccentric, lived alone with one maid and owned no less than eight cats.'

'I see,' said Mr Mayherne. 'The question of her being well off came up as early as that?'

'If you mean that I inquired—' began Leonard Vole hotly, but Mr Mayherne stilled him with a gesture.

'I have to look at the case as it will be presented by the other side. An ordinary observer would not have supposed Miss French to be a lady of means. She lived poorly, almost humbly. Unless you had been told the contrary, you would in all probability have considered her to be in poor circumstances—at any rate to begin with. Who was it exactly who told you that she was well off?'

'My friend, George Harvey, at whose house the party took place.'

'Is he likely to remember having done so?'

'I really don't know. Of course it is some time ago now.'

'Quite so, Mr Vole. You see, the first aim of the prosecution will be to establish that you were in low water financially—that is true, is it not?'

Leonard Vole flushed.

'Yes,' he said, in a low voice. 'I'd been having a run of infernal bad luck just then.'

'Quite so,' said Mr Mayherne again. 'That being, as I say, in low water financially, you met this rich old lady and cultivated her acquaintance assiduously. Now if we are in a position to say that you had no idea she was well off, and that you visited her out of pure kindness of heart—'

'Which is the case.'

'I dare say. I am not disputing the point. I am looking at it from the outside point of view. A great deal depends on the memory of Mr Harvey. Is he likely to remember that conversation or is he not? Could he be confused by counsel into believing that it took place later?'

Leonard Vole reflected for some minutes. Then he said steadily enough, but with a rather paler face:

'I do not think that that line would be successful, Mr Mayherne. Several of those present heard his remark, and one or two of them chaffed me about my conquest of a rich old lady.'

The solicitor endeavoured to hide his disappointment with a wave of the hand.

'Unfortunate,' he said. 'But I congratulate you upon your plain speaking, Mr Vole. It is to you I look to guide me. Your judgement is quite right. To persist in the line I spoke of would have been disastrous. We must leave that point. You made the acquaintance of Miss French, you called upon her, the acquaintanceship progressed. We want a clear reason for all this. Why did you, a young man of thirty-three, good-looking, fond of sport, popular with your friends, devote so much of your time to an elderly woman with whom you could hardly have anything in common?'

Leonard Vole flung out his hands in a nervous gesture.

'I can't tell you—I really can't tell you. After the first visit, she pressed me to come again, spoke of being lonely and unhappy. She made it difficult for me to refuse. She showed so plainly her fondness and affection for me that I was placed in an awkward position. You see, Mr Mayherne, I've got a weak nature— I drift—I'm one of those people who can't say "No". And believe me or not, as you like, after the third or fourth visit I paid her I found myself getting genuinely fond of the old thing. My mother died when I was young, an aunt brought me up, and she too died before I was fifteen. If I told you that I genuinely enjoyed being mothered and pampered, I dare say you'd only laugh.'

Mr Mayherne did not laugh. Instead he took off his pince-nez again and polished them, always a sign with him that he was thinking deeply.

'I accept your explanation, Mr Vole,' he said at last. 'I believe it to be psychologically probable. Whether a jury would take that view of it is another matter. Please continue your narrative. When was it that Miss French first asked you to look into her business affairs?'

'After my third or fourth visit to her. She understood very little of money matters, and was worried about some investments.'

Mr Mayherne looked up sharply.

'Be careful, Mr Vole. The maid, Janet Mackenzie, declares that her mistress was a good woman of business and transacted all her own affairs, and this is borne out by the testimony of her bankers.'

'I can't help that,' said Vole earnestly. 'That's what she said to me.'

Mr Mayherne looked at him for a moment or two in silence. Though he had no intention of saying so, his belief in Leonard Vole's innocence was at that moment strengthened. He knew something of the mentality of elderly ladies. He saw Miss French, infatuated with the good-looking young man, hunting about for pretexts that should bring him to the house. What more likely than that she should plead ignorance of business, and beg him to help her with her money affairs? She was enough of a woman of the world to realize that any man is slightly flattered by such an admission of his superiority. Leonard Vole had been flattered. Perhaps, too, she had not been averse to letting this young man know that she was wealthy. Emily French had been a strong-willed old woman, willing to pay her price for what she wanted. All this passed rapidly through Mr Mayherne's mind, but he gave no indication of it, and asked instead a further question.

'And you did handle her affairs for her at her request?'

'I did.'

'Mr Vole,' said the solicitor. 'I am going to ask you a very serious question, and one to which it is vital I should have a truthful answer. You were in low water financially. You had the handling of an old lady's affairs—an old lady who, according to her own statement, knew little or nothing of business. Did you at any time, or in any manner, convert to your own use the securities which you handled? Did you engage in any transaction for your own pecuniary advantage which will not bear the light of day?' He quelled the other's response. 'Wait a minute before you answer. There are two courses open to us. Either we can make a feature of your probity and honesty in conducting her affairs whilst pointing out how unlikely it is that you would commit murder to obtain money which you might have obtained by such infinitely easier means. If, on the other hand, there is anything in your dealings which the prosecution will get hold of—if, to put it baldly, it can be proved that you swindled the old lady in any way, we must take the line that you had no motive for the murder, since she was already a profitable source of income to you. You perceive the distinction. Now, I beg of you, take your time before you reply.'

But Leonard Vole took no time at all.

'My dealings with Miss French's affairs are all perfectly fair and above board. I acted for her interests to the very best of my ability, as anyone will find who looks into the matter.'

'Thank you,' said Mr Mayherne. 'You relieve my mind very much. I pay you the compliment of believing that you are far too clever to lie to me over such an important matter.'

'Surely,' said Vole eagerly, 'the strongest point in my favour is the lack of motive. Granted that I cultivated the acquaintanceship of a rich old lady in the hopes of getting money out of her—that, I gather, is the substance of what you have been saying—surely her death frustrates all my hopes?'

The solicitor looked at him steadily. Then, very deliberately, he repeated his unconscious trick with his pince-nez. It was not until they were firmly replaced on his nose that he spoke.

'Are you not aware, Mr Vole, that Miss French left a will under which you are the principal beneficiary?'

'What?' The prisoner sprang to his feet. His dismay was obvious and unforced. 'My God! What are you saying? She left her money to me?'

Mr Mayherne nodded slowly. Vole sank down again, his head in his hands.

'You pretend to know nothing of this will?'

'Pretend? There's no pretence about it. I knew nothing about it.'

'What would you say if I told you that the maid, Janet Mackenzie, swears that you *did* know? That her mistress told her distinctly that she had consulted you in the matter, and told you of her intentions?'

'Say? That she's lying! No, I go too fast. Janet is an elderly woman. She was a faithful watchdog to her mistress, and she didn't like me. She was jealous and suspicious. I should say that Miss French confided her intentions to Janet, and that Janet either mistook something she said, or else was convinced in her own mind that I had persuaded the old lady into doing it. I dare say that she believes herself now that Miss French actually told her so.'

'You don't think she dislikes you enough to lie deliberately about the matter?'

Leonard Vole looked shocked and startled.

'No, indeed! Why should she?'

'I don't know,' said Mr Mayherne thoughtfully. 'But she's very bitter against you.'

The wretched young man groaned again.

'I'm beginning to see,' he muttered. 'It's frightful. I made up to her, that's what they'll say. I got her to make a will leaving her money to me, and then I go there that night, and there's nobody in the house—they find her the next day—oh! my God, it's awful!'

'You are wrong about there being nobody in the house,' said Mr Mayherne. 'Janet, as you remember, was to go out for the evening. She went, but about half-past nine she returned to fetch the pattern of a blouse sleeve which she had promised to a friend. She let herself in by the back door, went upstairs and fetched it, and went out again. She heard voices in the sitting-room, though she could not distinguish what they said, but she will swear that one of them was Miss French's and one was a man's.'

'At half-past nine,' said Leonard Vole. 'At half-past nine . . . ' He sprang to his feet. 'But then I'm saved—saved—'

'What do you mean, saved?' cried Mr Mayherne, astonished.

'*By half-past nine I was at home again!* My wife can prove that. I left Miss French about five minutes to nine. I arrived home about twenty past nine. My wife was there waiting for me. Oh! Thank God—thank God! And bless Janet Mackenzie's sleeve pattern.'

In his exuberance, he hardly noticed that the grave expression of the solicitor's face had not altered. But the latter's words brought him down to earth with a bump.

'Who, then, in your opinion, murdered Miss French?'

'Why, a burglar, of course, as was thought at first. The window was forced, you remember. She was killed with a heavy blow from a crowbar, and the crowbar was found lying on the floor beside the body. And several articles were missing. But for Janet's absurd suspicions and dislike of me, the police would never have swerved from the right track.'

'That will hardly do, Mr Vole,' said the solicitor. 'The things that were missing were mere trifles of no value, taken as a blind. And the marks on the window were not at all conclusive. Besides, think for yourself. You say you were no longer in the house by half-past nine. Who, then, was the man Janet heard talking to Miss French in the sitting-room? She would hardly be having an amicable conversation with a burglar?'

'No,' said Vole. 'No—' He looked puzzled and discouraged. 'But anyway,' he added with reviving spirit, 'it lets me out. I've got an alibi. You must see Romaine—my wife—at once.'

'Certainly,' acquiesced the lawyer. 'I should already have seen Mrs Vole but for her being absent when you were arrested. I wired to Scotland at once, and I understand that she arrives back tonight. I am going to call upon her immediately I leave here.'

Vole nodded, a great expression of satisfaction settling down over his face.

'Yes, Romaine will tell you. My God! it's a lucky chance that.'

'Excuse me, Mr Vole, but you are very fond of your wife?'

'Of course.'

'And she of you?'

'Romaine is devoted to me. She'd do anything in the world for me.'

He spoke enthusiastically, but the solicitor's heart sank a little lower. The testimony of a devoted wife—would it gain credence?

'Was there anyone else who saw you return at nine-twenty? A maid, for instance?'

'We have no maid.'

'Did you meet anyone in the street on the way back?'

'Nobody I knew. I rode part of the way in a 'bus. The conductor might remember.'

Mr Mayherne shook his head doubtfully.

'There is no one, then, who can confirm your wife's testimony?'

'No. But it isn't necessary, surely?'

'I dare say not. I dare say not,' said Mr Mayherne hastily. 'Now there's just one thing more. Did Miss French know that you were a married man?'

'Oh, yes.'

'Yet you never took your wife to see her. Why was that?'

For the first time, Leonard Vole's answer came halting and uncertain.

'Well—I don't know.'

'Are you aware that Janet Mackenzie says her mistress believed you to be single, and contemplated marrying you in the future?'

Vole laughed.

'Absurd! There was forty years difference in age between us.'

'It has been done,' said the solicitor drily. 'The fact remains. Your wife never met Miss French?'

'No—' Again the constraint.

'You will permit me to say,' said the lawyer, 'that I hardly understand your attitude in the matter.'

Vole flushed, hesitated, and then spoke.

'I'll make a clean breast of it. I was hard up, as you know. I hoped that Miss French might lend me some money. She was fond of me, but she wasn't at all interested in the struggles of a young couple. Early on, I found that she had taken it for granted that my wife and I didn't get on—were living apart. Mr Mayherne—I wanted the money—for Romaine's sake. I said nothing, and allowed the old lady to think what she chose. She spoke of my being an adopted son to her. There was never any question of marriage—that must be just Janet's imagination.'

'And that is all?'

'Yes—that is all.'

Was there just a shade of hesitation in the words? The lawyer fancied so. He rose and held out his hand.

'Goodbye, Mr Vole.' He looked into the haggard young face and spoke with an unusual impulse. 'I believe in your innocence in spite of the multitude of facts arrayed against you. I hope to prove it and vindicate you completely.'

Vole smiled back at him.

'You'll find the alibi is all right,' he said cheerfully.

Again he hardly noticed that the other did not respond.

'The whole thing hinges a good deal on the testimony of Janet Mackenzie,' said Mr Mayherne. 'She hates you. That much is clear.'

'She can hardly hate me,' protested the young man.

The solicitor shook his head as he went out.

'Now for Mrs Vole,' he said to himself.

He was seriously disturbed by the way the thing was shaping.

The Voles lived in a small shabby house near Paddington Green. It was to this house that Mr Mayherne went.

In answer to his ring, a big slatternly woman, obviously a char-woman, answered the door.

'Mrs Vole? Has she returned yet?'

'Got back an hour ago. But I dunno if you can see her.'

'If you will take my card to her,' said Mr Mayherne quietly, 'I am quite sure that she will do so.'

The woman looked at him doubtfully, wiped her hand on her apron and took the card. Then she closed the door in his face and left him on the step outside.

In a few minutes, however, she returned with a slightly altered manner.

'Come inside, please.'

She ushered him into a tiny drawing-room. Mr Mayherne, examining a drawing on the wall, started up suddenly to face a tall pale woman who had entered so quietly that he had not heard her.

'Mr Mayherne? You are my husband's solicitor, are you not? You have come from him? Will you please sit down?'

Until she spoke he had not realized that she was not English. Now, observing her more closely, he noticed the high cheekbones, the dense blue-black of the hair, and an occasional very slight movement of the hands that was distinctly foreign. A strange woman, very quiet. So quiet as to make one uneasy. From the very first Mr Mayherne was conscious that he was up against something that he did not understand.

'Now, my dear Mrs Vole,' he began, 'you must not give way—'

He stopped. It was so very obvious that Romaine Vole had not the slightest intention of giving way. She was perfectly calm and composed.

'Will you please tell me all about it?' she said. 'I must know everything. Do not think to spare me. I want to know the worst.' She hesitated, then repeated in a lower tone, with a curious emphasis which the lawyer did not understand: 'I want to know the worst.'

Mr Mayherne went over his interview with Leonard Vole. She listened attentively, nodding her head now and then.

'I see,' she said, when he had finished. 'He wants me to say that he came in at twenty minutes past nine that night?'

'He did come in at that time?' said Mr Mayherne sharply.

'That is not the point,' she said coldly. 'Will my saying so acquit him? Will they believe me?'

Mr Mayherne was taken aback. She had gone so quickly to the core of the matter.

'That is what I want to know,' she said. 'Will it be enough? Is there anyone else who can support my evidence?'

There was a suppressed eagerness in her manner that made him vaguely uneasy.

'So far there is no one else,' he said reluctantly.

'I see,' said Romaine Vole.

She sat for a minute or two perfectly still. A little smile played over her lips. The lawyer's feeling of alarm grew stronger and stronger.

'Mrs Vole—' he began. 'I know what you must feel—'

'Do you?' she said. 'I wonder.'

'In the circumstances—'

'In the circumstances—I intend to play a lone hand.'

He looked at her in dismay.

'But, my dear Mrs Vole—you are overwrought. Being so devoted to your husband—'

'I beg your pardon?'

The sharpness of her voice made him start. He repeated in a hesitating manner:

'Being so devoted to your husband—'

Romaine Vole nodded slowly, the same strange smile on her lips.

'Did he tell you that I was devoted to him?' she asked softly. 'Ah! yes, I can see he did. How stupid men are! Stupid—stupid—stupid—'

She rose suddenly to her feet. All the intense emotion that the lawyer had been conscious of in the atmosphere was now concentrated in her tone.

'I hate him, I tell you! I hate him. I hate him. I hate him! I would like to see him hanged by the neck till he is dead.'

The lawyer recoiled before her and the smouldering passion in her eyes.

She advanced a step nearer, and continued vehemently:

'Perhaps I *shall* see it. Supposing I tell you that he did not come in that night at twenty past nine, but at twenty past *ten*? You say that he tells you he knew nothing about the money coming to him. Supposing I tell you he knew all about it, and counted on it, and committed murder to get it? Supposing I tell you that he admitted to me that night when he came in what he had done? That there was blood on his coat? What then? Supposing that I stand up in court and say all these things?'

Her eyes seemed to challenge him. With an effort, he concealed his growing dismay, and endeavoured to speak in a rational tone.

'You cannot be asked to give evidence against your husband—'

'He is not my husband!'

The words came out so quickly that he fancied he had misunderstood her.

'I beg your pardon? I—'

'He is not my husband.'

The silence was so intense that you could have heard a pin drop.

'I was an actress in Vienna. My husband is alive but in a madhouse. So we could not marry. I am glad now.'

She nodded defiantly.

'I should like you to tell me one thing,' said Mr Mayherne. He contrived to appear as cool and unemotional as ever. 'Why are you so bitter against Leonard Vole?'

She shook her head, smiling a little.

'Yes, you would like to know. But I shall not tell you. I will keep my secret ...'

Mr Mayherne gave his dry little cough and rose.

'There seems no point in prolonging this interview,' he remarked. 'You will hear from me again after I have communicated with my client.'

She came closer to him, looking into his eyes with her own wonderful dark ones.

'Tell me,' she said, 'did you believe—honestly—that he was innocent when you came here today?'

'I did,' said Mr Mayherne.

'You poor little man,' she laughed.

'And I believe so still,' finished the lawyer. 'Good evening, madam.'

He went out of the room, taking with him the memory of her startled face.

'This is going to be the devil of a business,' said Mr Mayherne to himself as he strode along the street.

Extraordinary, the whole thing. An extraordinary woman. A very dangerous woman. Women were the devil when they got their knife into you.

What was to be done? That wretched young man hadn't a leg to stand upon. Of course, possibly he did commit the crime ...

'No,' said Mr Mayherne to himself. 'No—there's almost too much evidence against him. I don't believe this woman. She was trumping up the whole story. But she'll never bring it into court.'

He wished he felt more conviction on the point.

The police court proceedings were brief and dramatic. The principal witnesses for the prosecution were Janet Mackenzie, maid to the dead woman, and Romaine Heilger, Austrian subject, the mistress of the prisoner.

Mr Mayherne sat in court and listened to the damning story that the latter told. It was on the lines she had indicated to him in their interview.

The prisoner reserved his defence and was committed for trial.

Mr Mayherne was at his wits' end. The case against Leonard Vole was black beyond words. Even the famous KC who was engaged for the defence held out little hope.

'If we can shake the Austrian woman's testimony, we might do something,' he said dubiously. 'But it's a bad business.'

Mr Mayherne had concentrated his energies on one single point. Assuming Leonard Vole to be speaking the truth, and to have left the murdered woman's house at nine o'clock, who was the man whom Janet heard talking to Miss French at half-past nine?

The only ray of light was in the shape of a scapegrace nephew who had in bygone days cajoled and threatened his aunt out of various sums of money. Janet Mackenzie, the solicitor learned, had always been attached to this young man, and had never ceased urging his claims upon her mistress. It certainly seemed possible that it was this nephew who had been with Miss French after Leonard Vole left, especially as he was not to be found in any of his old haunts.

In all other directions, the lawyer's researches had been negative in their result. No one had seen Leonard Vole entering his own house, or leaving that of Miss French. No one had seen any other man enter or leave the house in Cricklewood. All inquiries drew blank.

It was the eve of the trial when Mr Mayherne received the letter which was to lead his thoughts in an entirely new direction.

It came by the six o'clock post. An illiterate scrawl, written on common paper and enclosed in a dirty envelope with the stamp stuck on crooked.

Mr Mayherne read it through once or twice before he grasped its meaning.

DEAR MISTER:

Youre the lawyer chap wot acks for the young feller. If you want that painted foreign hussy showd up for wot she is an her pack of lies you come to 16 Shaw's Rents Stepney tonight It ull cawst you 2 hundred quid Arsk for Missis Mogson.

The solicitor read and re-read this strange epistle. It might, of course, be a hoax, but when he thought it over, he became increasingly convinced that it was genuine, and also convinced that it was the one hope for the prisoner. The evidence of Romaine Heilger damned him completely, and the line the defence meant to pursue, the line that the evidence of a woman who had admittedly lived an immoral life was not to be trusted, was at best a weak one.

Mr Mayherne's mind was made up. It was his duty to save his client at all costs. He must go to Shaw's Rents.

He had some difficulty in finding the place, a ramshackle building in an evil-smelling slum, but at last he did so, and on inquiry for Mrs Mogson was sent up to a room on the third floor. On this door he knocked, and getting no answer, knocked again.

At this second knock, he heard a shuffling sound inside, and presently the door was opened cautiously half an inch and a bent figure peered out.

Suddenly the woman, for it was a woman, gave a chuckle and opened the door wider.

'So it's you, dearie,' she said, in a wheezy voice. 'Nobody with you, is there? No playing tricks? That's right. You can come in—you can come in.'

With some reluctance the lawyer stepped across the threshold into the small dirty room, with its flickering gas jet. There was an untidy unmade bed in a corner, a plain deal table and two rickety chairs. For the first time Mr Mayherne had a full view of the tenant of this unsavoury apartment. She was a woman of middle age, bent in figure, with a mass of untidy grey hair and a scarf wound tightly round her face. She saw him looking at this and laughed again, the same curious toneless chuckle.

'Wondering why I hide my beauty, dear? He, he, he. Afraid it may tempt you, eh? But you shall see—you shall see.'

She drew aside the scarf and the lawyer recoiled involuntarily before the almost formless blur of scarlet. She replaced the scarf again.

'So you're not wanting to kiss me, dearie? He, he, I don't wonder. And yet I was a pretty girl once—not so long ago as you'd think, either. Vitriol, dearie, vitriol—that's what did that: Ah! but I'll be even with 'em—'

She burst into a hideous torrent of profanity which Mr Mayherne tried vainly to quell. She fell silent at last, her hands clenching and unclenching themselves nervously.

'Enough of that,' said the lawyer sternly. 'I've come here because I have reason to believe you can give me information which will clear my client, Leonard Vole. Is that the case?'

Her eyes leered at him cunningly.

'What about the money, dearie?' she wheezed. 'Two hundred quid, you remember.'

'It is your duty to give evidence, and you can be called upon to do so.'

'That won't do, dearie. I'm an old woman, and I know nothing. But you give me two hundred quid, and perhaps I can give you a hint or two. See?'

'What kind of hint?'

'What should you say to a letter? A letter from *her*. Never mind how I got hold of it. That's my business. It'll do the trick. But I want my two hundred quid.'

Mr Mayherne looked at her coldly, and made up his mind.

'I'll give you ten pounds, nothing more. And only that if this letter is what you say it is.'

'Ten pounds?' She screamed and raved at him.

'Twenty,' said Mr Mayherne, 'and that's my last word.'

He rose as if to go. Then, watching her closely he drew out a pocket-book, and counted out twenty one-pound notes.

'You see,' he said. 'That is all I have with me. You can take it or leave it.'

But already he knew that the sight of the money was too much for her. She cursed and raved impotently, but at last she gave in. Going over to the bed, she drew something out from beneath the tattered mattress.

'Here you are, damn you!' she snarled. 'It's the top one you want.'

It was a bundle of letters that she threw to him, and Mr Mayherne untied them and scanned them in his usual cool, methodical manner. The woman, watching him eagerly, could gain no clue from his impassive face.

He read each letter through, then returned again to the top one and read it a second time. Then he tied the whole bundle up again carefully.

They were love letters, written by Romaine Heilger, and the man they were written to was not Leonard Vole. The top letter was dated the day of the latter's arrest.

'I spoke true, dearie, didn't?' whined the woman. 'It'll do for her, that letter?'

Mr Mayherne put the letters in his pocket, then he asked a question.

'How did you get hold of this correspondence?'

'That's telling,' she said with a leer. 'But I know something more. I heard in court what that hussy said. Find out where *she* was at twenty past ten, the time she says she was at home. Ask at the Lion Road Cinema. They'll remember—a fine upstanding girl like that—curse her!

'Who is the man?' asked Mr Mayherne. 'There's only a Christian name here.'

The other's voice grew thick and hoarse, her hands clenched and unclenched. Finally she lifted one to her face.

'He's the man that did this to me. Many years ago now. She took him away from me—a chit of a girl she was then. And when I went after him—and went for him too—he threw the cursed stuff at me! And she laughed—damn her! I've had it in for her for years. Followed her, I have, spied upon her. And now I've got her! She'll suffer for this, won't she, Mr Lawyer? She'll suffer?'

'She will probably be sentenced to a term of imprisonment for perjury,' said Mr Mayherne quietly.

'Shut away—that's what I want. You're going, are you? Where's my money? Where's that good money?'

Without a word, Mr Mayherne put down the notes on the table. Then, drawing a deep breath, he turned and left the squalid room. Looking back, he saw the old woman crooning over the money.

He wasted no time. He found the cinema in Lion Road easily enough, and, shown a photograph of Romaine Heilger, the commissionaire recognized her at once. She had arrived at the cinema with a man some time after ten o'clock on the evening in question. He had not noticed her escort particularly, but he remembered the lady who had spoken to him about the picture that was showing. They stayed until the end, about an hour later.

Mr Mayherne was satisfied. Romaine Heilger's evidence was a tissue of lies from beginning to end. She had evolved it out of her passionate hatred. The lawyer wondered whether he would ever know what lay behind that hatred. What had Leonard Vole done to her? He had seemed dumbfounded when the solicitor had reported her attitude to him. He had declared earnestly that such a thing was incredible—yet it had seemed to Mr Mayherne that after the first astonishment his protests had lacked sincerity.

He *did* know. Mr Mayherne was convinced of it. He knew, but he had no intention of revealing the fact. The secret between those two remained a secret. Mr Mayherne wondered if some day he should come to learn what it was.

The solicitor glanced at his watch. It was late, but time was everything. He hailed a taxi and gave an address.

'Sir Charles must know of this at once,' he murmured to himself as he got in.

The trial of Leonard Vole for the murder of Emily French aroused widespread interest. In the first place the prisoner was young and good-looking, then he was accused of a particularly dastardly crime, and there was the further interest of Romaine Heilger, the principal witness for the prosecution. There had been pictures of her in many papers, and several fictitious stories as to her origin and history.

The proceedings opened quietly enough. Various technical evidence came first. Then Janet Mackenzie was called. She told substantially the same story as before. In cross-examination counsel for the defence succeeded in getting her to contradict herself once or twice over her account of Vole's association with Miss French; he emphasized the fact that though she had heard a man's voice in the sitting-room that night, there was nothing to show that it was Vole who was there, and he managed to drive home a feeling that jealousy and dislike of the prisoner were at the bottom of a good deal of her evidence.

Then the next witness was called.

'Your name is Romaine Heilger?'

'Yes.'

'You are an Austrian subject?'

'Yes.'

'For the last three years you have lived with the prisoner and passed yourself off as his wife?'

Just for a moment Romaine Heilger's eyes met those of the man in the dock. Her expression held something curious and unfathomable.

'Yes.'

The question went on. Word by word the damning facts came out. On the night in question the prisoner had taken out a crowbar with him. He had returned at twenty minutes past ten, and had confessed to having killed the old lady. His cuffs had been stained with blood, and he had burned them in the kitchen stove. He had terrorized her into silence by means of threats.

As the story proceeded, the feeling of the court which had, to begin with, been slightly favourable to the prisoner, now set dead against him. He himself sat with downcast head and moody air, as though he knew he were doomed.

Yet it might have been noted that her own counsel sought to restrain Romaine's animosity. He would have preferred her to be a more unbiased witness.

Formidable and ponderous, counsel for the defence arose.

He put it to her that her story was a malicious fabrication from start to finish, that she had not even been in her own house at the time in question, that she was in love with another man and was deliberately seeking to send Vole to his death for a crime he did not commit.

Romaine denied these allegations with superb insolence.

Then came the surprising denouement, the production of the letter. It was read aloud in court in the midst of a breathless stillness.

> Max, beloved, the Fates have delivered him into our hands! He has been arrested for murder—but, yes, the murder of an old lady! Leonard who would not hurt a fly! At last I shall have my revenge. The poor chicken! I shall say that he came in that night with blood upon him—that he confessed to me. I shall hang him, Max—and when he hangs he will know and realize that it was Romaine who sent him to his death. And then—happiness, Beloved! Happiness at last!

There were experts present ready to swear that the handwriting was that of Romaine Heilger, but they were not needed. Confronted with the letter, Romaine broke down utterly and confessed everything. Leonard Vole had returned to the house at the time he said, twenty past nine. She had invented the whole story to ruin him.

With the collapse of Romaine Heilger, the case for the Crown collapsed also. Sir Charles called his few witnesses, the prisoner himself went into the box and told his story in a manly straightforward manner, unshaken by cross-examination.

The prosecution endeavoured to rally, but without great success. The judge's summing up was not wholly favourable to the prisoner, but a reaction had set in and the jury needed little time to consider their verdict.

'We find the prisoner not guilty.'

Leonard Vole was free!

Little Mr Mayherne hurried from his seat. He must congratulate his client.

He found himself polishing his pince-nez vigorously, and checked himself. His wife had told him only the night before that he was getting a habit of it. Curious things, habits. People themselves never knew they had them.

An interesting case—a very interesting case. That woman, now, Romaine Heilger.

The case was dominated for him still by the exotic figure of Romaine Heilger. She had seemed a pale quiet woman in the house at Paddington, but in court she had flamed out against the sober background. She had flaunted herself like a tropical flower.

If he closed his eyes he could see her now, tall and vehement, her exquisite body bent forward a little, her right hand clenching and unclenching itself unconsciously all the time.

Curious things, habits. That gesture of hers with the hand was her habit, he supposed. Yet he had seen someone else do it quite lately. Who was it now? Quite lately—

He drew in his breath with a gasp as it came back to him. *The woman in Shaw's Rents* . . .

He stood still, his head whirling. It was impossible—impossible—Yet, Romaine Heilger was an actress.

The KC came up behind him and clapped him on the shoulder.

'Congratulated our man yet? He's had a narrow shave, you know, Come along and see him.'

But the little lawyer shook off the other's hand.

He wanted one thing only—to see Romaine Heilger face to face.

He did not see her until some time later, and the place of their meeting is not relevant.

'So you guessed,' she said, when he had told her all that was in his mind. 'The face? Oh! that was easy enough, and the light of that gas jet was too bad for you to see the make-up.'

'But why—why—'

'Why did I play a lone hand?' She smiled a little, remembering the last time she had used the words.

'Such an elaborate comedy!'

'My friend—I had to save him. The evidence of a woman devoted to him would not have been enough—you hinted as much yourself. But I know something of the psychology of crowds. Let my evidence be wrung from me, as an admission, damning me in the eyes of the law, and a reaction in favour of the prisoner would immediately set in.'

'And the bundle of letters?'

'One alone, the vital one, might have seemed like a—what do you call it?— put-up job.'

'Then the man called Max?'

'Never existed, my friend.'

'I still think,' said little Mr Mayherne, in an aggrieved manner, 'that we could have got him off by the—er—normal procedure.'

'I dared not risk it. You see, you *thought* he was innocent—'

'And you *knew* it? I see,' said little Mr Mayherne.

'My dear Mr Mayherne,' said Romaine, 'you do not see at all. I knew—he was guilty!'

DOROTHY L. SAYERS

1893–1957

Known as the creator of Lord Peter Wimsey, one of detective fiction's best-known and most enduring aristocratic amateur detectives, Dorothy Leigh Sayers was born in Oxford, England. Although she completed work for a degree in modern languages at Sommerville College, Oxford, in 1915, Oxford did not grant degrees to women until 1920. In that year she received both her B.A. and M.A. degrees, one of the first women officially to graduate from Oxford. In 1924 she gave birth to a son, who was raised from infancy by a cousin and the secret kept from family and friends. Two years later she married Oswald Arthur Fleming. Sayers knew early on that she wanted to write. She taught school briefly and worked at an advertising agency, where she promoted Coleman's mustard using cartoon figures of a British colonel, which later inspired the creation of Colonel Mustard for the board game *Clue*. She was also a noted scholar and translator of literary classics.

Sayers was arguably the greatest and most widely read author of detective fiction during the Golden Age between the two World Wars; her novels were a significant reason for the era's reputation and title. She believed in the "fair play" rule that every clue should be as perceptible to the reader as to the detective. A founding member of the Detection Club in 1927, she coauthored several works with other members. Her own first novel, *Whose Body?* (1923) introduced Lord Peter Wimsey as the erudite and witty aristocrat whose hobby is criminal investigation. His relationship with strong-minded Harriet Vane begins in *Strong Poison* (1930) and culminates in their marriage in the final novel, *Busman's Honeymoon* (1937). After a short story collection, *In the Teeth of the Evidence* (1939), in which Wimsey appears in the title story, Sayers devoted the rest of her life to religious writings and literary translations. Following her death, a Wimsey manuscript was found among her papers, a novel completed by Jill Paton

Walsh (*Thrones, Dominations*, 1998). "The Haunted Policeman" was first published in *Harper's Bazaar*, February, 1938.

Recommended Sayers works: *Gaudy Night, Strong Poison, Lord Peter: A Collection of all the Lord Peter Wimsey Stories.*

Other recommended authors: Amanda Cross, Elizabeth Daly, Veronica Stallwood.

The Haunted Policeman

"GOOD GOD!" said his lordship. "Did I do that?"

"All the evidence points that way," replied his wife.

"Then I can only say that I never knew so convincing a body of evidence produce such an inadequate result."

The nurse appeared to take this reflection personally. She said in a tone of rebuke: "He's a *beautiful* boy."

"H'm," said Peter. He adjusted his eyeglass carefully. "Well, you're the expert witness. Hand him over."

The nurse did so, with a dubious air. She was relieved to see that this disconcerting parent handled the child competently; as, in a man who was an experienced uncle, was not, after all, so very surprising. Lord Peter sat down gingerly on the bed.

"Do you feel it's up to standard?" he inquired with some anxiety. "Of course, *your* workmanship's always sound—but you never know with these collaborate efforts."

"I think it'll do," said Harriet.

"Good." He turned abruptly to the nurse. "All right; we'll keep it. Take it and put it away, and tell 'em to invoice it to me. It's a very interesting addition to you, Harriet; but it would have been a hell of a rotten substitute." His voice wavered a little, for in the last twenty-four hours he had had the fright of his life.

The doctor, who had been doing something in the other room, entered in time to catch the last words.

"There was never any likelihood of that, you goop," he said, cheerfully. "Now, you've seen all there is to be seen, and you'd better run away and play." He led his charge firmly to the door. "Go to bed," he advised him in kindly accents; "you look all in."

"I'm all right," said Peter. "I haven't been doing anything. And look here—" He stabbed a belligerent finger in the direction of the adjoining room. "Tell those nurses of yours, if I want to pick my son up, I'll pick him up. If his mother wants to kiss him, she can kiss him. I'll have none of your infernal hygiene in my house."

"Very well," said the doctor, "just as you like. Anything for a quiet life. I rather believe in a few healthy germs myself. Builds up resistance. No, thanks, I won't have a drink. I've got to go to another one, and an alcoholic breath impairs confidence."

"Another one?" said Peter, aghast.

"One of my hospital mothers. You're not the only fish in the sea by a long chalk. One born every minute."

"God! what a world." They passed down the great curved stair. In the hall a sleepy footman clung, yawning, to his post of duty.

"All right, William," said Peter. "Buzz off now; I'll lock up." He let the doctor out. "Good night—and thanks very much, old man. I'm sorry I swore at you."

"They mostly do," replied the doctor philosophically. "Well, bung-ho, Flim. I'll look in again later, just to earn my fee, but I shan't be wanted. You've married into a good tough family, and I congratulate you."

The car, spluttering and protesting a little after its long wait in the cold, drove off, leaving Peter alone on the doorstep. Now that it was all over and he could go to bed, he felt extraordinarily wakeful. He would have liked to go to a party. He leaned back against the wrought-iron railings and lit a cigarette, staring vaguely into the lamp-lit dusk of the square. It was thus that he saw the policeman.

The blue-uniformed figure came up from the direction of South Audley Street. He too was smoking, and he walked, not with the firm tramp of a constable on his beat, but with the hesitating step of a man who has lost his bearings. When he came in sight he had pushed back his helmet and was rubbing his head in a puzzled manner. Official habit made him look sharply at the bare-headed gentleman in evening dress, abandoned on a doorstep at three in the morning, but since the gentleman appeared to be sober and bore no signs of being about to commit a felony, he averted his gaze and prepared to pass on.

" 'Morning, officer," said the gentleman, as he came abreast with him.

" 'Morning, sir," said the policeman.

"You're off duty early," pursued Peter, who wanted somebody to talk to. "Come in and have a drink."

This offer reawakened all the official suspicion.

"Not just now, sir, thank you," replied the policeman guardedly.

"Yes, now. That's the point." Peter tossed away his cigarette. It described a fiery arc in the air and shot out a little train of sparks as it struck the pavement. "I've got a son."

"Oh, ah!" said the policeman, relieved by this innocent confidence. "Your first, eh?"

"And last, if I know anything about it."

"That's what my brother says, every time," said the policeman. "Never no more, he says. He's got eleven. Well, sir, good luck to it. I see how you're situated, and thank you kindly, but after what the sergeant said I dunno as I better. Though if I was to die this moment, not a drop 'as passed me lips since me supper beer."

Peter put his head on one side and considered this.

"The sergeant said you were drunk?"

"He did, sir."

"And you were not?"

"No, sir. I saw everything just the same as I told him, though what's become of it now is more than I can say. But drunk I was not, sir."

"Then," said Peter, "as Mr. Joseph Surface remarked to Lady Teazle, what is troubling you is the consciousness of your own innocence. He insinuated that you had looked on the wine when it was red—you'd better come in and make it so. You'll feel better."

The policeman hesitated.

"Well, sir, I dunno. Fact is, I've had a bit of a shock."

"So've I," said Peter. "Come in for God's sake and keep me company."

"Well, sir—" said the policeman again. He mounted the steps.

The logs in the hall-chimney were glowing a deep red through their ashes. Peter raked them apart, so that the young flame shot up between them. "Sit down," he said; "I'll be back in a moment."

The policeman sat down, removed his helmet, and stared about him, trying to remember who occupied the big house at the corner of the Square. The engraved coat-of-arms upon the great silver bowl on the chimney-piece told him nothing, even though it was repeated in color upon the backs of two tapestried chairs: three white mice skipping upon a black ground. Peter, returning from the shadows beneath the stair, caught him as he traced the outlines with a thick finger.

"A student of heraldry?" he said. "Seventeenth-century work and not very graceful. You're new to this beat, aren't you? My name's Wimsey."

He put down a tray on the table.

"If you'd rather have beer or whisky, say so. These bottles are only a concession to my mood."

The policeman eyed the long necks and bulging silver-wrapped corks with curiosity. "Champagne?" he said. "Never tasted it, sir. But I'd like to try the stuff."

"You'll find it thin," said Peter, "but if you drink enough of it, you'll tell me the story of your life." The cork popped, and the wine frothed out into the wide glasses, glinting as it caught the firelight.

"Well!" said the policeman. "Here's to your good lady, sir, and the new young gentleman. Long life and all the best. A bit in the nature of cider, ain't it, sir?"

"Just a trifle. Give me your opinion after the third glass, if you can put up with it so long. And thanks for your good wishes. You a married man?"

"Not yet, sir. Hoping to be when I get promotion. If only the sergeant—but that's neither here nor there. You been married long, sir, if I may ask?"

"Just over a year."

"Ah! and do you find it comfortable, sir?"

Peter laughed.

"I've spent the past twenty-four hours wondering why, when I'd had the blazing luck to get onto a perfectly good thing, I should be fool enough to risk the whole show on a silly experiment."

The policeman nodded sympathetically.

"I see what you mean, sir. Seems to me, life's like that. If you don't take risks, you get nowhere. If you do, they may go wrong, and then where are you? And 'alf the time, when things happen, they happen first, before you can even think about 'em."

"Quite right," said Peter, and filled the glasses again. He found the policeman soothing. True to his class and training, he turned naturally in moments of emotion to the company of the common man. Indeed, when the recent domestic crisis had threatened to destroy his nerve, he had headed for the butler's pantry with the swift instinct of the homing pigeon. There, they had treated him with great humanity, and allowed him to clean the silver.

With a mind oddly clarified by champagne and lack of sleep, he watched the constable's reaction to Pol Roger 1926. The first glass had produced a philosophy of life; the second produced a name—Alfred Burt—and further hints of some mysterious grievance against the station sergeant; the third glass, as prophesied, produced the story.

"You were right, sir" (said the policeman) "when you spotted I was new to the beat. I only come on it at the beginning of the week, and that acounts for me not being acquainted with you, sir, nor with most of the residents about here. Jessop, now, he knows everybody, and so did Pinker—but he's been took off to another division. You'd remember Pinker—big chap, make two o' me, with a sandy mustache. Yes, I thought you would.

"Well, sir, as I was saying, me knowing the district in a general way, but not, so to speak, like the palm o' me 'and, might account for me making a bit of a fool of myself, but it don't account for me seeing what I did see. See it I did, and not drunk nor nothing like it. And as for making a mistake in the number, well, that might happen to anybody. All the same, sir, thirteen was the number I see, plain as the nose on your face."

"You can't put it stronger than that," said Peter, whose nose was of a kind difficult to overlook.

"You know Merriman's End, sir?"

"I think I do. Isn't it a long cul-de-sac running somewhere at the back of South Audley Street, with a row of houses on one side and a high wall on the other?"

"That's right, sir. Tall, narrow houses they are, all alike, with deep porches and pillars to them."

"Yes. Like an escape from the worst square in Pimlico. Horrible. Fortunately, I believe the street was never finished, or we should have had another row of the monstrosities on the opposite side. This house is pure eighteenth century. How does it strike you?"

P. C. Burt contemplated the wide hall—the Adam fireplace and paneling with their graceful shallow moldings, the pedimented doorways, the high roundheaded window lighting hall and gallery, the noble proportions of the stair. He sought for a phrase.

"It's a gentleman's house," he pronounced at length. "Room to breathe, if you see what I mean. Seems like you couldn't act vulgar in it." He shook his head. "Mind you, I wouldn't call it cosy. It ain't the place I'd choose to sit down to a kipper in me shirtsleeves. But it's got class. I never thought about it before, but now you mention it I see what's wrong with them other houses in Merriman's End. They're sort of squeezed-like. I been into more'n one o' them tonight, and that's what they are; they're squeezed. But I was going to tell you about that.

"Just upon midnight it was" (pursued the policeman) "when I turns into Merriman's End in the ordinary course of my dooties. I'd got pretty near down towards the far end, when I see a fellow lurking about in a suspicious way under the wall. There's back gates there, you know, sir, leading into some gardens, and this chap was hanging about inside one of the gateways. A rough-looking fellow, in a baggy old coat—might a-been a tramp off the Embankment. I turned my light on him—that street's not very well lit, and it's a dark night—but I couldn't see much of his face, because he had on a ragged old hat and a big scarf round his neck. I thought he was up to no good, and I was about to ask him what he was doing there, when I hear a most awful yell come out o' one o' them houses opposite. Ghastly it was, sir, 'Help!' it said. 'Murder! help!' fit to freeze your marrow."

"Man's voice or woman's?"

"Man's, sir, I think. More of a roaring kind of yell, if you take my meaning. I says, 'Hullo! What's up there? Which house is it?' The chap says nothing, but he points, and him and me runs across together. Just as we gets to the house, there's a noise like as if someone was being strangled just inside, and a thump, as it might be something falling against the door."

"Good God!" said Peter.

"I gives a shout and rings the bell. 'Hoy!' I says. 'What's up here?' and then I knocks on the door. There's no answer, so I rings and knocks again. Then the chap who was with me, he pushes open the letter-flap and squints through it."

"Was there a light in the house?"

"It was all dark, sir, except the fanlight over the door. That was lit up bright, and when I looks up, I see the number of the house—Number Thirteen, painted plain as you like on the transom. Well, this chap peers in, and all of a sudden he gives a kind of gurgle and falls back. 'Here!' I says, 'what's amiss? Let me have a look. So I puts me eye to the flap and I looks in.'"

P. C. Burt paused and drew a long breath. Peter cut the wire of the second bottle.

"Now, sir," said the policeman. "believe me or believe me not, I was as sober at that moment as I am now. I can tell you everything I see in that house, same as if it was wrote up there on that wall. Not as it was a great lot, because the flap wasn't all that wide, but by squinnying a bit, I could make shift to see right across the hall and a piece on both sides and part way up the stairs. And here's what I see, and you take notice of every word, on account of what came after."

He took another gulp of the Pol Roger to loosen his tongue and continued:

"There was the floor of the hall. I could see that very plain. All black and white squares it was, like marble, and it stretched back a good long way. About halfway along, on the left, was the staircase, with a red carpet, and the statue of a white naked woman at the foot, carrying a big pot full of blue and yellow flowers. In the wall next the stairs there was an open door, and a room all lit up. I could just see the end of a table, with a lot of glass and silver on it. Between that door and the front door there was a big black cabinet, shiny with gold figures painted on it, like them things they had at the Exhibition. Right at the back of the hall there was a place like a conservatory, but I couldn't see what was in it, only it looked very gay. There was a door on the right, and that was open, too. A very pretty drawing-room, by what I could see of it, with pale-blue paper and pictures on the walls. There were pictures in the hall, too, and a table on the right with copper bowl, like as it might be for visitors' cards to be put in. Now, I see all that, sir, and I put it to you, if it hadn't a' been there, how could I describe it so plain?"

"I have known people describe what wasn't there," said Peter thoughtfully, "but it was seldom anything of that kind. Rats, cats, and snakes I have heard of and occasionally naked female figures; but delirious lacquer cabinets and hall-tables are new to me."

"As you say, sir," agreed the policeman, "and I see you believe me so far. But here's something else, what you mayn't find quite so easy. There was a man laying in that hall, sir, as sure as I sit here, and he was dead. He was a big man and clean-shaven, and he wore evening dress. Somebody had stuck a knife into his throat. I could see the handle of it—it looked like a carving-knife, and the blood had run out, all shiny, over the marble squares."

The policeman looked at Peter, passed his handkerchief over his forehead, and finished the fourth glass of champagne.

"His head was up against the end of the hall table," he went on, "and his feet must have been up against the door, but I couldn't see anything quite close to me, because of the letter-box. You understand, sir, I was looking through the wire cage of the box, and there was something inside—letters, I suppose—that cut off my view downwards. But I see all the rest—in front and a bit of both sides; and it must have been regularly burnt in upon me brain, as they say, for I don't suppose I was looking more than a quarter of a minute or so. Then all the lights went out at once, same as if somebody had turned off the main switch. So I looks round, and I don't mind telling you I felt a bit queer. And *when* I looks round, lo and behold! my bloke in the muffler had hopped it."

"The devil he had," said Peter.

"Hopped it," repeated the policeman, "and there I was. And just there, sir, is where I made my big mistake, for I thought he couldn't a-got far, and I started off up the street after him. But I couldn't see him, and I couldn't see nobody. All the houses was dark, and it come over me what a sight of funny things may go on and nobody take a mite o' notice. The way I'd shouted and banged on the door, you'd a-thought it'd a-brought out every soul in the street, not to mention that awful yelling. But there—you may have noticed it yourself, sir. A man may leave his ground-floor windows open, or have his chimney afire, and you may make noise enough to wake the dead, trying to draw his attention, and nobody give no heed. He's fast asleep, and the neighbors say, 'Blast that row, but it's no business of mine,' and stick their 'eads under the bedclothes."

"Yes," said Peter. "London's like that."

"That's right, sir. A village is different. You can't pick up a pin there without somebody coming up to ask where you got it from—but London keeps itself to itself. . . . Well, something'll have to be done, I thinks to myself, and I blows me whistle. They heard that all right. Windows started to go up all the street. That's London, too."

Peter nodded. "London will sleep through the last trump. Puddley-in-the-Rut and Doddering-in-the-Dumps will look down their noses and put on virtuous airs. But God, Who is never surprised, will say to His angel, 'Whistle 'em up, Michael, whistle 'em up; East and West will rise from the dead at the sound of the policeman's whistle.' "

"Quite so, sir," said P. C. Burt; and wondered for the first time whether there might not be something in this champagne stuff after all. He waited for a moment and then resumed:

"Well, it so happened that just when I sounded my whistle, Withers—that's the man on the other beat—was in Audley Square, coming to meet me. You know, sir, we has times for meeting one another, arranged different-like every night; and twelve o'clock in the square was our rendyvoos tonight. So up he comes in, you might say, no time at all, and finds me there, with everyone a-hollering at me from the windows to know what was up. Well, naturally I didn't want the whole bunch of 'em running out into the street and our man getting away in the crowd, so I just tells 'em there's nothing, only a bit of an accident farther along. And then I see Withers and glad enough I was. We stands there at the top o' the street, and I tells him there's a dead man laying in the hall at Number Thirteen, and it looks to me like murder. 'Number Thirteen' he says, 'you can't mean Number Thirteen. There ain't no Number

Thirteen in Merriman's End, you fathead; it's all even numbers.' And so it is, sir, for the houses on the other side were never built, so there's no odd numbers at all.

"Well, that give me a bit of a jolt. I wasn't so much put out at not having remembered about the numbers, for as I tell you, I never was on the beat before this week. No; but I knew I'd seen that there number writ up plain as pie on the fanlight, and I didn't see how I could have been mistaken. But when Withers heard the rest of the story, he thought maybe I'd misread it for Number Twelve. It couldn't be Eighteen, for there's only the eight houses in the road; nor it couldn't be Sixteen neither, for I knew it wasn't the end house. But we thought it might be Twelve or Ten; so away we goes to look.

"We didn't have no difficulty about getting in at Number Twelve. There was a very pleasant old gentleman came down in his dressing-gown, asking what the disturbance was, and could he be of use. I apologized for disturbing him, and said I was afraid there'd been an accident in one of the houses, and had he heard anything. Of course, the minute he opened the door I could see it wasn't Number Twelve we wanted; there was only a little hall with polished boards, and the walls plain paneled—all very bare and neat and no black cabinet nor naked woman nor nothing. The old gentleman said, yes, his son had heard somebody shouting and knocking a few minutes earlier. He'd got up and put his head out of the window, but couldn't see nothing, but they thought from the sound it was Number Fourteen forgotten his latch-key again. So we thanked him very much and went on to Number Fourteen.

"We had a bit of a job to get Number Fourteen downstairs. A fiery sort of gentleman he was, something in the military way, I thought, but he turned out to be a retired Indian Civil Servant. A dark gentleman, with a big voice, and his servant was dark, too. The gentleman wanted to know what the blazes all this row was about, and why a decent citizen wasn't allowed to get his proper sleep. He supposed that young fool at Number Twelve was drunk again. Withers had to speak a bit sharp to him; but at last the servant came down and let us in. Well, we had to apologize once more. The hall was not a bit like—the staircase was on the wrong side, for one thing and though there was a statue at the foot of it, it was some kind of a heathen idol with a lot of heads and arms, and the walls were covered with all sorts of brass stuff and native goods—you know the kind of thing. There was a black-and-white linoleum on the floor and that was about all there was to it. The servant had a soft sort of way with him I didn't half like. He said he slept at the back and had heard nothing till his master rang for him. Then the gentleman came to the top of the stairs and shouted out it was no use disturbing him; the noise came from Number Twelve as usual, and if that young man didn't stop his blanky Bohemian goings-on, he'd have the law on his father. I asked if he'd seen anything, and he said, no, he hadn't. Of course, sir, me and that other chap was inside the porch, and you can't see anything what goes on inside those porches from the other houses, because they're filled in at the sides with colored glass—all the lot of them."

Lord Peter Wimsey looked at the policeman and then looked at the bottle, as though estimating the alcoholic content of each. With deliberation, he filled both glasses again.

"Well, sir," said P. G. Burt, after refreshing himself, "by this time Withers was looking at me in rather an old-fashioned manner. However, he said nothing, and we went back to Number Ten, where there was two maiden ladies and a hall full of stuffed birds and wallpaper like a florist's catalogue. The one who slept in the front was deaf as a post, and the one who slept at the back hadn't heard nothing. But we got hold of their maids, and the cook said she'd heard the voice calling 'Help!' and thought it was in Number Twelve, and she'd hid her head in the pillow and said her prayers. The housemaid was a sensible girl. She'd looked out when she'd heard me knocking. She couldn't see anything at first, owing to us being in the porch, but she thought something must be going on, so, not wishing to catch cold, she went back to put on her bedroom slippers. When she got back to the window, she was just in time to see a man running up the road. He went very quick and very silent, as if he had galoshes on, and she could see the ends of his muffler flying out behind him. She saw him run out of the street and turn to the right, and then she heard me coming along after him. Unfortunately, her eye being on the man, she didn't notice which porch I came out of. Well, that showed I wasn't inventing the whole story at any rate, because there was my bloke in the muffler. The girl didn't recognize him at all, but that wasn't surprising, because she'd only just entered the old ladies' service. Besides, it wasn't likely the man had anything to do with it, because he was outside with me when the yelling started. My belief is, he was the sort as doesn't care to have his pockets examined too close, and the minute my back was turned he thought he'd be better and more comfortable elsewhere.

"Now there ain't no need" (continued the policeman), "for me to trouble you, sir, with all them houses what we went into. We made inquiries at the whole lot, from Number Two to Number Sixteen, and there wasn't one of them had a hall in any ways conformable to what that chap and I saw through the letter-box. Nor there wasn't a soul in 'em could give us any help more than what we'd had already. You see, sir, though it took me a bit o' time telling, it all went very quick. There was the yells; they didn't last beyond a few seconds or so, and before they was finished, we was across the road and inside the porch. Then there was me shouting and knocking; but I hadn't been long at that afore the chap with me looks through the box. Then I has my look inside, for fifteen seconds it might be, and while I'm doing that, my chap's away up the street. Then I runs after him, and then I blows me whistle. The whole thing might take a minute or a minute and a half. Not more.

"Well, sir; by the time we'd been into every house in Merriman's End, I was feeling a bit queer again, I can tell you, and Withers, he was looking queerer. He says to me, 'Burt,' he says, 'is this your idea of a joke? Because if so, the 'Olborn Empire's where you ought to be, not the police force.' So I tells him over again, most solemn, what I seen—'and,' I says, 'if only we could lay hands on that chap in the muffler, he could tell you he seen it, too. And what's more,' I says, 'do you think I'd risk me job, playing a silly trick like that?' He says, 'Well, it beats me,' he says. 'If I didn't know you was a sober kind of chap. I'd say you was seein' things.'

"'Things?' I says to him. 'I see that there corpse a-layin' there with the knife in his neck, and that was enough for me. 'Orrible, he looked, and the blood all over the floor.' 'Well,' he says, 'maybe he wasn't dead after all, and they've cleared him out of the way.' 'And cleared the house away too, I suppose,' I said to him. So Withers says, in an odd sort o' voice, 'You're sure about the house? You wasn't letting your imagination run away with you over naked females and such?' That was a nice thing to say. I said, 'No, I wasn't. There's been some mon-key business going on in this street and I'm going to get to the bottom of it, if we has to comb out London for that chap in the muffler.' 'Yes,' says Withers, nasty like, 'it's a pity he cleared off so sudden.' 'Well,' I says, 'you can't say I imagined *him*, anyhow, because that there girl saw him, and a mercy she did,' I said, 'or you'd be saying next I ought to be in Colney Hatch.' 'Well,' he says, 'I dunno what you think you're going to do about it. You better ring up the sta-tion and ask for instructions.'

"Which I did. And Sergeant Jones, he come down himself, and he listens attentive-like to what we both has to say, and then he walks along the street, slow-like, from end to end. And then he comes back and says to me, 'Now, Burt,' he says, 'just you describe that hall to me again, careful.' Which I does, same as I described it to you, sir. And he says, 'You're sure there was the room on the left of the stairs with the glass and silver on the table; and the room on the right with the pictures in it?' And I says, 'Yes, Sergeant, I'm quite sure of that.' And Withers says, 'Ah!' in a kind of got-you-now-voice, if you take my meaning. And the sergeant says, 'Now, Burt,' he says, 'pull yourself together and take a look at these here houses. Don't you see they're all single-fronted? There ain't one of 'em has rooms *both* sides o' the front hall. Look at the windows, you fool,' he says."

Lord Peter squinted at the bottle and poured out the last of the champagne.

"I don't mind telling you, sir" (went on the policeman) "that I was fair knocked silly. To think of me never noticing that! Withers had noticed it all right, and that's what made him think I was drunk or barmy. But I stuck to what I'd seen. I said, there must be two of them houses knocked into one, somewhere; but that didn't work, because we'd been into all of them, and there wasn't no such thing—not without there was one o'them concealed doors like you read about in crook stories. 'Well, anyhow,' I says to the sergeant, 'the yells was real all right, because other people heard 'em. Just you ask, and they'll tell you.' So the sergeant says, 'Well, Burt, I'll give you every chance.'

"So he knocks up Number Twelve again—not wishing to annoy Number Fourteen any more than he was already—and this time the son come down. An agreeable gentleman he was, too; not a bit put out. He says, Oh, yes, he'd heard the yells and his father'd heard them too. 'Number Fourteen,' he says, 'that's where the trouble is. A very old bloke, is Number Fourteen, and I shouldn't be surprised if he beats that unfortunate servant of his. The Englishman abroad, you know! The outposts of Empire and all that kind of thing. They're rough and ready—and then the curry in them parts is bad for the liver.' So I was for inquiring at Number Fourteen again; but the sergeant, he loses patience, and says, 'You know quite well,' he says, 'it ain't Number Fourteen, and, in my opinion, Burt, you're either dotty or drunk. You best go home straight away,' he says, 'and sober up, and I'll see you again when you can give a better account of yourself.' So I argues a bit, but it ain't no use, and away he goes, and Withers goes back to his beat. And I walks up and down a bit till Jessop comes to take over, and then I comes away, and that's when I sees you, sir.

"But I ain't drunk, sir—at least, I wasn't then, though there do seem to be a kind of a swimming in me head at this moment. Maybe that stuff's stronger than it tastes. But I wasn't drunk then, and I'm pretty sure I'm not dotty. I'm haunted, sir, that's what it is—haunted. It might be there was someone killed in one of them houses a many years ago, and that's what I see tonight. Perhaps they changed the numbering of the street on account of it—I've heard tell of such things—and when the same night come round, the house goes back to what it was before. But there I am, with a black mark against me, and it ain't a fair trick for no ghost to go getting a plain man into trouble. And I'm sure, sir, you'll agree with me."

The policeman's narrative had lasted some time, and the hands of the grandfather clock stood at a quarter to five. Peter Wimsey gazed benevolently at his companion, for whom he was beginning to feel a positive affection. He was, if anything, slightly more drunk than the policeman, for he had missed tea and had no appetite for his dinner; but the wine had not clouded his wits; it had only increased excitability and postponed sleep. He said:

"When you looked through the letter-box, could you see any part of the ceiling, or the lights?"

"No, sir; on account, you see, of the flap. I could see right and left and straight forward; but not upwards, and none of the near part of the floor."

"When you looked at the house from outside, there was no light except through the fanlight. But when you looked through the flap, all the rooms were lit, right and left and at the back?"

"That's so, sir."

"Are there back doors to the houses?"

"Yes, sir. Coming out of Merriman's End, you turn to the right, and there's an opening a little way along which takes you to the back doors."

"You seem to have a very distinct visual memory. I wonder if your other kinds of memory are as good. Can you tell me, say, whether any of the houses you went into had any particular smell? Especially Ten, Twelve, and Fourteen?"

"Smell, sir?" The policeman closed his eyes to stimulate recollection. "Why, yes, sir. Number Ten, where the two ladies live, that had a sort of an old-fashioned smell. I can't put me tongue to it. Not lavender—but something as ladies keeps in bowls and such—rose leaves and what not. Potpourri, that's the stuff. Potpourri. And Number Twelve—well, no, there was nothing particular there, except I remember thinking they must keep pretty good servants, though we didn't see anybody except the family. All that floor and paneling was polished beautiful—you could see your face in it. Beeswax and turpentine, I says to meself. And elbow-grease. What you'd call a clean house with a good, clean smell. But Number Fourteen—that was different. I didn't like the smell of that. Stuffy, like as if the servant had been burning some o' that there incense to his idols, maybe."

"Ah!" said Peter. "What you say is very suggestive." He placed his fingertips together and shot his last question over them:

"Ever been inside the National Gallery?"

"No, sir," said the policeman, astonished. "I can't say as I ever was."

"That's London again," said Peter. "We're the last people in the world to know anything of our great metropolitan institutions. Now, what is the best way to tackle this bunch of toughs, I wonder? It's a little early for a call. Still, there's nothing like doing one's good deed before breakfast, and the sooner you're set right with the sergeant, the better. Let me see. Yes—I think that may do it. Costume pieces are not as a rule in my line, but my routine has been so much upset already, one way and another, that an irregularity more or less will hardly matter. Wait here for me while I have a bath and change. I may be a little time; but it would hardly be decent to get there before six."

The bath had been an attractive thought, but was perhaps ill-advised, for a curious languor stole over him with the touch of the hot water. The champagne was losing its effervescence. It was with an effort that he dragged himself out and reawakened himself with a cold shower.

The matter of dress required a little thought. A pair of gray flannel trousers was easily found, and though they were rather too well creased for the part he meant to play, he thought that with luck they would probably pass unnoticed. The shirt was a difficulty. His collection of shirts was a notable one, but they were mostly of an inconspicuous and gentlemanly sort. He hesitated for some time over a white shirt with an open sports collar, but decided at length upon a blue one, bought as an experiment and held to be not quite successful. A red tie, if he had possessed such a thing, would have been convincing. After some consideration, he remembered that he had seen his wife in a rather wide Liberty tie, whose prevailing color was orange. That, he felt, would do if he could find it. On her it had looked rather well; on him, it would be completely abominable.

He went through into the next room; it was queer to find it empty. A peculiar sensation came over him. Here *he* was, rifling his wife's drawers, and there *she* was, spirited out of reach at the top of the house with a couple of nurses and an entirely new baby, which might turn into goodness knew what. He sat down before the glass and stared at himself. He felt as though he ought to have changed somehow in the night; but he only looked unshaven and, he thought, a trifle intoxicated. Both were quite good things to look at the moment, though hardly suitable for the father of a family. He pulled out all the drawers in the dressing-table; they emitted vaguely familiar smells of face-powder and handkerchief sachet. He tried the big built-in wardrobe: frocks, costumes, and trays full of underwear, which made him feel sentimental. At last he struck a promising vein of gloves and stockings. The next tray held ties, the orange of the desired Liberty creation gleaming in a friendly way among them. He put it on, and observed with pleasure that the effect was Bohemian beyond description.

He wandered out again, leaving all the drawers open behind him as though a burglar had passed through the room. An ancient tweed jacket of his own, of a very countrified pattern, suitable only for fishing in Scotland, was next unearthed, together with a pair of brown canvas shoes. He secured his trousers by a belt, searched for and found an old soft-brimmed felt hat of no recognizable color, and, after removing a few trout-flies from the hat-band and tucking his shirt-sleeves well up inside the coat-sleeve, decided that he would do. As an afterthought, he returned to his wife's room and selected a wide woolen scarf in a shade of greenish blue. Thus equipped, he came downstairs again, to find P. C. Burt fast asleep, with his mouth open and snoring.

Peter was hurt. Here he was, sacrificing himself in the interests of this policeman, and the man hadn't the common decency to appreciate it. However, there was no point in waking him yet. He yawned horribly and sat down. . . .

It was the footman who wakened the sleepers at half-past six. If he was surprised to see his master, very strangely attired, slumbering in the hall in company with a large policeman, he was too well trained to admit the fact even to himself. He merely removed the tray. The faint clink of glass roused Peter, who slept like a cat at all times.

"Hullo, William," he said. "Have I overslept myself? What's the time?"

"Five and twenty to seven, my lord."

"Just about right." He remembered that the footman slept on the top floor. "All quiet on the Western Front, William?"

"Not altogether quiet, my lord." William permitted himself a slight smile. "The young master was lively about five. But all satisfactory, I gather from Nurse Jenkyn."

"Nurse Jenkyn? Is that the young one? Don't let yourself be run away with, William. I say, just give P. C. Burt a light prod in the ribs, would you? He and I have business together."

In Merriman's End, the activities of the morning were beginning. The milkman came jingling out of the cul-de-sac; lights were twinkling in upper rooms; hands were withdrawing curtains; in front of Number Ten, the housemaid was already scrubbing the steps. Peter posted his policeman at the top of the street.

"I don't want to make my first appearance with official accompaniment," he said. "Come along when I beckon. What, by the way, is the name of the agreeable gentleman in Number Twelve? I think he may be of some assistance to us."

"Mr. O'Halloran, sir."

The policeman looked at Peter expectantly. He seemed to have abandoned all initiative and to place implicit confidence in this hospitable and eccentric gentleman. Peter slouched down the street with his hands in his trousers pockets and his shabby hat pulled rakishly over his eyes. At Number Twelve he paused and examined the windows. Those on the ground floor were open; the house was awake. He marched up the steps, took a brief glance through the flap of the letter-box, and rang the bell. A maid in a neat blue dress and white cap and apron opened the door.

"Good morning," said Peter, slightly raising the shabby hat; "is Mr. O'Halloran in?" He gave the r a soft continental roll. "Not the old gentleman, I mean young Mr. O'Halloran?"

"He's in," said the maid, doubtfully, "but he isn't up yet."

"Oh!" said Peter. "Well, it is a little early for a visit. But I desire to see him urgently. I am—there is a little trouble where I live. Could you entreat him— would you be so kind? I have walked all the way," he added, pathetically, and with perfect truth.

"Have you, sir?" said the maid. She added kindly. "You do look tired, sir, and that's a fact."

"It is nothing," said Peter. "It is only that I forgot to have any dinner. But if I can see Mr. O'Halloran it will be all right."

"You'd better come in, sir," said the maid. "I'll see if I can wake him." She conducted the exhausted stranger in and offered him a chair. "What name shall I say, sir?"

"Petrovinsky," said his lordship, hardily. As he had rather expected, neither the unusual name nor the unusual clothes of this unusually early visitor seemed to cause very much surprise. The maid left him in the tidy little paneled hall and went upstairs without so much as a glance at the umbrella stand.

Left to himself, Peter sat still, noticing that the hall was remarkably bare of furniture, and was lit by a single electric pendant almost immediately inside the front door. The letterbox was the usual wire-cage, the bottom of which had been carefully lined with brown paper. From the back of the house came a smell of frying bacon.

Presently there was the sound of somebody running downstairs. A young man appeared in a dressing-gown. He called out as he came: "Is that you, Stefan? Your name came up as Mr. Whiskey. Has Marfa run away again, or— What the hell? Who the devil are you, sir?"

"Wimsey," said Peter, mildly, "not Whiskey; Wimsey the policeman's friend. I just looked in to congratulate you on a mastery of the art of false perspective which I thought had perished with the ingenious Van Hoogstraaten, or at least with Grace and Lambelet."

"Oh!" said the young man. He had a pleasant countenance, with humorous eyes and ears pointed like a faun's. He laughed a little ruefully. "I suppose my beautiful murder is out. It was too good to last. Those bobbies! I hope to

God they gave Number Fourteen a bad night. May I ask you how you come to be involved in the matter?"

"I," said Peter, "am the kind of person in whom distressed constables confide—I cannot imagine why. And when I had the picture of that sturdy blue-clad figure, led so persuasively by a Bohemian stranger and invited to peer through a hole, I was irresistibly transported in mind to the National Gallery. Many a time have I squinted sideways through those holes into the little black box, and admired that Dutch interior of many vistas painted so convincingly on the four flat sides of the box. How right you were to preserve your eloquent silence! Your Irish brogue would have given you away. The servants, I gather, were purposely kept out of sight."

"Tell me," said Mr. O'Halloran, seating himself sideways upon the hall table, "do you know by heart the occupation of every resident in this quarter of London? I do not paint under my own name."

"No," said Peter. "Like the good Dr. Watson, the constable could observe, though he could not reason from his observation; it was the smell of turpentine that betrayed you. I gather that at the time of his first call the apparatus was not far off."

"It was folded together and lying under the stairs," replied the painter. "It has since been removed to the studio. My father had only just had time to get it out of the way and hitch down the 'Number Thirteen' from the fanlight before the police reinforcements arrived. He had not even time to put back this table I am sitting on; a brief search would have discovered it in the dining-room. My father is a remarkable sportsman; I cannot too highly recommend the presence of mind he displayed while I was haring round the houses and leaving him to hold the fort. It would have been so simple and so unenterprising to explain; but my father, being an Irishman, enjoys treading on the coattails of authority."

"I should like to meet your father. The only thing I do not thoroughly understand is the reason of this elaborate plot. Were you by any chance executing a burglary round the corner, and keeping the police in play while you did it?"

"I never thought of that," said the young man, with regret in his voice. "No. The bobby was not the predestined victim. He happened to be present at a full-dress rehearsal, and the joke was too good to be lost. The fact is, my uncle is Sir Lucius Preston, the R.A."

"Ah!" said Peter. "The light begins to break."

"My own style of draftsmanship," pursued Mr. O'Halloran, "is modern. My uncle has on several occasions informed me that I draw like that only because I do not know how to draw. The idea was that he should be invited to dinner tomorrow and regaled with a story of the mysterious 'Number Thirteen,' said to appear from time to time in this street and to be haunted by strange noises. Having thus detained him till close upon midnight, I should have set out to see him to the top of the street. As we went along, the cries would have broken out. I should have led him back—"

"Nothing," said Peter, "could be clearer. After the preliminary shock he would have been forced to confess that your draftsmanship was a triumph of academic accuracy."

"I hope," said Mr. O'Halloran. "the performance may still go forward as originally intended." He looked at Peter, who replied:

"I hope so, indeed. I also hope that your uncle's heart is a strong one. But may I, in the meantime, signal to my unfortunate policeman and relieve his mind? He is in danger of losing his promotion, through a suspicion that he was drunk on duty."

"Good God!" said Mr. O'Halloran. "No—I don't want that to happen. Fetch him in."

The difficulty was to make P.C. Burt recognize in the day-light what he had seen by night through the letter-flap. Of the framework of painted canvas, with its forms and figures oddly foreshortened and distorted, he could make little. Only when the thing was set up and lighted in the curtained studio was he at length reluctantly convinced.

"It's wonderful." he said. "It's like Maskelyne and Devant. I wish the sergeant could a-seen it."

"Lure him down here tomorrow night," said Mr. O'Halloran. "Let him come as my uncle's bodyguard. You—" he turned to Peter—"you seem to have a way with policemen. Can't you inveigle the fellow along? Your impersonation of starving and disconsolate Bloomsbury is fully as convincing as mine. How about it?"

"I don't know," said Peter. "The costume gives me pain. Besides, is it kind to a poor policeman? I give you the R.A., but when it comes to the guardian of the law—Blast it all! I'm a family man, and I must have *some* sense of responsibility."

JOHN DICKSON CARR
1906–1977

Master of the "locked-room" mystery, John Dickson Carr was born in Uniontown, Pennsylvania. Carr was the son of a distinguished lawyer who specialized in criminal cases. Therefore, his interest in crime began at an early age. At fifteen he wrote his first detective stories, and continued this pursuit at Haverford College in Pennsylvania. His first detective novel, *It Walks By Night*, was published by Harper in 1930. In 1932 Carr married an English woman, Clarice Cleaves, and moved to England to write mysteries. They did not return permanently to the United States until 1965. Carr was the first American to be elected to the exclusive London Detective Club in 1936. He received the Edgar Award for his official biography of Sir Arthur Conan Doyle (1949), twice received the Ellery Queen Prize for short stories, and served as the President of the Mystery Writers of America. Carr was named a Grand Master by the Mystery Writers of America in 1962.

Carr, also writing under the pseudonyms Carr Dickson, Carter Dickson, and Roger Fairbairn, is considered the undisputed genius of the "impossible crime" story, a mystery where the victim is murdered in an inaccessible place: a locked room, the top of a tower, etc. He introduces into detective fiction the amateur detectives Dr. Gideon Fell, whom he patterned after the well-known mystery writer G.K. Chesterton, and Sir Henry Merrivale, who has recognizable touches of Sir Winston Churchill, the famous Prime Minister of England. He writes other works that feature Henri Bencolin of the French Sureté and Colonel March of Scotland Yard. Although best known for his intricate and ingenious "locked-room" puzzles, he also is a pioneer in the writing of historical mysteries, "laugh-out-loud" detective novels, and stories with a touch of the supernatural. His writing career in detective fiction included 71 novels, four short novels, and seven collections of short stories and radio plays. In 1954 Carr coauthored a very fine series of Sherlock Holmes stories, *The Exploits of Sherlock Holmes*, with Adrian Conan Doyle, Conan Doyle's youngest son. "The House in Goblin Wood" first appeared in the *Strand* magazine in November of 1947.

Recommended Carr works: *The Mad Hatter Mystery, The Plague Court Murders, A Graveyard To Let.*

Other recommended authors: Georgette Heyer, Ellery Queen, Minette Walters.

The House in Goblin Wood

In Pall Mall, that hot July afternoon three years before the war, an open saloon car was drawn up to the curb just opposite the Senior Conservatives' Club.

And in the car sat two conspirators.

It was the drowsy post-lunch hour among the clubs, where only the sun remained brilliant. The Rag lay somnolent; the Athenæum slept outright. But these two conspirators, a dark-haired young man in his early thirties and a fair-haired girl perhaps half a dozen years younger, never moved. They stared intently at the Gothic-like front of the Senior Conservatives'.

'Look here, Eve,' muttered the young man, and punched at the steering-wheel, 'do you think this is going to work?'

'I don't know,' the fair-haired girl confessed. 'He absolutely *loathes* picnics.'

'Anyway, we've probably missed him.'

'Why so?'

'He can't have taken as long over lunch as that!' her companion protested, looking at a wrist-watch. The young man was rather shocked. 'It's a quarter to four! Even if . . .'

'Bill! There! Look there!'

Their patience was rewarded by an inspiring sight.

Out of the portals of the Senior Conservatives' Club, in awful majesty, marched a large, stout, barrel-shaped gentleman in a white linen suit.

His corporation preceded him like the figurehead of a man-of-war. His shell-rimmed spectacles were pulled down on a broad nose, all being shaded by a Panama hat. At the top of the stone steps he surveyed the street, left and right, with a lordly sneer.

'Sir Henry!' called the girl.

'Hey?' said Sir Henry Merrivale.

'I'm Eve Drayton. Don't you remember me? You knew my father!'

'Oh, ah,' said the great man.

'We've been waiting here a terribly long time,' Eve pleaded. 'Couldn't you see us for just five minutes?—The thing to do,' she whispered to her companion, 'is to keep him in a good humour. Just keep him in a good humour!'

As a matter of fact, H. M. was in a good humour, having just triumphed over the Home Secretary in an argument. But not even his own mother could have guessed it. Majestically, with the same lordly sneer, he began in grandeur to descend the steps of the Senior Conservatives'. He did this, in fact, until his foot encountered an unnoticed object lying some three feet from the bottom.

It was a banana skin.

'Oh, dear!' said the girl.

Now it must be stated with regret that in the old days certain urchins, of what were then called the 'lower orders', had a habit of placing such objects on the steps in the hope that some eminent statesman would take a toss on his way to Whitehall. This was a venial but deplorable practice, probably accounting for what Mr Gladstone said in 1882.

In any case, it accounted for what Sir Henry Merrivale said now.

From the pavement, where H. M. landed in a seated position, arose in H. M.'s bellowing voice such a torrent of profanity, such a flood of invective and vile obscenities, as has seldom before blasted the holy calm of Pall Mall. It brought the hall porter hurrying down the steps, and Eve Drayton flying out of the car.

Heads were now appearing at the windows of the Athenæum across the street.

'Is it all right?' cried the girl, with concern in her blue eyes. 'Are you hurt?'

H. M. merely looked at her. His hat had fallen off, disclosing a large bald head; and he merely sat on the pavement and looked at her.

'Anyway, H. M., get up! Please get up!'

'Yes, sir,' begged the hall porter, 'for heaven's sake get up!'

'Get up?' bellowed H. M., in a voice audible as far as St James's Street. 'Burn it all, how *can* I get up?'

'But why not?'

'My behind's out of joint,' said H. M. simply. 'I'm hurt awful bad. I'm probably goin' to have spinal dislocation for the rest of my life.'

'But, sir, people are looking!'

H. M. explained what these people could do. He eyed Eve Drayton with a glare of indescribable malignancy over his spectacles.

'I suppose, my wench, *you're* responsible for this?'

Eve regarded him in consternation.

'You don't mean the banana skin?' she cried.

'Oh, yes, I do,' said H. M., folding his arms like a prosecuting counsel.

'But we—we only wanted to invite you to a picnic!'

H. M. closed his eyes.

'That's fine,' he said in a hollow voice. 'All the same, don't you think it'd have been a subtler kind of hint just to pour mayonnaise over my head or shove ants down the back of my neck? Oh, lord love a duck!'

'I didn't mean that! I meant . . .'

'Let me help you up, sir,' interposed the calm, reassuring voice of the dark-haired and blue-chinned young man who had been with Eve in the car.

'So you want to help too, hey? And who are *you*?'

'I'm awfully sorry!' said Eve. 'I should have introduced you! This is my fiancé. Dr William Sage.'

H. M.'s face turned purple.

'I'm glad to see,' he observed, 'you had the uncommon decency to bring along a doctor. I appreciate that, I do. And the car's there. I suppose, to assist with the examination when I take off my pants?'

The hall porter uttered a cry of horror.

Bill Sage, either from jumpiness and nerves or from sheer inability to keep a straight face, laughed loudly.

'I keep telling Eve a dozen times a day,' he said, 'that I'm not to be called "doctor". I happen to be a surgeon——'

(Here H. M. really did look alarmed.)

'—but I don't think we need operate. Nor, in my opinion,' Bill gravely addressed the hall porter, 'will it be necessary to remove Sir Henry's trousers in front of the Senior Conservatives' Club.'

'Thank you very much, sir.'

'We had an infernal nerve to come here,' the young man confessed to H. M. 'But I honestly think, Sir Henry, you'd be more comfortable in the car. What about it? Let me give you a hand up?'

Yet even ten minutes later, when H. M. sat glowering in the back of the car and two heads were craned round towards him, peace was not restored.

'All right!' said Eve. Her pretty, rather stolid face was flushed; her mouth looked miserable. 'If you won't come to the picnic, you won't. But I did believe you might do it to oblige me.'

'Well . . . now!' muttered the great man uncomfortably.

'And I did think, too, you'd be interested in the other person who was coming with us. But Vicky's—difficult. She won't come either, if you don't.'

'Oh? And who's this other guest?'

'Vicky Adams.'

H. M.'s hand, which had been lifted for an oratorical gesture, dropped to his side.

'Vicky Adams? That's not the gal who . . . ?'

'Yes!' Eve nodded. 'They say it was one of the great mysteries, twenty years ago, that the police failed to solve.'

'It was, my wench,' H. M. agreed sombrely. 'It was.'

'And now Vicky's grown up. And we thought if you of all people went along, and spoke to her nicely, she'd tell us what really happened on that night.'

H. M.'s small, sharp eyes fixed disconcertingly on Eve.

'I say, my wench. What's your interest in all this?'

'Oh, reasons.' Eve glanced quickly at Bill Sage, who was again punching moodily at the steering-wheel, and checked herself. 'Anyway, what difference does it make now? If you won't go with us . . .'

H. M. assumed a martyred air.

'I never said I *wasn't* goin' with you, did I?' he demanded. (This was inaccurate, but no matter.) 'Even after you practically made a cripple of me, I never said I *wasn't* goin'?' His manner grew flurried and hasty. 'But I got to leave now,' he added apologetically. 'I got to get back to my office.'

'We'll drive you there, H. M.'

'No, no, no,' said the practical cripple, getting out of the car with surprising celerity. 'Walkin' is good for my stomach if it's not so good for my behind. I'm a forgiven' man. You pick me up at my house tomorrow morning. G'bye.'

And he lumbered off in the direction of the Haymarket.

It needed no close observer to see that H. M. was deeply abstracted. He remained so abstracted, indeed, as to be nearly murdered by a taxi at the Admiralty Arch; and he was half-way down Whitehall before a familiar voice stopped him.

'Afternoon, Sir Henry!'

Burly, urbane, buttoned up in blue serge, with his bowler hat and his boiled blue eye, stood Chief Inspector Masters.

'Bit odd,' the Chief Inspector remarked affably, 'to see you taking a constitutional on a day like this. And how are you, sir?'

'Awful,' said H. M. instantly. 'But that's not the point. Masters, you crawlin' snake! You're the very man I wanted to see.'

Few things startled the Chief Inspector. This one did.

'You', he repeated, 'wanted to see *me*?'

'Uh-huh.'

'And what about?'

'Masters, do you remember the Victoria Adams case about twenty years ago?'

The Chief Inspector's manner suddenly changed and grew wary.

'Victoria Adams case?' he ruminated. 'No, sir, I can't say I do.'

'Son, you're lyin'! You were sergeant to old Chief Inspector Rutherford in those days, and well I remember it!'

Masters stood on his dignity.

'That's as may be, sir. But twenty years ago . . . '

'A little girl of twelve or thirteen, the child of very wealthy parents, disappeared one night out of a country cottage with all the doors and windows locked on the inside. A week later, while everybody was havin' screaming hysterics, the child reappeared again: through the locks and bolts, tucked up in her bed as usual. And to this day nobody's ever known what really happened.'

There was a silence, while Masters shut his jaws hard.

'This family, the Adamses,' persisted H. M., 'owned the cottage, down Aylesbury way, on the edge of Goblin Wood, opposite the lake. Or was it?'

'Oh, ah,' growled Masters. 'It was.'

H. M. looked at him curiously.

'They used the cottage as a base for bathin' in summer, and ice-skatin' in winter. It was black winter when the child vanished, and the place was all locked up inside against drafts. They say her old man nearly went loopy when he found her there a week later, lying asleep under the lamp. But all she'd say, when they asked her where she'd been, was, "*I don't know.*"'

Again there was a silence, while red buses thundered through the traffic press of Whitehall.

'You've got to admit, Masters, there was a flaming public rumpus. I say: did you ever read Barrie's *Mary Rose?*'

'No.'

'Well, it was a situation straight out of Barrie. Some people, y'see, said that Vicky Adams was a child of faerie who'd been spirited away by the pixies . . . '

Whereupon Masters exploded.

He removed his bowler hat and wiped his forehead. He made remarks about pixies, in detail, which could not have been bettered by H. M. himself.

'I know, son, I know.' H. M. was soothing. Then his big voice sharpened. 'Now tell me. Was all this talk strictly true?'

'What talk?'

'Locked windows? Bolted doors? No attic-trap? No cellar? Solid walls and floor?'

'Yes, sir,' answered Masters, regaining his dignity with a powerful effort, 'I'm bound to admit it *was* true.'

'Then there wasn't any jiggery-pokery about the cottage?'

'In your eye there wasn't,' said Masters.

'How d'ye mean?'

'Listen, sir.' Masters lowered his voice. 'Before the Adamses took over that place, it was a hideout for Chuck Randall. At that time he was the swellest of the swell mob; we lagged him a couple of years later. Do you think Chuck wouldn't have rigged up some gadget for a getaway? Just so! Only . . . '

'Well? Hey?'

'We couldn't find it,' grunted Masters.

'And I'll bet that pleased old Chief Inspector Rutherford?'

'I tell you straight: he was fair up the pole. Especially as the kid herself was a pretty kid, all big eyes and dark hair. You couldn't help trusting her.'

'Yes,' said H. M. 'That's what worries me.'

'Worries you?'

'Oh, my son!' said H. M. dismally. 'Here's Vicky Adams, the spoiled daughter of dotin' parents. She's supposed to be "odd" and "fey". She's even encouraged to be. During her adolescence, the most impressionable time of her life, she gets wrapped round with the gauze of a mystery that people talk about even yet. What's that woman like now, Masters? What's that woman like now?'

'Dear Sir Henry!' murmured Miss Vicky Adams in her softest voice.

She said this just as William Sage's car, with Bill and Eve Drayton in the front seat, and Vicky and H. M. in the back seat, turned off the main road. Behind them lay the smoky-red roofs of Aylesbury, against a brightness of late afternoon. The car turned down a side road, a damp tunnel of greenery, and into another road which was little more than a lane between hedgerows.

H. M.—though cheered by three good-sized picnic hampers from Fortnum & Mason, their wickerwork lids bulging with a feast—did not seem happy. Nobody in that car was happy, with the possible exception of Miss Adams herself.

Vicky, unlike Eve, was small and dark and vivacious. Her large light-brown eyes, with very black lashes, could be arch and coy; or they could be dreamily intense. The late Sir James Barrie might have called her a sprite. Those of more sober views would have recognized a different quality: she had an inordinate sex appeal, which was as palpable as a physical touch to any male within yards. And despite her smallness, Vicky had a full voice like Eve's. All these qualities she used even in so simple a matter as giving traffic directions.

'First right,' she would say, leaning forward to put her hands on Bill Sage's shoulders. 'Then straight on until the next traffic light. Ah, clever boy!'

'Not at all, not at all!' Bill would disclaim, with red ears and rather an erratic style of driving.

'Oh, yes, you are!' And Vicky would twist the lobe of his ear, playfully, before sitting back again.

(Eve Drayton did not say anything. She did not even turn round. Yet the atmosphere, even of that quiet English picnic party, had already become a trifle hysterical.)

'Dear Sir Henry!' murmured Vicky, as they turned down into the deep lane between the hedgerows. 'I do wish you wouldn't be so materialistic! I do, really. Haven't you the tiniest bit of spirituality in your nature?'

'Me?' said H. M. in astonishment. 'I got a very lofty spiritual nature. But what I want just now, my wench, is grub.—Oi!'

Bill Sage glanced round.

'By that speedometer,' H. M. pointed, 'we've now come forty-six miles and a bit. We didn't even leave town until people of decency and sanity were having their tea. Where are we *goin'*?'

'But didn't you know?' asked Vicky, with wide-open eyes. 'We're going to the cottage where I had such a dreadful experience when I was a child.'

'Was it such a dreadful experience, Vicky dear?' inquired Eve.

Vicky's eyes seemed far away.

'I don't remember, really. I was only a child, you see. I didn't understand. I hadn't developed the power for myself then.'

'What power?' H. M. asked sharply.

'To dematerialize,' said Vicky. 'Of course.'

In that warm, sun-dusted lane, between the hawthorn hedges, the car jolted over a rut. Crockery rattled.

'Uh-huh. I see,' observed H. M. without inflection. 'And where do you go, my wench, when you dematerialize?'

'Into a strange country. Through a little door. You wouldn't understand. Oh, you *are* such Philistines!' moaned Vicky. Then, with a sudden change of mood, she leaned forward and her whole physical allurement flowed again towards Bill Sage. '*You* wouldn't like me to disappear, would you, Bill?'

(Easy! Easy!)

'Only', said Bill, with a sort of wild gallantry, 'if you promised to reappear again straightaway.'

'Oh, I should have to do that.' Vicky sat back. She was trembling. 'The power wouldn't be strong enough. But even a poor little thing like me might be able to teach you a lesson. Look there!'

And she pointed ahead.

On their left, as the lane widened, stretched the ten-acre gloom of what is fancifully known as Goblin Wood. On their right lay a small lake, on private property and therefore deserted.

The cottage—set well back into a clearing of the wood so as to face the road, screened from it by a line of beeches—was in fact a bungalow of rough-hewn stone, with a slate roof. Across the front of it ran a wooden porch. It had a seedy air, like the long, yellow-green grass of its front lawn. Bill parked the car at the side of the road, since there was no driveway.

'It's a bit lonely, ain't it?' demanded H. M. His voice boomed out against that utter stillness, under the hot sun.

'Oh, yes!' breathed Vicky. She jumped out of the car in a whirl of skirts. 'That's why *they* were able to come and take me. When I was a child.'

'They?'

'Dear Sir Henry! Do I need to explain?'

Then Vicky looked at Bill.

'I must apologize,' she said, 'for the state the house is in. I haven't been out here for months and months. There's a modern bathroom, I'm glad to say. Only paraffin lamps, of course. But then,' a dreamy smile flashed across her face, 'you won't need lamps, will you? Unless . . .'

'You mean,' said Bill, who was taking a black case out of the car, 'unless you disappear again?'

'Yes, Bill. And promise me you won't be frightened when I do.'

The young man uttered a ringing oath which was shushed by Sir Henry Merrivale, who austerely said he disapproved of profanity. Eve Drayton was very quiet.

'But in the meantime.' Vicky said wistfully, 'let's forget it all, shall we? Let's laugh and dance and sing and pretend we're children! And surely our guest must be even more hungry by this time?'

It was in this emotional state that they sat down to their picnic.

H. M., if the truth must be told, did not fare too badly. Instead of sitting on some hummock of ground, they dragged a table and chairs to the shaded porch. All spoke in strained voices. But no word of controversy was said. It was only afterwards, when the cloth was cleared, the furniture and hampers pushed indoors, the empty bottles flung away, that danger tapped a warning.

From under the porch Vicky fished out two half-rotted deck chairs, which she set up in the long grass of the lawn. These were to be occupied by Eve and H. M., while Vicky took Bill Sage to inspect a plum tree of some remarkable quality she did not specify.

Eve sat down without comment. H. M., who was smoking a black cigar opposite her, waited some time before he spoke.

'Y' know,' he said, taking the cigar out of his mouth, 'you're behaving remarkably well.'

'Yes,' Eve laughed. 'Aren't I?'

'Are you pretty well acquainted with this Adams gal?'

'I'm her first cousin,' Eve answered simply. 'Now that her parents are dead, I'm the only relative she's got. I know *all* about her.'

From far across the lawn floated two voices saying something about wild strawberries. Eve, her fair hair and fair complexion vivid against the dark line of Goblin Wood, clenched her hands on her knees.

'You see, H. M.,' she hesitated, 'there was another reason why I invited you here. I—I don't quite know how to approach it.'

'I'm the old man,' said H. M., tapping himself impressively on the chest. 'You tell me.'

'Eve, darling!' interposed Vicky's voice, crying across the ragged lawn. 'Coo-ee! Eve!'

'Yes, dear?'

'I've just remembered,' cried Vicky, 'that I haven't shown Bill over the cottage! You don't mind if I steal him away from you for a little while?'

'No, dear! Of course not!'

It was H. M., sitting so as to face the bungalow, who saw Vicky and Bill go in. He saw Vicky's wistful smile as she closed the door after them. Eve did not even look round. The sun was declining, making fiery chinks through the thickness of Goblin Wood behind the cottage.

'I won't let her have him.' Eve suddenly cried. 'I won't! I won't! I won't!'

'Does she want him, my wench? Or, which is more to the point, does he want her?'

'He never has,' Eve said with emphasis. 'Not really. And he never will.'

H. M., motionless, puffed out cigar smoke.

'Vicky's a faker,' said Eve. 'Does that sound catty?'

'Not necessarily. I was just thinkin' the same thing myself.'

'I'm patient,' said Eve. Her blue eyes were fixed. 'I'm terribly, terribly patient. I can wait years for what I want. Bill's not making much money now, and I haven't got a bean. But Bill's got great talent under that easy-going manner of his. He *must* have the right girl to help him. If only . . .

'If only the elfin sprite would let him alone. Hey?'

'Vicky acts like that,' said Eve, 'towards practically every man she ever meets. That's why she never married. She says it leaves her soul free to commune with other souls. This occultism—'

Then it all poured out, the family story of the Adamses. This repressed girl spoke at length, spoke as perhaps she had never spoken before. Vicky Adams, the child who wanted to attract attention, her father, Uncle Fred, and her mother, Aunt Margaret, seemed to walk in vividness as the shadows gathered.

'I was too young to know her at the time of the "disappearance", of course. But, oh, I knew her afterwards! And I thought . . . '

'Well?'

'If I could get *you* here,' said Eve, 'I thought she'd try to show off with some game. And then you'd expose her. And Bill would see what an awful faker she is. But it's hopeless! It's hopeless!'

'Looky here,' observed H. M., who was smoking his third cigar. He sat up. 'Doesn't it strike you those two are being a rummy-awful long time just in lookin' through a little bungalow?'

Eve, roused out of a dream, stared back at him. She sprang to her feet. She was not now, you could guess, thinking of any disappearance.

'Excuse me a moment,' she said curtly.

Eve hurried across to the cottage, went up on the porch, and opened the front door. H. M. heard her heels rap down the length of the small passage inside. She marched straight back again, closed the front door, and rejoined H. M.

'All the doors of the rooms are shut,' she announced in a high voice. 'I really don't think I ought to disturb them.'

'Easy, my wench!'

'I have absolutely no interest,' declared Eve, with the tears coming into her eyes, 'in what happens to either of them now. Shall we take the car and go back to town without them?'

H. M. threw away his cigar, got up, and seized her by the shoulders.

'I'm the old man,' he said, with a leer like an ogre. 'Will you listen to me?'

'No!'

'If I'm any reader of the human dial,' persisted H. M., 'that young feller's no more gone on Vicky Adams than I am. He was scared, my wench. Scared.' Doubt, indecision crossed H. M.'s face. 'I dunno what he's scared of. Burn me, I don't! But . . .'

'Hoy!' called the voice of Bill Sage.

It did not come from the direction of the cottage.

They were surrounded on three sides by Goblin Wood, now blurred with twilight. From the north side the voice bawled at them, followed by crackling in dry undergrowth. Bill, his hair and sports coat and flannels more than a little dirty, regarded them with a face of bitterness.

'Here are her blasted wild strawberries,' he announced, extending his hand. Three of 'em. The fruitful (excuse me) result of three-quarters of an hour's hard labour. I absolutely refuse to chase 'em in the dark.'

For a moment Eve Drayton's mouth moved without speech.

'Then you weren't . . . in the cottage all this time?'

'In the cottage?' Bill glanced at it. 'I was in that cottage,' he said, 'about five minutes. Vicky had a woman's whim. She wanted some wild strawberries out of what she called the "forest".'

'Wait a minute, son!' said H. M. very sharply. 'You didn't come out that front door. Nobody did.'

'No! I went out the back door! It opens straight on the wood.'

'Yes. And what happened then?'

'Well, I went to look for these damned . . .'

'No, no! What did *she* do?'

'Vicky? She locked and bolted the back door on the inside. I remember her grinning at me through the glass panel. She—'

Bill stopped short. His eyes widened, and then narrowed, as though at the impact of an idea. All three of them turned to look at the rough-stone cottage.

'By the way,' said Bill. He cleared his throat vigorously. 'By the way, have you seen Vicky since then?'

'No.'

'This couldn't be . . . ?'

'It could be, son,' said H. M. 'We'd all better go in there and have a look.'

They hesitated for a moment on the porch. A warm, moist fragrance breathed up from the ground after sunset. In half an hour it would be completely dark.

Bill Sage threw open the front door and shouted Vicky's name. That sound seemed to penetrate, reverberating, through every room. The intense heat and stuffiness of the cottage, where no window had been raised in months, blew out at them. But nobody answered.

'Get inside,' snapped H. M. 'And stop yowlin.' 'The Old Maestro was nervous. 'I'm dead sure she didn't get out by the front door, but we'll just make certain there's no slippin out now.'

Stumbling over the table and chairs they had used on the porch, he fastened the front door. They were in a narrow passage, once handsome with parquet floor and pine-panelled walls, leading to a door with a glass panel at the rear. H. M. lumbered forward to inspect this door, and found it locked and bolted, as Bill had said.

Goblin Wood grew darker.

Keeping well together, they searched the cottage. It was not large, having two good-sized rooms on one side of the passage, and two small rooms on the other side, so as to make space for bathroom and kitchenette. H. M., raising fogs of dust, ransacked every inch where a person could possibly hide.

And all the windows were locked on the inside. And the chimney-flues were too narrow to admit anybody.

And Vicky Adams wasn't there.

'Oh, my eye!' breathed Sir Henry Merrivale.

They had gathered, by what idiotic impulse not even H. M. could have said, just outside the open door of the bathroom. A bath-tap dripped monotonously. The last light through a frosted-glass window showed three faces hung there as though disembodied.

'Bill,' said Eve in an unsteady voice, 'this is a trick. Oh, I've longed for her to be exposed! This is a trick!'

'Then where is she?'

'H. M. can tell us! Can't you, H. M.?'

'Well . . . now,' muttered the great man.

Across H. M.'s Panama hat was a large black handprint, made there when he had pressed down the hat after investigating the chimney. He glowered under it.

'Son,' he said to Bill, 'there's just one question I want you to answer in all this hokey-pokey. When you went out pickin' wild strawberries, will you swear Vicky Adams didn't go with you?'

'As God is my Judge, she didn't,' returned Bill, with fervency and obvious truth. 'Besides, how the devil could she? Look at the lock and bolt on the back door!'

H. M. made two more violent black handprints on his hat.

He lumbered forward, his head down, two or three paces in the narrow passage. His foot half skidded on something that had been lying there unnoticed, and he picked it up. It was a large, square section of thin, waterproof oilskin, jagged at one corner.

'Have you found anything?' demanded Bill in a strained voice.

'No. Not to make any sense, that is. But just a minute!'

At the rear of the passage, on the left-hand side, was the bedroom from which Vicky Adams had vanished as a child. Though H. M. had searched this room once before, he opened the door again.

It was now almost dark in Goblin Wood.

He saw dimly a room twenty years before: a room of flounces, of lace curtains, of once-polished mahogany, its mirrors glimmering against white-papered walls. H. M. seemed especially interested in the windows.

He ran his hands carefully round the frame of each, even climbing laboriously up on a chair to examine the tops. He borrowed a box of matches from Bill; and the little spurts of light, following the rasp of the match, rasped against nerves as well. The hope died out of his face, and his companions saw it.

'H. M.,' Bill said for the dozenth time, 'where is she?'

'Son,' replied H. M. despondently, 'I don't know.'

'Let's get out of here,' Eve said abruptly. Her voice was a small scream. 'I kn-know it's all a trick! I know Vicky's a faker! But let's get out of here. For God's sake let's get out of here!'

'As a matter of fact,' Bill cleared his throat, 'I agree. Anyway, we won't hear from Vicky until tomorrow morning.'

'Oh, *yes*, *you will*,' whispered Vicky's voice out of the darkness.

Eve screamed.

They lighted a lamp.

But there was nobody there.

Their retreat from the cottage, it must be admitted, was not very dignified.

How they stumbled down that ragged lawn in the dark, how they piled rugs and picnic hampers into the car, how they eventually found the main road again, is best left undescribed.

Sir Henry Merrivale has since sneered at this—'a bit of a goosy feeling; nothin' much'—and it is true that he has no nerves to speak of. But he can be worried, badly worried, and that he was worried on this occasion may be deduced from what happened later.

H. M., after dropping in at Claridge's for a modest late supper of lobster and *Pêche Melba*, returned to his house in Brook Street and slept a hideous sleep. It was three o'clock in the morning, even before the summer dawn, when the ringing of the bedside telephone roused him.

What he heard sent his blood pressure soaring.

'Dear Sir Henry!' crooned a familiar and sprite-like voice.

H. M. was himself again, full of gall and bile. He switched on the bedside lamp and put on his spectacles with care, so as adequately to address the phone.

'Have I got the honour,' he said with dangerous politeness, 'of addressin' Miss Vicky Adams?'

'Oh, yes!'

'I sincerely trust,' said H. M., 'you've been havin' a good time? Are you materialized yet?'

'Oh, yes!'

'Where are you now?'

'I'm afraid'—there was coy laughter in the voice—'that must be a little secret for a day or two. I want to teach you a really *good* lesson. Blessings, dear.'

And she hung up the receiver.

H. M. did not say anything. He climbed out of bed. He stalked up and down the room, his corporation majestic under an old-fashioned nightshirt stretching to his heels. Then, since he himself had been waked up at three o'clock in the morning, the obvious course was to wake up somebody else; so he dialled the home number of Chief Inspector Masters.

'No, sir,' retorted Masters grimly, after coughing the frog out of his throat, 'I do *not* mind you ringing up. Not a bit of it!' He spoke with a certain pleasure. 'Because I've got a bit of news for you.'

H. M. eyed the phone suspiciously.

'Masters, are you trying to do me in the eye again?'

'It's what you always try to do to me, isn't it?'

'All right, all right!' growled H. M. 'What's the news?'

'Do you remember mentioning the Vicky Adams case to me yesterday?'

'Sort of. Yes.'

'Oh, ah! Well, I had a word or two round among our people. I was tipped the wink to go and see a certain solicitor. He was old Mr Fred Adams's solicitor before Mr Adams died about six or seven years ago.'

Here Masters's voice grew suave with triumph.

'I always said, Sir Henry, that Chuck Randall had planted some gadget in that cottage for a quick get-away. And I was right. The gadget was . . .'

'You were quite right, Masters. The gadget was a trick window.'

The telephone so to speak, gave a start.

'What's that?'

'A trick window.' H. M. spoke patiently. 'You press a spring. And the whole frame of the window, two leaves locked together, slides down between the walls far enough so you can climb over. Then you push it back up again.'

'*How in lum's name do you know that?*'

'Oh, my son! They used to build windows like it in country houses during the persecution of Catholic priests. It was a good enough *second* guess. Only. . . it won't work.'

Masters seemed annoyed. 'It won't work now,' Masters agreed. 'And do you know why?'

'I can guess. Tell me.'

'Because, just before Mr Adams died, he discovered how his darling daughter had flummoxed him. He never told anybody except his lawyer. He took a handful of four-inch nails, and sealed up the top of that frame so tight an orangoutang couldn't move it, and painted 'em over so they wouldn't be noticed.'

'Uh-huh. You can notice 'em now.'

'I doubt if the young lady herself ever knew. But, by George!' Masters said savagely, 'I'd like to see anybody try the same game now!'

'You would, hey? Then will it interest you to know that the same gal has just disappeared out of the same house AGAIN?'

H. M. began a long narrative of the facts, but he had to break off because the telephone was raving.

'Honest, Masters,' H. M. said seriously, 'I'm not joking. She didn't get out through the window. But she did get out. You'd better meet me'—he gave directions—'tomorrow morning. In the meantime, son, sleep well.'

It was, therefore, a worn-faced Masters who went into the Visitors' Room at the Senior Conservatives' Club just before lunch on the following day.

The Visitors' Room is a dark, sepulchral place, opening on an air-well, where the visitor is surrounded by pictures of dyspeptic-looking gentlemen with beards. It has a pervading mustiness of wood and leather. Though whisky and soda stood on the table, H. M. sat in a leather chair far away from it, ruffling his hands across his bald head.

'Now, Masters, keep your shirt on!' he warned. 'This business may be rummy. But it's not a police matter—yet.'

'I know it's not a police matter,' Masters said grimly. 'All the same, I've had a word with the Superintendent at Aylesbury.'

'Fowler?'

'You know him?'

'Sure. I know everybody. Is he goin' to keep an eye out?'

'He's going to have a look at that ruddy cottage. I've asked for any telephone calls to be put through here. In the meantime, sir—'

It was at this point, as though diabolically inspired, that the telephone rang. H. M. reached it before Masters.

'It's the old man,' he said, unconsciously assuming a stance of grandeur. 'Yes, yes! Masters is here, but he's drunk. You tell me first. What's that?'

The telephone talked thinly.

'Sure I looked in the kitchen cupboard,' bellowed H. M. 'Though I didn't honestly expect to find Vicky Adams hidin' there. What's that? Say it again! Plates? Cups that had been . . .'

An almost frightening change had come over H. M.'s expression. He stood motionless. All the posturing went out of him. He was not even listening to the voice that still talked thinly, while his eyes and his brain moved to put together facts. At length (though the voice still talked) he hung up the receiver.

H. M. blundered back to the centre table, where he drew out a chair and sat down.

'Masters,' he said very quietly. 'I've come close to makin' the silliest mistake of my life.'

Here he cleared his throat.

'I shouldn't have made it, son, I really shouldn't. But don't yell at me for cuttin' off Fowler. I can tell you now how Vicky Adams disappeared. And she said one true thing when she said she was going into a strange country.'

'How do you mean?'

'She's dead,' answered H. M.

The word fell with heavy weight into that dingy room, where the bearded faces look down.

'Y'see,' H. M. went on blankly, 'a lot of us were right when we thought Vicky Adams was a faker. She was. To attract attention to herself, she played that trick on her family with the hocused window. She's lived and traded on it ever since. That's what sent me straight in the wrong direction. I was on the alert for some *trick* Vicky Adams might play. So it never occurred to me that this elegant pair of beauties, Miss Eve Drayton and Mr William Sage, were deliberately conspirin' to murder *her*.'

Masters got slowly to his feet.

'Did you say . . . murder?'

'Oh, yes.'

Again H. M. cleared his throat.

'It was all arranged beforehand for me to be a witness. They knew Vicky Adams couldn't resist a challenge to disappear, especially as Vicky always believed she could get out by the trick window. They wanted Vicky to *say* she was goin' to disappear. They never knew anything about the trick window, Masters. But they knew their own plan very well.

'Eve Drayton even told me the motive. She hated Vicky, of course. But that wasn't the main point. She was Vicky Adam's only relative; she'd inherit an awful big scoopful of money. Eve said she could be patient. (And, burn me, how her eyes meant it when she said that!) Rather than risk any slightest suspicion of murder, she was willing to wait seven years until a disappeared person can be presumed dead.

'Our Eve, I think, was the fiery drivin' force of that conspiracy. She was only scared part of the time. Sage was scared all of the time. But it was Sage who did the real dirty work. He lured Vicky Adams into that cottage, while Eve kept me in close conversation on the lawn . . . '

H. M. paused.

Intolerably vivid in the mind of Chief Inspector Masters, who had seen it years before, rose the picture of the rough-stone bungalow against the darkening wood.

'Masters,' said H. M., 'why should a bath-tap be dripping in a house that hadn't been occupied for months?'

'Well?'

'Sage, y'see, is a surgeon. I saw him take his black case of instruments out of the car. He took Vicky Adams into that house. In the bathroom he stabbed her, he stripped her, and *he dismembered her body in the bath-tub.—Easy, son!*'

'Go on,' said Masters, without moving.

'The head, the torso, the folded arms and legs, were wrapped up in three large square pieces of thin, transparent oilskin. Each was sewed up with coarse thread so the blood wouldn't drip. Last night I found one of the oilskin pieces he'd ruined when his needle slipped at the corner. Then he walked out of the house, with the back door still standin' unlocked, to get his wild-strawberry alibi.'

'Sage went out of there,' shouted Masters, 'leaving the body in the house?'

'Oh, yes,' agreed H. M.

'But where did he leave it?'

H. M. ignored this.

In the meantime, son, what about Eve Drayton? At the end of the arranged three-quarters of an hour, she indicated there was hanky-panky between her fiancé and Vicky Adams. She flew into the house. But what did she do?

'She walked to the back of the passage. I heard her. *There she simply locked and bolted the back door.* And then she marched out to join me with tears in her eyes. And these two beauties were ready for investigation.'

'Investigation?' said Masters. '*With that body still in the house?*'

'Oh, yes.'

Masters lifted both fists.

'It must have given young Sage a shock,' said H. M., 'when I found that piece of waterproof oilskin he'd washed but dropped. Anyway, these two had only two more bits of hokey-pokey. The "vanished" gal had to speak—to show she was still alive. If you'd been there, son, you'd have noticed that Eve Drayton's got a voice just like Vicky Adams's. If somebody speaks in a dark room, carefully imitatin' a coy tone she never uses herself, the illusion's goin' to be pretty good. The same goes for a telephone.

'It was finished, Masters. All that had to be done was remove the body from the house, and get it far away from there . . . '

'But that's just what I'm asking you, sir! Where was the body all this time? And who in blazes *did* remove the body from the house?'

'All of us did,' answered H. M.

'What's that?'

'Masters,' said H. M., 'aren't you forgettin' the picnic hampers?'

And now, the Chief Inspector saw, H. M. was as white as a ghost. His next words took Masters like a blow between the eyes.

'Three good-sized wickerwork hampers, with lids. After our big meal on the porch, those hampers were shoved inside the house, where Sage could get at 'em. He had to leave most of the used crockery behind, in the kitchen cupboard. But three wickerwork hampers from a picnic, and three butcher's parcels to go inside 'em. I carried one down to the car myself. It felt a bit funny . . .'

H. M. stretched out his hand, not steadily, towards the whisky.

'Y'know,' he said, 'I'll always wonder whether I was carrying the—head.'

ELLERY QUEEN

The pseudonym of cousins Manfred B. Lee (1905–1971) and Frederic Dannay (1905–1982) who created America's arguably most popular fictional male detective, also named Ellery Queen. Both cousins were born in Brooklyn. Dannay had experience as a copywriter and Lee as a writer of advertising material before they turned to writing mysteries. The cousins decided to enter a mystery novel contest sponsored by *McClure's* magazine and Stokes's Publishing. As the result, the first Ellery Queen novel, *The Roman Hat Mystery*, was published in 1929. In the beginning, the identity of "Ellery Queen" was kept secret with one of the cousins appearing before the public masked, generating great reader appeal. Only later was the identity of the writing team revealed. The Ellery Queen novels are among the best of the American "puzzle" mysteries, always following the "fair-play" rule, and using many variations of "the dying message" plot, in which the victim leaves some clue about the murderer. The cousins also promoted the mystery short-story form by creating *Ellery Queen's Mystery Magazine*, the most prestigious magazine of its kind. The Ellery Queen series is the recipient of five Edgars from the Mystery Writers of America, and the organization's special award, the Raven. In 1939 the first Ellery Queen radio series began, followed by four television series featuring Ellery Queen and numerous Hollywood films.

Ellery Queen, the amateur detective, is a mystery writer who writes novels based on the crimes he has solved. He is a somewhat condescending, arrogant young man as the books begin, but grows and mellows throughout the series. Tall and thin, with unsettling silver eyes, Queen is intelligent, perceptive, and observant of the smallest detail. He appreciates smart and attractive women. His cases range in setting from New York to Hollywood to small town New England, and are filled with social commentary and criticism. He is famous for his "challenge to the reader" to solve the crime before the last chapter of the book. He has access to the police and important information through his father Inspector Richard Queen of the New York police. Writing under another pseudonym, Barnaby Ross, the Lee-Dannay team also created amateur detective Drury Lane, a deaf former Shakespearean actor, who is the sleuth for four novels. This academic mystery, "'My Queer Dean!,'" featuring Ellery Queen, demonstrates his use of wordplay to solve a murder. It was first published in *Queen's Bureau of Investigation* (1955).

Recommended Queen works: *The Egyptian Cross Mystery, Calamity Town, Cat of Many Tails.*

Other recommended authors: Anthony Boucher, John Dickson Carr, S.S. Van Dine.

'My Queer Dean!'

The queerness of Matthew Arnold Hope, beloved teacher of Ellery's Harvard youth and lately dean of liberal arts in a New York university, is legendary.

The story is told, for instance, of baffled students taking Dr Hope's Shakespeare course for the first time. 'History advises us that Richard II died peacefully at Pontefract, probably of pneumonia,' Dr Hope scolds. 'But what does Shakespeare say, Act V, Scene V? That Exton struck him down,' and here the famous authority on Elizabethan literature will pause for emphasis, 'with a blushing crow!'

Imaginative sophomores have been known to suffer nightmares as a result of this remark. Older heads nod intelligently, of course, knowing that Dr Hope meant merely to say—in fact, thought he was saying—'a crushing blow.'

The good dean's unconscious spoonerisms, like the sayings of Miss Parker and Mr Goldwyn, are reverently preserved by aficionados, among whom Ellery counts himself a charter member. It is Ellery who has saved for posterity that deathless pronouncement of Dr Hope's to a freshman class in English composition: 'All those who persist in befouling their theme papers with cant and other low expressions not in good usage are warned for the last time: Refine your style or be exiled from this course with the rest of the vanished Bulgarians!'

But perhaps Dean Hope's greatest exploit began recently in the faculty lunchroom. Ellery arrived at the dean's invitation to find him waiting impatiently at one of the big round tables with three members of the English Department.

'Dr Agnes Lovell, Professor Oswald Gorman, Mr Morgan Naseby,' the dean said rapidly. 'Sit down, Ellery. Mr Queen will have the cute frocktail and the horned beef cash—only safe edibles on the menu today, my boy—Will, go fetch, young man! Are you dreaming that you're back in class?' The waiter, a harried-looking freshman, fled. Then Dr Hope said solemnly, 'My friends, prepare for a surprise.'

Dr Lovell, a very large woman in a tight suit, said roguishly: 'Wait, Matthew! Let me guess. Romance?'

'And who'd marry—in Macaulay's imperishable phrase—a living concordance?' said Professor Gorman in a voice like an abandoned winch. He was a tall freckled man with strawberry eyebrows and a quarrelsome jaw. 'A real surprise, Dr Hope, would be a departmental salary rise.'

'A consummation devoutly et cetera,' said Mr Naseby, immediately blushing. He was a stout young man with an eager manner, evidently a junior in the department.

'May I have your attention?' Dean Hope looked about cautiously. 'Suppose I tell you,' he said in a trembling voice, 'that by tonight I may have it within my power to deliver the death-blow—I repeat, the death-blow!—to the cocky-pop that Francis Bacon wrote Shakespeare's plays?'

There were two gasps, a snort, and one inquiring hum.

'Matthew!' squealed Dr Lovell. 'You'd be famous!'

'Immortal, Dean Hope,' said Mr Naseby adoringly.

'Deluded,' said Professor Gorman, the snorter. 'The Baconian benightedness, like the Marlowe mania, has no known specific.'

'Ah, but even a fanatic,' cried the dean, 'would have to yield before the nature of this evidence.'

'Sounds exciting, Doc,' murmured Ellery. 'What is it?'

'A man called at my office this morning, Ellery. He produced credentials identifying him as a London rare-book dealer, Alfred Mimms. He has in his possession, he said, a copy of the 1613 edition of *The Essaies of Sir Francis Bacon Knight the kings solliciter generall*, an item ordinarily bringing four or five hundred dollars. He claims that this copy, however, is unique, *being inscribed on the title page in Bacon's own hand to Will Shakespeare*.'

Amid the cries, Ellery asked: 'Inscribed how?'

'In an encomium,' quavered Dean Hope, 'an encomium to Shakespeare expressing Bacon's admiration and praise for—and I quote—"*the most excellent plaies of your sweet wit and hand*"!'

'Take that!' whispered Mr Naseby to an invisible Baconian.

'That does it,' breathed Dr Lovell.

'That would do it,' said Professor Gorman, 'if.'

'Did you actually see the book, Doc?' asked Ellery.

'He showed me a photostat of the title-page. He'll have the original for my inspection tonight, in my office.'

'And Mimm's asking price is—?'

'Ten thousand dollars.'

'Proof positive that it's a forgery,' said Professor Gorman rustily. 'It's far too little.'

'Oswald,' hissed Dr Lovell, 'you creak, do you know that?'

'No, Gorman is right,' said Dr Hope. 'An absurd price if the inscription is genuine, as I pointed out to Mimms. However, he had an explanation. He is acting, he said, at the instructions of the book's owner, a tax-poor British nobleman whose identity he will reveal tonight if I purchase the book. The owner, who has just found it in a castle room boarded up and forgotten for two centuries, prefers an American buyer in a confidential sale—for tax reasons, Mimms hinted. But, as a cultivated man, the owner wishes a scholar to have it rather than some ignorant Croesus. Hence the relatively low price.'

'Lovely,' glowed Mr Naseby. 'And so typically British.'

'Isn't it?' said Professor Gorman. 'Terms cash, no doubt? On the line? Tonight?'

'Well, yes.' The old dean took a bulging envelope from his breast pocket and eyed it ruefully. Then, with a sigh, he tucked it back. 'Very nearly my life's savings. . . . But I'm not altogether senile,' Dr Hope grinned. 'I'm asking you to be present, Ellery—with Inspector Queen. I shall be working at my desk on administrative things into the evening. Mimms is due at eight o'clock.'

'We'll be here at seven-thirty,' promised Ellery. 'By the way, Doc, that's a lot of money to be carrying around in your pocket. Have you confided this business to anyone else?'

'No, no.'

'Don't. And may I suggest that you wait behind a locked door? Don't admit Mimms—or anyone else you don't trust—until we get here. I'm afraid, Doc, I share the professor's scepticism.'

'Oh, so do I,' murmured the dean. 'The odds on this being a swindle are, I should think, several thousand to one. But one can't help saying to oneself . . . suppose it's not?'

It was nearly half-past seven when the Queens entered the Arts Building. Some windows on the upper floors were lit up where a few evening classes were in session, and the dean's office was bright. Otherwise the building was dark.

The first thing Ellery saw as they stepped out of the self-service elevator on to the dark third floor was the door of Dean Hope's ante-room . . . wide open.

They found the old scholar crumpled on the floor just inside the doorway. His white hairs dripped red.

'Crook came early,' howled Inspector Queen. 'Look at the dean's wristwatch, Ellery—smashed in his fall at 7.15.'

'I warned him not to unlock his door,' wailed Ellery. Then he bellowed. 'He's breathing! Call an ambulance!'

He had carried the dean's frail body to a couch in the inner office and was gently wetting the blue lips from a paper cup when the Inspector turned from the telephone.

The eyes fluttered open. 'Ellery . . . '

'Doc, what happened?'

'Book . . . taken . . . ' The voice trailed off in a mutter.

'Book taken?' repeated the Inspector incredulously. 'That means Mimms not only came early, but Dr Hope found the book was genuine! Is the money on him, son?'

Ellery searched the dean's pockets, the office, the ante-room. 'It's gone.'

'Then he did buy it. Then somebody came along, cracked him on the skull, and lifted the book.'

'Doc!' Ellery bent over the old man again. 'Doc, who struck you? Did you see?'

'Yes ... Gorman ...' Then the battered head rolled to one side and Dr Hope lost consciousness.

'Gorman? Who's Gorman, Ellery?'

'Professor Oswald Gorman,' Ellery said through his teeth, 'one of the English faculty at the lunch today. *Get him.*'

When Inspector Queen returned to the dean's office guiding the agitated elbow of Professor Gorman, he found Ellery waiting behind the dean's flower-vase as if it were a bough from Birnam Wood.

The couch was empty.

'What did the ambulance doctor say, Ellery?'

'Concussion. How bad they don't know yet.' Ellery rose, fixing Professor Gorman with a Macduffian glance. 'And where did you find this pedagogical louse, Dad?'

'Upstairs on the seventh floor, teaching a Bible class.'

'The title of my course, Inspector Queen,' said the Professor furiously, 'is *The Influence of the Bible on English Literature.*'

'Trying to establish an alibi, eh?'

'Well, son,' said his father in a troubled voice, 'the professor's more than just tried. He's done it.'

'Established an alibi?' Ellery cried.

'It's a two-hour seminar, from six to eight. He's alibied for every second from 6 p.m. on by the dozen people taking the course—including a minister, a priest, and a rabbi. What's more,' mused the Inspector, 'even assuming the 7.15 on the dean's broken watch was a plant, Professor Gorman can account for every minute of his day since your lunch broke up. Ellery, something is rotten in New York County.'

'I beg your pardon,' said a British voice from the ante-room. 'I was to meet Dr Hope here at eight o'clock.'

Ellery whirled. Then he swooped down upon the owner of the voice, a pale skinny man in a bowler hat carrying a package under one arm.

'Don't tell me you're Alfred Mimms and you're just bringing the Bacon!'

'Yes, but I'll—I'll come back,' stammered the visitor, trying to hold on to his package. But it was Ellery who won the tug of war, and as he tore the wrappings away the pale man turned to run.

And there was Inspector Queen in the doorway with his pistol showing. 'Alfred Mimms, is it?' said the Inspector genially. 'Last time, if memory serves, it was Lord Chalmerston. Remember, Dink, when you were sent up for selling a phony First Folio to that Oyster Bay millionaire? Ellery, this is Dink Chalmers of Flatbush, one of the cleverest confidence men in the rare-book game.' Then the Inspector's geniality faded. 'But, son, this leaves us in more of a mess than before.'

'No, dad,' said Ellery. 'This clears the mess up.'

From Inspector Queen's expression, it did nothing of the kind.

'Because what did Doc Hope reply when I asked him what happened?' Ellery said. 'He replied, "Book taken." Well, obviously, the book wasn't taken. The book was never here. Therefore he didn't mean to say "book taken". Professor, you're a communicant of the Matthew Arnold Hope Cult of Spoonerisms: What must the dean have meant to say?'

' "Took . . . Bacon"!' said Professor Gorman.

'Which makes no sense, either, unless we recall, Dad, that his voice trailed off. As if he meant to add a word, but failed. Which word? The word "money"— "took Bacon *money*". Because while the Bacon book wasn't here to be taken, the ten thousand dollars Doc Hope was toting around all day to pay for it was.

'And who took the Bacon money? The one who knocked on the dean's door just after seven o'clock and asked to be let in. The one who, when Dr Hope unlocked the door—indicating the knocker was someone he knew and trusted— promptly clobbered the old man and made off with his life's savings.'

'But when you asked who hit him,' protested the Inspector, 'he answered "Gorman".'

'Which he couldn't have meant, either, since the professor has an alibi of granite. Therefore—'

'Another spoonerism!' exclaimed Professor Gorman.

'I'm afraid so. And since the only spoonerism possible from the name "Gorman" is "Morgan", hunt up Mr Morgan Naseby of the underpaid English department, Dad, and you'll have Doc's assailant and his ten grand back, too.'

Later, at Bellevue Hospital, an indestructible Elizabethan scholar squeezed the younger Queen's hand feebly. Conversation was forbidden, but the good pedagogue and spoonerist extraordinary did manage to whisper, 'My queer Dean . . .'

MARGARET MARON

Creator of two well-known mystery series, featuring amateur detective Deborah Knott and police lieutenant Sigrid Harald, Margaret Maron was born in rural North Carolina, the locale she captures so insightfully in the popular series featuring Judge Deborah Knott. Maron, like Deborah Knott, left the area and lived for several years in the North before returning to her home state. Maron had plans to be a poet, but she began selling short stories, mostly mysteries, starting with "The Death of Me" in *Alfred Hitchcock's Mystery Magazine* in 1968. After twelve years she switched to novels, starting with *One Coffee With* (1981), which introduced the well-received series set in New York City with Lieutenant Sigred Harald, a policewoman who continues to grow and change throughout the novels. *Corpus Christmas* (1989), the sixth in the series, was an Agatha Award and an American Mystery Award nominee.

After Maron returned to the South in the early 1980s, she published a non-series novel *Bloody Kin* (1985). The North Carolina setting and a few of her characters in the novel were subsequently used in the Deborah Knott series, but Deborah herself does not appear until the short story "Deborah's Judgment" (1991). Detective fiction author Sara Paretsky asked Maron to contribute a short story to *A Woman's Eye*, a collection Paretsky was editing, and Maron reports that at that point Deborah Knott strolled into her head and began telling this story. "Deborah's Judgment" won the Agatha Award for Best Short Story. The following year Deborah Knott appeared in *Bootlegger's Daughter* (1992), which won the Edgar, Anthony, Agatha, and Macavity Awards for Best Novel, an unprecedented honor making Maron the only writer ever to receive all four major American mystery awards for one novel. Throughout the series, Deborah searches for a way to promote her own sense of justice in an area still entrenched in patriarchal control and the conflicting attitudes of the "Old South" and the "New South." Maron is a keen social critic in all her works, and, like Lieutenant Sigred Harald, Deborah is a continuously evolving character. "Deborah's Judgment" first appeared in *A Woman's Eye* in 1991 and later was included in Maron's short story collection *Shoveling Smoke* (1997).

Recommended Maron works: *Bootlegger's Daughter, Home Fires, Shoveling Smoke: Selected Mystery Stories*.

Other recommended authors: Nevada Barr, Erle Stanley Gardner, Sharyn McCrumb.

Deborah's Judgment

"And Deborah judged Israel at that time."

An inaudible ripple of cognizance swept through the congregation as the pastor of Bethel Baptist Church paused in his reading of the text and beamed down at us.

I was seated on the aisle near the front of the church, and when Barry Blackman's eyes met mine, I put a modest smile on my face, then tilted my head in ladylike acknowledgment of the pretty compliment he was paying me by his choice of subject for this morning's sermon. A nice man but hardly Christianity's most original preacher. I'd announced my candidacy back in December, so this wasn't the first time I'd heard that particular text, and my response had become almost automatic.

He lowered his eyes to the huge Bible and continued to read aloud, "*And she dwelt under the palm tree of Deborah, between Ramah and Bethel in Mount Ephraim; and the children of Israel came up to her for judgment.*"

From your mouth to God's ear, Barry, I thought.

Eight years of courtroom experience let me listen to the sermon with an outward show of close attention while inwardly my mind jumped on and off a dozen trains of thought. I wondered, without really caring, if Barry was still the terrific kisser he'd been the summer after ninth grade when we both drove tractors for my oldest brother during tobacco-barning season.

There was an S curve between the barns and the back fields where the lane dipped past a stream and cut through a stand of tulip poplars and sweetgum trees. Our timing wasn't good enough to hit every trip, but at least two or three times a day it'd work out that we passed each other there in the shady coolness, one on the way out to the field with empty drags, the other headed back to the barn with drags full of heavy green tobacco leaves.

Nobody seemed to notice that I occasionally returned to the barn more flushed beneath the bill of my baseball cap than even the August sun would merit, although I did have to endure some teasing one day when a smear of tobacco tar appeared on my pink T-shirt right over my left breast. "Looks like somebody tried to grab a handful," my sister-in-law grinned.

I muttered something about the tractor's tar-gummy steering wheel, but I changed shirts at lunchtime and for the rest of the summer I wore the darkest T-shirts in my dresser drawer.

Now Barry Blackman was a preacher man running to fat, the father of two little boys and a new baby girl, while Deborah Knott was a still-single attorney running for a seat on the court bench, a seat being vacated against his will by old Harrison Hobart, who occasionally fell asleep these days while charging his own juries.

As Barry drew parallels between Old Testament Israel and modern Colleton County, I plotted election strategy. After the service, I'd do a little schmoozing among the congregation—

Strike "schmoozing," my subconscious stipulated sternly, and I was stricken myself to realize that Lev Schuster's Yiddish phrases continued to infect my vocabulary. Here in rural North Carolina schmoozing's still called socializing, and I'd better not forget it before the primary. I pushed away errant thoughts of Lev and concentrated on lunch at Beulah's. For that matter, where was Beulah and why weren't she and J.C. seated there beside me?

Beulah had been my mother's dearest friend, and her daughter-in-law, Helen, is president of the local chapter of Mothers Against Drunk Driving. They were sponsoring a meet-the-candidates reception at four o'clock in the fellowship hall of a nearby Presbyterian church, and three of the four men running for Hobart's seat would be there too. (The fourth was finishing up the community service old Hobart had imposed in lieu of a fine for driving while impaired, but he really didn't expect to win many MADD votes anyhow.)

Barry's sermon drew to an end just a hair short of equating a vote for Deborah Knott as a vote for Jesus Christ. The piano swung into the opening chords of "Just as I Am," and the congregation stood to sing all five verses. Happily, no one accepted the hymn's invitation to be saved that morning, and after a short closing prayer we were dismissed.

I'm not a member at Bethel, but I'd been a frequent visitor from the month I was born; so I got lots of hugs and howdies and promises of loyal support when the primary rolled around. I hugged and howdied right back and thanked them kindly, all the time edging toward my car.

It was starting to bother me that neither Beulah nor J.C. had come to church. Then Miss Callie Ogburn hailed me from the side door, talking sixty to the yard as she bustled across the grass.

"Beulah called me up first thing this morning and said tell you about J.C. and for you to come on anyhow. She phoned all over creation last night trying to let you know she's still expecting you to come for dinner."

That explained all those abortive clicks on my answering machine. Beulah was another of my parents' generation who wouldn't talk to a tape. I waited till Miss Callie ran out of breath, then asked her what it was Beulah wanted to tell me about J.C.

"He fell off the tractor and broke his leg yesterday, and he's not used to the crutches yet, so Beulah didn't feel like she ought to leave him this morning. You know how she spoils him."

I did. J.C. was Beulah's older brother, and he'd lived with her and her husband Sam almost from the day they were married more than forty years ago. J.C. was a born bachelor, and except for the war years when he worked as a carpenter's helper at an air base over in Goldsboro, he'd never had much ambition beyond helping Sam farm. Sam always said J.C. wasn't much of a leader but he was a damn good follower and earned every penny of his share of the crop profits.

Although I'd called them Cousin Beulah and Cousin Sam till I was old enough to drop the courtesy title, strictly speaking, only Sam Johnson was blood kin. But Beulah and my mother had been close friends since childhood, and Beulah's two children fit into the age spaces around my older brothers, which was why we'd spent so many Sundays at Bethel Baptist.

When Sam died seven or eight years ago, Sammy Junior took over, and J.C. still helped out even though he'd slowed down right much. At least, J.C. called it right much. I could only hope I'd feel like working half days on a tractor when I reached seventy-two.

Five minutes after saying good-bye to Miss Callie, I was turning off the paved road into the sandy lane that ran past the Johnson home place. The doors there were closed and none of their three cars were in the yard, but Helen's

Methodist and I'd heard Beulah mention the long-winded new preacher at her daughter-in-law's church.

Helen and Sammy Junior had remodeled and painted the shabby old two-story wooden farmhouse after old Mrs. Johnson died, and it was a handsome place these days: gleaming white aluminum siding and dark blue shutters, sitting in a shady grove of hundred-year-old white oaks.

Beulah's brick house—even after forty years, everyone in the family still calls it the "new house"—was farther down the lane and couldn't be seen from the road or the home place.

My car topped the low ridge that gave both generations their privacy, then swooped down toward a sluggish creek that had been dredged out into a nice-size irrigation pond beyond the house. As newlyweds, Sam and Beulah had planted pecans on each side of the lane, and mature nut trees now met in a tall arch.

The house itself was rooted in its own grove of pecans and oaks, with under-plantings of dogwoods, crepe myrtles, redbuds, and flowering pears. Pink and white azaleas lined the foundation all around. On this warm day in late April, the place was a color illustration out of *Southern Living*. I pulled up under a chinaball tree by the back porch and tapped my horn, expecting to see Beulah appear at the screen door with her hands full of biscuit dough and an ample print apron protecting her Sunday dress against flour smudges.

A smell of burning paper registered oddly as I stepped from the car. It wasn't cool enough for a fire, and no one on this farm would break the fourth commandment by burning trash on the Sabbath.

There was no sign of Beulah when I crossed the wide planks of the wooden porch and called through the screen, but the kitchen was redolent of baking ham. J.C.'s old hound dog crawled out from under the back steps and wagged his tail at me hopefully. The screen door was unhooked, and the inner door stood wide.

"Beulah?" I called again. "J.C.?"

No answer. Yet her Buick and J.C.'s Ford pickup were both parked under the barn shelter at the rear of the yard.

The kitchen, dining room, and den ran together in one large L-shaped space, and when a quick glance into the formal, seldom-used living room revealed no one there either, I crossed to the stairs in the center hall. Through an open door at the far end of the hall, I could see into Donna Sue's old bedroom, now the guest room.

The covers on the guest bed had been straightened, but the spread was folded down neatly and pillows were piled on top of the rumpled quilt as if J.C. had rested there after Beulah made the bed. He wouldn't be able to use the stairs until his leg mended, so he'd probably moved in here for the duration. A stack of *Field and Stream* magazines and an open pack of his menthol cigarettes on the nightstand supported my hypothesis.

The house remained silent as I mounted the stairs.

"Anybody home?"

Beulah's bedroom was deserted and as immaculate as downstairs except for the desk. She and Sam had devoted a corner of their bedroom to the paper work connected with the farm. Although Sammy Junior did most of the farm records now on a computer over at his house, Beulah had kept the oak desk. One of my own document binders lay on its otherwise bare top. I'd drawn up her new will less than a month ago and had brought it out to her myself in this very same binder. I lifted the cover. The holographic distribution of small personal keepsakes she had insisted on was still there, but the will itself was missing.

For the first time since I'd entered this quiet house, I felt a small chill of foreboding.

Sammy Junior's old bedroom had been turned into a sewing room, and it was as empty as the bathroom. Ditto J.C.'s. As a child I'd had the run of every room in the house except this one, so I'd never entered it alone.

From the doorway, it looked like a rerun of the others: everything vacuumed and polished and tidy; but when I stepped inside, I saw the bottom drawer of the wide mahogany dresser open. Inside were various folders secured by brown cords, bundles of tax returns, account ledgers, bank statements, and two large flat candy boxes, which I knew held old family snapshots. More papers and folders were loosely stacked on the floor beside a low footstool, as if someone had sat there to sort through the drawer and had then been interrupted before the task was finished. Beulah would never leave a clutter like that.

Thoroughly puzzled, I went back down to the kitchen. The ham had been in the oven at least a half hour too long, so I turned it off and left the door cracked. The top burners were off, but each held a pot of cooked vegetables, still quite hot. Wherever Beulah was, she hadn't been gone very long.

Year round, she and J.C. and Sam, too, when he was alive, loved to walk the land, and if they weren't expecting company, it wasn't unusual to find them out at the pond or down in the woods. But with me invited for Sunday dinner along with Sammy Junior and Helen and their three teenagers? And with J.C.'s broken leg?

Not hardly likely, as my daddy would say.

Nevertheless, I went out to my car and blew the horn long and loud.

Buster, the old hound, nuzzled my hand as I stood beside the car indecisively. And that was another thing. If J.C. were out stumping across the farm on crutches, Buster wouldn't be hanging around the back door. He'd be right out there with J.C. It didn't make sense, yet if there's one thing the law has taught me, it's that it doesn't pay to formulate a theory without all the facts. I headed back inside to phone and see if Helen and Sammy Junior were home yet, and as I lifted the receiver from the kitchen wall, I saw something I'd missed before.

At the far end of the den, beyond the high-backed couch, the fireplace screen had been moved to one side of the hearth, and there were scraps of charred paper in the grate.

I remembered the smell of burning paper that had hung in the air when I first arrived. I started to ward the fireplace, and now I could see the coffee table strewn with the Sunday edition of the Raleigh *News and Observer*.

As I rounded the high couch, I nearly tripped on a pair of crutches, but they barely registered, so startled was I by seeing J.C. lying there motionless, his eyes closed.

"Glory, J.C.!" I exclaimed. "You asleep? That must be some painkiller the doctor—"

I suddenly realized that the brightly colored sheet of Sunday comics over his chest was drenched in his own bright blood.

I knelt beside the old man and clutched his callused, work-worn hand. It was still warm. His faded blue eyes opened, rolled back in his head, then focused on me.

"Deb'rah?" His voice was faint and came from far, far away. "I swear I plumb forgot . . . "

He gave a long sigh and his eyes closed again.

Dwight Bryant is detective chief of the Colleton County Sheriff's Department. After calling the nearest rescue squad, I'd dialed his mother's phone number on the off chance that he'd be there in the neighborhood and not twenty-two miles away at Dobbs, the county seat. Four minutes flat after I hung up the phone, I saw his Chevy pickup zoom over the crest of the lane and tear through the arch of pecan trees. He was followed by a bright purple TR, and even in this ghastly situation, I had to smile at his exasperation as Miss Emily Bryant bounded from the car and hurried up the steps ahead of him.

"Damn it all, Mother, if you set the first foot inside that house, I'm gonna arrest you, and I mean it!"

She turned on him, a feisty little carrottop Chihuahua facing down a sandy-brown Saint Bernard. "If you think I'm going to stay out here when one of my oldest and dearest friends may be lying in there—"

"She's not, Miss Emily," I said tremulously. J.C.'s blood was under my fingernails from where I'd staunched his chest wound. "I promise you. I looked in every room."

"And under all the beds and in every closet?" She stamped her small foot imperiously on the porch floor. "I won't touch a thing, Dwight, but I've got to look."

"No." That was the law talking, not her son; and she huffed but quit arguing.

"Okay, Deborah," said Dwight, holding the screen door open for me. "Show me."

Forty-five minutes later we knew no more than before. The rescue squad had arrived and departed again with J.C., who was still unconscious and barely clinging to life.

Sammy Junior and Helen were nearly frantic over Beulah's disappearance and were torn between following the ambulance and staying put till there was word of her. Eventually they thought to call Donna Sue, who said she'd meet the ambulance at the hospital and stay with J.C. till they heard more.

A general APB had been issued for Beulah, but since nobody knew how she left, there wasn't much besides her physical appearance to put on the wire.

Dwight's deputies processed the den and J.C.'s room like a crime scene. After they finished, Dwight and I walked through the house with Sammy Junior and Helen; but they, too, saw nothing out of the ordinary except for the papers strewn in front of J.C.'s bedroom dresser.

Sammy Junior's impression was the same as mine. "It's like Mama was interrupted."

"Doing what?" asked Dwight.

"Probably getting Uncle J.C.'s insurance papers together for him. I said I'd take 'em over to the hospital tomorrow. In all the excitement yesterday when he broke his leg, we didn't think about 'em."

He started to leave the room, then hesitated. "Y'all find his gun?"

"Gun?" said Dwight.

Sammy Junior pointed to a pair of empty rifle brackets over the bedroom door. "That's where he keeps his .22."

Much as we'd all like to believe this is still God's country, everything peaceful and nice, most people now latch their doors at night, and they do keep loaded guns around for more than rats and snakes and wild dogs.

Helen shivered and instinctively moved closer to Sammy Junior. "The back door's always open, Dwight. I'll bet you anything some burglar or rapist caught her by surprise and forced her to go with him. And then J.C. probably rared up on the couch and they shot him like you'd swat a fly."

I turned away from the pain on Sammy Junior's face and stared through the bedroom window as Dwight said, "Been too many cars down the lane and through the yard for us to find any tread marks."

Any lawyer knows how easily the lives of good decent people can be shattered, but I'll never get used to the abruptness of it. Trouble seldom comes creeping up gently, giving a person time to prepare or get out of the way. It's always the freakish bolt of lightning out of a clear blue sky, the jerk of a steering wheel, the collapse of something rock solid only a second ago.

From the window I saw puffy white clouds floating serenely over the farm. The sun shone as brightly as ever on flowering trees and new-planted corn, warming the earth for another round of seedtime and harvest. A soft wind smoothed the field where J.C. had been disking before his accident yesterday, and in the distance the pond gleamed silver-green before a stand of willows.

My eye was snagged by what looked like a red-and-white cloth several yards into the newly disked field. Probably something Buster had pulled off the clothesline, I thought, and was suddenly aware that the others were waiting for my answer to a question I'd barely heard.

"No," I replied. "I'd have noticed another car or truck coming out of the lane. Couldn't have missed them by much, though, because the vegetables on the stove were still hot. Beulah must have turned them off just before going upstairs."

"It's a habit with her," Sammy Junior said. He had his arm around Helen and was kneading her shoulder convulsively. It would probably be bruised tomorrow, but Helen didn't seem to notice.

"Mama burned so many pots when we were kids that she got to where she wouldn't leave the kitchen without turning off the vegetables. She'd mean to come right back, but then there was always something that needed doing, and you know how Mama is."

We did. We surely did. "Whatsoever thy hand findeth to do" must have been written with Beulah in mind. She always reacted impulsively and couldn't pass a dusty surface or a dirty windowpane or anything out of place without cleaning it or taking it back to its rightful spot in the house.

Maybe that's why that scrap of red-and-white cloth out in the field bothered me. If I could see it, so would Beulah. She wouldn't let it lie out there ten minutes if she could help it, and it was with a need to restore some of her order that I slipped away from the others.

Downstairs, the crime scene crew had finished with the kitchen; and for lack of anything more useful to do, Miss Emily had decided that everybody'd fare better on a full stomach. She'd put bowls of vegetables on the counter, sliced the ham, and set out glasses and a jug of sweet iced tea. At this returning semblance of the ordinary, Helen and Sammy Junior's three anxious teenagers obediently filled their plates and went outside under the trees to eat. Their parents and Dwight weren't enthusiastic about food at the moment, but Miss Emily bullied them into going through the motions. Even Dwight's men had to stop and fix a plate.

No one noticed as I passed through the kitchen and down the back steps, past the Johnson grandchildren, who were feeding ham scraps to Buster and talking in low worried tones.

The lane cut through the yard, skirted the end of the field, then wound circuitously around the edge of the woods and on down to the pond; but the red-and-white rag lay on a beeline from the back door to the pond and I hesitated about stepping off the grass. My shoes were two-inch sling-back pumps, and they'd be wrecked if I walked out into the soft dirt of the newly disked field.

As I dithered, I saw that someone else had recently crossed the field on foot. A single set of tracks.

With growing horror I remembered the red-and-white hostess aprons my aunt Zell had sewed for all her friends last Christmas.

I ran back to my car, grabbed the sneakers I keep in the trunk, and then rushed to call Dwight.

It was done strictly by the book.

Dwight's crime scene crew would later methodically photograph and measure and take pains not to disturb a single clod till every mark Beulah had left on the soft dirt was thoroughly documented; but the rest of us hurried through the turned field, paralleling the footprints from a ten-foot distance and filled with foreboding by the steady, unwavering direction those footsteps had taken.

Beulah's apron lay about two hundred feet from the edge of the yard. She must have untied the strings and just let it fall as she walked away from it.

The rifle, though, had been deliberately pitched. We could see where she stopped, the depth of her footprints where she heaved it away from her as if it were something suddenly and terribly abhorrent.

After that, there was nothing to show that she'd hesitated a single second. Her footprints went like bullets, straight down to the pond and into the silent, silver-green water.

As with most farm ponds dredged for irrigation, the bottom dropped off steeply from the edge to discourage mosquito larvae.

"How deep is it there?" Dwight asked when we arrived breathless and panting.

"Twelve feet," said Sammy Junior. "And she never learned how to swim."

His voice didn't break, but his chest was heaving, his face got red, and tears streamed from his eyes. "Why? In God's name, *why*, Dwight? Helen? Deb'rah? You all *know* Uncle J.C. near 'bout worships Mama. And we've always teased her that J.C. stood for Jesus Christ the way she's catered to him."

It was almost dark before they found Beulah's body.

No one tolled the heavy iron bell at the home place. The old way of alerting the neighborhood to fire or death has long since been replaced by the telephone, but the reaction hasn't changed much in two hundred years.

By the time that second ambulance passed down the lane, this one on its way to the state's medical examiner in Chapel Hill, cars filled the yard and lined the ditch banks on either side of the road. And there was no place in Helen's kitchen or dining room to set another plate of food. It would have taken a full roll of tinfoil to cover all the casseroles, biscuits, pies, deviled eggs, and platters of fried chicken, sliced turkey, and roast pork that had been brought in by shocked friends and relatives.

My aunt Zell arrived, white-faced and grieving, the last of three adventuresome country girls who'd gone off to Goldsboro during World War II to work at the air base. I grew up on stories of those war years; how J.C. had been sent over by his and Beulah's parents to keep an eye on my mother, Beulah, and Aunt Zell and protect them from the dangers of a military town, how they'd tried to fix him up with a WAC from New Jersey, the Saturday night dances, the innocent flirtations with that steady stream of young airmen who passed through the Army Air Forces Technical Training School at Seymour Johnson Field on their way to the airfields of Europe.

It wasn't till I was eighteen, the summer between high school and college, the summer Mother was dying, that I learned it hadn't all been lighthearted laughter.

We'd been sorting through a box of old black-and-white snapshots that Mother was determined to date and label before she died. Among the pictures of her or Aunt Zell or Beulah perched on the wing of a bomber or jitterbugging with anonymous, interchangeable airmen, there was one of Beulah and a young man. They had their arms around each other, and there was a sweet solemnity in their faces that separated this picture from the other clowning ones.

"Who's that?" I asked, and Mother sat staring into the picture for so long that I had to ask again.

"His name was Donald," she finally replied. Then her face took on an earnest look I'd come to know that summer, the look that meant I was to be entrusted with another secret, another scrap of her personal history that she couldn't bear to take to her grave untold even though each tale began, "Now you mustn't ever repeat this, but—"

"Donald Farraday came from Norwood, Nebraska," she said. "Exactly halfway between Omaha and Lincoln on the Platte River. That's what he always said. After he shipped out, Beulah used to look at the map and lay her finger halfway between Omaha and Lincoln and make Zell and me promise that we'd come visit her."

"I thought Sam was the only one she ever dated seriously," I protested.

"Beulah was the only one *Sam* ever dated seriously," Mother said crisply. "He had his eye on her from the time she was in grade school and he and J.C. used to go hunting together. She wrote to him while he was fighting the Japs, but they weren't going steady or anything. And she'd have never married Sam if Donald hadn't died."

"Oh," I said, suddenly understanding the sad look that sometimes shadowed Beulah's eyes when only minutes before she and Mother and Aunt Zell might have been giggling over some Goldsboro memory.

Donald Farraday was from a Nebraska wheat farm, Mother told me, on his way to fight in Europe. Beulah met him at a jitterbug contest put on by the canteen, and it'd been love at first sight. Deep and true and all-consuming. They had only sixteen days and fifteen nights together, but that was enough to know this wasn't a passing wartime romance. Their values, their dreams, everything meshed.

"And they had so much fun together. You've never seen two people laugh so much over nothing. She didn't even cry when he shipped out because she was so happy thinking about what marriage to him was going to be like after the war was over."

"How did he die?"

"We never really heard," said Mother. "She had two of the sweetest, most beautiful letters you could ever hope to read, and then nothing. That was near the end when fighting was so heavy in Italy—we knew he was in Italy though it was supposed to be secret. They weren't married so his parents would've gotten the telegram, and of course, not knowing anything about Beulah, they couldn't write her."

"So what happened?"

"The war ended. We all came home. I married your daddy, Zell married James. Sam came back from the South Pacific and with Donald dead, Beulah didn't care who she married."

"Donna Sue!" I said suddenly.

"Yes," Mother agreed. "Sue for me, Donna in memory of Donald. She doesn't know about him, though, and don't you ever tell her." Her face was sad as she looked at the photograph in her hand of the boy and girl who'd be forever young, forever in love. "Beulah won't let us mention his name, but I know she still grieves for what might have been."

After Mother was gone, I never spoke to Beulah about what I knew. The closest I ever came was my junior year at Carolina when Jeff Creech dumped me for a psych major and I moped into the kitchen where Beulah and Aunt Zell were drinking coffee. I moaned about how my heart was broken and I couldn't go on and Beulah had smiled at me, "You'll go on, sugar. A woman's body doesn't quit just because her heart breaks."

Sudden tears had misted Aunt Zell's eyes—we Stephensons can cry over telephone commercials—and Beulah abruptly left.

"She was remembering Donald Farraday, wasn't she?" I asked.

"Sue told you about him?"

"Yes."

Aunt Zell had sighed then. "I don't believe a day goes by that she doesn't remember him."

The endurance of Beulah's grief had suddenly put Jeff Creech into perspective, and I realized with a small pang that losing him probably wasn't going to blight the rest of my life.

As I put my arms around Aunt Zell, I thought of her loss: Mother gone, now Beulah. Only J.C. left to remember those giddy girlhood years. At least the doctors were cautiously optimistic that he'd recover from the shooting.

"Why did she do it?" I asked.

But Aunt Zell was as perplexed as the rest of us. The house was crowded with people who'd known and loved Beulah and J.C. all their lives, and few could recall a true cross word between older brother and younger sister.

"Oh, Mama'd get fussed once in a while when he'd try to keep her from doing something new," said Donna Sue.

Every wake I've ever attended, the survivors always alternate between sudden paroxysms of tears and a need to remember and retell. For all the pained bewilderment and unanswered questions that night, Beulah's wake was no different.

"Remember, Sammy, how Uncle J.C. didn't want her to buy that place at the beach?"

"He never liked change," her brother agreed. "He talked about jellyfish and sharks—"

"—and sun poisoning," Helen said with a sad smile as she refilled his glass of iced tea. "Don't forget the sun poisoning."

"Changed his tune soon enough once he got down there and the fish started biting," said a cousin as he bit into a sausage biscuit.

One of Dwight's deputies signaled me from the hallway, and I left them talking about how J.C.'d tried to stop Beulah from touring England with one of her alumnae groups last year, and how he'd fretted the whole time she was gone, afraid her plane would crash into the Atlantic or be hijacked by terrorists.

"Dwight wants you back over there," said the deputy and drove me through the gathering dark, down the lane to where Beulah's house blazed with lights.

Dwight was waiting for me in the den. They'd salvaged a few scraps from the fireplace, but the ashes had been stirred with a poker and there wasn't much left to tell what had been destroyed. Maybe a handful of papers, Dwight thought. "And this. It fell behind the grate before it fully burned."

The sheet was crumpled and charred, but enough remained to see the words *Last Will and Testament of Beulah Ogburn Johnson* and the opening paragraph about revoking all earlier wills.

"You were her lawyer," said Dwight. "Why'd she burn her will?"

"I don't know," I answered, honestly puzzled. "Unless—"

"Unless what?"

"I'll have to read my copy tomorrow, but there's really not going to be much difference between what happens if she died intestate and—" I interrupted myself, remembering. "In fact, if J.C. dies, it'll be exactly the same, Dwight. Sammy Junior and Donna Sue still split everything."

"And if he lives?"

"If this were still a valid instrument," I said, choosing my words carefully, "J.C. would have a lifetime right to this house and Beulah's share of the farm income, with everything divided equally between her two children when he died; without the will, he's not legally entitled to stay the night."

"They'd never turn him out."

I didn't respond and Dwight looked at me thoughtfully.

"But without the will, they could if they wanted to," he said slowly.

Dwight Bryant's six or eight years older than I, and he's known me all my life, yet I don't think he'd ever looked at me as carefully as he did that night in

Beulah's den, in front of that couch soaked in her brother's blood. "And if he'd done something bad enough to make their mother shoot him and then go drown herself . . . "

"They could turn him out and not a single voice in the whole community would speak against it," I finished for him.

Was that what Beulah wanted? Dead or alive, she was still my client. But I wondered: when she shot J.C. and burned her will, had she been of sound mind?

By next morning, people were beginning to say no. There was no sane reason for Beulah's act, they said, so it must have been a sudden burst of insanity, and wasn't there a great-aunt on her daddy's side that'd been a little bit queer near the end?

J.C. regained consciousness, but he was no help.

"I was resting on the couch," he said, "and I never heard a thing till I woke up hurting and you were there, Deb'rah."

He was still weak, but fierce denial burned in his eyes when they told him that Beulah had shot him. "She never!"

"Her fingerprints are on your rifle," said Dwight.

"She never!" He gazed belligerently from Donna Sue to Sammy Junior. "She never. Not her own brother. Where is she? You better not've jailed her, Dwight!"

He went into shock when they told him Beulah was dead. Great sobbing cries of protest racked his torn and broken body. It was pitiful to watch. Donna Sue petted and hugged him, but the nurse had to inject a sedative to calm him, and she asked us to leave.

I was due in court anyhow, and afterwards there was a luncheon speech at the Jaycees and a pig-picking that evening to raise funds for the children's hospital. I fell into bed exhausted, but instead of sleeping, my mind began to replay everything that had happened Sunday, scene by scene. Suddenly there was a freeze-frame on the moment I discovered J.C.

Next morning I was standing beside his hospital bed before anyone else got there.

"What was it you forgot?" I asked him.

The old man stared at me blankly. "Huh?"

"When I found you, you said, 'Deborah, I swear I plumb forgot.' Forgot what, J.C.?"

His faded blue eyes shifted to the shiny get-well balloons tethered to the foot of his bed by colorful streamers.

"I don't remember saying that," he lied.

From the hospital, I drove down to the town commons and walked along the banks of our muddy river. It was another beautiful spring day, but I was harking back to Sunday morning, trying to think myself into Beulah's mind.

You're a sixty-six-year-old widow, I thought. You're cooking Sunday dinner for your children and for the daughter of your dead friend. (*She's running for judge, Sue. Did you ever imagine it?*) And there's J.C. calling from the den about his insurance papers. So you turn off the vegetables and go upstairs and look in his drawer for the policies and you find—

What do you find that sends you back downstairs with a rifle in your hands and papers to burn? Why bother to burn anything after you've shot the person who loves you best in all the world?

And why destroy a will that would have provided that person with a dignified and independent old age? Was it because the bequest had been designated "To my beloved only brother who has always looked after me," and on this beautiful Sunday morning J.C. has suddenly stopped being beloved and has instead become someone to hurt? Maybe even to kill?

Why, *why*, WHY?

I shook my head impatiently. What in God's creation could J.C. have kept in that drawer that would send Beulah over the edge?

Totally baffled, I deliberately emptied my mind and sat down on one of the stone benches and looked up into a dogwood tree in full bloom. With the sun above them, the white blossoms glowed with a paschal translucence. Mother had always loved dogwoods.

Mother. Aunt Zell. Beulah.

A spring blossoming more than forty-five years ago.

I thought of dogwoods and spring love, and into my emptied mind floated a single *what if—*?

I didn't force it. I just sat and watched while it grew from possibility to certainty, a certainty reinforced as I recalled something Mother had mentioned about shift work at the airfield.

It was such a monstrous certainty that I wanted to be dissuaded, so I went to my office and called Aunt Zell and asked her to think back to the war years.

"When you all were in Goldsboro," I said, "did you work days or nights?"

"Days, of course," she answered promptly.

The weight started to roll off my chest.

"Leastways, we three girls did," she added. "J.C. worked nights. Why?"

For a moment I thought the heaviness would smother me before I could stammer out a reason and hang up.

Sherry, my secretary, came in with some papers to sign, but I waved her away. "Bring me the phone book," I told her, "and then leave me alone unless I buzz you."

Astonishingly, it took only one call to Information to get the number I needed. He answered on the second ring and we talked for almost an hour. I told him I was a writer doing research on the old Army Air Forces technical schools.

He didn't seem to think it odd when my questions got personal.

He sounded nice.

He sounded lonely.

"You look like hell," Sherry observed when I passed through the office. "You been crying?"

"Anybody wants me, I'll be at the hospital," I said without breaking stride.

Donna Sue and Helen were sitting beside J.C.'s bed when I got there, and it took every ounce of courtroom training for me not to burst out with it. Instead I made sympathetic conversation like a perfect Southern lady, and when they broke down again about Beulah, I said, "You all need to get out in the spring sunshine for a few minutes. Go get something with ice in it and walk around the parking lot twice. I'll keep J.C. company till you get back."

J.C. closed his eyes as they left, but I let him have it with both barrels.

"You bastard!" I snarled. "You filthy bastard! I just got off the phone to Donald Farraday. He still lives in Norwood, Nebraska, J.C. Halfway between Omaha and Lincoln."

The old man groaned and clenched his eyes tighter.

"He didn't die. He wasn't even wounded. Except in the heart. By you." So much anger roiled up inside me, I was almost spitting my words at him.

"He wrote her every chance he got till it finally sank in she was never going to answer. He thought she'd changed her mind, realized that she didn't really love him. And every day Beulah must have been coming home, asking if she'd gotten any mail, and you only gave her Sam's letters, you rotten, no-good—"

"Sam was homefolks," J.C. burst out. "That other one, he'd have taken her way the hell away to Nebraska. She didn't have any business in Nebraska! Sam loved her."

"She didn't love *him*," I snapped.

"Sure, she did. Oh, it took her a bit to get over the other one, but she settled."

"Only because she thought Farraday was dead! You had no right, you sneaking, sanctimonious Pharisee! You wrecked her whole life!"

"Her life wasn't wrecked," he argued. "She had Donna Sue and Sammy Junior and the farm and—"

"If it was such a star-spangled life," I interrupted hotly, "why'd she take a gun to you the minute she knew what you'd done to her?"

The fight went out of him and he sank back into the pillow, sobbing now and holding himself where the bullet had passed through his right lung.

"Why in God's name did you keep the letters? That's what she found, wasn't it?"

Still sobbing, J.C. nodded.

"I forgot they were still there. I never opened them, and she didn't either. She said she couldn't bear to. She just put them in the grate and put a match to them and she was crying. I tried to explain about how I'd done what was best for her, and all at once she had the rifle in her hands and she said she'd never forgive me, and then I reckon she shot me."

He reached out a bony hand and grasped mine. "You won't tell anyone, will you?"

I jerked my hand away as if it'd suddenly touched filth.

"Please, Deb'rah?"

"Donald Farraday has a daughter almost the same age as Donna Sue," I said. "Know what he named her, J.C.? He named her Beulah."

Dwight Bryant was waiting when I got back from court that afternoon and he followed me into my office.

"I hear you visited J.C. twice today."

"So?" I slid off my high heels. They were wickedly expensive and matched the power red of my linen suit. I waggled my stockinged toes at him, but he didn't smile.

"Judge not," he said sternly.

"Is that with an *N* or a *K*?" I parried.

"Sherry tells me you never give clients the original of their will."

"Never's a long time, and Sherry may not know as much about my business as she thinks she does."

"But it *was* a copy that Beulah burned, wasn't it?"

"I'm prepared to go to court and swear it was the original if I have to. It won't be necessary though. J.C. won't contest it."

Dwight stared at me a long level moment. "Why're you doing this to him?"

I matched his stare with one about twenty degrees colder. "Not me, Dwight. Beulah."

"He swears he doesn't know why she shot him, but you know, don't you?"

I shrugged.

He hauled himself to his feet, angry and frustrated. "If you do this, Deborah, J.C.'ll have to spend the rest of his life depending on Donna Sue and Sammy Junior's good will. You don't have the right. Nobody elected you judge yet."

"Yes, they did," I said, thinking of the summer I was eighteen and how Mother had told me all her secrets so that if I ever needed her eye-witness testimony I'd have it.

And Deborah was a judge in the land.

Damn straight.

SHARYN MCCRUMB

1948–

Acclaimed for her lyrical novels and short stories celebrating the Appalachian Mountain region in the Southeastern United States, Sharyn McCrumb was born in Wilmington, North Carolina. She received a B.A. degree from the University of North Carolina, Chapel Hill, in 1970 and an M.A. from Virginia Tech in 1985. McCrumb has spent most of her adult life in Virginia, creating popular characters in several genres and becoming a well-known voice of Appalachian culture and folklore. In 1997 she was honored with an award for Outstanding Contribution to Appalachian

Literature. She is the first mystery writer to win an Anthony Award in two categories in the same year (1995), for best novel *She Walks These Hills* (1994) and best short story "The Monster of Glamis" (1994). She is also one of the few writers to have received all the major American mystery awards for her works: the Edgar, Agatha, Anthony, and Macavity.

McCrumb's first novel, *Sick of Shadows* (1984), introduced forensic anthropologist Elizabeth MacPherson as her amateur detective, and this rather lighthearted series continues through nine novels, including the memorably titled *If I'd Killed Him When I Met Him . . .* (1995) and *The PMS Outlaws* (2000). In another series, Dr. James Owens Mega, a college professor and science-fiction author, is the protagonist in the science-fiction satire *Bimbos of the Death Sun* (1988), which won the Edgar for Best Original Paperback, and a second novel, *Zombies of the Gene Pool* (1992). In 1990 McCrumb started a third series featuring Appalachian sheriff Spencer Arrowood in *If Ever I Return, Pretty Peggy-O*, a Macavity Award winner, followed by others including *She Walks These Hills* (1994), which won the Agatha, Anthony, and Macavity Awards for Best Novel. This series is often referred to as the "Ballad Novels" for their evocative characters and narratives of the southern Appalachian locale. A collection of short stories, *Foggy Mountain Breakdown and Other Stories* (1997), showcases McCrumb's wit and wisdom and the range of writing that has brought her international acclaim. "Nine Lives to Live," featuring a most unusual amateur detective, appears in this collection. It was first published in *Cat Crimes II*, edited by Martin H. Greenberg and Ed Gorman, in 1992.

Recommended McCrumb works: *Sick of Shadows, She Walks These Hills, Foggy Mountain Breakdown and Other Stories*.

Other recommended authors: Carolyn Hart, Jane Langton, Nancy Pickard.

Nine Lives to Live

It had seemed like a good idea at the time. Of course, Philip Danby had only been joking, but he had said it in a serious tone in order to humor those idiot New Age clients who actually seemed to believe in the stuff. "I want to come back as a cat," he'd said, smiling facetiously into the candlelight at the Eskeridge dinner table. He had to hold his breath to keep from laughing as the others babbled about reincarnation. The women wanted to come back blonder and thinner, and the men wanted to be everything from Dallas Cowboys to oak trees. *Oak trees?* And he had to keep a straight face through it all, hoping these dodos would give the firm some business.

The things he had to put up with to humor clients. His partner, Giles Eskeridge, seemed to have no difficulties in that quarter, however. Giles often said that rich and crazy went together, therefore, architects who wanted a lucrative business had to be prepared to put up with eccentrics. They also had to put up with long hours, obstinate building contractors, and capricious zoning boards. Perhaps that was why Danby had plumped for life as a cat next time. As he had explained to his dinner companions that night, "Cats are independent. They don't have to kowtow to anybody; they sleep sixteen hours a day; and yet they get fed and sheltered and even loved—just for being their contrary little selves. It sounds like a good deal to me."

Julie Eskeridge tapped him playfully on the cheek. "You'd better take care to be a pretty, pedigreed kitty, Philip." She laughed. "Because life isn't so pleasant for an ugly old alley cat!"

"I'll keep that in mind," he told her. "In fifty years or so."

It had been more like fifty days. The fact that Giles had wanted to come back as a shark should have tipped him off. When they found out that they'd just built a three-million-dollar building on top of a toxic landfill, the contractor was happy to keep his mouth shut about it for a mere ten grand, and Giles was perfectly prepared to bury the evidence to protect the firm from lawsuits and EPA fines.

Looking back on it, Danby realized that he should not have insisted that they report the landfill to the authorities. In particular, he should not have insisted on it at six P.M. at the building site with no one present but himself and Giles. That was literally a fatal error. Before you could say "philosophical differences," Giles had picked up a shovel lying near the offending trench, and with one brisk swing, he had sent the matter to a higher court. As he pitched headlong into the reeking evidence, Danby's last thought was a flicker of cold anger at the injustice of it all.

His next thought was that he was watching a black-and-white movie, while his brain seemed intent upon sorting out a flood of olfactory sensations. *Furniture polish . . . stale coffee . . . sweaty socks . . . Prell shampoo . . . potting soil . . .* He shook his head, trying to clear his thoughts. Where was he? The apparent answer to that was: lying on a gray sofa inside the black-and-white movie, because everywhere he looked he saw the same colorless vista. A concussion, maybe? The memory of Giles Eskeridge swinging a shovel came back in a flash. Danby decided to call the police before Giles turned up to try again. He stood up, and promptly fell off the sofa.

Of course, he landed on his feet.

All four of them.

Idly, to keep from thinking anything more ominous for the moment, Danby wondered what *else* the New Age clients had been right about. Was Stonehenge a flying saucer landing pad? Did crystals lower cholesterol? He was in no position to doubt anything just now. He sat twitching his plume of a tail and wishing he hadn't been so flippant about the afterlife at the Eskeridge dinner party. He didn't even particularly like cats. He also wished that he could get his paws on Giles in retribution for the shovel incident. First he would bite Giles's neck, snapping his spine, and then he would let him escape for a few seconds. Then he'd sneak up behind him and pounce. Then bat him into a corner. Danby began to purr in happy contemplation.

The sight of a coffee table looming a foot above his head brought the problem into perspective. At present Danby weighed approximately fifteen furry pounds, and he was unsure of his exact whereabouts. Under those circumstances avenging his murder would be difficult. On the other hand, he didn't have any other pressing business, apart from an eight-hour nap which he felt in need of. First things first, though. Danby wanted to know what he looked like, and then he needed to find out where the kitchen was, and whether Sweaty Socks and Prell Shampoo had left anything edible on the countertops. There would be time enough for philosophical thoughts and revenge plans when he was cleaning his whiskers.

The living room was enough to make an architect shudder. Clunky Early American sofas and clutter. He was glad he couldn't see the color scheme.

There was a mirror above the sofa, though, and he hopped up on the cheap upholstery to take a look at his new self. The face that looked back at him was definitely feline, and so malevolent that Danby wondered how anyone could mistake cats for pets. The yellow (or possibly green) almond eyes glowered at him from a massive triangular face, tiger-striped, and surrounded by a ruff of gray-brown fur. Just visible beneath the ruff was a dark leather collar equipped with a little brass bell. That would explain the ringing in his ears. The rest of his body seemed massive, even allowing for the fur, and the great plumed tail swayed rhythmically as he watched. He resisted a silly urge to swat at the reflected movement. So he was a tortoiseshell, or tabby, or whatever they called those brown-striped cats, and his hair was long. And he was still male. He didn't need to check beneath his tail to confirm that. Besides, the reek of ammonia in the vicinity of the sofa suggested that he was not shy about proclaiming his masculinity in various corners of his domain.

No doubt it would have interested those New Age clowns to learn that he was not a kitten, but a fully grown cat. Apparently the arrival had been instantaneous as well. He had always been given to understand that the afterlife would provide some kind of preliminary orientation before assigning him a new identity. A deity resembling John Denver, in rimless glasses and a Sierra Club T-shirt, should have been on hand with some paperwork regarding his case, and in a nonthreatening conference they would decide what his karma entitled him to become. At least, that's what the New Agers had led him to believe. But it hadn't been like that at all. One minute he had been tumbling into a sewage pit, and the next, he had a craving for Meow Mix. Just like that. He wondered what sort of consciousness had been flickering inside that narrow skull prior to his arrival. Probably not much. A brain with the wattage of a lightning bug could control most of the items on the feline agenda: eat, sleep, snack, doze, dine, nap, and so on. Speaking of eating . . .

He made it to the floor in two moderate bounds, and jingled toward the kitchen, conveniently signposted by the smell of lemon-scented dishwashing soap and stale coffee. The floor could do with a good sweeping, too, he thought, noting with distaste the gritty feel of tracked-in dirt on his velvet paws.

The cat dish, tucked in a corner beside the sink cabinet, confirmed his worst fears about the inhabitants' instinct for tackiness. Two plastic bowls were inserted into a plywood cat model, painted white, and decorated with a cartoonish cat face. If his food hadn't been at stake, Danby would have sprayed *that* as an indication of his professional judgment. As it was, he summoned a regal sneer and bent down to inspect the offering. The water wasn't fresh; there were bits of dry catfood floating in it. Did they expect him to drink *that*? Perhaps he ought to dump it out so that they'd take the hint. And the dry cat-food hadn't been stored in an airtight container, either. He sniffed contemptuously: the cheap brand, mostly cereal. He supposed he'd have to go out and kill something just to keep his ribs from crashing together. Better check out the counters for other options. It took considerable force to launch his bulk from floor to countertop, and for a moment he teetered on the edge of the sink fighting to regain his balance, while his bell tolled ominously, but once he righted himself he strolled onto the counter with an expression of nonchalance suggesting that his dignity had never been imperiled. He found two breakfast plates stacked in the sink. The top one was a trove of congealing egg yolk and bits of buttered toast. He finished it off, licking off every scrap of egg with his rough tongue, and thinking what a favor he was doing the people by cleaning the plate for them.

While he was on the sink, he peeked out the kitchen window to see if he could figure out where he was. The lawn outside was thick and luxurious, and a spreading oak tree grew beside a low stone wall. Well, it wasn't Albuquerque. Probably not California, either, considering the healthy appearance of the grass. Maybe he was still in Maryland. It certainly looked like home. Perhaps the transmigration of souls has a limited geographic range, like AM radio stations.

After a few moments' consideration, while he washed an offending forepaw, it occurred to Danby to look at the wall phone above the counter. The numbers made sense to him, so apparently he hadn't lost the ability to read. Sure enough, the telephone area code was 301. He wasn't far from where he started. Theoretically, at least, Giles was within reach. He must mull that over, from the vantage point of the window sill, where the afternoon sun was marvelously warm, and soothing … zzzzz.

Danby awakened several hours later to a braying female voice calling out, "Tigger! Get down from there this minute! Are you glad Mommy's home, sweetie?"

Danby opened one eye, and regarded the woman with an insolent stare. *Tigger?* Was there no limit to the indignities he must bear? A fresh wave of Prell shampoo told him that the self-proclaimed *mommy* was chatelaine of this bourgeois bungalow. And didn't she look the part, too, with her polyester pants suit and her cascading chins! She set a grocery bag and a stack of letters on the countertop, and held out her arms to him. "And is my snookums ready for din-din?" she cooed.

He favored her with an extravagant yawn, followed by his most forbidding Mongol glare, but his hostility was wasted on the besotted Mrs.—he glanced down at the pile of letters—Sherrod. She continued to beam at him as if he had fawned at her feet. As it was, he was so busy studying the address on the Sherrod junk mail that he barely glanced at her. He hadn't left town! His tail twitched triumphantly. Morning Glory Lane was not familiar to him, but he'd be willing to bet that it was a street in Sussex Garden Estates, just off the bypass. That was a couple of miles from Giles Eskeridge's mock-Tudor monstrosity, but with a little luck and some common sense about traffic he could walk there in a couple of hours. If he cut through the fields, he might be able to score a mouse or two on the way.

Spurred on by the thought of a fresh, tasty dinner that would beg for its life, Danby/Tigger trotted to the back door and began to meow piteously, putting his forepaws as far up the screen door as he could reach.

"Now, Tigger!" said Mrs. Sherrod in her most arch tone. "You know perfectly well that there's a litter box in the bathroom. You just want to get outdoors so that you can tomcat around, don't you?" With that she began to put away groceries, humming tunelessly to herself.

Danby fixed a venomous stare at her retreating figure, and then turned his attention back to the problem at hand. Or rather, at paw. That was just the trouble: *Look, Ma, no hands!* Still, he thought, there ought to be a way. Because it was warm outside, the outer door was open, leaving only the metal storm door between himself and freedom. Its latch was the straight-handled kind that you pushed down to open the door. Danby considered the factors: door handle three feet above floor, latch opens on downward pressure, one fifteen-pound cat intent upon going out. With a vertical bound that Michael Jordan would have envied, Danby catapulted himself upward and caught onto the handle, which obligingly twisted downward, as the door swung open at the weight of the feline cannon-ball. By the time gravity took over and returned him to the ground, he was claw-deep in scratchy, sweet-smelling grass.

As he loped off toward the street, he could hear a plaintive voice wailing, "Ti-iii-gerrr!" It almost drowned out the jingling of that damned little bell around his neck.

Twenty minutes later Danby was sunning himself on a rock in an abandoned field, recovering from the exertion of moving faster than a stroll. In the distance he could hear the drone of cars from the interstate, as the smell of gasoline wafted in on a gentle breeze. As he had trotted through the neighborhood, he'd read street signs, so he had a better idea of his whereabouts now. Windsor Forest, that pretentious little suburb that Giles called home, was only a few miles away, and once he crossed the interstate, he could take a shortcut through the woods. He hoped that La Sherrod wouldn't put out an all-points bulletin for her missing kitty. He didn't want any SPCA interruptions once he reached his destination. He ought to ditch the collar as well, he thought. He couldn't very well pose as a stray with a little bell under his chin.

Fortunately, the collar was loose, probably because the ruff around his head made his neck look twice as large. Once he determined that, it took only a few minutes of concentrated effort to work the collar forward with his paws until it slipped over his ears. After that, a shake of the head—jingle! jingle!—rid him of Tigger's identity. He wondered how many pets who "just disappeared one day," had acquired new identities and gone off on more pressing business.

He managed to reach the bypass before five o'clock, thus avoiding the commuter traffic of rush hour. Since he understood automobiles, it was a relatively simple matter for Danby to cross the highway during a lull between cars. He didn't see what the possums found so difficult about road crossing. Sure enough, there was a ripe gray corpse on the white line, mute testimony to the dangers of indecision on highways. He took a perfunctory sniff, but the roadkill was too far gone to interest anything except the buzzards.

Once across the road, Danby stuck to the fields, making sure that he paralleled the road that led to Windsor Forest. His attention was occasionally diverted by a flock of birds overhead, or an enticing rustle in the grass that might have been a field mouse, but he kept going. If he didn't reach the Eskeridge house by nightfall, he would have to wait until morning to get himself noticed.

In order to get at Giles, Danby reasoned, he would first have to charm Julie Eskeridge. He wondered if she was susceptible to needy animals. He couldn't remember whether they had a cat or not. An unspayed female would be nice, he thought. A Siamese, perhaps, with big blue eyes and a sexy voice.

Danby reasoned that he wouldn't have too much trouble finding Giles's house. He had been there often enough as a guest. Besides, the firm had designed and built several of the overwrought mansions in the spacious subdivision. Danby had once suggested that they buy Palladian windows by the gross, since every nouveau riche home-builder insisted on having a brace of them, no matter what style of house he had commissioned. Giles had not been amused by Danby's observation. He seldom was. What Giles lacked in humor, he also lacked in scruples and moral restraint, but he compensated for these deficiencies with a highly developed instinct for making and holding on to money. While he'd lacked Danby's talent in design and execution, he had a genius for turning up wealthy clients, and for persuading these tasteless yobbos to spend a fortune on their showpiece homes. Danby did draw the line at carving up antique Sheraton sideboards to use as bathroom sink cabinets, though. When he also drew the line at environmental crime, Giles had apparently found his conscience an expensive luxury that the firm could not afford. Hence, the shallow grave at the new construction site, and Danby's new lease on life. It was really quite unfair of Giles, Danby reflected. They'd been friends since college, and after Danby's parents died, he had drawn up a will leaving his share of the business to Giles. And how had Giles repaid this friendship? With the blunt end of a shovel. Danby stopped to sharpen his claws on the bark of a handy pine tree. Really, he thought, Giles deserved no mercy whatsoever. Which was just as well, because, catlike, Danby possessed none.

The sun was low behind the surrounding pines by the time Danby arrived at the Eskeridge's mock-Tudor home. He had been delayed en route by the scent of another cat, a neutered orange male. (Even to his color-blind eyes, an orange cat was recognizable. It might be the shade of gray, or the configuration of white at the throat and chest.) He had hunted up this fellow feline, and made considerable efforts to communicate, but as far as he could tell, there was no higher intelligence flickering behind its blank green eyes. There was no intelligence at all, as far as Danby was concerned; he'd as soon try talking to a shrub. Finally tiring of the eunuch's unblinking stare, he'd stalked off, forgoing more social experiments in favor of his mission.

He sat for a long time under the forsythia hedge in Giles's front yard, studying the house for signs of life. He refused to be distracted by a cluster of sparrows cavorting on the birdbath, but he realized that unless a meal was coming soon, he would be reduced to foraging. The idea of hurling his bulk at a few ounces of twittering songbird made his scowl even more forbidding than usual. He licked a front paw and glowered at the silent house.

After twenty minutes or so, he heard the distant hum of a car engine, and smelled gasoline fumes. Danby peered out from the hedge in time to see Julie Eskeridge's Mercedes rounding the corner from Windsor Way. With a few hasty licks to smooth down his ruff, Danby sauntered toward the driveway just as the car pulled in. Now for the hard part: how do you impress Julie Eskeridge without a checkbook?

He had never noticed before how much Giles's wife resembled a giraffe. He blinked at the sight of her huge feet swinging out of the car perilously close to his nose. They were followed by two replicas of the Alaska pipeline, both encased in nylon. Better not jump up on her; one claw on the stockings, and he'd have an enemy for life. Julie was one of those people who air-kissed because she couldn't bear to spoil her makeup. Instead of trying to attract her attention at the car (where she could have skewered him with one spike heel), Danby loped to the steps of the side porch, and began meowing piteously. As Julie approached the steps, he looked up at her with wide-eyed supplication, waiting to be admired.

"Shoo, cat!" said Julie, nudging him aside with her foot.

As the door slammed in his face, Danby realized that he had badly miscalculated. He had also neglected to devise a backup plan. A fine mess he was in now. It wasn't enough that he was murdered and reassigned to cathood. Now he was also homeless.

He was still hanging around the steps twenty minutes later when Giles came home, mainly because he couldn't think of an alternate plan just yet. When he saw Giles's black sports car pull up behind Julie's Mercedes, Danby's first impulse was to run, but then he realized that, while Giles might see him, he certainly wouldn't recognize him as his old business partner. Besides, he was curious to see how an uncaught murderer looked. Would Giles be haggard with grief and remorse? Furtive, as he listened for police sirens in the distance?

Giles Eskeridge was whistling. He climbed out of his car, suntanned and smiling, with his lips pursed in a cheerfully tuneless whistle. Danby trotted forward to confront his murderer with his haughtiest scowl of indignation. The reaction was not quite what he expected.

Giles saw the huge, fluffy cat, and immediately knelt down, calling, "Here, kitty, kitty!"

Danby looked at him as if he had been propositioned.

"Aren't you a beauty!" said Giles, holding out his hand to the strange cat. "I'll bet you're a pedigreed animal, aren't you, fella? Are you lost, boy?"

Much as it pained him to associate with a remorseless killer, Danby sidled over to the outstretched hand, and allowed his ears to be scratched. He reasoned that Giles's interest in him was his one chance to gain entry to the house. It was obvious that Julie wasn't a cat fancier. Who would have taken heartless old Giles for an animal lover? Probably similarity of temperament, Danby decided.

He allowed himself to be picked up and carried into the house, while Giles stroked his back and told him what a pretty fellow he was. This was an indignity, but still an improvement over Giles's behavior toward him during their last encounter. Once inside Giles called out to Julie, "Look what I've got, honey!"

She came in from the kitchen, scowling. "That nasty cat!" she said. "Put him right back outside!"

At this point Danby concentrated all his energies toward making himself purr. It was something like snoring, he decided, but it had the desired effect on his intended victim, for at once Giles made for his den and plumped down in an armchair, arranging Danby in his lap, with more petting and praise. "He's a wonderful cat, Julie," Giles told his wife. "I'll bet he's a purebred Maine coon. Probably worth a couple of hundred bucks."

"So are my wool carpets," Mrs. Eskeridge replied. "So are my new sofas! And who's going to clean up his messes?"

That was Danby's cue. He had already thought out the pièce de résistance in his campaign of endearment. With a trill that meant "This way, folks!," Danby hopped off his ex-partner's lap and trotted to the downstairs bathroom. He had used it often enough at dinner parties, and he knew that the door was left ajar. He had been saving up for this moment. With Giles and his missus watching from the doorway, Danby hopped up on the toilet seat, twitched his elegant plumed tail, and proceeded to use the toilet in the correct manner.

He felt a strange tingling in his paws, and he longed to scratch at something and cover it up, but he ignored these urges, and basked instead in the effusive praise from his self-appointed champion. Why couldn't Giles have been that enthusiastic over his design for the Jenner building, Danby thought resentfully.

Some people's sense of values was so warped. Meanwhile, though, he might as well savor the Eskeridges' transports of joy over his bowel control; there weren't too many ways for cats to demonstrate superior intelligence. He couldn't quote a little Shakespeare or identify the dinner wine. Fortunately, among felines toilet training passed for genius, and even Julie was impressed with his accomplishments. After that, there was no question of Giles turning him out into the cruel world. Instead, they carried him back to the kitchen and opened a can of tuna fish for his dining pleasure. He had to eat it in a bowl on the floor, but the bowl was Royal Doulton, which was some consolation. And while he ate, he could still hear Giles in the background, raving about what a wonderful cat he was. He was in.

"No collar, Julie. Someone must have abandoned him on the highway. What shall we call him?"

"Varmint," his wife suggested. She was a hard sell.

Giles ignored her lack of enthusiasm for his newfound prodigy. "I think I'll call him Merlin. He's a wizard of a cat."

Merlin? Danby looked up with a mouthful of tuna. Oh well, he thought, Merlin and tuna were better than Tigger and cheap dry cat food. You couldn't have everything.

After that, he quickly became a full-fledged member of the household, with a newly purchased plastic feeding bowl, a catnip mouse toy, and another little collar with another damned bell. Danby felt the urge to bite Giles's thumb off while he was attaching this loathsome neckpiece over his ruff, but he restrained himself. By now he was accustomed to the accompaniment of a maniacal jingling with every step he took. What was it with human beings and bells?

Of course, that spoiled his plans for songbird hunting outdoors. He'd have to travel faster than the speed of sound to catch a sparrow now. Not that he got out much, anyhow. Giles seemed to think that he might wander off again, so he was generally careful to keep Danby housebound.

That was all right with Danby, though. It gave him an excellent opportunity to become familiar with the house, and with the routine of its inhabitants— all useful information for someone planning revenge. So far he (the old Danby, that is) had not been mentioned in the Eskeridge conversations. He wondered what story Giles was giving out about his disappearance. Apparently the body had not been found. It was up to him to punish the guilty, then.

Danby welcomed the days when both Giles and Julie left the house. Then he would forgo his morning, mid-morning, and early afternoon naps in order to investigate each room of his domain, looking for lethal opportunities: medicine bottles or perhaps a small appliance that he could push into the bathtub.

So far, though, he had not attempted to stage any accidents, for fear that the wrong Eskeridge would fall victim to his snare. He didn't like Julie any more than she liked him, but he had no reason to kill her. The whole business needed careful study. He could afford to take his time analyzing the opportunities for revenge. The food was good, the job of house cat was undemanding, and he rather enjoyed the irony of being doted on by his intended victim. Giles was certainly better as an owner than he was as a partner.

An evening conversation between Giles and Julie convinced him that he must accelerate his efforts. They were sitting in the den, after a meal of baked chicken. They wouldn't give him the bones, though. Giles kept insisting that they'd splinter in his stomach and kill him. Danby was lying on the hearth rug, pretending to be asleep until they forgot about him, at which time he would sneak back into the kitchen and raid the garbage. He'd given up smoking, hadn't he? And although he'd lapped up a bit of Giles's scotch one night, he seemed to have lost the taste for it. How much prudence could he stand?

"If you're absolutely set on keeping this cat, Giles," said Julie Eskeridge, examining her newly polished talons, "I suppose I'll have to be the one to take him to the vet."

"The vet. I hadn't thought about it. Of course, he'll have to have shots, won't he?" murmured Giles, still studying the newspaper. "Rabies, and so on."

"And while we're at it, we might as well have him neutered," said Julie. "Otherwise, he'll start spraying the drapes and all."

Danby rocketed to full alert. To keep them from suspecting his comprehension, he centered his attention on the cleaning of a perfectly tidy front paw. It was time to step up the pace on his plans for revenge, or he'd be meowing in soprano. And forget the scruples about innocent bystanders: now it was a matter of self-defense.

That night he waited until the house was dark and quiet. Giles and Julie usually went to bed about eleven-thirty, turning off all the lights, which didn't faze him in the least. He rather enjoyed skulking about the silent house using his infrared vision, although he rather missed late night television. He had once considered turning the set on with his paw, but that seemed too precocious, even for a cat named Merlin. Danby didn't want to end up in somebody's behavior lab with wires coming out of his head.

He examined his collection of cat toys, stowed by Julie in his cat basket because she hated clutter. He had a mouse-shaped catnip toy, a rubber fish, and a little red ball. Giles had bought the ball under the ludicrous impression that Danby could be induced to play catch. When he'd rolled it across the floor, Danby lay down and gave him an insolent stare. He had enjoyed the next quarter of an hour, watching Giles on his hands and knees, batting the ball and trying to teach Danby to fetch. But finally Giles gave up, and the ball had been tucked in the cat basket ever since. Danby picked it up with his teeth, and carried it upstairs. Giles and Julie came down the right side of the staircase, didn't they? That's where the bannister was. He set the ball carefully on the third step, in the approximate place that a human foot would touch the stair. A trip wire would be more reliable, but Danby couldn't manage the technology involved.

What else could he devise for the Eskeridges' peril? He couldn't poison their food, and since they'd provided him with a flea collar, he couldn't even hope to get bubonic plague started in the household. Attacking them with tooth and claw seemed foolhardy, even if they were sleeping. The one he wasn't biting could always fight him off, and a fifteen-pound cat can be killed with relative ease by any human determined to do it. Even if they didn't kill him on the spot, they'd get rid of him immediately, and then he'd lose his chance forever. It was too risky.

It had to be stealth, then. Danby inspected the house, looking for lethal opportunities. There weren't any electrical appliances close to the bathtub, and besides, Giles took showers. In another life Danby might have been able to rewire the electric razor to shock its user, but such a feat was well beyond his present level of dexterity. No wonder human beings had taken over the earth; they were so damned hard to kill.

Even his efforts to enlist help in the task had proved fruitless. On one of his rare excursions out of the house (Giles had gone golfing, and Danby slipped out without Julie's noticing), Danby had roamed the neighborhood, looking for . . . well . . . pussy. Instead he'd found dimwitted tomcats, and a Doberman pinscher, who was definitely Somebody. Danby had kept conversation to a minimum, not quite liking the look of the beast's prominent fangs. Danby suspected that the Doberman had previously been an IRS agent. Of course, the dog had *said* that it had been a serial killer, but that was just to lull Danby into a false sense of security. Anyhow, much as the dog approved of Danby's plan to kill his humans, he wasn't interested in forming a conspiracy. Why should he go to the gas chamber to solve someone else's problem?

Danby himself had similar qualms about doing anything too drastic—such as setting fire to the house. He didn't want to stage an accident that would include himself among the victims. After puttering about the darkened house for a wearying few hours, he stretched out on the sofa in the den to take a quick nap before resuming his plotting. He'd be able to think better after he rested.

The next thing Danby felt was a ruthless grip on his collar, dragging him forward. He opened his eyes to find that it was morning, and that the hand at his throat belonged to Julie Eskeridge, who was trying to stuff him into a metal cat carrier. He tried to dig his claws into the sofa, but it was too late. Before he could blink, he had been hoisted along by his tail, and shoved into the box. He barely got his tail out of the way before the door slammed shut behind him. Danby crouched in the plastic carrier, peeking out the side slits, and trying to figure out what to do next. Obviously the rubber ball on the steps had been a dismal failure as a murder weapon. Why couldn't he have come back as a mountain lion?

Danby fumed about the slings and arrows of outrageous fortune all the way out to the car. It didn't help to remember where he was going, and what was scheduled to be done with him shortly thereafter. Julie Eskeridge set the cat carrier on the backseat and slammed the door. When she started the car, Danby howled in protest.

"Be quiet back there!" Julie called out. "There's nothing you can do about it."

We'll see about that, thought Danby, turning to peer out the door of his cage. The steel bars of the door were about an inch apart, and there was no mesh or other obstruction between them. He found that he could easily slide one paw sideways out of the cage. Now, if he could just get a look at the workings of the latch, there was a slight chance that he could extricate himself. He lay down on his side and squinted up at the metal catch. It seemed to be a glorified bolt. To lock the carrier, a metal bar was slid into a socket, and then rotated downward to latch. If he could push the bar back up and then slide it back . . .

It wasn't easy to maneuver with the car changing speed and turning corners. Danby felt himself getting quite dizzy with the effort of concentrating as the carrier gently rocked. But finally, when the car reached the interstate and sped along smoothly, he succeeded in positioning his paw at the right place on the bar, and easing it upward. Another three minutes of tense probing allowed him to slide the bar a fraction of an inch, and then another. The bolt was now clear of the latch. There was no getting out of the car, of course. Julie had rolled up the windows, and they were going sixty miles an hour. Danby spent a full minute pondering the implications of his dilemma. But no matter which way he looked at the problem, the alternative was always the same: do something desperate or go under the knife. It wasn't as if dying had been such a big deal, after all. There was always next time.

Quickly, before the fear could stop him, Danby hurled his furry bulk against the door of the cat carrier, landing in the floor of the backseat with a solid thump. He sprang back up on the seat, and launched himself into the air with a heartfelt snarl, landing precariously on Julie Eskeridge's right shoulder, and digging his claws in to keep from falling.

The last things he remembered were Julie's screams and the feel of the car swerving out of control.

When Danby opened his eyes, the world was still playing in black-and-white. He could hear muffled voices, and smell a jumble of scents: blood, gasoline, smoke. He struggled to get up, and found that he was still less than a foot off the ground. Still furry. Still the Eskeridges' cat. In the distance he could see the crumpled wreckage of Julie's car.

A familiar voice was droning on above him. "He must have been thrown free of the cat carrier during the wreck, officer. That's definitely Merlin, though. My poor wife was taking him to the vet."

A burly policeman was standing next to Giles, nodding sympathetically. "I guess it's true what they say about cats, sir. Having nine lives, I mean. I'm very sorry about your wife. She wasn't so lucky."

Giles hung his head. "No. It's been a great strain. First my business partner disappears, and now I lose my wife." He stooped and picked up Danby. "At least I have my beautiful kitty-cat for consolation. Come on, boy. Let's go home."

Danby's malevolent yellow stare did not waver. He allowed himself to be carried away to Giles's waiting car without protest. He could wait. Cats were good at waiting. And life with Giles wasn't so bad, now that Julie wouldn't be around to harass him. Danby would enjoy a spell of being doted on by an indulgent human, fed gourmet catfood, and given the run of the house. Meanwhile he could continue to leave the occasional ball on the stairs, and think of other ways to toy with Giles, while he waited to see if the police ever turned up to ask Giles about his missing partner. If not, Danby could work on more ways to kill humans. Sooner or later he would succeed. Cats are endlessly patient at stalking their prey.

"It's just you and me, now, fella," said Giles, placing his cat on the seat beside him.

And after he killed Giles, perhaps he could go in search of the building contractor that Giles bribed to keep his dirty secret. He certainly deserved to die. And that nasty woman Danby used to live next door to, who used to complain about his stereo and his crabgrass. And perhaps the surly headwaiter at Chantage. Stray cats can turn up anywhere.

Danby began to purr.

DIANE MOTT DAVIDSON
1949–

One of the many successful writers of culinary mysteries, whose protagonists are involved with food and cooking, Diane Mott Davidson was born in Honolulu, Hawaii, and grew up in Washington, D.C., and Charlottesville, Virginia. She received a B.A. from Stanford and an MFA from Johns Hopkins University. She taught at a prep school and did other work prior to moving to Evergreen, Colorado. Her writing success began with the publication of *Catering to Nobody* (1990), which was nominated for the Anthony, Agatha, and Macavity Awards. Since then she has published ten more novels in the mystery series featuring amateur detective Goldy Bear, owner of Goldilock's Catering. The novels are set in Colorado, most around the fictitious Aspen Meadow.

Part of the appeal of the novels is the titles, for example, *Dying for Chocolate* (1992), *The Cereal Killers* (1993), *The Main Corpse* (1996), and *Chopping Spree* (2002). Another important quality is the recurring cast surrounding Goldy: an abusive medical doctor ex-husband, his second ex-wife Marla who becomes Goldy's close friend, county homicide detective Tom Schulz whom Goldy eventually marries, and her young son Arch who grows up in the course of the series. The plots tend to be fast-paced and intricate as Goldy goes about her catering business. She often finds herself in frightening situations and readily admits to being scared. She is not a "tough cookie" (another of Davidson's titles) in the sense of being all-powerful, but she is good at thinking about people and situations and deducing cause and effect in relation to the crimes. Another appeal of the novels is that original recipes created for the series are included in the books, along with descriptions of Goldy preparing them. Goldy is featured in "Cold Turkey," one of only two Davidson short stories. It received the Anthony for Best Short Story when it was first published in *Sisters in Crime 5* in 1992.

Recommended Davidson works: *Dying for Chocolate, The Last Suppers, Chopping Spree.*

Other recommended authors: Susan Wittig Albert, Claudia Bishop, Virginia Rich.

Cold Turkey

I did not expect to find Edith Blanton's body in my walk-in refrigerator. The day had been bad enough already. My first thought after the shock was *I'm going to have to throw all this food away.*

My mind reeled. I couldn't get a dial tone to call for help. Reconstruct, I ordered myself as I ran to a neighbor's. The police are going to want to know everything. My neighbor pressed 9-1-1. I talked. Hung up. I immediately worried about my eleven-year-old son, Arch. Where was he? I looked at my watch: ten past eight. He was spending the night somewhere. Oh yes, Dungeons and Dragons weekend party at a friend's house. I made a discreet phone call to make sure he was okay. I did not mention the body. If I had, he and his friends would have wanted to troop over to see it.

Then I flopped down in a wing-back chair and tried to think.

I had talked to Edith Blanton that morning. She had called with a batch of demanding questions. Was I ready to cater the Episcopal Church Women's Luncheon, to be held the next day? Irritation had blossomed like a headache. Butterball Blanton, as she was known everywhere but to her face, was a busybody. I'd given the shortest possible answers. The menu was set, the food prepared. Chicken and artichoke heart pot pie. Molded strawberry salad. Tossed greens with vinaigrette. Parkerhouse rolls. Lemon sponge cake. Not on your diet, I had wanted to add, but did not.

Now Goldy, she'd gone on, *you have that petition we're circulating around the church, don't you?* I checked for raisins for a Waldorf salad and said, Which petition is that? Edith made an impatient noise in her throat. *The one outlawing guitar music.* Sigh. I said I had it around somewhere. . . . Actually, I kind of liked ecclesiastical folk music, as long as I personally did not have to sing it. *And Goldy, you're not serving that Japanese raw fish, are you? To the churchwomen?* Never. *And you didn't use anything from the local farm where they found salmonella, did you?* Oh, enough. Absolutely not, Butt—er . . . Mrs. Blanton, I promised before hanging up.

The phone had rung again immediately: our priest, Father Olson. I said, Surely you're not calling about the luncheon. He said, *Don't call me Shirley.* A comic in a clerical collar. After pleasantries we had gotten around to the real stuff: *How's Marla?* I said that Marla Korman, my best friend, was fine. As far as I knew. *Why? Oh, just checking, hadn't seen her in a while.* Haha, sure. I involuntarily glanced at my appointments calendar. After the churchwomen's luncheon, I was doing a dinner party for Marla. I didn't mention this to the uninvited Father Olson. You see, Episcopal priests can marry. Father Olson was unmarried, which made him interested in Marla. The reverse was not the case, however, which was why he had to call me to find out how she was. But none of this did I mention to Father O., as we called him. Didn't want to hurt his feelings.

My neighbor handed me a cup of tea. I thought again of Edith Blanton's pale calves, of the visible side of her pallid face, of the blood on the refrigerator floor. I pushed the image out of my mind and tried to think again about the day. The police were going to ask a lot of questions. Had I heard from anyone in the church again? Had anyone mentioned a current crisis? What had happened after Father Olson called?

Oh yes. Next had come a frantic knock at the door: something else to do with Marla. This time it was her soon-to-be-ex-boyfriend—lanky, strawberry-blond David McAllister. He had desperation in his voice. *What can I do to show Marla I love her?* Sheesh! Did I look like Ann Landers? I ushered him out to the kitchen, where I started to chop pecans, *also* for the Waldorf salad, *also* for Marla's dinner party, to which the wealthy-but-boring David McAllister *also* had not been invited. Not only that, but he was driving me crazy cracking his knuckles. When he took a breath while talking about how much he adored Marla, I said I was in the middle of a crisis involving petitions, raw eggs and the churchwomen, and ushered him out.

About an hour later I'd left the house. I lifted my head from my neighbor's chair and looked at my watch: quarter after eight. When had I left the house? Around one, only to return seven hours later. The entire afternoon and early evening had been taken up with the second unsuccessful meeting between me, my lawyer, and the people suing me to change the name of my catering business. George Pettigrew and his wife own Three Bears Catering down in Denver. In June it came to their attention that my real, actual name is Goldy (a nickname that has stuck like epoxy glue since childhood) Bear (Germanic in origin, but lamentable nonetheless). What was worse in the Pettigrews' eyes was that my business in the mountain town of Aspen Meadow was called Goldilocks' Catering, Where Everything Is Just Right! We began negotiating three weeks ago, at the beginning of September. The Pettigrews screamed copyright infringement. I tried to convince them that all of us could successfully capitalize on, if not inhabit, the same fairy tale. The meeting this afternoon was another failure, except from the viewpoint of my lawyer, who gets his porridge no matter what.

I nestled my head against one of the wings of my neighbor's chair. Just thinking about the day again was exhausting. For as if all this had not been enough, when I got home I heard a dog in my outdoor trash barrels. At least I thought it was a dog. When I went around the side of the house to check, a *real* bear, large and black, shuffled away from the back of the house and up toward the woods. This is not an uncommon sight in the Colorado high country when fall weather sets in. But combined with the nagging from Edith and the fight with the Pettigrews, it was enough to send me in search of a parfait left over from an elementary school faculty party.

Not on your diet, I thought with a measure of guilt, the diet you just undertook with all sorts of good intentions. Oh well. Diets aren't good for you. Too much deprivation. But on this plan I didn't have to give up sweets; I could have one dessert a day. Of course the brownie I'd had after the lawyer's office fiasco was only a memory. Besides, I was under so much stress. I could just imagine that tall chilled crystal glass, those thick layers of chocolate and vanilla pudding. I opened the refrigerator door full of anticipation. And there in the dark recesses of the closetlike space was Edith, fully clothed, lying limp, sandwiched between the congealed strawberry salad and marinating T-bones.

I'd screamed. Rushed over to the neighbor's where I now sat, staring into a cup of lukewarm tea. I looked at my watch again. 8:20.

My neighbor was scurrying around looking for a blanket in case I went into shock. I was not going into shock; I just needed to talk to somebody. So I phoned Marla. That's what best friends are for, right? To get you through crises? Besides, Marla and I went way back. We had both made the mistake of marrying the same man, not simultaneously. We had survived the divorces from The Jerk and become best friends. I had even coached her in figuring her monetary settlement, sort of like when an NFL team in the playoffs gets films from another team's archenemy.

When Marla finally picked up the phone, I told her Edith Blanton was dead and in my refrigerator. I must have still been incoherent because I added the bit about the bear.

There was a pause while Marla tried to apply logic. Finally she said. "Goldy. I'm on my way over."

"Okay, okay! I'll meet you at my front door. Just be careful."

"Of what? Is this homicide or is it a frigging John Irving novel?"

Before I could say anything she hung up.

My neighbor and I walked slowly back to my house. The police arrived first: two men in uniforms. They took my name and Edith Blanton's. They asked how and when I'd found the body. When they tried to call for an investigative team, they discovered that the reason I hadn't been able to get a dial tone was that my phone was dead. The wires outside had been cut. This would explain why my brand-new, horrendously expensive security system had not worked when Edith and . . . whoever . . . had broken in. The police used their radio. While I was bemoaning my fate, Marla arrived. She was dressed in a sweatsuit sewn with gold spangles: I think they were supposed to represent aspen leaves.

The team arrived and took pictures. The coroner, gray-haired and grim-faced, signaled the removal company to cart out the body bag holding Edith. Marla murmured, "The Butterball bagged."

I said, "Stop."

Marla closed her eyes and fluttered her plump hands. "I know. I'm sorry. But she *was* a bitch. Everybody in the church disliked her."

I harrumphed. The two uniformed policemen told us to quit talking. They told me to go into the living room so the team leader, a female homicide investigator I did not know, could ask some questions. Marla flounced out. She said she was going home to make up the guest bed for me; no way was she allowing me to stay in that house.

The team leader and I settled ourselves on the two chairs in my living room. Out in the kitchen the lab technicians and other investigators were having a field day spreading black graphite fingerprint powder over the food for the churchwomen's luncheon.

The investigator was a burly woman with curly blond hair held back with black barrettes. Her eyes were light brown and impassive, her voice even. She wanted to know my name, if I knew the victim and for how long, was I having problems with her and where I'd been all day. I told her about my activities, about the following day's luncheon and Edith's questions. At their leader's direction, the team took samples of all the food. They also took what they'd found on the refrigerator floor: an anti-guitar-music petition. Through the blobs of congealed strawberry salad and raw egg yolk, you could see there were no names on it. Edith was still clutching the paper after she'd been hit on the head and dragged into the refrigerator.

I said, "Dragged . . . ?"

The investigator bit the inside of her cheek. Then she said, "Please tell me every single thing about your conversation with Edith Blanton."

So we went through it all again, including the bit about the petition. I added that I had not been due to see Edith, er, the deceased until the next day. Moreover, I was not having more problems with her than anybody else in town, especially Father Olson, who, unlike Edith, thought every liturgy should sound like a hootenanny.

The investigator's next question confused me. Did I have a pet? Yes, I had a cat that I had inherited from former employers. However, I added, strangers spooked him. Poor Scout would be cowering under a bed for at least the next three days.

She said, "And the color of the cat is . . . ?"

"Light brown, dark brown and white," I said. "Sort of a Burmese-Siamese mix. I think."

The investigator held out a few strands of hair.

"Does this look familiar? Look like your cat's hair?" It was dark brown and did not look like anything that grew on Scout. In fact, it looked fake.

" 'Fraid not," I said.

"Synthetic, anyway, we think. You got any of this kind of material around?"

I shook my head no. "Oh gosh," I said, "the bear." I started to tell her about what I'd seen around the back of the house, but she was looking at her clipboard. She shifted in her chair.

She said, "Wait. Is this a *relative* of yours? Er, Ms. Bear?"

"No, no, no. Have you heard of Three Bears Catering?"

The investigator looked more confused. "Is that you, too? I wouldn't know. They did the policemen's banquet down in Denver last year, and they all wore bear . . . suits. . . . "

She eyed me, the corners of her mouth turned down. She said, "Any chance this bear-person might have been waiting to attack you in your refrigerator? Over the name change problem? And attacked Edith instead? Do they know what you look like?"

"I told you. I spent the afternoon with the Pettigrews," I said through clenched teeth. "They're suing me; why would they want to kill me?"

"You tell me."

At that moment, Marla poked her head into the living room. "I'm back. Can we leave? Or do you have to stay until the kitchen demolition team finishes?"

I looked at the investigator, who shook her head. She said, "We have a lot to do. Should be finished by midnight. At the latest. Also, we gotta take the cut wires from out back and, uh, your back door."

I said, "My back door? Great." I gave Marla a pained look. "I have to stay until they go. Just do me a favor and call somebody to come put in a piece of plywood for the door hole. Also, see if you can find my cat cage. I'm bringing Scout to your house."

Marla nodded and disappeared. The investigator then asked me to go through the whole thing *backward*, beginning with my discovery of Edith. This I did meticulously, as I know the backward-story bit is one way investigators check for lies.

Finally she said, " 'Haven't I seen you around? Aren't you a friend of Tom Schulz's?"

I smiled. "Homicide Investigator Schulz is a good friend of mine. Unfortunately, he's up snagging inland salmon at Green Lake Reservoir. Now, tell me. Am I a suspect in this or not?"

The investigator's flat brown eyes revealed nothing. After a moment she said, "At this time we don't have enough information to tell about any suspects. But this hair we found in the victim's hand isn't yours. You didn't know your phone lines were cut. And you probably didn't break down your own back door."

Well. I guess that was police talk for *No you're not a suspect*.

The investigator wrote a few last things on her clipboard, then got up to finish with her cohorts in the kitchen. I didn't see her for the next three hours. Marla appeared with the cat cage, and I found Scout crouched under Arch's bed. I coaxed him out while Marla welcomed the emergency fix-it people at the stroke of midnight. The panel on their truck said: *Felony Fix-up—They Trash It, We Patch It*. How comforting. Especially the twenty-four-hour service part.

An hour after the police and Felony Fix-up had left my kitchen looking like a relic of the scorched-earth policy, I sat in Marla's kitchen staring down one of Marla's favorite treats—imported *baba au rhum*. There's something about being awake at one A.M. that makes you think you need something to eat. Still, guilt reared its hideous head.

"What's the matter?" Marla asked. "I thought you loved those. Eat up. It'll help you stop thinking about Edith Blanton."

"Not likely, but I'll try." I inhaled the deep buttered-rum scent. "I shouldn't. I ate Lindt Lindors all summer and I'm supposed to be on a diet."

"One dessert won't hurt you."

"I've already had one dessert."

"So? *Two* won't hurt you." She shook her peaches-and-cream cheeks. "If I'd had to go through what you just did, I'd have six." So saying, she delicately loaded two *babas* onto a Wedgwood dessert plate. "Tomorrow's going to be even worse," she warned. "You'll have to phone the president of the churchwomen first thing and cancel the luncheon. You'll have to call Father Olson. No, never mind, I'll make both calls."

"Why?"

"Because, my dear, I am still hopeful that you'll be able to do my dinner party tomorrow night." Marla pushed away from the table to sashay over to her refrigerator for an aerosol can of whipped cream. "I know it's crass," she said as she shook the can vigorously, "but I still have three people, one of whom is a male I am very interested in, expecting dinner. Shrimp cocktail, steaks, potato soufflé, green beans, Waldorf salad, and chocolate cake. Remember? Beginning at six o'clock. I can't exactly call them up and say, Well, my caterer found this body in her refrigerator—"

"All right! If I can finish cleaning up the mess tomorrow, we're on." I took a bite of the *baba* and said, "The cops ruined the salad and the cake. You'll have to give me some more of your Jonathan apples. Gee, I don't feel so hot—"

"Don't worry. Sleep in. I have lots of apples. And I'll send a maid over to help you."

"Just not in a bear suit."

"Hey! Speaking of which! Should we give the Pettigrews a call in the morning? Just to hassle them?" She giggled. "Should we give them a call right now?"

"No, no, no," I said loudly over the sound of Marla hosing her *babas* with cream. "The police are bound to talk to them. If they're blameless, I can't afford to have them any angrier at me than they already are. I'm so tired, I don't even want to think about it."

Marla gave me a sympathetic look, got up and made me a cup of espresso laced with rum.

I said, "So who's this guy tomorrow night?"

"Fellow named Tony Kaplan. Just moved here from L.A., where he sold his house for over a million dollars. And it was a small house, too. He's cute. Wants to open a bookstore."

"Not another newcomer who's fantasized about running a bookstore in a mountain town," I said as I took the whipped cream bottle and pressed out a blob on top of my coffee. Immigrants from either coast always felt they had a mission to bring culture to us cowpokes. "Gee," I said. "Almost forgot. Regarding your busy social life, Father Olson called and asked me how you were."

"I hope you told him I was living in sin with a chocolate bar."

"Well, I didn't have time because then David McAllister showed up at my front door. Wanted to know if there was anything he could do to show you he loved you."

Marla tsked. "He asked me the same thing, and I said, Well, you can start with a nice bushel of apples."

"You are cruel." I sipped the coffee. With the rum and the whipped cream, it was sort of like hot ice cream. "You shouldn't play with his feelings."

"Excuse me, but jealousy is for seventh-graders."

"Too cruel," I said as we got up and placed the dishes in the sink. She escorted me with Scout the cat up to her guest room, then gave me towels; I handed over a key to my front door for her maid. Then I said, "Tell me about Edith Blanton."

Marla plunked down a pair of matching washcloths. She said, "Edith knew everything about everybody. Who in the church had had affairs with whom . . . "

"Oh, that's nice."

Marla pulled up her shoulders in an exaggerated gesture of nonchalance. The sweat-suit spangles shook. "Well, it was," she said. "I mean, everybody was nice to her because they were afraid of what she had on them. They didn't want her to talk. And she got what she wanted, until she took up arms against Father Olson over the guitar music."

"Too bad she couldn't get anything on him."

"Oh, honey," Marla said with an elaborate swirl of her eyes before she turned away and swaggered down the hall to her room. "Don't think she wasn't trying."

The next day Scout and I trekked to the church before going back to my house. Scout meowed morosely the whole way. I told him I had to leave a big sign on the church door, saying that the luncheon had been canceled. He only howled louder when I said it was just in case someone hadn't gotten the word. If I hadn't been concentrating so hard on trying to comfort him, I would have noticed George Pettigrew's truck in the church parking lot. Then I would have been prepared for Pettigrew's smug grin, his hands clutched under his armpits, his foot tapping as I vaulted out of my van. As it was, I nearly had a fit.

"Were you around my house in a bear suit last night?" I demanded. He opened his eyes wide, as if I were crazy. "And *what* are you doing here? Haven't you got enough catering jobs down in Denver?"

"We don't use the bear suits anymore," he replied in a superior tone. "We had a hygiene problem with the hair getting into the food. And as a matter of fact I am doing lunches for two Skyboxes at Mile High Stadium tomorrow. But I can still offer to help out the churchwomen, since their local caterer canceled." His eyes bugged out as he raised his eyebrows. "Bad news travels fast."

Well, the luncheon was not going to happen. To tell him this, I was tempted to use some very unchurchlike language. But at that moment Father Olson pulled up in his 300E Mercedes 4matic. Father O. had told the vestry that a priest needed a four-wheel-drive vehicle to visit parishioners in the mountains; he'd also petitioned for folk-music tapes to give to shut-ins. The vestry had refused to purchase the tapes, but they'd sprung fifty thou for the car.

Father O. came up and put his hands on my shoulders. He gave me his Serious Pastoral Look. "Goldy," he said, "I've been so concerned for you."

"So have I," I said ruefully, with a sideways glance at George Pettigrew, who shrank back in the presence of clerical authority.

I turned my attention back to Father Olson. Marla might want to reconsider. An ecclesiastical career suited Father O., who had come of age in the sixties. He had sincere brown eyes, dark skin and a beard, a cross between Moses and Ravi Shankar.

" . . . feel terrible about what's happened to Edith," he was saying, "of course. How can this possibly . . . Oh, you probably don't want to talk about it. . . . "

I said, "You're right."

Fancy cars were pulling into the church parking lot. George Pettigrew unobtrusively withdrew just as a group of women disentangled themselves from their Cadillacs and Mercedes.

"Listen," I said, "I have to split. Can you take care of these women who haven't gotten the bad news? I have a dinner party tonight that I simply can't cancel."

I almost didn't make it. Cries of *Oh here she is; I wonder what she's fixed* erupted like birdcalls. Father Olson gave me the Pastoral Nod. I sidled past the women, hopped back in the van, and managed to get out of the church parking lot without getting into a single conversation.

To my surprise, the maid Marla had sent over had done a superb job cleaning my kitchen. It positively sparkled. Unfortunately, right around the corner was the plywood nailed over the back-door opening: a grim reminder of last night's events.

I set about thawing and marinating more steaks, then got out two dozen frozen Scout's Brownies, my patented contribution to the chocoholics of the world. I had first developed the recipe under the watchful eye of the cat, so I'd named them after him. Marla adored them.

Edith Blanton came to mind as I again got out my recipe for Waldorf salad. Someone, dressed presumably as a bear, had taken the time to cut the phone wires and break in. Why? Had that person been following Edith, meaning to kill her at his first opportunity? Or had Edith surprised a robber? Had he killed her intentionally or accidentally?

I knew one thing for sure. Homicide Investigator Tom Schulz was my friend—well, more than a friend—and he often talked to me about cases up in Aspen Meadow. This would not be true with the current investigator working the Edith Blanton case, no question about it. If I was going to find out what happened, I was on my own.

While washing and cutting celery into julienne sticks, I conjured up a picture of Edith Blanton with her immaculately coiffed head of silver hair, dark green skirt, and Loden jacket. Despite being an energetic busybody, Edith had been a lady. She never would have broken into my house.

I held my breath and opened my refrigerator door. All clean. I reached for a bag of nuts. Although classic Waldorfs called for walnuts, I was partial to fresh, sweet pecans that I mail-ordered from Texas. I chopped a cupful and then softened some raisins in hot water. The bear-person had been in my refrigerator. Why? If you're going to steal food, why wear a disguise?

Because if I had caught him, stealing food or attacking Edith Blanton, I would have recognized him.

So it was someone I knew? Probably.

I went back into the refrigerator. Although only a quarter cup of mayonnaise was required for the Waldorf, it was imperative to use *homemade* mayonnaise, which I would make with a nice fresh raw egg. I would mix the mayonnaise with a little lemon juice, sugar, and heavy cream. . . . Wait a minute.

Two days ago my supplier had brought me eggs from a salmonella-free source in eastern Colorado. I was sure they were brown. So why was I starting at a half dozen nice white eggs?

I picked one up and looked at it. It was an egg, all right. I brought it out into the kitchen and called Alicia, my supplier. The answering service said she was out on a delivery.

"Well, do you happen to know what color eggs she delivered on her run two days ago?"

There was a long pause. The operator finally said, "Is this some kind of *yolk?*"

Oh, hilarious. I hung up. So funny I forgot to laugh.

I would have called a neighbor and borrowed an egg, but I didn't have any guarantees about hers, either. Many locals bought their eggs from a farm outside of town where they *had* found salmonella, and hers might be tainted too.

I felt so frustrated I thawed a brownie in the microwave. This would be my one dessert of the day. Oh, and was it wonderful—thick and dark and chewy. Fireworks of good feeling sparked through my veins.

Okay, I said firmly to my inner self, yesterday when you came into this refrigerator you found a body. There is no way you could possibly remember the color of eggs or anything else that Alicia delivered two days ago. So make the mayo and quit bellyaching.

With this happy thought, I started the food processor whirring and filched another brownie. Mm, mm. When the mayonnaise was done, I finished the Waldorf salad, put in the refrigerator, and then concentrated on shelling and cooking fat prawns for the shrimp cocktail. When I put the shrimp in to chill, I stared at the refrigerator floor. I still had not answered the first question. Why had Edith been at my house in the first place?

She had been carrying a petition. A *blank* petition. So?

My copy had had a few names on it. Edith was carrying a blank petition because I had said I didn't know where my copy was. She came over with a new one.

So? That still didn't explain how she got in.

When she got here, she didn't get any answer at the front door. But she saw the light filtering from the kitchen, and being the busybody she was, she went around back. The door was open, and she surprised the bear in mid-heist. . . .

Well. Go figure. I packed up all the food and hustled off to Marla's.

"Oh darling, *enfin!*" Marla cried when she swung open her heavy front door. She was wearing a multilayered yellow-and-red chiffon dress that looked like sewn-together scarves. Marla always dressed to match the season, and I was pretty sure I was looking at the designer version of Autumn.

"You don't need to be so dramatic," I said as I trudged past her with the first box.

"Oh! I thought you were Tony." She giggled. "Just kidding."

To my relief she had already set her cherry dining room table with her latest haul from Europe: Limoges china and Baccarat crystal. I started boiling potatoes for the soufflé and washed the beans.

"I want to taste!" Marla cried as she got out a spoon to attack the Waldorf.

"Not on your life!" I said as I snatched the covered bowl away from her. "If we get started eating and chatting there'll be nothing left for your guests."

To my relief the front doorbell rang. Disconsolate, Marla slapped the silver spoon down on the counter and left. From the front hall came the cry "Oh darling, *enfin!*" Tony Kaplan, would-be bookstore proprietor.

The evening was warm, which was a good thing, as Marla and I had decided to risk an outdoor fire on her small barbecue. There were six T-bones—one for each guest and two extra for big appetites. I looked at my watch: six o'clock. Marla had said to serve at seven. The coals would take a bit longer after the sun went down, but since we were near the solstice, that wouldn't be until half past six. The things a caterer has to know.

Tony Kaplan meandered out to the kitchen. Marla was welcoming the other couple. He needed ice for his drink, he said with a laugh. He was a tall, sharp-featured man who hunched his shoulders over when he walked, as if his height bothered him. I introduced myself. He laughed. "Is that your real name?" I told him there was a silver ice bucket in the living room. He just might not have recognized it, as it was in the shape of a sundae. You had to lift up the ice cream part to get to the ice. "Oh, I get it!" There was another explosive laugh, his third. He may have been rich, but his personality left a lot to be desired.

When the coals were going and I had put the soufflé in the oven, my mind turned again to Edith. Who could have possibly wanted to break into my refrigerator? Why not steal the computer I had right there on the counter to keep track of menus?

"We're ready for the shrimp cocktail," Marla stage-whispered into the kitchen.

"Already? But I thought you said—"

"Tony's driving me crazy. If I give him some shrimp, maybe he'll stop chuckling at everything I have to say."

While Marla and her guests were bathing their shrimp with cocktail sauce, I hustled out to check on the coals. To my surprise, a nice coat of white ash had developed. Sometimes things do work. The steaks sizzled enticingly when I placed them on the grill. I ran back inside and got out the salad and started the beans. When I came back out to turn the T-bones, the sun had slid behind the mountains and the air had turned cool.

"Come on, let's go," I ordered the steaks. After a long five minutes the first four were done. I slapped them down on the platter, put the last two on the grill, and came in. In a crystal bowl, I made a basket of lettuce and then spooned the Waldorf salad on top. This I put on a tray along with the butter and rolls. The soufflé had puffed and browned; I whisked it out to the dining room. While I was putting the beans in a china casserole dish, I remembered that I had neglected to get the last two steaks off the fire.

Cancel the *things working* idea, I thought. I ferried the rest of the dishes out to Marla's sideboard, invited the guests to serve themselves buffet-style, and made a beeline back to the kitchen.

I looked out the window: around the steaks the charcoal fire was merrily send-ing up foot-high flames and clouds of smoke. Bad news. At this dry time of year, sparks were anathema. There was no fire extinguisher in Marla's kitchen. Why should there be? She never cooked. I grabbed a crystal pitcher, started water spurting into it, looked back out the window to check the fire again.

Judas priest. A bear was lurching from one bush in Marla's backyard to the next. In the darkening twilight, I could not tell if it was the same one that had been in my backyard. All I could see was him stopping and then holding his hands as if he were cheering.

I sidestepped to get beside one of Marla's cabinets, then peeked outside. I knew bravery was in order; I just didn't know what that was going to look like. Too bad Scout had never made it as an attack-cat.

The bear-person shows up at my house. The bear-person shows up at Marla's. Why?

Oh damn. The eggs.

"Marla!" I shrieked. I ran out to the dining room. "Don't eat the Wal-dorf salad! There's a bear in your backyard . . . but I just know it's not a real one . . . . Somebody needs to call the cops! Quick! Tony, could you please go grab this person? It's not a real bear, just somebody in a bear suit. I'm sure he killed Edith Blanton."

For once, Tony did not laugh. He said, "You've got a killer dressed as a bear in the backyard. You want me to go grab him with my bare hands?"

"Yes," I said, "of course! Hurry up!"

"This is a weird dinner party," said Tony.

"Oh, I'll do it!" I shrieked.

I sprinted to the kitchen and vaulted full tilt out Marla's back door. Maybe it *was* a real bear. Then I'd be in trouble for sure. I started running down through the tall grass toward the bush where the bear was hidden. The bear stood up. He made his cheering motion again. But . . .

Ordinary black bears have bad eyesight.

Ordinary black bears don't grow over five feet tall.

This guy was six feet if he was an inch, and his eyes told him I was coming after him.

He turned and trundled off in the opposite direction. I sped up, hampered only by tall grass and occasional rocks. Behind me I could hear shouts—Marla, Tony, whoever. I was not going to turn around. I was bent on my prey.

The bear howled: a gargled human howl. Soon he was at the end of Marla's property, where an enormous rock formation was the only thing between us and the road. The bear ran up on the rocks. Then, unsure of what to do, he jumped down the other side. Within a few seconds I had scrambled up to where he had stood. The bear had landed in the center of the road.

I launched myself. When I landed on his right shoulder, he crumpled. Amazing. The last time I'd seen a bear successfully tackled was when Randy

Gradishar had thrown Walter Payton for a six-yard loss in the Chicago backfield.

I leapt up. "You son of a bitch!" I screamed. Then I kicked him in the stomach for good measure.

I reached down to pull off his bear mask. Of course, I was fully expecting to see the no-longer-smug face of George Pettigrew.

But it wasn't George.

Looking up at me was the tormented face of David McAllister. I was stunned. But of course. The hand-paw motion. David McAllister had been doing what he always did when he was nervous: cracking his knuckles.

"David? David? What's going on?"

"I'm sorry, I'm sorry," he blubbered, "I didn't mean to hurt that old woman in your house. I just needed Marla. . . . I thought I was going to lose my mind. . . . I wanted to hurt her . . . and whoever she was seeing. . . . I wanted to make them pay. . . . I'm just so sorry. . . . "

Marla and Tony Kaplan appeared at the top of the rocks.

"Goldy!" Maria shrieked. "Are you okay? The police are on their way. What's that, a person?"

Later, much later, Maria and I sat in her kitchen and started in on the untouched platter of brownies. David McAllister had said he figured Marla had asked for the apples for Waldorf salad because she was having somebody else over. (*He knew you better than you thought*, I told her.) He was crazy with jealousy, and I had been no help. Worse, when he was in my kitchen, he had seen "Marla—dinner party" on my appointments calendar. And here I'd thought all he'd been doing was cracking his knuckles. He cut my wires and broke through my back door. He knew I made everything from scratch. (*He knew us all better than we thought*, Marla said.) So he substituted salmonella-tainted eggs for the mayonnaise, to make Marla and her dinner guests sick. When Edith Blanton surprised him, they struggled, and she fell back on the corner of the marble slab I used for kneading. It was an accident. But because David McAllister had broken into my house before his struggle with Edith, the charge was going to be murder in the first degree.

Marla sank her teeth into her first brownie. "Ooo-ooo," she said. "Yum. I feel better already. Have one."

"I shouldn't. I can't." In fact, I couldn't even look at the brownies; my knees were scraped and my chest hurt where I'd fallen on David McAllister.

"Well, you're probably right. If you hadn't gone after that parfait, you never would have found Butterball, I mean Mrs. Blanton. Which just goes to show, if you're going to give up deserts, you have to do it cold—"

"Don't say it. Don't even think it. And no matter how you cajole, I'm not going to join you in this chocolate indulgence."

Her eyes twinkled like the rings on her fingers. "But that's what I wanted all along!" she protested. "Leave more for me that way! Dark, fudgy, soothing . . . "

"Oh all right," I said. "Just one."

JAN BURKE
1953–

A highly-respected and versatile master of both the detective novel and short story, Jan Burke was born in Houston, Texas, but has lived most of her life in southern California. She earned a degree in history from the University of California, Long Beach, and worked as a manager in a manufacturing firm and as a columnist for a Long Beach newspaper before becoming a full-time writer. Her first novel, *Goodnight, Irene* (1993), features amateur detective Irene Kelly, who often butts heads with the local police in her work as a crime reporter for the *Las Piernas News Express*. As the series continues, Kelly's involvement with police detective Frank Harriman causes her to switch her reporting to the political beat, though she still has an interest in Frank's cases. Kelly is a tough, aggressive, but humane reporter who takes on many of the political and social issues of the day. Burke is a master at handling the love-hate relationship between the press and the police and the interdependency of the two. The seventh novel in the series, *Bones* (1999), won the Edgar for Best Novel. After *Flight* (2001), which centers on Irene's husband, and the standalone thriller *Nine* (2002), Burke returned to the Irene series. Burke is also an associate editor and contributor to *Writing Mysteries* (2000), edited by Sue Grafton.

Burke's short fiction presents a variety of amateur sleuths in both historical and contemporary settings. Many of the stories have been nominated for major awards. "Unharmed" (1994) won the Ellery Queen Mystery Magazine Readers Award and the Macavity for Best Short Story of that year, and "The Abbey Ghosts," (2001) won the Macavity and was nominated for an Edgar. "Revised Endings," which does not exactly feature a "detective" at all, is an excellent example of one of Burke's "what if" stories.

Included in Burke's collection *Eighteen* (2004), "Revised Endings" was first published in *Viva*, a Dutch language magazine, in 1994, and first appeared in English in *Mysterious Intent* mystery magazine, Summer/Fall issue, 1998.

Recommended Burke works: *Bones, Eighteen, Goodnight, Irene*.

Other recommended authors: Anne Perry, Sarah Shankman, Mary Willis Walker.

Revised Endings

Harriet read the letter again. She wasn't sure why; each re-reading upset her as much if not more than the first.

"Once again, I must tell you that the ending of this story positively reeks," Kitty Craig had written. "I can't imagine any reader believing Lord Harold Wiggins would choose this method of killing off his enemy, nor would any reader believe he could manage to mask the taste of antimony by mixing it into the braunschweiger. Rewrite."

Harriet Bently had been writing the popular Lord Harold Wiggins series for ten years now. She knew exactly what dearest Harry (as only Harriet had liberty to call him) would choose to do in *any* given situation, even if her editor did not. After all, Harry had moved into Harriet's life—lock, stock and barrel. No, she didn't invite him to tea like a child's imaginary friend; but she thought of him constantly, and had grown comfortable with his presence in her life. Like any series character and his author, they had become quite attached to each other.

It was more than Kitty Craig's rude tone that upset her. Kitty was notorious in the publishing industry for her biting, sarcastic remarks; Harriet told herself (not entirely successfully) that she shouldn't take Kitty's insults personally. What upset Harriet was Kitty's disregard for Lord Harold Wiggins's intelligence. His trademark was to effect justice without costing the English taxpayers a farthing for an imprisonment or a trial; once Lord Wiggins knew who the guilty party was, he cleverly killed the villain. In this book, Lord Wiggins made sure the poisoner Monroe would never age another day by slipping him a lethal dose of antimony. Monroe was a villain of the first water, and certainly deserved the punishment Lord Wiggins meted out. Harriet couldn't help but feel proud of her protagonist.

Her previous editor, Linda Lucerne, had loved Lord Harold almost as much as she did. Linda never changed much more than a punctuation mark; Kitty used industrial strength black markers to X through pages of manuscript at a time. Pages that had taken hours of research, planning, writing, and rewriting before they were ever mailed to Shoehorn, Dunstreet and Matthews (known affectionately as SDM), the esteemed publishers of the Lord Harold Wiggins series.

Yes, Linda Lucerne had loved Harriet's style, and said so from the moment she accepted the first novel, *Lord Wiggins Makes Hay While the Sun Shines*. And make hay he did. Linda's faith was proved justified, and the success of *Makes Hay* was repeated in *Lord Wiggins Beards the Lion in His Den* and the next seven Lord Harold Wiggins books. Alas, Linda had suffered a heart attack just after the tenth book, *Lord Wiggins Throws Pearls Before Swine*, had been mailed off to SDM. Upon her recovery, she had opted for retirement from the publishing industry.

Harriet tried hard to remember a sin she might have committed that would have justified so mean a punishment as having Kitty Craig become her new editor.

She had known other writers who had suffered under Kitty's abuses. Upon learning that Kitty would be her editor, Harriet had complained long and loud to her agent. But Wendall had pointed out that Kitty had been personally chosen for Harriet by Mr. William Shoehorn III. He had also mentioned that unless she was willing to come up with a new main character, they had no hope of moving to another publishing house. SDM owned Lord Harold. Wendall urged her to be open-minded.

Harriet loved Lord Wiggins too much to forsake him, and so she had tried to follow Wendall's advice. Tried, that is, until she received her first editorial letter from Kitty Craig. A long list of changes were demanded, each demand phrased in abusive language. The one that bothered Harriet the most was the demand to change the ending:

"How absolutely boring! Monroe dies when he swallows lemonade laced with strychnine. Strychnine! That old saw? Is your imagination so limited? Formula writer though you are, I would hope you could come up with something a tad more original."

Old saw indeed! Strychnine was a classic poison, she lamented, famous throughout detective fiction. But Kitty would hear none of it.

Harriet decided to be big about it; after all, she didn't want a reputation as the sort of writer who simply couldn't let go of a word she'd written. She was no rank amateur. She could bear the burden of criticism; being showered with the unwanted opinions of others was inevitable in her profession. And so she set herself to the painful task of revising the ending of *Pearls Before Swine*. That in turn meant that she had to revise a number of passages in the story, but she did not complain.

In fact, by the time she mailed off her new version, she was quite pleased with it. This time, Lord Wiggins offered Monroe a piece of chocolate cake chock-full of Catapres. It had been a bit tricky for dear Harry to obtain the drug, but she had managed it. Monroe had suffered heart failure thirty minutes after eating his dessert, allowing Lord Harold all the time in the world to leave the scene. It was certainly not as popular in fiction as strychnine, so Harriet thought Kitty might be contented.

Kitty hated it.

"You are going to have to do better than this. Catapres? Could you possibly devise anything more obscure? No reader is going to recognize this as a poison. Crimeny, it sounds like a resort that would appeal to people from the Bronx."

Not being from New York, Harriet couldn't guess what Kitty meant by her last remark. She steamed and stewed for a while and then went back to work. Now it was a challenge.

In version three, Lord Harold arranged for Monroe to be bitten repeatedly by a Gila monster.

"What utter nonsense!" Kitty wrote. "How the heck does an English lord happen to have a twenty-inch Arizona desert lizard hanging about?"

Even Harriet had to admit that the Gila monster wasn't her best effort. She spent a little more time on version four. There might not be many Gila monsters roaming about the English countryside, but she knew that rhododendrons weren't so rare. And so it was that Lord Harold made tea from the deadly leaves, and served it with scones to the unsuspecting Monroe.

"Harriet, please. You are trying my patience. This is so unimaginative. If you want this to sell anywhere outside of the East Lansing Lawn and Garden Club, rewrite."

Harriet wasn't even sure how she found the nerve to try a fifth time. She needed to publish annually to maintain the lifestyle to which she had become accustomed, and Kitty's demands were delaying the publication date of *Pearls Before Swine*. She had arranged to attend the annual Mystery World Awards Banquet, the Whodundunits. Her flight from Los Angeles to New York was booked, the hotel arrangements made. But now she wasn't sure she could face the inquires of her fellow authors; they were bound to notice that the next Lord Harold Wiggins book had not arrived on schedule.

She had grown more bitter about this trial by rewrite as each day passed. But once more she devised an ending, this time with antimony, arranging elaborate plot devices to allow Lord Harold Wiggins access to an industrial poison. And still Kitty wasn't satisfied.

As she held Kitty's fifth nasty letter, something snapped inside Harriet. She began to see Kitty as the root of all evil in her life. Before Kitty, she had been happy. Nothing much had disturbed the world dear Harry had shared with her; he had paid her way, she had kept him alive. It seemed to Harriet that Kitty wanted to kill them both. Well, Harriet decided, we'll see who kills whom.

The idea began to comfort her. She would attend the Whodundunits, slip a little something into Kitty's wine and sit back and enjoy her evening, knowing that her troubles would soon be over. In a room full of people who were constantly dreaming up ways for other people to die, the death of a woman who was almost universally despised by them would present a monumental problem for New York's Finest.

Harriet became quite delighted at the prospect. She did not doubt that she would be able to kill. After all, she had already murdered over thirty characters. (Three was Harriet's lucky number, and so she made it the average body count in her books.) Among those thirty characters were a great many individuals she liked better than Kitty Craig.

For her first real life murder, she would need something special. For weeks, she consulted her reference works on poison. She searched the pages of *A Panorama of Poisonous Plants, Powders, and Potions*. She studied the listings in *Lyle's Lethal Liquids*, even considered *Conroy's Compendium of Caustics*. But her most promising candidates were found in *Everyday Toxic Substances: Our Dangerous Friends*.

She made a long list of factors to consider. Reaction time. What would dear Harry say? Quick, she decided. Very quick and highly toxic. Kitty in prolonged, relentless pain was a tempting picture, but she concluded that having Ms. Craig dead before the salads were served was preferable; attention-getting though agonizing death throes are, it might put a bit of a damper on the evening's festivities.

The poison would need to be something that could be transported easily; if discovered among her belongings, it could not seem out of place. Her final prerequisite was that it be something she could obtain without raising suspicions.

After hours of concentrated effort, she finally had the means in hand and the logistics of delivering it well planned.

She hummed a happy little tune as she latched her suitcase closed and carried it to the front door. She sat in the entry, lovingly caressing the corners of her carry-on bag. Harriet was far too careful to have her plans spoiled by the possibility of lost luggage. She could hardly contain her excitement when the taxicab pulled up in her driveway and tooted its horn.

She was pleased to learn that she was not the type to get the pre-homicidal jitters. Dear Harry would be thrilled to find his creator so calm, so poised, so at ease with this new role. Indeed, both flight attendants and Mr. Johnson, the gentleman seated next to her in first class, found her a charming traveling companion.

Harriet couldn't remember the last time she had really noticed or been noticed by a man, and she gloried in the handsome Mr. Johnson's attentions. At first she wondered if deadly intentions might somehow serve as an aphrodisiac. But then Mr. Johnson confessed himself to be a great fan of Lord Harold Wiggins, and said he recognized Harriet from her cover photo. This was sheer flattery, she was certain, as she hadn't updated that photo in ten years.

In New York, he accompanied her to baggage claim, and helped her to retrieve her suitcase. As he carried it for her, she learned that he was staying at the same hotel. Harriet was sure at that moment that this was her lucky day.

It was as they stood waiting for a taxi that Harriet saw the young woman. Ticket jacket in hand, no doubt late for a plane, she ran across the opposite sidewalk. Looking directly at Harriet, she took two quick steps off the curb; Harriet screamed a warning in her mind that never reached her lips—the driver had even less of a chance to stop the car in time. The car struck the young woman and hurled her several yards down the street.

Harriet experienced the moments of intense awareness that come to those who are caught as unwilling spectators to such events: with absolute clarity she heard the grating screech of the car's brakes, saw the disbelief on the woman's face at the moment of impact, heard the dull thud as it launched her into an unnatural and graceless flight, watched the awful landing.

Harriet rushed toward the woman and stood frozen above her. There could be no doubt that the woman was dead. Heads and necks are not configured in the same way on the living. Harriet had never before stood so close to the dead.

In contrast to the clarity of those few moments was the enveloping confusion which followed. Somehow, she ended up back inside the terminal, sitting on a plastic chair next to Mr. Johnson, who held her as she cried.

He didn't question Harriet's purchase of an immediate return flight; he took the same one back to Los Angeles. She left her carry-on bag on the plane.

Mrs. Johnson opened the envelope from Shoehorn, Dunstreet and Matthews without the sense of dread she had come to expect.

Dear Harriet,

    You are no doubt as saddened as we are about the unfortunate incident at the Whodundunits. Why no one who knew the Heimlich manuever could have been there at the moment Ms. Craig choked on that chicken bone is beyond me. We're all brushing up on our CPR here at SDM.

    I look forward to serving as your new editor. I've browsed through several of the drafts you sent to Ms. Craig, and I hope you won't mind my saying that I believe your first effort was the best. Will you be too angry with me if I send it along as is?

Lord Harold's Biggest Fan,
Lana Dunstreet

    P.S. Best wishes on your recent marriage. I hope Mr. Johnson realizes how lucky he is.

PART II

THE PRIVATE INVESTIGATOR

The second major classification of detective fiction features the private investigator as the detective. Unlike the amateur detective, who is a fictional creation, the private investigator has a counterpart in real life. The term "private eye," often applied to this fictional detective, was originally used in connection with the operatives of the Pinkerton Detective Agency, the first national private detective agency in the United States, based in Chicago. The Pinkerton logo was a wide-open eye, and the motto was "We Never Sleep." Thus the "private eye" was created.

"Private-eye" or tough "hard-boiled" detective fiction is the classification most dominated by American writers. Authors originally found their subject matter in a post-World War I America filled with chaos and violence. The Great Depression of the 1930s created poverty and crime. Prohibition nurtured gangster mobs with gun battles in the city streets. The American public at the time was fascinated by the likes of gangsters Al Capone and John Dillinger, and the outlaw team of Bonnie Parker and Clyde Barrow.

Hard-boiled detective writers portrayed this side of American life first in the inexpensive action pulp magazines that appeared en masse soon after World War I. The pulp reading audience devoured this new type of detective fiction, filled with rapid action, colloquial language, violent crimes, and graphic violence. *Black Mask* magazine was the best-known of the pulps, followed by *Dime Detective*, *Thrilling Detective*, and many more.

The major creators of the hard-boiled school of detective fiction were Dashiell Hammett and Raymond Chandler. Both writers began by writing for the pulps, especially *Black Mask*. Hammett, who worked as an operative for the Pinkerton Detective Agency for eight years, knew the "private eye" world first hand. Many of his characters and plots were based on his own field experiences. It is Hammett who gives mystery readers Sam Spade in *The Maltese Falcon* (1930), the Continental Op in *The Dain Curse* (1928), and Nick and Nora Charles in *The Thin Man* (1934), all private eyes who help establish the characteristics of the hard-boiled sleuth. Raymond Chandler follows in Hammett's footsteps with Philip Marlowe, the tough, wise-cracking P.I. introduced in *The Big Sleep* (1939). Hammett and Chandler were joined by other outstanding writers of the hard-boiled school: John D. MacDonald, Ross Macdonald, John Daly, Chester Himes, James M. Cain, and others.

These writers established a clear set of characteristics for the hard-boiled school of writing. The setting of the stories was always the city, filled with temptations, corruption, and dangers. The personality of the city, whether Los Angeles, San Francisco, or New York, was strong enough to make it a major character in the story. The only way a person can survive in the city is to know it better than anyone else. The man who does this is the private eye.

The private investigator, almost always male at this time, is also strictly defined by these authors. He is a loner, free from all social and family ties, who prefers to isolate himself from regular human relationships. He is intelligent, sometimes even college educated, which allows him to rapidly size up people and situations. He is in very good physical condition, and expected to take lots of physical punishment. He is good with his fists and a gun, and prefers to go armed in the city. Insults and wisecracks are his way of dealing with problems, and he never allows himself to show pain or fear.

This type of operative is both cynical and idealistic, a complex character. He distrusts the police, whom he sees as brutal and corrupt; the rich, whom he blames for most of society's problems; and beautiful women, whom he believes are potentially destructive or corrupt. Yet he is often the champion of the outcast, the vulnerable, and the downtrodden. He will carry an investigation through to the end, regardless of the cost, to insure justice. He is basically honorable, has a strict sense of duty, and is often motivated by compassion. This is the typical P.I. as created by the founders of the hard-boiled category.

However, later writers in the P.I. tradition expand the perimeters and deviate from the original characteristics in innovative ways. Erle Stanley Gardner presents the male-female private-eye partnership of Donald Lam and Bertha Cool. Rex Stout gives the P.I. a sidekick or "legman" when he introduces private investigator Nero Wolfe and his narrator sidekick Archie Goodwin. More contemporary authors, such as Robert B. Parker, Harlan Coben, Robert Crais, Dennis Lehane, and Rick Riordan allow their P.I.s to have valuable friendships, necessary sidekicks, adopted family members, and even long-term relationships with intelligent and strong women.

And perhaps the best innovation in the private-eye world has to do with women. The original world of the hard-boiled detective was clearly a male one, where women were suspect and dangerous. In 1937, Rex Stout changed that by introducing Dol Bonner, a female private investigator of considerable talent, in *The Hand in the Glove*. However, it was not until the 1970s, an era that encouraged the empowerment of women, that the tough, modern female P.I. finally emerged. P.D. James establishes the criteria for this type of character in her creation of Cordelia Grey in *An Unsuitable Job for a Woman* (1972). But she is quickly followed by other female writers who present their own version of the female P.I. Best known are Marcia Muller for Sharon McCone, Sue Grafton for Kinsey Milhone, Liza Cody for Anna Lee, Karen Kijewski for Kat Colorado, Carolina Garcia-Aguilera for Lupe Solano, and Sara Paretsky for her powerful creation, V. I. Warshawski.

In V. I. Warshawski the contemporary female private eye is defined. She is both intelligent and in excellent physical condition, running miles a day to stay in shape. She is good with a gun and in other areas of self-defense. She has relationships with men, but on her own terms, and never really trusts them. The job comes first. She has great personal courage, and sees the investigation through to the end, so justice can be done. She has trustworthy but eccentric friends. And in V. I.'s case, she is a terrible housekeeper and not necessarily good with children.

However, like her male counterparts, she knows her city, in this case Chicago, and survives as a private eye in a world where many cannot survive at all, proving that these female P.I.s are not suspect, but they are dangerous.

This type of detective fiction is often compared with the Western genre by critics, having a lone figure who must stand for justice without the aid of the society that needs protection. However, the main issues the contemporary private eye must deal with center around the destructive/corruptive powers of the city, the privilege of the upper classes, the manipulation of important institutions, and the constantly shifting power base of big business, whether legal or illegal.

Readers of this classification of detective fiction come to know both the glamour and the grimness of the city streets. It is the private investigator, male or female, who must walk these streets, defend the victims, hunt down the killers, and insure justice.

CRITICAL ESSAYS AND COMMENTARIES

RAYMOND CHANDLER

The Simple Art of Murder

Fiction in any form has always intended to be realistic. Old-fashioned novels which now seem stilted and artificial to the point of burlesque did not appear that way to the people who first read them. Writers like Fielding and Smollett could seem realistic in the modern sense because they dealt largely with uninhibited characters, many of whom were about two jumps ahead of the police, but Jane Austen's chronicles of highly inhibited people against a background of rural gentility seem real enough psychologically. There is plenty of that kind of social and emotional hypocrisy around today. Add to it a liberal dose of intellectual pretentiousness and you get the tone of the book page in your daily paper and the earnest and fatuous atmosphere breathed by discussion groups in little clubs. These are the people who make best-sellers, which are promotional jobs based on a sort of indirect snob-appeal, carefully escorted by the trained seals of the critical fraternity, and lovingly tended and watered by certain much too powerful pressure groups whose business is selling books, although they would like you to think they are fostering culture. Just get a little behind in your payments and you will find out how idealistic they are.

The detective story for a variety of reasons can seldom be promoted. It is usually about murder and hence lacks the element of uplift. Murder, which is a frustration of the individual and hence a frustration of the race, may, and in fact has, a good deal of sociological implication. But it has been going on too long for it to be news. If the mystery novel is at all realistic (which it very seldom is) it is written in a certain spirit of detachment; otherwise nobody but a psychopath would want to write it or read it. The murder novel has also a depressing way of minding its own business, solving its own problems and answering its own questions. There is nothing left to discuss, except whether it was well enough written to be good fiction, and the people who make up the half-million sales wouldn't know that anyway. The detection of quality in writing is difficult enough even for those who make a career of the job, without paying too much attention to the matter of advance sales.

The detective story (perhaps I had better call it that, since the English formula still dominates the trade) has to find its public by a slow process of distillation. That it does do this, and holds on thereafter with such tenacity, is a fact; the reasons for it are a study for more patient minds than mine. Nor is it any part of my thesis to maintain that it is a vital and significant form of art. There are no vital and significant forms of art; there is only art, and precious little of that. The growth of populations has in no way increased the amount; it has merely increased the adeptness with which substitutes can be produced and packaged.

Yet the detective story, even in its most conventional form, is difficult to write well. Good specimens of the art are much rarer than good serious novels. Rather second-rate items outlast most of the high velocity fiction, and a great many that should never have been born simply refuse to die at all. They are as durable as the statues in public parks and just about that dull. This is very annoying to people of what is called discernment. They do not like it that penetrating and important works of fiction of a few years back stand on their special shelf in the library marked "Best-Sellers of Yesteryear," and nobody goes near them but an occasional shortsighted customer who bends down, peers briefly and hurries away; while old ladies jostle each other at the mystery shelf to grab off some item of the same vintage with a title like *The Triple Petunia Murder Case*, or *Inspector Pinchbottle to the Rescue*. They do not like it that "really important books" get dusty on the reprint counter, while *Death Wears Yellow Garters* is put out in editions of fifty or one hundred thousand copies on the news-stands of the country, and is obviously not there just to say goodbye.

To tell you the truth, I do not like it very much myself. In my less stilted moments I too write detective stories, and all this immortality makes just a little too much competition. Even Einstein couldn't get very far if three hundred treatises of the higher physics were published every year, and several thousand others in some form or other were hanging around in excellent condition, and being read too. Hemingway says somewhere that the good writer competes only with the dead. The good detective story writer (there must after all be a few) competes not only with all the unburied dead but with all the hosts of the living as well. And on almost equal terms; for it is one of the qualities of this kind of writing that the thing that makes people read it never goes out of style. The hero's tie may be a little off the mode and the good gray inspector may arrive in a dogcart instead of a streamlined sedan with siren screaming, but what he does when he gets there is the same old futzing around with timetables and bits of charred paper and who trampled the jolly old flowering arbutus under the library window.

I have, however, a less sordid interest in the matter. It seems to me that production of detective stories on so large a scale, and by writers whose immediate reward is small and whose need of critical praise is almost nil, would not be possible at all if the job took any talent. In that sense the raised eyebrow of the critic and the shoddy merchandizing of the publisher are perfectly logical. The average detective story is probably no worse than the average novel, but you never see the average novel. It doesn't get published. The average—or only slightly above average—detective story does. Not only is it published but it is sold in small quantities to rental libraries, and it is read. There are even a few optimists who buy it at the full retail price of two dollars, because it looks so fresh and new, and there is a picture of a corpse on the cover. And the strange thing is that this average, more than middling dull, pooped-out piece of utterly unreal and mechanical fiction is not terribly different from what are called the masterpieces of the art. It drags on a little more slowly, the dialogue is a little grayer, the cardboard out of which the characters are cut is a shade thinner, and the cheating is a little more obvious; but it is the same kind of book. Whereas the good novel is not at all the same kind of book as the bad novel. It is about entirely different things. But the good detective story and the bad detective story are about exactly the same things, and they are about them in very much the same way. There are reasons for this too, and reasons for the reasons; there always are.

I suppose the principal dilemma of the traditional or classic or straight-deductive or logic—and—deduction novel of detection is that for any approach to perfection it demands a combination of qualities not found in the same mind. The cool-headed constructionist does not also come across with lively characters, sharp dialogue, a sense of pace and an acute use of observed detail. The grim logician has as much atmosphere as a drawing-board. The scientific sleuth has a nice new shiny laboratory, but I'm sorry I can't remember the face. The fellow who can write you a vivid and colorful prose simply won't be bothered with the coolie labor of breaking down unbreakable alibis. The master of rare knowledge is living psychologically in the age of the hoop skirt. If you know all you should know about ceramics and Egyptian needle-work, you don't know anything at all about the police. If you know that platinum won't melt under about 2800 degrees F. by itself, but will melt at the glance of a pair of deep blue eyes when put close to a bar of lead, then you don't know how men make love in the twentieth century. And if you know enough about the elegant flânerie of the pre-war French Riviera to lay your story in that locale, you don't know that a couple of capsules of barbital small enough to be swallowed will not only not kill a man—they will not even put him to sleep, if he fights against them.

Every detective story writer makes mistakes, and none will ever know as much as he should. Conan Doyle made mistakes which completely invalidated some of his stories, but he was a pioneer, and Sherlock Holmes after all is mostly an attitude and a few dozen lines of unforgettable dialogue. It is the ladies and gentlemen of what Mr. Howard Haycraft (in his book *Murder for Pleasure*) calls the Golden Age of detective fiction that really get me down. This age is not remote. For Mr. Haycraft's purpose it starts after the first World War and lasts up to about 1930. For all practical purposes it is still here. Two-thirds or three-quarters of all the detective stories published still adhere to the formula the giants of this era created, perfected, polished and sold to the world as problems in logic and deduction. These are stern words, but be not alarmed. They are only words. Let us glance at one of the glories of the literature, an acknowledged masterpiece of the art of fooling the reader without cheating him. It is called *The Red House Mystery*, was written by A. A. Milne, and has been named by Alexander Woollcott (rather a fast man with a superlative) "one of the three best mystery stories of all time." Words of that size are not spoken lightly. The book was published in 1922, but is quite timeless, and might as easily have been published in July 1939, or, with a few slight changes, last week. It ran thirteen editions and seems to have been in print, in the original format, for about sixteen years. That happens to few books of any kind. It is an agreeable book, light, amusing in the *Punch* style, written with a deceptive smoothness that is not as easy as it looks.

It concerns Mark Ablett's impersonation of his brother Robert, as a hoax on his friends. Mark is the owner of the Red House, a typical laburnum-and-lodge-gate English country house, and he has a secretary who encourages him and abets him in this impersonation, because the secretary is going to murder him, if he pulls it off. Nobody around the Red House has ever seen Robert, fifteen years absent in Australia, known to them by repute as a no-good. A letter from Robert is talked about, but never shown. It announces his arrival, and Mark hints it will not be a pleasant occasion. One afternoon, then, the supposed Robert arrives, identifies himself to a couple of servants, is shown into the study, and Mark (according to testimony at the inquest) goes in after him. Robert is then found dead on the floor with a bullet hole in his face, and of course Mark has vanished into thin air. Arrive the police, suspect Mark must be the murderer, remove the debris and proceed with the investigation, and in due course, with the inquest.

Milne is aware of one very difficult hurdle and tries as well as he can to get over it. Since the secretary is going to murder Mark once he has established himself as Robert, the impersonation has to continue on and fool the police. Since, also, everybody around the Red House knows Mark intimately, disguise is necessary. This is achieved by shaving off Mark's beard, roughening his hands ("not the hands of a manicured gentlemen"—testimony) and the use of a gruff voice and rough manner. But this is not enough. The cops are going to have the body and the clothes on it and whatever is in the pockets. Therefore none of this must suggest Mark. Milne therefore works like a switch engine to put over the motivation that Mark is such a thoroughly conceited performer that he dresses the part down to the socks and underwear (from all of which the secretary has removed the maker's labels), like a ham blacking himself all over to play Othello. If the reader will buy this (and the sales record shows he must have) Milne figures he is solid. Yet, however light in texture the story may be, it is offered as a problem of logic and deduction. If it is not that, it is nothing at all. There is nothing else for it to be. If the situation is false, you cannot even accept it as a light novel, for there is no story for the light novel to be about. If the problem does not contain the elements of truth and plausibility, it is no problem; if the logic is an illusion, there is nothing to deduce. If the impersonation is impossible once the reader is told the conditions it must fulfill, then the whole thing is a fraud. Not a deliberate fraud, because Milne would not have written the story if he had known what he was up against. He is up against a number of deadly things, none of which he even considers. Nor, apparently, does the casual reader, who wants to like the story, hence takes it at its face value. But the reader is not called upon to know the facts of life; it is the author who is the expert in the case. Here is what this author ignores:

1. The coroner holds formal jury inquest on a body for which no competent legal identification is offered. A coroner, usually in a big city, will sometimes hold inquest on a body that *cannot* be identified, if the record of such an inquest has or may have a value (fire, disaster, evidence of murder, etc.). No such reason exists here, and there is no one to identify the body. A couple of witnesses said the man said he was Robert Ablett. This is mere presumption, and has weight only if nothing conflicts with it. Identification is a condition precedent to an inquest. Even in death a man has a right to his own identity. The coroner will, wherever humanly possible, enforce that right. To neglect it would be a violation of his office.

2. Since Mark Ablett, missing and suspected of the murder, cannot defend himself, all evidence of his movements before and after the murder is vital (as also whether he has money to run away on); yet all such evidence is given by the man closest to the murder, and is without corroboration. It is automatically suspect until proved true.

3. The police find by direct investigation that Robert Ablett was not well thought of in his native village. Somebody there must have known him. No such person was brought to the inquest. (The story couldn't stand it.)

4. The police know there is an element of threat in Robert's supposed visit, and that it is connected with the murder must be obvious to them. Yet they make no attempt to check Robert in Australia, or find out what character he had there, or what associates, or even if he actually came to England, and with whom. (If they had, they would have found out he had been dead three years.)

5. The police surgeon examines the body with a recently shaved beard (exposing unweathered skin), artificially roughened hands, yet the body of a wealthy, soft-living man, long resident in a cool climate. Robert was a rough individual and had lived fifteen years in Australia. That is the surgeon's information. It is impossible he would have noticed nothing to conflict with it.

6. The clothes are nameless, empty, and have had the labels removed. Yet the man wearing them asserted an identity. The presumption that he was not what he said he was is overpowering. Nothing whatever is done about this peculiar circumstance. It is never even mentioned as being peculiar.

7. A man is missing, a well-known local man, and a body in the morgue closely resembles him. It is impossible that the police should not at once eliminate the chance that the missing man *is* the dead man. Nothing would be easier than to prove it. Not even to think of it is incredible. It makes idiots of the police, so that a brash amateur may startle the world with a fake solution.

The detective in the case is an insouciant gent named Antony Gillingham, a nice lad with a cheery eye, a cozy little flat in London, and that airy manner. He is not making any money on the assignment, but is always available when the local gendarmerie loses its notebook. The English police seem to endure him with their customary stoicism; but I shudder to think of what the boys down at the Homicide Bureau in my city would do to him.

There are less plausible examples of the art than this. In *Trent's Last Case* (often called "the perfect detective story") you have to accept the premise that a giant of international finance, whose lightest frown makes Wall Street quiver like a chihuahua, will plot his own death so as to hang his secretary, and that the secretary when pinched will maintain an aristocratic silence; the old Etonian in him maybe. I have known relatively few international financiers, but I rather think the author of this novel has (if possible) known fewer. There is one by Freeman Wills Crofts (the soundest builder of them all when he doesn't get too fancy) wherein a murderer by the aid of makeup, split second timing, and some very sweet evasive action, impersonates the man he has just killed and thereby gets him alive and distant from the place of the crime. There is one of Dorothy Sayers' in which a man is murdered alone at night in his house by a mechanically released weight which works because he always turns the radio on at just such a moment, always stands in just such a position in front of it, and always bends over just so far. A couple of inches either way and the customers would get a rain check. This is what is vulgarly known as having God sit in your lap; a murderer who needs that much help from Providence must be in the wrong business. And there is a scheme of Agatha Christie's featuring M. Hercule Poirot, that ingenius Belgian who talks in a literal translation of school-boy French, wherein, by duly messing around with his "little gray cells," M. Poirot decides that nobody on a certain through sleeper could have done the murder alone, therefore everybody did it together, breaking the process down into a series of simple operations, like assembling an egg-beater. This is the type that is guaranteed to knock the keenest mind for a loop. Only a halfwit could guess it.

There are much better plots by these same writers and by others of their school. There may be one somewhere that would really stand up under close scrutiny. It would be fun to read it, even if I did have to go back to page 47 and refresh my memory about exactly what time the second gardener potted the prize-winning tearose begonia. There is nothing new about these stories and nothing old. The ones I mentioned are all English only because the authorities (such as they are) seem to feel the English writers had an edge in this dreary routine, and that the Americans, (even the creator of Philo Vance—probably the most asinine character in detective fiction) only made the Junior Varsity.

This, the classic detective story, has learned nothing and forgotten nothing. It is the story you will find almost any week in the big shiny magazines, handsomely illustrated, and paying due deference to virginal love and the right kind of luxury goods. Perhaps the tempo has become a trifle faster, and the dialogue a little more glib. There are more frozen daiquiris and stingers ordered, and fewer glasses of crusty old port; more clothes by *Vogue*, and décors by the *House Beautiful*, more chic, but not more truth. We spend more time in Miami hotels and Cape Cod summer colonies and go not so often down by the old gray sundial in the Elizabethan garden. But fundamentally it is the same careful grouping of suspects, the same utterly incomprehensible trick of how somebody stabbed Mrs. Pottington Postlethwaite III with the solid platinum poignard just as she flatted on the top note of the Bell Song from *Lakmé* in the presence of fifteen ill-assorted guests; the same ingenue in fur-trimmed pajamas screaming in the night to make the company pop in and out of doors and ball up the timetable; the same moody silence next day as they sit around sipping Singapore slings and sneering at each other, while the flat-feet crawl to and fro under the Persian rugs, with their derby hats on.

Personally I like the English style better. It is not quite so brittle, and the people as a rule, just wear clothes and drink drinks. There is more sense of background, as if Cheesecake Manor really existed all around and not just the part the camera sees; there are more long walks over the Downs and the characters don't all try to behave as if they had just been tested by MGM. The English may not always be the best writers in the world, but they are incomparably the best dull writers.

There is a very simple statement to be made about all these stories: they do not really come off intellectually as problems, and they do not come off artistically as fiction. They are too contrived, and too little aware of what goes on in the world. They try to be honest, but honesty is an art. The poor writer is dishonest without knowing it, and the fairly good one can be dishonest because he doesn't know what to be honest about. He thinks a complicated murder scheme which baffles the lazy reader, who won't be bothered itemizing the details, will also baffle the police, whose business is with details. The boys with their feet on the desks know that the easiest murder case in the world to break is the one somebody tried to get very cute with; the one that really bothers them is the murder somebody only thought of two minutes before he pulled it off. But if the writers of this fiction wrote about the kind of murders that happen, they would also have to write about the authentic flavor of life as it is lived. And since they cannot do that, they pretend that what they do is what should be done. Which is begging the question—and the best of them know it.

In her introduction to the first *Omnibus of Crime*, Dorothy Sayers wrote: "It (the detective story) does not, and by hypothesis never can, attain the loftiest level of literary achievement." And she suggested somewhere else that this is because it is a "literature of escape" and not "a literature of expression." I do not know what the loftiest level of literary achievement is: neither did Aeschylus or Shakespeare; neither does Miss Sayers. Other things being equal, which they never are, a more powerful theme will provoke a more powerful performance. Yet some very dull books have been written about God, and some very fine ones about how to make a living and stay fairly honest. It is always a matter of who writes the stuff, and what he has in him to write it with. As for literature of expression and literature of escape, this is critics' jargon, a use of abstract words as if they had absolute meanings. Everything written with vitality expresses that vitality; there are no dull subjects, only dull minds. All men who read escape from something else into what lies behind the printed page; the quality of the dream may be argued, but its release has become a functional necessity. All men must escape at times from the deadly rhythm of their private thoughts. It is part of the process of life among thinking beings. It is one of the things that distinguish them from the three-toed sloth; he apparently—one can never be quite sure—is perfectly content hanging upside down on a branch, and not even reading Walter Lippman. I hold no particular brief for the detective story as the ideal escape. I merely say that *all* reading for pleasure is escape, whether it be Greek, mathematics, astronomy, Benedetto Croce, or *The Diary of the Forgotten Man.* To say otherwise is to be an intellectual snob, and a juvenile at the art of living.

I do not think such considerations moved Miss Dorothy Sayers to her essay in critical futility.

I think what was really gnawing at her mind was the slow realization that her kind of detective story was an arid formula which could not even satisfy its own implications. It was second-grade literature because it was not about the things that could make first-grade literature. If it started out to be about real people (and she could write about them—her minor characters show that), they must very soon do unreal things in order to form the artificial pattern required by the plot. When they did unreal things, they ceased to be real themselves. They became puppets and cardboard lovers and papier mâché villains and detectives of exquisite and impossible gentility. The only kind of writer who could be happy with these properties was the one who did not know what reality was. Dorothy Sayers' own stories show that she was annoyed by this triteness; the weakest element in them is the part that makes them detective stories, the strongest the part which could be removed without touching the "problem of logic and deduction." Yet she could not or would not give her characters their heads and let them make their own mystery. It took a much simpler and more direct mind than hers to do that.

In the *Long Week-End*, which is a drastically competent account of English life and manners in the decade following the first World War, Robert Graves and Alan Hodge gave some attention to the detective story. They were just as traditionally English as the ornaments of the Golden Age, and they wrote of the time in which these writers were almost as well-known as any writers in the world. Their books in one form or another sold into the millions, and in a dozen languages. These were the people who fixed the form and established the rules and founded the famous Detection Club, which is a Parnassus of English writers of mystery. Its roster includes practically every important writer of detective fiction since Conan Doyle. But Graves and Hodge decided that during this whole period only one first-class writer had written detective stories at all. An American, Dashiell Hammett. Traditional or not, Graves and Hodge were not fuddy-duddy connoisseurs of the second rate; they could see what went on in the world and that the detective story of their time didn't; and they were aware that writers who have the vision and the ability to produce real fiction do not produce unreal fiction.

How original a writer Hammett really was, it isn't easy to decide now, even if it mattered. He was one of a group, the only one who achieved critical recognition, but not the only one who wrote or tried to write realistic mystery fiction. All literary movements are like this; some one individual is picked out to represent the whole movement; he is usually the culmination of the movement. Hammett was the ace performer, but there is nothing in his work that is not implicit in the early novels and short stories of Hemingway. Yet for all I know, Hemingway may have learned something from Hammett, as well as from writers like Dreiser, Ring Lardner, Carl Sandburg, Sherwood Anderson and himself. A rather revolutionary debunking of both the language and material of fiction had been going on for some time. It probably started in poetry; almost everything does. You can take it clear back to Walt Whitman, if you like. But Hammett applied it to the detective story, and this, because of its heavy crust of English gentility and American pseudo-gentility, was pretty hard to get moving. I doubt that Hammett had any deliberate artistic aims whatever; he was trying to make a living by writing something he had first hand information about. He made some of it up; all writers do; but it had a basis in fact; it was made up out of real things. The only reality the English detection writers knew was the conversational accent of Surbiton and Bognor Regis. If they wrote about dukes and Venetian vases, they knew no more about them out of their own experience than the well-heeled Hollywood character knows about the French Modernists that hang in his Bel-Air château or the semi-antique Chippendale-cum-cobbler's bench that he uses for a coffee table. Hammett took murder out of the Venetian vase and dropped it into the alley; it doesn't have to stay there forever, but it was a good idea to begin by getting as far as possible from Emily Post's idea of how a well-bred debutante gnaws a chicken wing. He wrote at first (and almost to the end) for people with a sharp, aggressive attitude to life. They were not afraid of the seamy side of things; they lived there. Violence did not dismay them; it was right down their street.

Hammett gave murder back to the kind of people that commit it for reasons, not just to provide a corpse; and with the means at hand, not with hand-wrought duelling pistols, curare, and tropical fish. He put these people down on paper as they are, and he made them talk and think in the language they customarily used for these purposes. He had style, but his audience didn't know it, because it was in a language not supposed to be capable of such refinements. They thought they were getting a good meaty melodrama written in the kind of lingo they imagined they spoke themselves. It was, in a sense, but it was much more. All language begins with speech, and the speech of common men at that, but when it develops to the point of becoming a literary medium it only looks like speech. Hammett's style at its worst was almost as formalized as a page of Marius the Epicurean; at its best it could say almost anything. I believe this style, which does not belong to Hammett or to anybody, but is the American language (and not even exclusively that any more), can say things he did not know how to say or feel the need of saying. In his hands it had no overtones, left no echo, evoked no image beyond a distant hill. He is said to have lacked heart, yet the story he thought most of himself is the record of a man's devotion to a friend. He was spare, frugal, hardboiled, but he did over and over again what only the best writers can ever do at all. He wrote scenes that seemed never to have been written before.

With all this he did not wreck the formal detective story. Nobody can; production demands a form that can be produced. Realism takes too much talent, too much knowledge, too much awareness. Hammett may have loosened it up a little here, and sharpened it a little there. Certainly all but the stupidest and most meretricious writers are more conscious of their artificiality than they used to be. And he demonstrated that the detective story can be important writing. *The Maltese Falcon* may or may not be a work of genius, but an art which is capable of it is not "by hypothesis" incapable of anything. Once a detective story can be as good as this, only the pedants will deny that it *could* be even better. Hammett did something else, he made the detective story fun to write, not an exhausting concatenation of insignificant clues. Without him there might not have been a regional mystery as clever as Percival Wilde's *Inquest*, or an ironic study as able as Raymond Postgate's *Verdict of Twelve*, or a savage piece of intellectual double-talk like Kenneth Fearing's *The Dagger of the Mind*, or a tragi-comic idealization of the murderer as in Donald Henderson's *Mr. Bowling Buys a Newspaper*, or even a gay and intriguing Hollywoodian gambol like Richard Sale's *Lazarus No. 7*.

The realistic style is easy to abuse: from haste, from lack of awareness, from inability to bridge the chasm that lies between what a writer would like to be able to say and what he actually knows how to say. It is easy to fake; brutality is not strength, flipness is not wit, edge-of-the-chair writing can be as boring as flat writing; dalliance with promiscuous blondes can be very dull stuff when described by goaty young men with no other purpose in mind than to describe dalliance with promiscuous blondes. There has been so much of this sort of thing that if a character in a detective story says, "Yeah," the author is automatically a Hammett imitator.

And there are still quite a few people around who say that Hammett did not write detective stories at all, merely hard-boiled chronicles of mean streets with a perfunctory mystery element dropped in like the olive in a martini. These are the flustered old ladies—of both sexes (or no sex) and almost all ages—who like their murders scented with magnolia blossoms and do not care to be reminded that murder is an act of infinite cruelty, even if the perpetrators sometimes look like playboys or college professors or nice motherly women with softly graying hair. There are also a few badly-scared champions of the formal or the classic mystery who think no story is a detective story which does not pose a formal and exact problem and arrange the clues around it with neat labels on them. Such would point out, for example, that in reading *The Maltese Falcon* no one concerns himself with who killed Spade's partner, Archer (which is the only formal problem of the story) because the reader is kept thinking about something else. Yet in *The Glass Key* the reader is constantly reminded that the question is who killed Taylor Henry, and exactly the same effect is obtained; an effect of movement, intrigue, cross-purposes and the gradual elucidation of character, which is all the detective story has any right to be about anyway. The rest is spillikins in the parlor.

But all this (and Hammett too) is for me not quite enough. The realist in murder writes of a world in which gangsters can rule nations and almost rule cities, in which hotels and apartment houses and celebrated restaurants are owned by men who made their money out of brothels, in which a screen star can be the fingerman for a mob, and the nice man down the hall is a boss of the numbers racket; a world where a judge with a cellar full of bootleg liquor can send a man to jail for having a pint in his pocket, where the mayor of your town may have condoned murder as an instrument of money-making, where no man can walk down a dark street in safety because law and order are things we talk about but refrain from practising; a world where you may witness a hold-up in broad daylight and see who did it, but you will fade quickly back into the crowd rather than tell anyone, because the hold-up men may have friends with long guns, or the police may not like your testimony, and in any case the shyster for the defense will be allowed to abuse and vilify you in open court, before a jury of selected morons, without any but the most perfunctory interference from a political judge.

It is not a very fragrant world, but it is the world you live in, and certain writers with tough minds and a cool spirit of detachment can make very interesting and even amusing patterns out of it. It is not funny that a man should be killed, but it is sometimes funny that he should be killed for so little, and that his death should be the coin of what we call civilization. All this still is not quite enough.

In everything that can be called art there is a quality of redemption. It may be pure tragedy, if it is high tragedy, and it may be pity and irony, and it may be the raucous laughter of the strong man. But down these mean streets a man must go who is not himself mean, who is neither tarnished nor afraid. The detective in this kind of story must be such a man. He is the hero, he is everything. He must be a complete man and a common man and yet an unusual man. He must be, to use a rather weathered phrase, a man of honor, by instinct, by inevitability, without thought of it, and certainly without saying it. He must be the best man in his world and a good enough man for any world. I do not care much about his private life; he is neither a eunuch nor a satyr; I think he might seduce a duchess and I am quite sure he would not spoil a virgin; if he is a man of honor in one thing, he is that in all things. He is a relatively poor man, or he would not be a detective at all. He is a common man or he could not go among common people. He has a sense of character, or he would not know his job. He will take no man's money dishonestly and no man's insolence without a due and dispassionate revenge. He is a lonely man and his pride is that you will treat him as a proud man or be very sorry you ever saw him. He talks as the man of his age talks, that is, with rude wit, a lively sense of the grotesque, a disgust for sham, and a contempt for pettiness. The story is his adventure in search of a hidden truth, and it would be no adventure if it did not happen to a man fit for adventure. He has a range of awareness that startles you, but it belongs to him by right, because it belongs to the world he lives in.

If there were enough like him, I think the world would be a very safe place to live in, and yet not too dull to be worth living in.

NATALIE HEVENER KAUFMAN AND CAROL MCGINNIS KAY

From "Grafton's Place in the Development of the Detective Novel"

"The story's not over yet."

... In their house filled with enthusiastic readers, Sue [Grafton] was allowed to read anything she found on the packed bookshelves, and she turned most often to detective fiction. "In my early teens, on the occasions when my parents went out for the evening, I'd be left alone in the house with its tall, narrow windows and gloomy high ceilings. ... Usually I sat downstairs in the living room in my mother's small upholstered rocking chair, reading countless mystery novels with a bone-handled butcher knife within easy reach. ... I worked my way from Nancy

Drew through Agatha Christie and on to Mickey Spillane," a wildly diverse set of twentieth-century detective writers. "From Mickey Spillane, I turned to James M. Cain, then to Raymond Chandler, Dashiell Hammett, Ross Macdonald, Richard Prather, and John D. MacDonald, a baptism by immersion in the dark poetry of murder" ("An Eye" 99–100).

. . .

Interestingly, the word "detective" did not appear in the English language until 1842, according to the *Oxford English Dictionary*, when its first recorded use was in the name of a new department of the Metropolitan Police Force in London: the Detective Division. (We should remember that the concept of a *public* police force was itself less than two decades old in England at that time and was just beginning in America. The enormous growth in population and attendant problems with crime in both countries had necessitated the establishment of the first publicly funded police forces.) The word "detected" had been in existence as far back as the fourteenth century, when it meant "disclosed," "open," or "exposed" (*Oxford English Dictionary*). Put simply, during the medieval and Renaissance periods, crime tended to be solved by confession, usually obtained by torture, or by the testimony of a witness or an informant, also frequently obtained by torture. For centuries, self-revelation of guilt by the criminal was the basic method of solving a crime.

Transformation of the adjective "detected" into the noun "detective" indicates the nineteenth century's recognition that there was a new method of solving crime. This new method centered around the abilities of someone to think through the details of the crime and rationally conclude the identity of the criminal. Exposure of the criminal was done by the detective, not by the criminal. This new method, which seems blindingly obvious to contemporary readers, was a radical consequence of a great modern shift in popular thinking about the way in which the world originated, operated, and could be understood.

The shift had begun in the eighteenth century with the Enlightenment and its reliance on rational thought instead of divine revelation as a way to comprehend the universe. People came to believe that an individual was not merely a passive receptacle of divine knowledge but was instead capable of *generating* knowledge (hence the development of the concepts of plagiarism and copyright during the eighteenth century). This increased awareness that a single human being could observe the natural world, postulate a theory to explain a phenomenon, and prove that theory through experimentation and analysis reached a logical apotheosis in the publication of Charles Darwin's *On the Origin of Species* in 1859.

Darwin's techniques aboard the *Beagle* would remind any mystery reader of Sherlock Holmes, or Auguste Dupin, or Hercule Poirot at work. The scientist-detective observes the scene in minute detail, notices the unexpected, speculates about the possible causes of the anomaly, and then tests out each theory until only one is left. The process is highly rational, orderly, and thorough. Success occurs because one brilliant and tenacious individual finds the solution to a puzzle.

. . .

The Holmesian model of the brilliant, eccentric, rational amateur detective dominated the mystery genre throughout the nineteenth and early twentieth centuries in both England and America. In this country, Anna Katherine Green's *The Leavenworth Case* (1878) predated the first Sherlock Holmes novel by nearly ten years; her novels featuring police detective Ebenezer Gryce, and later the nosy spinster, Amelia Butterworth—prototype for Miss Marple—were wildly popular in both England and America. . . .

According to many critics, the detective genre peaked in England in the 1920s and '30s with the novels of Dorothy Sayers, Agatha Christie, and Margery Allingham, and continuing through the '40s with the novels of Ngaio Marsh. The period is often called the Golden Age of detective fiction, a term coined by Howard Haycraft in *Murder for Pleasure*. The age deserves its title in more ways than one: it established the basic formula of the genre and, additionally, married the English comedy of manners with a strong sense of nostalgia for a "golden" past that post–World War I English readers feared would never come again. If, in fact, it had ever existed at all.

The typical Golden Age novels offer a slew of murders in nice quiet English villages or lovely aristocratic country homes where such aberrant acts might never be expected to occur. They do, however, and, in a further demonstration of their abnormality, they occur in the most bizarre ways possible—through touching a poisoned walking cane, or being caught in a wool baler, for example. The witty and arch aristocrats are suitably shocked, and they do so hope "the butler did it" and not one of their own people. (The number of times a fictional murder was done by the butler was virtually nil— the cliché represents a class-based hope of considerable intensity.) What follows is formulaic: a brilliant man, or occasionally a shrewd spinster, takes a logical look at a string of clues that bewilder the local policemen and deduces the identity of the murderer, who turns out to be the one bad apple in an otherwise pristine aristocratic barrel. The clever detective traps the murderer, who is promptly arrested by the (finally useful) police, and the ripples in the village pond can smooth out again. Class, order, and tranquility are restored.

What a lovely concept. What complete balderdash.

The latter reaction was the response of Raymond Chandler and Dashiell Hammett, the leading writers of detective stories for the popular American pulp magazine *Black Mask*.

. . .

Chandler summarized his irritation with Americanized versions of the British Golden Age mystery in "The Simple Art of Murder," a landmark article in *The Atlantic Monthly* (1944) in which he described Hammett's transformation of the genre and his, own aims in writing detective fiction. . . .

Recalling her own reading of detective fiction as a teenager, Grafton says, "I can still remember the astonishment I felt the night I leapt from the familiarity of Miss Marple into the pagan sensibilities of *I, the Jury*" ("An Eye" 99) by Mickey Spillane, one of the hardest of the hard-boiled writers. It must have been a shock. The two worlds—Golden Age and hard-boiled—had been created from very different sensibilities and to this day have widely differing appeal to readers.

. . .

In the same year that Christie began writing *The Body in the Library*—1939— Chandler's *The Big Sleep* was published. About the only things the two novels appear to share is that murders do occur in both and some of the action takes place in the homes of wealthy men. But these two homes—Colonel Bantry's aristocratic home, where the major noise in the morning is the maid opening the curtains before she serves tea, and General Sternwood's *nouveau riche* L.A. house, where the major noise is the screaming of one of his daughters high on drugs—might as well be on separate planets.

Chandler's shabby, sunbaked Los Angeles is filled with the mean streets of contemporary American life: ugly, corrupt, unstable, replete with violence and confusion. In this setting, wealthy men may be as wicked as the gang boss and one must not make assumptions about who the good guys are. This is a world, Chandler says, "where the mayor of your town may have condoned murder as an instrument of money-making, where no man can walk down a dark street in safety because law and order are things we talk about but refrain from practicing" ("Simple Art" 59). Murder is no longer the result of one rotten apple; in this world one suspects that almost the whole damn barrelful of apples is rotten, and termites are probably gnawing on the barrel itself.

In *The Big Sleep*, Chandler introduced Philip Marlowe as his prototypical hard-boiled detective. There is as yet no accepted source for the term "hard-boiled," although there are two possibilities: in an after-dinner speech to the Army and Navy Club of Connecticut in 1887, Mark Twain used the term to indicate a tough style of speech* and, according to mystery novelist Donald E. Westlake, it was later routinely applied to tough drill sergeants during World War I (DeAndrea 153), Whatever the origin, "hard-boiled" as applied to a detective, such as Sam Spade, Philip Marlowe, and later Lew Archer and a legion of others, meant a tough male professional private eye who tells the story of the investigation himself. No admiring Dr. Watsons here. This detective works alone to fight crime because he is good at it, and someone needs to do it. The investigation is a job, not an intellectual game. The hard-boiled detective makes no claim to being the great rational puzzle-solver; indeed, one has the impression that in this world a Hercule Poirot would promptly be tossed into the river

---

*We are indebted to Matthew J. Bruccoli, University of South Carolina, for calling our attention to this early usage. For the Twain passage, see Louis J. Budd (ed.), *Mark Twain: Collected Tales, Sketches, Speeches, and Essay.*

wearing concrete booties. Instead, in order to survive in a world without controls, this detective must use his fists, guns, wits, luck, physical bravery—anything he can—in order to remove whatever evil force he can. As Grafton sees him, "He smoked too much, drank too much, screwed and punched his way through molls and mobsters with devastating effect. In short, he kicked ass" ("An Eye" 100).

. . .

Understandably, hard-boiled novels don't end with a general sense of order restored, because the basic systems are themselves flawed. Instead, the novels conclude with a highly limited sense of satisfaction that one specific source of human evil has been contained. Until Thursday, at least. And assuming the novel concludes on a Wednesday.

. . .

Grafton began planning her detective series with the intention of playing against the character of hard-boiled Philip Marlowe. Her first step was to try out the role in the hands and voice of a woman. Her original introduction of Kinsey for "A" *Is for Alibi* began: "My name is Kinsey Millhone." . . .

If Chandler gives us a loner hero, so does Grafton, but she takes it one step farther by explaining *why* Kinsey is a loner. If Chandler gives us a hero who does investigative work because he's good at it and he needs to earn money on which to live, so does Grafton, but she explains *why and how* Kinsey turns to investigation for a career. If Chandler gives us a hero who lives simply, so does Grafton, but, again, she explains *the history behind* Kinsey's fondness for small living quarters and for sandwiches. The list could go on. All the major characteristics of the hard-boiled detective appear in Kinsey. What Grafton does that is different is emphasize the psychology behind those characteristics. As Grafton points out, "Kinsey keeps nothing back—she is irrepressible."

Grafton also says she wanted to try her hand at writing detective fiction because she likes "the rules of the genre." Her toying with the nature of the central character did not come from any disdain for the form. On the contrary, Grafton believes a detective novel offers "the perfect blend of ingenuity and intellect, action and artifice" ("An Eye" 100). . . . Because, says Grafton, *all* fiction writing is the unfolding of a story with some key elements withheld until the conclusion, mysteries are actually superior to the so-called mainstream novels because they force an author to allow the plot to blossom in a way that must be simultaneously codified and natural. The process is both real and a game. As Grafton sees it, "Mystery at its best is the most divine form of manipulation."

. . .

At the time Grafton decided she wanted into the game, female private eyes were scarce creatures in novels and only occasionally found in short stories. Fictional women detectives had existed as far back as the 1860s in both England

and America, but the most popular ones were usually amateurs of the Miss Amelia Butterworth or Miss Jane Marple variety of genteel spinster, or professionals of the equally genteel Miss Maud Silver variety, and almost never of the hard-hitting, fast-action professional mold of the American male private eyes. Marcia Muller is credited with being first to create a popular female private eye in a novel: Sharon McCone, who first appeared in *Edwin of the Iron Shoes* in 1977. Significantly, Muller had a difficult time getting the book accepted for publication because publishers assumed that a tough-talking and tough-acting female private eye would not be accepted by the reading public. And, indeed, Muller's earliest books, though popular, were not runaway best-sellers, and she continued for several years to have trouble finding a willing publisher. Not until Sue Grafton and Sara Paretsky published their initial ventures in 1982 was the new wave of women private eyes firmly established. With the appearance of "A" *Is for Alibi* and *Indemnity Only*, the genre of detective fiction was significantly reshaped, and bookstore shelves are now packed with novels featuring women private eyes.

. . .

The game board on which the author and reader play was established from the beginning by such playful devices as Grafton's use of the alphabet in every title and by the supporting use of the alphabet for the locales and families involved in most cases. If "B" *Is for Burglar*, then part of the story takes place in Boca Raton and the family involved is named Boldt; if "F" *Is for Fugitive*, then the story takes place in Floral Beach and involves the Fowler family, and so on.

Even the center of the novels' game board—Santa Teresa—is part of the fun shared by author and reader. "Santa Teresa" is the fictitious name Ross Macdonald gave to Santa Barbara for his detective series. Grafton says she chose the name as an appreciative "way of tipping my hat" to Macdonald, whose work she greatly admires, and to "let the town live on." Grafton's nod to Dashiell Hammett is more amusing: in "A" *Is for Alibi*, when Kinsey goes to interview Gwen File at the dog-clipping parlor, she finds Gwen clipping a poodle named "Dashiell"—and in good hard-boiled fashion, he steps right in a pile of dog shit.

The basic device of titling the novels with the letters of the alphabet is an obvious call to game playing. What prompted Grafton to use this device? She was aware, she says, that publishers were very interested in series novels, and she was deliberately looking for a device to signal that she was beginning a series. Two of her father's mysteries had used lines from a children's nursery rhyme, *The Rat Began to Gnaw the Rope* and *The Rope Began to Hang the Butcher*. She was actively looking for something similar. One night she was reading one of her favorite books, Edward Gorey's *The Gashlycrumb Tinies*, a lovely little book of poetry about Victorian children being maimed and killed(!), when she had a "Eureka" moment. In typical Gorey fashion, *The Gashlycrumb Tinies* is funny, irreverent, bloody, and importantly for our story, it is organized alphabetically: "A is for Amy who fell down the stairs. B is for Basil assaulted by bears." Thinking this device might work for mystery novels, Grafton sat right down and began to make a list of all the words associated with murder that she could use if she based a series on the alphabet.

. . .

Grafton's concern for the psychology of her characters and the human richness of her central detective obviously strike a responsive chord in contemporary readers. Of course, fully realized fictional characters have always found a receptive readership, but the popularity of Grafton and many other writers of detective fiction, especially the women authors who as a group spend more time developing richly textured characters than devising shocking methods of murder, seems to us to require a little more comment than relegating it simply to "strong characterization."

It is in the last thirty years or so that we have witnessed an absolute onslaught of *series* of detective novels. Why would this be the case?

This is the same period in American social history that has seen a growing sense of isolation and loneliness in all our lives, a trend brought to our attention in the past five years by an increasing number of articles in professional journals and popular newsprint about the subject. For example, *Time* ran a feature article about the topic, which included a set of photos of people in urban settings, each one looking away from the others, alone in the middle of a crowd. This loss of a sense of community is attributed to many forces, including a number of initiatives that had seemed innately good at first: for example, the widespread introduction of air-conditioning was certainly a welcome relief, but it moved entire families from the front porch or the fire escape, where they talked with neighbors, into the privacy of their own homes. Here they talked only to each other, or with the arrival of television, not even each other. Later they turned to that great magic box in the study—the computer—which was normally used by only one person at a time.

Now, we doubt that many people would willingly forgo any of today's gadgetry—the more we get, the more we want. Certainly neither of us is willing to give up the dishwasher in order to regain the family unit gathering to wash dishes together, or the clothes drier in order to return to conversations with neighbors as we hang out the clothes on the line. But that loss of opportunity for human interaction is very real and quite serious. Psychologists tell us that we all need human contact in order to be emotionally healthy. And most of us figure out some way to have that contact.

. . .

Interestingly, what is one of the first uses we human beings have made of the computer's Internet? We've created "chat rooms," so that while we sit in isolation in our studies, we can still have the illusion of maintaining personal relationships. Just as we can delight in driving our gadget-laden cars on the highway—alone, moving fast, but with an ear glued to the cell phone.

Talk with any group of detective fiction readers and they will tell you that they can hardly wait for the next one so that they can see what *their friend* Kinsey Millhone (or V. I. Warshawski, or Sharon McCone, or Neil Hamel, or

Carlotta Carlyle, or Anna Pigeon, or whoever) is up to now. This warmth with which readers talk about their favorite detectives reveals the importance of these characters in the readers' lives. They fill a genuine void in contemporary American life. We're tempted to draw a parallel to the current popularity of soap operas, now prevalent on the evening as well as the afternoon television schedules, but we would not want this misunderstood to suggest a parallel in the quality of writing. . . .

Detective fiction has always been intensely responsive to, and reflective of, the needs of its own time. Detective fiction is almost obsessively *au courant*. When Anna Katherine Green wrote the first American detective novel in 1878, *The Leavenworth Case*, she presented inquest testimony about new techniques in ballistics that was right out of contemporary newspaper headlines. The entire novel, in fact, was based on current events; it was a fictionalized account of a celebrated unsolved murder case in New York on which her attorney father had worked. Raymond Chandler's scene was the dark crime-laden world of gangsters that dominated L.A. newspaper headlines and those of most cities in the U.S. at the time. It is unsurprising, then, that contemporary detective fiction—again, especially that written by women—touches time and again on current American fears. Patricia Cornwell makes us face our fears of that modern phenomenon, the serial killer, and of loss of personal privacy through someone else's manipulation of the computer sitting on our desk. Judith Van Geison, Karen McQuillen, Dana Stabenow, and Nevada Barr play on our fears that the environment will be vandalized beyond repair. Grafton, Muller, Paretsky, as well as Linda Barnes, Barbara Neely, Barbara D'Amato, Sandra Scoppotone, Julie Smith, Grace Edwards, and a host of others touch our deep-seated fears that the social and legal systems, which should enable our society to function, are themselves so essentially corrupt that we may never be able to put Humpty Dumpty together again.

Grafton's novels explore a variety of troubling contemporary social issues: class distinctions, prostitution, real-estate scams, corrupt lawyers and politicians, sexism, the strangle-hold of bureaucracy and flaws in the basic structures of government, the church, and, even closer to home, the family. Grafton says she reads several newspapers each day, looking for ideas for her novels. She does not want to use an actual case for her novels—she won't name real names—but she likes to borrow the motive or the murder or the method of discovery that she sees in current news. Contemporaneousness is a deliberate emphasis on the part of the author of detective fiction, then, and an important reason for enthusiastic reader response.

Part of being contemporary is being realistic, making the characters and the action seem natural. Chandler praised Hammett—and he himself was praised—for creating a fictional world that was much more natural than the artificial world of the Golden Age British "cozies." Yet, when a reader in the early twenty-first century reads a Chandler or a Hammett novel, much of it seems enormously dated, even artificial, as precious in its own way as anything by Arthur Conan Doyle or Dorothy Sayers.

The contemporary nature of the genre leads, of course, to a wealth of superficial detail about dress, or slang, or drinks that can make a novel appear out-of-date very quickly, but it seems to us that there is a more profound outdating process going on, one that is indigenous to the genre itself. By this, we mean that much of what we fear as a society changes as social conditions change. The sheer numbers of the rapid population growth frightened nineteenth-century readers, who feared loss of public order and control. The horrors of trench warfare in World War I made the English afraid that there was not a benign deity in charge after all. The economic chaos of the thirties, coupled with the threat of another war, made Americans despair that anyone could ever put the world right again. The complacency of the fifties made many people apprehensive that there were no more adventures to be had. For each shift in popular consciousness, there is a corresponding shift in the character of the detective and the world in which the detective operates. The one action humanity has *always* feared is murder; it is the one fear that requires no social construct. Thus, this is the action that becomes the generic metaphor for all the specific fears for our individual time. It becomes freighted with all of society's current worries and apprehensions. Chandler seems dated to us, then, not only because gangster talk has changed, but also because what frightens us is not what frightened his readers in the thirties. The terrors offered by crooks and dirty postcard dealers that were natural then seem odd, artificial, and even laughable to us now. We have our own fears ("our" drug lords are *much* worse than "their" bootleggers), which doubtless will appear equally odd to the readers of 2040.

One of the key reasons for the popularity of Sue Grafton—and for many of her colleagues—is her ability to give voice to our contemporary fears, while, at the same time, giving us the reassurance of a central figure, credible by current standards, who can hold back the darkness for one more day. In Grafton's own words, "The hard-boiled private eye in current fiction represents a clarity and vigor, the immediacy of a justice no longer evident in the courts, an antidote to our confusion and our fearfulness. In a country where violence is out of control, the hard-boiled private eye exemplifies containment, order, and hope, with the continuing, unspoken assertion that the individual can still make a difference. . . . The hard-boiled private-eye novel is still the classic struggle between good and evil played out against the backdrop of our social interactions" ("An Eye" 101–2).

. . .

While Grafton's Kinsey is similar to several other women detectives in some of her strengths, her kick-ass manner, and her effective detective abilities, she is unique and especially admirable for the way in which she has learned an important lesson about life: the solution to a problem lies within the problem itself—*if* one has the ability to see it and act on it. This concept colors everything about Kinsey's life and work. The concept was vividly illustrated in the quick snapshot in *"B" Is for Burglar* of the poison oak and its antidote, mugwort, grow-ing side by side. We see it developed more fully every time we learn more about Kinsey's childhood or personal life. The tragic loss of her parents could have been an excuse for collapsing into victimhood, but given her innate courage (and her aunt's nudges), Kinsey turned the problem into the core of her strength. She is tough, strong, and self-reliant, not because of a tragedy, but because of what she created out of a tragedy.

. . .

This powerful sense of responsibility and self-creation is greatly appealing to a reading public awash in newspaper headlines that suggest rampant apathy and random violence throughout the country. . . .

Stylistically, the novels are appealing for then clarity of expression, satisfy-ing plot twists, vivid figures of speech, and striking characters. They are easy to read, but this does not mean they are simple. Far from it. Grafton creates a fic-tional world for Kinsey in which contradiction, complexity, and balance are the keynotes, and readers are constantly teased into rethinking something in the novels or their own lives they had taken for granted. The grace note hovering above everything—the line that keeps the serious moments from becoming preachy or depressing and keeps readers coming back for more—is Grafton's sar-donic sense of humor.

Grafton is a leader for changing the genre, then, because she creates an entire world that is credible, thought provoking, and amusing. We believe her creation of complex Kinsey Millhone and we accept the validity of the world in which Kinsey operates. We can see ourselves reflected in Kinsey and our fears embodied in her world. In Grafton's detective novels of humanity and com-plexity, we like being puzzled and frightened and then escaping unscathed; we like being teased—not pushed—into thinking; we like being challenged to find our own strengths; and we just love being verbally tickled into laughing out loud.

Works Cited

Chandler, Raymond. "The Simple Art of Murder." *The Atlantic Monthly*, December 1944: 53–59.

DeAndrea, William L. "The Hard-Boiled Dectective." In *Encyclopedia Mysteriosa: A Comprehensive Guide to the Art of Detection in Print, Film, Radio, and Television.* New York: Prentice Hall, 1994.

Grafton, Sue. "An Eye for an I: Justice, Morality, the Nature of the Hard-Boiled Private Detec-tive, and All That Existential Stuff." In *The Crown Crime Companion.* Ed. Otto Penzler. New York: Random House Crown Trade Paperbacks, 1995: 97–102.

STORIES

DASHIELL HAMMETT
1894–1961

The most influential figure in the structuring of hard-boiled detective fiction, Samuel Dashiell Hammett was born in St. Mary's County, Maryland, in 1894. A school dropout at 13, Hammett traveled the country working at numerous jobs and found permanent work in both Baltimore and San Francisco as a detective for the Pinkerton National Detective Agency. Later he contracted tuberculosis while in the army in World War I and could not resume work with the Pinkerton Agency. However, he took his eight years as a Pinkerton investigator and created characters and plots for his detective fiction. He published his first stories in *Black Mask* magazine; his first novels were serialized in that magazine as well.

Hammett's first tough-guy detective was the Continental Op, a nameless San Francisco operative, based on James Wright, Hammett's boss in the Baltimore Pinkerton office. Although often described as fat and middle-aged, the Op is tough and professional, often enjoying the violence he inflicts. In *The Maltese Falcon* (1939), Hammett presents Sam Spade, who becomes one of the most famous P.I.s in all of detective fiction. Spade lives by his own code, moves easily between the legal and illegal worlds, is both idealistic and cynical, and fights crime while refusing to carry a gun. San Francisco is his home turf. Hammett's other detective creations include Nick and Nora Charles, the husband-wife investigators from *The Thin Man* (1934). Nick is a hard-drinking, witty, ex-playboy who worked for the Trans-American Detective Agency of San Francisco until he marries the extremely wealthy Nora. It is Nora, a character Hammett said he based on playwright Lillian Hellman, his long-time companion, who involves them in a case to solve together. All the Hammett detectives move through a violent world of con men and blackmailers, corrupt politicians and hit men, slumming socialites and crooked cops. "The Gutting of Couffignal," one of the best of the Continental Op stories, first appeared in *Black Mask* in December 1925.

Recommended Hammett works: *The Maltese Falcon, The Thin Man, The Dain Curse.*

Other recommended authors: Raymond Chandler, Carroll John Daly, Mickey Spillane.

The Gutting of Couffignal

Wedge-shaped Couffignal is not a large island, and not far from the mainland, to which it is linked by a wooden bridge. Its western shore is a high, straight cliff that jumps abruptly up out of San Pablo Bay. From the top of this cliff the island slopes eastward, down to a smooth pebble beach that runs into the water again, where there are piers and a club-house and moored pleasure boats.

Couffignal's main street, paralleling the beach, has the usual bank, hotel, moving-picture theater, and stores. But it differs from most main streets of its size in that it is more carefully arranged and preserved. There are trees and hedges and strips of lawn on it, and no glaring signs. The buildings seem to belong beside one another, as if they had been designed by the same architect, and in the stores you will find goods of a quality to match the best city stores.

The intersecting streets—running between rows of neat cottages near the foot of the slope—become winding hedged roads as they climb toward the cliff. The higher these roads get, the farther apart and larger are the houses they lead to. The occupants of these higher houses are the owners and rulers of the island. Most of them are well-fed old gentlemen who, the profits they took from the world with both hands in their younger days now stowed away at safe percentages, have bought into the island colony so they may spend what is left of their lives nursing their livers and improving their golf among their kind. They admit to the island only as many storekeepers, working-people, and similar riffraff as are needed to keep them comfortably served.

That is Couffignal.

It was some time after midnight. I was sitting in a second-story room in Couffignal's largest house, surrounded by wedding presents whose value would add up to something between fifty and a hundred thousand dollars.

Of all the work that comes to a private detective (except divorce work, which the Continental Detective Agency doesn't handle) I like weddings as little as any. Usually I manage to avoid them, but this time I hadn't been able to. Dick Foley, who had been slated for the job, had been handed a black eye by an unfriendly pickpocket the day before. That let Dick out and me in. I had come up to Couffignal—a two-hour ride from San Francisco by ferry and auto stage—that morning, and would return the next.

This had been neither better nor worse than the usual wedding detail. The ceremony had been performed in a little stone church down the hill. Then the house had begun to fill with reception guests. They had kept it filled to overflowing until some time after the bride and groom had sneaked off to their eastern train.

The world had been well represented. There had been an admiral and an earl or two from England; an ex-president of a South American country; a Danish baron; a tall young Russian princess surrounded by lesser titles, including a fat, bald, jovial and black-bearded Russian general who had talked to me for a solid hour about prize fights, in which he had a lot of interest, but not so much knowledge as was possible; an ambassador from one of the Central European countries; a justice of the Supreme Court; and a mob of people whose prominence and near-prominence didn't carry labels.

In theory, a detective guarding wedding presents is supposed to make himself indistinguishable from the other guests. In practice, it never works out that way. He has to spend most of his time within sight of the booty, so he's easily spotted. Besides that, eight or ten people I recognized among the guests were clients or former clients of the Agency, and so knew me. However, being known doesn't make so much difference as you might think, and everything had gone off smoothly.

Shortly after dark a wind smelling of rain began to pile storm clouds up over the bay. Those guests who lived at a distance, especially those who had water to cross, hurried off for their homes. Those who lived on the island stayed until the first raindrops began to patter down. Then they left.

The Hendrixson house quieted down. Musicians and extra servants left. The weary house servants began to disappear in the direction of their bedrooms. I found some sandwiches, a couple of books and a comfortable armchair, and took them up to the room where the presents were now hidden under grey-white sheeting.

Keith Hendrixson, the bride's grandfather—she was an orphan—put his head in at the door.

"Have you everything you need for your comfort?" he asked.

"Yes, thanks."

He said good night and went off to bed—a tall old man, slim as a boy.

The wind and the rain were hard at it when I went downstairs to give the lower windows and doors the up-and-down. Everything on the first floor was tight and secure, everything in the cellar. I went upstairs again.

Pulling my chair over by a floor lamp, I put sandwiches, books, ash tray, gun and flashlight on a small table beside it. Then I switched off the other lights, set fire to a Fatima, sat down, wriggled my spine comfortably into the chair's padding, picked up one of the books, and prepared to make a night of it.

The book was called *The Lord of the Sea*, and had to do with a strong, tough and violent fellow named Hogarth, whose modest plan was to hold the world in one hand. There were plots and counterplots, kidnappings, murders, prison-breakings, forgeries and burglaries, diamonds large as hats and floating forts larger than Couffignal. It sounds dizzy here, but in the book it was as real as a dime.

Hogarth was still going strong when the lights went out.

In the dark, I got rid of the glowing end of my cigarette by grinding it in one of the sandwiches. Putting the book down, I picked up gun and flashlight, and moved away from the chair.

Listening for noises was no good. The storm was making hundreds of them. What I needed to know was why the lights had gone off.

I waited. My job was to watch the presents. Nobody had touched them yet. There was nothing to get excited about.

Minutes went by, perhaps ten of them.

The floor swayed under my feet. The windows rattled with a violence beyond the strength of the storm. The dull boom of a heavy explosion blotted out the sounds of wind and falling water. The blast was not close at hand, but not far enough away to be off the island.

Crossing to the window, peering through the wet glass, I could see nothing. I should have seen a few misty lights far down the hill. Not being able to see them settled one point. The lights had gone out all over Couffignal, not only in the Hendrixson house.

That was better. The storm could have put the lighting system out of whack, could have been responsible for the explosion—maybe.

Staring through the black window, I had an impression of great excitement down the hill, of movement in the night. But all was too far away for me to have seen or heard even had there been lights, and all too vague to say what was moving. The impression was strong but worthless. It didn't lead anywhere. I told myself I was getting feeble-minded, and turned away from the window.

Another blast spun me back to it. This explosion sounded nearer than the first, maybe because it was stronger. Peering through the glass again, I still saw nothing. And still had the impression of things that were big moving down there.

Bare feet pattered in the hall. A voice was anxiously calling my name. Turning from the window again, I pocketed my gun and snapped on the flashlight. Keith Hendrixson, in pajamas and bathrobe, looking thinner and older than anybody could be, came into the room.

"Is it—"

"I don't think it's an earthquake," I said, since that is the first calamity your Californian thinks of. "The lights went off a little while ago. There have been a couple of explosions down the hill since the—"

I stopped. Three shots, close together, had sounded. Rifleshots, but of the sort that only the heaviest of rifles could make. Then, sharp and small in the storm, came the report of a far-away pistol.

"What is it?" Hendrixson demanded.

"Shooting."

More feet were pattering in the halls, some bare, some shod. Excited voices whispered questions and exclamations. The butler, a solemn, solid block of a man, partly dressed, and carrying a lighted five-pronged candlestick, came in.

"Very good, Brophy," Hendrixson said as the butler put the candlestick on the table. "Will you try to learn what is the matter?"

"I have tried, sir. The telephone seems to be out of order, sir. Shall I send Oliver down to the village?"

"No-o. I don't suppose it's that serious. Do you think it is anything serious?" he asked me.

I said I didn't think so, but I was paying more attention to the outside than to him. I had heard a thin screaming that could have come from a distant woman, and a volley of small-arms shots. The racket of the storm muffled these shots, but when the heavier firing we had heard before broke out again, it was clear enough.

To have opened the window would have been to let in gallons of water without helping us to hear much clearer. I stood with an ear tilted to the pane, trying to arrive at some idea of what was happening outside.

Another sound took my attention from the window—the ringing of the doorbell. It rang loudly and persistently.

Hendrixson looked at me. I nodded.

"See who it is, Brophy," he said.

The butler went solemnly away, and came back even more solemnly.

"Princess Zhukovski," he announced.

She came running into the room—the tall Russian girl I had seen at the reception. Her eyes were wide and dark with excitement. Her face was very white and wet. Water ran in streams down her blue waterproof cape, the hood of which covered her dark hair.

"Oh, Mr. Hendrixson!" She had caught one of his hands in both of hers. Her voice, with nothing foreign in its accents, was the voice of one who is excited over a delightful surprise. "The bank is being robbed, and the—what do you call him?—marshal of police has been killed!"

"What's that?" the old man exclaimed, jumping awkwardly, because water from her cape had dripped down on one of his bare feet. "Weegan killed? And the bank robbed?"

"Yes! Isn't it terrible?" She said it as if she were saying wonderful. "When the first explosion woke us, the general sent Ignati down to find out what was the matter, and he got down there just in time to see the bank blown up. Listen!"

We listened, and heard a wild outbreak of mixed gunfire.

"That will be the general arriving!" she said. "He'll enjoy himself most wonderfully. As soon as Ignati returned with the news, the general armed every male in the household from Aleksandr Sergyeevich to Ivan the cook, and led them out happier than he's been since he took his division to East Prussia in 1914."

"And the duchess?" Hendrixson asked.

"He left her at home with me, of course, and I furtively crept out and away from her while she was trying for the first time in her life to put water in a samovar. This is not the night for one to stay at home!"

"H-m-m," Hendrixson said, his mind obviously not on her words. "And the bank!"

He looked at me. I said nothing. The racket of another volley came to us.

"Could you do anything down there?" he asked.

"Maybe, but—" I nodded at the presents under their covers.

"Oh, those!" the old man said. "I'm as much interested in the bank as in them; and, besides, we will be here."

"All right!" I was willing enough to carry my curiosity down the hill. "I'll go down. You'd better have the butler stay in here, and plant the chauffeur inside the front door. Better give them guns if you have any. Is there a raincoat I can borrow! I brought only a light overcoat."

Brophy found a yellow slicker that fitted me. I put it on, stowed gun and flashlight conveniently under it, and found my hat while Brophy was getting and loading an automatic pistol for himself and a rifle for Oliver, the mulatto chauffeur.

Hendrixson and the princess followed me downstairs. At the door I found she wasn't exactly following me—she was going with me.

"But, Sonya!" the old man protested.

"I'm not going to be foolish, though I'd like to," she promised him. "But I'm going back to my Irinia Androvana, who will perhaps have the samovar watered by now."

"That's a sensible girl!" Hendrixson said, and let us out into the rain and the wind.

It wasn't weather to talk in. In silence we turned downhill between two rows of hedging, with the storm driving at our backs. At the first break in the hedge I stopped, nodding toward the black blot a house made.

"That is your—"

Her laugh cut me short. She caught my arm and began to urge me down the road again.

"I only told Mr. Hendrixson that so he would not worry," she explained. "You do not think I am not going down to see the sights."

She was tall. I am short and thick. I had to look up to see her face—to see as much of it as the rain-grey night would let me see.

"You'll be soaked to the hide, running around in this rain," I objected.

"What of that? I am dressed for it."

She raised a foot to show me a heavy waterproof boot and a woolen-stockinged leg.

"There's no telling what we'll run into down there, and I've got work to do," I insisted. "I can't be looking out for you."

"I can look out for myself."

She pushed her cape aside to show me a square automatic pistol in one hand.

"You'll be in my way."

"I will not," she retorted. "You'll probably find I can help you. I'm as strong as you, and quicker, and I can shoot."

The reports of scattered shooting had punctuated our argument, but now the sound of heavier firing silenced the dozen objections to her company that I could still think of. After all, I could slip away from her in the dark if she became too much of a nuisance.

"Have it your own way," I growled, "but don't expect anything from me."

"You're so kind," she murmured as we got under way again, hurrying now, with the wind at our backs speeding us along.

Occasionally dark figures moved on the road ahead of us, but too far away to be recognizable. Presently a man passed us, running uphill—a tall man whose nightshirt hung out of his trousers, down below his coat, identifying him as a resident.

"They've finished the bank and are at Medcraft's!" he yelled as he went by.

"Medcraft is the jeweler," the girl informed me.

The sloping under our feet grew less sharp. The houses—dark but with faces vaguely visible here and there at windows—came closer together. Below, the flash of a gun could be seen now and then.

Our road put us into the lower end of the main street just as a staccato rat-tat-tat broke out.

I pushed the girl into the nearest doorway, and jumped in after her.

Bullets ripped through walls with the sound of hail tapping on leaves.

That was the thing I had taken for an exceptionally heavy rifle—a machine gun.

The girl had fallen back in a corner, all tangled up with something. I helped her up. The something was a boy of seventeen or so, with one leg and a crutch.

"It's the boy who delivers papers," Princess Zhukovski said, "and you've hurt him with your clumsiness."

The boy shook his head, grinning as he got up.

"No'm, I ain't hurt none, but you kind of scared me, jumping on me."

She had to stop and explain that she hadn't jumped on him, that she had been pushed into him by me, and that she was sorry and so was I.

"What's happening?" I asked the newsboy when I could get a word in.

"Everything," he boasted, as if some of the credit were his. "There must be a hundred of them, and they've blowed the bank wide open, and now some of 'em is in Medcraft's, and I guess they'll blow that up, too. And they killed Tom Weegan. They got a machine gun on a car in the middle of the street."

"Where's everybody—all the merry villagers?"

"Most of 'em are up behind the Hall. They can't do nothing, though, because the machine gun won't let 'em get near enough to see what they're shooting at, and that smart Bill Vincent told me to clear out, 'cause I've only got one leg, as if I couldn't shoot as good as the next one, if I only had something to shoot with!"

"That wasn't right of them," I sympathized. "But you can do something for me. You can stick here and keep your eye on this end of the street, so I'll know if they leave in this direction."

"You're not just saying that so I'll stay here out of the way, are you?"

"No," I lied. "I need somebody to watch. I was going to leave the princess here, but you'll do better."

"Yes," she backed me up, catching the idea. "This gentleman is a detective, and if you do what he asks you'll be helping more than if you were up with the others."

The machine gun was still firing, but not in our direction now.

"I'm going across the street," I told the girl. "If you—"

"Aren't you going to join the others?"

"No. If I can get around behind the bandits while they're busy with the others, maybe I can turn a trick."

"Watch sharp now!" I ordered the boy, and the princess and I made a dash for the opposite sidewalk.

We reached it without drawing lead, sidled along a building for a few yards, and turned into an alley. From the alley's other end came the smell and wash and the dull blackness of the bay.

While we moved down this alley I composed a scheme by which I hoped to get rid of my companion, sending her off on a safe wild-goose chase. But I didn't get a chance to try it out.

The big figure of a man loomed ahead of us.

Stepping in front of the girl, I went on toward him. Under my slicker I held my gun on the middle of him.

He stood still. He was larger than he had looked at first. A big, slope-shouldered, barrel-bodied husky. His hands were empty. I spotted the flashlight on his face for a split second. A flat-cheeked, thick-featured face, with high cheekbones.

"Ignati!" the girl exclaimed over my shoulder.

He began to talk what I supposed was Russian to the girl. She laughed and replied. He shook his big head stubbornly, insisting on something. She stamped her foot and spoke sharply. He shook his head again and addressed me.

"General Pleshskev, he tell me bring Princess Sonya to home."

His English was almost as hard to understand as his Russian. His tone puzzled me. It was as if he was explaining some absolutely necessary thing that he didn't want to be blamed for, but that nevertheless he was going to do.

While the girl was speaking to him again, I guessed the answer. This big Ignati had been sent out by the general to bring the girl home, and he was going to obey his orders if he had to carry her. He was trying to avoid trouble with me by explaining the situation.

"Take her," I said, stepping aside.

The girl scowled at me, laughed.

"Very well, Ignati," she said in English, "I shall go home," and she turned on her heel and went back up the alley, the big man close behind her.

Glad to be alone, I wasted no time in moving in the opposite direction until the pebbles of the beach were under my feet. The pebbles ground harshly under my heels. I moved back to more silent ground and began to work my way as swiftly as I could up the shore toward the center of action. The machine gun barked on. Smaller guns snapped. Three concussions, close together—bombs, hand grenades, my ears and my memory told me.

The stormy sky glared pink over a roof ahead of me and to the left. The boom of the blast beat my eardrums. Fragments I couldn't see fell around me. That, I thought, would be the jeweler's safe blowing apart.

I crept on up the shore line. The machine gun went silent. Lighter guns snapped, snapped, snapped. Another grenade went off. A man's voice shrieked pure terror.

Risking the crunch of pebbles, I turned down to the water's edge again. I had seen no dark shape on the water that could have been a boat. There had been boats moored along this beach in the afternoon. With my feet in the water of the bay I still saw no boat. The storm could have scattered them, but I didn't think it had. The island's western height shielded this shore. The wind was strong here, but not violent.

My feet sometimes on the edge of the pebbles, sometimes in the water, I went on up the shore line. Now I saw a boat. A gently bobbing black shape ahead. No light was on it. Nothing I could see moved on it. It was the only boat on that shore. That made it important.

Foot by foot, I approached.

A shadow moved between me and the dark rear of a building. I froze. The shadow, man-size, moved again, in the direction from which I was coming.

Waiting, I didn't know how nearly invisible, or how plain, I might be against my background. I couldn't risk giving myself away by trying to improve my position.

Twenty feet from me the shadow suddenly stopped.

I was seen. My gun was on the shadow.

"Come on," I called softly. "Keep coming. Let's see who you are."

The shadow hesitated, left the shelter of the building, drew nearer. I couldn't risk the flashlight. I made out dimly a handsome face, boyishly reckless, one cheek dark-stained.

"Oh, how d'you do?" the face's owner said in a musical baritone voice. "You were at the reception this afternoon."

"Yes."

"Have you seen Princess Zhukovski? You know her?"

"She went home with Ignati ten minutes or so ago."

"Excellent!" He wiped his stained cheek with a stained handkerchief, and turned to look at the boat. "That's Hendrixson's boat," he whispered. "They've got it and they've cast the others off."

"That would mean they are going to leave by water."

"Yes, he agreed, "unless—Shall we have a try at it?"

"You mean jump it?"

"Why not?" he asked. "There can't be very many aboard. God knows there are enough of them ashore. You're armed. I've a pistol."

"We'll size it up first," I decided, "so we'll know what we're jumping."

"That is wisdom," he said, and led the way back to the shelter of the buildings.

Hugging the rear walls of the buildings, we stole toward the boat.

The boat grew clearer in the night. A craft perhaps forty-five feet long, its stern to the shore, rising and falling beside a small pier. Across the stern something protruded. Something I couldn't quite make out. Leather soles scuffled now and then on the wooden deck. Presently a dark head and shoulders showed over the puzzling thing in the stern.

The Russian lad's eyes were better than mine.

"Masked," he breathed in my ear. "Something like a stocking over his head and face."

The masked man was motionless where he stood. We were motionless where we stood.

"Could you hit him from here?" the lad asked.

"Maybe, but night and rain aren't a good combination for sharpshooting. Our best bet is to sneak as close as we can, and start shooting when he spots us."

"That is wisdom," he agreed.

Discovery came with our first step forward. The man in the boat grunted. The lad at my side jumped forward. I recognized the thing in the boat's stern just in time to throw out a leg and trip the young Russian. He tumbled down, all sprawled out on the pebbles. I dropped behind him.

The machine gun in the boat's stern poured metal over our heads.

"No good rushing that!" I said. "Roll out of it!"

I set the example by revolving toward the back of the building we had just left.

The man at the gun sprinkled the beach, but sprinkled it at random, his eyes no doubt spoiled for night-seeing by the flash of his gun.

Around the corner of the building, we sat up.

"You saved my life by tripping me," the lad said coolly.

"Yes. I wonder if they've moved the machine gun from the street, or if—"

The answer to that came immediately. The machine gun in the street mingled its vicious voice with the drumming of the one in the boat.

"A pair of them!" I complained. "Know anything about the layout?"

"I don't think there are more than ten or twelve of them," he said, "although it is not easy to count in the dark. The few I have seen are completely masked—like the man in the boat. They seem to have disconnected the telephone and light lines first and then to have destroyed the bridge. We attacked them while they were looting the bank, but in front they had a machine gun mounted in an automobile, and we were not equipped to combat on equal terms."

"Where are the islanders now?"

"Scattered, and most of them in hiding, I fancy, unless General Pleshskev has succeeded in rallying them again."

I frowned and beat my brains together. You can't fight machine guns and hand grenades with peaceful villagers and retired capitalists. No matter how well led and armed they are, you can't do anything with them. For that matter, how could anybody do much against that tough a game?

"Suppose you stick here and keep your eye on the boat," I suggested. "I'll scout around and see what's doing farther up, and if I can get a few good men together, I'll try to jump the boat again, probably from the other side. But we can't count on that. The getaway will be by boat. We can count on that, and try to block it. If you lie down you can watch the boat around the corner of the building without making much of a target of yourself. I wouldn't do anything to attract attention until the break for the boat comes. Then you can do all the shooting you want."

"Excellent!" he said. "You'll probably find most of the islanders up behind the church. You can get to it by going straight up the hill until you come to an iron fence, and then follow that to the right."

"Right."

I moved off in the direction he had indicated.

At the main street I stopped to look around before venturing across. Everything was quiet there. The only man I could see was spread out face-down on the sidewalk near me.

On hands and knees I crawled to his side. He was dead. I didn't stop to examine him further, but sprang up and streaked for the other side of the street.

Nothing tried to stop me. In a doorway, flat against a wall, I peeped out. The wind had stopped. The rain was no longer a driving deluge, but a steady down-pouring of small drops. Couffignal's main street, to my senses, was a deserted street.

I wondered if the retreat to the boat had already started. On the sidewalk, walking swiftly toward the bank, I heard the answer to that guess.

High up on the slope, almost up to the edge of the cliff, by the sound, a machine gun began to hurl out its stream of bullets.

Mixed with the racket of the machine gun were the sounds of smaller arms, and a grenade or two.

At the first crossing, I left the main street and began to run up the hill. Men were running toward me. Two of them passed, paying no attention to my shouted, "What's up now?"

The third man stopped because I grabbed him—a fat man whose breath bubbled, and whose face was fish-belly white.

"They've moved the car with the machine gun on it up behind us," he gasped when I had shouted my question into his ear again.

"What are you doing without a gun?" I asked.

"I—I dropped it."

"Where's General Pleshskev?"

"Back there somewhere. He's trying to capture the car, but he'll never do it. It's suicide!"

Other men had passed us, running downhill, as we talked. I let the white-faced man go, and stopped four men who weren't running so fast as the others.

"What's happening now?" I questioned them.

"They's going through the houses up the hill," a sharp-featured man with a small mustache and a rifle said.

"Has anybody got word off the island yet?" I asked.

"Can't," another informed me. "They blew up the bridge first thing."

"Can't anybody swim?"

"Not in that wind. Young Catlan tried it and was lucky to get out again with a couple of broken ribs."

"The wind's gone down," I pointed out.

The sharp-featured man gave his rifle to one of the others and took off his coat.

"I'll try it," he promised.

"Good! Wake up the whole country, and get word through to the San Francisco police boat and to the Mare Island Navy Yard. They'll lend a hand if you tell 'em the bandits have machine guns. Tell 'em the bandits have an armed boat waiting to leave in. It's Hendrixson's."

The volunteer swimmer left.

"A boat?" two of the men asked together.

"Yes. With a machine gun on it. If we're going to do anything, it'll have to be now, while we're between them and their getaway. Get every man and every gun you can find down there. Tackle the boat from the roofs if you can. When the bandits' car comes down there, pour it into it. You'll do better from the buildings than from the street."

The three men went on downhill. I went uphill, toward the crackling of firearms ahead. The machine gun was working irregularly. It would pour out its rat-tat-tat for a second or so, and then stop for a couple of seconds. The answering fire was thin, ragged.

I met more men, learned from them that the general, with less than a dozen men, was still fighting the car. I repeated the advice I had given the other men. My informants went down to join them. I went on up.

A hundred yards farther along, what was left of the general's dozen broke out of the night, around and past me, flying downhill, with bullets hailing after them.

The road was no place for mortal man. I stumbled over two bodies, scratched myself in a dozen places getting over a hedge. On soft, wet sod I continued my uphill journey.

The machine gun on the hill stopped its clattering. The one in the boat was still at work.

The one ahead opened again, firing too high for anything near at hand to be its target. It was helping its fellow below, spraying the main street.

Before I could get closer it had stopped. I heard the car's motor racing. The car moved toward me.

Rolling into the hedge, I lay there, straining my eyes through the spaces between the stems. I had six bullets in a gun that hadn't yet been fired.

When I saw wheels on the lighter face of the road, I emptied my gun, holding it low.

The car went on.

I sprang out of my hiding-place.

The car was suddenly gone from the empty road.

There was a grinding sound. A crash. The noise of metal folding on itself. The tinkle of glass.

I raced toward those sounds.

Out of a black pile where an engine sputtered, a black figure leaped—to dash off across the soggy lawn. I cut after it, hoping that the others in the wreck were down for keeps.

I was less than fifteen feet behind the fleeing man when he cleared a hedge. I'm no sprinter, but neither was he. The wet grass made slippery going.

He stumbled while I was vaulting the hedge. When we straightened out again I was not more than ten feet behind him.

Once I clicked my gun at him, forgetting I had emptied it. Six cartridges were wrapped in a piece of paper in my vest pocket, but this was not time for loading.

A building loomed ahead. My fugitive bore off to the right, to clear the corner.

To the left a heavy shotgun went off.

The running man disappeared around the house corner.

"Sweet God!" General Pleshskev's mellow voice complained. "That with a shotgun I should miss all of a man at that distance!"

"Go round the other way!" I yelled, plunging around the corner.

His feet thudded ahead. I could not see him. The general puffed around from the other side of the house.

"You have him?"

"No."

In front of us was a stone-faced bank, on top of which ran a path. On either side of us was a high and solid hedge.

"But, my friend," the general protested. "How could he have—?"

A pale triangle showed on the path above—a triangle that could have been a bit of shirt showing above the opening of a vest.

"Stay here and talk!" I whispered to the general, and crept forward.

"It must be that he has gone the other way," the general carried out my instructions, rambling on as if I were standing beside him, "because if he had come my way I should have seen him, and if he had raised himself over either of the hedges or the embankment, one of us would surely have seen him against . . . "

He talked on and on while I gained the shelter of the bank on which the path sat, while I found places for my toes in the rough stone facing.

The man on the road, trying to make himself small with his back in a bush, was looking at the talking general. He saw me when I had my feet on the path.

He jumped, and one hand went up.

I jumped, with both hands out.

A stone, turning under my foot, threw me sidewise, twisting my ankle, but saving my head from the bullet he sent at it.

My outflung left arm caught his legs as I spilled down. He came over on top of me. I kicked him once, caught his gun arm, and had just decided to bite it when the general puffed up over the edge of the path and prodded the man off me with his shotgun.

When it came my turn to stand up, I found it not so good. My twisted ankle didn't like to support its share of my hundred-and-eighty-some pounds. Putting most of my weight on the other leg, I turned my flashlight on the prisoner.

"Hello, Flippo!" I exclaimed.

"Hello!" he said without joy in the recognition.

He was a roly-poly Italian youth of twenty-three or -four. I had helped send him to San Quentin four years ago for his part in a payroll stick-up. He had been out on parole for several months now.

"The prison board isn't going to like this," I told him.

"You got me wrong," he pleaded. "I ain't been doing a thing. I was up here to see some friends. And when this thing busted loose I had to hide, because I got a record, and if I'm picked up I'll be railroaded for it. And now you got me, and you think I'm in on it!"

"You're a mind reader," I assured him, and asked the general, "Where can we pack this bird away for awhile, under lock and key?"

"In my house there is a lumber room with a strong door and not a window."

"That'll do it. March, Flippo!"

General Pleshskev collared the youth, while I limped along behind them, examining Flippo's gun, which was loaded except for the one shot he had fired at me, and reloading my own.

We had caught our prisoner on the Russian's grounds, so we didn't have far to go.

The general knocked on the door and called out something in his language. Bolts clicked and grated, and the door was swung open by a heavily mustached Russian servant. Behind him the princess and a stalwart older woman stood.

We went in while the general was telling his household about the capture, and took the captive up to the lumber room. I frisked him for his pocketknife and matches—he had nothing else that could help him get out—locked him in and braced the door solidly with a length of board. Then we went downstairs again.

"You are injured!" the princess, seeing me limp across the floor, cried.

"Only a twisted ankle," I said. "But it does bother me some. Is there any adhesive tape around?"

"Yes," and she spoke to the mustached servant, who went out of the room and presently returned, carrying rolls of gauze and tape and a basin of steaming water.

"If you'll sit down," the princess said, taking these things from the servant.

But I shook my head and reached for the adhesive tape.

"I want cold water, because I've got to go out in the wet again. If you'll show me the bathroom, I can fix myself up in no time."

We had to argue about that, but I finally got to the bathroom, where I ran cold water on my foot and ankle, and strapped it with adhesive tape, as tight as I could without stopping the circulation altogether. Getting my wet shoe on again was a job, but when I was through I had two firm legs under me, even if one of them did hurt some.

When I rejoined the others I noticed that the sound of firing no longer came up the hill, and that the patter of rain was lighter, and a grey streak of coming daylight showed under a drawn blind.

I was buttoning my slicker when the knocker sounded on the front door. Russian words came through, and the young Russian I had met on the beach came in.

"Aleksandr, you're—" the stalwart older woman screamed, when she saw the blood on his cheek, and fainted.

He paid no attention to her at all, as if he was used to having her faint.

"They've gone in the boat," he told me while the girl and two men servants gathered up the woman and laid her on an ottoman.

"How many?" I asked.

"I counted ten, and I don't think I missed more than one or two, if any."

"The men I sent down there couldn't stop them?"

He shrugged.

"What would you? It takes a strong stomach to face a machine gun. Your men had been cleared out of the buildings almost before they arrived."

The woman who had fainted had revived by now and was pouring anxious questions in Russian at the lad. The princess was getting into her blue cape. The woman stopped questioning the lad and asked her something.

"It's all over," the princess said. "I am going to view the ruins."

That suggestion appealed to everybody. Five minutes later all of us, including the servants, were on our way downhill. Behind us, around us, in front of us, were other people going downhill, hurrying along in the drizzle that was very gentle now, their faces tired and excited in the bleak morning light.

Halfway down, a woman ran out of a crosspath and began to tell me something. I recognized her as one of Hendrixson's maids.

I caught some of her words.

"Presents gone. . . . Mr. Brophy murdered. . . . Oliver. . . . "

"I'll be down later," I told the others, and set out after the maid.

She was running back to the Hendrixson house. I couldn't run, couldn't even walk fast. She and Hendrixson and more of his servants were standing on the front porch when I arrived.

"They killed Oliver and Brophy," the old man said.

"How?"

"We were in the back of the house, the rear second story, watching the flashes of the shooting down in the village. Oliver was down here, just inside the front door, and Brophy in the room with the presents. We heard a shot in there, and immediately a man appeared in the doorway of our room, threatening us with two pistols, making us stay there for perhaps ten minutes. Then he shut and locked the door and went away. We broke the door down—and found Brophy and Oliver dead."

"Let's look at them."

The chauffeur was just inside the front door. He lay on his back, with his brown throat cut straight across the front, almost back to the vertebræ. His rifle was under him. I pulled it out and examined it. It had not been fired.

Upstairs, the butler Brophy was huddled against a leg of one of the tables on which the presents had been spread. His gun was gone. I turned him over, straightened him out, and found a bullet hole in his chest. Around the hole his coat was charred in a large area.

Most of the presents were still here. But the most valuable pieces were gone. The others were in disorder, lying around any which way, their covers pulled off.

"What did the one you saw look like?" I asked.

"I didn't see him very well," Hendrixson said. "There was no light in our room. He was simply a dark figure against the candle burning in the hall. A large man in a black rubber raincoat, with some sort of black mask that covered his whole head and face."

As we went downstairs again I gave Hendrixson a brief account of what I had seen and heard and done since I had left him. There wasn't enough of it to make a long tale.

"Do you think you can get information about the others from the one you caught?" he asked, as I prepared to go out.

"No. But I expect to bag them just the same."

Couffignal's main street was jammed with people when I limped into it again. A detachment of Marines from Mare Island was there, and men from a San Francisco police boat. Excited citizens in all degrees of partial nakedness boiled around them. A hundred voices were talking at once, recounting their personal adventures and braveries and losses and what they had seen. Such words as machine gun, bomb, bandit, car, shot, dynamite, and killed sounded again and again, in every variety of voice and tone.

The bank had been completely wrecked by the charge that had blown the vault. The jewelry store was another ruin. A grocer's across the street was serving as a field hospital. Two doctors were toiling there, patching up damaged villagers.

I recognized a familiar face under a uniform cap—Sergeant Roche of the harbor police—and pushed through the crowd to him.

"Just get here?" he asked as we shook hands. "Or were you in on it?"

"In on it."

"What do you know?"

"Everything."

"Who ever heard of a private detective that didn't," he joshed as I led him out of the mob.

"Did you people run into an empty boat out in the bay?" I asked when we were away from audiences.

"Empty boats have been floating around the bay all night," he said.

I hadn't thought of that.

"Where's your boat now?" I asked.

"Out trying to pick up the bandits. I stayed with a couple of men to lend a hand here."

"You're in luck," I told him. "Now sneak a look across the street. See the stout old boy with the black whiskers? Standing in front of the druggist's."

General Pleshskev stood there, with the woman who had fainted, the young Russian whose bloody cheek had made her faint, and a pale, plump man of forty-something who had been with them at the reception. A little to one side stood big Ignati, the two menservants I had seen at the house, and another who was obviously one of them. They were chatting together and watching the excited antics of a red-faced property owner who was telling a curt lieutenant of Marines that it was his own personal private automobile that the bandits had stolen to mount their machine gun on.

"Yes," said Roche, "I see your fellow with the whiskers."

"Well, he's your meat. The woman and two men with him are also your meat. And those four Russians standing to the left are some more of it. There's another missing, but I'll take care of that one. Pass the word to the lieutenant, and you can round up those babies without giving them a chance to fight back. They think they're safe as angels."

"Sure, are you?" the sergeant asked.

"Don't be silly!" I growled, as if I had never made a mistake in my life.

I had been standing on my one good prop. When I put my weight on the other to turn away from the sergeant, it stung me all the way to the hip. I pushed my back teeth together and began to work painfully through the crowd to the other side of the street.

The princess didn't seem to be among those present. My idea was that, next to the general, she was the most important member of the push. If she was at their house, and not yet suspicious, I figured I could get close enough to yank her in without a riot.

Walking was hell. My temperature rose. Sweat rolled out on me.

"Mister, they didn't none of 'em come down that way."

The one-legged newsboy was standing at my elbow. I greeted him as if he were my pay check.

"Come on with me," I said, taking his arm. "You did fine down there, and now I want you to do something else for me."

Half a block from the main street I led him up on the porch of a small yellow cottage. The front door stood open, left that way when the occupants ran down to welcome police and Marines, no doubt. Just inside the door, beside a hall rack, was a wicker porch chair. I committed unlawful entry to the extent of dragging that chair out on the porch.

"Sit down, son," I urged the boy.

He sat, looking up at me with a puzzled freckled face. I took a firm grip on his crutch and pulled it out of his hand.

"Here's five bucks for rental," I said, "and if I lose it I'll buy you one of ivory and gold."

And I put the crutch under my arm and began to propel myself up the hill.

It was my first experience with a crutch. I didn't break any records. But it was a lot better than tottering along on an unassisted bum ankle.

The hill was longer and steeper than some mountains I've seen, but the gravel walk to the Russian's house was finally under my feet.

I was still some dozen feet from the porch when Princess Zhukovski opened the door.

"Oh!" she exclaimed, and then, recovering from her surprise, "your ankle is worse!"

She ran down the steps to help me climb them. As she came I noticed that something heavy was sagging and swinging in the right-hand pocket of her grey flannel jacket.

With one hand under my elbow, the other arm across my back, she helped me up the steps and across the porch. That assured me she didn't think I had tumbled to the game. If she had, she wouldn't have trusted herself within reach of my hands. Why, I wondered, had she come back to the house after starting downhill with the others?

While I was wondering we went into the house, where she planted me in a large and soft leather chair.

"You must certainly be starving after your strenuous night," she said. "I will see if—"

"No, sit down," I nodded at a chair facing mine. "I want to talk to you."

She sat down, clasping her slender white hands in her lap. In neither face nor pose was there any sign of nervousness, not even of curiosity. And that was overdoing it.

"Where have you cached the plunder?" I asked.

The whiteness of her face was nothing to go by. It had been white as marble since I had first seen her. The darkness of her eyes was as natural. Nothing happened to her other features. Her voice was smoothly cool.

"I am sorry," she said. "The question doesn't convey anything to me."

"Here's the point," I explained. "I'm charging you with complicity in the gutting of Couffignal, and in the murders that went with it. And I'm asking you where the loot has been hidden."

Slowly she stood up, raised her chin, and looked at least a mile down at me.

"How dare you? How dare you speak so to me, a Zhukovski!"

"I don't care if you're one of the Smith Brothers!" Leaning forward, I had pushed my twisted ankle against a leg of the chair, and the resulting agony didn't improve my disposition. "For the purpose of this talk you are a thief and a murderer."

Her strong slender body became the body of a lean crouching animal. Her white face became the face of an enraged animal. One hand—claw now—swept to the heavy pocket of her jacket.

Then, before I could have batted an eye—though my life seemed to depend on my not batting it—the wild animal had vanished. Out of it—and now I know where the writers of the old fairy stories got their ideas—rose the princess again, cool and straight and tall.

She sat down, crossed her ankles, put an elbow on an arm of her chair, propped her chin on the back of that hand, and looked curiously into my face.

"However," she murmured, "did you chance to arrive at so strange and fanciful a theory?"

"It wasn't chance, and it's neither strange nor fanciful," I said. "Maybe it'll save time and trouble if I show you part of the score against you. Then you'll know how you stand and won't waste your brains pleading innocence."

"I should be grateful," she smiled, "very!"

I tucked my crutch in between one knee and the arm of my chair, so my hands would be free to check off my points on my fingers.

"First—whoever planned the job knew the island—not fairly well, but every inch of it. There's no need to argue about that. Second—the car on which the machine gun was mounted was local property, stolen from the owner here. So was the boat in which the bandits were supposed to have escaped. Bandits from the outside would have needed a car or a boat to bring their machine guns, explosives, and grenades here, and there doesn't seem to be any reason why they shouldn't have used that car or boat instead of stealing a fresh one. Third—there wasn't the least hint of the professional bandit touch on this job. If you ask me, it was a military job from beginning to end. And the worst safe-burglar in the world could have got into both the bank vault and the jeweler's safe without wrecking the buildings. Fourth—bandits from the outside wouldn't have destroyed the bridge. They might have blocked it, but they wouldn't have destroyed it. They'd have saved it in case they had to make their getaway in that direction. Fifth—bandits figuring on a getaway by boat would have cut the job short, wouldn't have spread it over the whole night. Enough racket was made here to wake up California all the way from Sacramento to Los Angeles. What you people did was to send one man out in the boat, shooting, and he didn't go far. As soon as he was at a safe distance, he went overboard, and swam back to the island. Big Ignati could have done it without turning a hair."

That exhausted my right hand. I switched over, counting on my left.

"Sixth—I met one of your party, the lad, down on the beach, and he was coming from the boat. He suggested that we jump it. We were shot at, but the man behind the gun was playing with us. He could have wiped us out in a second if he had been in earnest, but he shot over our heads. Seventh—that same lad is the only man on the island, so far as I know, who saw the departing bandits. Eighth—all of your people that I ran into were especially nice to me, the general even spending an hour talking to me at the reception this afternoon. That's a distinctive amateur crook trait. Ninth—after the machine gun car had been wrecked I chased its occupant. I lost him around this house. The Italian boy I picked up wasn't him. He couldn't have climbed up on the path without my seeing him. But he could have run around to the general's side of the house and vanished indoors there. The general liked him, and would have helped him. I know that, because the general performed a downright miracle by missing him at some six feet with a shotgun. Tenth—you called at Hendrixson's house for no other purpose than to get me away from there."

That finished the left hand. I went back to the right.

"Eleventh—Hendrixson's two servants were killed by someone they knew and trusted. Both were killed at close quarters and without firing a shot. I'd say you got Oliver to let you into the house, and were talking to him when one of your men cut his throat from behind. Then you went upstairs and probably shot the unsuspecting Brophy yourself. He wouldn't have been on his guard against you. Twelfth—but that ought to be enough, and I'm getting a sore throat from listing them."

She took her chin off her hand, took a fat white cigarette out of a thin black case, and held it in her mouth while I put a match to the end of it. She took a long pull at it—a draw that accounted for a third of its length—and blew the smoke down at her knees.

"That would be enough," she said when all these things had been done, "if it were not that you yourself know it was impossible for us to have been so engaged. Did you not see us—did not everyone see us—time and time again?"

"That's easy!" I argued. "With a couple of machine guns, a trunkful of grenades, knowing the island from top to bottom, in the darkness and in a storm, against bewildered civilians—it was duck soup. There are nine of you that I know of, including two women. Any five of you could have carried on the work, once it was started, while the others took turns appearing here and there, establishing alibis. And that is what you did. You took turns slipping out to alibi yourselves. Everywhere I went I ran into one of you. And the general! That whiskered old joker running around leading the simple citizens to battle! I'll bet he led 'em plenty! They're lucky there are any of 'em alive this morning!"

She finished her cigarette with another inhalation, dropped the stub on the rug, ground out the light with one foot, sighed wearily, and asked:

"And now what?"

"Now I want to know where you have stowed the plunder."

The readiness of her answer surprised me.

"Under the garage, in a cellar we dug secretly there some months ago."

I didn't believe that, of course, but it turned out to be the truth.

I didn't have anything else to say. When I fumbled with my borrowed crutch, preparing to get up, she raised a hand and spoke gently:

"Wait a moment, please. I have something to suggest."

Half standing, I leaned toward her, stretching out one hand until it was close to her side.

"I want the gun," I said.

She nodded, and sat still while I plucked it from her pocket, put it in one of my own, and sat down again.

"You said a little while ago that you didn't care who I was," she began immediately. "But I want you to know. There are so many of us Russians who once were somebodies and who now are nobodies that I won't bore you with the repetition of a tale the world has grown tired of hearing. But you must remember that this weary tale is real to us who are its subjects. However, we fled from Russia with what we could carry of our property, which fortunately was enough to keep us in bearable comfort for a few years.

"In London we opened a Russian restaurant, but London was suddenly full of Russian restaurants, and ours became, instead of a means of livelihood, a source of loss. We tried teaching music and languages, and so on. In short, we hit on all the means of earning our living that other Russian exiles hit upon, and so always found ourselves in over-crowded, and thus unprofitable, fields. But what else did we know—could we do?

"I promised not to bore you. Well, always our capital shrank, and always the day approached on which we should be shabby and hungry, the day when we should become familiar to readers of your Sunday papers—charwomen who had been princesses, dukes who now were butlers. There was no place for us in the world. Outcasts easily become outlaws. Why not? Could it be said that we owed the world any fealty? Had not the world sat idly by and seen us despoiled of place and property and country?

"We planned it before we had heard of Couffignal. We could find a small settlement of the wealthy, sufficiently isolated, and, after establishing ourselves there, we would plunder it. Couffignal, when we found it, seemed to be the ideal place. We leased this house for six months, having just enough capital remaining to do that and to live properly here while our plans matured. Here we spent four months establishing ourselves, collecting our arms and our explosives, mapping our offensive, waiting for a favorable night. Last night seemed to be that night, and we had provided, we thought, against every eventuality. But we had not, of course, provided against your presence and your genius. They were simply others of the unforeseen misfortunes to which we seem eternally condemned."

She stopped, and fell to studying me with mournful large eyes that made me feel like fidgeting.

"It's no good calling me a genius," I objected. "The truth is you people botched your job from beginning to end. Your general would get a big laugh out of a man without military training who tried to lead an army. But here are you people with absolutely no criminal experience trying to swing a trick that needed the highest sort of criminal skill. Look at how you all played around with me! Amateur stuff! A professional crook with any intelligence would have either let me alone or knocked me off. No wonder you flopped! As for the rest of it—your troubles—I can't do anything about them."

"Why?" very softly. "Why can't you?"

"Why should I?" I made it blunt.

"No one else knows what you know." She bent forward to put a white hand on my knee. "There is wealth in that cellar beneath the garage. You may have whatever you ask."

I shook my head.

"You aren't a fool!" she protested. "You know—"

"Let me straighten this out for you," I interrupted. "We'll disregard whatever honesty I happen to have, sense of loyalty to employers, and so on. You might doubt them, so we'll throw them out. Now I'm a detective because I happen to like the work. It pays me a fair salary, but I could find other jobs that would pay more. Even a hundred dollars more a month would be twelve hundred a year. Say twenty-five or thirty thousand dollars in the years between now and my sixtieth birthday.

"Now I pass up about twenty-five or thirty thousand of honest gain because I like being a detective, like the work. And liking work makes you want to do it as well as you can. Otherwise there'd be no sense to it. That's the fix I am in. I don't know anything else, don't enjoy anything else, don't want to know or enjoy anything else. You can't weigh that against any sum of money. Money is good stuff. I haven't anything against it. But in the past eighteen years I've been getting my fun out of chasing crooks and tackling puzzles, my satisfaction out of catching crooks and solving riddles. It's the only kind of sport I know anything about, and I can't imagine a pleasanter future than twenty-some years more of it. I'm not going to blow that up!"

She shook her head slowly, lowering it, so that now her dark eyes looked up at me under the thin arcs of her brows.

"You speak only of money," she said. "I said you may have whatever you ask."

That was out. I don't know where these women get their ideas.

"You're still all twisted up," I said brusquely, standing now and adjusting my borrowed crutch. "You think I'm a man and you're a woman. That's wrong. I'm a man hunter and you're something that has been running in front of me. There's nothing human about it. You might just as well expect a hound to play tiddlywinks with the fox he's caught. We're wasting time anyway. I've been thinking the police or Marines might come up here and save me a walk. You've been waiting for your mob to come back and grab me. I could have told you they were being arrested when I left them."

That shook her. She had stood up. Now she fell back a step, putting a hand behind her for steadiness, on her chair. An exclamation I didn't understand popped out of her mouth. Russian, I thought, but the next moment I knew it had been Italian.

"Put your hands up."

It was Flippo's husky voice. Flippo stood in the doorway, holding an automatic.

I raised my hands as high as I could without dropping my supporting crutch, meanwhile cursing myself for having been too careless, or too vain, to keep a gun in my hand while I talked to the girl.

So this is why she had come back to the house. If she freed the Italian, she had thought, we would have no reason for suspecting that he hadn't been in on the robbery, and so we would look for the bandits among his friends. A prisoner, of course, he might have persuaded us of his innocence. She had given him the gun so he could either shoot his way clear, or, what would help her as much, get himself killed trying.

While I was arranging these thoughts in my head, Flippo had come up behind me. His empty hand passed over my body, taking away my own gun, his, and the one I had taken from the girl.

"A bargain, Flippo," I said when he had moved away from me, a little to one side, where he made one corner of a triangle whose other corners were the girl and I. "You're out on parole, with some years still to be served. I picked you up with a gun on you. That's plenty to send you back to the big house. I know you weren't in on this job. My idea is that you were up here on a smaller one of your own, but I can't prove that and don't want to. Walk out of here, alone and neutral, and I'll forget I saw you."

Little thoughtful lines grooved the boy's round, dark face.

The princess took a step toward him.

"You heard the offer I just now made him?" she asked. "Well, I make that offer to you, if you will kill him."

The thoughtful lines in the boy's face deepened.

"There's your choice, Flippo," I summed up for him. "All I can give you is freedom from San Quentin. The princess can give you a fat cut of the profits in a busted caper, with a good chance to get yourself hanged."

The girl, remembering her advantage over me, went at him hot and heavy in Italian, a language in which I know only four words. Two of them are profane and the other two obscene. I said all four.

The boy was weakening. If he had been ten years older, he'd have taken my offer and thanked me for it. But he was young and she—now that I thought of it—was beautiful. The answer wasn't hard to guess.

"But not to bump him off," he said to her, in English, for my benefit. "We'll lock him up in there where I was at."

I suspected Flippo hadn't any great prejudice against murder. It was just that he thought this one unnecessary, unless he was kidding me to make the killing easier.

The girl wasn't satisfied with his suggestion. She poured more hot Italian at him. Her game looked sure-fire, but it had a flaw. She couldn't persuade him that his chances of getting any of the loot away were good. She had to depend on her charms to swing him. And that meant she had to hold his eye.

He wasn't far from me.

She came close to him. She was singing, chanting, crooning Italian syllables into his round face.

She had him.

He shrugged. His whole face said yes. He turned—

I knocked him on the noodle with my borrowed crutch.

The crutch splintered apart. Flippo's knees bent. He stretched up to his full height. He fell on his face on the floor. He lay there, dead still, except for a thin worm of blood that crawled out of his hair to the rug.

A step, a tumble, a foot or so of hand-and-knee scrambling put me within reach of Flippo's gun.

The girl, jumping out of my path, was halfway to the door when I sat up with the gun in my hand.

"Stop!" I ordered.

"I shan't," she said, but she did, for the time at least. "I am going out."

"You are going out when I take you."

She laughed, a pleasant laugh, low and confident.

"I'm going out before that," she insisted good-naturedly.

I shook my head.

"How do you purpose stopping me?" she asked.

"I don't think I'll have to," I told her. "You've got too much sense to try to run while I'm holding a gun on you."

She laughed again, an amused ripple.

"I've got too much sense to stay," she corrected me. "Your crutch is broken, and you're lame. You can't catch me by running after me, then. You pretend you'll shoot me, but I don't believe you. You'd shoot me if I attacked you, of course, but I shan't do that. I shall simply walk out, and you know you won't shoot me for that. You'll wish you could, but you won't. You'll see."

Her face turned over her shoulder, her dark eyes twinkling at me, she took a step toward the door.

"Better not count on that!" I threatened.

For answer to that she gave me a cooing laugh. And took another step.

"Stop, you idiot!" I bawled at her.

Her face laughed over her shoulder at me. She walked without haste to the door, her short skirt of grey flannel shaping itself to the calf of each grey wool-stockinged leg as its mate stepped forward.

Sweat greased the gun in my hand.

When her right foot was on the doorsill, a little chuckling sound came from her throat.

"Adieu!" she said softly.

And I put a bullet in the calf of her left leg.

She sat down—plump! Utter surprise stretched her white face. It was too soon for pain.

I had never shot a woman before. I felt queer about it.

"You ought to have known I'd do it!" My voice sounded harsh and savage and like a stranger's in my ears. "Didn't I steal a crutch from a cripple?"

RAYMOND CHANDLER
1888–1959

Considered one of the most important developers of the hard-boiled detective, Raymond Thornton Chandler was born in Chicago but at an early age moved to England with his mother. He was educated at British schools, including Dulwich College in London. His early writing experience was as a freelance journalist in England before returning to the United States in 1912. During World War I he served in the Canadian Army and the Royal Air Force. When the war ended, he moved to Los Angeles, California, and began a business career in the oil industry. In 1933 he became a full-time writer and sold his first short story to *Black Mask* magazine. He continued to write stories for *Black Mask* and other pulp magazines, but his enduring reputation as a great writer of hard-boiled detective fiction began with the publication of his first novel, *The Big Sleep* (1939). Chandler is one of the most written about of all American mystery writers. He received the Edgar Award in 1955 for *The Long Goodbye* (1954) and was President of the Mystery Writers of America briefly in 1959, just previous to his death.

Philip Marlowe is the Los Angeles private investigator who appears in all of Chandler's novels. Marlowe is full of contradictions. He is educated and tough, sophisticated and physical. He likes to solve chess puzzles and enjoys classical music and art, but he also has a good eye for women and enjoys his liquor. He is his own man, honorable, reliable, and willing to take a beating rather than betray a client. Chandler gives Marlowe some of the best descriptive one-liners in all of American literature. Through Marlowe, Chandler presents "the mean streets," an undaunted look at urban violence, corrupt politicians, and brutal police. Not only a detective fiction writer but a critic as well, Chandler provides possibly the best critical essay on the private-eye novel in "The Simple Art of Murder," published in *The Atlantic Monthly* in 1944. "Trouble Is My Business" was first published in August 1939, in *Dime Detective* magazine.

Recommended Chandler works: *The Big Sleep, Farewell, My Lovely, The Long Goodbye.*

Other recommended authors: Dashiell Hammett, John D. MacDonald, Robert B. Parker.

Trouble Is My Business

One

Anna Halsey was about two hundred and forty pounds of middle-aged putty-faced woman in a black tailor-made suit. Her eyes were shiny black shoe buttons, her cheeks were as soft as suet and about the same color. She was sitting behind a black glass desk that looked like Napoleon's tomb and she was smoking a cigarette in a black holder that was not quite as long as a rolled umbrella. She said: "I need a man."

I watched her shake ash from the cigarette to the shiny top of the desk where flakes of it curled and crawled in the draft from an open window.

"I need a man good-looking enough to pick up a dame who has a sense of class, but he's got to be tough enough to swap punches with a power shovel. I need a guy who can act like a bar lizard and backchat like Fred Allen, only better, and get hit on the head with a beer truck and think some cutie in the legline topped him with a breadstick."

"It's a cinch," I said. "You need the New York Yankees, Robert Donat, and the Yacht Club Boys."

"You might do," Anna said, "cleaned up a little. Twenty bucks a day and ex's. I haven't brokered a job in years, but this one is out of my line. I'm in the smooth-angles of the detecting business and I make money without getting my can knocked off. Let's see how Gladys likes you."

She reversed the cigarette holder and tipped a key on a large black-and-chromium annunciator box. "Come in and empty Anna's ash tray, honey."

We waited.

The door opened and a tall blonde dressed better than the Duchess of Windsor strolled in.

She swayed elegantly across the room, emptied Anna's ash tray, patted her fat cheek, gave me a smooth rippling glance and went out again.

"I think she blushed," Anna said when the door closed. "I guess you still have It."

"She blushed—and I have a dinner date with Darryl Zanuck," I said. "Quit horsing around. What's the story?"

"It's to smear a girl. A redheaded number with bedroom eyes. She's shill for a gambler and she's got her hooks into a rich man's pup."

"What do I do to her?"

Anna sighed. "It's kind of a mean job, Philip, I guess. If she's got a record of any sort, you dig it up and toss it in her face. If she hasn't, which is more likely as she comes from good people, it's kind of up to you. You get an idea once in a while, don't you?"

"I can't remember the last one I had. What gambler and what rich man?"

"Marty Estel."

I started to get up from my chair, then remembered that business had been bad for a month and that I needed the money.

I sat down again.

"You might get into trouble, of course," Anna said. "I never heard of Marty bumping anybody off in the public square at high noon, but he don't play with cigar coupons."

"Trouble is my business." I said. "Twenty-five a day and guarantee of two-fifty, if I pull the job."

"I gotta make a little something for myself," Anna whined.

"O.K. There's plenty of coolie labor around town. Nice to have seen you looking so well. So long, Anna."

I stood up this time. My life wasn't worth much, but it was worth that much. Marty Estel was supposed to be pretty tough people, with the right

helpers and the right protection behind him. His place was out in West Hollywood, on the Strip. He wouldn't pull anything crude, but if he pulled at all,
something would pop.

"Sit down, it's a deal," Anna sneered. "I'm a poor old broken-down woman
trying to run a high-class detective agency on nothing but fat and bad health,
so take my last nickel and laugh at me."

"Who's the girl?" I had sat down again.

"Her name is Harriet Huntress—a swell name for the part too. She lives in the
El Milano, nineteen-hundred block on North Sycamore, very high-class. Father
went broke back in thirty-one and jumped out of his office window. Mother dead.
Kid sister in boarding school back in Connecticut. That might make an angle."

"Who dug up all this?"

"The client got a bunch of photostats of notes the pup had given to Marty.
Fifty grand worth. The pup—he's an adopted son to the old man—denied the
notes, as kids will. So the client had the photostats experted by a guy named
Arbogast, who pretends to be good at that sort of thing. He said O.K. and dug
around a bit, but he's too fat to do legwork, like me, and he's off the case now."

"But I could talk to him?"

"I don't know why not." Anna nodded several of her chins.

"This client—does he have a name?"

"Son, you have a treat coming. You can meet him in person—right now."
She tipped the key of her call box again. "Have Mr. Jeeter come in, honey."

"That Gladys," I said, "does she have a steady?"

"You lay off Gladys!" Anna almost screamed at me. "She's worth eighteen
grand a year in divorce business to me. Any guy that lays a finger on her, Philip
Marlowe, is practically cremated."

"She's got to fall some day," I said. "Why couldn't I catch her?"

The opening door stopped that.

I hadn't seen him in the paneled reception room, so he must have been
waiting in a private office. He hadn't enjoyed it. He came in quickly, shut the
door quickly, and yanked a thin octagonal platinum watch from his vest and
glared at it. He was a tall white-blond type in pin-striped flannel of youthful cut.
There was a small pink rosebud in his lapel. He had a keen frozen face, a little
pouchy under the eyes, a little thick in the lips. He carried an ebony cane with
a silver knob, wore spats and looked a smart sixty, but I gave him close to ten
years more. I didn't like him.

"Twenty-six minutes, Miss Halsey," he said icily. "My time happens to be valuable. By regarding it as valuable I have managed to make a great deal of money."

"Well, we're trying to save you some of the money," Anna drawled. She
didn't like him either. "Sorry to keep you waiting, Mr. Jeeter, but you wanted
to see the operative I selected and I had to send for him."

"He doesn't look the type to me," Mr. Jeeter said, giving me a nasty glance.
"I think more of a gentleman—"

"You're not the Jeeter of *Tobacco Road*, are you?" I asked him.

He came slowly towards me and half lifted the stick. His icy eyes tore at me like claws. "So you insult me," he said. "Me—a man in my position."

"Now wait a minute," Anna began.

"Wait a minute nothing," I said. "This party said I was not a gentleman. Maybe that's O.K. for a man in his position, whatever it is—but a man in my position doesn't take a dirty crack from anybody. He can't afford to. Unless, of course, it wasn't intended."

Mr. Jeeter stiffened and glared at me. He took his watch out again and looked at it. "Twenty-eight minutes," he said. "I apologize, young man. I had no desire to be rude."

"That's swell," I said. "I knew you weren't the Jeeter in *Tobacco Road* all along."

That almost started him again, but he let it go. He wasn't sure how I meant it.

"A question or two while we are together," I said. "Are you willing to give this Huntress girl a little money—for expenses?"

"Not one cent," he barked. "Why should I?"

"It's got to be a sort of custom. Suppose she married him. What would he have?"

"At the moment a thousand dollars a month from a trust fund established by his mother, my late wife." He dipped his head. "When he is twenty-eight years old, far too much money."

"You can't blame the girl for trying," I said. "Not these days. How about Marty Estel? Any settlement there?"

He crumpled his gray gloves with a purple-veined hand. "The debt is uncollectible. It is a gambling debt."

Anna sighed wearily and flicked ash around on her desk.

"Sure," I said. "But gamblers can't afford to let people welsh on them. After all, if your son had won, Marty would have paid *him*."

"I'm not interested in that," the tall thin man said coldly.

"Yeah, but think of Marty sitting there with fifty grand in notes. Not worth a nickel. How will he sleep nights?"

Mr. Jeeter looked thoughtful. "You mean there is danger of violence?" he suggested, almost suavely.

"That's hard to say. He runs an exclusive place, gets a good movie crowd. He has his own reputation to think of. But he's in a racket and he knows people. Things can happen—a long way off from where Marty is. And Marty is no bathmat. He gets up and walks."

Mr. Jeeter looked at his watch again and it annoyed him. He slammed it back into his vest. "All that is your affair," he snapped. "The district attorney is a personal friend of mine. If this matter seems to be beyond your powers—"

"Yeah," I told him. "But you came slumming down our street just the same. Even if the D.A. is in your vest pocket—along with that watch."

He put his hat on, drew on one glove, tapped the edge of his shoe with his stick, walked to the door and opened it.

"I ask results and I pay for them," he said coldly. "I pay promptly. I even pay generously sometimes, although I am not considered a generous man. I think we all understand one another."

He almost winked then and went on out. The door closed softly against the cushion of air in the door-closer. I looked at Anna and grinned.

"Sweet, isn't he?" she said. "I'd like eight of him for my cocktail set."

I gouged twenty dollars out of her—for expenses.

Two

The Arbogast I wanted was John D. Arbogast and he had an office on Sunset near Ivar. I called him up from a phone booth. The voice that answered was fat. It wheezed softly, like the voice of a man who had just won a pie-eating contest.

"Mr. John D. Arbogast?"

"Yeah."

"This is Philip Marlowe, a private detective working on a case you did some experting on. Party named Jeeter."

"Yeah?"

"Can I come up and talk to you about it—after I eat lunch?"

"Yeah." He hung up. I decided he was not a talkative man.

I had lunch and drove out there. It was east of Ivar, an old two-story building faced with brick which had been painted recently. The street floor was stores and a restaurant. The building entrance was the foot of a wide straight stairway to the second floor. On the directory at the bottom I read: John D. Arbogast, Suite 212. I went up the stairs and found myself in a wide straight hall that ran parallel with the street. A man in a smock was standing in an open doorway down to my right. He wore a round mirror strapped to his forehead and pushed back, and his face had a puzzled expression. He went back to his office and shut the door.

I went the other way, about half the distance along the hall. A door on the side away from Sunset was lettered: JOHN D. ARBOGAST, EXAMINER OF QUES-TIONED DOCUMENTS. PRIVATE INVESTIGATOR. ENTER. The door opened without resistance onto a small windowless anteroom with a couple of easy chairs, some magazines, two chromium smoking stands. There were two floor lamps and a ceiling fixture, all lighted. A door on the other side of the cheap but thick new rug was lettered: JOHN D. ARBOGAST, EXAMINER OF QUESTIONED DOCU-MENTS. PRIVATE.

A buzzer had rung when I opened the outer door and gone on ringing until it closed. Nothing happened. Nobody was in the waiting room. The inner door didn't open. I went over and listened at the panel—no sound of conversation inside. I knocked. That didn't buy me anything either. I tried the knob. It turned, so I opened the door and went in.

This room had two north windows, both curtained at the sides and both shut tight. There was dust on the sills. There was a desk, two filing cases, a carpet which was just a carpet, and walls which were just walls. To the left another door with a glass panel was lettered: JOHN D. ARBOGAST. LABORATORY. PRIVATE.

I had an idea I might be able to remember the name.

The room in which I stood was small. It seemed almost too small even for the pudgy hand that rested on the edge of the desk, motionless, holding a fat pencil like a carpenter's pencil. The hand had a wrist, hairless as a plate. A buttoned shirt cuff, not too clean, came down out of a coat sleeve. The rest of the sleeve dropped over the far edge of the desk out of sight. The desk was less than six feet long, so he couldn't have been a very tall man. The hand and the ends of the sleeves were all I saw of him from where I stood. I went quietly back through the anteroom and fixed its door so that it couldn't be opened from the outside and put out the three lights and went back to the private office. I went around an end of the desk.

He was fat all right, enormously fat, fatter by far than Anna Halsey. His face, what I could see of it, looked about the size of a basket ball. It had a pleasant pinkness, even now. He was kneeling on the floor. He had his large head against the sharp inner corner of the kneehole of the desk, and his left hand was flat on the floor with a piece of yellow paper under it. The fingers were outspread as much as such fat fingers could be, and the yellow paper showed between. He looked as if he were pushing hard on the floor, but he wasn't really. What was holding him up was his own fat. His body was folded down against his enormous thighs, and the thickness and fatness of them held him that way, kneeling, poised solid. It would have taken a couple of good blocking backs to knock him over. That wasn't a very nice idea at the moment, but I had it just the same. I took time out and wiped the back of my neck, although it was not a warm day.

His hair was gray and clipped short and his neck had as many folds as a concertina. His feet were small, as the feet of fat men often are, and they were in black shiny shoes which were sideways on the carpet and close together and neat and nasty. He wore a dark suit that needed cleaning. I leaned down and buried my fingers in the bottomless fat of his neck. He had an artery in there somewhere, probably, but I couldn't find it and he didn't need it any more anyway. Between his bloated knees on the carpet a dark stain had spread and spread—

I knelt in another place and lifted the pudgy fingers that were holding down the piece of yellow paper. They were cool, but not cold, and soft and a little sticky. The paper was from a scratch pad. It would have been very nice if it had had a message on it, but it hadn't. There were vague meaningless marks, not words, not even letters. He had tried to write something after he was shot— perhaps even thought he *was* writing something—but all he managed was some hen scratches.

He had slumped down then, still holding the paper, pinned it to the floor with his fat hand, held on to the fat pencil with his other hand, wedged his torso against his huge thighs, and so died. John D. Arbogast. Examiner of Questioned Documents. Private. Very damned private. He had said "yeah" to me three times over the phone.

And here he was.

I wiped doorknobs with my handkerchief, put off the lights in the anteroom, left the outer door so that it was locked from the outside, left the hallway, left the building and left the neighborhood. So far as I could tell nobody saw me go. So far as I could tell.

Three

The El Milano was, as Anna had told me, in the 1900 block on North Sycamore. It was most of the block. I parked fairly near the ornamental forecourt and went along to the pale blue neon sign over the entrance to the basement garage. I walked down a railed ramp into a bright space of glistening cars and cold air. A trim light-colored Negro in a spotless coverall suit with blue cuffs came out of a glass office. His black hair was as smooth as a bandleader's.

"Busy?" I asked him.

"Yes and no, sir."

"I've got a car outside that needs a dusting. About five bucks worth of dusting."

It didn't work. He wasn't the type. His chestnut eyes became thoughtful and remote. "That is a good deal of dusting, sir. May I ask if anything else would be included?"

"A little. Is Miss Harriet Huntress' car in?"

He looked. I saw him look along the glistening row at a canary-yellow convertible which was about as inconspicuous as a privy on the front lawn.

"Yes, sir. It is in."

"I'd like her apartment number and a way to get up there without going through the lobby. I'm a private detective." I showed him a buzzer. He looked at the buzzer. It failed to amuse him.

He smiled the faintest smile I ever saw. "Five dollars is nice money, sir, to a working man. It falls a little short of being nice enough to make me risk my position. About from here to Chicago short, sir. I suggest that you save your five dollars, sir, and try the customary mode of entry."

"You're quite a guy," I said. "What are you going to be when you grow up—a five-foot shelf?"

"I am already grown up, sir. I am thirty-four years old, married happily, and have two children. Good afternoon, sir."

He turned on his heel. "Well, goodbye," I said. "And pardon my whiskey breath. I just got in from Butte."

I went back up along the ramp and wandered along the street to where I should have gone in the first place. I might have known that five bucks and a buzzer wouldn't buy me anything in a place like the El Milano.

The Negro was probably telephoning the office right now.

The building was a huge white stucco affair, Moorish in style, with great fretted lanterns in the forecourt and huge date palms. The entrance was at the inside corner of an L, up marble steps, through an arch framed in California or dishpan mosaic.

A doorman opened the door for me and I went in. The lobby was not quite as big as the Yankee Stadium. It was floored with a pale blue carpet with sponge rubber underneath. It was so soft it made me want to lie down and roll. I waded over to the desk and put an elbow on it and was stared at by a pale thin clerk with one of those mustaches that get stuck under your fingernail. He toyed with it and looked past my shoulder at an Ali Baba oil jar big enough to keep a tiger in.

"Miss Huntress in?"

"Who shall I announce?"

"Mr. Marty Estel."

That didn't take any better than my play in the garage. He leaned on something with his left foot. A blue-and-gilt door opened at the end of the desk and a large sandy-haired man with cigar ash on his vest came out and leaned absently on the end of the desk and stared at the Ali Baba oil jar, as if trying to make up his mind whether it was a spittoon.

The clerk raised his voice. "You are Mr. Marty Estel?"

"From him."

"Isn't that a little different? And what is your name, sir, if one may ask?"

"One may ask," I said. "One may not be told. Such are my orders. Sorry to be stubborn and all that rot."

He didn't like my manner. He didn't like anything about me. "I'm afraid I can't announce you," he said coldly. "Mr. Hawkins, might I have your advice on a matter?"

The sandy-haired man took his eyes off the oil jar and slid along the desk until he was within blackjack range of me.

"Yes, Mr. Gregory?" he yawned.

"Nuts to both of you," I said. "And that includes your lady friends."

Hawkins grinned. "Come into my office, bo. We'll kind of see if we can get you straightened out."

I followed him into the doghole he had come out of. It was large enough for a pint-sized desk, two chairs, a knee-high cuspidor, and an open box of cigars. He placed his rear end against the desk and grinned at me sociably.

"Didn't play it very smooth, did you, bo? I'm the house man here. Spill it."

"Some days I feel like playing smooth," I said, "and some days I feel like playing it like a waffle iron." I got my wallet out and showed him the buzzer and the small photostat of my license behind a celluloid window.

"One of the boys, huh?" He nodded. "You ought to of asked for me in the first place."

"Sure. Only I never heard of you. I want to see this Huntress frail. She doesn't know me, but I have business with her, and it's not noisy business."

He made a yard and half sideways and cocked his cigar in the other corner of his mouth. He looked at my right eyebrow. "What's the gag? Why try to apple-polish the dinge downstairs? You gettin' any expense money?"

"Could be."

"I'm nice people," he said. "But I gotta protect the guests."

"You're almost out of cigars," I said, looking at the ninety or so in the box. I lifted a couple, smelled them, tucked a folded ten-dollar bill below them and put them back.

"That's cute," he said. "You and me could get along. What you want done?"

"Tell her I'm from Marty Estel. She'll see me."

"It's the job if I get a kickback."

"You won't. I've got important people behind me."

I started to reach for my ten, but he pushed my hand away. "I'll take a chance," he said. He reached for his phone and asked for Suite 814 and began to hum. His humming sounded like a cow being sick. He leaned forward suddenly and his face became a honeyed smile. His voice dripped.

"Miss Huntress? This is Hawkins, the house man. Hawkins. Yeah . . . Hawkins. Sure, you meet a lot of people, Miss Huntress. Say, there's a gentleman in my office wanting to see you with a message from Mr. Estel. We can't let him up without your say so, because he don't want to give us no name . . . Yeah, Hawkins, the house detective, Miss Huntress. Yeah, he says you don't know him personal, but he looks O.K. to me . . . O.K. Thanks a lot, Miss Huntress. Serve him right up."

He put the phone down and patted it gently.

"All you needed was some background music," I said.

"You can ride up," he said dreamily. He reached absently into his cigar box and removed the folded bill. "A darb," he said softly. "Every time I think of that dame I have to go out and walk around the block. Let's go."

We went out to the lobby again and Hawkins took me to the elevator and highsigned me in.

As the elevator doors closed I saw him on his way to the entrance, probably for his walk around the block.

The elevator had a carpeted floor and mirrors and indirect lighting. It rose as softly as the mercury in a thermometer. The doors whispered open, I wandered over the moss they used for a hall carpet and came to a door marked 814. I pushed a little button beside it, chimes rang inside and the door opened.

She wore a street dress of pale green wool and a small cock-eyed hat that hung on her ear like a butterfly. Her eyes were wide-set and there was thinking room between them. Their color was lapis-lazuli blue and the color of her hair was dusky red, like a fire under control but still dangerous. She was too tall to be cute. She wore plenty of make-up in the right places and the cigarette she was poking at me had a built-on mouthpiece about three inches long. She didn't look hard, but she looked as if she had heard all the answers and remembered the ones she thought she might be able to use sometime.

She looked me over coolly. "Well, what's the message, brown-eyes?"

"I'd have to come in," I said. "I never could talk on my feet."

She laughed disinterestedly and I slid past the end of her cigarette into a long rather narrow room with plenty of nice furniture, plenty of windows, plenty of drapes, plenty of everything. A fire blazed behind a screen, a big log on top of a gas teaser. There was a silk Oriental rug in front of a nice rose davenport in front of the nice fire, and beside that there was Scotch and swish on a tabouret, ice in a bucket, everything to make a man feel at home.

"You'd better have a drink," she said. "You probably can't talk without a glass in your hand."

I sat down and reached for the Scotch. The girl sat in a deep chair and crossed her knees. I thought of Hawkins walking around the block. I could see a little something in his point of view.

"So you're from Marty Estel," she said, refusing a drink.

"Never met him."

"I had an idea to that effect. What's the racket, bum? Marty will love to hear how you used his name."

"I'm shaking in my shoes. What made you let me up?"

"Curiosity. I've been expecting lads like you any day. I never dodge trouble. Some kind of a dick, aren't you?"

I lit a cigarette and nodded. "Private. I have a little deal to propose."

"Propose it." She yawned.

"How much will you take to lay off young Jeeter?"

She yawned again. "You interest me—so little I could hardly tell you."

"Don't scare me to death. Honest, how much are you asking? Or is that an insult?"

She smiled. She had a nice smile. She had lovely teeth. "I'm a bad girl now," she said. "I don't have to ask. They bring it to me, tied up with ribbon."

"The old man's a little tough. They say he draws a lot of water."

"Water doesn't cost much."

I nodded and drank some more of my drink. It was good Scotch. In fact it was perfect. "His idea is you get nothing. You get smeared. You get put in the middle. I can't see it that way."

"But you're working for him."

"Sounds funny, doesn't it? There's probably a smart way to play this, but I just can't think of it at the moment. How much would you take—or would you?"

"How about fifty grand?"

"Fifty grand for you and another fifty for Marty?"

She laughed. "Now, you ought to know Marty wouldn't like me to mix in his business. I was just thinking of my end."

She crossed her legs the other way. I put another lump of ice in my drink.

"I was thinking of five hundred," I said.

"Five hundred what?" She looked puzzled.

"Dollars—not Rolls-Royces."

She laughed heartily. "You amuse me. I ought to tell you to go to hell, but I like brown eyes. Warm brown eyes with flecks of gold in them."

"You're throwing it away. I don't have a nickel."

She smiled and fitted a fresh cigarette between her lips. I went over to light it for her. Her eyes came up and looked into mine. Hers had sparks in them.

"Maybe I have a nickel already," she said softly.

"Maybe that's why he hired the fat boy—so you couldn't make him dance." I sat down again.

"Who hired what fat boy?"

"Old Jeeter hired a fat boy named Arbogast. He was on the case before me. Didn't you know? He got bumped off this afternoon."

I said it quite casually for the shock effect, but she didn't move. The provocative smile didn't leave the corners of her lips. Her eyes didn't change. She made a dim sound with her breath.

"Does it have to have something to do with me?" she asked quietly.

"I don't know. I don't know who murdered him. It was done in his office, around noon or a little later. It may not have anything to do with the Jeeter case. But it happened pretty pat—just after I had been put on the job and before I got a chance to talk to him."

She nodded. "I see. And you think Marty does things like that. And of course you told the police?"

"Of course I did not."

"You're giving away a little weight there, brother."

"Yeah. But let's get together on a price and it had better be low. Because whatever the cops do to me they'll do plenty to Marty Estel and you when they get the story—if they get it."

"A little spot of blackmail," the girl said coolly. "I think I might call it that. Don't go too far with me, brown-eyes. By the way, do I know your name?"

"Philip Marlowe."

"Then listen, Philip. I was in the Social Register once. My family were nice people. Old man Jeeter ruined my father—all proper and legitimate, the way that kind of heel ruins people—but he ruined him, and my father committed suicide, and my mother died and I've got a kid sister back East in school and perhaps I'm not too damn particular how I get the money to take care of her. And maybe I'm going to take care of old Jeeter one of these days, too—even if I have to marry his son to do it."

"Stepson, adopted son," I said. "No relation at all."

"It'll hurt him just as hard, brother. And the boy will have plenty of the long green in a couple of years. I could do worse—even if he does drink too much."

"You wouldn't say that in front of him, lady."

"No? Take a look behind you, gumshoe. You ought to have the wax taken out of your ears."

I stood up and turned fast. He stood about four feet from me. He had come out of some door and sneaked across the carpet and I had been too busy being clever with nothing on the ball to hear him. He was big, blond, dressed in a rough sporty suit, with a scarf and open-necked shirt. He was red-faced and his eyes glittered and they were not focusing any too well. He was a bit drunk for that early in the day.

"Beat it while you can still walk," he sneered at me. "I heard it. Harry can say anything she likes about me. I like it. Dangle, before I knock your teeth down your throat!"

The girl laughed behind me. I didn't like that. I took a step towards the big blond boy. His eyes blinked. Big as he was, he was a pushover.

"Ruin him, baby," the girl said coldly behind my back. "I love to see these hard numbers bend at the knees."

I looked back at her with a leer. That was a mistake. He was wild, probably, but he could still hit a wall that didn't jump. He hit me while I was looking back over my shoulder. It hurts to be hit that way. He hit me plenty hard, on the back end of the jawbone.

I went over sideways, tried to spread my legs, and slid on the silk rug. I did a nose dive somewhere or other and my head was not as hard as the piece of furniture it smashed into.

For a brief blurred moment I saw his red face sneering down at me in triumph. I think I was a little sorry for him—even then.

Darkness folded down and I went out.

Four

When I came to, the light from the windows across the room was hitting me square in the eyes. The back of my head ached. I felt it and it was sticky. I moved around slowly, like a cat in a strange house, got up on my knees and reached for the bottle of Scotch on the tabouret at the end of the davenport. By some miracle I hadn't knocked it over. Falling I had hit my head on the clawlike leg of a chair. That had hurt me a lot more than young Jeeter's haymaker. I could feel the sore place on my jaw all right, but it wasn't important enough to write in my diary.

I got up on my feet, took a swig of the Scotch and looked around. There wasn't anything to see. The room was empty. It was full of silence and the memory of a nice perfume. One of those perfumes you don't notice until they are almost gone, like the last leaf on a tree. I felt my head again, touched the sticky place with my handkerchief, decided it wasn't worth yelling about, and took another drink.

I sat down with the bottle on my knees, listening to traffic noise somewhere, far off. It was a nice room. Miss Harriet Huntress was a nice girl. She knew a few wrong numbers, but who didn't? I should criticize a little thing like that. I took another drink. The level in the bottle was a lot lower now. It was smooth and you hardly noticed it going down. It didn't take half your tonsils with it, like some of the stuff I had to drink. I took some more. My head felt all right now. I felt fine. I felt like singing the Prologue to *Pagliacci*. Yes, she was a nice girl. If she was paying her own rent, she was doing right well. I was for her. She was swell. I used some more of her Scotch.

The bottle was still half full. I shook it gently, stuffed it in my overcoat pocket, put my hat somewhere on my head and left. I made the elevator without hitting the walls on either side of the corridor, floated downstairs, strolled out into the lobby.

Hawkins, the house dick, was leaning on the end of the desk again, staring at the Ali Baba oil jar. The same clerk was nuzzling at the same itsy-bitsy mustache. I smiled at him. He smiled back. Hawkins smiled at me. I smiled back. Everybody was swell.

I made the front door the first time and gave the doorman two bits and floated down the steps and along the walk to the street and my car. The swift California twilight was falling. It was a lovely night. Venus in the west was as bright as a street lamp, as bright as life, as bright as Miss Huntress' eyes, as bright as a bottle of Scotch. That reminded me. I got the square bottle out and tapped it with discretion, corked it, and tucked it away again. There was still enough to get home on.

I crashed five red lights on the way back but my luck was in and nobody pinched me. I parked more or less in front of my apartment house and more or less near the curb. I rode to my floor in the elevator, had a little trouble opening the doors and helped myself out with my bottle. I got the key into my door and unlocked it and stepped inside and found the light switch. I took a little more of my medicine before exhausting myself any further. Then I started for the kitchen to get some ice and ginger ale for a real drink.

I thought there was a funny smell in the apartment—nothing I could put a name to offhand—a sort of medicinal smell. I hadn't put it there and it hadn't been there when I went out. But I felt too well to argue about it. I started for the kitchen, got about halfway there.

They came out at me, almost side by side, from the dressing room beside the wall bed—two of them—with guns. The tall one was grinning. He had his hat low on his forehead and he had a wedge-shaped face that ended in a point, like the bottom half of the ace of diamonds. He had dark moist eyes and a nose so bloodless that it might have been made of white wax. His gun was a Colt Woodsman with a long barrel and the front sight filed off. That meant he thought he was good.

The other was a little terrierlike punk with bristly reddish hair and no hat and watery blank eyes and bat ears and small feet in dirty white sneakers. He had an automatic that looked too heavy for him to hold up, but he seemed to like holding it. He breathed open-mouthed and noisily and the smell I had noticed came from him in waves—menthol.

"Reach, you bastard," he said.

I put my hands up. There was nothing else to do.

The little one circled around to the side and came at me from the side. "Tell us we can't get away with it," he sneered.

"You can't get away with it," I said.

The tall one kept on grinning loosely and his nose kept on looking as if it was made of white wax. The little one spat on my carpet. "Yah!" He came close to me, leering, and made a pass at my chin with the big gun.

I dodged. Ordinarily that would have been just something which, in the circumstances, I had to take and like. But I was feeling better than ordinary. I was a world-beater. I took them in sets, guns and all. I took the little man around the throat and jerked him hard against my stomach, put a hand over his little gun hand and knocked the gun to the floor. It was easy. Nothing was bad about it but his breath. Blobs of saliva came out on his lips. He spit curses.

The tall man stood and leered and didn't shoot. He didn't move. His eyes looked a little anxious, I thought, but I was too busy to make sure. I went down behind the little punk, still holding him, and got hold of his gun. That was wrong. I ought to have pulled my own.

I threw him away from me and he reeled against a chair and fell down and began to kick the chair savagely. The tall man laughed.

"It ain't got any firing pin in it," he said.

"Listen," I told him earnestly, "I'm half full of good Scotch and ready to go places and get things done. Don't waste much of my time. What do you boys want?"

"It still ain't got any firing pin in it," Waxnose said. "Try and see. I don't never let Frisky carry a loaded rod. He's too impulsive. You got a nice arm action there, pal. I will say that for you."

Frisky sat up on the floor and spat on the carpet again and laughed. I pointed the muzzle of the big automatic at the floor and squeezed the trigger. It clicked dryly, but from the balance it felt as if it had cartridges in it.

"We don't mean no harm," Waxnose said. "Not this trip. Maybe next trip? Who knows? Maybe you're a guy that will take a hint. Lay off the Jeeter kid is the word. See?"

"No."

"You won't do it?"

"No, I don't see. Who's the Jeeter kid?"

Waxnose was not amused. He waved his long .22 gently. "You oughta get your memory fixed, pal, about the same time you get your door fixed. A pushover that was. Frisky just blew it in with his breath."

"I can understand that," I said.

"Gimme my gat," Frisky yelped. He was up off the floor again, but this time he rushed his partner instead of me.

"Lay off, dummy," the tall one said. "We just got a message for a guy. We don't blast him. Not today."

"Says you!" Frisky snarled and tried to grab the .22 out of Waxnose's hand. Waxnose threw him to one side without trouble but the interlude allowed me to switch the big automatic to my left hand and jerk out my Luger. I showed it to Waxnose. He nodded, but did not seem impressed.

"He ain't got no parents," he said sadly. "I just let him run around with me. Don't pay him no attention unless he bites you. We'll be on our way now. You get the idea. Lay off the Jeeter kid."

"You're looking at a Luger," I said. "Who is the Jeeter kid? And maybe we'll have some cops before you leave."

He smiled wearily. "Mister, I pack this small-bore because I can shoot. If you think you can take me, go to it."

"O.K.," I said. "Do you know anybody named Arbogast?"

"I meet such a lot of people," he said, with another weary smile. "Maybe yes, maybe no. So long, pal. Be pure."

He strolled over to the door, moving a little sideways, so that he had me covered all the time, and I had him covered, and it was just a case of who shot first and straightest, or whether it was worthwhile to shoot at all, or whether I could hit anything with so much nice warm Scotch in me. I let him go. He didn't look like a killer to me, but I could have been wrong.

The little man rushed me again while I wasn't thinking about him. He clawed his big automatic out of my left hand, skipped over to the door, spat on the carpet again, and slipped out. Waxnose backed after him—long sharp face, white nose, pointed chin, weary expression. I wouldn't forget him.

He closed the door softly and I stood there, foolish, holding my gun. I heard the elevator come up and go down again and stop. I still stood there. Marty Estel wouldn't be very likely to hire a couple of comics like that to throw a scare into anybody. I thought about that, but thinking got me nowhere. I remembered the half-bottle of Scotch I had left and went into executive session with it.

An hour and a half later I felt fine, but I still didn't have any ideas. I just felt sleepy.

The jarring of the telephone bell woke me. I had dozed off in the chair, which was a bad mistake, because I woke up with two flannel blankets in my mouth, a splitting headache, a bruise on the back of my head and another on my jaw, neither of them larger than a Yakima apple, but sore for all that. I felt terrible. I felt like an amputated leg.

I crawled over to the telephone and humped myself in a chair beside it and answered it. The voice dripped icicles.

"Mr. Marlowe? This is Mr. Jeeter. I believe we met this morning. I'm afraid I was a little stiff with you."

"I'm a little stiff myself. Your son poked me in the jaw. I mean your stepson, or your adopted son—or whatever he is."

"He is both my stepson and my adopted son. Indeed?" He sounded interested. "And where did you meet him?"

"In Miss Huntress' apartment."

"Oh I see." There had been a sudden thaw. The icicles had melted. "Very interesting. What did Miss Huntress have to say?"

"She liked it. She liked him poking me in the jaw."

"I see. And why did he do that?"

"She had him hid out. He overheard some of our talk. He didn't like it."

"I see. I have been thinking that perhaps some consideration—not large, of course—should be granted to her for her co-operation. That is, if we can secure it."

"Fifty grand is the price."

"I'm afraid I don't—"

"Don't kid me," I snarled. "Fifty thousand dollars. Fifty grand. I offered her five hundred—just for a gag."

"You seem to treat this whole business in a spirit of considerable levity," he snarled back. "I am not accustomed to that sort of thing and I don't like it."

I yawned. I didn't give a damn if school kept in or not. "Listen, Mr. Jeeter, I'm a great guy to horse around, but I have my mind on the job just the same. And there are some very unusual angles to this case. For instance a couple of gunmen just stuck me up in my apartment here and told me to lay off the Jeeter case. I don't see why it should get so tough."

"Good heavens!" He sounded shocked. "I think you had better come to my house at once and we will discuss matters. I'll send my car for you. Can you come right away?"

"Yeah. But I can drive myself, I—"

"No. I'm sending my car and chauffeur. His name is George; you may rely upon him absolutely. He should be there in about twenty minutes."

"O.K.," I said. "That just gives me time to drink my dinner. Have him park around the corner of Kenmore, facing towards Franklin." I hung up.

When I'd had a hot-and-cold shower and put on some clean clothes I felt more respectable. I had a couple of drinks, small ones for a change, and put a light overcoat on and went down to the street.

The car was there already. I could see it half a block down the side street. It looked like a new market opening. It had a couple of headlamps like the one on the front end of a streamliner, two amber foglights hooked to the front fender, and a couple of sidelights as big as ordinary headlights. I came up beside it and stopped and a man stepped out of the shadows, tossing a cigarette over his shoulder with a neat flip of the wrist. He was tall, broad, dark, wore a peaked cap, a Russian tunic with a Sam Browne belt, shiny leggings and breeches that flared like an English staff major's whipcords.

"Mr. Marlowe?" He touched the peak of his cap with a gloved forefinger.

"Yeah," I said. "At ease. Don't tell me that's old man Jeeter's car."

"One of them." It was a cool voice that could get fresh.

He opened the rear door and I got in and sank down into the cushions and George slid under the wheel and started the big car. It moved away from the curb and around the corner with as much noise as a bill makes in a wallet. We went west. We seemed to be drifting with the current, but we passed everything. We slid through the heart of Hollywood, the west end of it, down to the Strip and along the glitter of that to the cool quiet of Beverly Hills where the bridle path divides the boulevard.

We gave Beverly Hills the swift and climbed along the foothills, saw the distant lights of the university buildings and swung north into Bel-Air. We began to slide up long narrow streets with high walls and no sidewalks and big gates. Lights on mansions glowed politely through the early night. Nothing stirred. There was no sound but the soft purr of the tires on concrete. We swung left again and I caught a sign which read Calvello Drive. Halfway up this George started to swing the car wide to make a left turn in at a pair of twelve-foot wrought-iron gates. Then something happened.

A pair of lights flared suddenly just beyond the gates and a horn screeched and a motor raced. A car charged at us fast. George straightened out with a flick of the wrist, braked the car and slipped off his right glove, all in one motion.

The car came on, the lights swaying. "Damn drunk," George swore over his shoulder.

It could be. Drunks in cars go all kinds of places to drink. It could be. I slid down onto the floor of the car and yanked the Luger from under my arm and reached up to open the catch. I opened the door a little and held it that way, looking over the sill. The headlights hit me in the face and I ducked, then came up again as the beam passed.

The other car jammed to a stop. Its door slammed open and a figure jumped out of it, waving a gun and shouting. I heard the voice and knew.

"Reach, you bastards!" Frisky screamed at us.

George put his left hand on the wheel and I opened my door a little more. The little man in the street was bouncing up and down and yelling. Out of the small dark car from which he had jumped came no sound except the noise of its motor.

"This is a heist!" Frisky yelled. "Out of there and line up, you sons of bitches!"

I kicked my door open and started to get out, the Luger down at my side.

"You asked for it!" the little man yelled.

I dropped—fast. The gun in his hand belched flame. Somebody must have put a firing pin in it. Glass smashed behind my head. Out of the corner of my eye, which oughtn't to have had any corners at that particular moment, I saw George make a movement as smooth as a ripple of water. I brought the Luger up and started to squeeze the trigger, but a shot crashed beside me—George.

I held my fire. It wasn't needed now.

The dark car lurched forward and started down the hill furiously. It roared into the distance while the little man out in the middle of the pavement was still reeling grotesquely in the light reflected from the walls.

There was something dark on his face that spread. His gun bounded along the concrete. His little legs buckled and he plunged sideways and rolled and then, very suddenly, became still.

George said. "Yah!" and sniffed at the muzzle of his revolver.

"Nice shooting." I got out of the car, stood there looking at the little man— a crumpled nothing. The dirty white of his sneakers gleamed a little in the side glare of the car's lights.

George got out beside me. "Why me, brother?"

"I didn't fire. I was watching that pretty hip draw of yours. It was sweeter than honey."

"Thanks, pal. They were after Mister Gerald, of course. I usually ferry him home from the club about this time, full of liquor and bridge losses."

We went over to the little man and looked down at him. He wasn't anything to see. He was just a little man who was dead, with a big slug in his face and blood on him.

"Turn some of those damn lights off." I growled. "And let's get away from here fast."

"The house is just across the street." George sounded as casual as if he had just shot a nickel in a slot machine instead of a man.

"The Jeeters are out of this, if you like your job. You ought to know that. We'll go back to my place and start all over."

"I get it," he snapped, and jumped back into the big car. He cut the foglights and the sidelights and I got in beside him in the front seat.

We straightened out and started up the hill, over the brow. I looked back at the broken window. It was the small one at the extreme back of the car and it wasn't shatterproof. A large piece was gone from it. They could fit that, if they got around to it, and make some evidence. I didn't think it would matter, but it might.

At the crest of the hill a large limousine passed us going down. Its dome light was on and in the interior, as in a lighted showcase, an elderly couple sat stiffly, taking the royal salute. The man was in evening clothes, with a white scarf and a crush hat. The woman was in furs and diamonds.

George passed them casually, gunned the car and we made a fast right turn into a dark street. "There's a couple of good dinners all shot to hell," he drawled, "and I bet they don't even report it."

"Yeah. Let's get back home and have a drink," I said. "I never really got to like killing people."

Five

We sat with some of Miss Harriet Huntress' Scotch in our glasses and looked at each other across the rims. George looked nice with his cap off. His head was clustered over with wavy dark-brown hair and his teeth were very white and clean. He sipped his drink and nibbled a cigarette at the same time. His snappy black eyes had a cool glitter in them.

"Yale?" I asked.

"Dartmouth, if it's any of your business."

"Everything's my business. What's a college education worth these days?"

"Three squares and a uniform," he drawled.

"What kind of guy is young Jeeter?"

"Big blond bruiser, plays a fair game of golf, thinks he's hell with the women, drinks heavy but hasn't sicked up on the rugs so far."

"What kind of guy is old Jeeter?"

"He'd probably give you a dime—if he didn't have a nickel with him."

"Tsk, tsk, you're talking about your boss."

George grinned. "He's so tight his head squeaks when he takes his hat off. I always took chances. Maybe that's why I'm just somebody's driver. This is good Scotch."

I made another drink, which finished the bottle. I sat down again.

"You think those two gunnies were stashed out for Mister Gerald?"

"Why not? I usually drive him home about that time. Didn't today. He had a bad hangover and didn't go out until late. You're a dick, you know what it's all about, don't you?"

"Who told you I was a dick?"

"Nobody but a dick ever asked so goddam many questions."

I shook my head. "Uh-uh. I've asked you just six questions. Your boss has a lot of confidence in you. He must have told you."

The dark man nodded, grinned faintly and sipped. "The whole set-up is pretty obvious," he said. "When the car started to swing for the turn into the driveway these boys went to work. I don't figure they meant to kill anybody, somehow. It was just a scare. Only that little guy was nuts."

I looked at George's eyebrows. They were nice black eyebrows, with a gloss on them like horsehair.

"It doesn't sound like Marty Estel to pick that sort of helpers."

"Sure. Maybe that's why he picked that sort of helpers."

"You're smart. You and I can get along. But shooting that little punk makes it tougher. What will you do about that?"

"Nothing."

"O.K. If they get to you and tie it to your gun, if you still have the gun, which you probably won't, I suppose it will be passed off as an attempted stick-up. There's just one thing."

"What?" George finished his second drink, laid the glass aside, lit a fresh cigarette and smiled.

"It's pretty hard to tell a car from in front—at night. Even with all those lights. It might have been a visitor."

He shrugged and nodded. "But if it's a scare, that would do just as well. Because the family would hear about it and the old man would guess whose boys they were—and why."

"Hell, you really are smart," I said admiringly, and the phone rang.

It was an English-butler voice, very clipped and precise, and it said that if I was Mr. Philip Marlowe, Mr. Jeeter would like to speak to me. He came on at once, with plenty of frost.

"I must say that you take your time about obeying orders," he barked. "Or hasn't that chauffeur of mine—"

"Yeah, he got here, Mr. Jeeter," I said. "But we ran into a little trouble. George will tell you."

"Young man, when I want something done—"

"Listen, Mr. Jeeter, I've had a hard day. Your son punched me on the jaw and I fell and cut my head open. When I staggered back to my apartment, more dead than alive, I was stuck up by a couple of hard guys with guns who told me to lay off the Jeeter case. I'm doing my best but I'm feeling a little frail, so don't scare me."

"Young man—"

"Listen," I told him earnestly, "if you want to call all the plays in this game, you can carry the ball yourself. Or you can save yourself a lot of money and hire an order taker. I have to do things my way. Any cops visit you tonight?"

"Cops?" he echoed in a sour voice. "You mean policemen?"

"By all means—I mean policemen."

"And why should I see any policemen?" he almost snarled.

"There was a stiff in front of your gates half an hour ago. Stiff meaning dead man. He's quite small. You could sweep him up in a dustpan, if he bothers you."

"My God! Are you serious?"

"Yes. What's more he took a shot at George and me. He recognized the car. He must have been all set for your son, Mr. Jeeter."

A silence with barbs on it. "I thought you said a dead man," Mr. Jeeter's voice said very coldly. "Now you say he shot at you."

"That was while he wasn't dead," I said. "George will tell you. George—"

"You come out here at once!" he yelled at me over the phone. "At once, do you hear? At once!"

"George will tell you," I said softly and hung up.

George looked at me coldly. He stood up and put his cap on. "O.K., pal," he said. "Maybe some day I can put you on to a soft thing." He started for the door.

"It had to be that way. It's up to him. He'll have to decide."

"Nuts," George said, looking back over his shoulder. "Save your breath, shamus. Anything you say to me is just so much noise in the wrong place."

He opened the door, went out, shut it, and I sat there still holding the telephone, with my mouth open and nothing in it but my tongue and a bad taste on that.

I went out to the kitchen and shook the Scotch bottle, but it was still empty. I opened some rye and swallowed a drink and it tasted sour. Something was bothering me. I had a feeling it was going to bother me a lot more before I was through.

They must have missed George by a whisker. I heard the elevator come up again almost as soon as it had stopped going down. Solid steps grew louder along the hallway. A fist hit the door. I went over and opened it.

One was in brown, one in blue, both large, hefty and bored.

The one in brown pushed his hat back on his head with a freckled hand and said: "You Philip Marlowe?"

"Me," I said.

They rode me back into the room without seeming to. The one in blue shut the door. The one in brown palmed a shield and let me catch a glint of the gold and enamel.

"Finlayson, Detective Lieutenant working out of Central Homicide," he said. "This is Sebold, my partner. We're a couple of swell guys not to get funny with. We hear you're kind of sharp with a gun."

Sebold took his hat off and dusted his salt-and-pepper hair back with the flat of his hand. He drifted noiselessly out to the kitchen.

Finlayson sat down on the edge of a chair and flicked his chin with a thumbnail as square as an ice cube and yellow as a mustard plaster. He was older than Sebold, but not so good-looking. He had the frowsy expression of a veteran cop who hadn't got very far.

I sat down. I said: "How do you mean, sharp with a gun?"

"Shooting people is how I mean."

I lit a cigarette. Sebold came out of the kitchen and went into the dressing room behind the wall bed.

"We understand you're a private-license guy." Finlayson said heavily.

"That's right."

"Give." He held his hand out. I gave him my wallet. He chewed it over and handed it back. "Carry a gun?"

I nodded. He held out his hand for it. Sebold came out of the dressing room. Finlayson sniffed at the Luger, snapped the magazine out, cleared the breech and held the gun so that a little light shone up through the magazine opening into the breech end of the barrel. He looked down the muzzle, squinting. He handed the gun to Sebold. Sebold did the same thing.

"Don't think so," Sebold said. "Clean, but not that clean. Couldn't have been cleaned within the hour. A little dust."

"Right."

Finlayson picked the ejected shell off the carpet, pressed it into the magazine and snapped the magazine back in place. He handed me the gun. I put it back under my arm.

"Been out anywhere tonight?" he asked tersely.

"Don't tell me the plot," I said. "I'm just a bit-player."

"Smart guy," Sebold said dispassionately. He dusted his hair again and opened a desk drawer. "Funny stuff. Good for a column. I like 'em that way—with my blackjack."

Finlayson sighed. "Been out tonight, shamus?"

"Sure. In and out all the time. Why?"

He ignored the question. "Where you been?"

"Out to dinner. Business call or two."

"Where at?"

"I'm sorry, boys. Every business has its private files."

"Had company, too," Sebold said, picking up George's glass and sniffing it. "Recent—within the hour."

"You're not that good," I told him sourly.

"Had a ride in a big Caddy?" Finlayson bored on, taking a deep breath. "Over West L. A. direction?"

"Had a ride in a Chrysler—over Vine Street direction."

"Maybe we better just take him down," Sebold said, looking at his fingernails.

"Maybe you better skip the gang-buster stuff and tell me what's stuck in your nose. I get along with cops—except when they act as if the law is only for citizens."

Finlayson studied me. Nothing I had said made an impression on him. Nothing Sebold said made any impression on him. He had an idea and he was holding it like a sick baby.

"You know a little rat named Frisky Lavon?" he sighed. "Used to be a dummy-chucker, then found out he could bug his way outa raps. Been doing that for say twelve years. Totes a gun and acts simple. But he quit acting tonight at seven-thirty about. Quit cold—with a slug in his head."

"Never heard of him," I said.

"You bumped anybody off tonight?"

"I'd have to look at my notebook."

Sebold leaned forward politely. "Would you care for a smack in the kisser?" he inquired.

Finlayson held his hand out sharply. "Cut it, Ben, Cut it. Listen, Marlowe. Maybe we're going at this wrong. We're not talking about murder. Could have been legitimate. This Frisky Lavon got froze off tonight on Calvello Drive in Bel Air. Out in the middle of the street. Nobody seen or heard anything. So we kind of want to know."

"All right," I growled. "What makes it my business? And keep that piano tuner out of my hair. He has a nice suit and his nails are clean, but he bears down on his shield too hard."

"Nuts to you," Sebold said.

"We got a funny phone call," Finlayson said. "Which is where you come in. We ain't just throwing our weight around. And we want a forty-five. They ain't sure what kind yet."

"He's smart. He threw it under the bar at Levy's," Sebold sneered.

"I never had a forty-five," I said. "A guy who needs that much gun ought to use a pick."

Finlayson scowled at me and counted his thumbs. Then he took a deep breath and suddenly went human on me. "Sure, I'm just a dumb flatheel," he said. "Anybody could pull my ears off and I wouldn't even notice it. Let's all quit horsing around and talk sense.

"This Frisky was found dead after a no-name phone call to West L. A. police. Found dead outside a big house belonging to a man named Jeeter who owns a string of investment companies. He wouldn't use a guy like Frisky for a penwiper, so there's nothing in that. The servants didn't hear nothing, nor the servants at any of the four houses on the block. Frisky is lying in the street and somebody run over his foot, but what killed him was a forty-five slug smack in his face. West L. A. ain't hardly started the routine when some guy calls up Central and says to tell Homicide if they want to know who got Frisky Lavon, ask a private eye named Philip Marlowe, complete with address and everything, then a quick hang-up.

"O.K. The guy on the board gives me the dope and I don't know Frisky from a hole in my sock, but I ask Identification and sure enough they have him and just about the time I'm looking it over the flash comes from West L. A. and the description seems to check pretty close. So we get together and it's the same guy all right and the chief of detectives has us drop around here. So we drop around."

"So here you are," I said. "Will you have a drink?"

"Can we search the joint, if we do?"

"Sure. It's a good lead—that phone call, I mean—if you put in about six months on it."

"We already got that idea," Finlayson growled. "A hundred guys could have chilled this little wart, and two-three of them maybe could have thought it was a smart rib to pin it on you. Them two-three is what interests us."

I shook my head.

"No ideas at all, huh?"

"Just for wisecracks," Sebold said.

Finlayson lumbered to his feet. "Well, we gotta look around."

"Maybe we had ought to have brought a search warrant," Sebold said, tickling his upper lip with the end of his tongue.

"I don't *have* to fight this guy, do I?" I asked Finlayson. "I mean, is it all right if I leave him his gag lines and just keep my temper?"

Finlayson looked at the ceiling and said dryly: "His wife left him day before yesterday. He's just trying to compensate, as the fellow says."

Sebold turned white and twisted his knuckles savagely. Then he laughed shortly and got to his feet.

They went at it. Ten minutes of opening and shutting drawers and looking at the backs of shelves and under seat cushions and letting the bed down and peering into the electric refrigerator and the garbage pail fed them up.

They came back and sat down again. "Just a nut," Finlayson said wearily. "Some guy that picked your name outa the directory maybe. Could be anything."

"Now I'll get that drink."

"I don't drink," Sebold snarled.

Finlayson crossed his hands on his stomach. "That don't mean any liquor gets poured in the flowerpot, son."

I got three drinks and put two of them beside Finlayson. He drank half of one of them and looked at the ceiling. "I got another killing, too," he said thoughtfully. "A guy in your racket, Marlowe. A fat guy on Sunset. Name of Arbogast. Ever hear of him?"

"I thought he was a handwriting expert," I said.

"You're talking about police business," Sebold told his partner coldly.

"Sure. Police business that's already in the morning paper. This Arbogast was shot three times with a twenty-two. Target gun. You know any crooks that pack that kind of heat?"

I held my glass tightly and took a long slow swallow. I hadn't thought Waxnose looked dangerous enough, but you never knew.

"I did," I said slowly. "A killer named Al Tessilore. But he's in Folsom. He used a Colt Woodsman."

Finlayson finished the first drink, used the second in about the same time, and stood up. Sebold stood up, still mad.

Finlayson opened the door. "Come on, Ben." They went out.

I heard their steps along the hall, the clang of the elevator once more. A car started just below in the street and growled off into the night.

"Clowns like that don't kill," I said out loud. But it looked as if they did.

I waited fifteen minutes before I went out again. The phone rang while I was waiting, but I didn't answer it.

I drove towards the El Milano and circled around enough to make sure I wasn't followed.

Six

The lobby hadn't changed any. The blue carpet still tickled my ankles while I ambled over to the desk, the same pale clerk was handing a key to a couple of horse-faced females in tweeds, and when he saw me he put his weight on his left foot again and the door at the end of the desk popped open and out popped the fat and erotic Hawkins, with what looked like the same cigar stub in his face.

He hustled over and gave me a big warm smile this time, took hold of my arm. "Just the guy I was hoping to see," he chuckled. "Let's us go upstairs a minute."

"What's the matter?"

"Matter?" His smile became broad as the door to a two-car garage. "Nothing ain't the matter. This way."

He pushed me into the elevator and said "Eight" in a fat cheerful voice and up we sailed and out we got and slid along the corridor. Hawkins had a hard hand and knew where to hold an arm. I was interested enough to let him get away with it. He pushed the buzzer beside Miss Huntress' door and Big Ben chimed inside and the door opened and I was looking at a deadpan in a derby hat and a dinner coat. He had his right hand in the side pocket of the coat, and under the derby a pair of scarred eyebrows and under the eyebrows a pair of eyes that had as much expression as the cap on a gas tank.

The mouth moved enough to say: "Yeah?"

"Company for the boss," Hawkins said expansively.

"What company?"

"Let me play too," I said. "Limited Liability Company. Gimme the apple."

"Huh?" The eyebrows went this way and that and the jaw came out. "Nobody ain't kiddin' anybody, I hope."

"Now, now, gents—" Hawkins began.

A voice behind the derby hatted man interrupted him. "What's the matter, Beef?"

"He's in a stew," I said.

"Listen, mugg—"

"Now, now, gents—" as before.

"Ain't nothing the matter," Beef said, throwing his voice over his shoulder as if it were a coil of rope. "The hotel dick got a guy up here and he says he's company."

"Show the company in, Beef." I liked this voice. It was smooth quiet, and you could have cut your name in it with a thirty-pound sledge and a cold chisel.

"Lift the dogs," Beef said, and stood to one side.

We went in. I went first, then Hawkins, then Beef wheeled neatly behind us like a door. We went in so close together that we must have looked like a three-decker sandwich.

Miss Huntress was not in the room. The log in the fireplace had almost stopped smoldering. There was still that smell of sandalwood on the air. With it cigarette smoke blended.

A man stood at the end of the davenport, both hands in the pockets of a blue camel's hair coat with the collar high to a black snap-brim hat. A loose scarf hung outside his coat. He stood motionless, the cigarette in his mouth lisping smoke. He was tall, black-haired, suave, dangerous. He said nothing.

Hawkins ambled over to him. "This is the guy I was telling you about, Mr. Estel," the fat man burbled. "Come in earlier today and said he was from you. Kinda fooled me."

"Give him a ten, Beef."

The derby hat took its left hand from somewhere and there was a bill in it. It pushed the bill at Hawkins. Hawkins took the bill, blushing.

"This ain't necessary, Mr. Estel. Thanks a lot just the same."

"Scram."

"Huh?" Hawkins looked shocked.

"You heard him," Beef said truculently. "Want your fanny out the door first, huh?"

Hawkins drew himself up. "I gotta protect the tenants. You gentlemen know how it is. A man in a job like this."

"Yeah. Scram," Estel said without moving his lips.

Hawkins turned and went out quickly, softly. The door clicked gently shut behind him. Beef looked back at it, then moved behind me.

"See if he's rodded, Beef."

The derby hat saw if I was rodded. He took the Luger and went away from me. Estel looked casually at the Luger, back at me. His eyes held an expression of indifferent dislike.

"Name's Philip Marlowe, eh? A private dick."

"So what?" I said.

"Somebody's goin' to get somebody's face pushed into somebody's floor," Beef said coldly.

"Aw, keep that crap for the boiler room." I told him. "I'm sick of hard guys for this evening. I said 'so what,' and 'so what' is what I said."

Marty Estel looked mildly amused. "Hell, keep your shirt in. I've got to look after my friends, don't I? You know who I am. O.K., I know what you talked to Miss Huntress about. And I know something about you that you don't know I know."

"All right." I said. "This fat slob Hawkins collected ten from me for letting me up here this afternoon—knowing perfectly well who I was—and he has just collected ten from your iron man for slipping me the nasty. Give me back my gun and tell me what makes my business your business."

"Plenty. First off, Harriet's not home. We're waiting for her on account of a thing that happened. I can't wait any longer. Got to go to work at the club. So what did you come after this time?"

"Looking for the Jeeter boy. Somebody shot at his car tonight. From now on he needs somebody to walk behind him."

"You think I play games like that?" Estel asked me coldly.

I walked over to a cabinet and opened it and found a bottle of Scotch. I twisted the cap off, lifted a glass from the tabouret and poured some out. I tasted it. It tasted all right.

I looked around for ice, but there wasn't any. It had all melted long since in the bucket.

"I asked you a question," Estel said gravely.

"I heard it. I'm making my mind up. The answer is, I wouldn't have thought it—no. But it happened. I was there. I was in the car—instead of young Jeeter. His father had sent for me to come to the house to talk things over."

"What things?"

I didn't bother to look surprised. "You hold fifty grand of the boy's paper. That looks bad for you, if anything happens to him."

"I don't figure it that way. Because that way I would lose my dough. The old man won't pay—granted. But I wait a couple of years and I collect from the kid. He gets his estate out of trust when he's twenty-eight. Right now he gets a grand a month and he can't even will anything, because it's still in trust. Savvy?"

"So you wouldn't knock him off," I said, using my Scotch. "But you might throw a scare into him."

Estel frowned. He discarded his cigarette into a tray and watched it smoke a moment before he picked it up again and snubbed it out. He shook his head.

"If you're going to bodyguard him, it would almost pay me to stand part of your salary, wouldn't it? Almost. A man in my racket can't take care of everything. He's of age and it's his business who he runs around with. For instance, women. Any reason why a nice girl shouldn't cut herself a piece of five million bucks?"

I said: "I think it's a swell idea. What was it you knew about me that I didn't know you knew?"

He smiled, faintly. "What was it you were waiting to tell Miss Huntress—the thing that happened?"

He smiled faintly again.

"Listen, Marlowe, there are lots of ways to play any game. I play mine on the house percentage, because that's all I need to win. What makes me get tough?"

I rolled a fresh cigarette around in my fingers and tried to roll it around my glass with two fingers. "Who said you were tough? I always heard the nicest things about you."

Marty Estel nodded and looked faintly amused. "I have sources of information," he said quietly. "When I have fifty grand invested in a guy, I'm apt to find out a little about him. Jeeter hired a man named Arbogast to do a little work. Arbogast was killed in his office today—with a twenty-two. That could have nothing to do with Jeeter's business. But there was a tail on you when you went there and you didn't give it to the law. Does that make you and me friends?"

I licked the edge of my glass, nodded. "It seems it does."

"From now on just forget about bothering Harriet, see?"

"O.K."

"So we understand each other real good, now."

"Yeah."

"Well, I'll be going. Give the guy back his Luger, Beef."

The derby hat came over and smacked my gun into my hand hard enough to break a bone.

"Staying?" Estel asked, moving towards the door.

"I guess I'll wait a little while. Until Hawkins comes up to touch me for another ten."

Estel grinned. Beef walked in front of him wooden-faced to the door and opened it. Estel went out. The door closed. The room was silent. I sniffed at the dying perfume of sandalwood and stood motionless, looking around.

Somebody was nuts. I was nuts. Everybody was nuts. None of it fitted together worth a nickel. Marty Estel, as he said, had no good motive for murdering anybody, because that would be the surest way to kill chances to collect his money. Even if he had a motive for murdering anybody, Waxnose and Frisky didn't seem like the team he would select for the job. I was in bad with the police, I had spent ten dollars of my twenty expense money, and I didn't have enough leverage anywhere to lift a dime off a cigar counter.

I finished my drink, put the glass down, walked up and down the room, smoked a third cigarette, looked at my watch, shrugged and felt disgusted. The inner doors of the suite were closed. I went across to the one out of which young Jeeter must have sneaked that afternoon. Opening it I looked into a bedroom done in ivory and ashes of roses. There was a big double bed with no footboard, covered with figured brocade. Toilet articles glistened on a built-in dressing table with a panel light. The light was lit. A small lamp on a table beside the door was lit also. A door near the dressing table showed the cool green of bathroom tiles.

I went over and looked in there. Chromium, a glass stall shower, monogrammed towels on a rack, a glass shelf for perfume and bath salts at the foot of the tub, everything nice and refined. Miss Huntress did herself well. I hoped she was paying her own rent. It didn't make any difference to me—I just liked it that way.

I went back towards the living room, stopped in the doorway to take another pleasant look around, and noticed something I ought to have noticed the instant I stepped into the room. I noticed the sharp tang of cordite on the air, almost, but not quite gone. And then I noticed something else.

The bed had been moved over until its head overlapped the edge of a closet door which was not quite closed. The weight of the bed was holding it from opening. I went over there to find out why it wanted to open. I went slowly and about halfway there I noticed that I was holding a gun in my hand.

I leaned against the closet door. It didn't move. I threw more weight against it. It still didn't move. Braced against it I pushed the bed away with my foot, gave ground slowly.

A weight pushed against me hard. I had gone back a foot or so before anything else happened. Then it happened suddenly. He came out—sideways, in a sort of roll. I put some more weight back on the door and held him like that a moment, looking at him.

He was still big, still blond, still dressed in tough sporty material, with scarf and open necked shirt. But his face wasn't red any more.

I gave ground again and he rolled down the back of the door, turning a little like a swimmer in the surf, thumped the floor and lay there, almost on his back, still looking at me. Light from the bedside lamp glittered on his head. There was a scorched and soggy stain on the rough coat—about where his heart would be. So he wouldn't get that five million after all. And nobody would get anything and Marty Estel wouldn't get his fifty grand. Because young Mister Gerald was dead.

I looked back into the closet where he had been. Its door hung wide open now. There were clothes on racks, feminine clothes, nice clothes. He had been backed in among them, probably with his hands in the air and a gun against his chest. And then he had been shot dead, and whoever did it hadn't been quite quick enough or quite strong enough to get the door shut. Or had been scared and had just yanked the bed over against the door and left it that way.

Something glittered down on the floor. I picked it up. A small automatic, .25 caliber, a woman's purse gun with a beautifully engraved butt inlaid with silver and ivory. I put the gun in my pocket. That seemed a funny thing to do, too.

I didn't touch him. He was as dead as John D. Arbogast and looked a whole lot deader. I left the door open and listened, walked quickly back across the room and into the living room and shut the bedroom door, smearing the knob as I did it.

A lock was being tinkled at with a key. Hawkins was back again, to see what delayed me. He was letting himself in with his passkey.

I was pouring a drink when he came in.

He came well into the room, stopped with his feet planted and surveyed me coldly.

"I seen Estel and his boy leave," he said. "I didn't see you leave. So I come up. I gotta—"

"You gotta protect the guests," I said.

"Yeah. I gotta protect the guests. You can't stay up here, pal. Not without the lady of the house home."

"But Marty Estel and his hard boy can."

He came a little closer to me. He had a mean look in his eye. He had always had it, probably, but I noticed it more now.

"You don't want to make nothing of that, do you?" he asked me.

"No. Every man to his own chisel. Have a drink."

"That ain't your liquor."

"Miss Huntress gave me a bottle. We're pals. Marty Estel and I are pals. Everybody is pals. Don't you want to be pals?"

"You ain't trying to kid me, are you?"

"Have a drink and forget it."

I found a glass and poured him one. He took it.

"It's the job if anybody smells it on me," he said.

"Uh-huh."

He drank slowly, rolling it around on his tongue. "Good Scotch."

"Won't be the first time you tasted it, will it?"

He started to get hard again, then relaxed. "Hell, I guess you're just a kidder." He finished the drink, put the glass down, patted his lips with a large and very crumpled handkerchief and sighed.

"O.K.," he said. "But we'll have to leave now."

"All set. I guess she won't be home for a while. You see them go out?"

"Her and the boy friend. Yeah, long time ago."

I nodded. We went towards the door and Hawkins saw me out. He saw me downstairs and off the premises. But he didn't see what was in Miss Huntress' bedroom. I wondered if he would go back up. If he did, the Scotch bottle would probably stop him.

I got into my car and drove off home—to talk to Anna Halsey on the phone. There wasn't any case any more—for us. I parked close to the curb this time. I wasn't feeling gay any more. I rode up in the elevator and unlocked the door and clicked the light on.

Waxnose sat in my best chair, an unlit hand-rolled brown cigarette between his fingers, his bony knees crossed, and his long Woodsman resting solidly on his leg. He was smiling. It wasn't the nicest smile I ever saw.

"Hi, pal," he drawled. "You still ain't had that door fixed. Kind of shut it, huh?" His voice, for all the drawl, was deadly.

I shut the door, stood looking across the room at him.

"So you killed my pal," he said.

He stood up slowly, came across the room slowly and leaned the .22 against my throat. His smiling thin-lipped mouth seemed as expressionless, for all its smile, as his wax-white nose. He reached quietly under my coat and took the Luger. I might as well leave it home from now on. Everybody in town seemed to be able to take it away from me.

He stepped back across the room and sat down again in the chair.

"Steady does it," he said almost gently. "Park the body, friend. No false moves. No moves at all. You and me are at the jumping-off place. The clock's tickin' and we're waiting to go."

I sat down and stared at him. A curious bird. I moistened my dry lips. "You told me his gun had no firing pin," I said.

"Yeah. He fooled me on that, the little so-and-so. And I told you to lay off the Jeeter kid. That's cold now. It's Frisky I'm thinking about. Crazy, ain't it? Me bothering about a dimwit like that, packin' him around with me, and letting him get hisself bumped off." He sighed and added simply, "He was my kid brother."

"I didn't kill him," I said.

He smiled a little more. He had never stopped smiling. The corners of his mouth just tucked in a little deeper.

"Yeah?"

He slid the safety catch off the Luger, laid it carefully on the arm of the chair at his right, and reached into his pocket. What he brought out made me as cold as an ice bucket.

It was a metal tube, dark and rough-looking, about four inches long and drilled with a lot of small holes. He held his Woodsman in his left hand and began to screw the tube casually on the end of it.

"Silencer," he said. "They're the bunk, I guess you smart guys think. This one ain't the bunk—not for three shots. I oughta know. I made it myself."

I moistened my lips again. "It'll work for one shot," I said. "Then it jams your action. That one looks like cast-iron. It will probably blow your hand off."

He smiled his waxy smile, screwed it on, slowly, lovingly, gave it a last hard turn and sat back relaxed. "Not this baby. She's packed with steel wool and that's good for three shots, like I said. Then you got to repack it. And there ain't enough back pressure to jam the action on this gun. You feel good? I'd like you to feel good."

"I feel swell, you sadistic son of a bitch," I said.

"I'm having you lie down on the bed after a while. You won't feel nothing. I'm kind of fussy about my killings. Frisky didn't feel nothing, I guess. You got him neat."

"You don't see good," I sneered. "The chauffeur got him with a Smith & Wesson forty-four. I didn't even fire."

"Uh-huh."

"O.K., you don't believe me," I said. "What did you kill Arbogast for? There was nothing fussy about that killing. He was just shot at his desk, three times with a twenty-two and he fell down on the floor. What did he ever do to your filthy little brother?"

He jerked the gun up, but his smile held. "You got guts," he said. "Who is this here Arbogast?"

I told him. I told him slowly and carefully, in detail. I told him a lot of things. And he began in some vague way to look worried. His eyes flickered at me, away, back again, restlessly, like a hummingbird.

"I don't know any party named Arbogast, pal," he said slowly. "Never heard of him. And I ain't shot any fat guys today."

"You killed him," I said. "And you killed young Jeeter—in the girl's apartment at the El Milano. He's lying there dead right now. You're working for Marty Estel. He's going to be awfully damn sorry about that kill. Go ahead and make it three in a row."

His face froze. The smile went away at last. His whole face looked waxy now. He opened his mouth and breathed through it, and his breath made a restless worrying sound. I could see the faint glitter of sweat on his forehead, and I could feel the cold from the evaporation of sweat on mine.

Waxnose said very gently: "I ain't killed anybody at all, friend. Not anybody. I wasn't hired to kill people. Until Frisky stopped that slug I didn't have no such ideas. That's straight."

I tried not to stare at the metal tube on the end of the Woodsman.

A flame flickered at the back of his eyes, a small, weak, smoky flame. It seemed to grow larger and clearer. He looked down at the floor between his feet. I looked around at the light switch, but it was too far away. He looked up again. Very slowly he began to unscrew the silencer. He had it loose in his hand. He dropped it back into his pocket, stood up, holding the two guns, one in each hand. Then he had another idea. He sat down again, took all the shells out of the Luger quickly and threw it on the floor after them.

He came towards me softly across the room. "I guess this is your lucky day," he said. "I got to go a place and see a guy."

"I knew all along it was my lucky day. I've been feeling so good."

He moved delicately around me to the door and opened it a foot and started through the narrow opening, smiling again.

"I gotta see a guy," he said very gently, and his tongue moved along his lips.

"Not yet," I said, and jumped.

His gun hand was at the edge of the door, almost beyond the edge. I hit the door hard and he couldn't bring it in quickly enough. He couldn't get out of the way. I pinned him in the doorway, and used all the strength I had. It was a crazy thing. He had given me a break and all I had to do was to stand still and let him go. But I had a guy to see too—and I wanted to see him first.

Waxnose leered at me. He grunted. He fought with his hand beyond the door edge. I shifted and hit his jaw with all I had. It was enough. He went limp. I hit him again. His head bounced against the wood. I heard a light thud beyond the door edge. I hit him a third time. I never hit anything any harder.

I took my weight back from the door then and he slid towards me, blank-eyed, rubber-kneed and I caught him and twisted his empty hands behind him and let him fall. I stood over him panting. I went to the door. His Woodsman lay almost on the sill. I picked it up, dropped it into my pocket—not the pocket that held Miss Huntress' gun. He hadn't even found that.

There he lay on the floor. He was thin, he had no weight, but I panted just the same. In a little while his eyes flickered open and looked up at me.

"Greedy guy," he whispered wearily. "Why did I ever leave Saint Looey?"

I snapped handcuffs on his wrists and pulled him by the shoulders into the dressing room and tied his ankles with a piece of rope. I left him laying on his back, a little sideways, his nose as white as ever, his eyes empty now, his lips moving a little as if he were talking to himself. A funny lad, not all bad, but not so pure I had to weep over him either.

I put my Luger together and left with my three guns. There was nobody out-side the apartment house.

Seven

The Jeeter mansion was on a nine- or ten-acre knoll, a big colonial pile with fat white columns and dormer windows and magnolias and a four-car garage. There was a circular parking space at the top of the driveway with two cars parked in it—one was the big dreadnaught in which I'd ridden and the other a canary-yellow sports convertible I had seen before.

I rang a bell the size of a silver dollar. The door opened and a tall narrow cold-eyed bird in dark clothes looked out at me.

"Mr. Jeeter home? Mr. Jeeter, Senior?"

"May I arsk who is calling?" The accent was a little too thick, like cut Scotch.

"Philip Marlowe. I'm working for him. Maybe I had ought to of gone to the servant's entrance."

He hitched a finger at a wing collar and looked at me without pleasure. "Aw, possibly. You may step in. I shall inform Mr. Jeeter. I believe he is engaged at the moment. Kindly wait 'ere in the 'all."

"The act stinks," I said. "English butlers aren't dropping their h's this year."

"Smart guy, huh?" he snarled, in a voice from not any farther across the Atlantic than Hoboken. "Wait here." He slid away.

I sat down in a carved chair and felt thirsty. After a while the butler came cat-footing back along the hall and jerked his chin at me unpleasantly.

We went along a mile of hallway. At the end it broadened without any doors into a huge sunroom. On the far side of the sunroom the butler opened a wide door and I stepped past him into an oval room with a black-and-silver oval rug, a black marble table in the middle of the rug, stiff high-backed carved chairs against the walls, a huge oval mirror with a rounded surface that made me look like a pygmy with water on the brain, and in the room three people.

By the door opposite where I came in, George the chauffeur stood stiffly in his neat dark uniform, with his peaked cap in his hand. In the least uncom-fortable of the chairs sat Miss Harriet Huntress holding a glass in which there was half a drink. And around the silver margin of the oval rug, Mr. Jeeter, Senior, was trying his legs out in a brisk canter, still under wraps, but mad inside. His face was red and the veins on his nose were distended. His hands were in the pockets of a velvet smoking jacket. He wore a pleated shirt with a black pearl in the bosom, a batwing black tie and one of his patent-leather oxfords was unlaced.

He whirled and yelled at the butler behind me: "Get out and keep those doors shut! And I'm not at home to anybody, understand? Nobody!"

The butler closed the doors. Presumably, he went away. I didn't hear him go.

George gave me a cool one-sided smile and Miss Huntress gave me a bland stare over her glass. "You made a nice comeback," she said demurely.

"You took a chance leaving me alone in your apartment," I told her. "I might have sneaked some of your perfume."

"Well, what do you want?" Jeeter yelled at me. "A nice sort of detective you turned out to be. I put you on a confidential job and you walk right in on Miss Huntress and explain the whole thing to her."

"It worked, didn't it?"

He stared. They all stared. "How do you know that?" he barked.

"I know a nice girl when I see one. She's here telling you she had an idea she got not to like, and for you to quit worrying about it. Where's Mister Gerald?"

Old man Jeeter stopped and gave me a hard level stare. "I still regard you as incompetent," he said. "My son is missing."

"I'm not working for you. I'm working for Anna Halsey. Any complaints you have to make should be addressed to her. Do I pour my own drink or do you have a flunky in a purple suit to do it? And what do you mean, your son is missing?"

"Should I give him the heave, sir?" George asked quietly.

Jeeter waved his hand at a decanter and siphon and glasses on the black marble table and started around the rug again. "Don't be silly," he snapped at George.

George flushed a little, high on his cheekbones. His mouth looked tough.

I mixed myself a drink and sat down with it and tasted it and asked again: "What do you mean your son is missing, Mr. Jeeter?"

"I'm paying you good money," he started to yell at me, still mad. "When?"

He stopped dead in his canter and looked at me again. Miss Huntress laughed lightly. George scowled.

"What do you suppose I mean—my son is missing?" he snapped. "I should have thought that would be clear enough even to you. Nobody knows where he is. Miss Huntress doesn't know. I don't know. No one at any of the places where he might be known."

"But I'm smarter than they are," I said. "I know."

Nobody moved for a long minute. Jeeter stared at me fish-eyed. George stared at me. The girl stared at me. She looked puzzled. The other two just stared.

I looked at her. "Where did you go when you went out, if you're telling?"

Her dark blue eyes were water-clear. "There's no secret about it. We went out together—in a taxi. Gerald had had his driving license suspended for a month. Too many tickets. We went down towards the beach and I had a change of heart, as you guessed. I decided I was just being a chiseler after all. I didn't want Gerald's money really. What I wanted was revenge. On Mr. Jeeter here for ruining my father. Done all legally of course, but done just the same. But I got myself in a spot where I couldn't have my revenge and not look like a cheap chiseler. So I told George to find some other girl to play with. He was sore and we quarreled. I stopped the taxi and got out in Beverly Hills. He went on. I don't know where. Later I went back to the El Milano and got my car out of the garage and came here. To tell Mr. Jeeter to forget the whole thing and not bother to sick sleuths on to me."

"You say you went with him in a taxi," I said. "Why wasn't George driving him, if he couldn't drive himself?"

I stared at her, but I wasn't talking to her. Jeeter answered me, frostily. "George drove me home from the office, of course. At that time Gerald had already gone out. Is there anything important about that?"

I turned to him. "Yeah. There's going to be. Mister Gerald is at the El Milano. Hawkins the house dick told me. He went back there to wait for Miss Huntress and Hawkins let him into her apartment. Hawkins will do you those little favors—for ten bucks. He may be there still and he may not."

I kept on watching them. It was hard to watch all three of them. But they didn't move. They just looked at me.

"Well—I'm glad to hear it," old man Jeeter said. "I was afraid he was off somewhere getting drunk."

"No. He's not off anywhere getting drunk," I said. "By the way, among these places you called to see if he was there, you didn't call the El Milano?"

George nodded. "Yes, I did. They said he wasn't there. Looks like this house peeper tipped the phone girl off not to say anything."

"He wouldn't have to do that. She'd just ring the apartment and he wouldn't answer—naturally." I watched old man Jeeter hard then, with a lot of interest. It was going to be hard for him to take that up, but he was going to have to do it.

He did. He licked his lips first. "Why—naturally, if I may ask?" he said coldly.

I put my glass down on the marble table and stood against the wall, with my hands hanging free. I still tried to watch them—all three of them.

"Let's go back over this thing a little," I said. "We're all wise to the situation. I know George is, although he shouldn't be, being just a servant. I know Miss Huntress is. And of course *you* are, Mr. Jeeter. So let's see what we have got. We have a lot of things that don't add up, but I'm smart. I'm going to add them up anyhow. First-off a handful of photostats of notes from Marty Estel. Gerald denies having given these and Mr. Jeeter won't pay them, but he has a handwriting man named Arbogast check the signatures, to see if they look genuine. They do. They are. This Arbogast may have done other things. I don't know. I couldn't ask him. When I went to see him, he was dead—shot three times—as I've since heard—with a twenty-two. No, I didn't tell the police, Mr. Jeeter."

The tall silver-haired man looked horribly shocked. His lean body shook like a bullrush. "Dead?" he whispered. "Murdered?"

I looked at George. George didn't move a muscle. I looked at the girl. She sat quietly, waiting, tight-lipped.

I said: "There's only one reason to suppose his killing had anything to do with Mr. Jeeter's affairs. He was shot with a twenty-two—and there is a man in this case who wears a twenty-two."

I still had their attention. And their silence.

"Why he was shot I haven't the faintest idea. He was not a dangerous man to Miss Huntress or Marty Estel. He was too fat to get around much. My guess is he was a little too smart. He got a simple case of signature identification and he went on from there to find out more than he should. And after he had found out more than he should—he guessed more than he ought—and maybe he even tried a little blackmail. And somebody rubbed him out this afternoon with a twenty-two. O.K., I can stand it. I never knew him.

"So I went over to see Miss Huntress and after a lot of finagling around with this itchy-handed house dick I got to see her and we had a chat, and then Mister Gerald stepped neatly out of hiding and bopped me a nice one on the chin and over I went and hit my head on a chair leg. And when I came out of that the joint was empty. So I went on home.

"And home I found the man with the twenty-two and with him a dimwit called Frisky Lavon, with a bad breath and a very large gun, neither of which matters now as he was shot dead in front of your house tonight, Mr. Jeeter—shot trying to stick up your car. The cops know about that one—they came to see me about it—because the other guy, the one that packs the twenty-two, is the little dimwit's brother and he thought I shot Dimwit and tried to put the bee on me. But it didn't work. That's two killings.

"We now come to the third and most important. I went back to the El Milano because it no longer seemed a good idea for Mister Gerald to be running around casually. He seemed to have a few enemies. It even seemed that he was supposed to be in the car this evening when Frisky Lavon shot at it—but of course that was just a plant."

Old Jeeter drew his white eyebrows together in an expression of puzzlement. George didn't look puzzled. He didn't look anything. He was as wooden faced as a cigar-store Indian. The girl looked a little white now, a little tense. I plowed on.

"Back at the El Milano I found that Hawkins had let Marty Estel and his bodyguard into Miss Huntress' apartment to wait for her. Marty had something to tell her—that Arbogast had been killed. That made it a good idea for her to lay off young Jeeter for a while—until the cops quieted down anyhow. A thoughtful guy, Marty. A much more thoughtful guy than you would suppose. For instance, he knew about Arbogast and he knew Mr. Jeeter went to Anna Halsey's office this morning and he knew somehow—Anna might have told him herself, I wouldn't put it past her—that I was working on the case now. So he had me tailed to Arbogast's place and away, and he found out later from his cop friends that Arbogast had been murdered, and he knew I hadn't given it out. So he had me there and that made us pals. He went away after telling me this and once more I was left alone in Miss Huntress' apartment. But this time for no reason at all I poked around. And I found young Mister Gerald, in the bedroom, in a closet."

I stepped quickly over to the girl and reached into my pocket and took out the small fancy .25 automatic and laid it down on her knee.

"Ever see this before?"

Her voice had a curious tight sound, but her dark blue eyes looked at me levelly.

"Yes. It's mine."

"You kept it where?"

"In the drawer of a small table beside the bed."

"Sure about that?"

She thought. Neither of the two men stirred.

George began to twitch the corner of his mouth. She shook her head suddenly, sideways.

"No. I have an idea now I took it out to show somebody—because I don't know much about guns—and left it lying on the mantel in the living room. In fact, I'm almost sure I did. It was Gerald I showed it to."

"So he might have reached for it there, if anybody tried to make a wrong play at him?"

She nodded, troubled. "What do you mean—he's in the closet?" she asked in a small quick voice.

"You know. Everybody in this room knows what I mean. They know that I showed you that gun for a purpose." I stepped away from her and faced George and his boss. "He's dead, of course. Shot through the heart—probably with this gun. It was left there with him. That's why it would be left."

The old man took a step and stopped and braced himself against the table. I wasn't sure whether he had turned white or whether he had been white already. He stared stonily at the girl. He said very slowly, between his teeth: "You damned murderess!"

"Couldn't it have been suicide?" I sneered.

He turned his head enough to look at me. I could see that the idea interested him. He half nodded.

"No." I said. "It couldn't have been suicide."

He didn't like that so well. His face congested with blood and the veins on his nose thickened. The girl touched the gun lying on her knee, then put her hand loosely around the butt. I saw her thumb slide very gently towards the safety catch. She didn't know much about guns, but she knew that much.

"It couldn't be suicide," I said again, very slowly. "As an isolated event—maybe. But not with all the other stuff that's been happening. Arbogast, the stick-up down on Calvello Drive outside this house, the thugs planted in my apartment, the job with the twenty-two."

I reached into my pocket again and pulled out Waxnose's Woodsman. I held it carelessly on the flat of my left hand. "And curiously enough, I don't think it was *this* twenty-two—although this happens to be the gunman's twenty-two. Yeah, I have the gunman, too. He's tied up in my apartment. He came back to knock me off, but I talked him out of it. I'm a swell talker."

"Except that you overdo it," the girl said coolly, and lifted the gun a little.

"It's obvious who killed him, Miss Huntress," I said. "It's simply a matter of motive and opportunity. Marty Estel didn't, and didn't have it done. That would spoil his chances to get his fifty grand. Frisky Lavon's pal didn't, regardless of who he was working for, and I don't think he was working for Marty Estel. He couldn't have got into the El Milano to do the job, and certainly not into Miss Huntress' apartment. Whoever did it had something to gain by it and an opportunity to get to the place where it was done. Well, who had something to gain? Gerald had five million coming to him in two years out of a trust fund. He couldn't will it until he got it. So if he died, his natural heir got it. Who's his natural heir? You'd be surprised. Did you know that in the state of California and some others, but not in all, a man can by his own act become a natural heir? Just by adopting somebody who has money and no heirs!"

George moved then. His movement was once more as smooth as a ripple of water. The Smith & Wesson gleamed dully in his hand, but he didn't fire it. The small automatic in the girl's hand cracked. Blood spurted from George's brown hard hand. The Smith & Wesson dropped to the floor. He cursed. She didn't know much about guns—not very much.

"Of course!" she said grimly. "George could get into the apartment without any trouble, if Gerald was there. He would go in through the garage, a chauffeur in uniform, ride up in the elevator and knock at the door. And when Gerald opened it, George would back him in with that Smith & Wesson. But how did he know Gerald was there?"

I said: "He must have followed your taxi. We don't know where he has been all evening since he left me. He had a car with him. The cops will find out. How much was in it for you, George?"

George held his right wrist with his left hand, held it tightly, and his face was twisted, savage. He said nothing.

"George would back him in with the Smith & Wesson," the girl said wearily. "Then he would see my gun on the mantel-piece. That would be better. He would use that. He would back Gerald into the bedroom, away from the corridor, into the closet, and there, quietly, calmly, he would kill him and drop the gun on the floor."

"George killed Arbogast, too. He killed him with a twenty-two because he knew that Frisky Lavon's brother had a twenty-two, and he knew that because he had hired Frisky and his brother to put over a big scare on Gerald—so that when he was murdered it would look as if Marty Estel had had it done. That was why I was brought out here tonight in the Jeeter car—so that the two thugs who had been warned and planted could pull their act and maybe knock me off, if I got too tough. Only George likes to kill people. He made a neat shot at Frisky. He hit him in the face. It was so good a shot I think he meant it to be a miss. How about it, George?"

Silence.

I looked at old Jeeter at last. I had been expecting him to pull a gun himself, but he hadn't. He just stood there, open-mouthed, appalled, leaning against the black marble table, shaking.

"My God!" he whispered. "My God!"

"You don't have one—except money."

A door squeaked behind me. I whirled, but I needn't have bothered. A hard voice, about as English as Amos and Andy, said: "Put 'em up, bud."

The butler, the very English butler, stood there in the doorway, a gun in his hand, tight-lipped. The girl turned her wrist and shot him just kind of casually, in the shoulder or something. He squealed like a stuck pig.

"Go away, you're intruding," she said coldly.

He ran. We heard his steps running.

"He's going to fall," she said.

I was wearing my Luger in my right hand now, a little late in the season, as usual. I came around with it. Old man Jeeter was holding on to the table, his face gray as a paving block. His knees were giving. George stood cynically, holding a handkerchief around his bleeding wrist, watching him.

"Let him fall," I said. "Down is where he belongs."

He fell. His head twisted. His mouth went slack. He hit the carpet on his side and rolled a little and his knees came up. His mouth drooled a little. His skin turned violet.

"Go call the law, angel," I said. "I'll watch them now."

"All right," she said standing up. "But you certainly need a lot of help in your private-detecting business, Mr. Marlowe."

Eight

I had been in there for a solid hour, alone. There was the scarred desk in the middle, another against the wall, a brass spittoon on a mat, a police loudspeaker box on the wall, three squashed flies, a smell of cold cigars and old clothes. There were two hard armchairs with felt pads and two hard straight chairs without pads. The electric-light fixture had been dusted about Coolidge's first term.

The door opened with a jerk and Finlayson and Sebold came in. Sebold looked as spruce and nasty as ever, but Finlayson looked older, more worn, mousier. He held a sheaf of papers in his hand. He sat down across the desk from me and gave me a hard bleak stare.

"Guys like you get in a lot of trouble," Finlayson said sourly. Sebold sat down against the wall and tilted his hat over his eyes and yawned and looked at his new stainless-steel wrist watch.

"Trouble is my business," I said. "How else would I make a nickel?"

"We oughta throw you in the can for all this cover-up stuff. How much you making on this one?"

"I was working for Anna Halsey who was working for old man Jeeter. I guess I made a bad debt."

Sebold smiled his blackjack smile at me. Finlayson lit a cigar and licked at a tear on the side of it and pasted it down, but it leaked smoke just the same when he drew on it. He pushed papers across the desk at me.

"Sign three copies."

I signed three copies.

He took them back, yawned and rumpled his old gray head. "The old man's had a stroke," he said. "No dice there. Probably won't know what time it is when he comes out. This George Hasterman, this chauffeur guy, he just laughs at us. Too bad he got pinked. I'd like to wrastle him a bit."

"He's tough," I said.

"Yeah. O.K., you can beat it for now."

I got up and nodded to them and went to the door. "Well, good night, boys."

Neither of them spoke to me.

I went out, along the corridor and down in the night elevator to the City Hall lobby. I went out the Spring Street side and down the long flight of empty steps and the wind blew cold. I lit a cigarette at the bottom. My car was still out at the Jeeter place. I lifted a foot to start walking to a taxi half a block down across the street. A voice spoke sharply from a parked car.

"Come here a minute."

It was a man's voice, tight, hard. It was Marty Estel's voice. It came from a big sedan with two men in the front seat. I went over there. The rear window was down and Marty Estel leaned a gloved hand on it.

"Get in." He pushed the door open. I got in. I was too tired to argue. "Take it away, Skin."

The car drove west through dark, almost quiet streets, almost clean streets. The night air was not pure but it was cool. We went up over a hill and began to pick up speed.

"What they get?" Estel asked coolly.

"They didn't tell me. They didn't break the chauffeur yet."

"You can't convict a couple million bucks of murder in this man's town." The driver called Skin laughed without turning his head. "Maybe I don't even touch my fifty grand now . . . she likes you."

"Uh-huh. So what?"

"Lay off her."

"What will it get me?"

"It's what it'll get you if you don't."

"Yeah, sure," I said. "Go to hell, will you please. I'm tired." I shut my eyes and leaned in the corner of the car and just like that went to sleep. I can do that sometimes, after a strain.

A hand shaking my shoulder woke me. The car had stopped. I looked out at the front of my apartment house.

"Home," Marty Estel said. "And remember. Lay off her."

"Why the ride home? Just to tell me that?"

"She asked me to look out for you. That's why you're loose. She likes you. I like her. See? You don't want any more trouble."

"Trouble—" I started to say, and stopped. I was tired of that gag for that night. "Thanks for the ride, and apart from that, nuts to you." I turned away and went into the apartment house and up.

The door lock was still loose but nobody waited for me this time. They had taken Waxnose away long since. I left the door open and threw the windows up and I was still sniffing at policemen's cigar butts when the phone rang. It was her voice, cool, a little hard, not touched by anything, almost amused. Well, she'd been through enough to make her that way, probably.

"Hello, brown-eyes. Make it home all right?"

"Your pal Marty brought me home. He told me to lay off you. Thanks with all my heart, if I have any, but don't call me up any more."

"A little scared, Mr. Marlowe?"

"No. Wait for me to call you," I said. "Good night, angel."

"Good night, brown-eyes."

The phone clicked. I put it away and shut the door and pulled the bed down. I undressed and lay on it for a while in the cold air.

Then I got up and had a drink and a shower and went to sleep.

They broke George at last, but not enough. He said there had been a fight over the girl and young Jeeter had grabbed the gun off the mantel and George had fought with him and it had gone off. All of which, of course, looked possible—in the papers. They never pinned the Arbogast killing on him or on anybody. They never found the gun that did it, but it was not Waxnose's gun. Waxnose disappeared—I never heard where. They didn't touch old man Jeeter, because he never came out of his stroke, except to lie on his back and have nurses and tell people how he hadn't lost a nickel in the depression.

Marty Estel called me up four times to tell me to lay off Harriet Huntress. I felt kind of sorry for the poor guy. He had it bad. I went out with her twice and sat with her twice more at home, drinking her Scotch. It was nice, but I didn't have the money, the clothes, the time or the manners. Then she stopped being at the El Milano and I heard she had gone to New York.

I was glad when she left—even though she didn't bother to tell me goodbye.

SUE GRAFTON

1940–

One of the major creators in the United States of the contemporary tough woman P.I., Grafton was born in Louisville, Kentucky, and graduated from the University of Louisville with a degree in English in 1961. Her father, C. W. Grafton, published three mystery novels. Grafton began writing when she was twenty-two and spent two decades writing screenplays, television scripts, and two non-mystery novels before publishing "A" is for Alibi (1982) featuring private investigator Kinsey Millhone. Grafton jokes that it was better to write the well-plotted murder than to kill an ex-husband with whom she was involved in a bitter child-custody suit. The book was a successful start to her best-selling Kinsey Millhone "alphabet" series, which has won numerous awards, including three Anthony Awards and three Shamus Awards for Best Novel. Grafton served as President of the Private Eye Writers of America (PWA) 1989-90 and President of Mystery Writers of America (MWA) 1994-95. In 2003, Grafton received the Eye Award, the highest recognition by the PWA for an author's lifetime achievement.

Grafton is widely recognized as one of the Big Three, along with Marcia Muller and Sara Paretsky, who in the early 1980s created and popularized the tough female P.I. Grafton's Kinsey Millhone lives and works in the fictitious Santa Teresa, California, a thinly veiled version of Santa Barbara, California. Grafton thus pays tribute to writer Ross Macdonald, who used "Santa Teresa" as the pseudonym for his hometown, Santa Barbara, in his Lew Archer mysteries. Tough and sassy Kinsey is one of the best-known women P.I.s in detective fiction, and she has her own biography, in "G" is for Grafton: The World of Kinsey Millhone (1997), written by Natalie Hevener Kaufman and Carol McGinnis Kay. Grafton's series is published in at least 28 countries and 26 languages, including Estonian, Bulgarian, and Indonesian. "The Parker Shotgun," featuring Kinsey Millhone, was first published in 1986 in Mean Streets, edited by Robert J. Randisi. The story received both the Macavity and the Anthony Awards for Best Short Story in 1987 and is included in The Best American Mystery Short Stories of the Century (2000), edited by Tony Hillerman.

Recommended Grafton works: "B" is for Burglar, "G" is for Gumshoe, "P" is for Peril.

Other recommended authors: Susan Dunlap, Marcia Muller, Sara Paretsky.

The Parker Shotgun

The Christmas holidays had come and gone, and the new year was underway. January, in California, is as good as it gets—cool, clear, and green, with a sky the color of wisteria and a surf that thunders like a volley of gunfire in a distant field. My name is Kinsey Millhone. I'm a private investigator, licensed, bonded, insured; white, female, age thirty-two, unmarried, and physically fit.

That Monday morning, I was sitting in my office with my feet up, wondering what life would bring, when a woman walked in and tossed a photograph on my desk. My introduction to the Parker shotgun began with a graphic view of its apparent effect when fired at a formerly nice-looking man at close range. His face was still largely intact, but he had no use now for a pocket comb. With effort, I kept my expression neutral as I glanced up at her.

"Somebody killed my husband."

"I can see that," I said.

She snatched the picture back and stared at it as though she might have missed some telling detail. Her face suffused with pink, and she blinked back tears. "Jesus. Rudd was killed five months ago, and the cops have done shit. I'm so sick of getting the runaround I could scream."

She sat down abruptly and pressed a hand to her mouth, trying to compose herself. She was in her late twenties, with a gaudy prettiness. Her hair was an odd shade of brown, like cherry Coke, worn shoulder length and straight. Her eyes were large, a lush mink brown; her mouth was full. Her complexion was all warm tones, tanned, and clear. She didn't seem to be wearing makeup, but she was still as vivid as a magazine illustration, a good four-color run on slick paper. She was seven months pregnant by the look of her; not voluminous yet, but rotund. When she was calmer, she identified herself as Lisa Osterling.

"That's a crime lab photo. How'd you come by it?" I said when the preliminaries were disposed of.

She fumbled in her handbag for a tissue and blew her nose. "I have my little ways," she said morosely. "Actually I know the photographer and I stole a print. I'm going to have it blown up and hung on the wall just so I won't forget. The police are hoping I'll drop the whole thing, but I got news for *them*." Her mouth was starting to tremble again, and a tear splashed onto her skirt as though my ceiling had a leak.

"What's the story?" I said. "The cops in this town are usually pretty good." I got up and filled a paper cup with water from my Sparklett's dispenser, passing it over to her. She murmured a thank you and drank it down, staring into the bottom of the cup as she spoke. "Rudd was a cocaine dealer until a month or so before he died. They haven't said as much, but I know they've written him off as some kind of small-time punk. What do they care? They'd like to think he was killed in a drug deal—a double cross or something like that. He wasn't, though. He'd given it all up because of this."

She glanced down at the swell of her belly. She was wearing a kelly green T-shirt with an arrow down the front. The word "Oops!" was written across her breasts in machine embroidery.

"What's your theory?" I asked. Already I was leaning toward the official police version of events. Drug dealing isn't synonymous with longevity. There's too much money involved and too many amateurs getting into the act. This was Santa Teresa—ninety-five miles north of the big time in L.A., but there are still standards to maintain. A shotgun blast is the underworld equivalent of a bad annual review.

"I don't have a theory. I just don't like theirs. I want you to look into it so I can clear Rudd's name before the baby comes."

I shrugged. "I'll do what I can, but I can't guarantee the results. How are you going to feel if the cops are right?"

She stood up, giving me a flat look. "I don't know why Rudd died, but it had nothing to do with drugs," she said. She opened her handbag and extracted a roll of bills the size of a wad of socks. "What do you charge?"

"Thirty bucks an hour plus expenses."

She peeled off several hundred-dollar bills and laid them on the desk.

I got out a contract.

My second encounter with the Parker shotgun came in the form of a dealer's appraisal slip that I discovered when I was nosing through Rudd Osterling's private possessions an hour later at the house. The address she'd given me was on the Bluffs, a residential area on the west side of town, overlooking the Pacific. It should have been an elegant neighborhood, but the ocean generated too much fog and too much corrosive salt air. The houses were small and had a temporary feel to them, as though the occupants intended to move on when the month was up. No one seemed to get around to painting the trim, and the yards looked like they were kept by people who spent all day at the beach. I followed her in my car, reviewing the information she'd given me as I urged my ancient VW up Capilla Hill and took a right on Presipio.

The late Rudd Osterling had been in Santa Teresa since the sixties, when he migrated to the West Coast in search of sunshine, good surf, good dope, and casual sex. Lisa told me he'd lived in vans and communes, working variously as a roofer, tree trimmer, bean picker, fry cook, and forklift operator—never with any noticeable ambition or success. He'd started dealing cocaine two years earlier, apparently netting more money than he was accustomed to. Then he'd met and married Lisa, and she'd been determined to see him clean up his act. According to her, he'd retired from the drug trade and was just in the process of setting himself up in a landscape maintenance business when someone blew the top of his head off.

I pulled into the driveway behind her, glancing at the frame and stucco bungalow with its patchy grass and dilapidated fence. It looked like one of those households where there's always something under construction, probably without permits and not up to code. In this case, a foundation had been laid for an addition to the garage, but the weeds were already growing up through cracks in the concrete. A wooden outbuilding had been dismantled, the old lumber tossed in an unsightly pile. Closer to the house, there were stacks of cheap pecan wood paneling, sunbleached in places and warped along one edge. It was all hapless and depressing, but she scarcely looked at it.

I followed her into the house.

"We were just getting the house fixed up when he died," she remarked.

"When did you buy the place?" I was manufacturing small talk, trying to cover my distaste at the sight of the old linoleum counter, where a line of ants stretched from a crust of toast and jelly all the way out the back door.

"We didn't really. This was my mother's. She and my stepdad moved back to the Midwest last year."

"What about Rudd? Did he have any family out here?"

"They're all in Connecticut, I think, real la-di-dah. His parents are dead, and his sisters wouldn't even come out to the funeral."

"Did he have a lot of friends?"

"All cocaine dealers have friends."

"Enemies?"

"Not that I ever heard about."

"Who was his supplier?"

"I don't know that."

"No disputes? Suits pending? Quarrels with the neighbors? Family arguments about the inheritance?"

She gave me a "no" on all four counts.

I had told her I wanted to go through his personal belongings, so she showed me into the tiny back bedroom, where he'd set up a card table and some cardboard file boxes. A real entrepreneur. I began to search while she leaned against the doorframe, watching.

I said, "Tell me about what was going on the week he died." I was sorting through cancelled checks in a Nike shoe box. Most were written to the neighborhood supermarket, utilities, telephone company.

She moved to the desk chair and sat down. "I can't tell you much because I was at work. I do alterations and repairs at a dry cleaner's up at Presipio Mall. Rudd would stop in now and then when he was out running around. He'd picked up a few jobs already, but he really wasn't doing the gardening full time. He was trying to get all his old business squared away. Some kid owed him money. I remember that."

"He sold cocaine on *credit?*"

She shrugged. "Maybe it was grass or pills. Somehow the kid owed him a bundle. That's all I know."

"I don't suppose he kept any records."

"Nuh-uh. It was all in his head. He was too paranoid to put anything down in black and white."

The file boxes were jammed with old letters, tax returns, receipts. It all looked like junk to me.

"What about the day he was killed? Were you at work then?"

She shook her head. "It was a Saturday. I was off work, but I'd gone to the market. I was out maybe an hour and a half, and when I got home police cars were parked in front, and the paramedics were here. Neighbors were standing out on the street." She stopped talking, and I was left to imagine the rest.

"Had he been expecting anyone?"

"If he was, he never said anything to me. He was in the garage, doing I don't know what. Chauncy, next door, heard the shotgun go off, but by the time he got here to investigate, whoever did it was gone."

I got up and moved toward the hallway. "Is this the bedroom down here?"

"Right. I haven't gotten rid of his stuff yet. I guess I'll have to eventually. I'm going to use his office for the nursery."

I moved into the master bedroom and went through his hanging clothes. "Did the police find anything?"

"They didn't look. Well, one guy came through and poked around some. About five minutes' worth."

I began to check through the drawers she indicated were his. Nothing remarkable came to light. On top of the chest was one of those brass and walnut caddies, where Rudd apparently kept his watch, keys, loose change. Almost idly, I picked it up. Under it there was a folded slip of paper. It was a partially completed appraisal form from a gun shop out in Colgate, a township to the north of us. "What's a Parker?" I said when I'd glanced at it. She peered over the slip.

"Oh. That's probably the appraisal on the shotgun he got."

"The one he was killed with?"

"Well, I don't know. They never found the weapon, but the homicide detective said they couldn't run it through ballistics, anyway—or whatever it is they do."

"Why'd he have it appraised in the first place?"

"He was taking it in trade for a big drug debt, and he needed to know if it was worth it."

"Was this the kid you mentioned before or someone else?"

"The same one, I think. At first, Rudd intended to turn around and sell the gun, but then he found out it was a collector's item so he decided to keep it. The gun dealer called a couple of times after Rudd died, but it was gone by then."

"And you told the cops all this stuff?"

"Sure. They couldn't have cared less."

I doubted that, but I tucked the slip in my pocket anyway. I'd check it out and then talk to Dolan in homicide.

The gun shop was located on a narrow side street in Colgate, just off the main thoroughfare. Colgate looks like it's made up of hardware stores, U-haul rentals, and plant nurseries; places that seem to have half their merchandise outside, surrounded by chain link fence. The gun shop had been set up in someone's front parlor in a dinky white frame house. There were some glass counters filled with gun paraphernalia, but no guns in sight.

The man who came out of the back room was in his fifties, with a narrow face and graying hair, gray eyes made luminous by rimless glasses. He wore a dress shirt with the sleeves rolled up and a long gray apron tied around his waist.

He had perfect teeth, but when he talked I could see the rim of pink where his upper plate was fit, and it spoiled the effect. Still, I had to give him credit for a certain level of good looks, maybe a seven on a scale of ten. Not bad for a man his age. "Yes ma'am," he said. He had a trace of an accent, Virginia, I thought.

"Are you Avery Lamb?"

"That's right. What can I help you with?"

"I'm not sure. I'm wondering what you can tell me about this appraisal you did." I handed him the slip.

He glanced down and then looked up at me. "Where did you get this?"

"Rudd Osterling's widow," I said.

"She told me she didn't have the gun."

"That's right."

His manner was a combination of confusion and wariness. "What's your connection to the matter?"

I took out a business card and gave it to him. "She hired me to look into Rudd's death. I thought the shotgun might be relevant since he was killed with one."

He shook his head. "I don't know what's going on. This is the second time it's disappeared."

"Meaning what?"

"Some woman brought it in to have it appraised back in June. I made an offer on it then, but before we could work out a deal, she claimed the gun was stolen."

"I take it you had some doubts about that."

"Sure I did. I don't think she ever filed a police report, and I suspect she knew damn well who took it but didn't intend to pursue it. Next thing I knew, this Osterling fellow brought the same gun in. It had a beavertail fore-end and an English grip. There was no mistaking it."

"Wasn't that a bit of a coincidence? His bringing the gun in to you?"

"Not really. I'm one of the few master gunsmiths in this area. All he had to do was ask around the same way she did."

"Did you tell her the gun had showed up?"

He shrugged with his mouth and a lift of his brows. "Before I could talk to her, he was dead and the Parker was gone again."

I checked the date on the slip. "That was in August?"

"That's right, and I haven't seen the gun since."

"Did he tell you how he acquired it?"

"Said he took it in trade. I told him this other woman showed up with it first, but he didn't seem to care about that."

"How much was the Parker worth?"

He hesitated, weighing his words. "I offered him six thousand."

"But what's its value out in the marketplace?"

"Depends on what people are willing to pay."

I tried to control the little surge of impatience he had sparked. I could tell he'd jumped into his crafty negotiator's mode, unwilling to tip his hand in case the gun showed up and he could nick it off cheap. "Look," I said, "I'm asking you in confidence. This won't go any further unless it becomes a police matter, and then neither one of us will have a choice. Right now, the gun's missing anyway, so what difference does it make?"

He didn't seem entirely convinced, but he got my point. He cleared his throat with obvious embarrassment. "Ninety-six."

I stared at him. "Thousand dollars?"

He nodded.

"Jesus. That's a lot for a gun, isn't it?"

His voice dropped. "Ms. Millhone, that gun is priceless. It's an A-1 Special 28-gauge with a two-barrel set. There were only two of them made."

"But why so much?"

"For one thing, the Parker's a beautifully crafted shotgun. There are different grades, of course, but this one was exceptional. Fine wood. Some of the most incredible scroll-work you'll ever see. Parker had an Italian working for him back then who'd spend sometimes five thousand hours on the engraving alone. The company went out of business around 1942, so there aren't any more to be had."

"You said there were two. Where's the other one, or would you know?"

"Only what I've heard. A dealer in Ohio bought the one at auction a couple years back for ninety-six. I understand some fella down in Texas has it now, part of a collection of Parkers. The gun Rudd Osterling brought in has been missing for years. I don't think he knew what he had on his hands."

"And you didn't tell him."

Lamb shifted his gaze. "I told him enough," he said carefully. "I can't help it if the man didn't do his homework."

"How'd you know it was the missing Parker?"

"The serial number matched, and so did everything else. It wasn't a fake, either. I examined the gun under heavy magnification, checking for fill-in welds and traces of markings that might have been overstamped. After I checked it out, I showed it to a buddy of mine, a big gun buff, and he recognized it, too."

"Who else knew about it besides you and this friend?"

"Whoever Rudd Osterling got it from, I guess."

"I'll want the woman's name and address if you've still got it. Maybe she knows how the gun fell into Rudd's hands."

Again he hesitated for a moment, and then he shrugged. "I don't see why not." He made a note on a piece of scratch paper and pushed it across the counter to me. "I'd like to know if the gun shows up," he said.

"Sure, as long as Mrs. Osterling doesn't object."

I didn't have any other questions for the moment. I moved toward the door, then glanced back at him. "How could Rudd have sold the gun if it was stolen property? Wouldn't he have needed a bill of sale for it? Some proof of ownership?"

Avery Lamb's face was devoid of expression. "Not necessarily. If an avid collector got hold of that gun, it would sink out of sight, and that's the last you'd ever see of it. He'd keep it in his basement and never show it to a soul. It'd be enough if he knew he had it. You don't need a bill of sale for that."

I sat out in my car and made some notes while the information was fresh. Then I checked the address Lamb had given me, and I could feel the adrenaline stir. It was right back in Rudd's neighborhood.

The woman's name was Jackie Barnett. The address was two streets over from the Osterling house and just about parallel; a big corner lot planted with avocado trees and bracketed with palms. The house itself was yellow stucco with flaking brown shutters and a yard that needed mowing. The mailbox read "Squires," but the house number seemed to match. There was a basketball hoop nailed up above the two-car garage and a dismantled motorcycle in the driveway.

I parked my car and got out. As I approached the house, I saw an old man in a wheelchair planted in the side yard like a lawn ornament. He was parchment pale, with baby-fine white hair and rheumy eyes. The left half of his face had been disconnected by a stroke, and his left arm and hand rested uselessly in his lap. I caught sight of a woman peering through the window, apparently drawn by the sound of my car door slamming shut. I crossed the yard, moving toward the front porch. She opened the door before I had a chance to knock.

"You must be Kinsey Millhone. I just got off the phone with Avery. He said you'd be stopping by."

"That was quick. I didn't realize he'd be calling ahead. Saves me an explanation. I take it you're Jackie Barnett."

"That's right. Come in if you like. I just have to check on him," she said, indicating the man in the yard.

"Your father?"

She shot me a look. "Husband," she said. I watched her cross the grass toward the old man, grateful for a chance to recover from my gaffe. I could see now that she was older than she'd first appeared. She must have been in her fifties—at that stage where women wear too much makeup and dye their hair too bold a shade of blonde. She was buxom, clearly overweight, but lush. In a seventeenth-century painting, she'd have been depicted supine, her plump naked body draped in sheer white. Standing over her, something with a goat's rear end would be poised for assault. Both would look coy but excited at the prospects. The old man was beyond the pleasures of the flesh, yet the noises he made—garbled and indistinguishable because of the stroke—had the same intimate quality as sounds uttered in the throes of passion, a disquieting effect.

I looked away from him, thinking of Avery Lamb instead. He hadn't actually told me the woman was a stranger to him, but he'd certainly implied as much. I wondered now what their relationship consisted of.

Jackie spoke to the old man briefly, adjusting his lap robe. Then she came back and we went inside.

"Is your name Barnett or Squires?" I asked.

"Technically it's Squires, but I still use Barnett for the most part," she said. She seemed angry, and I thought at first the rage was directed at me. She caught my look. "I'm sorry," she said, "but I've about had it with him. Have you ever dealt with a stroke victim?"

"I understand it's difficult."

"It's impossible! I know I sound hard-hearted, but he was always short-tempered and now he's frustrated on top of that. Self-centered, demanding. Nothing suits him. Nothing. I put him out in the yard sometimes just so I won't have to fool with him. Have a seat, hon."

I sat. "How long has be been sick?"

"He had the first stroke in June. He's been in and out of the hospital ever since."

"What's the story on the gun you took out to Avery's shop?"

"Oh, that's right. He said you were looking into some fellow's death. He lived right here on the Bluffs, too, didn't he?"

"Over on Whitmore . . . "

"That was terrible. I read about it in the papers, but I never did hear the end of it. What went on?"

"I wasn't given the details," I said briefly. "Actually, I'm trying to track down a shotgun that belonged to him. Avery Lamb says it was the same gun you brought in."

She had automatically proceeded to get out two cups and saucers, so her answer was delayed until she'd poured coffee for us both. She passed a cup over to me, and then she sat down, stirring milk into hers. She glanced at me self-consciously. "I just took that gun to spite *him*," she said with a nod toward the yard. "I've been married to Bill for six years and miserable for every one of them. It was my own damn fault. I'd been divorced for ages and I was doing fine, but somehow when I hit fifty, I got in a panic. Afraid of growing old alone, I guess. I ran into Bill, and he looked like a catch. He was retired, but he had loads of money, or so he said. He promised me the moon. Said we'd travel. Said he'd buy me clothes and a car and I don't know what all. Turns out he's a penny-pinching miser with a mean mouth and a quick fist. At least he can't do that anymore." She paused to shake her head, staring down at her coffee cup.

"The gun was his?"

"Well, yes, it was. He has a collection of shotguns. I swear he took better care of them than he did of me. I just despise guns. I was always after him to get rid of them. Makes me nervous to have them in the house. Anyway, when he got sick, it turned out he had insurance, but it only paid eighty percent. I was afraid his whole life savings would go up in smoke. I figured he'd go on for years, using up all the money, and then I'd be stuck with his debts when he died. So I just picked up one of the guns and took it out to that gun place to sell. I was going to buy me some clothes."

"What made you change your mind?"

"Well, I didn't think it'd be worth but eight or nine hundred dollars. Then Avery said he'd give me six thousand for it, so I had to guess it was worth at least twice that. I got nervous and thought I better put it back."

"How soon after that did the gun disappear?"

"Oh, gee, I don't know. I didn't pay much attention until Bill got out of the hospital the second time. He's the one who noticed it was gone," she said. "Of course, he raised pluperfect hell. You should have seen him. He had a connip- tion fit for two days, and then he had another stroke and had to be hospital- ized all over again. Served him right if you ask me. At least I had Labor Day weekend to myself. I needed it."

"Do you have any idea who might have taken the gun?"

She gave me a long, candid look. Her eyes were very blue and couldn't have appeared more guileless. "Not the faintest."

I let her practice her wide-eyed stare for a moment, and then I laid out a little bait just to see what she'd do. "God, that's too bad," I said. "I'm assuming you reported it to the police."

I could see her debate briefly before she replied. Yes or no. Check one. "Well, of course," she said.

She was one of those liars who blush from lack of practice.

I kept my tone of voice mild. "What about the insurance? Did you put in a claim?"

She looked at me blankly, and I had the feeling I'd taken her by surprise on that one. She said, "You know, it never even occurred to me. But of course he probably would have it insured, wouldn't he?"

"Sure, if the gun's worth that much. What company is he with?"

"I don't remember offhand. I'd have to look it up."

"I'd do that if I were you," I said. "You can file a claim, and then all you have to do is give the agent the case number."

"Case number?"

"The police will give you that from their report."

She stirred restlessly, glancing at her watch. "Oh, lordy, I'm going to have to give him his medicine. Was there anything else you wanted to ask while you were here?" Now that she'd told me a fib or two, she was anxious to get rid of me so she could assess the situation. Avery Lamb had told me she'd never reported it to the cops. I wondered if she'd call him up now to com- pare notes.

"Could I take a quick look at his collection?" I said, getting up.

"I suppose that'd be all right. It's in here," she said. She moved toward a small paneled den, and I followed, stepping around a suitcase near the door.

A rack of six guns was enclosed in a glass-fronted cabinet. All of them were beautifully engraved, with fine wood stocks, and I wondered how a priceless

Parker could really be distinguished. Both the cabinet and the rack were locked, and there were no empty slots. "Did he keep the Parker in here?"

She shook her head. "The Parker had its own case." She hauled out a handsome wood case from behind the couch and opened it for me, demonstrating its emptiness as though she might be setting up a magic trick. Actually, there was a set of barrels in the box, but nothing else.

I glanced around. There was a shotgun propped in one corner, and I picked it up, checking the manufacturer's imprint on the frame. L.C. Smith. Too bad. For a moment I'd thought it might be the missing Parker. I'm always hoping for the obvious. I set the Smith back in the corner with regret.

"Well, I guess that'll do," I said. "Thanks for the coffee."

"No trouble. I wish I could be more help." She started easing me toward the door.

I held out my hand. "Nice meeting you," I said. "Thanks again for your time."

She gave my hand a perfunctory shake. "That's all right. Sorry I'm in such a rush, but you know how it is when you have someone sick."

Next thing I knew, the door was closing at my back and I was heading toward my car, wondering what she was up to.

I'd just reached the driveway when a white Corvette came roaring down the street and rumbled into the drive. The kid at the wheel flipped the ignition key and cantilevered himself up onto the seat top. "Hi. You know if my mom's here?"

"Who, Jackie? Sure," I said, taking a flyer. "You must be Doug."

He looked puzzled. "No, Eric. Do I know you?"

I shook my head. "I'm just a friend passing through."

He hopped out of the Corvette. I moved on toward my car, keeping an eye on him as he headed toward the house. He looked about seventeen, blond, blue-eyed, with good cheekbones, a moody, sensual mouth, lean surfer's body. I pictured him in a few years, hanging out in resort hotels, picking up women three times his age. He'd do well. So would they.

Jackie had apparently heard him pull in, and she came out onto the porch, intercepting him with a quick look at me. She put her arm through his, and the two moved into the house. I looked over at the old man. He was making noises again, plucking aimlessly at his bad hand with his good one. I felt a mental jolt, like an interior tremor shifting the ground under me. I was beginning to get it.

I drove the two blocks to Lisa Osterling's. She was in the backyard, stretched out on a chaise in a sunsuit that made her belly look like a watermelon in a laundry bag. Her face and arms were rosy, and her tanned legs glistened with tanning oil. As I crossed the grass, she raised a hand to her eyes, shading her face from the winter sunlight so she could look at me. "I didn't expect to see you back so soon."

"I have a question," I said, "and then I need to use your phone. Did Rudd know a kid named Eric Barnett?"

"I'm not sure. What's he look like?"

I gave her a quick rundown, including a description of the white Corvette. I could see the recognition in her face as she sat up.

"Oh, him. Sure. He was over here two or three times a week. I just never knew his name. Rudd said he lived around here somewhere and stopped by to borrow tools so he could work on his motorcycle. Is he the one who owed Rudd the money?"

"Well, I don't know how we're going to prove it, but I suspect he was."

"You think he killed him?"

"I can't answer that yet, but I'm working on it. Is the phone in here?" I was moving toward the kitchen. She struggled to her feet and followed me into the house. There was a wall phone near the back door. I tucked the receiver against my shoulder, pulling the appraisal slip out of my pocket. I dialed Avery Lamb's gun shop. The phone rang twice.

Somebody picked up on the other end. "Gun shop."

"Mr. Lamb?"

"This is Orville Lamb. Did you want me or my brother, Avery?"

"Avery, actually. I have a quick question for him."

"Well, he left a short while ago, and I'm not sure when he'll be back. Is it something I can help you with?"

"Maybe so," I said. "If you had a priceless shotgun—say, an Ithaca or a Parker, one of the classics—would you shoot a gun like that?"

"You could," he said dubiously, "but it wouldn't be a good idea especially if it was in mint condition to begin with. You wouldn't want to take a chance on lowering the value. Now if it'd been in use previously, I don't guess it would matter much, but still I wouldn't advise it—just speaking for myself. Is this a gun of yours?"

But I'd hung up. Lisa was right behind me, her expression anxious. "I've got to go in a minute," I said, "but here's what I think went on. Eric Barnett's stepfather has a collection of fine shotguns, one of which turns out to be very, very valuable. The old man was hospitalized, and Eric's mother decided to hock one of the guns in order to do a little something for herself before he'd blown every asset he had on his medical bills. She had no idea the gun she chose was worth so much, but the gun dealer recognized it as the find of a lifetime. I don't know whether he told her that or not, but when she realized it was more valuable than she thought, she lost her nerve and put it back."

"Was that the same gun Rudd took in trade?"

"Exactly. My guess is that she mentioned it to her son, who saw a chance to square his drug debt. He offered Rudd the shotgun in trade, and Rudd decided he'd better get the gun appraised, so he took it out to the same place. The gun dealer recognized it when he brought it in."

She stared at me. "Rudd was killed over the gun itself, wasn't he?" she said.

"I think so, yes. It might have been an accident. Maybe there was a struggle and the gun went off."

She closed her eyes and nodded. "Okay. Oh, wow. That feels better. I can live with that." Her eyes came open, and she smiled painfully. "Now what?"

"I have one more hunch to check out, and then I think we'll know what's what."

She reached over and squeezed my arm. "Thanks."

"Yeah, well, it's not over yet, but we're getting there."

When I got back to Jackie Barnett's, the white Corvette was still in the driveway, but the old man in the wheelchair had apparently been moved into the house. I knocked, and after an interval, Eric opened the door, his expression altering only slightly when he saw me.

I said, "Hello again. Can I talk to your mom?"

"Well, not really. She's gone right now."

"Did she and Avery go off together?"

"Who?"

I smiled briefly. "You can drop the bullshit, Eric. I saw the suitcase in the hall when I was here the first time. Are they gone for good or just for a quick jaunt?"

"They said they'd be back by the end of the week," he mumbled. It was clear he looked a lot slicker than he really was. I almost felt bad that he was so far outclassed.

"Do you mind if I talk to your stepfather?"

He flushed. "She doesn't want him upset."

"I won't upset him."

He shifted uneasily, trying to decide what to do with me.

I thought I'd help him out. "Could I just make a suggestion here? According to the California penal code, grand theft is committed when the real or personal property taken is of a value exceeding two hundred dollars. Now that includes domestic fowl, avocados, olives, citrus, nuts, and artichokes. Also shotguns, and it's punishable by imprisonment in the county jail or state prison for not more than one year. I don't think you'd care for it."

He stepped away from the door and let me in.

The old man was huddled in his wheelchair in the den. The rheumy eyes came up to meet mine, but there was no recognition in them. Or maybe there was recognition but no interest. I hunkered beside his wheelchair. "Is your hearing okay?"

He began to pluck aimlessly at his pant leg with his good hand, looking away from me. I've seen dogs with the same expression when they've done pottie on the rug and know you've got a roll of newspaper tucked behind your back.

"Want me to tell you what I think happened?" I didn't really need to wait. He couldn't answer in any mode that I could interpret. "I think when you came home from the hospital the first time and found out the gun was gone, the shit hit the fan. You must have figured out that Eric took it. He'd probably taken other things if he'd been doing cocaine for long. You probably hounded him until you found out what he'd done with it, and then you went over to Rudd's to get it. Maybe you took the L.C. Smith with you the first time, or maybe you came back for it when he refused to return the Parker. In either case, you blew his head off and then came back across the yards. And then you had another stroke."

I became aware of Eric in the doorway behind me. I glanced back at him. "You want to talk about this stuff?" I asked.

"Did he kill Rudd?"

"I think so," I said. I stared at the old man.

His face had taken on a canny stubbornness, and what was I going to do? I'd have to talk to Lieutenant Dolan about the situation, but the cops would probably never find any real proof, and even if they did, what could they do to him? He'd be lucky if he lived out the year.

"Rudd was a nice guy," Eric said.

"God, Eric. You *all* must have guessed what happened," I said snappishly.

He had the good grace to color up at that, and then he left the room. I stood up. To save myself, I couldn't work up any righteous anger at the pitiful remainder of a human being hunched in front of me. I crossed to the gun cabinet.

The Parker shotgun was in the rack, three slots down, looking like the other classic shotguns in the case. The old man would die, and Jackie would inherit it from his estate. Then she'd marry Avery and they'd all have what they wanted. I stood there for a moment, and then I started looking through the desk drawers until I found the keys. I unlocked the cabinet and then unlocked the rack. I substituted the L.C. Smith for the Parker and then locked the whole business up again. The old man was whimpering, but he never looked at me, and Eric was nowhere in sight when I left.

The last I saw of the Parker shotgun, Lisa Osterling was holding it somewhat awkwardly across her bulky midriff. I'd talk to Lieutenant Dolan all right, but I wasn't going to tell him everything. Sometimes justice is served in other ways.

SARA PARETSKY

1947–

A major influence in contemporary women's detective fiction with her creation of Chicago private investigator V. I. Warshawski, Paretsky was born in Ames, Iowa, and grew up in Lawrence, Kansas. She attended the University of Kansas and later the University of Chicago, where she received an M.B.A. in finance and a Ph.D. in history in 1977. She worked in the corporate world for fourteen years, during which she began her ground-breaking V. I. Warshawski series. She has had enormous impact on the mystery field. She was the founder of Sisters in Crime in 1986 and served as its first president. The organization to promote women mystery writers has grown to thousands of members and active chapters in several countries. Paretsky is a member of the Private Eye Writers of America, the Authors Guild, the Crime Writers Association, and the Mystery Writers of America, for which she served as vice-president in 1989. *Ms. Magazine* named her one of their thirteen Women of the Year in 1987. Among her awards are a Silver Dagger for *Blood Shot* (1987), an Anthony for Best Collection or Anthology for *A Woman's Eye* (1991), and the Cartier Diamond Dagger Award for lifetime achievement in 2002.

V. I. (Victoria Iphegenia) Warshawski's father was a Polish policeman in Chicago and her mother a Jewish-Italian opera singer who died when V. I. was in high school. A lawyer who saw that the legal system did not always lead to justice, Warshawski became a solo private investigator. She repeatedly takes on corruption in powerful institutions—giant business corporations, government, the Catholic Church. Her cases always involve major social issues. V. I. is tough and often exposed to violence, but unlike the male loner of the hardboiled tradition, she is aware of the importance of personal friendships and of the patriarchal structures that continue to oppress and marginalize much of society. "Skin Deep," featuring V. I. Warshawski, first appeared in *The New Black Mask 8* in 1987 and is included in Paretsky's short story collection *Windy City Blues* (1995).

Recommended Paretsky works: *Killing Orders, Bitter Medicine, Tunnel Vision*.

Other recommended authors: Sue Grafton, Val McDermid, Marcia Muller.

Skin Deep

I

The warning bell clangs angrily and the submarine dives sharply. Everyone to battle stations. The Nazis pursuing closely, the bell keeps up its insistent clamor, loud, urgent, filling my head. My hands are wet: I can't remember what my job is in this cramped, tiny boat. If only someone would turn off the alarm bell. I fumble with some switches, pick up an intercom. The noise mercifully stops.

"Vic! Vic, is that you?"

"What?"

"I know it's late. I'm sorry to call so late, but I just got home from work. It's Sal, Sal Barthele."

"Oh, Sal. Sure." I looked at the orange clock readout. It was four-thirty. Sal owns the Golden Glow, a bar in the south Loop I patronize.

"It's my sister, Vic. They've arrested her. She didn't do it. I know she didn't do it."

"Of course not, Sal— Didn't do what?"

"They're trying to frame her. Maybe the manager . . . I don't know."

I swung my legs over the side of the bed. "Where are you?"

She was at her mother's house, 95th and Vincennes. Her sister had been arrested three hours earlier. They needed a lawyer, a good lawyer. And they needed a detective, a good detective. Whatever my fee was, she wanted me to know they could pay my fee.

"I'm sure you can pay the fee, but I don't know what you want me to do," I said as patiently as I could.

"She—they think she murdered that man. She didn't even know him. She was just giving him a facial. And he dies on her."

"Sal, give me your mother's address. I'll be there in forty minutes."

The little house on Vincennes was filled with neighbors and relatives murmuring encouragement to Mrs. Barthele. Sal is very black, and statuesque. Close to six feet tall, with a majestic carriage, she can break up a crowd in her bar with a look and a gesture. Mrs. Barthele was slight, frail, and light-skinned. It was hard to picture her as Sal's mother.

Sal dispersed the gathering with characteristic firmness, telling the group that I was here to save Evangeline and that I needed to see her mother alone.

Mrs. Barthele sniffed over every sentence. "Why did they do that to my baby?" she demanded of me. "You know the police, you know their ways. Why did they come and take my baby, who never did a wrong thing in her life?"

As a white woman, I could be expected to understand the machinations of the white man's law. And to share responsibility for it. After more of this meandering, Sal took the narrative firmly in hand.

Evangeline worked at La Cygnette, a high-prestige beauty salon on North Michigan. In addition to providing facials and their own brand-name cosmetics at an exorbitant cost, they massaged the bodies and feet of their wealthy clients, stuffed them into steam cabinets, ran them through a Bataan-inspired exercise routine, and fed them herbal teas. Signor Giuseppe would style their hair for an additional charge.

Evangeline gave facials. The previous day she had one client booked after lunch, a Mr. Darnell.

"Men go there a lot?" I interrupted.

Sal made a face. "That's what I asked Evangeline. I guess it's part of being a yuppie—go spend a lot of money getting cream rubbed into your face."

Anyway, Darnell was to have had his hair styled before his facial, but the hairdresser fell behind schedule and asked Evangeline to do the guy's face first.

Sal struggled to describe how a La Cygnette facial worked—neither of us had ever checked out her sister's job. You sit in something like a dentist's chair, lean back, relax—you're naked from the waist up, lying under a big down comforter. The facial expert—cosmetician was Evangeline's official title—puts cream on your hands and sticks them into little electrically heated mitts, so your hands are out of commission if you need to protect yourself. Then she puts stuff on your face, covers your eyes with heavy pads, and goes away for twenty minutes while the face goo sinks into your hidden pores.

Apparently while this Darnell lay back deeply relaxed, someone had rubbed some kind of poison into his skin. "When Evangeline came back in to clean his face, he was sick—heaving, throwing up, it was awful. She screamed for help and started trying to clean his face—it was terrible, he kept vomiting on her. They took him to the hospital, but he died around ten tonight.

"They came to get Baby at midnight—you've got to help her, V. I.—even if the guy tried something on her, she never did a thing like that—she'd haul off and slug him, maybe, but rubbing poison into his face? You go help her."

II

Evangeline Barthele was a younger, darker edition of her mother. At most times, she probably had Sal's energy—sparks of it flared now and then during our talk—but a night in the holding cells had worn her down.

I brought a clean suit and makeup for her: justice may be blind but her administrators aren't. We talked while she changed.

"This Darnell—you sure of the name?—had he ever been to the salon before?"

She shook her head. "I never saw him. And I don't think the other girls knew him either. You know, if a client's a good tipper or a bad one they'll comment on it, be glad or whatever that he's come in. Nobody said anything about this man."

"Where did he live?"

She shook her head. "I never talked to the guy, V. I."

"What about the PestFree?" I'd read the arrest report and talked briefly to an old friend in the M.E.'s office. To keep roaches and other vermin out of their posh Michigan Avenue offices, La Cygnette used a potent product containing a wonder chemical called chorpyrifos. My informant had been awestruck—"Only an operation that didn't know shit about chemicals would leave chorpyrifos lying around. It's got a toxicity rating of five—it gets you through the skin—you only need a couple of tablespoons to kill a big man if you know where to put it."

Whoever killed Darnell had either known a lot of chemistry or been lucky—into his nostrils and mouth, with some rubbed into the face for good measure, the pesticide had made him convulsive so quickly that even if he knew who killed him he'd have been unable to talk, or even reason.

Evangeline said she knew where the poison was kept—everyone who worked there knew, knew it was lethal and not to touch it, but it was easy to get at. Just in a little supply room that wasn't kept locked.

"So why you? They have to have more of a reason than just that you were there."

She shrugged bitterly. "I'm the only black professional at La Cygnette—the other blacks working there sweep rooms and haul trash. I'm trying hard not to be paranoid, but I gotta wonder."

She insisted Darnell hadn't made a pass at her, or done anything to provoke an attack—she hadn't hurt the guy. As for anyone else who might have had opportunity, salon employees were always passing through the halls, going in and out of the little cubicles where they treated clients—she'd seen any number of people, all with legitimate business in the halls, but she hadn't seen anyone emerging from the room where Darnell was sitting.

When we finally got to bond court later that morning, I tried to argue circumstantial evidence—any of La Cygnette's fifty or so employees could have committed the crime, since all had access and no one had motive. The prosecutor hit me with a very unpleasant surprise: the police had uncovered evidence linking my client to the dead man. He was a furniture buyer from Kansas City who came to Chicago six times a year, and the doorman and the maids at his hotel had identified Evangeline without any trouble as the woman who accompanied him on his visits.

Bail was denied. I had a furious talk with Evangeline in one of the interrogation rooms before she went back to the holding cells.

"Why the hell didn't you tell me? I walked into the courtroom and got blindsided."

"They're lying," she insisted.

"Three people identified you. If you don't start with the truth right now, you're going to have to find a new lawyer and a new detective. Your mother may not understand, but for sure Sal will."

"You can't tell my mother. You can't tell Sal!"

"I'm going to have to give them some reason for dropping your case, and knowing Sal it's going to have to be the truth."

For the first time she looked really upset. "You're my lawyer. You should believe my story before you believe a bunch of strangers you never saw before."

"I'm telling you, Evangeline, I'm going to drop your case. I can't represent you when I know you're lying. If you killed Darnell we can work out a defense. Or if you didn't kill him and knew him we can work something out, and I can try to find the real killer. But when I know you've been seen with the guy any number of times, I can't go into court telling people you never met him before."

Tears appeared on the ends of her lashes. "The whole reason I didn't say anything was so Mama wouldn't know. If I tell you the truth, you've got to promise me you aren't running back to Vincennes Avenue talking to her."

I agreed. Whatever the story was, I couldn't believe Mrs. Barthele hadn't heard hundreds like it before. But we each make our own separate peace with our mothers.

Evangeline met Darnell at a party two years earlier. She liked him, he liked her—not the romance of the century, but they enjoyed spending time together. She'd gone on a two-week trip to Europe with him last year, telling her mother she was going with a girlfriend.

"First of all, she has very strict morals. No sex outside marriage. I'm thirty, mind you, but that doesn't count with her. Second, he's white, and she'd murder me. She really would. I think that's why I never fell in love with him—if we wanted to get married I'd never be able to explain it to Mama."

This latest trip to Chicago, Darnell thought it would be fun to see what Evangeline did for a living, so he booked an appointment at La Cygnette. She hadn't told anyone there she knew him. And when she found him sick and dying she'd panicked and lied.

"And if you tell my mother of this, V. I.—I'll put a curse on you. My father was from Haiti and he knew a lot of good ones."

"I won't tell your mother. But unless they nuked Lebanon this morning or murdered the mayor, you're going to get a lot of lines in the paper. It's bound to be in print."

She wept at that, wringing her hands. So after watching her go off with the sheriff's deputies, I called Murray Ryerson at the *Herald-Star* to plead with him not to put Evangeline's liaison in the paper. "If you do she'll wither your testicles. Honest."

"I don't know, Vic. You know the *Sun-Times* is bound to have some kind of screamer headline like DEAD MAN FOUND IN FACE-LICKING SEX ORGY. I can't sit on a story like this when all the other papers are running it."

I knew he was right, so I didn't push my case very hard.

He surprised me by saying, "Tell you what: you find the real killer before my deadline for tomorrow's morning edition and I'll keep your client's personal life out of it. The sex scoop came in too late for today's paper. The *Trib* prints on our schedule and they don't have it, and the *Sun-Times* runs older, slower presses, so they have to print earlier."

I reckoned I had about eighteen hours. Sherlock Holmes had solved tougher problems in less time.

III

Roland Darnell had been the chief buyer of living-room furnishings for Alexander Dumas, a high-class Kansas City department store. He used to own his own furniture store in the nearby town of Lawrence, but lost both it and his wife when he was arrested for drug smuggling ten years earlier. Because of some confusion about his guilt—he claimed his partner, who disappeared the night he was arrested, was really responsible—he'd only served two years. When he got out, he moved to Kansas City to start a new life.

I learned this much from my friends at the Chicago police. At least, my acquaintances. I wondered how much of the story Evangeline had known. Or her mother. If her mother didn't want her child having a white lover, how about a white ex-con, ex- (presumably) drug-smuggling lover?

I sat biting my knuckles for a minute. It was eleven now. Say they started printing the morning edition at two the next morning, I'd have to have my story by one at the latest. I could follow one line, and one line only—I couldn't afford to speculate about Mrs. Barthele—and anyway, doing so would only get me killed. By Sal. So I looked up the area code for Lawrence, Kansas, and found their daily newspaper.

The *Lawrence Daily Journal-World* had set up a special number for handling press inquiries. A friendly woman with a strong drawl told me Darnell's age (forty-four); place of birth (Eudora, Kansas); ex-wife's name (Ronna Perkins); and ex-partner's name (John Crenshaw). Ronna Perkins was living elsewhere in the country and the *Journal-World* was protecting her privacy. John Crenshaw had disappeared when the police arrested Darnell.

Crenshaw had done an army stint in Southeast Asia in the late sixties. Since much of the bamboo furniture the store specialized in came from the Far East, some people speculated that Crenshaw had set up the smuggling route when he was out there in the service. Especially since Kansas City immigration officials discovered heroin in the hollow tubes making up chair backs. If Darnell knew anything about the smuggling, he had never revealed it.

"That's all we know here, honey. Of course, you could come on down and try to talk to some people. And we can wire you photos if you want."

I thanked her politely—my paper didn't run too many photographs. Or even have wire equipment to accept them. A pity—I could have used a look at Crenshaw and Ronna Perkins.

La Cygnette was on an upper floor of one of the new marble skyscrapers at the top end of the Magnificent Mile. Tall, white doors opened onto a hushed waiting room reminiscent of a high-class funeral parlor. The undertaker, a middle-aged highly made-up woman seated at a table that was supposed to be French provincial, smiled at me condescendingly.

"What can we do for you?"

"I'd like to see Angela Carlson. I'm a detective."

She looked nervously at two clients seated in a far corner. I lowered my voice. "I've come about the murder."

"But—but they made an arrest."

I smiled enigmatically. At least I hoped it looked enigmatic. "The police never close the door on all options until after the trial." If she knew anything about the police she'd know that was a lie—once they've made an arrest you have to get a presidential order to get them to look at new evidence.

The undertaker nodded nervously and called Angela Carlson in a whisper on the house phone. Evangeline had given me the names of the key players at La Cygnette; Carlson was the manager.

She met me in the doorway leading from the reception area into the main body of the salon. We walked on thick, silver pile through a white maze with little doors opening onto it. Every now and then we'd pass a white-coated attendant who gave the manager a subdued hello. When we went by a door with a police order slapped to it, Carlson winced nervously.

"When can we take that off? Everybody's on edge and that sealed door doesn't help. Our bookings are down as it is."

"I'm not on the evidence team, Ms. Carlson. You'll have to ask the lieutenant in charge when they've got what they need."

I poked into a neighboring cubicle. It contained a large white dentist's chair and a tray covered with crimson pots and bottles, all with the cutaway swans which were the salon's trademark. While the manager fidgeted angrily I looked into a tiny closet where clients changed—it held a tiny sink and a few coat hangers.

Finally she burst out, "Didn't your people get enough of this yesterday? Don't you read your own reports?"

"I like to form my own impressions, Ms. Carlson. Sorry to have to take your time, but the sooner we get everything cleared up, the faster your customers will forget this ugly episode."

She sighed audibly and led me on angry heels to her office, although the thick carpeting took the intended ferocity out of her stride. The office was another of the small treatment rooms with a desk and a menacing phone console. Photographs of a youthful Mme. de Leon, founder of La Cygnette, covered the walls.

Ms. Carlson looked through a stack of pink phone messages. "I have an incredibly busy schedule, Officer. So if you could get to the point. . . . "

"I want to talk to everyone with whom Darnell had an appointment yesterday. Also the receptionist on duty. And before I do that I want to see their personnel files."

"Really! All these people were interviewed yesterday." Her eyes narrowed suddenly. "Are you really with the police? You're not, are you? You're a reporter. I want you out of here now. Or I'll call the real police."

I took my license photostat from my wallet. "I'm a detective. That's what I told your receptionist. I've been retained by the Barthele family. Ms. Barthele is not the murderer and I want to find out who the real culprit is as fast as possible."

She didn't bother to look at the license. "I can barely tolerate answering police questions. I'm certainly not letting some snoop for hire take up my time. The police have made an arrest on extremely good evidence. I suppose you think you can drum up a fee by getting Evangeline's family excited about her innocence, but you'll have to look elsewhere for your money."

I tried an appeal to her compassionate side, using half-forgotten arguments from my court appearances as a public defender. Outstanding employee, widowed mother, sole support, intense family pride, no prior arrests, no motive. No sale.

"Ms. Carlson, you the owner or the manager here?"

"Why do you want to know?"

"Just curious about your stake in the success of the place and your responsibility for decisions. It's like this: you've got a lot of foreigners working here. The immigration people will want to come by and check out their papers.

"You've got lots and lots of tiny little rooms. Are they sprinklered? Do you have emergency exits? The fire department can make a decision on that.

"And how come your only black professional employee was just arrested and you're not moving an inch to help her out? There are lots of lawyers around who'd be glad to look at a discrimination suit against La Cygnette.

"Now if we could clear up Evangeline's involvement fast, we could avoid having all these regulatory people trampling around upsetting your staff and your customers. How about it?"

She sat in indecisive rage for several minutes: how much authority did I have, really? Could I offset the munificent fees the salon and the building owners paid to various public officials just to avoid such investigations? Should she call headquarters for instruction? Or her lawyer? She finally decided that even if I didn't have a lot of power I could be enough of a nuisance to affect business. Her expression compounded of rage and defeat, she gave me the files I wanted.

Darnell had been scheduled with a masseuse, the hair expert Signor Giuseppe, and with Evangeline. I read their personnel files, along with that of the receptionist who had welcomed him to La Cygnette, to see if any of them might have hailed from Kansas City or had any unusual traits, such as an arrest record for heroin smuggling. The files were very sparse. Signor Giuseppe Fruttero hailed from Milan. He had no next-of-kin to be notified in the event of an accident. Not even a good friend. Bruna, the masseuse, was Lithuanian, unmarried, living with her mother. Other than the fact that the receptionist had been born as Jean Evans in Hammond but referred to herself as Monique from New Orleans, I saw no evidence of any kind of cover-up.

Angela Carlson denied knowing either Ronna Perkins or John Crenshaw or having any employees by either of those names. She had never been near Lawrence herself. She grew up in Evansville, Indiana, came to Chicago to be a model in 1978, couldn't cut it, and got into the beauty business. Angrily she gave me the names of her parents in Evansville and summoned the receptionist.

Monique was clearly close to sixty, much too old to be Roland Darnell's ex-wife. Nor had she heard of Ronna or Crenshaw.

"How many people knew that Darnell was going to be in the salon yesterday?"

"Nobody knew." She laughed nervously. "I mean, of course I knew—I made the appointment with him. And Signor Giuseppe knew when I gave him his schedule yesterday. And Bruna, the masseuse, of course, and Evangeline."

"Well, who else could have seen their schedules?"

She thought frantically, her heavily mascaraed eyes rolling in agitation. With another nervous giggle she finally said, "I suppose anyone could have known. I mean, the other cosmeticians and the makeup artists all come out for their appointments at the same time. I mean, if anyone was curious they could have looked at the other people's lists."

Carlson was frowning. So was I. "I'm trying to find a woman who'd be forty now, who doesn't talk much about her past. She's been divorced and she won't have been in the business long. Any candidates?"

Carlson did another mental search, then went to the file cabinets. Her mood was shifting from anger to curiosity and she flipped through the files quickly, pulling five in the end.

"How long has Signor Giuseppe been here?"

"When we opened our Chicago branch in 1980 he came to us from Miranda's—I guess he'd been there for two years. He says he came to the States from Milan in 1970."

"He a citizen? Has he got a green card?"

"Oh, yes. His papers are in good shape. We are very careful about that at La Cygnette." My earlier remark about the immigration department had clearly stung. "And now I really need to get back to my own business. You can look at those files in one of the consulting rooms—Monique, find one that won't be used today."

It didn't take me long to scan the five files, all uninformative. Before returning them to Monique I wandered on through the back of the salon. In the rear a small staircase led to an upper story. At the top was another narrow hall lined with small offices and storerooms. A large mirrored room at the back filled with hanging plants and bright lights housed Signor Giuseppe. A dark-haired man with a pointed beard and a bright smile, he was ministering gaily to a thin, middle-aged woman, talking and laughing while he deftly teased her hair into loose curls.

He looked at me in the mirror when I entered. "You are here for the hair, Signora? You have the appointment?"

"No, Signor Giuseppe. Sono qui perchè la sua fama se è sparsa di fronte a lei. Milano è una bella città, non è vero?"

He stopped his work for a moment and held up a deprecating hand. "Signora, it is my policy to speak only English in my adopted country."

"Una vera stupida e ignorante usanza io direi." I beamed sympathetically and sat down on a high stool next to an empty customer chair. There were seats for two clients. Since Signor Giuseppe reigned alone, I pictured him spinning at high speed between customers, snipping here, pinning there.

"Signora, if you do not have the appointment, will you please leave? Signora Dotson here, she does not prefer the audience."

"Sorry, Mrs. Dotson," I said to the lady's chin. "I'm a detective. I need to talk to Signor Giuseppe, but I'll wait."

I strolled back down the hall and entertained myself by going into one of the storerooms and opening little pots of La Cygnette creams and rubbing them into my skin. I looked in a mirror and could already see an improvement. If I got Evangeline sprung maybe she'd treat me to a facial.

Signor Giuseppe appeared with a plastically groomed Mrs. Dotson. He had shed his barber's costume and was dressed for the street. I followed them down the stairs. When we got to the bottom I said, "In case you're thinking of going back to Milan—or even to Kansas—I have a few questions."

Mrs. Dotson clung to the hairdresser, ready to protect him.

"I need to speak to him alone, Mrs. Dotson. I have to talk to him about bamboo."

"I'll get Miss Carlson, Signor Giuseppe," his guardian offered.

"No, no, Signora. I will deal with this crazed woman myself. A million thanks. *Grazie, grazie.*"

"Remember, no Italian in your adopted America," I reminded him nastily.

Mrs. Dotson looked at us uncertainly.

"I think you should get Ms. Carlson," I said. "Also a police escort. Fast."

She made up her mind to do something, whether to get help or flee I wasn't sure, but she scurried down the corridor. As soon as she had disappeared, he took me by the arm and led me into one of the consulting rooms.

"Now, who are you and what is this?" His accent had improved substantially.

"I'm V. I. Warshawski. Roland Darnell told me you were quite an expert on fitting drugs into bamboo furniture."

I wasn't quite prepared for the speed of his attack. His hands were around my throat. He was squeezing and spots began dancing in front of me. I didn't try to fight his arms, just kicked sharply at his shin, following with my knee to his stomach. The pressure at my neck eased. I turned in a half circle and jammed my left elbow into his rib cage. He let go.

I backed to the door, keeping my arms up in front of my face and backed into Angela Carlson.

"What on earth are you doing with Signor Giuseppe?" she asked.

"Talking to him about furniture." I was out of breath. "Get the police and don't let him leave the salon."

A small crowd of white-coated cosmeticians had come to the door of the tiny treatment room. I said to them, "This isn't Giuseppe Fruttero. It's John Crenshaw. If you don't believe me, try speaking Italian to him—he doesn't understand it. He's probably never been to Milan. But he's certainly been to Thailand, and he knows an awful lot about heroin."

IV

Sal handed me the bottle of Black Label. "It's yours, Vic. Kill it tonight or save it for some other time. How did you know he was Roland Darnell's ex-partner?"

"I didn't. At least not when I went to La Cygnette. I just knew it had to be someone in the salon who killed him, and it was most likely someone who knew him in Kansas. And that meant either Darnell's ex-wife or his partner. And Giuseppe was the only man on the professional staff. And then I saw he didn't know Italian—after praising Milan and telling him he was stupid in the same tone of voice and getting no response it made me wonder."

"We owe you a lot, Vic. The police would never have dug down to find that. You gotta thank the lady, Mama."

Mrs. Barthele grudgingly gave me her thin hand. "But how come those police said Evangeline knew that Darnell man? My baby wouldn't know some convict, some drug smuggler."

"He wasn't a drug smuggler, Mama. It was his partner. The police have proved all that now. Roland Darnell never did anything wrong." Evangeline, chic in red with long earrings that bounced as she spoke, made the point hotly.

Sal gave her sister a measuring look. "All I can say, Evangeline, is it's a good thing you never had to put your hand on a Bible in court about Mr. Darnell."

I hastily poured a drink and changed the subject.

GAR ANTHONY HAYWOOD
1954–

A versatile and popular writer known especially for his African-American private investigator Aaron Gunner, Gar Anthony Haywood was born and raised in Los Angeles, California. He was a voracious reader as a child and attributes his becoming a writer to his early love of reading. Haywood worked in computer maintenance for many years before becoming a full-time writer. He has written ten novels to date and several detective fiction short stories, television and film scripts, and articles for the *Los Angeles Times* and the *New York Times*. His first novel, *Fear of the Dark* (1988), was much anticipated, since two years earlier the manuscript had won the St. Martin's Press/Private Eye Writers of America contest for best unpublished novel. When it was published, it won the Shamus Award for Best First Novel and introduced countless readers to Los Angeles P. I. Aaron Gunner. In 1996, Haywood was presented the Chester Himes award, named for an important creator of African-American detective fiction.

Aaron Gunner is a tough but sensitive P. I. enmeshed in racial tensions and issues in a dark, contemporary Los Angeles. In the mid-1990s, after three novels in the Gunner series, Haywood created the husband and wife team Joe and Dottie Loudermilk. Joe is a retired police officer, ready to tour the country and leave behind their five grown children, but the couple finds murder wherever they go, whether Arizona's Grand Canyon in *Going Nowhere Fast* (1994) or Washington, D. C., in *Bad News Travels Fast* (1995). These books contrast sharply with the noir elements of Gunner in his urban chaos. Haywood wrote three more Gunner novels after these novels, and then made yet another sharp departure with the stand-alone thrillers *Man Eater* (2003) and *Firecracker* (2004), both written under the pseudonym Ray Shannon. "And Pray Nobody Sees You," Haywood's first Gunner short story, won both the Shamus and Anthony Awards for Best Short Story of 1995. It was first published in *Spooks, Spies and Private Eyes* (1995), edited by Paula L. Woods.

Recommended Haywood works: *Fear of the Dark, All the Lucky Ones Are Dead, Firecracker*.

Other recommended authors: Chester Himes, Walter Mosley, Gary Phillips.

And Pray Nobody Sees You

It doesn't happen often, but every now and then a good story will buy you a free drink at the Deuce. Lilly has to be feeling charitable and business has to be slow, say, down to three lifeless regulars and maybe another new face, somebody who likes to treat a single shot of *Meyer's* like a lover they're afraid to part with. Lilly will get tired of watching Howard Gaines slide dominoes across her bar, or listening to Eggy Jones whine about the latest indignity he's suffered at the hands of his wife Camille, and will demand that somebody tell her a story entertaining enough to hold her interest. She calls herself asking, Lilly, but she's too big to ask for anything; everything she says sounds like a demand, whether it comes with a "please" or not.

She was in the mood for a story a couple of Tuesdays back, and as usual, looked to me first to do the honors. I don't always take the prize on these occasions, but I manage to get my share. Maybe it's the line of work I'm in.

This particular evening, I answered Lilly's call with the following.

And watched the Wild Turkey flow afterward.

It started with a U-turn.

Brother driving a blue Chrysler did a one-eighty in the middle of Wilmington Avenue, two o'clock on a Thursday afternoon, in broad daylight. Mickey Moore, Weldon Foley, and me were standing outside Mickey's barber shop when we saw him go by on the eastbound side of the street, stop, then yank the Chrysler around like he'd just seen somebody who owed him money. We would have all ducked for cover, smelling the week's latest drive-by in the making, except that the driver looked too old to be a gangbanger and the three of us were the only people on the street. That left us nothing else to believe but that we'd just seen the act of a fool, nothing more and nothing less.

"You see that? That nigger's crazy," Mickey said.

"Sure is," Foley agreed, nodding his hairless head. I sometimes suspect Mickey keeps him around precisely for that purpose; he sure as hell never has to take his clippers to him.

"And look. Not a goddamn cop in sight. Now, if that was me—"

"Or me," I said, thinking the same thing my landlord was thinking. I'd never gotten away with a U-turn in my life.

The Chrysler was now headed back in our direction on the westbound side of the street, cruising in the right lane the way cars do when the people driving them are looking for a parking space. It was an old '71 Barracuda, a clean and chromed-out borderline classic with a throaty exhaust and tires you could hide a small country in. It was grumbling like a California earthquake when it finally pulled to a stop at the curb, directly in front of us.

The driver got out of the car and approached us, his left arm folded up in a white sling. We let him come without saying a word.

"One of you Aaron Gunner?" he asked. He was a wiry twenty-something, six-one or six-two, with razor lines cut all along the sides and back of his head, something I imagined he'd had done in hopes of drawing attention from his face. It was sad to say, but the boy looked like a black Mr. Potato Head with bad skin.

"That's me," I told him, before Weldon or Mickey could point me out. "What can I do for you?"

He openly examined the front of Mickey's shop, as if he were looking for the fine print on the sign above the door, and said, "This is your office, right?"

"That's right. I've got a room in the back."

He glanced at my companions briefly. "All right if we go back there to talk?"

I shrugged. "Sure. Come on in."

Mickey was insulted by the slight of not being introduced, but he didn't say anything.

I led my homely visitor past Mickey's three empty barber chairs, through the beaded curtains in the open doorway beyond, and into the near-vacant space that has passed for my office for the last four years. The lamp on my desk was already on, so all I had to do was sit down and wait for my friend to find the couch and do the same.

He never did.

He just stood in front of my desk and said, "You're a private detective."

"Yes. Can't you tell?"

"I want to hire you."

"To do what?"

"I want you to find a car for me."

"A car?"

"Yeah." He nodded. "Sixty-five Ford Mustang, tangerine orange. Two-plus-two fastback, fully restored and cherried out."

"A sixty-five?"

"Yeah. First year they were made. Probably ain't but fifty of 'em in the whole country still on the road."

"Two-eighty-nine, or six?"

"Come on. If it was the six, man, I'd let 'em have the damn car."

He had a point. A sixty-five Mustang two-plus-two without the V-8 under the hood might have been worth a few dollars to somebody, but any true collector would've considered it a stiff. Cherried out or no.

"It sounds nice," I told him.

"Man, fuck 'nice.' It's a classic. There ain't but fifty of 'em still in existence, like I said."

I nodded my head to show him I was finally paying attention. "And your name was . . . ?"

"Purdy. David Purdy. Look—"

"This car we're talking about, Mr. Purdy. I take it it belongs to you?"

"Does it belong to me? Hell, yes, it belongs to me. Why else would I be here talkin' to you?"

"I give up. Why *are* you here talking to me?"

"Because I got *jacked* last night, man. What else? Over on Imperial and Hoover, over by my girl's house. Little motherfucker shot me at the stoplight and took my goddamn car."

"You call the police?"

"The police? Of course. I told you, man, I got shot." He tried to gesture with his left arm, but just moving the sling an inch from his side seemed to bring tears to his eyes.

"So? What do you need with me?" I asked him.

Purdy answered the question with a crooked, toothy grin meant to convey incredulity. "Man, you're jokin', right? What do I need with *you*? I need you to get the goddamn car back for me. What do you think?"

He'd been looking for a foot in his ass since he'd stepped out of the Chrysler, and now he'd finally earned it. Still, I let the comment pass. I'd spent the retainers of rude jackasses before, and their money went just as far as anyone else's. Purdy's would be no different.

"You don't think the police can find the car?" I asked.

"Let's just say I'm not countin' on it," Purdy said. "Least, not until there ain't nothin' left of it but a goddamn frame."

"I take it you didn't have one of those electronic tracking devices on it—the kind the police can home in on?"

"No. I didn't."

"That's too bad."

"Yeah, it is. I fucked up. I put a lot of time and money in that car, then turned around and didn't protect it right. So it's gone. But that don't mean I gotta forget about it, like the cops said I should. Hell, no. I want that car back, Mr. Gunner, and I want it back *now*, 'fore some fuckin' chop shop can hack it all to pieces."

"If that's possible, you mean," I said.

"It's possible. It just ain't gonna be easy. I'd find the car myself if the shit was easy."

I fell silent, pretending to be mulling things over, when all I was really doing was deciding on a fee.

"Somebody said you were the man for the job, so I looked you up. But if you're not—"

"What do you figure the car's worth? Ten, fifteen grand?" I asked.

"Shit. Try twenty-five," Purdy said.

"Okay, twenty-five. Here's the deal. I locate the car within forty-eight hours, in its original condition, you owe me twenty-five hundred. Ten percent of its worth, cash on delivery. If I don't find it, or I do and it's already been chopped up, you only owe me for my time. Three hundred dollars a day, plus expenses, half of which you've got to pay me now, just to get me started."

"No problem," Purdy said. Nothing I'd said had made him so much as blink.

"No problem?"

"No, man, no problem. I told you: I want the car back, and you're supposed to be the man can get it for me." He was already peeling some bills off a wad of green he'd removed from his pocket.

"I'm gonna need a description of the carjacker and the license plate of the car. And a phone number where you can be reached at any time, day or night."

Purdy threw four hundred dollars on the desk in front of me and said, "You've got it."

I still had my reservations about the man, but now I was bought and paid for. It was time to go to work.

The first thing I did was go see Mopar.

Mopar used to steal cars. Lots of them. It was what he did for fifteen years, from the time we were in high school together right up until his last bust, when a fight in the joint left him crippled for life and scared the thief right out of him, for good. His mother still called him Jerome, but he was Mopar to everyone else; back in high school, he could steal any car you cared to name, but he did all his racing in Chryslers.

Today, Mopar was in the body shop business.

He had his own place over on Florence Avenue, between Denker and La Salle. He'd started out working there, hammering dents out of Buicks and Oldsmobiles, then slowly bought into the business, buying bigger and bigger chunks as the years went by until finally, little over a year ago, he became the man holding all the paper. And all with only one good leg.

He was standing behind the counter in the office when I came in, just hanging up the phone. He was damn near as fat as Lilly these days, and only twice as jolly. The sight of my approach brought a broad grin to his face, same one he used to wear as a kid.

"Tail Gunner! What it be like?"

That was what he used to call me back in school, Tail Gunner. I can't tell you how glad I was that the nickname never caught on with anyone else.

"It's your world, Mopar," I said, burying my right hand deep in his. "I'm just livin' in it."

"Shit, you ain't livin' in *my* world. Otherwise, I'd see you more often 'round here."

I shrugged apologetically. "What can I say? I'm a busy man."

Mopar just laughed. "So what can I do you, man? This business, or pleasure?"

"Afraid it's business. I'm looking for somebody I think you might be able to help me find."

"Yeah? Who's that?"

"A 'jacker. Boy about fifteen to eighteen years old, five-seven, five-eight, a hundred and thirty pounds. Dark skin and dark eyes, with braces on his teeth. Likes to wear striped clothes and a San Antonio Spurs baseball cap turned sideways on his head, bill facing east. At least, that's how he was dressed last night."

"A 'jacker? Why you wanna ask me about a 'jacker?"

"Because you used to be one, Mopar. It hasn't been that long ago, man."

"Man, I wasn't never a 'jacker! I never pulled nobody out of a car in my life!"

"No, but—"

"These kids today, man, they're crazy! Shootin' people to steal a goddamn car. Man, I never even owned a gun till I got this place!"

"Okay, so you weren't a 'jacker. You're right, that was the wrong thing for me to say."

"Damn right it was."

"But your objective was still the same, right? To steal cars?"

Mopar didn't say anything.

"Look. I'm not saying you know the kid. I just thought you might, that's all. Because I know you've put a few of 'em to work for you in the past, tryin' to help 'em go straight like you did, and I thought, maybe this kid I'm lookin' for was one of 'em. Or maybe you've seen him hanging around somewhere, I don't know. It was just a thought."

Mopar just glared at me, his jovial mood a thing of the past. "You say this boy 'jacked a car last night?"

I nodded. "Orange sixty-five Mustang fastback, in primo condition. Owner says it happened over on Imperial and Hoover, a few minutes past midnight."

"Sixty-five fastback? You shittin' me?"

"Afraid not. Now you know why the man wants it found before somebody takes an air wrench to it."

"You mean the fool don't know they already did that eight hours ago?"

"I guess he's the optimistic type. I tried to tell him to save his money, but he's emotionally attached. So . . ."

I waited for the big man to make up his mind, but he seemed in no hurry to do so.

"Did I mention the fact that my client got shot? Clipped in the left wing, but it could've been worse. This kid who 'jacked him isn't just in it for the rides, Mopar. He likes to shoot people, too."

Still, Mopar offered me nothing but silence.

"Tell you what. Forget it," I said. "This was a bad idea, bothering you with this. Come by and see us at the Deuce sometime, huh?"

I turned and started out of the room.

"You say the kid wears braces?" Mopar asked.

I turned back around. "That's right."

He hesitated a moment longer, then said, "I can't give you a name. But I can tell you where to look."

I told him that would be fine.

Mopar said the kid liked to hang out in front of a liquor store on Western and 81st Street. Mopar remembered him because he'd had to chase him out of his shop once, when the kid had come around looking for one of Mopar's employees and had taken the news of the employee's recent dismissal badly. Every now and then since, Mopar'd see him at the liquor store, kicking it with his homies out on the sidewalk.

But he wasn't there Thursday night.

I know. I waited there six hours for him to show up. Three members of his crew were there—teenage boys dressed in oversized khaki pants and giant plaid jackets—but they were all the wrong size for the kid I was looking for, and none of them had braces on their teeth. I sat in my car across the street and thought about approaching them, but I knew all they'd do with my questions was tell me where I could stick them, so I decided to spare myself the aggravation and just stayed put.

When I'd inevitably given up watching the liquor store, I cruised the 'hood indiscriminately, hitting all the major intersections I could think of, but my results were the same. No kid with braces looking like a 'jacker on the prowl, no classic Mustangs in tangerine orange. I saw a howling parade of black-and-whites cut a swath through traffic on Normandie and Manchester, an old man roll off a bus bench into the gutter on Slauson and Vermont, and two hookers change a flat tire on a run-down convertible

Pontiac on Prarie and One Hundred and Eighth—but I didn't see any car-jackers anywhere.

So I went home.

The next morning, I called Matthew Poole with the L.A.P.D. and asked him if he knew anybody in Auto. Poole doesn't owe me any favors, but the homicide man helps me out when he can all the same. I don't really know why. Maybe it's because he thinks we're friends.

The man Poole eventually put me in touch with was a cop named Link, first name Sam. Over the phone, he sounded like one of those cops who came out of the womb flashing a badge and reading the obstetrician his rights; he was cordial enough, but you could tell he was of the opinion I was standing between him and his pension. I got right to the point and told him about Purdy, then asked him afterward if the story sounded familiar. The Mustang had been stolen only two nights before. I figured he ought to have heard something about the investigation, even if he himself hadn't been called out on it.

But Link said it was all news to him.

Nothing about the Mustang or Purdy struck him as familiar. And if a shooting had taken place during a 'jacking Wednesday night, he assured me he'd have known about it. In fact, he would have convinced me altogether that the whole of Purdy's story was a lie had my description of the kid I'd spent the previous night looking for not rung a bell with him.

"Striped clothes?" he asked me.

"Yeah."

"That could be Squealer. He's into stripes. You want to talk to him?"

He was offering to go pick him up for me.

"Yeah, but not formally. I need him conversant," I said, hoping he wouldn't be insulted by the insinuation the kid wouldn't talk downtown.

"You just want to know where to find him, then."

"If that wouldn't be too much trouble."

Link said it wouldn't be any trouble at all.

It took me all day to find him.

He wasn't at home and he wasn't at school. Link had given me a list of about a half-dozen places he liked to frequent, from the Baldwin Hills Crenshaw Plaza to the basketball courts at Jesse Owens Park, but he never appeared at any of them until a few minutes after seven P.M., when he showed up at a Baskin and Robbins ice cream parlor in a mini-mall on Budlong and Fifty-sixth Street, during my second visit to the site. His pants were black denim, no stripes, but his shirt was an oversized tee with alternating blue-and-green horizontal bands, and the cap turned sideways on his head was silver and black, the primary colors of the San Antonio Spurs. He had arrived on foot with two other kids who looked roughly the same age, a boy and a girl, and I had to watch the three of them eat ice cream and throw napkins at each other for well over an hour before he was ready to leave again.

I had hoped when the time came he'd leave alone, but I wasn't that lucky. He left the same way he came, with his two friends in tow. The trio walked north-bound along Budlong and I trailed behind them in my car, keeping a good block, block-and-half between us at all times. I was prepared to go on like this all night if I had to, but I wasn't looking forward to it. Of the forty-eight hours I'd given myself to find Purdy's Mustang, more than thirty were already gone, and the clock was still running. I had to get the kid alone, or he had to lead me to the car, one or the other. And fast.

Things were looking dark when Squealer and his homies led me to a house on Fiftieth Street between Harvard and Denker, then disappeared inside. There was light in only one window, and the place was as quiet as an empty grave. The thought occurred to me they might have crashed there for the night, and an hour later, nothing had happened to rule that possibility out—until the porch light winked back on and Squealer emerged from the house again.

Alone.

I got out of my car on the passenger side and ducked low to hide behind it, waiting for the kid to saunter past on the opposite side of the street. I was going to make this quick. He'd already shot Purdy and I had no reason to think he wouldn't shoot me, given the chance, so getting the drop on him first seemed to be the wise thing to do. He was stepping off the curb to cross Harvard when I closed the distance between us and put him down, rapping the base of his skull with the butt of my Ruger P-85. He fell like a house of cards. I caught him on his way down, dragged him over to my car, and tossed him in.

Then we went somewhere to talk.

There was nobody on the beach.

It was too cold for romance, and too dark for sight-seeing. The moon was heavily shielded behind a thick mask of cloud cover, and a mist hung over the water like a frozen gray curse. The kid and I would not be disturbed.

I had him trussed up like a calf at a rodeo. He was bound, gagged, and blindfolded, stretched out flat upon the wooden-plank walkway that ran beneath the Santa Monica Pier. His gun was in my back pocket, a small .22 I'd found shoved into the waistband of his pants. Down here, the sound of the crashing waves echoed between the pier's pylons like thunder in a bottle, thoroughly directionless, and you could taste the salt of the ocean spray with every intake of breath.

When I was certain he was awake, I knelt down beside the kid and said, "I want my car."

He took that as a cue to start thrashing around, but it didn't take him long to see the futility in it. He wasn't going anywhere.

"You haven't guessed by now, we're on the Santa Monica Pier," I said. "Down at the beach. Hear the waves down there? Care for a swim?"

I rolled him over a little.

He got the gist of my phony threat right away, and bought into it completely. I had to hold him down with both hands to keep him still.

"Okay. You get the picture. You don't tell me where my car is, I push you off this fucking pier and into the Pacific. Understand?"

He started to struggle again. I put my hand on his throat and asked him one more time: "Understand?"

Finally, he grew quiet, and slowly nodded his head.

"Very good. Car I'm looking for is a sixty-five Ford Mustang. Orange. You shot me in the arm and stole it from me Wednesday night, out on the corner of Imperial and Hoover. Remember?"

Squealer made no move to answer, so I rolled him over again, one full revolution.

"You're runnin' out of pier, homeboy," I said. Then, after a while, I asked him again: "Do you remember the car?"

This time, he nodded his head.

"Good. Now—I'm going to take your gag off, and you're going to tell me where I can find it. You're not going to scream, or cry, or call for your mama—you're just going to tell me where my car is. Otherwise . . . "

I let him think about that a moment, then peeled his gag away from his mouth.

"*At the mall! At the mall, man!*" he said, gasping to get the words out.

"What mall?"

"Fox Hills Mall, man! The Fox Hills Mall!"

"What, in the parking lot?"

"Yeah! In the parkin' lot! You know, the buildin'!"

"The building?" I had to think about that a moment. "You mean the parking structure?"

He nodded his head frantically. "Yeah, that's it! The parkin' structure!"

"What floor?"

"What floor? I don't know, man. Four, I think. Don't kill me, man, please!"

"Why'd you put it there?"

"Why? I don't—"

"Why didn't you take it in for chopping? Why'd you park it instead?"

"Shit, I wasn't gonna chop that ride, man! It was too sweet!"

"Too sweet?"

He nodded his head again.

"What were you going to do with it, you weren't going to chop it?" I asked him.

"I was gonna *keep* it. Just . . . let it chill at the mall for a while, then change it up. Get new papers on it, an' shit, so's it could be *my* ride."

I should have guessed.

I put the gag back in his mouth and stood up. Where this kid had found the courage to shoot a man, I couldn't begin to guess. He was scared shitless and seemingly willing to do whatever was asked of him to stay alive.

Odd.

I was going to leave him as he was, anticipating the worst, bouncing about on the wooden walkway floor like a beached whale waiting to die . . . and then I thought of one more question to ask him.

Kneeling beside him again, I said, "Tell me something, junebug. What'd you shoot me for?"

And then he told me exactly what I'd thought he might.

He said I'd made him do it.

The Mustang was on the *third* floor.

Parked in a distant corner all by itself and covered with a tarp. I peeled the tarp off to look it over carefully, but I knew it was the car I was after inside of ten seconds. Everything about it matched Purdy's description: model, color, license plate number. With one notable exception.

It was a 'sixty-six.

'Sixty-fives had a crosshairs grill; this one had the eggcrate grill of a 'sixty-six. Which made it a rarity, yes, but not a classic. A man who knew cars might conceivably spend a small fortune to recover a stolen 'sixty-five, but a 'sixty-six? I didn't think so. Any more than I thought a man would take a bullet fighting to hold onto a 'sixty-six, as Squealer the 'jacker had claimed Purdy had done Wednesday night.

Obviously, there was more to this car than met the eye.

When I finally found out what it was, a little over ninety minutes later, I called Purdy to tell him the good news.

"It's over there," I said, pointing. "Across the street."

Purdy turned and saw the Mustang parked on the other side of La Brea Avenue, directly opposite the Pink's hot dog stand in Hollywood where we were sitting. I'd used the keys I'd taken off Squealer to come here, and had been well into my second chili dog when Purdy showed up.

"I don't believe it," he said now, eyeing the car.

"We were lucky," I said, feigning weary humility.

"Where did you find it?"

I shrugged. "Does it matter?"

"No. Not really. I just thought—"

"You have my money, Mr. Purdy?"

"Of course." He took an envelope from his coat pocket and opened it so I could see the bills inside, but didn't hand it over. "You mind if I look the car over first?" he asked.

"Not at all," I said, wiping chili from the sides of my mouth. "I'll just hold onto the keys."

That wasn't what he'd had in mind, but he could see the point was non-negotiable. Without saying another word, he left to inspect the car, then returned a few minutes later.

"Twenty-five hundred dollars," he said, handing me the envelope he'd shown me earlier. He seemed infinitely relieved.

I told him thanks and gave him his keys.

He stood there for a moment, wanting to say more, then just turned and went back to the car. He got in, started the engine, and pulled away from the curb.

Halfway down the block, he made a U-turn.

And then his rearview mirror turned red.

Some people would say I set him up, but I don't look at it that way.

Purdy had hidden a two-pound bag of crack cocaine behind the Mustang's driver's side door panel, and when I found it out at the Fox Hills Mall parking lot that night, I knew I owed him. He'd played me for a sucker. Fed me some line about his classic car getting 'jacked, just so I could run down the small fortune in rock he'd stashed inside it.

And yet . . .

Technically, no harm had been done. The man had hired me to do a job, and I'd done it. I'd found his car, delivered it on time, and been paid the agreed-upon fee. So what if the whole thing was a lie? I'd still held up my end of the bargain, and Purdy had held up his.

I owed him, and yet I didn't owe him.

So I let him go. Sort of.

I put a little of his stash in his glove compartment with his registration, then put the rest back where I'd found it. I parked the car on the same street, in the same place where, only six weeks before, I'd gotten my last ticket for making a U-turn, on La Brea Avenue near Pink's. And finally, I parked his car on the northbound side of the street, facing away from the Gardena address printed on the business card Purdy had given me.

A setup? Not hardly.

All Purdy would have had to do to get off that night was not make that U-turn.

See? He screwed himself.

All I did was watch.

Later, at the Deuce, Lilly nearly busted a gut laughing. In the proper frame of mind, the giant barkeep's as appreciative of my cleverness as I am myself. Sometimes even more so.

"Tell me one thing, Gunner," she said.

"Shoot."

"You made any U-turns yourself since then? Or you out of the habit for good?"

I grinned at her, winked, and downed the last of my free drink, though all it was by now was ice water. "Naw," I said.

"Naw, what?"

"Naw, I'm not out of the habit. I just know how to do 'em right now, that's all."

"Do 'em *right*? And what way is *that*?"

"That's where you turn the wheel," I said, demonstrating, "and pray nobody sees you."

I pushed myself away from the bar and called it a night.

S. J. ROZAN

1950–

Innovator of a New York–based series featuring two private investigators who alternate as narrators of the books in the series, Shira Judith Rozan was born and raised in the Bronx in New York City. She received a B.A. from Oberlin College and an M. Arch. from State University of New York (SUNY) Buffalo. She is an architect in a New York firm and runs an on going series on Crime Writing and the American Imagination in New York City. Her first published novel, *China Trade* (1994), introduced Lydia Chin and Bill Smith, two private investigators with separate detective agencies who often work together on the same case, and eventually they become professional partners. *Concourse* (1995) won the Shamus Award for Best Novel, *No Colder Place* (1997) the Anthony, and the seventh in the series, *Reflecting the Sky* (2001), won another Shamus. The widely anthologized short story "Hoops" (1996) was nominated for an Edgar, and "Double-Crossing Delancy" (2001) received the Edgar for Best Short Story in 2002.

Rozan's novel series is unique in switching the first person narrator from Lydia Chin to Bill Smith in alternate novels, starting with Lydia in the first novel, *China Trade* (1994). Bill Smith is a divorced middle-aged man with no family, and the personalities of the two P.I.'s contrast as sharply as their narrative voices in the alternating novels. Although Rozan's own background is Jewish, Lydia Chin is American-born Chinese with a big family, and the cases often involve residents of New York's Chinatown. Although most of the novels are set in New York City, Rozan traveled to Hong Kong for authentic details in *Reflecting the Sky,* her mystery novel set in China. "Going Home," a short story which shows a very different look at the work of the P.I., was first published in *The Mysterious North* (2002), edited by Dana Stabenow.

Recommended Rozan works: *Reflecting the Sky, A Bitter Feast, Stone Quarry.*

Recommended other authors: Leslie Glass, Faye Kellerman, Sujata Massey.

Going Home

Setting, the sun lays down a golden path across the snow and the water. You could follow it straight to Paradise if you were ready, but you're not: that's for another day. Now, this is enough. The air: sharp, new, and yours alone. The muffled crunch of packed snow under your boots. The silence, vast and complete when you stop. The cold bites but is not bitter; the cold, here, meets you as an equal, and when it fights you it fights fair. The years Outside, the years in New York, you met a different kind of cold: mean, sneaky, the damp its sneering toady as it slipped between your skin and your bones. In New York, snow was gray and thick and betrayed itself into slush and ragged water. In New York, people called you many different names, none of them yours. You lived in run-down rooms, caged above, below, around by other people's rooms, and you ate takeout food, greasy and indistinguishable, off soggy paper plates; but Kenai people know you, Kenai people call you Joe. Here, when you're hungry, you head through the long blue shadows that cut across the golden light, head back toward your cabin, a solid, square black home absolutely alone on the hill. You'll eat trout from the stream that wraps the slope, trout smoked and put by over the brief summer (two fresh, warm months, not the endless, glaring furnace you knew in New York, in those years). This morning, when the light was thin and white, Mom came by, sat and had coffee, left you some pickled beans from last summer's garden; maybe you'll eat them too, absolutely alone, sitting at the window in the spare, empty cabin, watching the ice on the distant river waiting for its chance to find the sea.

"Joe. Joe Craig!"

You look around. Whose voice? There's no one here. You hear knocking. The wind, slapping a shutter against the cabin wall, up on the hill? But the wind is still.

"Anyone in there?"

Your eyes open slowly. With a sadness so deep and soft it almost suffocates you, you know it's happened again. You were dreaming, again. You haven't gone home. You're still Outside: This is New York. This is that rancid room, that stinking summer. The whining fan blows thick, damp air across your sweating face. That's the shrieking of the TV upstairs; there goes the roar of the elevated train. You can hear it but not see it, you can't see anything through the soot-streaked glass but the crumbling brick wall four feet away, the pulled shade on your neighbor's window.

You're still here.

Your heart crashes against your chest, but you tell yourself: Someday. You tell yourself, as you always do: One day, you'll be able to go home. You'll find a way to go back to the emptiness, the vast stillness, where you can be alone, where you can be Joe.

You feel yourself calming; your racing blood slows. Someday. And until then, knowing it's there is enough.

But here, now, who's calling you? The knocking's turned into pounding, pounding on your door. Who is this?

"Open up, Joe. Come on, I know you're in there."

You rise from the bed, glance around at the nothing you have: sagging mattress, sprung couch, yesterday's coffee in a pot on the stove. There isn't anything here that's Joe; it's all another guy, one of those other names. You open the door.

There is a man, shorter than you are, younger, too. He wears a white polo shirt, the underarms darkened with sweat. You don't know him.

"Joe Craig? No, I know you haven't gone by that for a long time now," he says, "but it's Joe Craig, right?"

You shake your head.

"Yeah," he says. "I've been looking for you. Your brother sent me."

"Got no brother," you say.

"Uh-huh. Tom. He wants you to go home."

"This is home." The words almost choke you.

"To Alaska. I'm a private investigator, out of Anchorage. Mick Burke."

He puts out his hand. You reach for it slowly, shake it, tell him, "You got the wrong guy."

"No. Took me six months. That last guy, Lester, you gave him the slip, huh?" He grins.

"Don't know any Lester. What do you want?"

"Look." He holds up a briefcase. "I brought the paperwork. Tom thought maybe you don't believe it." He lifts his eyebrows, looks past you, so you step aside, let him in the room.

He pushes away a crumb-covered plate, a sticky spoon, opens the briefcase on the rickety card table. Back in the cabin, the table is heavy, solid: two thick slabs of fir you set on wide legs, sanded and rubbed and oiled.

The man—Burke, he said—pulls out a folder, starts handing you papers. "They dropped the charges," he's telling you. "That's why Lester came here, if you stayed still long enough to listen. Though I can see why you didn't. Twenty-eight years on the lam, must get to be a habit." He looks at you, right in your eyes.

A shadowy memory, like another dream: a different room, a different stranger.

You say, "You want some other guy."

He taps one of the papers in your hand. It rustles with a sound like dead leaves skidding across the ice. He says it again: "They dropped the charges." He tells you more: "A guy in Idaho, in prison, he was dying. Wanted to clear his conscience. He confessed. Alaska murder warrant for you's been voided. You can go back any time."

You look at the paper. You think you've seen it before.

He pulls out a file: news clippings. They tell the same story. He looks over your shoulder, points to a date. "A year ago," he says, as though you can't read that. "Couple of months after your mother died. Sorry," he says, seeing your face. "Didn't know if you knew. Lester, he swore up and down he found you, told you the whole thing, but Tom said it was crap. If he told you, you'd have gone back. So Tom hired me." He grins again. He doesn't stop talking. "I started with Lester's report. The way I figured it, Lester located you, but you got wise to him, scrammed before he actually got to you. Right?"

You shake your head again.

He shrugs. "Yeah, whatever. Anyway, Joe, you can go back. And man, that place's changed!" He shakes his head. "It's terrific. I hadn't been down to Kenai in what, twenty years? Until your brother called me. What I remember, it was a real nowhere, more moose than people. But now they got a great road there down from Anchorage, keep it plowed most of the year. Good airport, too. Now it's more tourists than people." He laughs at his own joke. "Houses everywhere, they got a new high school, it's a real town now, Joe. Population's maybe tripled since you left. Hill where your cabin used to be? Tom showed me. Beautiful development, just beautiful, nice big houses, know what I mean?"

You know what he means. The other stranger—that must have been Lester—told you. You remember him now, remember that time, in that other room. He told you a lot of things. The new roads, the new houses. Fishing licenses now, so many tourists fishing the river. And Mom—what had he said about Mom? Your head begins to pound.

Burke says, "Your brother, he got a lot for that land. Lives right in town now. Wants you to go stay with him. Real convenient, Joe, right near the new supermarket, the movie theater. Just like you're used to, all these years here." He grins again, and his teeth are white, like snow. Sweat crawls down your back.

"Yeah," Burke is saying, "that's how Tom knew Lester was lying. Lester said he came back the second day with the plane tickets and you were gone, but Tom said as much as you loved Kenai, if you knew you could have gone home you would've, first chance you got."

Another train rumbles by, screeching as it rounds the curve. Somewhere close, someone's frying fish, the smell tossed into your room by the fan. "Christ, it's hot in here." Burke wipes his forehead, takes out a cell phone. "Tom said, call him as soon as I found you." He presses in a number, saying, "You'll really like it up there, Joe. Place has really changed."

You look at the door, but he's between you and the door, and he's got the phone against his ear. You turn, reach into the sink. The knife that's there is dull, rusted. But it's enough.

It's quick, and after, you pick up the couple of things you need, step over what you've done, and leave this room behind, as you've left so many cramped and squalid places. You leave behind the name you used there, too, and take another as you hurry down the baking city streets. Your heart is kicking in your chest but begins to slow again as you think of home. Your cabin, alone on the silent hill. The stream, the ice breaking up, trout running soon, you can fish all day and see no one. Mom will come over, sit at your smooth, heavy table, drinking coffee, laughing. Your skin feels the cold. Your ears are filled with silence. In front of you is a city sidewalk but you don't see that; you see, as you have seen for so long, the hill, the cabin, the golden path and blue shadows. You will see them, and follow them, until the day—and you know it's coming—when you can go home.

PART III

THE POLICE

The third major classification of detective fiction features the police as detectives. Although the police appeared early in works dealing with crimes to be solved, like the enigmatic Inspector Bucket in Charles Dicken's *Bleak House* (1852), they were not seen as the central characters who investigated and solved the mysteries. Beginning with Poe's C. Auguste Dupin, who saw the police as incompetent or incapable of solving certain types of crimes, through the works of Hammett and Chandler, who picture the police as brutal and corrupt, the amateur detective or the private investigator succeeded in finding the criminal while the police failed.

Then British mystery writers such as Freeman Wills Crofts with his Inspector French of Scotland Yard and Ngaio Marsh with Superintendent Roderick Alleyn introduced successful policemen and an interest in police procedure into the mystery genre. However, it was not until 1945 that the first true police procedural novel was written, *V as in Victim*, by Lawrence Treat. Most writers of this classification agree that the radio program *Dragnet*, featuring Joe Friday of the Los Angeles police department, was the greatest influence on the emergence of the police novel. Through radio programs and later television series such as *Dragnet, Hill Street Blues, N.Y.P.D. Blue, Law and Order*, and *C.S.I.*, the public has become fascinated with the world of the police.

Writers such as Georges Simenon in France and Evan Hunter, a.k.a. Ed McBain, in the United States helped establish this type of detective story. In contrast to the amateur and private-eye mystery, the police procedural places the detective in the middle of a working police force, where he or she must abide by the rules and regulations established by the law. The reader goes inside the squad room and is shown how it operates, even being shown the forms of actual police reports. What police procedural writers strive for is realism. In amateur detective stories crimes are often solved by artificial means: a watch destroyed at the time of death, an expression on the corpse's face, a clear fingerprint under the mantel. In reality, an identifiable fingerprint is hard to come by, there is not really any expression on a corpse's face, and the time on watches can be changed. Amateur mysteries are willing to sacrifice reality to maintain the puzzle; police procedurals do not. The police story stresses the fact that murders are not usually cleverly plotted puzzles; they are violent, messy, and committed for any number of reasons.

Although in the private eye stories the violence of death is more accurately portrayed and the detective moves closer to the real "mean streets," reality is still sacrificed. Private investigators do not always report murders or cooperate with the police. They hide clues, tamper with evidence, and break the law whenever they feel like it in order to solve the case. They cannot count on the police to catch the murderer because they are stupid or corrupt or both, and the P.I.s must become a law unto themselves for the criminals to be caught. Like amateur detectives, they are types of attractive superheroes.

An amateur detective and a private investigator can be seen as someone set apart. The classic amateur detective is more intelligent than the average person. The amateur is eccentric, overweight, an aristocratic, collector of rare books, etc. Often this sleuth does not have family or money problems and can concentrate on solving crimes. The private investigator is usually a loner, who shares personal feelings with few people. The P.I. distrusts most people and is skeptical of almost all established institutions.

In contrast, the detective of the police procedural must function as part of the group. The detective must deal with the restrictions of the profession and abide by the law the police are sworn to uphold. Solving crimes is a matter of teamwork, and the answer to most cases comes from an accumulation of information. The police officer relies on both other police officers and informants. In general, crimes are investigated by more than one policeman or policewoman. In small towns the crime is usually handled by a legitimate police team of two or three. In the big-city procedurals there may be 20 or 30 detectives in a squad, although the story will focus on the team of detectives who actually "caught" the case, and sometimes the novels in a series will focus on a different team in the squad in separate books. In contemporary police procedural works, the use of forensic science, computerized information centers, and cooperation between police forces in other cities and other countries is also emphasized. In contrast to the amateur and private investigator formats, the police do not always solve the crime, or if they do, they may not have enough "hard" evidence to take it to a jury and get a conviction. That is the reality of the law.

The police procedural also examines the family life of the detectives with their ordinary human problems. The reader gets to know the personalities in the squad room and the relationships, both good and bad, among the men and women. The contemporary procedural makes it clear that women, not just men, rise in the ranks of the police and make excellent homicide detectives. In these mysteries the squad room comes alive, and with each book the reader becomes reacquainted with favorite characters.

Without question, the police procedural is the most demanding form of detective fiction to write in terms of research. In the amateur and private-eye classifications, research is only necessary if the author is dealing with a specialized subject matter. For example, if you want to make your amateur detective an English professor, you must know something about American and British literature. Otherwise writers can get away with a minimal amount of background reading. Not so with the police procedural. Writers must know the actual structure of police forces along with the proper ranks and the requirements to achieve those ranks. These vary from city to city and from country to country. Writers must know the law, rules of evidence, how an actual crime scene investigation is set up, calibers of guns, power of different types of ammunition, and even the correct forms of police reports.

Most police procedural writers spend time with the police, so they know their lives. Their fictional police go to the hospital if they are beaten up or shot; they sometimes vomit at the sight of a corpse; they want revenge when a fellow officer is killed; they get angry and frustrated and wonder why the system seems against them, but they keep on fighting crime and catching criminals. And the criminals are different too. They are not the masterminds of complicated plots or the spoiled daughters of rich businessmen; they resemble real murderers. They range from ignorant losers motivated by emotion and impulse to psychotic serial killers to coldly professional "hitmen." They are usually caught sooner or later because of the extended power of the police force.

Readers are attracted to the police novel because it allows them to enter the "closed" world of the police. They get an opportunity to see how the police operate at a crime scene, get information from the forensics team, interview suspects, and gather the information that can convict the guilty person in a court of law. Numerous details of the police detective's life, both professional and private, appear in these stories. Critics of this classification are concerned with the accuracy of the portrayal of police life. Therefore, writers of police stories must know about guns, various types of bullets, entry and exit wounds, autopsy reports, and an endless number of other details. The critics want to feel that a writer puts them at the crime scene with the smell of cordite still in the air.

Police forces all over the world are presented in contemporary detective fiction. England is the setting for police novels and stories created by Reginald Hill, Peter Robinson, Ian Rankin, Jonathan Ross, Colin Dexter, P. D. James, Martha Grimes, Elizabeth George, Deborah Crombie, and Catherine Aird. Arthur Upfield and Claire McNab examine the Australian police. Janwillem Van de Wetering describes police work in the Netherlands. The detectives of

Ireland come alive in the works of Bartholomew Gill. Georges Simenon gives us the famous French detective Maigret. James McClure shows us how difficult police work can be in South Africa, while Iain Pears creates the special Art Theft squad in Italy.

However, writers from the United States seem to dominate the police procedural genre. Although there are too many good writers to mention them all, the following authors are much respected in this field: Ed McBain, James Lee Burke, Michael Connelly, Tony Hillerman, Joseph Wambaugh, Michael McGarrity, Laurie R. King, Carol O'Connell, Julie Smith, Dana Stabenow, and John Ball.

Finally, what must be noted is that the police procedural is serious in intent. It examines the ills of society. It is both social commentary and social criticism. Who better to question the way that a society is run than the police who must deal with the worst of it?

CRITICAL ESSAYS AND COMMENTARIES

LEROY LAD PANEK

From "The Police Novel"

. . .

Police procedurals, to be sure, build upon earlier forms of the detective story. They owe much to the scientific story, the golden age plot, the thriller, and the hard-boiled story. Additionally, however, they respond to police shows on radio and television, they attempt to portray an oppressed minority group (police), and they react to a growing public perception in the 1950s and 1970s that we are witnessing the death of civilization.

To make all of this even more difficult to deal with, the term "police procedural" is an extremely loose label pasted by reviewers on a wide variety of books which have in common only police officers as their heroes. In some cases, the label distorts the character of books which are really hard-boiled stories, thrillers, and so on. In some cases, however, the term "police procedural" accurately describes writers' aims, as well as the new kind of detective fiction which differs significantly from earlier sorts of detective story. In the last thirty years, the police procedural has opened up new opportunities for the detective story writer, provided a real challenge to the underlying assumptions of the traditional detective story, and, in some cases, made contact with the realism toward which detective stories had been struggling since the 1920's.

One problem with the term "police procedural" is that all detective writers make some sort of comment about it. This is true even of pioneers like Poe. To illustrate the special capacity of his genius detective and to demonstrate the utility of genius, Poe makes special point of detailing police routine. In "The Purloined Letter," particularly, he notes the minute and painstaking examination the police make of Minister D—'s rooms to demonstrate that genius is not simply the infinite capacity for taking pains.

On a different level, Dickens, Collins, and other nineteenth century writers described the policeman's social routines, the tact with which they investigate and interrogate, to convince their readers that the police did not threaten privacy, decorum, or individual liberty. With Gaboriau's *romans policier*, moreover, we find books in part devoted to presenting apologies, defenses, and descriptions of police life.

Gaboriau's attention to the aura, the criminological routines, and personal problems generated by police work mark the real beginning of the police procedural. Evoking, as he does, the atmosphere of the cells and the police court, spotlighting special techniques the police use in their work against crime, and singling out the stress police work places on normal relationships establishes practices that lie at the foundation of the procedural. But Gaboriau never got to it; he grew tired of police heroes and grew too fond of chronicling the hardships of beautiful people.

After Gaboriau, Doyle and his successors blanked out the policeman in favor of the amateur, and passed over police themes in favor of presenting sentiment and sensation in the middle classes. But from the 1920's onward, the policeman has maintained a continuous presence as the hero of detective stories. Amateur detectives enjoyed a brief spurt of popularity during World War II, and private eyes flourished for a decade after the war, but the policeman has kept up a steady presence from the twenties through the eighties.

. . .

The problem, however, is that most earlier police detectives are only nominally policemen. By and large, police work makes no appreciable impact on their personalities, and the Coles' Superintendent Wilson, Marsh's Superintendent Alleyn, and Innes' Inspector Appleby have the same sort of character as their amateur contemporaries. They have ballet, opera, painting, books, servants, and upper class cronies to fall back on when things get too depressing. They are all bosses and act as individual agents. They always win. They are not real policemen, but were created as policemen because actual crime solving was becoming too scientific, taxing, and complicated for the private individual.

We do not get to the police procedural from the nominal British policeman in golden age novels. We get there from Georges Simenon's books about Maigret. In 1931, Simenon introduced Inspector Maigret in M. *Gallet Decede*, and developed him through bushels of subsequent books. These short novels probe the lives of petty, nasty, twisted criminals and present the wearying and depressing routine investigations conducted by Maigret and his police assistants. They show no bizarre crimes, no exalted mental triumphs, and the hero is a solid, persistent, middle class man who at the end of the day is happy just to put his feet up.

. . .

Maigret, however, did not immediately inspire a vogue for a particular brand of novel about policemen. That inspiration came from America, where various literary and social forces led writers to reevaluate the detective and the detective story.

. . .

The transformation of the hard-boiled private eye into the hard-boiled policeman happened on the radio. From the 1920's onward, American broadcasting, both on radio and then television, has been obsessed with crime. J. Fred MacDonald, in *Don't Touch That Dial* (1979), notes, for instance, that by 1945 crime shows took up an average of ninety minutes of every radio broadcast day.

At first, radio detective shows reflected the golden age's fascination with the puzzle story. In 1929, WMAQ in Chicago ran a detective program entitled "Unfinished Play" which broadcast an unfinished crime story and offered a $200 prize to the listener who furnished the best solution. *The Eno Crime Club*, a network program from 1931 to 1936, followed the same pattern: on Tuesday nights it aired an unfinished drama and presented the ending on Wednesday evening.

Moving away from the puzzle story, radio in the 1930's began to respond to the public's perception of and fears about a national crime wave and started to feature police officers in its crime programming. Frequently, radio shows framed their police dramas with comments by real police officers: Chief James Davis of the Los Angeles Police read introductions for *Calling All Cars*, Col. Norman Schwartzkopf narrated *Gangbusters* in 1936, and Sergeant Mary Sullivan of the New York Police added postscripts to *Policewoman* from 1946 to 1947. All of these shows demonstrate a move toward realism in radio crime drama. This move became documentary realism in the late 1940's.

In the late 1940's, radio shows like *Broadway Is My Beat*, *The Man from Homicide*, and *The Line Up* introduced radio audiences to dramas that combined sordid crime, petty criminals, real surroundings, police procedure, and hard-boiled cops, the principal ingredients of the police procedural novel. The most important of these radio shows was Jack Webb's *Dragnet*, which aired first in 1949. Hillary Waugh (1920–) notes "if there was a father of the procedural, I think it would have to be the radio program *Dragnet*." Webb's evocation of Sergeant Joe Friday's first person, terse, matter-of-fact toughness, set in a specific time and place ("It was Tuesday, November third, and I was working the day watch out of homicide"), and dotted with references to numbered police code ("We were answering a call on a 1014") while telling a story of crime and detection, played a formative role in the move toward the police procedural. Television programs followed, and programs like *Dragnet*, *Highway Patrol*, and *The Naked City* did their bit to combine the aura of official police investigation with some of the essentials of the hard-boiled story.

. . .

The first novel to be called a police procedural is Lawrence Treat's *V as in Victim* (1945). Attempting to fuse the golden age story with the hard-boiled tale, Treat created a pair of contrasting detectives. Job Freeman, like his namesake, is an enthusiastic, scientific detective who solves the crime with fancy scientific gadgets. Nothing was new about this. The second hero, Mitch Taylor, is a cop. Tutored in traditional police wisdom, overworked, cynical about his job, exhausted by the demands of police work, and rooted in the values and style of the middle class, Taylor is something new to detective fiction. Treat, however, never took full advantage of him, tied up as he was with years of routine detective writing behind him.

Hillary Waugh, however, did not have this problem. In *Last Seen Wearing* (1952), and in his series novels about Fred Fellows and Frank Sessions, Waugh wrote police procedurals intended to (and sometimes capable of) create an "aura of horror" by "the sense of authenticity of the reports." Ed McBain (1926–) began his 87th Precinct novels in 1956 with *Cop Hater*. His combination of humor, grisly realism, sentimentality with insistence on verisimilitude in police details, and the creation of the detailed parallel world of Isola made him the most influential police procedural writer.

. . .

The main feature which unites all police procedural writers is, very simply, that they chose policemen and policewomen as their heroes. Individually, they differ a great deal: some write clumsy prose and some are competent stylists; some examine the complex implications of their characters and themes while others do not; some use traditional detective plots while others invent unique structures to capture the essence of police life; some write stories as unreal as most television shows; and others create shockingly accurate portraits of violence and degradation. Dell Shannon's Luis Mendoza drives a Ferrari, while Wambaugh's Bumper Morgan pilots a beat-up old Ford. McBain's Steve Carella enjoys idyllic domestic bliss while Sjowall and Wahloo's Martin Beck has become alienated from his wife and family.

Yet, looking at the heroes of the police procedural, several definite patterns emerge. First of all, procedural writers insist police are average people. In police novels, the hero can have chronic stomach trouble, as Bumper Morgan has, trouble with child care, or periodontal problems. The hero can walk off and vomit when confronted with horror or befoul himself when threatened with death. Physically, the police hero is the normal person faced with the normal deterioration of the body and its natural responses to the unnatural job of policework. Procedurals, too, demonstrate the hero's average nature by providing domestic worries. Wilcox' Hastings, for example, worries about having to have his suit cleaned if a criminal bleeds all over him. From housekeeping details to family details, like Gideon's concerns for his children or Beck's consciousness of his failing marriage, procedural writers stress that their heroes are, fundamentally, average people.

Indeed, many police officers are not just normal or average people, they are common. Treat's Mitch Taylor, with his plodding nature and his lower middle class values and tastes, sets the stage for future writers. In *Ax*, McBain devotes several pages to Cotton Hawes describing the plot of a grade C science fiction film entitled *The Locusts*. Wambaugh's characters engage in puerile jokes and adolescent prurience. The level of taste on the police force does not run to James Joyce or *nouvelle cuisine*. Police officers reflect the tastes, concerns, and attitudes of the lower middle class, the traditional source of police recruits. Generally, egg-heads and college boys are not welcome on the force. Indeed, one of Wambaugh's themes is the unfitness of the intellectual for policework. Police heroes tend to be proletarian heroes, and while they are not quite "dumb cops," sophisticated and complex brain work plays little part in the police novel. That the heroes solve crimes by accident, by routine, or by the fact that most criminals are abysmally stupid, places the police hero in revolt against the hard-boiled or the soft-boiled hero of detective tradition.

If the common person as hero presents some challenges to the traditional detective hero, so does the other hero pattern that evolves in the police procedural. Police work is, by its nature, a communal enterprise. More than one officer works on a case and more than one shift of workers assembles and collates information. The individual police officer depends on others to do lab work, to provide records, and to supply technical advice; he or she operates in a system of structured authority which offers advice, demands progress, and sometimes hampers effective crime solving. Thus, some police procedural novels, like some war novels, introduce the multiple or corporate hero. Corporate heroes run from the picture of partners working together, to the description of a whole squad, precinct, or division working together on one case, to a description of many officers pursuing diverse cases. The last of these types is the most difficult to write, but the plot which shows many police officers working on many cases defines the police procedural in its purest state. When we find a group of officers like those in the Gideon novels or in Egan's *Scenes of Crime* (1976) or in Wambaugh's books, we can be sure it is a police procedural. Indeed, McBain's books, taken together, tell the continuing story not of one individual policeman, but of the corporate hero, the 87th Precinct.

Whether single or corporate, however, the hero of the police procedural comes out of and, in one way or another, responds to the tradition of the hard-boiled detective. The police hero has all of the essentials of the hard-boiled detective. He is big, tough, and sexy. Literally tutored in violence, he gives and receives a lot of punishment. All of this may be modified by authors' conscious efforts to point out the police officer is not a special or exceptional human being, but most police heroes start from a hard-boiled pattern. Some of them, too, talk like hard-boiled detectives. Take this passage from McBain's first 87th Precinct novel, *Cop Hater*:

> "Everybody wants to go home," Carella said, "Home is where you pack your rod."
>
> "I never understand detectives," Kling said.
>
> "Come in, we have a visit to make," Carella said.
>
> "Where?"
>
> "Up the street, Mama Luz. Just point the car; it knows the way."
>
> Kling took off his hat and ran one hand through his blond hair. "Phew," he said, and then he put on his hat and climbed in behind the wheel. "Who are we looking for?"

"Man named Dizzy Ordiz."

"Never heard of him."

"He never heard of you either," Carella said.

This clipped, tough, wise-cracking style ties the policeman to the hard-boiled hero, and police writers use it to develop for their heroes the same psychic defenses and outlook aimed at by hard-boiled writers. Police writers, however, go on to build up a special kind of diction, cynicism, hardness, and low humor which portrays not one individual, but a group of people, police officers, who define and protect themselves with their special language.

The same transference from the individual to the group takes place in the procedural's use of other hard-boiled qualities. Alienation from family, friends, and the public at large affects not only individual officers, but the police as a class. The job causes the huddling together of people shut out from the rest of society. It causes veterans to die of heart attacks or commit suicide in loneliness and despair. The procedural concerns a class of alienated people, not just one. Further, the parallel between the soldier and the detective holds much more firmly in the police novel, which deals with a quasi-military organization, than it does in the hard-boiled novel about a lone wolf. Police heroes combine toughness and sentimentality, as do hard-boiled heroes, but the common nature of the typical police officer justifies schmaltzy behavior far more than the unexplained sentimentality of the exceptional hard-boiled hero. Finally, the police officer walks down streets far meaner than those through which the hard-boiled heroes drive. Police heroes deal with literal human garbage and filth far more degrading and dangerous than anything which confronts the hard-boiled detective. If none of them is as well written as the best hard-boiled stories, the police procedural intensifies and makes more real certain elements which are only suggested or mythical in the hard-boiled novel.

. . .

Procedural writers assume police work is a unique occupation which colors all facets of an individual's character and which has never before been adequately or sympathetically described. Their principal techniques of showing what policemen really do are articulated through their plots or through descriptive digressions on how shifts are assigned, how records are kept, and so on. The human impact of police work, the particular kinds of stress with which police officers live, forms the most important procedure described by police writers. They picture police work as an unrewarding, soul-destroying alternation of boredom, coping with the ludicrous and trivial, coming to terms with the morbid and depraved, and facing rare moments of absolutely terrifying physical danger.

Every worker, of course, thinks himself worthy of his hire, and then some, and police novels begin with the assumption that we pay the police very little for collecting society's trash. This, however, hardly makes police work uniquely underpaid: firefighters, teachers, sanitation workers, and even physicians can argue they get little financial reward for doing dirty jobs. The difference with police work, and procedural novels point this out, is that by its very nature it not only denies the police officer generous pay, but it also withholds most incentive and gratifications which other jobs extend to the employee.

Over the course of the last thirty years, procedural writers have developed the unrewarding nature of the police officer's job into several conventions that not only describe police work, but portray its impact on the participants' characters. Thus, procedurals take pains to show that police officers have little in the way of external incentive or example. The theme of promotion in rank emphasizes not the competence of police forces, but their stupidity and, occasionally, corruption. The good officer spends his time making arrests and can not study for promotion exams, and the rest is Catch 22. Treat's Mitch Taylor only goes through the motions of working because he knows advancement only comes to those who have influence with the higher ups.

Why, then, work for a system that does not reward real merit? Often in the procedural, the system does not reward merit because it does not understand it. Upper echelon officers are, almost universally, anti-professional political brown nosers, boot-licking junior executives, or bird-brained efficiency experts. As in war novels, few characters above the rank of lieutenant receive much praise. Fame could make up for this, but no one remembers good and brave police officers except other police officers.

Instead, the police hero gets the reverse of fame. Procedurals invariably introduce vignettes of public contempt, fear, hostility, and indifference to the police. Police officers do not even have the satisfaction of working for justice. The dilemmas of applying abstract law to practical, immediate problems, and of ignoring shoals of lesser crimes and criminals for greater crimes and criminals erode police officers' confidence that they serve justice or that justice can be served at all. Having to choke down Supreme court rulings they perceive to be wrong and having to wink at pimps, pushers, and petty extortionists takes its toll.

This confusion and public ingratitude affects the hero of the police procedural and his or her fellow officers. It can make stupid and lumpish officers if not more stupid, then more lumpish. It can result in the violent vigilante officer who finds reward in gratifying the need for violence or in enforcing an individual's, not the Supreme Court's, notion of justice. Most often it provides material for gripes. Most police heroes respond to their unrewarding job with the same situational ethics and undefinable, indefensible romanticism characteristic of the hard-boiled detective. Somehow or other, the police novels say, exceptional people continue to work for peanuts.

On top of being unrewarding, the work of the police often grinds down to boring chores and mechanical and repetitive tasks. Here lies a real dilemma for police procedural writers. If they want to capture the actuality of police work, procedural writers must in one way or another acknowledge that it is dominated by triviality and routine. Most real crimes admit a simple solution, not the byzantine structure of fancy detective fiction: victims usually know their attackers, and criminals, on the whole, are stupid and careless people. Along the same lines, routine investigation takes up most of the police officer's time. A slice of the police officer's life, therefore, means showing a lot of trivial, routine, uninteresting activities.

No writer, of course, can set out to write a popular book centered on these things. So procedural writers have found ways around them. The digression helps here, allowing writers to note that most cases are easy and most police work is uninteresting. They can then go on to deal with the exceptional case in their plot. Sometimes writers convert trivial cases into difficult ones by demonstrating that the police have so much to do it is a wonder any crime is solved. The anonymity and complexity of urban life also complicates easy cases and allows the writer to deal with the significant theme of the city. Finally, even the simplest case brings police officers into contact with people and allows the writer to develop interest not only in the police hero, but also in minor characters.

In terms of routine, procedural writers, too, have developed various ways of lifting the potentially deadening into something else. Police routine, in procedural novels, reduces to leg work and paper work. Here again, writers tip their hats to police routine more than they really describe it. McBain, for instance, often introduces facsimile reports or forms that do not develop the plot or character but merely contribute to the aura of police work. Paper work, however, can develop into a variety of character-building points. It can indicate the bureaucratic hobbling of real police work, it can portray the cultural level of the police officer (Wambaugh speaks of "pencilographical errors" while Freeling's Van Der Valk writes masterly reports), and it can describe the hero's attitude toward authority and general rebelliousness. On top of these character points, routine can also become the basis of plot. In one type of procedural, the heroes need to discover or invent an effective routine for screening the myriad facts and people which confront them: they need to find the right sieves (people born in 1943, Mid-Westerners, lawyers, etc.) which will produce the criminal. With this sort of routine, we come closest to the old intellectual detective hero, but most procedural writers shy away from this label.

The boredom and triviality of most police work has its bright side, too. It can be funny and it can evoke the most human side of the police hero. The police come into frequent contact with kooks, loonies, and fanatics whom the law or God or personal obsessions have unhinged. Sociologically, these people embody petty and pathetic problems of the culture. Practically, they can be very funny. Some procedural writers, especially Wambaugh and McBain, turn these episodes from the police officer's life into comic vignettes: the man who paints himself red in *The Choirboys* or the old woman who imagines herself ravished by Dracula in McBain. Also, it is often with trivial, routine cases writers show their characters' compassion. From the cliche of the lost child in the station house with an ice-cream cone to the patient, polite and kind treatment of the distraught and dispossessed, procedural writers demonstrate the humanity of their heroes. They do this, in part, because they can not show it when the police come into contact with the elemental horrors of life.

Small instances of human folly and weakness inspire laughter and compassion, but the squalor and depravity of society needs other responses. Police officers sometimes have to act as garbage collectors of a society that tries to ignore its waste and septic products. This is one of the main points of many police procedurals. Procedurals drag into public view that the police must deal with the sickest, stupidest, most perverse, and depraved parts of modern life. Instead of the hidden criminal of fiction, the police befoul themselves by daily contact with drunks, pushers, addicts, child molesters, torturers, psychopaths, and rapists.

Procedural plots center on the most abhorrent of crimes. What sort of impact does this have on the character of the police hero? The job brings the hero into contact with the darkest parts of human nature, and it pokes away at elemental fears. Seeing arbitrary violence or violated innocence brings fears for one's own family; seeing, touching, smelling mutilated and putrefying corpses inspires the throbbing whisper which reminds the heroes of their own deaths. Thinking about these thing can incapacitate the best.

Consequently, writers develop ways for their heroes to deal with them. There is, first, the role of the hard-boiled police officer, in which the heroes simply accept the facts as facts and refuse to inquire into their personal, social, moral, or theological meaning. Akin to this stance, some writers develop the separate hero, who refuses relationships outside of the job because its horrors blight any normal relationship; these heroes find solace only in the camaraderie of other police officers who know what they know. The depravity, perverseness, and human impact of crime also serve to move some cops to philosophy: Freeling's Castang and Wambaugh's Kilvinsky both work their ways toward a social theory describing the worthlessness of civilization and the decline of the West. Finally, the occasional horror of police work inspires the compartmentalization many procedural writers fix in their characters. Thus, police heroes separate the boredom from the excitement and the pathetic from the horrific. Especially, they try to separate police work from their private lives. Babies and children fill the home lives of many police heroes: Castang's wife gives birth in *Castang's City* (1980), Mendoza's wife has twins, and cuddly Teddy Carella has cuddly kids. This is all Sergeant Cuff's roses updated, and often made more sentimental.

Some parts of police work, however, resist compartmentalization. The mental or moral fervor of criminal investigation can follow an officer home, but, more insidiously, the aftershocks of physical terror creep into the individual's whole consciousness. This is one of the effects of violence that becomes a convention in the procedural. There are others. While stressing that life-threatening situations rarely occur to the average officer, episodes of potential and real violence occur in most procedurals. These episodes, in turn, raise questions important to the writers' delineation of the police personality. The first of these is, how can a normal human being calmly face situations that palpably threaten violence or death? Who would voluntarily face down a drunken 280-pound laborer armed with a tire iron? Who would want to interrupt a drug deal or break into a room of armed urban terrorists? Who could stay cool and observe regulations about the use of force? Not many people.

Some procedural writers admit this and show the screw-ups and loosening of the bowels characteristic of normal, nervous people. They also lend perspective to police brutality before, during, and after arrests. While exceptional police officers never break heads or flip anyone with their saps, police brutality is the human, particularly the male, response to being threatened. Physical danger, too, connects to the notion of brothers in arms. The intimacy of shared terror, in the past, present, and future, causes police officers to support one another physically and emotionally. It moves them, encased in one of the most closed of closed societies, to cover up for their fellows who go on the rampage, and to go on the rampage when a brother officer is killed. Of course, the bookish or squeamish impulse moves some procedural writers to hymn police training and the fact that the police can face danger and violence simply because they have received thorough and effective training. Others explain that police officers can handle violence because of their on-the-job training of dealing with danger. Nevertheless, the physiological responses remain, the adrenalin, the increased heartbeat, etc., along with mute wonder at individuals who can calmly risk their lives while following a routine of calm and order.

Most of the character conventions developed by procedural writers show human urges interfering with police work. The hard-boiled police hero, of course, overcomes them, but in a sense the character description in procedurals moves decisively away from the psychology of detection and toward the psychology of the normal individual who does a job packed with stress. It moves away from the genius detective model and usually pictures average people solving crimes, not by powerful and original thought, but by accident, dumb luck, or dogged routine.

Procedural police officers, however, do have some character points to make out of detection. Collin Wilcox, for example, develops a minor character who is simply, inexplicably lucky. Other writers tell us police officers have a kind of sixth sense that aids them in solving crimes. This is, from the point of view of fiction, indefinable and has a ticklish legal status (*Terry v. Ohio* [1968], for example, is a police favorite but a lawyer's nightmare), but somehow good police officers have the ability to read the furtive look, the nervous shuffle, the slouching gait and myriad other signs of guilt. Usually they can not say how or why they can do this: they can just do it. The other crime-fighting tool built into the procedural police officer is his knowledge of criminals and how to deal with them.

Every hero has informers who detail news of the streets, and they also know most of the people involved in shady business in the precinct. As often as not, however, these police abilities offer little help in solving major crimes and simply add to the hero's knowledge of how rotten things can be.

Police procedurals define themselves by using the police officer as the hero, but they also use distinctive kinds of crime and criminals to set tone and motivate plot. With the exception of assorted picaresque stories, master criminal plots and terrorist tales, crime in the procedural builds on the trend toward realism begun by the hard-boiled story. But the procedural goes much farther than the hard-boiled story. Crime in the police procedural seems much more real. Like the hard-boiled story, the procedural uses cold, matter-of-fact narration to bring home the horrible aftermath of violent crime. We find detailed descriptions of bits of brain oozing through blood-matted hair, exit wounds as big as grapefruits, post mortem excretion, torn and bleeding sexual organs, and so on. Writers place these details not in the middle of the adventure story, to be quickly forgotten, but in realistic surroundings. Readers witness the graphic effects of violence in the gutter, in tenement rooms, or at the morgue during an autopsy. The grotesque facts, coupled with the clinical tone, and placed in real surroundings, go a long way toward making crime in the procedural seem more brutally actual.

Not only are the details more shocking in the procedural than in earlier kinds of detective stories, the crimes are also more heinous. Whether through self-censorship or societal pressure, before the procedural, certain crimes never occurred in detective stories. Procedural writers take it upon themselves to write about these unspoken, unspeakable crimes.

. . .

The shocking nature of the details, and the crime itself, impact on both readers and hero. They define the distastefulness of the police officer's job for the reader and affect the hero's consciousness. Abominations force heroes to be hard-boiled and compartmental. At the same time, they provide an affront to the heroes' sensibilities. Finally, they engage both the hero and the readers in the outrage and humiliation that are human responses to the suffering of innocents.

Non-police characters in procedural novels do not seem to be very nice people. As with the hard-boiled story, the comparison with the combat soldier explains much about the policeman's view of non-combatants. It is, further, more apt for police officers than private eyes, for they have few friends outside of the force and confront widespread public hostility and suspicion. As physicians see only people who are ill, police officers see people at their very worst. Most of their work is with the victimized, the destitute, or the deranged. Grieving parents and friends, balky or hostile witnesses, as well as criminals, fill the officer's day. Minor characters in the procedural, therefore, tend to be vulnerable, weak and frightened people.

For its criminals, the police procedural novel goes back to the hard-boiled story, but here again it accomplishes the intent far better than its predecessor.

Because they intend to write realistic stories, procedural writers avoid using criminals with the intelligence and nerve to plan and execute a well-wrought crime. Master criminal stories, like McBain's Deaf Man books, and plots involving political terrorism may exhibit the police procedures of organization and mobilization and therefore, form a sub-group themselves, but they are at variance with the usual aims of the procedural novel.

Criminals in police procedurals fit into several clear categories. Most criminals are stupid. They commit crimes for petty reasons. The murderer in McBain's *Ax* splits another man's skull for $7.50. These criminals usually do little to cover their own tracks; after the crime, they continue doing what they have always done. The criminal's genius does not hamper detection, but the complexity and anonymity of the city makes things difficult for the police. In addition to brutish criminals, procedural writers deal with average people who commit crimes because of psychological pressure. Like the twisted woman in McBain's *Calypso* (1979), psycho-sexual diseases erupt in individuals and move them to violent crime.

Often, too, procedural writers develop characters whose mental imbalance has distinct social causes. Police procedural novels bring a sociological point of view to the detective story. We can see this in the treatment of heroes who belong to an identifiable group formed by tangible sources and practicing its own customs and mores. Ed McBain, in *Let's Hear It for the Deaf Man*, identifies the police as a minority group, bringing them under the type of analysis and degree of scrutiny which other minority groups have received in the 1960's and 1970's. Some of the same kinds of attention go to criminals in police procedurals. Procedural criminals may be stupid and influenced by the same kind of mental disease as villains in hard-boiled stories, but frequently writers trace the criminal's acts to some kind of societal cause. Sjowall and Wahloo, for instance, portray a criminal pushed to act by the perverseness of capitalism and the depredations of the welfare state in *Murder at the Savoy*. Novels about prostitutes (Waugh's *Finish Me Off* [1971] or McBain's *Calypso*) and stories which turn on narcotics (Uhnak's *The Ledger*, 1970, or Van de Wetering's *Outsider in Amsterdam*) portray the roots of evil not in the individual, but in the blind bumpings of large social trends. In this sense, the city, important in other connections, causes as many crimes as mental imbalance and cretinous behavior. Thus, the procedural takes the reader from outrage at violent, obnoxious crimes to some degree of understanding of the dispossessed, sick, victimized, pathetic personalities of criminals. By accomplishing this change in attitude, it demonstrates what the police at their best can do.

The police procedural gains many of its effects from the creation of character, but it brings character across by means of plot and atmosphere, which can differ radically from the plot and atmosphere of traditional detective stories. In terms of plot, not all procedural novels differ from traditional detective stories. I have touched on this already. Some procedurals develop as hard-boiled stories, with the hero crashing against and overcoming one obstacle after another. Others are thrillers, "how-catch-ems," or golden age stories complete with clues and surprise endings. Lawrence Treat, the founder of the form, certainly plots like a golden age writer. One of the virtues of the police procedural book, then, is that it allows writers to use a wide variety of plots. All they absolutely need is a police hero and some material describing police procedure. Thus, they mandate the heroes' characters but not their acts, and they demand description, which can be added on to many different kinds of action.

Police procedural writers, however, do have some common aims when it comes to plotting. Like some golden age writers and hard-boiled writers, they want to avoid the artificial completeness of the traditional detective story: as McBain says in *Calypso*, the police procedural does not want to be a book in which "everything [is] wrapped up neatly and tied with a pretty little bow. All the pieces in place, just like a phony fucking mystery novel." In some cases, the lure of the mystery novel is too strong, and many procedurals have the same completeness as traditional novels.

But, procedural writers also try to give the impression their plots are different from traditional mysteries. One way of doing this is to do away with the convention of the present, but unidentified criminal. To get away from the button, button game of guessing the criminal, some writers give us his identity early on. Creasey and McBain use a double focus, following the acts of both criminal and police. Other writers, like Sjowall and Wahloo in *Roseanna* (1965), identify the criminal early and concentrate on the police problem of gathering evidence against him.

At the other extreme, some procedural writers have no aesthetic bias against the *deus ex machina* and drop the criminal into the plot at the last minute as soon as a bit of new information becomes available. Although procedurals do ask the who did it question, procedural writers would rather reveal or explain identity and motive than taunt readers with a guessing game.

Just as they purposely avoid the game of choosing the murderer from a limited number of contestants, procedural writers also veer away from the surprise at the end of the plot. Or, they rig the surprise to defeat the expectations established by the traditional detective story. In the usual procedural, the guilt of the criminal is established by arduous, exhausting investigation and carries with it no exhilarating triumph, but rather a simple, weary recognition that everything in this case is over. Little joy or triumph accrues to the discovery of the pathetic criminals typical to the form. More importantly, procedural writers stress the endlessness of police work, so that a case solved can not carry with it the accomplishment of a job done. Police work never ends.

Some depart from the pattern of one crime and one solution and revolve around many crimes, some of which are never solved. . . . The denouement, precious to Poe and Doyle as the heart of the detective story, shrinks in size and significance. Instead, procedural writers try to tell stories about, or with the air of, chaos and confusion, hard work, and everyday facts, which they perceive to be the reality of police procedure.

Any number of things make the action of a police novel different from that of a book about an amateur or private detective: the quasi-military nature of police forces, the bureaucracy, the definition of detection as a job rather than an avocation or obsession, the continuing nature of crime, the chaos of dealing with all crime instead of a single crime, and so on. All of these impact on the hero's character, but they also have specific implications for plotting which separate the procedural from other kinds of detective story. The most marked feature of the police novel appears in writers' attempts to create plots that evoke the organized confusion of police work. To really understand the job, the writers tell us, we must first understand that at any given time police departments work on a large number and variety of cases, and the solution to most cases involves the contributions of a group of people. Writers try to get this across in several ways. For procedural writers intent on using traditional, one crime, one hero plots, there are several ways of portraying the organized chaos of police work. The simplest is to use digressions. In his easier books, McBain, for instance, will stop the flow of the one hero, one problem story and give readers a snapshot of life outside the principal investigation. Thus in *Jigsaw* (1970), we get this:

> "I've got that dry-cleaning store holdup, and the muggings over on Ainsley . . . six in the past two weeks, same m.o. . . . I've also got a lead I want to run down on the pusher who's been working the junior high school on seventeenth. And there're two cases coming to trial this month."

Other writers accomplish the same effect in other ways. Collin Wilcox indicates the nature of police work by beginning novels with Hastings working on a case or two before settling down into the book's principal crime. In *The Young Prey*, Waugh uses policemen's anecdotes about past cases to convey the unstinting, continuous, and chaotic nature of police work.

All of these minor narrative devices get the point across, but procedural writers have also invented larger techniques to do the same thing. These change the nature of the plot-making in the police procedural, making it not only a form with a new kind of detective hero, but also one with a different kind of plot. These novels confront the reader with a number of criminal investigations carried on either simultaneously or consecutively.

. . .

Joseph Wambaugh has inspired other writers in his searches for novel ways of organizing a presentation of the diversity of police experience. *The New Centurions* follows a group of officers from the police academy to the Watts riots. *The Choirboys* goes to Joseph Heller's *Catch-22* (1964) and builds an organization out of repeated images, incremental repetition, and the gradual revelation of the novel's central incident. With these new kinds of plots, the police novel effectively leaves the realm of the detective story and becomes a class of fiction by itself.

Whether they follow the actions of several police officers or stick to the traditional one-hero plot, we can identify a police procedural novel by the atmosphere which the writer sets out to establish. Thus in the early fifties, when Waugh decided to try a new sort of novel, he said he "determined to write a fictional murder mystery that would *sound* as if it really happened." Making a police novel sound as if it really happened depends in large measure on building up details so its atmosphere differs from other, less real, varieties of detective fiction. The most obvious of these details, of course, are those that describe the environment in which the police work. In police novels, therefore, we find inserted paragraphs detailing how records are kept, how radio calls are answered, how witnesses are supposed to be interrogated, and how work schedules are set up. McBain starts his novels with an epigraph advertising "the police routine is based on established investigatory technique." All of these details serve to illustrate the process of police work for readers unfamiliar with it. The feel of these details, however, does something else. Treat begins *V as in Victim* by describing the down-at-the-heels look of the police station, and McBain describes the 87th Precinct station as being like "the office of a failing insurance company." Descriptions of police duty schedules evoke the hectic and exhausting hours officers work. All of the items that objectively portray the police officer's routines also give off an atmosphere that combines neglect, exhaustion, absurdity, and near squalor.

In addition to the strictly police details, other facts contribute to the atmosphere of the procedural. One of the most important of these is climate. The weather is always awful; it is always raining or snowing, bitterly cold, disgustingly damp, or unbearably hot. Frequently, the first sentence establishes the irritating nature of the weather: Sjowall and Wahloo's *Murder at the Savoy*, for instance, starts with "The day was hot and stifling, without a breath of air." This sense of discomfort pervades the police novel, replacing the gothic "it was a dark and stormy night." Although police writers do use night to establish atmosphere, they do not use it to tingle spines. Most crimes occur at night, so using night is realistic, but being dragged out of bed and investigating a crime in darkness provides added discomfort. Atmospheric details like the weather and the time set the basic tone for the procedural. Writers, of course, sprinkle their books with shocking details—splattered internal organs, ugly facts about autopsies, and so on—but the essential pattern of atmosphere and tone in the police procedural establishes a groundwork of irritation and discomfort splashed with occasional bursts of violence.

The city plays a particularly vital role in establishing the distinctive atmosphere of the police procedural. The procedural continues and expands upon the description of the real city in the hard-boiled story. In the police novel, however, the city serves slightly different purposes and attains a much larger importance than in the earlier form. Police novels about small towns are the variants: most procedurals take place in large cities. Realistically, writers select the city because most crime is urban crime. The major social problems and many individual problems of the mid-twentieth century—juvenile delinquency, drug addiction, racial conflict—fester more obviously in cities than in small-town or rural settings where they are often urban imports. Further, at mid-century, American politicians pushing "law and order," as well as groups fighting for civil liberties, focused on the problems of cities and, particularly, of big-city police departments. Finally, because of the scale and scope of managing urban crime and urban policing, it is the city that attracts the moral and descriptive talents of the procedural writer. As a consequence of all of this, procedural novels portray the modern city going down the drain. From grimy tenements and sleazy bars to prostitutes' rooms and narcotics "shooting galleries," readers see in the police procedural a vivid portrait of the decayed city.

And yet, in the police procedural, something else enters the portrait of the decaying metropolis; it assumes a significance far beyond mere realistic setting or the occasion for complicating police work. In a fairly large class of procedurals, the city becomes the exotic place, full of danger, but also packed with fascination.

. . .

In addition to this travelogue appeal, the city has other implications for the procedural. McBain, in a number of books, repeatedly describes the city as "a hairy bastard, but you get to love it." The city, in fact, ceases to be simply background and becomes a character in itself. Creasey's Gideon books, in a very real sense, show London as the most important character which the police repeatedly save from corruption or destruction. McBain's Isola, Riverhead, Clam's Point, and the rest are not, he insists, simply pseudonyms for Manhattan and environs; they are the archetypal city. They are ciphers out of a morality play in which the average man works for the salvation of the place that stands for the fruit of all human enterprise.

. . .

Since the 1950's, the police procedural has contributed significantly to the development of detective fiction. It has supplied the realistic challenge to traditional detective stories hard-boiled stories talked about but never achieved. It has evolved a hero who, although not quite new, was affected by a whole range of internal and external influences unique to police officers and neglected by earlier writers. It has departed from the spot-the-murderer plot and has developed settings and atmospheres which bring home both the depredations and the heroism of police work. Police procedurals, however, too often suffer from militancy and didacticism. They preach too ardently about the rigors of police work, and their sociology and psychology can be obtrusive, jejune, and predictable. They can also easily fall victim to sentimentality. Procedural writers, like other detective writers, often display weak wills, preferring to bend golden age or hard-boiled plots rather than to try to juggle multiple characters and diverse incidents. Only a few procedural writers have the confidence to adhere to the uncompromising realism that captures the police hero at his or her best and worst. Not many readers, I should add, have the stomach for a continued diet of police procedurals. But at its best, the form both plods, shocks, and portrays weak and fallible heroes faced with the very worst which life and society have to offer. The procedural story denies its readers the sophisticated stimulation of the classic detective story as well as the vicarious excitement of the hard-boiled tale. It is not the sort of book to take to the beach. At their best, procedurals can break out of the category of detective fiction and become mainstream literature. But not many of them have this potential. This comes from the manifold lures to compromise which face procedural writers. It also comes from the fact that, from the 1950's onward, the detective story has tended to homogenize itself. Fewer writers aim at pure, classic detective stories, hard-boiled pieces, or procedural novels; rather many writers produce books which at least touch on all of these traditions.

ED MCBAIN

The 87th Precinct

They keep telling me Carella is the hero of the series.

I keep telling them it isn't supposed to be that way. In fact, and hardly anyone will believe this, I actually *killed* Carella in the third book of the series. Not I, personally, but someone named Gonzo who, on page 116 of Permabooks' edition of *The Pusher* (in 1956, the series was published only in paperback), had the audacity to shoot Carella three times in the chest:

> The only warning was the tightening of Gonzo's eyes. Carella saw them squinch up, and he tried to move sideways, but the gun was already speaking. He did not see it buck in the boy's fist. He felt searing pain lash at his chest, and he heard the shocking declaration of three explosions and then he was falling, and he felt very warm, and he also felt very ridiculous because his legs simply would not hold him up, how silly, how very silly, and his chest was on fire, and the sky was tilting to meet the earth. . . . He opened his mouth, but no sound came from it. And then the waves of blackness came at him, and he fought to keep them away, unaware that Gonzo was running off through the trees, aware only of the engulfing blackness, and suddenly sure that he was about to die.

There is no self-respecting mystery writer who would dare write those words—"and suddenly sure that he was about to die"—unless he was using them to foreshadow an event in the pages ahead. Those words almost constituted a contract with the reader; and so (of course) I paid off the marker at the end of the book. At least, at the end of the book as it was delivered to my publishers.

The original scene took place in the hospital where Carella had been on the critical list since the shooting. Lieutenant Byrnes was there to visit him. Teddy Carella was coming down the corridor toward Byrnes.

> At first she was only a small figure at the end of the corridor, and then she walked closer and he watched her. Her hands were wrung together at her waist, and her head was bent, and Byrnes watched her and felt a new dread, a dread that attacked his stomach and his mind. There was defeat in the curve of her body, defeat in the droop of her head.
>
> *Carella,* he thought. *Oh God, Steve, no* . . .
>
> He rushed to her, and she looked up at him, and her face was streaked with tears, and when he saw the tears on the face of Steve Carella's wife, he was suddenly barren inside, barren and cold, and he wanted to break from her and run down the corridor, break from her and escape the pain in her eyes.

Outside the hospital, the church bells tolled.
It was Christmas day, and all was right with the world.
But Steve Carella was dead.

Now, I thought that was pretty classy. The original concept of the series as
I'd outlined it to Herb Alexander, my editor at Pocket Books, was to use a squadroom full of detectives as a conglomerate hero. I would try to portray accurately
the working day of a big-city cop, but I would do so in terms of a handful of
men whose diverse personalities and character traits, when combined, would
form a single hero—the 87th Squad. To my knowledge, this had never been done
before, and I felt it was unique. I felt, further, that the concept would enable
me to bring new men into the squadroom as needed, adding their particular
qualities or defects to the already existing mix, while at the same time dispos-
ing of characters who no longer seemed essential to the mix. The squad was the
hero, and no man on the squad was indispensable or irreplaceable. In real life,
detectives got shot and killed. So, in *The Pusher*, Detective Stephen Louis Carella
got shot, and on Christmas Day he died.

Ha.

The call came almost at once from Herb Alexander. He said, "You're not
serious, are you?"

I said, "About what?"

He said, "You can't kill Carella."

"Why not?" I said.

"He's the hero," Herb said. "He's the star of the series."

(Carella thus far had appeared in only one book, *Cop Hater*, the first book
in the series. In the second book, *The Mugger*, he was off on his honeymoon for
158 of 160 pages, returning to the squadroom only on page 159. But all at once,
he was the hero; he was the star.)

"Who says?" I said. "The concept is . . . "

Herb said, "Yes, I know the concept. But you can't kill Carella. He's the
hero."

We argued back and forth. I finally yielded, and brought Carella back to
life by adding three short paragraphs to the original ending, and by cutting the
last line that would have sent Carella to an early grave. I *still* did not believe he
was the hero. The concept of a conglomerate protagonist was firmly entrenched
in my mind—a splintered hero, if you will, a man of many parts because he was
in actuality many men, the men of the 87th Squad.

Years later, in a conversation about successful television series, Mel Brooks
said to me that the essential ingredients of any hit show were a family and a
house. The family could be doctors, in which case their house was a hospital.
The family could be teachers and students, in which case their house was a
school. The family could be interplanetary travelers, in which case their house

was a spaceship. Well, my family, in my series, was then (and is now) a family of working cops. Their house is the squadroom; their backyard is the precinct territory; their world is the city.

In this family, Lieutenant Peter Byrnes is the father. Detective Meyer Meyer is the patient older brother. Detective Steve Carella is next in succession, perhaps closest in age and temperament to the man who was presented with a double-barreled monicker at birth. Bert Kling is the youngest brother, learning constantly from his more experienced siblings—and by the way, you should have heard the *geschrei* that went up when, in *Lady, Lady, I Did It!* (the fourteenth book in the series), I killed off the girl who'd been Kling's fiancée since the second book in the series. But, damn it, they could try to tell me Steve Carella was the "hero," but they could not convince me Claire Townsend was the "heroine"—so dead she remained (you should pardon the pun), causing all sorts of later character mutations in Kling. Redheaded Cotton Hawes, the detective with the frightening white streak in his hair, is a cousin who came from the provinces (actually another precinct) to become an adopted brother. There are other members of this tight-knit clan—Hal Willis, with the diminutive size of a jockey and the hands of a judo expert; hard-luck Bob O'Brien who keeps getting into deadly shootouts he neither encourages nor desires; Arthur Brown, a huge black cop who fights prejudice in his own steady, unruffled manner; Captain Frick, in charge of the precinct and nominally the squad, the titular head of the family, going a bit senile in his most recent appearance. And, to stretch the metaphor to its outer limits, we can even consider stool pigeons like Danny Gimp or Fats Donner or Gaucho Palacios part of the family, like distant uncles on the outer fringes.

In this family, there is also a black sheep, a bad cop, a lousy cop, a rotten cop necessary to the balance of the squad. His name used to be Roger Havilland. In *Killer's Choice* (the fifth book in the series), in keeping with my concept of cops coming and going, and perhaps because I'd earlier been prevented from killing off Carella and still resented it, I killed off Havilland in a spectacularly satisfying way:

> Havilland knew only that he was flying backwards, off balance. He knew only that he collided with the plate glass window, and that the window shattered around him in a thousand flying fragments of sharp splinters. He felt sudden pain, and he yelled, with something close to tears in his voice, "You bastard! You dirty bastard! You can go and . . . " but that was all he said. He never said another word.
>
> One of the shards of glass had pierced his jugular vein and another had pierced his windpipe, and that was the end of Roger Havilland.

Much to my regret.

A family *has* to have a ne'er-do-well brother or uncle or cousin in it. If there are good cops, there have to be bad cops (as in real life) and they can't be bad cops working in some faraway precinct, they have to be bad cops in your own bailiwick. In a later book (and I can't honestly remember which one), I reincarnated Roger Havilland in the shape and form of Andy Parker. I promise (maybe) that I will never kill Andy Parker. He is too necessary to the mix. Similarly, Fat Ollie Weeks of the 83rd Precinct is another bad cop, a recent addition to the family, without whom the squad could not properly function. I'm not sure whether he'll ever succeed in getting transferred to the Eight-Seven, as he is constantly promising (or rather threatening) to do. He may be more effective where he is, a country cousin who causes the immediate family to wince, or sigh, or both, whenever he puts in an appearance.

That is the family, and this is their house, as described in *Cop Hater* in 1956; the house hasn't changed much over the years, but neither do real-life detective squadrooms:

> Where you were was a narrow, dimly-lighted corridor. There were two doors on the right of the open stairway, and a sign labeled them LOCKERS. If you turned left and walked down the corridor, you passed a wooden slatted bench on your left, a bench without a back on your right (set into a narrow alcove before the sealed doors of what had once been an elevator shaft), a door on your right marked MEN'S LAVATORY, and a door on your left over which a small sign hung, and the sign simply read CLERICAL.
>
> At the end of the corridor was the detective squadroom.
>
> You saw first a slatted rail divider. Beyond that, you saw desks and telephones, and a bulletin board with various photographs and notices on it, and a hanging light globe and beyond that more desks and the grilled windows that opened on the front of the building. You couldn't see very much that went on beyond the railing on your right because two huge metal filing cabinets blocked the desks on that side of the room.

This is where the men of the 87th spend part of their working day. The rest of their day is spent in the city. The city is a character in these books. As any reader of the series already knows (and as any *new* reader is promptly informed at once), the city is imaginary. This has not stopped a great many people from remarking on the fact that it strongly resembles New York City. It does. The similarity may be due to the fact that it *is* New York City—with a liberal dash of geographical license. When I began writing the series (and please remember that I *knew* from go that this was going to be a series, or at least I knew there were going to be three books about these cops because that's how many books were contracted for, the future being in the hands of the gods, who—thank God—smiled), I came to a decision about real cities as opposed to imaginary cities. I had done a lot of research on cops and police departments, and I knew they changed their rules and regulations as often as they changed their underwear—say once a year (come on, guys, you know I'm kidding). I knew that a series needed a familiar sameness to it, not only of character and of place, but also circumscribing the rules within which the hero (my squad) had to work while solving a mystery. (There *are* no mysteries, my cops are fond of repeating;

there are only crimes with motives.) I recognized at once that I could not change my police working procedure each time the cops in New York City changed theirs. Keeping up with the departmental or interdepartmental memos or directives would have been a full-time job that left me no time for writing. So I froze the procedure (except for scientific techniques, which are constantly changing, and which I keep up with and incorporate to the best of my ability) and I made my city imaginary because, Harold, the procedure here in this here city is *this* way, and it never changes, dig? And these are the rules of the game in this city, the same rules for the reader as for the cops. A cop can't search an apartment without a court order, and he can't interrogate a prisoner in custody without first reading off Miranda-Escobedo, and he can't expect the lab (which is run by former Lieutenant, now Captain, Sam Grossman, another member of the family) to come up with the identity of a murderer on the basis of a smudged fingerprint of the left thumb—and neither can the reader. Those are the rules. We play the game fair here. We're sometimes frustrated by this damn city with its complicated bureaucratic machinery and its geographical complexity, but it's there, as imaginary as it may be—and out there are killers.

> Take a look at this city.
> How can you possibly hate her?
> She is all walls, true, she flings up buildings like army stockades designed for protection against an Indian population long since cheated and departed. She hides the sky. She blocks her rivers from view. (Never perhaps in the history of mankind has a city so neglected the beauty of her waterways or treated them so casually. Were her rivers lovers, they would surely be unfaithful.) She forces you to catch glimpses of her in quick takes, through chinks in long canyons, here a wedge of water, there a slice of sky, never a panoramic view, always walls enclosing, constricting, yet how can you hate her, this flirtatious bitch with smoky hair?
> There are half a dozen *real* cities in this world, and this is one of them, and it's impossible to hate her when she comes to you with a suppressed female giggle about to burst on her silly face, bubbling up from some secret adolescent well to erupt in merriment on her unpredictable mouth. (If you can't personalize a city, you have never lived in one. If you can't get romantic and sentimental about her, you're a foreigner still learning the language. Try Philadelphia, you'll love it there.) To know a real city, you've got to hold her close, or not at all. You've got to breathe her.

That's from *Let's Hear It for the Deaf Man*, published in 1973. (The Deaf Man is my Moriarty, but also a member of the family, so to speak. Without him, the cops in my precinct would never be made to look like fools, and all families must appear foolish at times.) But take a look again at the city paragraphs above. Somebody there is talking about this "imaginary" city as if it were "real." Who is that person talking? Is it Carella? Is it Kling? Is it Meyer or Hawes? I'm glad you asked that question. It is the voice of another character in the series.

The character is omnipresent, like the characters that are the city and the weather. The character has no right to be there at all, because every writing instructor in the world will tell you author-intrusion is the cardinal sin. That character is Ed McBain. He likes to put his two cents in. I sometimes feel he is speaking for the reader as well as himself.

So how can anyone possibly say Carella is the hero of this series when there are so many other characters that go into its realization? Nobody can. But I'll tell you something. Sometimes, when somebody yells at me, or when I've had the oil burner repaired unsuccessfully twelve times, or when I've had to write six letters trying to get a change of address on a credit card, I find myself wondering what Carella would do in such a situation.

Does that make him a hero?

STORIES

FREEMAN WILLS CROFTS
1879–1957

Considered the father of the British police procedural, Freeman Wills Crofts was born in Dublin, Ireland. He was educated at Methodist and Campbell Colleges in Belfast, majoring in civil engineering. His early career was as a chief assistant engineer on the Belfast and Northern Counties Railway. He began writing as a way to entertain himself during a serious illness and that resulted in *The Cask* (1920), his first mystery. *The Cask*, which was immensely popular, and Agatha Christie's *The Mysterious Affair At Styles* (1920) launched the "Golden Age" of the British detective story. He then moved to England, became a full-time writer, and published a mystery novel almost every year, 30 of them featuring Inspector French of Scotland Yard. He was elected a Fellow of the Royal Society of Arts in 1939.

Inspector Joseph French, a C.I.D. detective for Scotland Yard, is an easygoing, amiable man who likes good food and dislikes official office routines. But he is also a determined investigator who specializes in deconstructing "unbreakable alibis." In more than 30 years on the force he never failed to solve a case. French's cases often involved complicated plots, intricate timetables, extensive travel to other countries, and precise, almost mathematical alibis. Crofts introduced the slow process of British police procedure and crime scene technology. His works emphasized the pure art of detection. "The Hunt Ball" appeared first in *The American Mercury*, 1943.

Recommended Crofts works: *Sir John Magill's Last Journey, The 12:30 from Croyden, Golden Ashes*.

Other recommended authors: Michael Innes, H. R. F. Keating, Patricia Moyes.

The Hunt Ball

Howard Skeffington had reached the end of his tether. He sat, hunched forward and staring unseeingly into the fire, as he faced the terrible conclusion to which inexorably he was being impelled: that his only escape from ruin lay in the death of his former friend, Justin Holt.

He, Howard Skeffington, must murder Holt! If he didn't, this pleasant life he was living, this fortune which seemed almost within his grasp, would be irretrievably lost. He would have to leave the country and everything he valued and look somewhere abroad for a job. And what sort of job could he get?

To a certain extent Skeffington was an adventurer. Possessed of a good appearance, charming manners and an admirable seat on a horse, he had made friends at Cambridge with some of the young men from this Seldon Sorby country, this center of the hunting life in England. At their homes he had spent vacations, riding their horses with skill, if not distinction. Alone in the world and not drawn to any career which involved hard work, he had conceived the idea of settling down at Seldon Sorby, and if possible marrying money.

The first part of this scheme he had carried out successfully. He had taken rooms in the district and been accepted as a member of the hunt. He had joined an associated and very select club and his social prospects seemed flourishing.

But he was up against one difficulty—money. His capital, he had estimated, would last him for four years, and on these four years he had staked his all. If before the end of that period he was unable to bring off the second part of his program, he would be finished: down and out.

His chances in this respect, however, he considered rosy. Elaine Goff-Powell, Sir Richard Goff-Powell's only daughter, would have enough for any husband. Moreover, he was sure she admired him, and he had made himself very agreeable to her father. Elaine was neither a beauty nor a wit: in fact, in moments of depression he realized she was, as he put it, damned plain and damned dull, too. But this gave him all the more hope. It wiped out the most dangerous of his potential competitors. As yet he had not risked a proposal, but he felt the time would soon be ripe and he had little fear of the result.

Unhappily, while the affair was moving, it was not moving quickly enough. Unless an engagement could be achieved soon, his resources would not stand the strain. Another five or six hundred would undoubtedly enable him to pull it off. As it was, the thing would be touch and go.

He had done what he could to borrow, but with indifferent success. Professional money-lenders would not touch him. Friends who might with luck be good for a tenner certainly would not stretch to anything more: and it would take a good many tenners to be of use to Skeffington.

In this difficulty he had embarked on a course which normally he would have avoided like the plague. He had taken to cheating at cards. He realized very fully the risk he ran, but he did not see that any other way was open to him.

For some weeks he had managed successfully, and he had determined to put his fortunes to the test at the Christmas Hunt Ball, which was to take place in a few days. With reasonable luck he would be accepted, and then this dreadfully wearing period of his life would be over.

But now, five days before the ball, disaster had overtaken him. His cheating had been discovered.

And yet not wholly discovered. What happened was this.

During a game at the club one of the men, this Justin Holt, suddenly ceased playing. His face took on an expression of agony, and after swaying about for a moment, his head pitched forward on the table, the cards dropping from his nerveless fingers. The others jumped to their feet, but before they could do anything Holt raised himself. He was covered with confusion and apologized profusely. He had, he explained, got a severe pain and giddiness. It had come so suddenly that for the moment it had bowled him over, but already it was better. Infinitely he regretted breaking up the party, but with the others' consent he would go home and lie down. When they wanted to help he hesitated, then asked Skeffington, who lived in his direction, if he would mind seeing him to his quarters.

The affair puzzled Skeffington, who had never before seen such a seizure. But for him the mystery was soon cleared up. When they were alone Holt suddenly found himself able to walk normally and the expression of pain vanished from his face.

He remained, however, looking extremely worried. "I did that little bit of play-acting for a reason, Skeffington," he said. "The truth is, I saw what you were doing. I've been suspicious for some time, and so, I may tell you, have been a number of the others. But tonight I watched you, and I saw the whole thing. Skeffington, you're finished at Seldon Sorby."

To Skeffington it sounded like a sentence of death, but he quickly pulled himself together. Staring at Holt as coolly as he could, he said: "Perhaps you'll kindly explain what you're talking about?"

Holt shook his head irritably. "Don't be a complete fool," he begged. "I tell you I saw it. There's no use in your pretending. I know."

"You can't know anything," Skeffington returned doggedly. "If you had seen anything at that table, you'd have said so at the time. You didn't."

"I didn't," Holt explained, "for an obvious reason. I have some thought for the hunt, if you haven't. I didn't want to make a scandal. If we had been by ourselves I would have spoken. But with outsiders present naturally I didn't."

"Very thoughtful," Skeffington sneered. "It hasn't occurred to you that your consideration has rendered your story useless? Even if you had seen anything, which I deny, you can't prove it."

"I can tell what I saw."

"That's not proof. I shall deny it and then where will you be? You will have made a libelous statement which you can't prove. I think, my dear Holt, you, and not I, will be the one to retire."

Again Holt shook his head. "That sounds all right, Skeffington, but you know as well as I do that I would be believed. You know, or you ought to, that several of the men suspect you as it is. If I describe what I saw you do, they will believe me."

"You just try it on," Skeffington said as contemptuously as he could. "It doesn't matter what anybody believes or doesn't believe privately. You can prove nothing, and you'll be the one who will suffer."

"That may be," Holt admitted, "but I'll tell you what I shall do. I'll give you three days to think it over. If by then you have sent in your resignation from the hunt, I will never refer to the matter again. If you have not resigned, I shall tell the committee. You do what you like."

Though Skeffington had attempted a mild bluff, he knew that Holt had the whip hand. It was true what the man said: he would be believed rather than Skeffington. Holt's transparent honesty was universally recognized, whereas Skeffington was aware that his own reputation was by no means too secure. His phenomenal luck had been remarked on jokingly—or was it jokingly?—by several members, and the somewhat spectacular wins which had produced these remarks would be remembered—if Holt told what he had seen.

Skeffington rapidly considered the matter. He must somehow get Holt to keep his silence. There must be no scandal, for scandal would mean complete ruin. The least breath and all chance of marrying Elaine Goff-Powell would be at an end. Indeed, if he didn't pull off an engagement at the ball next Tuesday, this last hope would be gone. He could not propose again for some weeks, and his money would not stretch to that.

But what could he do to restrain Holt? Nothing! Holt was one of those men who believed in doing what they considered was their duty. No, he could not hope to influence Holt.

Then first occurred to Skeffington the terrible idea that there was a way in which he could silence his enemy. One way, and only one.

Skeffington felt that he was at the most dreadful crisis of his life. To give up his present position, and practically penniless, to begin looking for a job—for which he had no training—would mean destitution, misery and death. And he could look forward to nothing else—if Holt were to live. But could he face the alternative; if Holt were to die? . . . Drops of sweat formed on his forehead.

He realized of course that his future did not depend solely on Holt. If Elaine turned him down he would equally be ruined. Therefore if Elaine turned him down there was no need to consider Holt any more. He was down and out in any case.

But if Elaine accepted him? Then Holt's actions would become vital. In this case . . .

All Skeffington's instincts were now prompting him to gain time. At all costs he must close Holt's mouth till after the ball. Then he, Skeffington, would either disappear and go under, or he would somehow deal with Holt. He turned to the man and spoke quietly and with more hesitation.

"Don't be in a hurry, Holt. I must think this over. Without admitting anything, I see you can do me a lot of harm. You have given me an ultimatum: resign or take the consequences. I want you to compromise."

"Compromise?" Holt was shocked. "How can I compromise on a thing of that sort? Why, it's fundamental You're not a fool, Skeffington: you must see that."

Skeffington shrugged. "I suppose you're right," he admitted presently. "Well, I'll tell you. I'll agree to your conditions provided you give me six days instead of three to make my arrangements. And what's more: during these six days I promise not to enter the card room. At the end of the six days, if I haven't resigned, you can go to the committee. Hang it all, Holt, that's not too much to ask. I must fix up some reason for the resignation. I'll have an uncle die in America and leave me money, or something of that kind. Then I'll go abroad and that will be the end of me so far as you're concerned."

Holt hesitated.

"Look here," went on Skeffington, "I'll not ask six days. Give me till the ball. We'll meet there and I'll let you have every satisfaction."

"But damn it, Skeffington, you mustn't come to the ball."

This was what Skeffington had feared. He shrugged, then turned away. "Oh well," he said coldly, "if you're going to be unreasonable I withdraw my offer. You tell the committee now, and when I am approached I shall deny everything and ask for your proof. And if you don't give it I shall press for your expulsion, and if you don't leave I shall start proceedings against you for defamation of character. A worse scandal, that, than my going to the ball!" He paused, then continued in a pleasanter tone. "But I don't want to do that. If you will wait till the ball it'll give me a chance to explain my departure. That's all I ask." He suddenly changed his tone. "I'm not attempting any extenuation, Holt, but try and imagine the ruin this means for me. It's not like you to kick a man when he's down."

There had been some further argument and Skeffington had triumphed. Holt had agreed to say nothing provided that at or before the ball Skeffington resigned.

Left alone, Skeffington hardened his heart and began to work out the solution of his terrible problem. First, if Elaine refused him. By borrowing from his friends and selling some of his stuff he could raise, he thought, a couple of hundred pounds. He had better do this at once and buy tickets to the Argentine, where he thought his knowledge of horses might stand him in good stead. No doubt before leaving he could borrow a little more. Enough to get past the immigration laws at all events. It would be hell after what he was accustomed to: but it would be at least a chance for life.

But if Elaine accepted him?

Then he was set up for life with all the money he could want: his future absolutely assured—if only Holt were dealt with.

Skeffington took care to speak to various members of the committee and others to whom Holt might have told his story, and in every case he was satisfied from their manner that they had heard nothing. Holt therefore was the only danger. If he were silenced, Skeffington would be safe.

For three days Skeffington thought over the problem and then at last he saw how the man might be eliminated, and with absolute secrecy. Admittedly there would be a little risk at one point, but that point once passed, no further hitch could arise. Carefully Skeffington made his preparations. He avoided the club on the excuse of private business and kept rigorously out of Holt's way.

At last the fateful night arrived, a dark and bitter evening with the ground like iron and a frosty fog in the air. The Christmas Hunt Ball was *the* social event of the year, when the local four hundred thronged the Seldon Sorby Town Hall and everyone who was anyone felt he must be present. The somewhat drab building was transformed out of all recognition with bunting and greenery, and the hunt colors made the gathering what the local paper invariably called a spectacle of sparkling brilliance.

The first two essentials of Skeffington's plan were to drive some people to the ball and to park his car in a secluded place near the back entrance of the hall. The former he managed by inviting a young married couple called Hatherley and a bachelor friend named Scarlett to accompany him, the second by a careful timing of his arrival, coupled with his knowledge of how the park filled. The market at the back of the hall was used as a park, and there he succeeded in placing the car in the corner he desired. He knew that before long it would be completely surrounded and that no one was likely to remain near it.

In the car, hooked up under the dash, was a heavy spanner round which he had wrapped a soft cloth. It was so fixed that he could lift it out by simply opening the door and putting in his hand.

He had taken just enough whisky to steady his nerves, and in spite of the terrible deed which was in front of him, he felt confident and in his best form.

To his delight Elaine had greeted him with more than her usual warmth. For half the evening he had danced exclusively with her, and now he led her to a deserted corner and with trepidation put the vital question. A thrill of overwhelming satisfaction shot through him when he heard the answer. Elaine would marry him, and further would agree to the engagement being announced at once.

But that thrill was accompanied by a pang of something not far removed from actual horror. To preserve what he had won he must now pass through the most hideous ten minutes of his life. Now also he realized that here would be more danger in the affair than he had anticipated. However, there was no alternative. The thing must be faced.

When he judged the time propitious—when the chauffeurs were at supper—he told Elaine that he wished to ask her father's blessing on the engagement. She suggested accompanying him, and he had to use all his tact to prevent her. However, by assuring her that he could speak more movingly of her goodness and charm if she were not present, he was able to leave her dancing with Scarlett.

Instead of seeking out Sir Richard Goff-Powell, Skeffington found Holt. Waiting till he had handed on his partner, he passed him, and without stopping, murmured: "Come to the cloak room. I've something to show you."

Skeffington hung about the passages till Holt hove in sight. "I've decided to resign," he said in a low voice, "but I've got a strange letter which I wish to show you. We can't talk here in private. Come out to my car and let me explain what has arisen."

Holt was unwilling, but Skeffington persuaded him by the argument that if they were seen discussing confidential matters, it might connect him with the resignation.

Skeffington passed out to the park, followed by his victim. Though the tops of the cars were faintly illuminated by distant lights, the spaces between them were dark as pitch. As they walked Skeffington removed his immaculate gloves, fearing tell-tale stains or even smears of blood. He was satisfied that they reached the car unobserved.

"Here's the letter," he said, opening the forward door and taking a paper from a cubby-hole. "My inside light has failed, but the letter's very short and you can read it by the side light. I'll switch it on. Then we can get in out of the cold and discuss it."

Holt, grumbling about being brought out of the warm hall, moved forward to the front of the wing to bring the paper to the lamp. In doing so he momentarily turned his back to Skeffington.

To produce this movement had been Skeffington's aim. Instead of switching on the light, his fingers grasped the spanner, and as Holt made that slight turn he brought the heavy tool down with all his force on the man's head. Holt dropped like a log.

With a tiny pocket torch Skeffington glanced at his victim's head. It was all right. There was no blood, but there was deformation of the bone. There could be no doubt that Holt was dead.

Hastily Skeffington completed his program. Opening the rear door of his car, he tried to lift the body in. This he found more difficult than he had expected. He had to leave it sitting on the floor propped up against the seat and go to the other side of the car and draw it in after him, returning to lift in the feet, one by one. He left it on the floor covered with a rug, then hastened back to the hall. This time also he was sure he was unobserved. A wash, a brush and a stiff glass of whisky, and he was once more in the ballroom.

He would have given anything to have slipped off to his rooms, but he daren't do so. Instead he found Sir Richard, and taking his courage in both hands, he went up to him.

"I have something to tell you, sir," he began, "and I most sincerely hope you will be pleased. Elaine has done me the honor to say she will marry me," and he expatiated on his news.

Sir Richard did not appear particularly pleased, but neither did he raise any objection. He shrugged and said the matter was one for Elaine. As soon as Skeffington could, he returned to the young woman.

How he endured to the end of the proceedings Skeffington scarcely knew. But at long last Elaine departed with her family and he went in search of his friends.

"I'll bring the car to the steps," he told the Hatherleys, then adding to Scarlett: "You might come and help me if you don't mind. It's a job to get out of such a jam."

Reaching the car, Skeffington opened the near forward door for Scarlett, then went round to the driver's side and got in himself. He thus had a witness of all his proceedings, while Scarlett had not seen the body.

As Skeffington pulled in to the steps a commissionaire opened the rear door for Mrs. Hatherley. He lifted away the rug, then swore hoarsely while Mrs. Hatherley gave a shrill scream.

What happened then seemed a confused muddle to Skeffington. He got out and tried to edge round to the door through the dense crowd which had instantly formed.

"What is it?" he heard himself shouting. "What's wrong?"

He heard murmurs all about him. "A man!" "Seems to be dead!" "There in the back of the car!"—then an authoritative voice which he recognized as that of the Chief Constable of the county: "Keep back everyone, please, and let Dr. Hackett pass. Doctor, will you please have a look here."

Everyone but Skeffington and Scarlett moved back. For a moment time seemed to stand still, then the doctor said slowly: "It's Holt and I'm afraid he's dead. A blow on the head. Must have been instantaneous."

Time began to move once more, in fact it now raced so quickly that Skeffington could hardly keep up with it.

As if by magic police appeared. The guests were politely herded back into the ballrooms. Skeffington was asked by a sharp-looking young inspector if he could give any explanation of the affair, and when he replied that he could not, he was told not so politely to wait where he was for a further interrogation.

The whole place buzzed as if a swarm of colossal bees had invaded it. Then gradually people began to leave, their names and addresses taken and a few questions put and answered. At long last the police returned to Skeffington.

He had taken a little more whisky, enough to subdue his fear and steady his hands, but not enough to make him stupid.

"Will you tell me what you know of this affair, Mr. Skeffington?" asked the local superintendent, who had now arrived and taken charge of the proceedings.

Skeffington replied without hesitation. He had driven Mr. and Mrs. Hatherley and Mr. Scarlett to the ball. He had parked in the corner of the market. All had then got out and gone into the hall. When Mrs. Hatherley was ready to go home he and Scarlett had gone for the car. He had driven it to the steps and when the rear door had been opened the body had been found. The affair was just as great a mystery to him as to the super.

It was a simple story and Skeffington told it well. Superintendent Redfern asked many questions, but he could not in any way shake the tale, and at last he thanked Skeffington and said that would be all.

Rather shakily Skeffington drove home.

During the next couple of days events moved quickly at police headquarters at Seldon Sorby. The place had been shaken to the core. Such a murder, taking place at the most fashionable event in the town's year, and involving the death of a relative of Lord Bonniton, the master of the most famous hunt in the country, seemed almost a national disaster. The Chief Constable was frantic and without delay had wired to Scotland Yard for help. A couple of hours later Chief Inspector French and Sergeant Carter had arrived to assist in the inquiry. French had heard all that had been done, had studied the various statements made, and had examined the Town Hall and market. As he had not thereupon laid his hand on the guilty party, the Chief Constable had asked querulous and suggestive questions.

"Silly fool," French grumbled to Carter that night at their hotel. "Does he think we're thought readers? If he was in all that hurry, why didn't he do the job himself?"

Later that evening French sat smoking over the lounge fire and imbibing cup after cup of strong coffee, as he puzzled his brains in the attempt to find some line of investigation which would give him his solution. He had put in train all the obvious inquiries: about Holt's career and recent activities, who had seen him at the ball, who had been in the market while the cars were parked, and such like, but he wanted to find some short-cut, some royal road almost, to the criminal. Sir Mortimer Ellison, the Assistant Commissioner at the Yard, had given him a hint before he started. "It's a society place," he had said, "and the big bugs are society people. You'll find them touchy down there because this case will get them on the raw. Hence the quicker you pull it off, the better for all concerned." And now he had been down for two days and he was no further on than when he arrived.

For three hours he considered the matter and then a point struck him, a very simple point. It might not lead to anything, but, on the other hand, it might. The following day he would try a reconstruction.

Accordingly next morning he demanded a man of the approximate build of the deceased and a car like Skeffington's. These he took to a secluded corner of the police yard.

The dummy was a young constable named Arthurs. He grinned when French explained that he wanted to smash in his head.

"Right, sir," he agreed. "I hope you'll remember the wife and kiddies when I'm gone."

"No one, I'm afraid, will know how it was done," French assured him. "Now, Arthurs, just where you're standing I hit you a bat on the head and stove in your skull. See?"

"Yes, sir."

"Well, go ahead. You don't want me to do it in reality, I suppose?"

"I'm afraid, sir, if my skull . . . "

French jerked round. "Good heavens, man, use your brains! Collapse!"

With a sudden look of comprehension Arthurs sank quietly on to the ground beside the car, while French adjured him to relax completely.

"Now, Carter, lift him into the position the dead man occupied."

Carter opened the rear door, and lifting the grinning Arthurs beneath the arms, tried to get him into the car. But, like Skeffington, he found he couldn't do it from where he was standing. He also had to go round to the other side and draw him in.

"Can't you pull in the legs?" French prompted.

Carter tried. "No, sir," he returned, "I'll have to go back and lift them in."

French watched him, a smile of satisfaction playing on his lips. "I rather thought that might happen," he declared. "Come along to the mortuary." He looked into the car. "Thank you, Arthurs, we've done with you. You made a good corpse."

On reaching the room where Holt's clothes lay, French took out his powdering apparatus and dusted the deceased's patent leather shoes. Several fingerprints showed up. French blew away the surplus, then photographed the prints.

"Now the deceased's fingers," he went on.

Soon the ten impressions were taken and photographed in their turn. A proper comparison would require enlargements and detailed observation, but a certain amount could be learned from mere casual inspection. French quickly satisfied himself. Most of the prints belonged to the deceased himself, but certain others were not his. From their position they might well have been caused by lifting the feet into a car.

Two hours later the club started a new waiter in the bar. Gradually a row of used glasses accumulated, each neatly labeled with name of the drinker. At intervals French tested and compared the fingerprints. Suddenly the affair clicked. Skeffington had lifted Holt's shoes.

The correct line of investigation was now indicated. Judicious inquiries brought to light Skeffington's financial position and mysterious luck at cards, Holt's strange illness, and the fact that Holt had asked Skeffington to accompany him to his rooms. The fact of the latter's engagement also became known. Here, French saw, was the motive.

"He thought putting the corpse in his own car would absolve him from suspicion, but the prints on the shoes are proof positive that he did it," he concluded to the Chief Constable. "We're ready for an arrest, I think?"

"Tonight," nodded the Chief Constable.

GEORGES SIMENON
1903–1989

Creator of the French police procedural mystery, Georges Joseph Christian Simenon was born in Liege, Belgium. Desiring to be a writer from an early age, he found work as a bookstore clerk and as a journalist covering the police beat to enhance his reading and writing. His first novel, *Au Pont Des Arches* (1920), published when he was 17, was written in ten days. Immigrating to France, he began a serious writing career in Paris which became very lucrative, even allowing him to buy a yacht, on which he cruised and wrote. In 1931 he published *The Death of Monsieur Gallet*, the novel that introduced French policeman Detective Jules Maigret, who in the 75 novels and 28 short stories of the "Maigret saga," rises to the rank of Commissioner. Simenon wrote the first 18 Maigret novels at the rate of one a month, and returned periodically throughout his writing career to create the others in the series. In Europe Maigret was often compared to Sherlock Holmes in popularity. Both a BBC television series and several movies featured the Maigret character.

Perhaps part of Maigret's appeal is that he is an unconventional policeman who challenges the image of the police detective. He is congenial and compassionate. A tall and heavyset man, he is well-dressed, likes to go home for lunch with his wife, enjoys movies, and finds smoking a pipe soothing. He prides himself on his intuitions about the crimes he investigates, and leaves basic police procedures to his younger investigative team of officers, Inspectors Lucas, Janvier, Lapointe, and Torrence. For Maigret the important thing is to capture the emotional atmosphere, the place, and the people where the crime occurred. By constant questions and infinite patience, he solves the case. He is a bourgeois policeman dealing with commonplace misdeeds that never fail to be psychologically compelling. "Inspector Maigret Deduces" was first presented in English in *The Short Cases of Inspector Maigret* (1959).

Recommended Simenon works: *The Crossroad Murders, A Battle of Nerves, The Strange Case of Peter The Lett.*

Other recommended authors: Bartholomew Gill, Arthur Upfield, Janwillem Van de Wetering.

Inspector Maigret Deduces

Dimly through A deep sleep Maigret heard a ringing sound, but he was not aware that it was the telephone bell and that his wife was leaning over him to answer.

"It's Paulie," she said, shaking her husband. "He wants to speak to you."

"You, Paulie?" Maigret growled, half awake.

"Is that you, Nunk?" came from the other end of the wire.

It was three in the morning. The bed was warm but the windowpanes were covered with frost flowers, for it was freezing outside. It was freezing even harder up at Jeumont, from where Paulie was telephoning.

"What's that you say? . . . Wait—I'll take the names . . . Otto . . . Yes, spell it, it's safer."

Madame Maigret, watching her husband, had only one question in her mind: whether he would have to get up or not. And, of course, he did, grumbling away. "Something very odd has happened," he explained, "over at Jeumont, and Paulie's taken it on himself to detain an entire railway car."

Paulie was Maigret's nephew, Paul Vinchon, and he was a police inspector at the Belgian frontier.

"Where are you going?" Madame Maigret asked.

"First to Headquarters to get some information. Then I'll probably hop on the first train."

When anything happens it is always on the 106—a train that leaves Berlin at 11:00 A.M. with one or two cars from Warsaw, reaches Liége at 11:44 P.M., when the station is empty—it closes as soon as the train leaves—and finally gets to Erquelinnes at 1:57 in the morning.

That evening the car steps had been white with frost, and slippery. At Erquelinnes the Belgian customs officials, who had virtually nothing to do as the train was on its way out, passed down the corridors, looking into a compartment here and there, before hurrying back to the warmth of the station stove.

By 2:14 the train got under way again to cross the frontier, and reached Jeumont at 2:17.

"Jeumont!" came the cry of a porter running along the platform with a lamp. "Fifty-one minutes' wait!"

In most of the compartments the passengers were still asleep, the lights were dimmed and the curtains drawn.

"Second- and third-class passengers off the train for customs," echoed down the train.

And Inspector Paul Vinchon stood frowning at the number of curtains that were drawn back and at the number of lights turned up. He went up to the conductor. "Why are there so many traveling first-class today?"

"Some international convention of dentists that starts in Paris tomorrow. We have at least twenty-five of them as well as the ordinary passengers."

Vinchon walked into the car at the head of the train, opened the doors one after the other, growling out mechanically, "Have your passports ready, please."

Wherever the passengers had not wakened and the light was still dimmed, he turned it up; faces rose out of the shadows, swollen with fatigue.

Five minutes later, on his way back up the corridor, he passed the customs men who were going through the first-class compartments, clearing the passengers into the corridor, while they examined the seats and searched every cranny.

"Passports, identity cards . . . "

He was in one of the red-upholstered German carriages. Usually these compartments held only four passengers, but because of the invasion of dentists this one had six.

Paulie threw an admiring glance at the pretty woman with the Austrian passport in the left corner seat by the corridor. The others he hardly looked at until he reached the far side of the compartment, where a man, covered with a thick rug, still had not moved.

"Passport," he said, touching him on the shoulder.

The other passengers were beginning to open their suitcases for the customs officials, who were now arriving. Vinchon shook his sleeping traveler harder; the man slid over on his side. A moment later Vinchon saw he was dead.

The scene was chaotic. The compartment was too narrow for all the people who crowded in, and when a stretcher was brought in, there was some difficulty in placing the extremely heavy body on it.

"Take him to the first-aid post," Inspector Vinchon ordered. A little later, he found a German doctor on the train.

At the same time he put a customs official on guard over the compartment. The young Austrian woman was the only one who wanted to leave the train to get some fresh air. When she was stopped, she gave a contemptuous shrug.

"Can you tell me what he died of?" Vinchon asked.

The doctor seemed puzzled; in the end, with Vinchon's help, he undressed the dead man. Even then there was no immediate sign of a wound; it took a full minute before the German pointed out, on the fleshy chest, a mark that could hardly be seen. "Someone stuck a needle in his heart," he said.

The train had still twelve or thirteen minutes before leaving again. The special Inspector was absent. Vinchon, feverish with excitement, had to make a snap decision: he ran to the stationmaster and gave orders for the murder car to be uncoupled.

The passengers were not sure what was happening. Those in the adjoining compartments protested when they were told that the car was staying at Jeumont and that they would have to find seats elsewhere. Those who had been traveling with the dead man protested even more when Vinchon told them he was obliged to keep them there till the next day.

However, there was nothing else for it, seeing that there was a murderer among them. All the same, once the train had left, one car and six passengers short, Vinchon began to feel weak at the knees, and rang up his uncle, the famous Inspector Maigret.

At a quarter to four in the morning Maigret was at the Quai des Orfèvres; only a few lights were burning and he asked a sergeant on duty to make him some coffee. By four o'clock, with his office already clouded with pipe smoke, he had Berlin on the line, and was dictating to a German colleague the names and addresses his nephew had given him.

Afterward he asked for Vienna, as one of the passengers in the compartment came from there, and then he wrote out a telegram for Warsaw, for there had also been a lady from Vilna by the name of Irvitch.

Meanwhile, in his office at the station at Jeumont, Paul Vinchon was taking a firm line with his five suspects, whose reactions varied according to their temperaments. At least there was a good fire on—one of those large station stoves that swallows up bucket after bucket of coal. Vinchon had chairs brought in from the neighboring offices, and good old administrative seats they were, too, with turned legs and shabby velvet upholstery.

"I assure you I am doing everything possible to speed things up, but in the circumstances I must detain you here."

He had not a minute to lose if he wanted to draw up anything like a suitable report for the morning. The passports were on his desk. The body of Otto Braun—the victim's name, according to the passport found in his pocket—was still at the first-aid post.

"I can, if you like, get you something to drink. But you will have to make up your minds quickly—the buffet is about to close."

At ten past four Vinchon was disturbed by a ring on the telephone. "Hello? Aulnoye? What's that? Of course. There's probably some connection, yes. Well, send him over by the first train. And the packet, too, of course."

Vinchon went into an adjoining office to put through another call to Maigret unheard.

"Is that you, Nunk? Something else, this time. A few minutes ago, as the train was drawing into the station at Aulnoye, a man was seen getting out from under a car. There was a bit of a chase, but they managed to get him in the end. He was carrying a waxed-paper packet of bearer bonds, mostly oil securities, for quite an amount. The man give his name as Jef Bebelmans, native of Antwerp, and his profession as an acrobat . . . Yes . . . They're bringing him over on the first train. You'll be on that one, too? . . . No? . . . At 10:20? Thanks, Nunk."

And he returned to his flock of sheep and goats, which is the way he thought of them . . .

When day broke, the frosty light made it seem even colder than the night before. Passengers for a local train started to arrive, and Vinchon worked on, deaf to the protests of the detained passengers, who eventually subsided, overwhelmed with fatigue.

No time was lost. This was essential, for it was the kind of business that could bring diplomatic complications. One could not go on indefinitely holding five travelers of different nationalities, all with their papers in order, just because a man had been killed in their railway compartment.

Maigret arrived at 10:20, as he had said he would. At 11:00, on a siding where the death car had been shunted, the reconstruction of the crime took place.

It was a little ghostly, with the gray light, the cold, and the general weariness. Twice a nervous laugh rang out, indicating that one of the lady passengers had helped herself too freely to the drinks to warm herself.

"First of all put the dead man back in his seat," Maigret ordered. "I suppose the curtains on the outside window were drawn?"

"Nothing's been touched," said his nephew.

Of course, it would have been better to wait until night, until the exact time of the affair. But as that was impossible—

Otto Braun, according to his passport, was fifty-eight, born at Bremen, and formerly a banker at Stuttgart. He certainly looked the part, neatly dressed, with his comfortable, heavy build and close-cropped hair.

The information that had just arrived from Berlin stated: *Had to stop his financial activities after the National Socialist revolution, but gave an undertaking of loyalty to the Government, and has never been disturbed. Said to be very rich. Contributed one million marks to party funds.*

In one of his pockets Maigret found a hotel bill from the Kaiserhof, in Berlin, where Otto Braun had stayed three days on his way from Stuttgart.

Meanwhile, the five passengers were standing in the corridor, watching, some dismally and others angrily, the comings and goings of Inspector Maigret. Pointing to the luggage rack above Braun, Maigret asked, "Are those his suitcases?"

"They're mine," came the sharp voice of Lena Leinbach, the Austrian.

"Will you please take the seat you had last night?"

She did so reluctantly, and her unsteady movements betrayed the effects of the drinks. She was beautifully dressed, and wore a mink coat, and a ring on every finger.

The report on her that was telegraphed from Vienna said: *Courtesan of the luxury class, who has had numerous affaires in the capitals of Central Europe, but has never come to the attention of the police. Was for a long time the mistress of a German prince.*

"Which of you got on at Berlin?" Maigret asked.

"If you will allow me," someone said in excellent French. And, in fact, it turned out to be a Frenchman, Adolphe Bonvoisin, from Lille.

"I can perhaps be of some help to you as I was on the train from Warsaw. There were two of us. I myself came from Lvov, where my firm—a textile concern—has a Polish subsidiary. Madame boarded the train at Warsaw at the same time as I did." He indicated a middle-aged woman in an astrakhan coat, dark and heavily built, with swollen legs.

"Madame Irvitch of Vilna?"

As she spoke no French, the interview was conducted in German. Madame Irvitch, the wife of a wholesale furrier, was coming to Paris to consult a specialist, and she wished to lodge a protest—

"Sit down in the place you were occupying last night."

Two passengers remained—two men.

"Name?" Maigret asked the first, a tall, thin, distinguished-looking man with an officer's bearing.

"Thomas Hauke, of Hamburg."

On Hauke, Berlin had had plenty to say: *Sentenced in 1924 to two years' imprisonment for dealing in stolen jewelry . . . closely watched since . . . frequents the pleasure spots of various European capitals . . . suspected of engaging in cocaine and morphine smuggling.*

Finally, the last one, a man of thirty-five, bespectacled, shaven-headed, severe. "Dr. Gellhorn," he said, "from Brussels."

A silly misunderstanding then arose. Maigret asked him why, when his fellow passenger was discovered unconscious, he had done nothing about it.

"Because I'm not a doctor of medicine. I'm an archeologist."

By now the compartment was occupied as it had been the previous night:

Otto Braun	Adolphe Bonvoisin	Madame Irvitch
Thomas Hauke	Dr. Gellhorn	Lena Leinbach

Naturally, except for Otto Braun, henceforth incapable of giving evidence one way or another, each one protested entire innocence. And each one claimed to know nothing.

Maigret had already spent a quarter of an hour in another room with Jef Bebelmans, the acrobat from Antwerp who had appeared from under a car at Aulnoye carrying more than two million in bearer bonds. At first, when confronted with the corpse, Bebelmans had betrayed no emotion, merely asking, "Who is it?"

Then he had been found to be in possession of a third-class ticket from Berlin to Paris, although that had not prevented him from spending part of the journey hiding under a car, no doubt to avoid declaring his bonds at the frontier.

Bebelmans, however, was not a talkative fellow. His one observation revealed a touch of humor: "It's your business to ask questions. Unfortunately, I have absolutely nothing to tell you."

The information on him was not too helpful, either: *Formerly an acrobat, he has since been a night-club waiter in Heidelberg, and later in Berlin.*

"Well, now," Maigret began, puffing away at his pipe, "you, Bonvoisin, and Madame Irvitch were already in the train at Warsaw. Who got in at Berlin?"

"Madame was first," Bonvoisin said, indicating Lena Leinbach.

"And your suitcases, madame?"

She pointed to the rack above the dead man, where there were three luxurious crocodile bags, each in a fawn cover.

"So you put your luggage over this seat and sat down in the other corner, diagonally opposite."

"The dead man—I mean, that gentleman—came in next." Bonvoisin asked nothing better than to go on talking.

"Without luggage?"

"All he had with him was a traveling rug."

This was the cue for a consultation between Maigret and his nephew. Quickly they made another inventory of the dead man's wallet, in which a luggage slip was found. As the heavy baggage had by then reached Paris, Maigret sent telephone instructions that these pieces should be opened at once.

"Good! Now, this gentleman—" He indicated Hauke.

"He got in at Cologne."

"Is that right, Monsieur Hauke?"

"To be precise, I changed compartments at Cologne. I was in a non-smoker."

Dr. Gellhorn, too, had got on at Cologne. While Maigret, hands in pockets, was putting his questions, muttering away to himself, watching each of them in turn, Paul Vinchon, like a good secretary, was taking notes at a rapid rate:

Bonvoisin: Until the German frontier, no one seemed to know anyone else, except for Madame Irvitch and myself. After the customs we all settled down to sleep as best we could, and the light was dimmed. At Liége I saw the lady opposite (Lena Leinbach) try to go out into the corridor. Immediately the gentleman in the other corner (Otto Braun) got up and asked her in German what she was doing. "I want a breath of air," she said. And I'm sure I heard him say, "Stay where you are."

Later in his statement Bonvoisin returned to this point:

At Namur she tried once more to get out of the train, but Otto Braun, who seemed to be asleep, suddenly moved, and she stayed where she was. At Charleron they spoke to each other again, but I was falling asleep and have only a hazy recollection.

So, somewhere between Charleroi and Jeumont, in that hour and a half or so, one of the passengers must have made the fatal move, must have approached Otto Braun and plunged a needle into his heart.

Only Bonvoisin would not have needed to get up. He had only to move slightly to the right to reach the German. Hauke's position, directly opposite the victim, was the next best, then Dr. Gellhorn's and finally the two women's.

Despite the cold, Maigret's forehead was bathed with sweat. Lena Leinbach watched him furiously, while Madame Irvitch complained of rheumatism and consoled herself by talking Polish to Bonvoisin.

Thomas Hauke was the most dignified of them all, and the most aloof, while Gellhorn claimed that he was missing an important appointment at the Louvre.

In Vinchon's notes the following dialogue appears:

Maigret, to Lena: Where were you living in Berlin?

Lena: I was only there for a week. I was staying as usual at the Kaiserhof.

M: Did you know Otto Braun?

L: No. I may have run across him in the hall or the lift.

M: Why, then, after the German frontier did he start talking to you as if he knew you?

L: (dryly) Perhaps because he grew bolder away from home.

M: *Was that why he forbade you to get off the train at Liége and Namur?*
L: *He merely said I'd catch cold.*

The questioning was still going on when there was a telephone call from Paris. Otto Braun's luggage—there were eight pieces—contained a great amount of clothing, and so much linen and personal stuff that one might have assumed the banker was going off on a long trip, if not forever. But no money—only four hundred marks in a wallet.

As for the other passengers: Lena Leinbach was carrying 500 French francs, 50 marks, 30 crowns; Dr. Gellhorn, 700 marks; Thomas Hauke, 40 marks and 20 French francs; Madame Irvitch, 30 marks, 100 francs, and letters of credit on a Polish bank in Paris; Bonvoisin, 12 zloty, 10 marks, 5000 francs.

They still had to search the hand luggage that was in the compartment. Hauke's bag held only one change of clothes, a dinner jacket, and some underwear. In Bonvoisin's there were two marked decks of cards.

But the real find came in Lena Leinbach's suitcases in which, under the crystal-and-gold bottles, the fragile lingerie, and the gowns, there were beautifully contrived false bottoms.

But the false bottoms were empty. When questioned, all Lena Leinbach said was, "I bought these from a lady who went in for smuggling. They were a great bargain. *I've* never used them for anything like that."

Who had killed Otto Braun in the bluish half light of the compartment between Charleroi and Jeumont?

Paris was beginning to get worried. Maigret was summoned to the telephone. This business was going to cause a stir, and there would be complications. The numbers of the bonds found on Jef Bebelmans had been transmitted to the lending banks, and everything was in order—there was no record of any large theft of bonds.

It was eleven o'clock when they had started this laborious reconstruction in the railway car. It was two o'clock before they got out, and then only because Madame Irvitch fainted after declaring in Polish she could no longer bear the smell of the corpse.

Vinchon was pale, for it seemed to him that his uncle was not showing his usual composure—that he was, in fact, dithering.

"It's not going well, Nunk?" he said in a low voice as they were crossing the tracks.

Maigret's only response was to sigh, "I wish I could find the needle. Hold them all another hour."

"But Madame Irvitch is ill!"

"What's that to do with me?"

"Dr. Gellhorn claims—"

"Let him," Maigret cut him short.

And he went off to lunch on his own at the station bar.

"Be quiet, I tell you!" Maigret snapped, an hour later. His nephew lowered his head. "All you do is bring me trouble. I'm going to tell you my conclusions. After that, I warn you, you can get yourself out of this mess, and if you don't, you needn't bother to ring up your nunk. Nunk's had enough."

Then, changing his tone, he went on, "Now! I've been looking for the one logical explanation of all the facts. It's up to you to prove it, or to obtain a confession. Try to follow me.

"First, Otto Braun, with all his wealth, would not have come to France with eight suitcases and goodness knows how many suits—and, on the other hand, with precisely four hundred marks.

"Second, there must have been some reason for him to pretend during the German part of the journey not to know Lena Leinbach, and then as soon as they were over the Belgian border for them to be on familiar terms.

"Third, he refused to let her get out of the train at Liége, at Namur, and at Charleroi.

"Fourth, in spite of that she made several desperate attempts to get out.

"Fifth, a certain Jef Bebelmans, a passenger from Berlin who had never seen Braun—or he would have shown some sign on seeing the corpse—was found carrying more than two million in bonds."

And, still in a very bad temper, Maigret rumbled on, "Now I'll explain. Otto Braun, for reasons of his own, wanted to smuggle his fortune, or part of it, out of Germany. Knowing that his luggage would be minutely searched, he came to an agreement with a demimondaine in Berlin, and had doublebottomed suitcases made for her, knowing that they would stand less chance of being closely examined, being full of feminine articles.

"But Lena Leinbach, like all self-respecting members of her calling, has one real love: Thomas Hauke. Hauke, who is a specialist in this line, arranged with Lena in Berlin—perhaps even in the Kaiserhof—to make off with the bonds hidden in her suitcases.

"She gets on the train first, and puts the cases where Braun, still suspicious, has told her to put them. She sits down in the opposite corner, for they are not supposed to know each other.

"At Cologne, Hauke, to keep an eye on things, comes to take his place in the compartment. Meanwhile, another accomplice, Jef Bebelmans, probably a professional burglar, is traveling third-class with the bonds, and at each frontier he has orders to hide for a while underneath the car.

"Once the Belgian frontier is crossed, Otto Braun obviously runs no further risk. He could at any moment take it into his head to open his companion's suitcases and remove his bonds. That is why, first at Liége, then at Namur, and again at Charleroi, Lena Leinbach tries to get off the train.

"Is Braun mistrustful? Does he suspect something? Or is he just in love with her? Whichever it is, he watches Lena closely, and she begins to panic, for in Paris he will inevitably discover the theft, the empty false bottoms.

"He may even notice it at the French frontier where, having no further reason to hide the bonds, he may want to open the suitcases. Thomas Hauke, too, must be aware of the danger of discovery—"

"And it's he who kills Braun?" Vinchon asked.

"I'm certain it is not. If Hauke had got up to do that, one or another of his traveling companions would have noticed. In my opinion Braun was killed when you went past the first time, calling, 'Have your passports ready, please.'

"At that moment everyone got up, in the dark, still half asleep. Only Lena Leinbach had a reason to go over to Braun, press close to him to take down her suitcases, and I am convinced that it was at that moment—"

"But the needle?"

"Look for it!" Maigret grunted. "A long brooch pin will do. If this woman had not happened on someone like you, who insisted on undressing the corpse, for a long time it would have seemed to be a death from natural causes.

"Now draw up your plan. Make Lena think Bebelmans has talked, make Bebelmans think Hauke has been broken—all the old dodges, eh?"

And he went off to have a beer while Vinchon did what his uncle had told him. Old dodges are good dodges because they work. In this case they worked because Lena Leinbach was wearing a long arrow-shaped pin of brilliants in her hat, and because Paulie, as Madame Maigret called him, pointing at it, said to her, "You can't deny it. There's blood on the pin!"

It wasn't true. But, for all that, she had a fit of hysterics and made a full confession.

ED MCBAIN

1926–

Creator of the most famous American police procedural series, the 87th Precinct, Ed McBain, the pseudonym for Evan Hunter, was born in New York. He graduated from Hunter College in 1950 with an English degree, and held various jobs as a high school teacher, a jazz band pianist, and an executive assistant to a literary agent who helped him get his first story published. Since then Hunter has written under the names Curt Cannon, Ezra Hannon, Hunt Collins, and Richard Marsten as well as his own legally adopted name, Evan Hunter (his birth name was Salvatore Lombino). Known as the author of *The Blackboard Jungle* (1954) and the screenwriter for Alfred Hitchcock's *The Birds* (1963), McBain is most famous for his two detective series, one featuring Matthew Hope and the other the 87th Precinct. These two series have sold over one hundred million copies worldwide. He received the Grand Master Award from the Mystery Writers of America in 1986, and was the first non-

British writer to win the Crime Writer's Association's Diamond Dagger Award in 1998, the most prestigious detective fiction award in Great Britain.

McBain is known as "the father of the American police procedural," which features the detectives of the 87th precinct in the fictional city of Isola, clearly New York. His focus is on the squad of detectives with the main detective varying from book to book. Homicide detective Steve Carella is most often featured, but the other members of the team, Meyer Meyer, Bert Kling, Cotton Hawes, Andy Parker, Arthur Brown, and Eileen Burke, are the main investigators in other books in the series. McBain's novels are noted for the accuracy of knowledge about police procedure in particular and the lives of police in general. McBain's police have few illusions about stopping crime or even keeping it under control. They do their job as skillfully as possible, murder after murder, knowing they will solve some, leave many unsolved, and too often see the murderer go free because of the legal system. It is their appreciation for the absurd, their sense of responsibility to the city's citizens, and their dedication as police officers that keep them on the job. This series which began with *Cop Hater* (1956) has now reached its 53rd novel with *The Frumptious Bandersnatch* (2004). "Sadie When She Died," an excellent 87th Precinct short story, first appeared in *Alfred Hitchcock's Mystery Magazine* in 1972.

Recommended McBain works: *Give the Boys a Great Big Hand, Let's Hear It for the Deaf Man, Eight Black Horses*.

Other recommended authors: Stephen Booth, James McClure, William Marshall.

Sadie When She Died

"I'm very glad she's dead," the man said.

He wore a homburg, muffler, overcoat, and gloves. He stood near the night table, a tall man with a narrow face, and a well-groomed grey moustache that matched the greying hair at his temples. His eyes were clear and blue and distinctly free of pain or grief.

Detective Steve Carella wasn't sure he had heard the man correctly. "Sir," Carella said, "I'm sure I don't have to tell you—"

"That's right," the man said, "you don't have to tell me. It happens. I'm a criminal lawyer and am well aware of my rights. My wife was no good, and I'm delighted someone killed her."

Carella opened his pad. This was not what a bereaved husband was supposed to say when his wife lay disemboweled on the bedroom floor in a pool of her own blood.

"Your name is Gerald Fletcher."

"That's correct."

"Your wife's name, Mr. Fletcher?"

"Sarah. Sarah Fletcher."

"Want to tell me what happened?"

"I got home about fifteen minutes ago. I called to my wife from the front door, and got no answer. I came into the bedroom and found her dead on the floor. I immediately called the police."

"Was the room in this condition when you came in?"

"It was."

"Touch anything?"

"Nothing. I haven't moved from this spot since I placed the call."

"Anybody in here when you came in?"

"Not a soul. Except my wife, of course."

"Is that your suitcase in the entrance hallway?"

"It is. I was on the Coast for three days. An associate of mine needed advice on a brief he was preparing. What's your name?"

"Carella. Detective Steve Carella."

"I'll remember that."

While the police photographer was doing his macabre little jig around the body to make sure the lady looked good in the rushes, or as good as any lady *can* look in her condition, a laboratory assistant named Marshall Davies was in the kitchen of the apartment, waiting for the medical examiner to pronounce the lady dead, at which time Davies would go into the bedroom and with delicate care remove the knife protruding from the blood and slime of the lady, in an attempt to salvage some good latent prints from the handle of the murder weapon.

Davies was a new technician, but an observant one, and he noticed that the kitchen window was wide open, not exactly usual on a December night when the temperature outside hovered at twelve degrees. Leaning over the sink, he further noticed that the window opened onto a fire escape on the rear of the building. He could not resist speculating that perhaps someone had climbed up the fire escape and then into the kitchen.

Since there was a big muddy footprint in the kitchen sink, another one on the floor near the sink, and several others fading as they traveled across the waxed kitchen floor to the living room, Davies surmised that he was onto something hot. Wasn't it possible that an intruder *had* climbed over the window sill, into the sink, and walked across the room, bearing the switchblade knife that had later been pulled viciously across the lady's abdomen from left to right? If the M.E. ever got through with the damn body, the boys of the 87th would be halfway home, thanks to Marshall Davies. He felt pretty good.

The three points of the triangle were Detective-Lieutenant Byrnes, and Detectives Meyer Meyer and Steve Carella. Fletcher sat in a chair, still wearing homburg, muffler, overcoat, and gloves as if he expected to be called outdoors at any moment. The interrogation was being conducted in a windowless cubicle labeled Interrogation Room.

The cops standing in their loose triangle around Gerald Fletcher were amazed but not too terribly amused by his brutal frankness.

"I hated her guts," he said.

"Mr. Fletcher," Lieutenant Byrnes said, "I *still* feel I must warn you that a woman has been murdered—"

"Yes. My dear, wonderful wife," Fletcher said sarcastically.

" . . . which is a serious crime . . . " Byrnes felt tongue-tied in Fletcher's presence. Bullet-headed, hair turning from iron-grey to ice-white, blue-eyed, built like a compact linebacker, Byrnes looked to his colleagues for support. Both Meyer and Carella were watching their shoelaces.

"You have warned me repeatedly," Fletcher said. "I can't imagine why. My wife is dead—someone killed her—but it was not I."

"Well, it's nice to have your assurance of that, Mr. Fletcher, but this alone doesn't necessarily still our doubts," Carella said, hearing the words and wondering where the hell they were coming from. He was, he realized, trying to impress Fletcher. He continued, "How do we know it *wasn't* you who stabbed her?"

"To begin with," Fletcher said, "there were signs of forcible entry in the kitchen and hasty departure in the bedroom, witness the wide-open window in the aforementioned room and the shattered window in the latter. The drawers in the dining-room sideboard were open—"

"You're very observant," Meyer said suddenly. "Did you notice all this in the four minutes it took you to enter the apartment and call the police?"

"It's my *job* to be observant," Fletcher said. "But to answer your question, no. I noticed all this *after* I had spoken to Detective Carella here."

Wearily, Byrnes dismissed Fletcher, who then left the room.

"What do you think?" Byrnes said.

"I think he did it," Carella said.

"Even with all those signs of a burglary?"

"*Especially* with those signs. He could have come home, found his wife stabbed—but not fatally—and finished her off by yanking the knife across her belly. Fletcher had four minutes, when all he needed was maybe four seconds."

"It's possible," Meyer said.

"Or maybe I just don't like the guy," Carella said.

"Let's see what the lab comes up with." Byrnes said.

The laboratory came up with good fingerprints on the kitchen window sash and on the silver drawer of the dining-room sideboard. There were good prints on some of the pieces of silver scattered on the floor near the smashed bedroom window. Most important, there were good prints on the handle of the switchblade knife. The prints matched; they had all been left by the same person.

Gerald Fletcher graciously allowed the police to take *his* fingerprints, which were then compared with those Marshall Davies had sent over from the police laboratory. The fingerprints on the window sash, the drawer, the silverware, and the knife did not match Gerald Fletcher's.

Which didn't mean a damn thing if he had been wearing his gloves when he'd finished her off.

On Monday morning, in the second-floor rear apartment of 721 Silvermine Oval, a chalked outline on the bedroom floor was the only evidence that a woman had lain there in death the night before. Carella sidestepped the outline and looked out the shattered window at the narrow alleyway below. There was a distance of perhaps twelve feet between this building and the one across from it.

Conceivably, the intruder could have leaped across the shaftway, but this would have required premeditation and calculation. The more probable likelihood was that the intruder had fallen to the pavement below.

"That's quite a long drop," Detective Bert Kling said, peering over Carella's shoulder.

"How far do you figure?" Carella asked.

"Thirty feet. At least."

"Got to break a leg taking a fall like that. You think he went through the window headfirst?"

"How else?"

"He might have broken the glass out first, then gone through," Carella suggested.

"If he was about to go to all that trouble, why didn't he just *open* the damn thing?"

"Well, let's take a look," Carella said.

They examined the latch and the sash. Kling grabbed both handles on the window frame and pulled up on them. "Stuck."

"Probably painted shut," Carella said.

"Maybe he did try to open it. Maybe he smashed it only when he realized it was stuck."

"Yeah," Carella said. "And in a big hurry, too. Fletcher was opening the front door, maybe already in the apartment by then."

"The guy probably had a bag or something with him, to put the loot in. He must have taken a wild swing with the bag when he realized the window was stuck, and maybe some of the stuff fell out, which would explain the silverware on the floor. Then he probably climbed through the hole and dropped down feet first. In fact, what he could've done, Steve, was drop the bag down first, and *then* climbed out and hung from the still before he jumped, to make it a shorter distance."

"I don't know if he had all that much time, Bert. He must have heard that front door opening, and Fletcher coming in and calling to his wife. Otherwise, he'd have taken his good, sweet time and gone out the kitchen window and down the fire escape, the way he'd come in."

Kling nodded reflectively. "Let's take a look at that alley," Carella said.

In the alleyway outside, Carella and Kling studied the concrete pavement, and then looked up at the shattered second-floor window of the Fletcher apartment.

"Where do you suppose he'd have landed?" Kling said.

"Right about where we're standing." Carella looked at the ground. "I don't know, Bert. A guy drops twenty feet to a concrete pavement, doesn't break anything, gets up, dusts himself off, and runs the fifty-yard dash, right?" Carella shook his head. "My guess is he stayed right where he was to catch his breath, giving Fletcher time to look out the window, which would be the natural thing to do, but which Fletcher didn't."

"He was anxious to call the police."

"I still think be did it."

"Steve, be reasonable. If a guy's fingerprints are on the handle of a knife, and the knife is still in the victim—"

"*And* if the victim's husband realizes what a sweet setup he's stumbled into, wife lying on the floor with a knife in her, place broken into and burglarized, why *not* finish the job and hope the burglar will be blamed?"

"Sure," Kling said, "Prove it."

"I can't," Carella said. "Not until we catch the burglar."

While Carella and Kling went through the tedious routine of retracing the burglar's footsteps, Marshall Davies called the 87th Precinct and got Detective Meyer.

"I think I've got some fairly interesting information about the suspect," Davies said. "He left latent fingerprints all over the apartment and footprints in the kitchen. A very good one in the sink, when he climbed in through the window, and some middling-fair ones tracking across the kitchen floor to the dining room. I got some excellent pictures and some good blowups of the heel."

"Good," Meyer said.

"But more important," Davies went on, "I got a good walking picture from the footprints on the floor. If a man is walking slowly, the distance between his footprints is usually about twenty-seven inches. Forty for running, thirty-five for fast walking. These were thirty-two inches. So we have a man's usual gait, moving quickly, but not in a desperate hurry, with the walking line normal and not broken."

"What does that mean?"

"Well, a walking line should normally run along the inner edge of a man's heelprints. Incidentally, the size and type of shoe and angle of the foot clearly indicate that this *was* a man."

"O.K., fine," Meyer said. He did not thus far consider Davies' information valuable nor even terribly important.

"Anyway, none of this is valuable nor even terribly important," Davies said, "until we consider the rest of the data. The bedroom window was smashed, and the Homicide men were speculating that the suspect had jumped through the window into the alley below. I went down to get some meaningful pictures, and got some pictures of where he must have landed—on both feet, incidentally—and I got another walking picture and direction line. He moved toward the basement door and into the basement. But the important thing is that our man is injured, and I think badly."

"How do you know?" Meyer asked.

"The walking picture downstairs is entirely different from the one in the kitchen. When he got downstairs he was leaning heavily on the left leg and dragging the right. I would suggest that whoever's handling the case put out a physicians' bulletin. If this guy hasn't got a broken leg, I'll eat the pictures I took."

A girl in a green coat was waiting in the apartment lobby when Carella and Kling came back in, still retracing footsteps, or trying to. The girl said, "Excuse me, are you the detectives?"

"Yes," Carella said.

"The super told me you were in the building," the girl said, "You're investigating the Fletcher murder, aren't you?" She was quite soft-spoken.

"How can we help you, miss?" Carella asked.

"I saw somebody in the basement last night, with blood on his clothes."

Carella glanced at Kling and immediately said, "What time was this?"

"About a quarter to eleven," the girl said.

"What were you doing in the basement?"

The girl looked surprised.

"That's where the washing machines are. I'm sorry, my name is Selma Bernstein. I live here in the building."

"Tell us what happened, will you?" Carella said.

"I was sitting by the machine, watching the clothes tumble, which is simply *fascinating*, you know, when the door leading to the back yard opened—the door to the alley. This man came down the stairs, and I don't even think he saw me. He went straight for the stairs at the other end, the ones that go up into the street. I never saw him before last night."

"Can you describe him?" Carella asked.

"Sure. He was about twenty-one or twenty-two, your height and weight, well, maybe a little bit shorter, five ten or eleven, brown hair."

Kling was already writing. The man was white, wore dark trousers, high-topped sneakers, and a poplin jacket with blood on the right sleeve and on the front. He carried a small red bag, "like one of those bags the airlines give you."

Selma didn't know if he had any scars. "He went by in pretty much of a hurry, considering he was dragging his right leg. I think he was hurt pretty badly."

What they had in mind, of course, was identification from a mug shot, but the I.S. reported that none of the fingerprints in their file matched the ones found in the apartment. So the detectives figured it was going to be a tough one, and they sent out a bulletin to all of the city's doctors just to prove it.

Just to prove that cops can be as wrong as anyone else, it turned out to be a nice easy one after all.

The call came from a physician in Riverhead at 4:37 that afternoon, just as Carella was ready to go home.

"This is Dr. Mendelsohn," he said. "I have your bulletin here, and I want to report treating a man early this morning who fits your description—a Ralph Corwin of 894 Woodside in Riverhead. He had a bad ankle sprain."

"Thank you, Dr. Mendelsohn," Carella said.

Carella pulled the Riverhead directory from the top drawer of his desk and quickly flipped to the C's. He did not expect to find a listing for Ralph Corwin. A man would have to be a rank amateur to burglarize an apartment without wearing gloves, then stab a woman to death, and then give his name when seeking treatment for an injury sustained in escaping from the murder apartment.

Ralph Corwin was apparently a rank amateur. His name was in the phone book, and he'd given the doctor his correct address.

Carella and Kling kicked in the door without warning, fanning into the room, guns drawn. The man on the bed was wearing only undershorts. His right ankle was taped.

"Are you Ralph Corwin?" Carella asked.

"Yes," the man said. His face was drawn, the eyes in pain.

"Get dressed, Corwin. We want to ask you some questions."

"There's nothing to ask," he said and turned his head into the pillow. "I killed her."

Ralph Corwin made his confession in the presence of two detectives of the 87th, a police stenographer, an assistant district attorney, and a lawyer appointed by the Legal Aid Society.

Corwin was the burglar. He'd entered 721 Silvermine Oval on Sunday night, December twelfth, down the steps from the street where the garbage cans were. He went through the basement, up the steps at the other end, into the back yard, and climbed the fire escape, all at about ten o'clock in the evening.

Corwin entered the Fletcher apartment because it was the first one he saw without lights. He figured there was nobody home. The kitchen window was open a tiny crack; Corwin squeezed his fingers under the bottom and opened it all the way. He was pretty desperate at the time because he was a junkie in need of cash. He swore that he'd never done anything like this before.

The man from the D.A.'s office was conducting the Q. and A. and asked Corwin if he hadn't been afraid of fingerprints, not wearing gloves. Corwin figured that was done only in the movies, and anyway, he said, he didn't own gloves.

Corwin used a tiny flashlight to guide him as he stepped into the sink and down to the floor. He made his way to the dining room, emptied the drawer of silverware into his airline bag. Then he looked for the bedroom, scouting for watches and rings, whatever he could take in the way of jewelry. "I'm not a pro," he said. "I was just hung up real bad and needed some bread to tide me over."

Now came the important part. The D.A.'s assistant asked Corwin what happened in the bedroom.

A.   There was a lady in bed. This was only like close to ten-thirty, you don't expect nobody to be asleep so early.

Q.   But there was a woman in bed.

A.   Yeah. She turned on the light the minute I stepped in the room.

Q.   What did you do?

A.   I had a knife in my pocket. I pulled it out to scare her. It was almost comical. She looks at me and says, "What are you doing here?"

Q.   Did you say anything to her?

A.   I told her to keep quiet, that I wasn't going to hurt her. But she got out of bed and I saw she was reaching for the phone. That's got to be crazy, right? A guy is standing there in your bedroom with a knife in his hand, so she reaches for the phone.

Q.   What did you do?

A.   I grabbed her hand before she could get it. I pulled her off the bed, away from the phone, you know? And I told her again that nobody was going to hurt her, that I was getting out of there right away, to just please calm down.

Q.   What happened next?

A.   She started to scream. I told her to stop. I was beginning to panic. I mean she was really yelling.

Q.   Did she stop?

A.   No.

Q.   What did you do?

A.   I stabbed her.

Q.   Where did you stab her?

A.   I don't know. It was a reflex. She was yelling, I was afraid the whole building would come down. I just . . . I just stuck the knife in her. I was very scared. I stabbed her in the belly. Someplace in the belly.

Q.   How many times did you stab her?

A.   Once. She . . . she backed away from me. I'll never forget the look on her face. And she . . . she fell on the floor.

Q.   Would you look at this photograph, please?

A.   Oh, no . . .

Q.   Is that the woman you stabbed?

A.   Oh, no . . . I didn't think . . . Oh, no!

A moment after he stabbed Sarah Fletcher, Corwin heard the door opening and someone coming in. The man yelled, "Sarah, it's me. I'm home." Corwin ran past Sarah's body on the floor, and tried to open the window, but it was stuck. He smashed it with his airline bag, threw the bag out first to save the swag because, no matter what, he knew he'd need another fix, and he climbed through the broken window, cutting his hand on a piece of glass. He hung from the sill, and finally let go, dropping to the ground. He tried to get up, and fell down again. His ankle was killing him, his hand bleeding. He stayed in the alley nearly fifteen minutes, then finally escaped via the route Selma Bernstein had described to Carella and Kling. He took the train to Riverhead and got to Dr. Mendelsohn at about nine in the morning. He read of Sarah Fletcher's murder in the newspaper on the way back from the doctor.

On Tuesday, December 14, which was the first of Carella's two days off that week, he received a call at home from Gerald Fletcher. Fletcher told the puzzled Carella that he'd gotten his number from a friend in the D.A.'s office, complimented Carella and the boys of the 87th on their snappy detective work, and invited Carella to lunch at the Golden Lion at one o'clock. Carella wasn't happy about interrupting his Christmas shopping, but this was an unusual opportunity, and he accepted.

Most policemen in the city for which Carella worked did not eat very often in restaurants like the Golden Lion. Carella had never been inside. A look at the menu posted on the window outside would have frightened him out of six months' pay. The place was a faithful replica of the dining room of an English coach house, circa 1627: huge oaken beams, immaculate white cloths, heavy silver.

Gerald Fletcher's table was in a secluded corner of the restaurant. He rose as Carella approached, extended his hand, and said, "Glad you could make it. Sit down, won't you?"

Carella shook Fletcher's hand, and then sat. He felt extremely uncomfortable, but he couldn't tell whether his discomfort was caused by the room or by the man with whom he was dining.

"Would you care for a drink?" Fletcher asked.

"Well, are you having one?" Carella asked.

"Yes, I am."

"I'll have a Scotch and soda," Carella said. He was not used to drinking at lunch.

Fletcher signaled the waiter and ordered the drinks, making his another whiskey sour.

When the drinks came, Fletcher raised his glass. "Here's to a conviction," he said.

Carella lifted his own glass. "I don't expect there'll be any trouble," he said. "It looks airtight to me."

Both men drank. Fletcher dabbed his lips with a napkin and said, "You never can tell these days. I hope you're right, though." He sipped at the drink. "I must admit I feel a certain amount of sympathy for him."

"Do you?"

"Yes. If he's an addict, he's automatically entitled to pity. And when one considers that the woman he murdered was nothing but a—"

"Mr. Fletcher . . ."

"Gerry, please. And I know: it isn't very kind of me to malign the dead. I'm afraid you didn't know my wife, though, Mr. Carella. May I call you Steve?"

"Sure."

"My enmity might be a bit more understandable if you had. Still, I shall take your advice. She's dead, and no longer capable of hurting me, so why be bitter. Shall we order, Steve?"

Fletcher suggested that Carella try either the trout *au meuniere* or the beef and kidney pie, both of which were excellent. Carella ordered prime ribs, medium rare, and a mug of beer.

As the men ate and talked, something began happening, or at least Carella *thought* something was happening; he might never be quite sure. The conversation with Fletcher seemed on the surface to be routine chatter, but rushing through this inane, polite discussion was an undercurrent that caused excitement, fear, and apprehension. As they spoke, Carella knew with renewed certainty that Gerald Fletcher had killed his wife. Without ever being told so, he knew it. *This* was why Fletcher had called this morning; *this* was why Fletcher had invited him to lunch; *this* was why he prattled on endlessly while every contradictory move of his body signaled on an almost extrasensory level that he *knew* Carella suspected him of murder, and was here to *tell* Carella (*without* telling him) that, "Yes, you stupid cop, I killed my wife. However much the evidence may point to another man, however many confessions you get, I killed her and I'm glad I killed her. And there isn't a damn thing you can do about it."

Ralph Corwin was being held before trial in the city's oldest prison, known to law enforcers and lawbreakers alike as Calcutta. Neither Corwin's lawyer nor the district attorney's office felt that allowing Carella to talk to the prisoner would be harmful to the case.

Corwin was expecting him. "What did you want to see me about?"

"I wanted to ask you some questions."

"My lawyer says I'm not supposed to add anything to what I already said. I don't even *like* that guy."

"Why don't you ask for another lawyer? Ask one of the officers here to call the Legal Aid Society. Or simply tell him. I'm sure he'd have no objection to dropping out."

Corwin shrugged. "I don't want to hurt his feelings. He's a little cockroach, but what the hell."

"You've got a lot at stake here, Corwin."

"But I killed her, so what does it matter *who* the lawyer is? You got it all in black and white."

"You feel like answering some questions?" Carella said.

"I feel like dropping dead, is what I feel like. Cold turkey's never good, and it's worse when you can't yell."

"If you'd rather I came back another time . . . "

"No, no, go ahead. What do you want to know?"

"I want to know exactly how you stabbed Sarah Fletcher."

"How do you *think* you stab somebody? You stick a knife in her."

"Where?"

"In the belly."

"Left-hand side of the body?"

"Yeah. I guess so."

"Where was the knife when she fell?"

"I don't know what you mean."

"Was the knife on the *right*-hand side of her body or the *left*?"

"I don't know. That was when I heard the front door opening and all I could think of was getting out of there."

"When you stabbed her, did she *twist* away from you?"

"No, she backed away, straight back, as if she couldn't believe what I done, and . . . and just wanted to get *away* from me."

"And then she fell?"

"Yes. She . . . her knees sort of gave way and she grabbed for her belly, and her hands sort of of—it was terrible—they just . . . they were grabbing *air*, you know? And she fell."

"In what position?"

"On her side."

"*Which* side?"

"I could still see the knife, so it must've been the opposite side. The side opposite from where I stabbed her."

"One last question, Ralph. Was she dead when you went through that window?"

"I don't know. She was bleeding and . . . she was very quiet. I . . . guess she was dead. I don't know. I guess so."

Among Sarah Fletcher's personal effects that were considered of interest to the police before they arrested Ralph Corwin, was an address book found in the dead woman's handbag on the bedroom dresser. In the Thursday afternoon stillness of the squad room, Carella examined the book.

There was nothing terribly fascinating about the alphabetical listings. Sarah Fletcher had possessed a good handwriting, and most of the listings were obviously married couples (Chuck and Nancy Benton, Harold and Marie Spander, and so on), some were girlfriends, local merchants, hairdresser, dentist, doctors, restaurants in town or across the river. A thoroughly uninspiring address book—until Carella came to a page at the end of the book, with the printed word MEMORANDA at its top.

Under the word, there were five names, addresses and telephone numbers written in Sarah's meticulous hand. They were all men's names, obviously entered at different times because some were in pencil and others in ink. The parenthetical initials following each entry were all noted in felt marking pens of various colors:

Andrew Hart, 1120 Hall Avenue, 622-8400 (PB&G) (TG)

Michael Thornton, 371 South Lindner, 881-9371 (TS)

Lou Kantor, 434 North 16 Street, FR 7-2346 (TPC) (TG)

Sal Decotto, 831 Grover Avenue, FR 5-3287 (F) (TG)

Richard Fenner, 110 Henderson, 593-6648 (QR) (TG)

If there was one thing Carella loved, it was a code. He loved a code almost as much as he loved German measles. He flipped through the phone book and the address for Andrew Hart matched the one in Sarah's handwriting. He found an address for Michael Thornton. It, too, was identical to the one in her book. He kept turning pages in the directory, checking names and addresses. He verified all five.

At a little past eight the next morning, Carella got going on them. He called Andrew Hart at the number listed in Sarah's address book. Hart answered, and was not happy. "I'm in the middle of shaving," he said. "I've got to leave for the office in a little while. What's this about?"

"We're investigating a homicide, Mr. Hart."

"A *what*? A homicide? Who's been killed?"

"A woman named Sarah Fletcher."

"I don't know anyone named Sarah Fletcher," he said.

"She seems to have known you, Mr. Hart."

"Sarah *who*? Fletcher, did you say?" Hart's annoyance increased.

"That's right."

"I don't know anybody by that name. Who says she knew me? I never heard of her in my life."

"Your name's in her address book."

"My name? That's impossible."

Nevertheless, Hart agreed to see Carella and Meyer Meyer at the office of Hart and Widderman, 480 Reed Street, sixth floor, at ten o'clock that morning.

At ten, Meyer and Carella parked the car and went into the building at 480 Reed, and up the elevator to the sixth floor. Hart and Widderman manufactured watchbands. A huge advertising display near the receptionist's desk in the lobby proudly proclaimed "H&W Beats the Band!" and then backed the slogan with more discreet copy that explained how Hart and Widderman had solved the difficult engineering problems of the expansion watch bracelet.

"Mr. Hart, please," Carella said.

"Who's calling?" the receptionist asked. She sounded as if she were chewing gum, even though she was not.

"Detectives Carella and Meyer."

"Just a minute, please," she said, and lifted her phone, pushing a button in the base. "Mr. Hart," she said, "there are some cops here to see you." She listened for a moment and then said, "Yes, sir." She replaced the receiver on its cradle, gestured toward the inside corridor with a nod of her golden tresses, said, "Go right in, please. Door at the end of the hall," and then went back to her magazine.

The grey skies had apparently infected Andrew Hart. "You didn't have to broadcast to the world that the police department was here," he said immediately.

"We merely announced ourselves," Carella said.

"Well, O.K., now you're here," Hart said, "let's get it over with." He was a big man in his middle fifties, with iron-grey hair and black-rimmed eyeglasses. "I told you I don't know Sarah Fletcher and I don't."

"Here's her book, Mr. Hart," Carella said. "That's your name, isn't it?"

"Yeah," Hart said, and shook his head. "But how it got there is beyond me."

"Is it possible she's someone you met at a party, someone you exchanged numbers with?"

"No."

"Are you married, Mr. Hart?"

"No."

"We've got a picture of Mrs. Fletcher. I wonder—"

"Don't go showing me any pictures of a corpse," Hart said.

"This was taken when she was still very much alive, Mr. Hart."

Meyer handed Carella a manila envelope. He opened the flap and removed from the envelope a framed picture of Sarah Fletcher which he handed to Hart. Hart looked at the photograph, and then immediately looked up at Carella.

"What is this?" he said. He looked at the photograph again, shook his head, and said, "Somebody killed her, huh?"

"Yes, somebody did," Carella answered. "Did you know her?"

"I knew her."

"I thought you said you didn't."

"I didn't know Sarah Fletcher, if that's who you think she was. But I knew *this* broad, all right."

"Who'd *you* think she was?" Meyer asked.

"Just who she told me she was. Sadie Collins. She introduced herself as Sadie Collins, and that's who I knew her as. Sadie Collins."

"Where was this, Mr. Hart? Where'd you meet her?"

"A singles bar. The city's full of them."

"Would you remember when?"

"At least a year ago."

"Ever go out with her?"

"I used to see her once or twice a week."

"When did you stop seeing her?"

"Last summer."

"Did you know she was married?"

"Who, Sadie? You're kidding."

"She never told you she was married?"

"Never."

Meyer asked, "When you were going out, where'd you pick her up? At her apartment?"

"No. She used to come to my place."

"Where'd you call her when you wanted to reach her?"

"I didn't. She used to call me."

"Where'd you go, Mr. Hart? When you went out?"

"We didn't go out too much."

"What *did* you do?"

"She used to come to my place. The truth is, we never went out. She didn't want to go out much."

"Didn't you think that was strange?"

"No," Hart shrugged. "I figured she liked to stay home."

"Why'd you stop seeing her, Mr. Hart?"

"I met somebody else. A nice girl. I'm very serious about her."

"Was there something wrong with Sadie?"

"No, no. She was a beautiful woman, beautiful."

"Then why would you be ashamed—"

"Ashamed? Who said anything about being ashamed?"

"I gathered you wouldn't want your girl friend—"

"Listen, what *is* this? I stopped seeing Sadie six months ago. I wouldn't even talk to her on the phone after that. If the crazy babe got herself killed—"

"Crazy?"

Hart suddenly wiped his hand over his face, wet his lips, and walked behind his desk. "I don't think I have anything more to say to you gentlemen."

"What did you mean by crazy?" Carella asked.

"Good day, gentlemen," Hart said.

Carella went to see Lieutenant Byrnes. In the lieutenant's corner office, Byrnes and Carella sat down over coffee. Byrnes frowned at Carella's request.

"Oh, come on, Pete!" Carella said. "If Fletcher *did* it—"

"That's only *your* allegation. Suppose he *didn't* do it, and suppose *you* do something to screw up the D.A.'s case?"

"Like what?"

"I don't know like what. The way things are going these days, if you spit on the sidewalk, that's enough to get a case thrown out of court."

"Fletcher hated his wife," Carella said calmly.

"Lots of men hate their wives. Half the men in this city hate their wives."

"But her little fling gives Fletcher a good reason for . . . Look, Pete, he had a motive; he had the opportunity, a golden one, in fact; and he had the means—another man's knife sticking in Sarah's belly. What more do you want?"

"Proof. There's a funny little system we've got here—it requires proof before we can arrest a man and charge him with murder."

"Right. And all I'm asking is the opportunity to *try* for it."

"Sure, by putting a tail on Fletcher. Suppose he sues the city?"

"Yes or no, Pete? I want permission to conduct a round-the-clock surveillance of Gerald Fletcher, starting Sunday morning. Yes or no?"

"I must be out of my mind," Byrnes said, and sighed.

Michael Thornton lived in an apartment building several blocks from the Quarter, close enough to absorb some of its artistic flavor, distant enough to escape its high rents. A blond man in his apartment, Paul Wendling, told Kling and Meyer that Mike was in his jewelry shop.

In the shop, Thornton was wearing a blue work smock, but the contours of the garment did nothing to hide his powerful build. His eyes were blue, his hair black. A small scar showed white in the thick eyebrow over his left eye.

"We understand you're working," Meyer said. "Sorry to break in on you this way."

"That's O.K.," Thornton said. "What's up?"

"You know a woman named Sarah Fletcher?"

"No," Thornton said.

"You know a woman named Sadie Collins?"

Thornton hesitated. "Yes," he said.

"What was your relationship with her?" Kling asked.

Thornton shrugged. "Why? Is she in trouble?"

"When's the last time you saw her?"

"You didn't answer my question," Thornton said.

"Well, you didn't answer ours either," Meyer said, and smiled. "What was your relationship with her, and when did you see her last?"

"I met her in July, in a joint called The Saloon, right around the corner. It's a bar, but they also serve sandwiches and soup. It gets a big crowd on weekends, singles, a couple of odd ones for spice—but not a gay bar. I saw her last in August, a brief, hot thing, and then goodbye."

"Did you realize she was married?" Kling said.

"No. Is she?"

"Yes," Meyer said. Neither of the detectives had yet informed Thornton that the lady in question was now unfortunately deceased. They were saving that for last, like dessert.

"Gee, I didn't know she was married." Thornton seemed truly surprised. "Otherwise, nothing would've happened."

"What *did* happen?"

"I bought her a few drinks and then I took her home with me. Later, I put her in a cab."

"When did you see her next?"

"The following day. It was goofy. She called me in the morning, said she was on her way downtown. I was still in bed. I said, 'So come on down, baby.' And she did. *Believe* me, she did."

"Did you see her again after that?" Kling asked.

"Two or three times a week."

"Where'd you go?"

"To my pad on South Lindner."

"Never went anyplace but there?"

"Never."

"Why'd you quit seeing her?"

"I went out of town for a while. When I got back, I just didn't hear from her again. She never gave me her number, and she wasn't in the directory, so I couldn't reach her."

"What do you make of this?" Kling asked, handing Thornton the address book.

Thornton studied it and said, "Yes, what about it? She wrote this down the night we met—we were in bed, and she asked my address."

"Did she write those initials at the same time, the ones in parentheses under your phone number?"

"I didn't actually see the page itself, I only saw her writing in the book."

"Got any idea what the initials mean?"

"None at all." Suddenly he looked thoughtful. "She *was* kind of special, I have to admit it." He grinned. "She'll call again, I'm sure of it."

"I wouldn't count on it," Meyer said. "She's dead."

His face did not crumble or express grief or shock. The only thing it expressed was sudden anger. "The stupid . . . " Thornton said. "That's all she ever was, a stupid, crazy . . . "

On Sunday morning, Carella was ready to become a surveillant, but Gerald Fletcher was nowhere in sight. A call to his apartment from a nearby phone booth revealed that he was not in his digs. He parked in front of Fletcher's apartment building until five P.M. when he was relieved by Detective Arthur Brown. Carella went home to read his son's latest note to Santa Claus, had dinner with his family, and was settling down in the living room with a novel he had bought a week ago and not yet cracked, when the telephone rang.

"Hello?" Carella said into the mouthpiece.

"Hello, Steve? This is Gerry. Gerry Fletcher."

Carella almost dropped the receiver. "How are you?"

"Fine, thanks. I was away for the weekend, just got back a little while ago, in fact. Frankly I find this apartment depressing as hell. I was wondering if you'd like to join me for a drink."

"Well," Carella said. "It's Sunday night, and it's late . . . "

"Nonsense, it's only eight o'clock. We'll do a little old-fashioned pub crawling."

It suddenly occurred to Carella that Gerald Fletcher had already had a few drinks before placing his call. It further occurred to him that if he played this too cozily, Fletcher might rescind his generous offer.

"Okay. I'll see you at eight-thirty, provided I can square it with my wife."

"Good," Fletcher said. "See you."

Paddy's Bar & Grill was on the Stem, adjacent to the city's theater district. Carella and Fletcher got there at about nine o'clock while the place was still relatively quiet. The action began a little later, Fletcher explained.

Fletcher lifted his glass in a silent toast. "What kind of person would you say comes to a place like this?"

"I would say we've got a nice lower-middle-class clientele bent on making contact with members of the opposite sex."

"What would you say if I told you the blonde in the clinging jersey is a working prostitute?"

Carella looked at the woman. "I don't think I'd believe you. She's a bit old for the young competition, and she's not *selling* anything. She's waiting for one of those two or three older guys to make their move. Hookers don't wait, Gerry. Is she a working prostitute?"

"I haven't the faintest idea," Fletcher said. "I was merely trying to indicate that appearances can sometimes be misleading. Drink up, there are a few more places I'd like to show you."

He knew Fletcher well enough by now to realize that the man was trying to tell him something. At lunch last Tuesday, Fletcher had transmitted a message and a challenge: *I killed my wife, what can you do about it?* Tonight, in a similar manner, he was attempting to indicate something else, but Carella could not fathom exactly what.

Fanny's was only twenty blocks away from Paddy's Bar and Grill, but as far removed from it as the moon. Whereas the first bar seemed to cater to a quiet crowd peacefully pursuing its romantic inclinations, Fanny's was noisy and raucous, jammed to the rafters with men and women of all ages, wearing plastic hippie gear purchased in head shops up and down Jackson Avenue.

Fletcher lifted his glass. "I hope you don't mind if I drink myself into a stupor," he said. "Merely pour me into the car at the end of the night." Fletcher drank. "I don't usually consume this much alcohol, but I'm very troubled about that boy."

"What boy?" Carella asked.

"Ralph Corwin," Fletcher said. "I understand he's having some difficulty with his lawyer and, well, I'd like to help him somehow."

"*Help* him?"

"Yes. Do you think the D.A.'s office would consider it strange if I suggested a good defense lawyer for the boy?"

"I think they might consider it passing strange, yes."

"Do I detect a note of sarcasm in your voice?"

"Not at all."

Fletcher squired Carella from Fanny's to, in geographical order, The Purple Chairs and Quigley's Rest. Each place was rougher, in its way, than the last. The Purple Chairs catered to a brazenly gay crowd, and Quigley's Rest was a dive, where Fletcher's liquor caught up with him, and the evening ended suddenly in a brawl. Carella was shaken by the experience, and still couldn't piece out Fletcher's reasons.

Carella received a further shock when he continued to pursue Sarah Fletcher's address book. Lou Kantor was simply the third name in a now wearying list of Sarah's bedmates, until she turned out to be a tough and striking woman. She confirmed Carella's suspicions immediately.

"I only knew her a short while," she said. "I met her in September, I believe. Saw her three or four times after that."

"Where'd you meet her?"

"In a bar called The Purple Chairs. That's right," she added quickly. "That's what I am."

"Nobody asked," Carella said. "What about Sadie Collins?"

"Spell it out, Officer, I'm not going to help you. I don't like being hassled."

"Nobody's hassling you, Miss Kantor. You practice your religion and I'll practice mine. We're here to talk about a dead woman."

"Then talk about her, spit it out. What do you want to know? Was she straight? Everybody's straight until they're *not* straight anymore, isn't that right? She was willing to learn. I taught her."

"Did you know she was married?"

"She told me. So what? Broke down in tears one night, and spent the rest of the night crying. I knew she was married."

"What'd you say about her husband?"

"Nothing that surprised me. She said he had another woman. Said he ran off to see her every weekend, told little Sadie he had out-of-town business. *Every* weekend, can you imagine that?"

"What do you make of this?" Carella said, and handed her Sarah's address book, opened to the MEMORANDA page.

"I don't know any of these people," Lou said.

"The initials under your name," Carella said. "TPC and then TG. Got any ideas?"

"Well, the TPC is obvious, isn't it? I met her at The Purple Chairs. What else could it mean?"

Carella suddenly felt very stupid. "Of course. What else could it mean?" He took back the book. "I'm finished," he said. "Thank you very much."

"I miss her," Lou said suddenly. "She was a wild one."

Cracking a code is like learning to roller-skate; once you know how to do it, it's easy. With a little help from Gerald Fletcher, who had provided a guided tour the night before, and a lot of help from Lou Kantor, who had generously provided the key, Carella was able to crack the code wide open—well, almost. Last night, he'd gone with Fletcher to Paddy's Bar and Grill, or PB&G under Andrew Hart's name; Fanny's, F under Sal Decotto; The Purple Chairs, Lou Kantor's TPC; and Quigley's Rest, QR for Richard Fenner on the list. Probably because of the fight, he hadn't taken Carella to The Saloon, TS under Michael Thornton's name—the place where Thornton had admitted first meeting Sarah.

Except, what the hell did TG mean, under all the names but Thornton's?

By Carella's own modest estimate, he had been in more bars in the past twenty-four hours than he had in the past twenty-four years. He decided, nevertheless, to hit The Saloon that night.

The Saloon was just that. A cigarette-scarred bar behind which ran a mottled, flaking mirror, wooden booths with patched, fake leather seat cushions; bowls of pretzels and potato chips; jukebox gurgling; steamy bodies.

"They come in here," the bartender said, "at all hours of the night. Take yourself. You're here to meet a girl, am I right?"

"There *was* someone I was hoping to see. A girl named Sadie Collins. Do you know her?"

"Yeah. She used to come in a lot, but I ain't seen her in months. What do you want to fool around with her for?"

"Why? What's the matter with her?"

"You want to know something?" the bartender said. "I thought she was a hooker at first. Aggressive. You know what that word means? Aggressive? She used to come dressed down to here and up to there, ready for action, selling everything she had, you understand? She'd come in here, pick out a guy she wanted, and go after him like the world was gonna end at midnight. And always the same type. Big guys. You wouldn't stand a chance with her, not that you ain't big, don't misunderstand me. But Sadie liked them gigantic, and mean: You know something?"

"What!"

"I'm glad she don't come in here anymore. There was something about her—like she was compulsive. You know what that word means, compulsive?"

Tuesday afternoon, Arthur Brown handed in his surveillance report on Gerald Fletcher. Much of it was not at all illuminating. From 4:55 P.M to 8:45 P.M. Fletcher had driven home, and then to 812 North Crane and parked. The report *did* become somewhat illuminating when, at 8:46 P.M., Fletcher emerged from that building with a redheaded woman wearing a black fur coat over a green dress. They went to Rudolph's restaurant, ate, and drove back to 812 Crane, arrived at 10:35 P.M. and went inside. Arthur Brown had checked the lobby mailboxes, which showed eight apartments on the eleventh floor, which was where the elevator indicator had stopped. Brown went outside to wait again, and Fletcher emerged alone at 11:40 P.M. and drove home. Detective O'Brien relieved Detective Brown at 12:15 A.M.

Byrnes said, "This woman could be important."

"That's just what I think," Brown answered.

Carella had not yet spoken to either Sal Decotto or Richard Fenner, the two remaining people listed in Sarah's book, but saw no reason to pursue that trail any further. If the place listings in her book had been chronological, she'd gone from bad to worse in her search for partners.

Why? To give it back to her husband in spades? Carella tossed Sarah's little black book into the manila folder bearing the various reports on the case, and turned his attention to the information Artie Brown had brought in last night. The redheaded woman's presence might be important, but Carella was still puzzling over Fletcher's behavior. Sarah's blatant infidelity provided Fletcher with a strong motive, so why take Carella to his wife's unhappy haunts, why *show* Carella that he had good and sufficient reason to kill her? Furthermore, why the offer to get a good defense attorney for the boy who had already been indicted for the slaying?

Sometimes Carella wondered who was doing what to whom.

At five o'clock that evening, Carella relieved Detective Hal Willis outside Fletcher's office building downtown, and then followed Fletcher to a department store in midtown Isola. Carella was wearing a false moustache stuck to his upper lip, a wig with hair longer than his own and of a different color, and a pair of sunglasses.

In the department store, he tracked Fletcher to the Intimate Apparel department. Carella walked into the next aisle, pausing to look at women's robes and kimonos, keeping one eye on Fletcher, who was in conversation with the lingerie salesgirl.

"May I help you, sir?" a voice said, and Carella turned to find a stocky woman at his elbow, with grey hair, black-rimmed spectacles, wearing Army shoes and a black dress. Her suspicious smile accused him of being a junkie shoplifter or worse.

"Thank you, no," Carella said. "I'm just looking."

Fletcher made his selections from the gossamer undergarments which the salesgirl had spread out on the counter, pointing first to one garment, then to another. The salesgirl wrote up the order and Fletcher reached into his wallet to give her either cash or a credit card; it was difficult to tell from an aisle away. He chatted with the girl a moment longer, and then walked off toward the elevator bank.

"Are you *sure* I can't assist you?" the woman in the Army shoes said, and Carella answered, "I'm positive," and moved swiftly toward the lingerie counter. Fletcher had left the counter without a package in his arms, which meant he was *sending* his purchases. The salesgirl was gathering up Fletcher's selections and looked up when Carella reached the counter.

"Yes, sir," she said. "May I help you?"

Carella opened his wallet and produced his shield. "Police officer," he said. "I'm interested in the order you just wrote up."

The girl was perhaps nineteen years old, a college girl working in the store during the Christmas rush. Speechlessly, she studied the shield, eyes bugging.

"Are these items being sent?" Carella asked.

"Yes, *sir*," the girl said. Her eyes were still wide. She wet her lips and stood up a little straighter, prepared to be a perfect witness.

"Can you tell me where?" Carella asked.

"Yes, *sir*," she said, and turned the sales slip toward him. "He wanted them wrapped separately, but they're all going to the same address. Miss Arlene Orton, 812 North Crane Street, right here in the city, and I'd guess it's a swell—"

"Thank you very much," Carella said.

It felt like Christmas day already.

The man who picked the lock on Arlene Orton's front door, ten minutes after she left her apartment on Wednesday morning, was better at it than any burglar in the city, and he happened to work for the Police Department. It took the technician longer to set up his equipment, but the telephone was the easiest of his jobs. The tap would become operative when the telephone company supplied the police with a list of so-called bridging points that located the pairs and cables for Arlene Orton's phone. The monitoring equipment would be hooked into these and whenever a call went out of or came into the apartment, a recorder would automatically tape both ends of the conversation. In addition, whenever a call was made from the apartment, a dial indicator would ink out a series of dots that signified the number being called.

The technician placed his bug in the bookcase on the opposite side of the room. The bug was a small FM transmitter with a battery-powered mike that needed to be changed every twenty-four hours. The technician would have pre-ferred running his own wires, but he dared not ask the building superinten-dent for an empty closet or workroom in which to hide his listener. A blabbermouth superintendent can kill an investigation more quickly than a squad of gangland goons.

In the rear of a panel truck parked at the curb some twelve feet south of the entrance to 812 North Crane, Steve Carella sat behind the recording equip-ment that was locked into the frequency of the bug. He sat hopefully, with a tuna sandwich and a bottle of beer, prepared to hear and record any sounds that emanated from Arlene's apartment.

At the bridging point seven blocks away and thirty minutes later, Arthur Brown sat behind equipment that was hooked into the telephone mike, and waited for Arlene Orton's phone to ring. He was in radio contact with Carella.

The first call came at 12:17 P.M. The equipment tripped in automatically and the spools of tape began recording the conversation, while Brown simul-taneously monitored it through his headphone.

"Hello?"

"Hello, Arlene?"

"Yes, who's this?"

"Nan."

"Nan? You sound so different. Do you have a cold or something?"

"Every year at this time. Just before the holidays. Arlene, I'm terribly rushed, I'll make this short. Do you know Beth's dress size?"

The conversation went on in that vein, and Arlene Orton spoke to three more girl friends in succession. She then called the local supermarket to order the week's groceries. She had a fine voice, deep and forceful, punctuated every so often (when she was talking to her girl friends) with a delightful giggle.

At four P.M., the telephone in Arlene's apartment rang again.

"Hello?"

"Arlene, this is Gerry."

"Hello, darling."

"I'm leaving here a little early. I thought I'd come right over."

"Good."

"I'll be there in, oh, half an hour, forty minutes."

"Hurry."

On Thursday morning, two days before Christmas, Carella sat at his desk in the squad room and looked over the transcripts of the five reels from the night before. The reel that interested him most was the second one. The con-versation on that reel had at one point changed abruptly in tone and content. Carella thought he knew why, but he wanted to confirm his suspicion.

Fletcher: I meant after the *holidays*, not the trial.

Miss Orton: I may be able to get away, I'm not sure. I'll have to check with my shrink.

Fletcher: What's he got to do with it?

Miss Orton: Well, I have to pay whether I'm there or not, you know.

Fletcher: Is he taking a vacation?

Miss Orton: I'll ask him.

Fletcher: Yes, ask him. Because I'd really like to get away.

Miss Orton: Ummm. When do you think the case (inaudible).

Fletcher: In March sometime. No sooner than that. He's got a new lawyer, you know.

Miss Orton: What does that mean, a new lawyer?

Fletcher: Nothing. He'll be convicted anyway.

Miss Orton: (Inaudible).

Fletcher: Because the trial's going to take a lot out of me.

Miss Orton: How soon after the trial . . .

Fletcher: I don't know.

Miss Orton: She's dead, Gerry, I don't see . . .

Fletcher: Yes, but . . .

Miss Orton: I don't see why we have to wait, do you?

Fletcher: Have you read this?

Miss Orton: No, not yet. Gerry, I think we ought to set a date now. A provisional date, depending on when the trial is. Gerry?

Fletcher: Mmmm?

Miss Orton: Do you think it'll be a terribly long, drawn-out trial?

Fletcher: What?

Miss Orton: Gerry?

Fletcher: Yes?

Miss Orton: Where are you?

Fletcher: I was just looking over some of these books.

Miss Orton: Do you think you can tear yourself away?

Fletcher: Forgive me, darling.

Miss Orton: If the trial starts in March, and we planned on April for it . . .

Fletcher: Unless they come up with something unexpected, of course.

Miss Orton: Like what?

Fletcher: Oh, I don't know. They've got some pretty sharp people investigating this case.

Miss Orton: What's there to investigate?

Fletcher: There's always the possibility he didn't do it.

Miss Orton: (Inaudible) a signed confession?

Ed McBain *Sadie When She Died* • 407

Fletcher: One of the cops thinks I killed her.

Miss Orton: You're not serious. Who?

Fletcher: A detective named Carella. He probably knows about us by now. He's a very thorough cop. I have a great deal of admiration for him. I wonder if he realizes that.

Miss Orton: Where'd he even get such an idea?

Fletcher: Well. I told him I hated her.

Miss Orton: What? Gerry, why the hell did you do that?

Fletcher: He'd have found out anyway. He probably knows by now that Sarah was sleeping around with half the men in this city. And he probably knows I knew it too.

Miss Orton: Who cares what he found out? Corwin's already confessed.

Fletcher: I can understand his reasoning. I'm just not sure he can understand mine.

Miss Orton: Some reasoning. If you were going to kill her, you'd have done it ages ago, when she refused to sign the separation papers. So let him investigate, who cares? Wishing your wife dead isn't the same thing as killing her. Tell that to Detective Copolla.

Fletcher: Carella. (Laughs). I'll tell him, darling.

According to the technician who had wired the Orton apartment, the living room bug was in the bookcase on the wall opposite the bar. Carella was interested in the tape from the time Fletcher had asked Arlene about a book—"Have you read this?"—and then seemed preoccupied. It was Carella's guess that Fletcher had discovered the bookcase bug. What interested Carella more, however, was what Fletcher had said *after* he knew the place was wired. Certain of an audience now, Fletcher had:

1. Suggested the possibility that Corwin was not guilty.

2. Flatly stated that a cop named Carella suspected him.

3. Expressed admiration for Carella, while wondering if Carella was aware of it.

4. Speculated that Carella had already doped out the purpose of the bar-crawling last Sunday night, was cognizant of Sarah's promiscuity, and knew Fletcher was aware of it.

5. Made a little joke about "telling" Carella.

Carella felt as eerie as he had when lunching with Fletcher and later when drinking with him. Now he'd spoken, through the bug, directly to Carella. But what was he trying to say? And why?

Carella wanted very much to hear what Fletcher would say when he *didn't* know he was being overhead. He asked Lieutenant Byrnes for permission to request a court order to put a bug in Fletcher's automobile. Byrnes granted permission, and the court issued the order.

Fletcher made a date with Arlene Orton to go to The Chandeliers across the river, and the bug was installed in Fletcher's 1972 car. If Fletcher left the city, the effective range of the transmitter on the open road would be about a quarter of a mile. The listener-pursuer had his work cut out for him.

By ten minutes to ten that night, Carella was drowsy and discouraged. On the way out to The Chandeliers, Fletcher and Arlene had not once mentioned Sarah nor the plans for their impending marriage. Carella was anxious to put them both to bed and get home to his family. When they finally came out of the restaurant and began walking toward Fletcher's automobile, Carella actually uttered an audible, "At last," and started his car.

They proceeded east on Route 701, heading for the bridge, and said nothing. Carella thought at first that something was wrong with the equipment, then finally Arlene spoke and Carella knew just what had happened. The pair had argued in the restaurant, and Arlene had been smoldering until this moment.

"Maybe you don't want to marry me at all," she shouted.

"That's ridiculous," Fletcher said.

"Then why won't you set a date?"

"I have set a date."

"You haven't set a date. All you've done is say after the trial. *When*, after the trial? Maybe this whole damn thing has been a stall. Maybe you *never* planned to marry me."

"You know that isn't true, Arlene."

"How do I know there really *were* separation papers?"

"There were. I told you there were."

"Then why wouldn't she sign them?"

"Because she loved me."

"If she loved you, then why did she do those horrible things?"

"To make me pay, I think."

"Is that why she showed you her little black book?"

"Yes, to make me pay."

"No. Because she was a slut."

"I guess. I guess that's what she became."

"Putting a little TG in her book every time she told you about a new one. *Told Gerry*, and marked a little TG in her book."

"Yes, to make me pay."

"A slut. You should have gone after her with detectives. Gotten pictures, threatened her, forced her to sign—"

"No, I couldn't have done that. It would have ruined me, Arl."

"Your precious career."

"Yes, my precious career."

They both fell silent again. They were approaching the bridge now. Carella tried to stay close behind them, but on occasion the distance between the two cars lengthened and he lost some words in the conversation.

"She wouldn't sign the papers and I ( ) adultery because ( ) have come out."

"And I thought ( )."

"I did everything I possibly could."

"Yes, Gerry, but now she's dead. So what's your excuse now?"

"I'm suspected of having *killed* her, damn it!"

Fletcher was making a left turn, off the highway. Carella stepped on the accelerator, not wanting to lose voice contact now.

"What difference does that make?" Arlene asked.

"None at all, I'm sure," Fletcher said. "I'm sure you wouldn't mind at all being married to a convicted murderer."

"What are you talking about?"

"I'm talking about the possibility . . . Never mind."

"Let me hear it."

"All right, Arlene. I'm talking about the possibility of someone accusing me of the murder. And of my having to stand trial for it."

"That's the most paranoid—"

"It's not paranoid."

"Then what is it? They've caught the murderer, they—"

"I'm only saying suppose. How could we get married if I killed her, if someone says I killed her?"

"No one has said that, Gerry."

"Well, *if* someone should."

Silence. Carella was dangerously close to Fletcher's car now, and risking discovery.

Carella held his breath and stayed glued to the car ahead.

"Gerry, I don't understand this," Arlene said, her voice low.

"Someone could make a good case for it."

"Why would anyone do that? They know that Corwin—"

"They could say I came into the apartment and . . . They could say she was still alive when I came into the apartment. They could say the knife was still in her and I . . . I came in and found her that way and . . . finished her off."

"Why would you do that?"

"To end it."

"You wouldn't kill anyone, Gerry."

"No."

"Then why are you even suggesting such a terrible thing?"

"If she wanted it . . . If someone accused me . . . If someone said I'd done it . . . that I'd finished the job, pulled the knife across her belly, they could claim she *asked* me to do it."

"What are you saying, Gerry?"

"I'm trying to explain that Sarah might have—"

"Gerry. I don't think I want to know."

"I'm only trying to tell you—"

"No. I don't want to know. Please, Gerry, you're frightening me."

"*Listen* to me, damn it! I'm trying to explain what *might* have happened. Is that so hard to accept? That she might have *asked* me to kill her?"

"Gerry, please, I—"

"I *wanted* to call the hospital, I was *ready* to call the hospital, don't you think I could *see* she wasn't fatally stabbed?"

"Gerry, please."

"She begged me to kill her, Arlene, she begged me to end it for her, she . . . Damn it, can't *either* of you understand that? I tried to show him, I took him to all the places, I thought he was a man who'd understand. Is it that difficult?"

"Oh, my God, *did* you kill her? *Did* you kill Sarah?"

"No. Not Sarah. Only the woman she'd become, the slut I'd forced her to become. She was Sadie, you see, when I killed her—when she died."

"Oh, my God," Arlene said, and Carella nodded in weary acceptance.

Carella felt neither elated nor triumphant. As he followed Fletcher's car into the curb in front of Arlene's building, he experienced only a familiar nagging sense of repetition and despair. Fletcher was coming out of his car now, walking around to the curb side, opening the door for Arlene, who took his hand and stepped onto the sidewalk, weeping. Carella intercepted them before they reached the front door of the building.

Quietly, he charged Fletcher with the murder of his wife, and made the arrest without resistance.

Fletcher did not seem at all surprised.

So it was finished, or at least Carella thought it was.

In the silence of his living room, the telephone rang at a quarter past one.

He caught the phone on the third ring.

"Hello?"

"Steve," Lieutenant Byrnes said. "I just got a call from Calcutta. Ralph Corwin hanged himself in his cell, just after midnight. Must have done it while we were still taking Fletcher's confession in the squad room."

Carella was silent.

"Steve?" Byrnes said.

"Yeah, Pete."

"Nothing," Byrnes said, and hung up.

Carella stood with the dead phone in his hands for several seconds and then replaced it on the hook. He looked into the living room, where the lights of the tree glowed warmly, and thought of a despairing junkie in a prison cell, who had taken his own life without ever having known he had not taken the life of another.

It was Christmas day.

Sometimes none of it made any sense at all.

TONY HILLERMAN
1925–

Author of the most popular mystery series featuring Native American police-men, Anthony Grove Hillerman was born in the small town of Sacred Heart, Oklahoma. Raised on a farm near Sacred Heart, Hillerman was educated at St. Mary's Academy, a boarding school for Native Americans. A much dec-orated soldier during World War II, he returned from the war to earn a B.A degree from the University of Oklahoma. He then pursued a career in jour-nalism in the Southwest and served as editor for the Santa Fe-based *New Mex-ican*. Returning to academics he received an M.A. from the University of New Mexico, where he taught journalism until 1987 when he left to write full-time. His mysteries, which began with *The Blessing Way* (1970), nominated for an Edgar, have earned him an Edgar Award for *Dance Hall of the Dead* (1973), the Mystery Writers of America Grandmaster Award (1991), and the Spe-cial Friends of the Dinee Award by the Navajo Nation, among many others. He has served as the president of Mystery Writers of America, and his auto-biography, *Seldom Disappointed* (2002), received the Agatha Award for Best Non-Fiction.

Drawing on his early background and fascination with Native Ameri-can cultures, Hillerman's detective series takes place on the Navajo reser-vation. His well-researched and accurate portrayal of traditional Navajo culture saturates his stories and provides one of the most intriguing set-tings found in contemporary mystery writing. The series introduces Joe Leaphorn and Jim Chee, both members of the Navajo Tribal police. The first three novels in the series featured Leaphorn and the next three focused on Chee. Loyal fans were delighted when the two first appeared together in the seventh novel, *Skinwalkers* (1986), and they have continued to solve crimes together in the rest of the books. In an unexpected twist, Leaphorn, the older of the policemen, takes a contemporary view of crimes on the reservation, while Chee, the younger member of the force, returns to tra-ditional concepts. "Chee's Witch" was first published in the *New Black Mask*, No.7, edited by Matthew J. Bruccoli and Richard Layman in 1986.

Recommended Hillerman works: *Dance Hall of the Dead, A Thief of Time, Coyote Waits.*

Other recommended authors: James D. Doss, J.A. Jance, Dana Stabenow.

Chee's Witch

Snow is so important to the Eskimos they have nine nouns to describe its variations. Corporal Jimmy Chee of the Navajo Tribal Police had heard that as an anthropology student at the University of New Mexico. He remembered it now because he was thinking of all the words you need in Navajo to account for the many forms of witchcraft. The word Old Woman Tso had used was "anti'l," which is the ultimate sort, the absolute worst. And so, in fact, was the deed which seemed to have been done. Murder, apparently. Mutilation, certainly, if Old Woman Tso had her facts right. And then, if one believed all the mythology of witchery told among the fifty clans who comprised The People, there must also be cannibalism, incest, even necrophilia.

On the radio in Chee's pickup truck, the voice of the young Navajo reading a Gallup used-car commercial was replaced by Willie Nelson singing of trouble and a worried mind. The ballad fit Chee's mood. He was tired. He was thirsty. He was sticky with sweat. He was worried. His pickup jolted along the ruts in a windless heat, leaving a white fog of dust to mark its winding passage across the Rainbow Plateau. The truck was gray with it. So was Jimmy Chee. Since sunrise he had covered maybe two hundred miles of half-graded gravel and unmarked wagon tracks of the Arizona-Utah-New Mexico border country. Routine at first—a check into a witch story at the Tsossie hogan north of Teec Nos Pos to stop trouble before it started. Routine and logical. A bitter winter, a sand storm spring, a summer of rainless, desiccating heat. Hopes dying, things going wrong, anger growing, and then the witch gossip. The logical. A bitter wind, a sand storm spring, a summer awry. The trouble at the summer hogan of the Tsossies was a sick child and a water well that had turned alkaline—nothing unexpected. But you didn't expect such a specific witch. The skinwalker, the Tsossies agreed, was The City Navajo, the man who had come to live in one of the government houses at Kayenta. Why the City Navajo? Because everybody knew he was a witch. Where had they heard that, the first time? The People who came to the trading post at Mexican Water said it. And so Chee had driven westward over Tohache Wash, past Red Mesa and Rabbit Ears to Mexican Water. He had spent hours on the shady porch giving those who came to buy, and to fill their water barrels, and to visit, a chance to know who he was until finally they might risk talking about witchcraft to a stranger. They were Mud Clan, and Many Goats People, and Standing Rock Clan—foreign to Chee's own Slow Talking People—but finally some of them talked a little.

A witch was at work on the Rainbow Plateau. Adeline Etcitty's mare had foaled a two-headed colt. Hosteen Musket had seen the witch. He'd seen a man walk into a grove of cottonwoods, but when he got there an owl flew away. Rudolph Bisti's boys lost three rams while driving their flocks up into the Chuska high pastures, and when they found the bodies, the huge tracks of a werewolf were all around them. The daughter of Rosemary Nashibitti had seen a big dog bothering her horses and had shot at it with her .22 and the dog had turned into a man wearing a wolfskin and had fled, half running, half flying. The old man they called Afraid of His Horses had heard the sound of the witch on the roof of his winter hogan, and saw the dirt falling through the smoke hole as the skinwalker tried to throw in his corpse powder. The next morning the old man had followed the tracks of the Navajo Wolf for a mile, hoping to kill him. But the tracks had faded away. There was nothing very unusual in the stories, except their number and the recurring hints that City Navajo was the witch. But then came what Chee hadn't expected. The witch had killed a man.

The police dispatcher at Window Rock had been interrupting Willie Nelson with an occasional blurted message. Now she spoke directly to Chee. He acknowledged. She asked his location.

"About fifteen miles south of Dennehotso," Chee said. "Homeward bound for Tuba City. Dirty, thirsty, hungry, and tired."

"I have a message."

"Tuba City," Chee repeated, "which I hope to reach in about two hours, just in time to avoid running up a lot of overtime for which I never get paid."

"The message is FBI Agent Wells needs to contact you. Can you make a meeting at Kayenta Holiday Inn at eight P.M.?"

"What's it about?" Chee asked. The dispatcher's name was Virgie Endecheenie, and she had a very pretty voice and the first time Chee had met her at the Window Rock headquarters of the Navajo Tribal Police he had been instantly smitten. Unfortunately, Virgie was a born-into Salt Cedar Clan, which was the clan of Chee's father, which put an instant end to that. Even thinking about it would violate the complex incest taboo of the Navajos.

"Nothing on what it's about," Virgie said, her voice strictly business. "It just says confirm meeting time and place with Chee or obtain alternate time."

"Any first name on Wells?" Chee asked. The only FBI Wells he knew was Jake Wells. He hoped it wouldn't be Jake.

"Negative on the first name," Virgie said.

"All right," Chee said. "I'll be there."

The road tilted downward now into the vast barrens of erosion which the Navajos call Beautiful Valley. Far to the west, the edge of the sun dipped behind a cloud—one of the line of thunderheads forming in the evening heat over the San Francisco Peaks and the Coconino Rim. The Hopis had been holding their Niman Kachina dances, calling the clouds to come and bless them.

Chee reached Kayenta just a little late. It was early twilight and the clouds had risen black against the sunset. The breeze brought the faint smells that rising humidity carry across desert country—the perfume of sage, creosote brush, and dust. The desk clerk said that Wells was in room 284 and the first name was Jake. Chee no longer cared. Jake Wells was abrasive but he was also smart. He had the best record in the special FBI Academy class Chee had attended, a quick, tough intelligence. Chee could tolerate the man's personality for a while to learn what Wells could make of his witchcraft puzzle.

"It's unlocked," Wells said. "Come on in." He was propped against the padded headboard of the bed, shirt off, shoes on, glass in hand. He glanced at Chee and then back at the television set. He was as tall as Chee remembered, and the eyes were just as blue. He waved the glass at Chee without looking away from the set. "Mix yourself one," he said, nodding toward a bottle beside the sink in the dressing alcove.

"How you doing, Jake?" Chee asked.

Now the blue eyes reexamined Chee. The question in them abruptly went away. "Yeah," Wells said. "You were the one at the Academy." He eased himself on his left elbow and extended a hand. "Jake Wells," he said.

Chee shook the hand. "Chee," he said.

Wells shifted his weight again and handed Chee his glass. "Pour me a little more while you're at it," he said, "and turn down the sound."

Chee turned down the sound.

"About 30 percent booze," Wells demonstrated the proportion with his hands. "This is your district then. You're in charge around Kayenta? Window Rock said I should talk to you. They said you were out chasing around in the desert today. What are you working on?"

"Nothing much," Chee said. He ran a glass of water, drinking it thirstily. His face in the mirror was dirty—the lines around his mouth and eyes whitish with dust. The sticker on the glass reminded guests that the laws of the Navajo Tribal Council prohibited possession of alcoholic beverages on the reservation. He refilled his own glass with water and mixed Wells's drink. "As a matter of fact, I'm working on a witchcraft case."

"Witchcraft?" Wells laughed. "Really?" He took the drink from Chee and examined it. "How does it work? Spells and like that?"

"Not exactly," Chee said. "It depends. A few years ago a little girl got sick down near Burnt Water. Her dad killed three people with a shotgun. He said they blew corpse powder on his daughter and made her sick."

Wells was watching him. "The kind of crime where you have the insanity plea."

"Sometimes," Chee said. "Whatever you have, witch talk makes you nervous. It happens more when you have a bad year like this. You hear it and you try to find out what's starting it before things get worse."

"So you're not really expecting to find a witch?"

"Usually not," Chee said.

"Usually?"

"Judge for yourself," Chee said. "I'll tell you what I've picked up today. You tell me what to make of it. Have time?"

Wells shrugged. "What I really want to talk about is a guy named Simon Begay." He looked quizzically at Chee. "You heard the name?"

"Yes," Chee said.

"Well, shit," Wells said. "You shouldn't have. What do you know about him?"

"Showed up maybe three months ago. Moved into one of those U.S. Public Health Service houses over by the Kayenta clinic. Stranger. Keeps to himself. From off the reservation somewhere. I figured you federals put him here to keep him out of sight."

Wells frowned. "How long you known about him?"

"Quite a while," Chee said. He'd known about Begay within a week after his arrival.

"He's a witness," Wells said. "They broke a car-theft operation in Los Angeles. Big deal. National connections. One of those where they have hired hands picking up expensive models and they drive 'em right on the ship and off-load in South America. This Begay is one of the hired hands. Nobody much. Criminal record going all the way back to juvenile, but all nickel-and-dime stuff. I gather he saw some things that help tie some big boys into the crime, so Justice made a deal with him."

"And they hide him out here until the trial?"

Something apparently showed in the tone of the question. "If you want to hide an apple, you drop it in with the other apples," Wells said. "What better place?"

Chee had been looking at Wells' shoes, which were glossy with polish. Now he examined his own boots, which were not. But he was thinking of Justice Department stupidity. The appearance of any new human in a country as empty as the Navajo Reservation provoked instant interest. If the stranger was a Navajo, there were instant questions. What was his clan? Who was his mother? What was his father's clan? Who were his relatives? The City Navajo had no answers to any of these crucial questions. He was (as Chee had been repeatedly told) unfriendly. It was quickly guessed that he was a "relocation Navajo," born to one of those hundreds of Navajo families which the federal government had tried to reestablish forty years ago in Chicago, Los Angeles, and other urban centers. He was a stranger. In a year of witches, he would certainly be suspected.

Chee sat looking at his boots, wondering if that was the only basis for the charge that City Navajo was a skinwalker. Or had someone seen something? Had someone seen the murder?

"The thing about apples is they don't gossip," Chee said.

"You hear gossip about Begay?" Wells was sitting up now, his feet on the floor.

"Sure," Chee said. "I hear he's a witch."

Wells produced a pro-forma chuckle. "Tell me about it," he said.

Chee knew exactly how he wanted to tell it. Wells would have to wait a while before he came to the part about Begay. "The Eskimos have nine nouns for snow," Chee began. He told Wells about the variety of witchcraft on the reservations and its environs: about frenzy witchcraft, used for sexual conquests, of witchery distortions, of curing ceremonials, of the exotic two-heart witchcraft of the Hopi Fog Clan, of the Zuni Sorcery Fraternity, of the Navajo "chindi," which is more like a ghost than a witch, and finally of the Navajo Wolf, the anti'l witchcraft, the werewolves who pervert every taboo of the Navajo Way and use corpse powder to kill their victims.

Wells rattled the ice in his glass and glanced at his watch.

"To get to the part about your Begay," Chee said, "about two months ago we started picking up witch gossip. Nothing much, and you expect it during a drought. Lately it got to be more than usual." He described some of the tales and how uneasiness and dread had spread across the plateau. He described what he had learned today, the Tsossies's naming City Navajo as the witch, his trip to Mexican Water, of learning there that the witch had killed a man.

"They said it happened in the spring—couple of months ago. They told me the ones who knew about it were the Tso outfit." The talk of murder, Chee noticed, had revived Wells's interest. "I went up there," he continued, "and found the old woman who runs the outfit. Emma Tso. She told me her son-in-law had been out looking for some sheep, and smelled something, and found the body under some chamiso brush in a dry wash. A witch had killed him."

"How—"

Chee cut off the question. "I asked her how he knew it was a witch killing. She said the hands were stretched out like this." Chee extended his hands, palms up. "They were flayed. The skin was cut off the palms and fingers."

Wells raised his eyebrows.

"That's what the witch uses to make corpse powder," Chee explained. "They take the skin that has the whorls and ridges of the individual personality—the skin from the palms and the finger pads, and the soles of the feet. They take that, and the skin from the glans of the penis, and the small bones where the neck joins the skull, and they dry it, and pulverize it, and use it as poison."

"You're going to get to Begay any minute now," Wells said. "That right?"

"We got to him," Chee said. "He's the one they think is the witch. He's the City Navajo."

"I thought you were going to say that," Wells said. He rubbed the back of his hand across one blue eye. "City Navajo. Is it that obvious?"

"Yes," Chee said. "And then he's a stranger. People suspect strangers."

"Were they coming around him? Accusing him? Any threats? Anything like that, you think?"

"It wouldn't work that way—not unless somebody had someone in their family killed. The way you deal with a witch is hire a singer and hold a special kind of curing ceremony. That turns the witchcraft around and kills the witch."

Wells made an impatient gesture. "Whatever," he said. "I think something has made this Begay spooky." He stared into his glass, communing with the bourbon. "I don't know."

"Something unusual about the way he's acting?"

"Hell of it is I don't know how he usually acts. This wasn't my case. The agent who worked him retired or some damn thing, so I got stuck with being the delivery man." He shifted his eyes from glass to Chee. "But if it was me, and I was holed up here waiting, and the guy came along who was going to take me home again, then I'd be glad to see him. Happy to have it over with. All that."

"He wasn't?"

Wells shook his head. "Seemed edgy. Maybe that's natural, though. He's going to make trouble for some hard people."

"I'd be nervous," Chee said.

"I guess it doesn't matter much anyway," Wells said. "He's small potatoes. The guy who's handling it now in the U.S. Attorney's Office said it must have been a toss-up whether to fool with him at all. He said the assistant who handled it decided to hide him out just to be on the safe side."

"Begay doesn't know much?"

"I guess not. That, and they've got better witnesses."

"So why worry?"

Wells laughed. "I bring this sucker back and they put him on the witness stand and he answers all the questions with I don't know and it makes the USDA look like a horse's ass. When a U.S. Attorney looks like that, he finds an FBI agent to blame it on." He yawned. "Therefore," he said through the yawn, "I want to ask you what you think. This is your territory. You are the officer in charge. Is it your opinion that someone got to my witness?"

Chee let the question hang. He spent a fraction of a second reaching the answer, which was they could have if they wanted to try. Then he thought about the real reason Wells had kept him working late without a meal or a shower. Two sentences in Wells's report. One would note that the possibility the witness had been approached had been checked with local Navajo Police. The next would report whatever Chee said next. Wells would have followed Federal Rule One—Protect Your Ass.

Chee shrugged. "You want to hear the rest of my witchcraft business?"

Wells put his drink on the lamp table and untied his shoe. "Does it bear on this?"

"Who knows? Anyway there's not much left. I'll let you decide. The point is we had already picked up this corpse Emma Tso's son-in-law found. Somebody had reported it weeks ago. It had been collected, and taken in for an autopsy. The word we got on the body was Navajo male in his thirties probably. No identification on him."

"How was this bird killed?"

"No sign of foul play," Chee said. "By the time the body was brought in, decay and the scavengers hadn't left a lot. Mostly bone and gristle, I guess. This was a long time after Emma Tso's son-in-law saw him."

"So why do they think Begay killed him?" Wells removed his second shoe and headed for the bathroom.

Chee picked up the telephone and dialed the Kayenta clinic. He got the night supervisor and waited while the supervisor dug out the file. Wells came out of the bathroom with his toothbrush. Chee covered the mouthpiece. "I'm having them read me the autopsy report," Chee explained. Wells began brushing his teeth at the sink in the dressing alcove. The voice of the night supervisor droned into Chee's ear.

"That all?" Chee asked. "Nothing added on? No identity yet? Still no cause?"

"That's him," the voice said.

"How about shoes?" Chee asked. "He have shoes on?"

"Just a sec," the voice said. "Yep. Size 10D. And a hat, and . . . "

"No mention of the neck or skull, right? I didn't miss that? No bones missing?" Silence. "Nothing about neck or skull bones."

"Ah," Chee said. "Fine. I thank you." He felt great. He felt wonderful. Finally things had clicked into place. The witch was exorcised. "Jake," he said. "Let me tell you a little more about my witch case."

Wells was rinsing his mouth. He spit out the water and looked at Chee, amused. "I didn't think of this before," Wells said, "but you really don't have a witch problem. If you leave that corpse a death by natural causes, there's no case to work. If you decide it's a homicide, you don't have jurisdiction anyway. Homicide on an Indian reservation, FBI has jurisdiction." Wells grinned. "We'll come in and find your witch for you."

Chee looked at his boots, which were still dusty. His appetite had left him, as it usually did an hour or so after he missed a meal. He still hungered for a bath. He picked up his hat and pushed himself to his feet.

"I'll go home now," he said. "The only thing you don't know about the witch case is what I just got from the autopsy report. The corpse had his shoes on and no bones were missing from the base of the skull."

Chee opened the door and stood in it, looking back. Wells was taking his pajamas out of his suitcase. "So what advice do you have for me? What can you tell me about my witch case?"

"To tell the absolute truth, Chee, I'm not into witches," Wells said. "Haven't been since I was a boy."

"But we don't really have a witch case now," Chee said. He spoke earnestly. "The shoes were still on, so the skin wasn't taken from the soles of his feet. No bones missing from the neck. You need those to make corpse powder."

Wells was pulling his undershirt over his head. Chee hurried.

"What we have now is another little puzzle," Chee said. "If you're not collecting stuff for corpse powder, why cut the skin off this guy's hands?"

"I'm going to take a shower," Wells said. "Got to get my Begay back to LA tomorrow."

Outside the temperature had dropped. The air moved softly from the west, carrying the smell of rain. Over the Utah border, over the Cococino Rim, over the Rainbow Plateau, lightning flickered and glowed. The storm had formed. The storm was moving. The sky was black with it. Chee stood in the darkness, listening to the mutter of thunder, inhaling the perfume, exulting in it.

He climbed into the truck and started it. How had they set it up, and why? Perhaps the FBI agent who knew Begay had been ready to retire. Perhaps an accident had been arranged. Getting rid of the assistant prosecutor who knew the witness would have been even simpler—a matter of hiring him away from the government job. That left no one who knew this minor witness was not Simon Begay. And who was he? Probably they had other Navajos from the Los Angeles community stealing cars for them. Perhaps that's what had suggested the scheme. To most white men all Navajos looked pretty much alike, just as in his first years at college all Chee had seen in white men was pink skin, freckles, and light-colored eyes. And what would the impostor say? Chee grinned. He'd say whatever was necessary to cast doubt on the prosecution, to cast the fatal "reasonable doubt," to make—as Wells had put it—the U.S. District Attorney look like a horse's ass.

Chee drove into the rain twenty miles west of Kayenta. Huge, cold drops drummed on the pickup roof and turned the highway into a ribbon of water. Tomorrow the backcountry roads would be impassable. As soon as they dried and the washouts had been repaired, he'd go back to the Tsossie hogan, and the Tso place, and to all the other places from which the word would quickly spread. He'd tell the people that the witch was in custody of the FBI and was gone forever from the Rainbow Plateau.

IAN RANKIN

1960–

Creator of the immensely popular Inspector Rebus series starting with *Knots and Crosses* (1987), Ian Rankin was born in Cardenden, Fife, Scotland. His family was working class, with few books available in their home. From early childhood Rankin started writing his own comic books and stories. He earned an M.A. in English Literature (specializing in American literature) from the University of Edinburgh and worked at various jobs while developing his skills as a writer. His first novel was *The Flood* (1986), followed shortly by the second, which introduced Inspector John Rebus, the character who continues in 13 subsequent novels, most recently *A Question of Blood* (2003), as well as in a British ITV series and television films. Rankin received a Crime Writers Association (CWA) Golden Dagger Award for Fiction for *Black and Blue* (1997), which was also nominated for an Edgar, and has won two Dagger Awards for short stories. He was the winner of the Chandler-Fulbright and was awarded the Order of the British Empire (OBE) in 2002. He has been recognized as the number one bestselling crime writer in the UK in the early twenty-first century, and his works are increasingly popular in the United States.

Inspector John Rebus is a member of the Criminal Investigation Department for the Lothian and Borders Police, whose "beat" covers Edinburgh, Scotland. He normally works out of the headquarters at Fetts Avenue in Edinburgh, often referred to as "the Big House." However, his investigative region extends all the way to the English border. He is a complex and often difficult personality, who sometimes rebels against the "system," but believes firmly in the law and the place of the police in society. The Rebus series is also enhanced by Detective Siobhan Clarke, a young female C.I.D. member who sees Rebus as her mentor. Whether Rebus and his police team are investigating serial killers, internet stalkers, political scandal, or crimes based in Edinburgh's dark past, Rankin produces some of the best police procedural novels. "The Dean's Curse," an Inspector Rebus story, first appeared in Rankin's collection of short stories *A Good Hanging and Other Stories (1992)*.

Recommended Rankin works: *Begger's Banquet* (short stories), *Black and Blue, A Question of Blood*.

Other recommended authors: Peter Robinson, Carolyn Graham, P. D. James.

The Dean Curse

The locals in Barnton knew him either as 'the Brigadier' or as 'that Army type who bought the West Lodge'. West Lodge was a huge but until recently neglected detached house set in a walled acre and a half of grounds and copses. Most locals were relieved that its high walls hid it from general view, the house itself being too angular, too gothic for modern tastes. Certainly, it was very large for the needs of a widower and his unsmiling daughter. Mrs MacLennan, who cleaned for the Brigadier, was pumped for information by curious neighbours, but could say only that Brigadier-General Dean had had some renovations done, that most of the house was habitable, that one room had become a library, another a billiard-room, another a study, another a makeshift gymnasium and so on. The listeners would drink this in deeply, yet it was never enough. What about the daughter? What about the Brigadier's background? What happened to his wife?

Shopkeepers too were asked for their thoughts. The Brigadier drove a sporty open-topped car which would pull in noisily to the side of the road to allow him to pop into this or that shop for a few things, including, each day at the same time, a bottle of something or other from the smarter of the two off-licences.

The grocer, Bob Sladden, reckoned that Brigadier-General Dean had been born nearby, even that he had lived for a few childhood years in West Lodge and so had retired there because of its carefree connections. But Miss Dalrymple, who at ninety-three was as old as anyone in that part of Barnton, could not recall any family named Dean living at West Lodge. Could not, indeed, recall any Deans ever living in this 'neck' of Barnton, with the exception of Sam Dean. But when pressed about Sam Dean, she merely shook her head and said. 'He was no good, that one, and got what he deserved. The Great War saw to him.' Then she would nod slowly, thoughtfully, and nobody would be any further forward.

Speculation grew wilder as no new facts came to light, and in The Claymore public bar one afternoon, a bar never patronised by the Brigadier (and who'd ever heard of an Army man not liking his drink?), a young out-of-work plasterer named Willie Barr came up with a fresh proposition.

'Maybe Dean isn't his real name.'

But everyone around the pool table laughed at that and Willie just shrugged, readying to play his next shot. 'Well,' he said, 'real name or not, I wouldn't climb over that daughter of his to get to any of you lot.'

Then he played a double off the cushion, but missed. Missed not because the shot was difficult or he'd had too many pints of Snakebite, but because his cue arm jerked at the noise of the explosion.

It was a fancy car all right, a Jaguar XJS convertible, its bodywork a startling red. Nobody in Barnton could mistake it for anyone else's car. Besides, everyone was used to it revving to its loud roadside halt, was used to its contented ticking-over while the Brigadier did his shopping. Some complained—though never to his face—about the noise, about the fumes from the exhaust. They couldn't say why he never switched off the ignition. He always seemed to want to be ready for a quick getaway. On this particular afternoon, the getaway was quicker even than usual, a squeal of tyres as the car jerked out into the road and sped past the shops. Its driver seemed ready actually to disregard the red stop light at the busy junction. He never got the chance. There was a ball of flames where the car had been and the heart-stopping sound of the explosion. Twisted metal flew into the air, then down again, wounding passers-by, burning skin. Shop windows blew in, shards of fine glass finding soft targets. The traffic lights turned to green, but nothing moved in the street.

For a moment, there was a silence punctuated only by the arrival on terra firma of bits of speedometer, headlamp, even steering-wheel. Then the screaming started, as people realised they'd been wounded. More curdling still though were the silences, the dumb horrified faces of people who would never forget this moment, whose shock would disturb each wakeful night.

And then there was a man, standing in a doorway, the doorway of what had been the wine merchant's. He carried a bottle with him, carefully wrapped in green paper, and his mouth was open in surprise. He dropped the bottle with a crash when he realised his car was not where he had left it, realising that the roaring he had heard and thought he recognised was that of his own car being driven away. At his feet, he saw one of his driving gloves lying on the pavement in front of him. It was still smouldering. Only five minutes before, it had been lying on the leather of his passenger seat. The wine merchant was standing beside him now, pale and shaking, looking in dire need of a drink. The Brigadier nodded towards the carcass of his sleek red Jaguar.

'That should have been me,' he said. Then: 'Do you mind if I use your telephone?'

John Rebus threw *The Dain Curse* up in the air, sending it spinning towards his living-room ceiling. Gravity caught up with it just short of the ceiling and pulled it down hard, so that it landed open against the uncarpeted floor. It was a cheap copy, bought secondhand and previously much read. But not by Rebus; he'd got as far as the beginning of the third section, 'Quesada', before giving up, before tossing what many regard as Hammett's finest novel into the air. Its pages fell away from the spine as it landed, scattering chapters. Rebus growled. The telephone had, as though prompted by the book's demise, started ringing. Softly, insistently. Rebus picked up the apparatus and studied it. It was six o'clock on the evening of his first rest-day in what seemed like months. Who would be phoning him? Pleasure or business? And which would he prefer it to be? He put the receiver to his ear.

'Yes?' His voice was non-committal.

'DI Rebus?' It was work then. Rebus grunted a response. 'DC Coupar here, sir. The Chief thought you'd be interested.' There was a pause for effect. 'A bomb's just gone off in Barnton.'

Rebus stared at the sheets of print lying all around him. He asked the Detective Constable to repeat the message.

'A bomb, sir. In Barnton.'

'What? A World War Two leftover you mean?'

'No, sir. Nothing like that. Nothing like that at all.'

There was a line of poetry in Rebus's head as he drove out towards one of Edinburgh's many quiet middle-class districts, the sort of place where nothing happened, the sort of place where crime was measured in a yearly attempted break-in or the theft of a bicycle. That was Barnton. The line of poetry hadn't been written about Barnton. It had been written about Slough.

It's my own fault, Rebus was thinking, for being disgusted at how far-fetched that Hammett book was. Entertaining, yes, but you could strain credulity only so far, and Dashiell Hammett had taken that strain like the anchor-man on a tug-o'-war team, pulling with all his might. Coincidence after coincidence, plot after plot, corpse following corpse like something off an assembly line.

Far-fetched, definitely. But then what was Rebus to make of his telephone call? He'd checked: it wasn't 1st April. But then he wouldn't put it past Brain Holmes or one of his other colleagues to pull a stunt on him just because he was having a day off, just because he'd carped on about it for the previous few days. Yes, this had Holmes' fingerprints all over it. Except for one thing.

The radio reports. The police frequency was full of it; and when Rebus switched on his car radio to the local commercial channel, the news was there, too. Reports of an explosion in Barnton, not far from the roundabout. It is thought a car has exploded. No further details, though there are thought to be many casualties. Rebus shook his head and drove, thinking of the poem again, thinking of anything that would stop him focussing on the truth of the news. A car bomb? A *car bomb*? In Belfast, yes, maybe even on occasion in London. But here in Edinburgh? Rebus blamed himself. If only he hadn't cursed Dashiell Hammett, if only he hadn't sneered at his book, at its exaggerations and its melodramas, if only . . . Then none of this would have happened.

But of course it would. It had.

The road had been blocked off. The ambulances had left with their cargo. Onlookers stood four deep behind the orange and white tape of the hastily erected cordon. There was just the one question: how many dead? The answer seemed to be: just the one. The driver of the car. An Army bomb disposal unit had materialised from somewhere and, for want of anything else to do, was checking the shops either side of the street. A line of policemen, aided so far as Rebus could judge by more Army personnel, was moving slowly up the road, mostly on hands and knees, in what an outsider might regard as some bizarre slow-motion race. They carried with them polythene bags, into which they dropped anything they found. The whole scene was one of brilliantly organised confusion and it didn't take Rebus longer than a couple of minutes to detect the mastermind behind it all—Superintendent 'Farmer' Watson. 'Farmer' only behind his back, of course, and a nickname which matched both his north-of-Scotland background and his at times agricultural methods. Rebus decided to skirt around his superior officer and glean what he could from the various less senior officers present.

He had come to Barnton with a set of preconceptions and it took time for these to be corrected. For example, he'd premised that the person in the car, the as-yet-unidentified deceased, would be the car's owner and that this person would have been the target of the bomb attack (the evidence all around most certainly pointed to a bomb, rather than spontaneous combustion, say, or any other more likely explanation). Either that or the car might be stolen or borrowed, and the driver some sort of terrorist, blown apart by his own device before he could leave it at its intended destination. There were certainly Army installations around Edinburgh: barracks, armouries, listening posts. Across the Forth lay what was left of Rosyth naval dockyard, as well as the underground installation at Pitreavie. There were targets. Bomb meant terrorist meant target. That was how it always was.

But not this time. This time there was an important difference. The apparent target escaped, by dint of leaving his car for a couple of minutes to nip into a shop. But while in the shop someone had tried to steal his car, and that person was now drying into the tarmac beneath the knees of the crawling policemen. This much Rebus learned before Superintendent Watson caught sight of him, caught sight of him smiling wryly at the car thief's luck. It wasn't every day you got the chance to steal a Jaguar XJS . . . but what a day to pick.

'Inspector!' Farmer Watson beckoned for Rebus to join him, which Rebus, ironing out his smile, did.

Before Watson could start filling him in on what he already knew, Rebus himself spoke.

'Who was the target, sir?'

'A man called Dean.' Meaningful pause. 'Brigadier-General Dean, retired.'

Rebus nodded. 'I thought there was a lot of Tommies about.'

'We'll be working with the Army on this one, John. That's how it's done, apparently. And then there's Scotland Yard, too. Their anti-terrorist people.'

'Too many cooks if you ask me, sir.'

Watson nodded. 'Still, these buggers are supposed to be specialised.'

'And we're only good for solving the odd drunk driving or domestic, eh, sir?'

The two men shared a smile at this. Rebus nodded towards the wreck of the car. 'Any idea who was behind the wheel?'

Watson shook his head. 'Not yet, and not much to go on either. We may have to wait till a mum or girlfriend reports him missing.'

'Not even a description?'

'None of the passers-by is fit to be questioned. Not yet anyway.'

'So what about Brigadier-General Whassisname?'

'Dean.'

'Yes. Where is he?'

'He's at home. A doctor's been to take a look at him, but he seems all right. A bit shocked.'

'A bit? Someone rips the arse out of his car and he's a *bit* shocked?' Rebus sounded doubtful. Watson's eyes were fixed on the advancing line of debris collectors.

'I get the feeling he's seen worse.' He turned to Rebus. 'Why don't you have a word with him, John? See what you think.'

Rebus nodded slowly. 'Aye, why not,' he said. 'Anything for a laugh, eh, sir?'

Watson seemed stuck for a reply, and by the time he'd formed one Rebus had wandered back through the cordon, hands in trouser pockets, looking for all the world like a man out for a stroll on a balmy summer's evening. Only then did the Superintendent remember that this was Rebus's day off. He wondered if it had been such a bright idea to send him off to talk to Brigadier-General Dean. Then he smiled, recalling that he had brought John Rebus out here precisely because something didn't quite feel right. If he could feel it, Rebus would feel it too, and would burrow deep to find its source—as deep as necessary and, perhaps, deeper than was seemly for a Superintendent to go.

Yes, there were times when even Detective Inspector John Rebus came in useful.

It was a big house. Rebus would go further. It was bigger than the last hotel he'd stayed in, though of a similar style: closer to Hammer Films than *House and Garden*. A hotel in Scarborough it had been; three days of lust with a divorced school-dinner lady. School-dinner ladies hadn't been like that in Rebus's day . . . or maybe he just hadn't been paying attention.

He paid attention now. Paid attention as an Army uniform opened the door of West Lodge to him. He'd already had to talk his way past a mixed guard on the gate—an apologetic PC and two uncompromising squaddies. That was why he'd started thinking back to Scarborough—to stop himself punching those squaddies in their square-chinned faces. The closer he came to Brigadier-General Dean, the more aggressive and unlovely the soldiers seemed. The two on the gate were like lambs compared to the one on the main door of the house, yet he in his turn was meekness itself compared to the one who led Rebus into a well-appointed living-room and told him to wait.

Rebus hated the Army—with good reason. He had seen the soldier's lot from the inside and it had left him with a resentment so huge that to call it a 'chip on the shoulder' was to do it an injustice. Chip? Right now it felt like a whole transport cafe! There was only one thing for it. Rebus made for the sideboard, sniffed the contents of the decanter sitting there and poured himself an inch of whisky. He was draining the contents of the glass into his mouth when the door opened.

Rebus had brought too many preconceptions with him today. Brigadier-Generals were squat, ruddy-faced men, with stiff moustaches and VSOP noses, a few silvered wisps of Brylcreemed hair and maybe even a walking stick. They retired in their seventies and babbled of campaigns over dinner.

Not so Brigadier-General Dean. He looked to be in his mid- to late-fifties. He stood over six feet tall, had a youthful face and vigorous dark hair. He was slim too, with no sign of a retirement gut or a port drinker's red-veined cheeks. He looked twice as fit as Rebus felt and for a moment the policeman actually caught himself straightening his back and squaring his shoulders.

'Good idea,' said Dean, joining Rebus at the sideboard, 'Mind if I join you?' His voice was soft, blurred at the edges, the voice of an educated man, a civilised man. Rebus tried hard to imagine Dean giving orders to a troop of hairy-fisted Tommies. Tried, but failed.

'Detective Inspector Rebus,' he said by way of introduction. 'Sorry to bother you like this, sir, but there are a few questions—'

Dean nodded, finishing his own drink and offering to replenish Rebus's.

'Why not?' agreed Rebus. Funny thing though: he could swear this whisky wasn't whisky at all but whiskey—Irish whiskey. Softer than the Scottish stuff, lacking an edge.

Rebus sat on the sofa, Dean on a well-used armchair. The Brigadier-General offered a toast of *slainte* before starting on his second drink, then exhaled noisily.

'Had to happen sooner or later, I suppose,' he said.

'Oh?'

Dean nodded slowly. 'I worked in Ulster for a time. Quite a long time. I suppose I was fairly high up in the tree there. I always knew I was a target. The Army knew, too, of course, but what can you do? You can't put bodyguards on every soldier who's been involved in the conflict, can you?'

'I suppose not, sir. But I assume you took precautions?'

Dean shrugged. 'I'm not in *Who's Who* and I've got an unlisted telephone number. I don't even use my rank much, to be honest.'

'But some of your mail might be addressed to Brigadier-General Dean?'

A wry smile. 'Who gave you that impression?'

'What impression, sir?'

'The impression of rank. I'm not a Brigadier-General. I retired with the rank of Major.'

'But the—'

'The what? The locals? Yes, I can see how gossip might lead to exaggeration. You know how it is in a place like this, Inspector. An incomer who keeps himself to himself. A military air. They put two and two together then multiply it by ten.'

Rebus nodded thoughtfully. 'I see.' Trust Watson to be wrong even in the fundamentals. 'But the point I was trying to make about your mail still stands, sir. What I'm wondering, you see, is how they found you.'

Dean smiled quietly. 'The IRA are quite sophisticated these days, Inspector. For all I know, they could have hacked into a computer, bribed someone

in the know, or maybe it was just a fluke, sheer chance.' He shrugged. 'I suppose we'll have to think of moving somewhere else now, starting all over again.
Poor Jacqueline.'

'Jacqueline being?'

'My daughter. She's upstairs, terribly upset. She's due to start university in
October. It's her I feel sorry for.'

Rebus looked sympathetic. He felt sympathetic. One thing about Army life
and police life—both could have a devastating effect on your personal life.

'And your wife, sir?'

'Dead, Inspector. Several years ago.' Dean examined his now empty glass.
He looked his years now, looked like someone who needed a rest. But there was
something other about him, something cool and hard. Rebus had met all types
in the Army—and since. Veneers could no longer fool him, and behind Major
Dean's sophisticated veneer he could glimpse something other, something from
the man's past. Dean hadn't just been a good soldier. At one time he'd been
lethal.

'Do you have any thoughts on how they might have found you, sir?'

'Not really.' Dean closed his eyes for a second. There was resignation in his
voice. 'What matters is that they *did* find me.' His eyes met Rebus's. 'And they
can find me again.'

Rebus shifted in his seat. Christ, what a thought. What a, well, time-bomb.
To always be watching, always expecting, always fearing. And not just for
yourself.

'I'd like to talk to Jacqueline, sir. It may be that she'll have some inkling as
to how they were able to—'

But Dean was shaking his head. 'Not just now, Inspector. Not yet. I don't
want her—well, you understand. Besides, I'd imagine that this will all be out of
your hands by tomorrow. I believe some people from the Anti-Terrorist Branch
are on their way up here. Between them and the Army . . . well, as I say, it'll be
out of your hands.'

Rebus felt himself prickling anew. But Dean was right, wasn't he? Why
strain yourself when tomorrow it would be someone else's weight? Rebus pursed
his lips, nodded, and stood up.

'I'll see you to the door,' said the Major, taking the empty glass from Rebus's
hand.

As they passed into the hallway, Rebus caught a glimpse of a young woman—
Jacqueline Dean presumably. She had been hovering by the telephone-table at
the foot of the staircase, but was now starting up the stairs themselves, her hand
thin and white on the bannister. Dean, too, watched her go. He half-smiled,
half-shrugged at Rebus.

'She's upset,' he explained unnecessarily. But she hadn't looked upset to
Rebus. She had looked like she was moping.

The next morning, Rebus went back to Barnton. Wooden boards had been placed over some of the shop windows, but otherwise there were few signs of yesterday's drama. The guards on the gate to West Lodge had been replaced by beefy plainclothes men with London accents. They carried portable radios, but otherwise might have been bouncers, debt collectors or bailiffs. They radioed the house. Rebus couldn't help thinking that a shout might have done the job for them, but they were in love with technology; you could see that by the way they held their radio-sets. He'd seen soldiers holding a new gun the same way.

'The guvnor's coming down to see you,' one of the men said at last. Rebus kicked his heels for a full minute before the man arrived.

'What do you want?'

'Detective Inspector Rebus, Central CID. I talked with Major Dean yesterday and—'

The man snapped. 'Who told you his rank?'

'Major Dean himself. I just wondered if I might—'

'Yes, well there's no need for that, Inspector. We're in charge now. Of course you'll be kept informed.'

The man turned and walked back through the gates with a steady, determined stride. The guards were smirking as they closed the gates behind their 'guvnor'. Rebus felt like a snubbed schoolboy, left out of the football game. Sides had been chosen and there he stood, unwanted. He could smell London on these men, that cocky superiority of a self-chosen elite. What did they call themselves? C13 or somesuch, the Anti-Terrorist Branch. Closely linked to Special Branch, and everyone knew the trade name for Special Branch—Smug Bastards.

The man had been a little younger than Rebus, well-groomed and accountant-like. More intelligent, for sure, than the gorillas on the gate, but probably well able to handle himself. A neat pistol might well have been hidden under the arm of his close-fitting suit. None of that mattered. What mattered was that the captain was leaving Rebus out of his team. It rankled; and when something rankled, it rankled hard.

Rebus had walked half a dozen paces away from the gates when he half-turned and stuck his tongue out at the guards. Then, satisfied with this conclusion to his morning's labours, he decided to make his own inquiries. It was eleven-thirty. If you want to find out about someone, reasoned a thirsty Rebus, visit his local.

The reasoning, in this case, proved false: Dean had never been near The Claymore.

'The daughter came in though,' commented one young man. There weren't many people in the pub at this early stage of the day, save a few retired gentlemen who were in conversation with three or four reporters. The barman, too, was busy telling his life story to a young female hack, or rather, into her tape recorder. This made getting served difficult, despite the absence of a lunchtime scrum. The young man had solved this problem, however, reaching behind the bar to refill his glass with a mixture of cider and lager, leaving money on the bartop.

'Oh?' Rebus nodded towards the three-quarters full glass. 'Have another?'

'When this one's finished I will.' He drank greedily, by which time the barman had finished with his confessions—much (judging by her face) to the relief of the reporter. 'Pint of Snakebite, Paul,' called the young man. When the drink was before him, he told Rebus that his name was Willie Barr and that he was unemployed.

'You said you saw the daughter in here?' Rebus was anxious to have his questions answered before the alcohol took effect on Barr.

'That's right. She came in pretty regularly.'

'By herself?'

'No, always with some guy.'

'One in particular, you mean?'

But Willie Barr laughed, shaking his head. 'A different one every time. She's getting a bit of a name for herself. And,' he raised his voice for the barman's benefit, 'she's not even eighteen, I'd say.'

'Were they local lads?'

'None I recognised. Never really spoke to them.' Rebus swirled his glass, creating a foamy head out of nothing.

'Any Irish accents among them?'

'In here?' Barr laughed. 'Not in here. Christ, no. Actually, she hasn't been in for a few weeks, now that I think of it. Maybe her father put a stop to it, eh? I mean, how would it look in the Sunday papers? Brigadier's daughter slumming it in Barnton.'

'Rebus smiled. 'It's not exactly a slum though, is it?'

'True enough, but her boyfriends . . . I mean, there was more of the car mechanic than the estate agent about them. Know what I mean?' He winked. 'Not that a bit of rough ever hurt *her* kind, eh?' Then he laughed again and suggested a game or two of pool, a pound a game or a fiver if the detective were a betting man.

But Rebus shook his head. He thought he knew now why Willie Barr was drinking so much: he was flush. And the reason he was flush was that he'd been telling his story to the papers—for a price. *Brigadier's Daughter Slumming It.* Yes, he'd been telling tales all right, but there was little chance of them reaching their intended audience. The Powers That Be would see to that.

Barr was helping himself to another pint as Rebus made to leave the premises.

It was late in the afternoon when Rebus received his visitor, the Anti-Terrorist accountant.

'A Mr. Matthews to see you,' the Desk Sergeant had informed Rebus, and 'Matthews' he remained, giving no hint of rank or proof of identity. He had come, he said, to 'have it out' with Rebus.

'What were you doing in The Claymore?'

'Having a drink.'

'You were asking questions. I've already told you, Inspector Rebus, we can't have—'

'I know, I know.' Rebus raised his hands in a show of surrender. 'But the more furtive you lot are, the more interested I become.'

Matthews stared silently at Rebus. Rebus knew that the man was weighing up his options. One, of course, was to go to Farmer Watson and have Rebus warned off. But if Matthews were as canny as he looked, he would know this might have the opposite effect from that intended. Another option was to talk to Rebus, to ask him what he wanted to know.

'What do you want to know?' Matthews said at last.

'I want to know about Dean.'

Matthews sat back in his chair. 'In strictest confidence?'

Rebus nodded. 'I've never been known as a clipe.'

'A clipe?'

'Someone who tells tales,' Rebus explained. Matthews was thoughtful.

'Very well then,' he said. 'For a start, Dean is an alias, a very necessary one. During his time in the Army Major Dean worked in Intelligence, mostly in West Germany but also for a time in Ulster. His work in both spheres was very important, crucially important. I don't need to go into details. His last posting was West Germany. His wife was killed in a terrorist attack, almost certainly IRA. We don't think they had targeted her specifically. She was just in the wrong place with the wrong number plates.'

'A car bomb?'

'No, a bullet. Through the windscreen, point-blank. Major Dean asked to be . . . he was invalided out. It seemed best. We provided him with a change of identity, of course.'

'I thought he looked a bit young to be retired. And the daughter, how did she take it?'

'She was never told the full details, not that I'm aware of. She was in boarding school in England.' Matthews paused. 'It was for the best.'

Rebus nodded. 'Of course, nobody'd argue with that. But why did—Dean—choose to live in Barnton?'

Matthews rubbed his left eyebrow, then pushed his spectacles back up his sharply sloping nose. 'Something to do with an aunt of his,' he said. 'He spent holidays there as a boy. His father was Army, too, posted here, there and everywhere. Never the most stable upbringing. I think Dean had happy memories of Barnton.'

Rebus shifted in his seat. He couldn't know how long Matthews would stay, how long he would continue to answer Rebus's questions. And there were so many questions.

'What about the bomb?'

'Looks like the IRA, all right. Standard fare for them, all the hallmarks. It's still being examined, of course, but we're pretty sure.'

'And the deceased?'

'No clues yet. I suppose he'll be reported missing sooner or later. We'll leave that side of things to you.'

'Gosh, thanks.' Rebus waited for his sarcasm to penetrate, then, quickly. 'How does Dean get on with his daughter?'

Matthews was caught off-guard by the question. He blinked twice, three times, then glanced at his wristwatch.

'All right, I suppose,' he said at last, making a show of scratching a mark from his cuff. 'I can't see what . . . Look, Inspector, as I say, we'll keep you fully informed. But meantime—'

'Keep out of your hair?'

'If you want to put it like that.' Matthews stood up. 'Now I really must be getting back—'

'To London?'

Matthews smiled at the eagerness in Rebus's voice. 'To Barnton. Don't worry, Inspector, the more *you* keep out of my *hair*, the quicker I can get out of yours. Fair enough?' He shot a hand out towards Rebus, who returned the almost painful grip.

'Fair enough,' said Rebus. He ushered Matthews from the room and closed the door again, then returned to his seat. He slouched as best he could in the hard, uncomfortable chair and put his feet up on the desk, examining his scuffed shoes. He tried to feel like Sam Spade, but failed. His legs soon began to ache and he slid them from the surface of the desk. The coincidences in Dashiell Hammett had nothing on the coincidence of someone nicking a car seconds before it exploded. Someone must have been watching, ready to detonate the device. But if they were watching, how come they didn't spot that Dean, the intended victim, wasn't the one to drive off?

Either there was more to this than met the eye, or else there was less. Rebus was wary—very wary. He'd already made far too many prejudgments, had already been proved wrong too many times. Keep an open mind, that was the secret. An open mind and an inquiring one. He nodded his head slowly, his eyes on the door.

'Fair enough,' he said quietly. 'I'll keep out of your hair, Mr Matthews, but that doesn't necessarily mean I'm leaving the barber's.'

The Claymore might not have been Barnton's most salubrious establishment, but it was as Princes Street's Caledonian Hotel in comparison with the places

Rebus visited that evening. He began with the merely seedy bars, the ones where each quiet voice seemed to contain a lifetime's resentment, and then moved downwards, one rung of the ladder at a time. It was slow work; the bars tended to be in a ring around Edinburgh, sometimes on the outskirts or in the distant housing schemes, sometimes nearer the centre than most of the population would care to think.

Rebus hadn't made many friends in his adult life, but he had his network of contacts and he was as proud of it as any grandparent would be of their extended family. They were like cousins, these contacts; mostly they knew each other, at least by reputation, but Rebus never spoke to one about another, so that the extent of the chain could only be guessed at. There were those of his colleagues who, in Major Dean's words, added two and two, then multiplied by ten. John Rebus, it was reckoned, had as big a net of 'snitches' as any copper on the force bar none.

It took four hours and an outlay of over forty pounds before Rebus started to catch a glimpse of a result. His basic question, though couched in vague and imprecise terms, was simple; have any car thieves vanished off the face of the earth since yesterday?

One name was uttered by three very different people in three distinct parts of the city: Brian Cant. The name meant little to Rebus.

'It wouldn't,' he was told. 'Brian only shifted across here from the west a year or so ago. He's got form from when he was a nipper, but he's grown smart since then. When the Glasgow cops started sniffing, he moved operations.' The detective listened, nodded, drank a watered-down whisky, and said little. Brian Cant grew from a name into a description, from a description into a personality. But there was something more.

'You're not the only one interested in him,' Rebus was told in a bar in Gorgie. 'Somebody else was asking questions a wee while back. Remember Jackie Hanson?'

'He used to be CID, didn't he?'

'That's right, but not any more . . . '

Not just any old banger for Brian Cant: he specialised in 'quality motors'. Rebus eventually got an address: a third-floor tenement flat near Powderhall race-track. A young man answered the door. His name was Jim Cant, Brian's younger brother. Rebus saw that Jim was scared, nervous. He chipped away at the brother quickly, explaining that he was there because he thought Brian might be dead. That he knew all about Cant's business, but that he wasn't interested in pursuing this side of things, except insofar as it might shed light on the death. It took a little more of this, then the brother opened up.

'He said he had a customer interested in a car,' Jim Cant explained. 'An Irishman, he said.'

'How did he know the man was Irish?'

'Must have been the voice. I don't think they met. Maybe they did. The man was interested in a specific car.'

'A red Jaguar?'

'Yeah, convertible. Nice cars. The Irishman even knew where there was one. It seemed a cinch, that's what Brian kept saying. A cinch.'

'He didn't think it would be hard to steal?'

'Five seconds' work, that's what he kept saying. I thought it sounded too easy. I told him so.' He bent over in his chair, grabbing at his knees and sinking his head between them. 'Ach, Brian, what the hell have you done?'

Rebus tried to comfort the young man as best he could with brandy and tea. He drank a mug of tea himself, wandering though the flat, his mind thrumming. Was he blowing things up out of all proportion? Maybe. He'd made mistakes before, not so much errors of judgment as errors of jumping the gun. But there was something about all of this . . . Something.

'Do you have a photo of Brian?' he asked as he was leaving. 'A recent one would be best.' Jim Cant handed him a holiday snap.

'We went to Crete last summer,' he explained. 'It was magic.' Then, holding the door open for Rebus: 'Don't I have to identify him or something?'

Rebus thought of the scrapings which were all that remained of what may or may not have been Brian Cant. He shook his head. 'I'll let you know,' he said. 'If we need you, we'll let you know.'

The next day was Sunday, day of rest. Rebus rested in his car, parked fifty yards or so along the road from the gates to West Lodge. He put his radio on, folded his arms and sank down into the driver's seat. This was more like it. The Hollywood private eye on a stakeout. Only in the movies, a stakeout could be whittled away to a few minutes' footage. Here, it was measured in a slow ticking of seconds . . . minutes . . . quarter hours.

Eventually, the gates opened and a figure hurried out, fairly trotting along the pavement as though released from bondage. Jacqueline Dean was wearing a denim jacket, short black skirt and thick black tights. A beret sat awkwardly on her cropped dark hair and she pressed the palm of her hand to it from time to time to stop it sliding off altogether. Rebus locked his car before following her. He kept to the other side of the road, wary not so much from fear that she might spot him but because C13 might have put a tail on her, too.

She stopped at the local newsagent's first and came out heavy-laden with Sunday papers. Rebus, making to cross the road, a Sunday-morning stroller, studied her face. What was the expression he'd thought of the first time he'd seen her? Yes, *moping*. There was still something of that in her liquid eyes, the dark shadows beneath. She was making for the corner shop now. Doubtless she would appear with rolls or bacon or butter or milk. All the things Rebus seemed to find himself short of on a Sunday, no matter how hard he planned.

He felt in his jacket pockets, but found nothing of comfort there, just the photograph of Brian Cant. The window of the corner shop, untouched by the blast, contained a dozen or so personal ads, felt-tipped onto plain white post-cards. He glanced at these, and past them, through the window itself to where Jacqueline was making her purchases. Milk and rolls: elementary, my dear Conan Doyle. Waiting for her change, she half-turned her head towards the window. Rebus concentrated on the postcards. 'Candy, Masseuse' vied for atten-tion with 'Pram and carry-cot for sale', 'Babysitting considered', and 'Lada, sel-dom used'. Rebus was smiling, almost despite himself, when the door of the shop tinkled open.

'Jacqueline?' he said. She turned towards him. He was holding open his ID. 'Mind if I have a word, Miss Dean?'

Major Dean was pouring himself a glass of Irish whiskey when the drawing-room door opened.

'Mind if I come in?' Rebus's words were directed not at Dean but at Matthews, who was seated in a chair by the window, one leg crossed over the other, hands gripping the arm-rests. He looked like a nervous businessman on an airplane, trying not to let his neighbour see his fear.

'Inspector Rebus,' he said tonelessly. 'I thought I could feel my scalp tingle.'

Rebus was already in the room. He closed the door behind him. Dean ges-tured with the decanter, but Rebus shook his head.

'How did you get in?' Matthews asked.

'Miss Dean was good enough to escort me through the gate. You've changed the guard detail again. She told them I was a friend of the family.'

Matthews nodded. 'And are you, Inspector? Are you a friend of the family?'

'That depends on what you mean by friendship.'

Dean had seated himself on the edge of his chair, steadying the glass with both hands. He didn't seem quite the figure he had been on the day of the explosion. A reaction, Rebus didn't doubt. There had been a quiet euphoria on the day; now came the aftershock.

'Where's Jacqui?' Dean asked, having paused with the glass to his lips.

'Upstairs,' Rebus explained. 'I thought it would be better if she didn't hear this.'

Matthews fingers plucked at the arm-rests. 'How much does she know?'

'Not much, Not yet. Maybe she'll work it out for herself.'

'So, Inspector, we come to the reason why you're here.'

'I'm here.' Rebus began, 'as part of a murder inquiry. I thought that's why you were here, too, Mr Matthews. Maybe I'm wrong. Maybe you're here to cover up rather than bring to light.'

Matthews' smile was momentary. But he said nothing.

'I didn't go looking for the culprits,' Rebus went on. 'As you said, Mr Matthews, that was *your* department. But I did wonder who the victim was. The accidental victim, as I thought. A young car thief called Brian Cant, that would be my guess. He stole cars to order. A client asked him for a red open-top Jag, even told him where he might find one. The client told him about Major Dean. Very specifically about Major Dean, right down to the fact that every day he'd nip into the wine-shop on the main street.' Rebus turned to Dean. 'A bottle of Irish a day, is it, sir?'

Dean merely shrugged and drained his glass.

'Anyway, that's what your daughter told me. So all Brian Cant had to do was wait near the wine-shop. You'd get out of your car, leave it running, and while you were in the shop he could drive the car away. Only it bothered me that the client—Cant's brother tells me he spoke with an Irish accent—knew so much, making it easy for Cant. What was stopping this person from stealing the car himself?'

'And the answer came to you?' Matthews suggested, his voice thick with irony.

Rebus chose to avoid his tone. He was still watching Dean. 'Not straight away, not even then. But when I came to the house, I couldn't help noticing that Miss Dean seemed a bit strange. Like she was waiting for a phone call from someone and that someone had let her down. It's easy to be specific now, but at the time it just struck me as odd. I asked her about it this morning and she admitted it's because she's been jilted. A man she'd been seeing, and seeing regularly, had suddenly stopped calling. I asked her about him, but she couldn't be very helpful. They never went to his flat, for example. He drove a flashy car and had plenty of money, but she was vague about what he did for a living.'

Rebus took a photograph from his pocket and tossed it into Dean's lap. Dean froze, as though it were some hair-trigger grenade.

'I showed her a photograph of Brian Cant. Yes, that was the name of her boyfriend—Brian Cant. So you see, it was small wonder she hadn't heard from him.'

Matthews rose from the chair and stood before the window itself, but nothing he saw there seemed to please him, so he turned back into the room. Dean had found the courage to lift the photograph from his leg and place it on the floor. He got up too, and made for the decanter.

'For Christ's sake,' Matthews hissed, but Dean poured regardless.

Rebus's voice was level. 'I always thought it was a bit of a coincidence, the car being stolen only seconds before exploding. But then the IRA use remote control devices, don't they? So that someone in the vicinity could have triggered the bomb any time they liked. No need for all these long-term timers and what have you. I was in the SAS once myself.'

Matthews raised an eyebrow. 'Nobody told me that,' he said, sounding impressed for the first time.

'So much for Intelligence, eh?' Rebus answered. 'Speaking of which, you told me that Major Dean here was in Intelligence. I think I'd go further. Covert operations, that sort of thing? Counter-intelligence, subversion?'

'Now you're speculating, Inspector.'

Rebus shrugged. 'It doesn't really matter. What matters is that someone had been spying on Brian Cant, an ex-policeman called Jackie Hanson. He's a private detective these days. He won't say anything about his clients, of course, but I think I can put two and two together without multiplying the result. He was working for you, Major Dean, because you were interested in Brian Cant. Jacqueline was serious about him, wasn't she? So much so that she might have forsaken university. She tells me they were even talking of moving in together. You didn't want her to leave. When you found out what Cant did for a . . . a living, I suppose you'd call it, you came up with a plan.' Rebus was enjoying himself now, but tried to keep the pleasure out of his voice.

'You contacted Cant,' he went on, 'putting on an Irish accent. Your Irish accent is probably pretty good, isn't it, Major? It would need to be, working in counter-intelligence. You told him all about a car—your car. You offered him a lot of money if he'd steal it for you and you told him precisely when and where he might find it. Cant was greedy. He didn't think twice.' Rebus noticed that he was sitting very comfortably in his own chair, whereas Dean looked . . . the word that sprang to mind was 'rogue'. Matthews, too, was sparking internally, though his surface was all metal sheen, cold bodywork.

'You'd know how to make a bomb, that goes without saying. Wouldn't you, Major? Know thine enemy and all that. Like I say, I was in the SAS myself. What's more, you'd know how to make an IRA device, or one that looked like the work of the IRA. The remote was in your pocket. You went into the shop, bought your whiskey, and when you heard the car being driven off, you simply pressed the button.'

'Jacqueline.' Dean's voice was little more than a whisper. 'Jacqueline.' He rose to his feet, walked softly to the door and left the room. He appeared to have heard little or nothing of Rebus's speech. Rebus felt a pang of disappointment and looked towards Matthews, who merely shrugged.

'You cannot, of course, prove any of this, Inspector.'

'If I put my mind to it I can.'

'Oh, I've no doubt, no doubt.' Matthews paused. 'But will you?'

'He's mad, you've got to see that.'

'Mad? Well, he's unstable. Ever since his wife . . . '

'No reason for him to murder Brian Cant.' Rebus helped himself to a whiskey now, his legs curiously shaky. 'How long have you known?'

Matthews shrugged again. 'He tried a similar trick in Germany, apparently. It didn't work that time. So what do we do now? Arrest him? He'd be unfit to plead.'

'However it happens,' Rebus said, 'he's got to be made safe.'

'Absolutely.' Matthews was nodding agreement. He came to the sideboard. 'A hospital, somewhere he can be treated. He was a good soldier in his day. I've read his record. A good soldier. Don't worry, Inspector Rebus, he'll be "made safe" as you put it. He'll be taken care of.' A hand landed on Rebus's forearm. 'Trust me.'

Rebus trusted Matthews—about as far as he could spit into a Lothian Road headwind. He had a word with a reporter friend, but the man wouldn't touch the story. He passed Rebus on to an investigative journalist who did some ferreting, but there was little or nothing to be found. Rebus didn't know Dean's real name. He didn't know Matthews' first name or rank or even, to be honest, that he had been C13 at all. He might have been Army, or have inhabited that indefinite smear of operations somewhere between Army, Secret Service and Special Branch.

By the next day, Dean and his daughter had left West Lodge and a fortnight later it appeared in the window of an estate agent on George Street. The asking price seemed surprisingly low, if your tastes veered towards *The Munsters*. But the house would stay in the window for a long time to come.

Dean haunted Rebus's dreams for a few nights, no more. But how did you make safe a man like that? The Army had designed a weapon and that weapon had become misadjusted, its sights all wrong. You could dismantle a weapon. You could dismantle a man, too, come to that. But each and every piece was still as lethal as the whole. Rebus put aside fiction, put aside Hammett and the rest and of an evening read psychology books instead. But then they too, in their way, were fiction, weren't they? And so, too, in time became the case that was not a case of the man who had never been.

CLARK HOWARD
1934–

A prolific and eclectic writer of mystery, Western, true crime genres, Clark Howard grew up in the lower West Side of Chicago. He was a ward of the county and habitual runaway who was eventually sent to a state reformatory for what he calls being "recalcitrant." He joined the Marines and served in combat in the Korean War. He began writing shortly afterwards. The number of his publications keeps rapidly increasing, including writing for Crime Library electronic publishing (www.crimelibrary.com), a rapidly growing collection of award-winning short stories by prominent writers as well as hundreds of nonfiction feature articles on crime and crime-related topics.

Howard has written over 20 novels and over 200 short stories. He has five Ellery Queen Readers' Awards and a dozen award nominations by Mystery Writers of America, Western Writers of America, and Private Eye Writers of America. His work has been adapted for film and television. "Horn Man," (available at Crime Library online) won the Edgar

Award in 1981 for Best Short Story, and "To Live and Die in Midland, Texas," which appeared in *Ellery Queen's Mystery Magazine* (EQMM) Sept./Oct. 2002, was nominated for an Anthony Award. His mystery stories regularly appear in "best of" collections, including "Horn Man" in *The 50 Greatest Mysteries of All Time* (1998), edited by Otto Penzler. "Under Suspicion" was selected for *The Best American Mystery Stories 2001*, edited by Lawrence Block, and *The World's Finest Mystery and Crime Stories: Second Annual Collection* (2001), edited by Ed Gorman. Much of Howard's work is set in the streets of Chicago, the city he remembers from his boyhood as the place of great fun and challenge despite an underprivileged and deprived youth. "Under Suspicion," which deals with the Chicago police department and officer Frank Dell, was first published in *Ellery Queen's Mystery Magazine*, March 2000.

Recommended Howard works: *Challenge the Widow-Maker and Other Stories of People in Peril, Crowded Lives and Other Stories of Desperation and Danger, Hard City*.

Other recommended authors: James Lee Burke, Michael Connelly, Ed McBain.

Under Suspicion

Frank Dell walked into the Three Corners Club shortly after five, as he usually did every day, and took a seat at the end of the bar. The bartender, seeing him, put together, without being told, a double Tanqueray over two ice cubes with two large olives, and set it in front of him on a cork coaster. Down at the middle of the bar, Dell saw two minor stickup men he remembered from somewhere and began staring at them without touching his drink. Frank Dell's stare was glacial and unblinking. After three disconcerting minutes of it, the two stickup men paid for their drinks and left. Only then did Dell lift his own glass.

Tim Callan, the club owner, came over and sat opposite Dell. "Well, I see you just cost me a couple more customers, Frankie," he said wryly.

"Hoodlums," Dell replied. "I'm just helping you keep the place respectable, Timmy."

"Bring some of your policemen buddies in to drink," Callan suggested. "That'll keep me respectable *and* profitable."

"You're not hurting for profits," Dell said. "Not with that after-hours poker game you run in the apartment upstairs."

Callan laughed. "Ah, Frankie, Frankie. Been quick with the answers all your life. You should've been a lawyer. Even my old dad, rest his soul, used to say that."

"I'm not crooked enough to be a lawyer," Dell said, sipping his drink.

"Not crooked *enough*! Hell, you're not crooked at all, Frankie. You're probably the straightest cop in Chicago." Callan leaned forward on one elbow. "How long we known each other, Frank?"

"What's on your mind, Tim?" Dell asked knowingly. Reminiscing, he had learned, frequently led to other things.

"We go back thirty years, do you realize that, Frank?" Callan replied, ignoring Dell's suspicion. "First grade at St. Mel's school out on the West Side."

"What's on your mind, Tim?" Dell's expression hardened just a hint. He hated asking the same question twice.

"Remember my baby sister, Francie?" Callan asked, lowering his voice.

"Sure. Cute little kid. Carrot-red hair. Freckles. Eight or ten years younger than us."

"Nine. She's twenty-seven now. She married this Guinea a few years ago, name of Nicky Santore. They moved up to Milwaukee where the guy's uncle got him a job in a brewery. Well, they started having problems. You know the greaseballs, they're all Don Juans, chasing broads all the time—"

"Get to the point, Tim," said Dell. He hated embellishment.

"OK. Francie left him and came back to live with my brother, Dennis—you know him, the fireman. Anyhow, after she got back, she found out she's expecting. Then Nicky finds out, and he comes back too. Guy begs Francie to take him back, and she does. Now, the only job he can get down here is pumping gas at a Texaco station, which only pays minimum wage. He's worried about doctor bills and everything with the baby coming, so he agrees, for a cut, to let a cousin of his use the station storeroom to stash hot goods. It works OK for a while, but then the cousin gets busted and leads the cops to the station. They find a load of laptop computers. Nick gets charged with receiving stolen property. He comes up for a preliminary hearing in three weeks."

"Tough break," Dell allowed, sipping again. "But he should get probation if he's got no priors."

"He's got a prior," Callan said, looking down at the bar.

"What is it?"

"Burglary. Him and that same cousin robbed some hotel rooms down at the Hilton when they was working as bellmen. Years ago. Both of them got probation on that."

"Then he's looking at one-to-four on this fall," Dell said.

Callan swallowed. "Can you help me out on this, Frankie?"

Dell gave him the stare. "You don't mean help you, Tim. You mean help Nicky Santore. What do you think I can do?"

"Give your personal voucher for him."

"Are you serious? You want me to go to an assistant state's attorney handling an RSP case and personally vouch for some Guinea with a prior that I don't even know?"

"Frank, it's for Francie—"

"No, it isn't. If Francie was charged, I'd get her off in a heartbeat. But it's not Francie; it's some two-bit loser she married."

"Frank, please, listen—"

"No. Forget it."

There was a soft buzzing signal from the pager clipped to Dell's belt. Reaching under his coat, he got it out and looked at it. It was a 911 page from the Lakeside station house out on the South Side, where he was assigned.

"I have to answer this," he told Callan. Taking a cellular phone from his coat pocket, he opened it and dialed one of the station house's unlisted numbers. When someone answered, he said, "This is Dell. I got a nine-one-one page."

"Yeah, it's Captain Larne. Hold on."

A moment later, an older, huskier voice spoke. "Dell? Mike Larne. Where's Dan?" He was asking about Dan Malone, Dell's partner, a widower in his fifties.

"Probably at home," Dell told the captain. "I dropped him off there less than an hour ago. What's up, Cap?"

"Edie Malone was found dead in her apartment a little while ago. It looks like she's been strangled."

Dell said nothing. He froze, absolutely still, the little phone at his ear. Edie was Dan's only child.

"Dell? Did you hear me?"

"Yessir, I heard you. Captain, I can't tell him—"

"You won't have to. The department chaplain and Dan's parish priest get that dirty job. What I want you to do is help me keep Dan from going off the deep end over this. You know how he is. We can't have *him* going wild thinking he'll solve this himself."

"What do you want me to do?"

"I'm going to assign you temporary duty to the homicide team working the case. If Dan knows you're on it, he might stay calm. Understand where I'm coming from?"

"Yessir." Dell was still frozen, motionless.

"Take down this address," Larne said. Dell animated, taking a small spiral notebook and ballpoint from his shirt pocket. He wrote down the address Larne gave him. "The homicide boys have only been there a little while. Kenmare and Garvan. Know them?"

"Yeah, Kenmare, slightly. They know I'm coming?"

"Absolutely. This has all been cleared with headquarters." Larne paused a beat, then said, "You knew the girl, did you?"

"Yessir."

"Well," Larne sighed heavily. "I hate to do this to you, Frank—"

"It's all right, Cap. I understand."

"Call me at home later."

"Right."

Dell closed the phone and slipped it back into his pocket. He walked away from the bar and out of the club without another word to Tim Callan.

Edie Malone's address was one of the trendy new apartment buildings remodeled from old commercial high-rises on the near North Side. The sixth floor had been cordoned off to permit only residents of that floor to exit the elevator, and they were required to go directly to their apartments. Edie Malone's apartment was posted as a crime scene. In addition to homicide detectives Kenmare and Garvan, there were half a dozen uniformed officers guarding the hallways and stairwells, personnel from the city crime lab in the apartment itself, and a deputy coroner and Cook County morgue attendants waiting to transport the victim to the county hospital complex for autopsy.

When Frank Dell arrived, Kenmare and Garvan took him into the bedroom to view the body. Edie Malone was wearing a white cotton sweatshirt with MONICA FOR PRESIDENT lettered on it, and a pair of cutoff denim shorts. Barefoot, she was lying on her back, elbows bent, hands a few inches from her ears, feet apart as if she were resting, with her long, dark red hair splayed out on the white shag carpet like spilled paint. Her eyes were wide open in a bloated face, the neck below it ringed with ugly purplish bruises. Looking at her, Dell had to blink back tears.

"I guess you knew her, your partner's daughter and all," said Kenmare. Dell nodded.

"Who found her?"

"Building super," said Garvan. "She didn't show up for work today and didn't answer the phone when her boss called. Then a coworker got nervous about it and told the boss that the victim had just broken up with a guy who she was afraid was going to rough her up over it. They finally came over and convinced the super to take a look in the apartment. The boss and the coworker were down in his office when we got here. We questioned them briefly, then sent them home. They've been instructed not to talk about it until after we see them tomorrow."

The three detectives went into the kitchen and sat at Edie's table, where the two from homicide continued to share their notes with Dell.

"Coroner guy says she looks like she's been dead sixteen, eighteen hours, which would mean sometime late last night, early this morning," said Garvan.

"She worked for Able, Bennett, and Crain Advertising Agency in the Loop," said Kenmare, then paused, adding, "Maybe you know some of this stuff already, from your partner."

Dell shook his head. "Dan and his daughter hadn't been close, for a while. He didn't approve of Edie's lifestyle. He and his wife had saved for years to send her to the University of Chicago so she could become a teacher, but then Dan's wife died, and a little while after that Edie quit school and moved out to be on her own. Dan didn't talk much about her after that."

"But Captain Larne still thinks Dan might jump ranks and try to work the case himself?"

"Sure." Dell shrugged. "She was still his daughter, his only kid."

"OK," Kenmare said, "we'll give you everything, then. Her boss was a Ronald Deever, one of the ad agency execs. The coworker who tipped him about the ex-boyfriend is a copywriter named Sally Simms."

"Did she know the guy's name?" Dell asked.

"Yeah." Kenmare flipped a page in his notebook. "Bob Pilcher. He's some kind of redneck. Works as a bouncer at one of those line-dancing clubs over in Hee-Haw town. The Simms woman met him a couple times on double dates with the victim." He closed his notebook. "That's it so far."

"Where do we go from here?" Dell asked.

Kenmare and Garvan exchanged glances. "We haven't figured that out yet," said the former. "You've been assigned by a district captain, with headquarters approval and a nod from our own commander, and the victim is the daughter of a veteran cop who's your senior partner. We'll be honest, Dell. We're not sure what your agenda is here."

Dell shook his head. "No agenda," he said. "I'm here to make it look good to Dan Malone so he'll get through this thing as calmly as possible. But it's your case. You two tell me what I can do to help and I'll do it. Or I'll just stand around and watch, if that's how you want it. Your call."

Kenmare and Garvan looked at each other for a moment, then both nodded. "OK," said Kenmare, "we can live with that. We'll work together on it." The two homicide detectives shook hands with Dell, the first time they had done so. Then Kenmare, who was the senior officer, said, "Let's line it up. First thing is to toss the bedroom as soon as the body is out and the crime lab guys are done. Maybe we'll get lucky, find a diary, love letters, stuff like that. You do the bedroom, Frank. You knew her; you might tumble to something that we might not think was important. While you're doing that, we'll work this floor, the one above, and the one below, canvassing the neighbors. We'll have uniforms working the other floors. Then we'll regroup."

With that agreed to, the detectives split up.

It was after ten when they got back together.

"Bedroom?" asked Kenmare. Dell handed him a small red address book.

"Just this. Looks like it might be old. Lot of neighborhood names where Dan still lives. None of the new telephone exchanges in it."

"That's it?"

"Everything else looks normal to me," Dell nodded. "Clothes, makeup, couple of paperback novels, Valium and birth-control pills in the medicine cabinet, that kind of stuff. But I'd feel better if one of you guys would do a follow-up toss."

"Good idea." Kenmare motioned to Garvan, who went into the bedroom.

"Neighbors?" Dell asked.

"Zilch," said Kenmare.

Kenmare and Dell cruised the living room and small kitchen, studying everything again, until Garvan came back out of the bedroom and announced, "It's clean." Then the men sat back down at the kitchen table.

"Let's line up tomorrow," Kenmare said. "Dell, you and I will work together, and I'll have Garvan sit in on the autopsy; he can also work some of the names in the address book by phone before and after. You and I will go see Ronald Deever and Sally Simms at the ad agency, maybe interview some of the other employees there also. We need to track down this guy Pilcher, too. Let's meet at seven for breakfast and see if there's anything we need to do before that. Frank, there's a little diner called Wally's just off Thirteenth and State. We can eat, then walk over to headquarters and set up a temporary desk for you in our bullpen."

"Sounds good," Dell said.

Kenmare left a uniformed officer at the door to Edie Malone's apartment, one at each end of the sixth-floor hallway, one at the elevator, and two in the lobby. When the detectives parted outside, Dell drove back to the South Side, where he lived. When he got into his own apartment, a little after midnight, he called Mike Larne at home.

"It's Dell, Captain," he said when Larne answered sleepily.

"How's it look?" Larne asked.

"Not good," Dell told him. "Only one possible lead so far: an ex-boyfriend who threatened to slap her around. We'll start doing some deeper work on it tomorrow."

"Was she raped?"

"Didn't look like it."

"Thank God for that much."

"I'll let you know for sure after the autopsy."

"All right. How's it setting with Kenmare and Garvan? You getting any resistance?"

"No, it's fine. They're OK. They're giving me a temp desk downtown tomorrow. What's the word on Dan?"

"The poor man is completely undone. The chaplain and the parish priest managed to get him drunk and put him to bed. Jim Keenan and some of the other boys are staying at the house until Dan's sisters arrive from Florida. Listen, you get some sleep. I'll talk to you tomorrow."

"OK, Cap."

Dell hung up and went directly to the cabinet where he kept his bottle of gin.

At the Able, Bennett, and Crain advertising agency the next day, on the fortieth floor of a Loop building, Kenmare sat in Ronald Deever's private office to interview him while Dell talked with Sally Simms in a corner of the firm's coffee room. Sally was a pert blonde who wrote copy for a dental products account. She told Dell that Edie Malone had been employed by the agency for about eight months as a receptionist and was well liked by everyone she worked with. Sally had double dated with her half a dozen times, twice with the man named Bob Pilcher.

"He's from North Carolina, a heavy smoker," she said. "That was the main reason Edie quit going out with him; she didn't like smokers. Said kissing them was like licking an ashtray."

"What's the name of the club where he works?" Dell asked.

"It's called Memphis City Limits. Kind of a hillbilly joint. Over on Fullerton near Halsted."

"What made you tell your boss that you were afraid Pilcher might rough Edie up?"

"That's what Edie told me. She said Bob told her he wasn't used to women dumping him, and maybe she just needed a little slapping around to get her act together. Edie wasn't sure he meant it, but I was. I mean, this is one of those guys that doesn't just walk, he *struts*. And he wears those real tight Wranglers to show off his package. Got real wavy hair with one little curl always down on his forehead. Ask me, he's definitely the kind would slap a woman around. I told Edie she was better off sticking with guys like Bart Mason."

"Who's he?" Dell asked.

"Bart? He's a nice young exec works for the home office of an insurance company down on twenty-two. They dated for a while, then broke up when Edie started seeing someone else."

"Who did she start seeing?"

Sally shrugged. "I don't know. She went out a lot."

"Have you told Bart Mason that Edie's dead?"

"Why, no. That detective in Ron Deever's office told both of us not to mention it."

"We appreciate that you didn't," "Dell said. "Besides this Bart Mason, do you know of any other men in the building that Edie went out with?"

"No," Sally said, shaking her head.

Just then, Kenmare came into the room. He said nothing, not wishing to interrupt the flow of Dell's interview. But Dell rose, saying, "OK, thanks very much, Miss Simms. We'll be in touch if we need anything else."

"Do I still have to not talk about it?" Sally asked.

"No, you can talk about it now. It'll be in the afternoon papers anyway. But don't call Bart Mason yet. We want to talk to him first." When Sally left the room, Dell said to Kenmare, "Bart Mason, guy works for an insurance company down on twenty-two, used to date Edie. Supposedly doesn't know she's dead yet."

"Let's see," said Kenmare.

Going down in the elevator, Dell asked, "Anything with Deever?"

"Nothing interesting."

The insurance company occupied the entire twenty-second floor, and the detectives had a receptionist show them to Bart Mason's office without announcing them. Once there, Kenmare thanked her and closed the door behind them. They identified themselves and Kenmare said, "Mr. Mason, do you know a woman named Edie Malone?"

"Sure. She works for an ad agency up on forty," Mason said. "We used to date." He was a pleasant-looking young man, neat as a drill instructor. "Why, what's the matter?"

"She was found murdered in her apartment."

"*Edie?*" The color drained from Bart Mason's face, and his eyes widened almost to bulging. "I don't believe it—"

"Can you tell us your whereabouts for the last forty-eight hours, Mr. Mason?"

Mason was staring incredulously at them. "Edie—murdered—?"

"We need to know where you've been for the last couple of days," Kenmare said.

"What? Oh, sure—" Mason picked up his phone and dialed a three-number extension. When his call was answered, he said, "Jenny, will you come over to my office right away? It's important."

"Who's that?" Dell asked when Mason hung up.

"My fiancée. Jenny Paula. She works over in claims. We live together. We're together all the time: eat breakfast together, come to work together, eat lunch, go home, eat dinner, sleep together. We haven't been apart since a week ago Sunday when Jen went to spend the day with her mother." He took a deep breath. "My God, Edie—"

A pretty young woman, Italian-looking, came into the office. She looked curiously at the two detectives. Mason introduced them.

"They need to know my whereabouts for the last few days," he said.

"But why?" she asked.

"Just tell them where I've been, hon."

Jenny shrugged, "With me."

"All the time?" asked Kenmare.

"Yes, all the time."

"Like I said, we do everything together," Mason reiterated. "We work together, shop for groceries together, stay in or go out together, we even shower together."

"Bart!" Jenny Paula said, chagrined. "What's this all about anyway?"

"I'll explain later. Can she go now, Officers?"

"Sure," said Kenmare. Thank you, Miss Paula." She left, somewhat piqued, and Kenmare said to Mason, "We may need to talk to her again, in a little more depth."

"We're both available anytime," Mason assured him.

"How long did you date Edie Malone?" Dell asked.

"About six months, I guess."

"Were you intimate?"

"Sure," Mason shrugged.

"When did you break up?"

"Late last summer sometime. Around Labor Day, I think."

"What caused you to break up?"

"Edie began seeing someone else. I didn't like it. So I split with her."

"Do you know who she started seeing?"

"Yeah, Ron Deever, her boss upstairs at the ad agency."

Dell and Kenmare exchanged quick glances. They continued to question Mason for several more minutes, then got his apartment address and left.

On the way back up to the fortieth floor, an annoyed Kenmare, referring to Ron Deever, said, "That son of a bitch. He never mentioned once that he went out with her. I think I'll haul his ass in and take a formal statement."

"He'll lawyer up on you," Dell predicted.

"Let him."

When they got back to Able, Bennett, and Crain, Kenmare went into Ron Deever's office again while Dell took Sally Simms back into the coffee room.

"Did you know that Edie Malone had dated Ron Deever?" he asked bluntly.

Sally lowered her eyes.

"Yes."

"I asked you if you knew of any other men in the building that Edie had gone out with and you said no. Why did you lie?"

"I'm sorry," she said, her hands beginning to tremble. "Look, this guy is my boss. I'm a single parent with a little boy in day care. I didn't want to take a chance of losing my job." She started tearing up. "First thing he asked me after you left was whether I told you about him and Edie."

"Why was he so concerned?"

"He's married."

"Did Edie know that when she was seeing him?"

"Sure. It was no big thing for her."

Dell sighed quietly. Reaching out, he patted the young woman's trembling hands. "Okay. Relax. I'll make sure Deever knows it wasn't you who told us. But if I have to question you again, don't lie to me about anything. Understand?"

"Sure." Sally dabbed at her eyes with a paper napkin. "Listen, thanks."

Dell sent her back to work and went into Deever's office, where Kenmare was reading the riot act to him.

"What the hell do you think this is, a TV show? This is a *homicide* investigation, Mister! When you withhold relevant information, you're obstructing justice!" He turned to Dell. "He's married. That's why he didn't come clean."

"I just chewed out Miss Simms, too," Dell said. "Told her how much trouble she could get into covering for him."

"All right," said Kenmare, "we're going to start all over, Mr. Deever, and I want the full and complete truth this time."

A shaky Ron Deever nodded compliance.

When they got back to the squad room, Garvan was waiting for them and a spare desk had been set up for Dell.

"She wasn't raped or otherwise sexually assaulted," he reported. "Cause of death was strangulation—from behind. Coroner fixed time of death at between nine at night and one in the morning. Best bet: between eleven and midnight." He tossed Edie's address book onto the desk. "You were right about this, Dell: It's old. Some of these people haven't seen or heard from her in three or four years. The ones who have couldn't tell me anything about her personal life. You guys make out?"

"Not really," said Kenmare. "We've got one guy who could have slipped out while his fiancée was asleep and gone over and done it—but it's not likely. Another guy, married, was at his son's basketball game earlier in the evening, then at home with his family out in Arlington Heights the rest of the night. One of us will have to go out and interview his wife on that this afternoon."

"I'll do it," Garvan said. "I need the fresh air after that autopsy. Oh, I almost forgot." He tossed five telephone messages to Dell. "These were forwarded from Lakeside. Three are from your partner, two from your captain."

"If you need some privacy to return the calls," Kenmare said, "Garvan and I can go for coffee."

Dell shook his head. "Nothing I can't say in front of you guys. You both know the situation." He could tell by their expressions, as he dialed Mike Larne's number first, that they were pleased at not being excluded. "It's Dell, Captain," he said when Larne answered. "I told you I'd check in when I had the autopsy results. Edie wasn't raped or anything like that. Somebody strangled her from behind, between nine Tuesday night and one on Wednesday morning." He listened for a moment, then said, "Couple of soft leads, is all. Very soft." Then: "Yeah, he's called me three times. I guess I better get back to him."

When he finished his call to Larne, Dell dialed Dan Malone's home. The phone was answered on the third ring. "Hello."

"Yeah, who's this?" Dell asked.

"Who are *you?*" the voice asked back.

"Frank Dell. Is that you, Keenan?"

"Oh, Frank. Yeah, it's me. Sorry, I didn't recognize your voice. How's it going?"

"Very slow. Dan's been calling me, I guess. How is he?"

"Thrashed, inside and out. But the boys and me have him under control. And his two sisters are here with him. He's sleeping right now. It means a lot to him that you're working the case, Frank. He's got a couple of names that he wants checked: old boyfriends of Edie's that he didn't like. Wasn't for you being on the case, he'd probably be out doing it hisself. Pistol-whipping them, maybe."

"You have the names?"

"Yeah, he wrote them down here by the phone." Dell took down the names and told Keenan to tell Dan that he'd see him tomorrow with a full report of the case's progress. After he hung up, he handed the names to Kenmare. "Old boyfriends," he said.

Kenmare gave them to Garvan. "Start a check on them before you go out to interview Deever's wife. Frank and I are going out to that line-dancing joint—it's called Memphis City Limits—to interview Bob Pilcher. We'll meet back here at end of shift."

Memphis City Limits did not have live music until after seven, but even in midafternoon there was a jukebox playing country-and-western and a few people on the dance floor around which the club was laid out. It was a big barn of a building that had once been a wholesale furniture outlet, then remained vacant for several years until some entrepreneurial mind decided there might be a profit in a club catering to the area's large influx of Southerners come north to find work.

Dell and Kenmare found Bob Pilcher drinking beer at a table with two cowgirl types and a beefy man in a lumberjack shirt. Identifying themselves, Kenmare asked if they could speak with Pilcher in private to ask him a few questions. Pilcher shook his head.

"Anything you want to ask me about Edie Malone, do it right here in front of witnesses."

"What makes you think it's about Edie Malone?" Kenmare asked.

"No other reason for you to be talking to me. Story's been on TV news all morning about her being murdered." Pilcher spoke with a heavily accented drawl that sounded purposefully exaggerated.

"When did you see her last?" Dell asked.

"'Bout a week ago." He winked at Dell. "She was alive, too."

"Can you account for your time during the past seventy-two hours?" Kenmare wanted to know, expanding the time period more than he had to because of Pilcher's attitude.

"Most of it, I reckon," Pilcher replied. "I'm here ever' day 'cept Sundays from no later than six of an evening to closing time at two A.M. Usually I'm here an hour or two *before* six, as you can see today. As for the rest of my time, you'd have to give me specific times and I'd see what I could come up with." His expression hardened a little. "Tell you one thing, though, boys, you wasting good po-lice time on me. I didn't off the gal."

"We have reason to believe you slapped her around now and then," Dell tried.

"So what if I did?" Pilcher challenged. "You can't arrest me for that. She's *dead*, fellers, hell!" He took a long swallow of beer. "Anyways, one of the reasons women like me is that I treat 'em rough. That one wasn't no different."

"So you did slap her around?"

"Yeah, I did," Pilcher defied him, lighting a cigarette. "Go on and do something about it if you can."

"Where can we find your employer," Kenmare asked, "to verify that you've been here the last three nights?"

Pilcher smiled what was really a nasty half-smirk. "So she was offed at night, huh? For sure you'll have to pin it on somebody else." He nodded across the club. "Manager's office is that door to the right of the bar."

Pilcher blew smoke rings at the two detectives as they left him at the table with his friends and sought out the club manager. He confirmed that Pilcher had indeed been on duty from at least six until two every night since the club had been closed the previous Sunday.

"Brother, would I like to nail that hillbilly for this," Kenmare groused as they walked back to their car. "I'd plant evidence to get that son of a bitch."

"So would I," Dell admitted. "Only there's no evidence to plant. Anyway, the timeline doesn't jibe. A second-year law student could get him off."

When they got back to the squad room, Garvan had already returned. "Struck out," he announced. "Deever's wife puts him at home from about ten-thirty, after their son's basketball game, until the next morning about eight when he left for work." He turned to Dell. "And those two boyfriends your partner didn't like: One of them's in the navy stationed on Okinawa; the other's married, lives in Oregon, hasn't been out of that state since last July. You guys?"

"Pilcher's a scumbag, but his alibi's tight," Kenmare said. He looked at his watch. "Let's call it a day. Thursday's a big night for my wife and me," he told Dell. "We get a sitter, go out for Chinese, and see a movie."

Dell just nodded, but Garvan said, "Go see a good cop picture tonight. Something with Bruce Willis in it. Maybe you can pick up some tips on how to be a detective."

"Up yours, you perennial rookie," Kenmare said, and left.

Garvan turned to Dell. "Buy you a drink, Lakeside?"

"Why not?" said Dell. "Lead the way, Homicide."

At two o'clock the next morning, Dell was in his car, parked at the alley entrance to the rear parking lot of the Memphis City Limits club. He was wearing dark trousers and a back windbreaker, and had black Nikes on his feet. Both hands were gloved, and he wore a wool navy watch cap low on his forehead, and a dark scarf around his neck. The fuse for the interior lights on his car had been removed.

He had been there for half an hour, watching as the last patrons of the night exited the club, got into their vehicles, and left. By ten past two, there were only a few cars left, belonging to club employees who were straggling out to go home. The lot was not particularly well lit, but the rear door to the club was, so it was easy for Dell to distinguish people as they left.

It was a quarter past two when Bob Pilcher came out and swaggered across the parking lot toward a Dodge Ram pickup. Dell got out of his car without the light going on and, in his Nikes, walked briskly, silently toward him from the left rear, tying the scarf over his lower face as he went. When he was within arm's length of Pilcher, he said, "Hey, stud."

Pilcher turned, a half-smile starting, and Dell cracked him across the face with a leather-covered lead sap. He heard part of Pilcher's face crack. Catching him before he dropped to the ground, Dell dragged the unconscious man around the truck, out of sight of the club's back door. Dropping him, he rolled him over, face-down. Pulling both arms above his head, he pressed each of Pilcher's palms, in turn, against the asphalt, held each down at the wrist, and with the sap used short, snapping blows to systematically break the top four finger knuckles and top thumb knuckle of each hand.

Then he walked quickly back to the alley, got into his car, and drove away. The whole thing had taken less than two minutes.

Be a long time before you slap another woman around, he thought grimly as he left. Or even hold a toothbrush.

Then he thought: That was for you, Edie.

The next day, Dell went to be with Dan Malone when he came to the funeral parlor to see Edie in her casket for the first time. The undertaker had picked up her body when the coroner was through with it, and one of Edie's aunts and two cousins had gone to Marshall Field's and bought her a simple mauve dress to be laid out in.

There were a number of aunts, uncles, cousins, and other collateral family members in attendance when the slumber room was opened, and groups of neighbors gathered outside, easily outnumbered by groups of police officers, in uniform and out, who had known Dan Malone for all or part of his thirty-two years on the force and had come from half the police districts in the city to offer their condolences.

Dell was shocked by the sight of Dan when the grieving man arrived. He looked as if he had aged ten years in the three days since Dell had seen him. A couple of male relatives helped him out of the car and were assisting him in an unsteady walk toward the entrance when Dan's eyes fell on Dell and he pulled away, insisting on a moment with his partner. Dell hurried to him, the two men embraced, then stepped up close to the building where people cleared a space for them to speak privately.

"Did you find those two bastards Keenan gave you the names of?" Dan asked hoarsely.

"Yeah, Dan, but they're clean," Dell told him. "They're not even around anymore."

"Are you sure? I never liked either one of em."

"They're clean, Dan. I promise you. Listen," Dell said to placate him, speaking close to his ear, "I did find one guy. He's clean for the killing, but he'd slapped Edie around a couple of times."

"The son of a bitch. Who is he?" The older man's teary eyes became fiery with rage.

"It's OK, Dan. I already took care of it."

"You did? What'd you do?"

"Fixed his hands. With a sap."

"Good, good." Malone wet his dry, whiskey-puffed lips. "I knew I could count on you, Frankie. Listen, come on inside and see my little girl."

"You go in with your family, Dan. I've already seen her," Dell lied. He had no intention of looking at Edie Malone's body again.

Dell gestured and several relatives hurried over to get Dan. Then Dell returned to a group of policemen that included Mike Larne, a couple of lieutenants, Keenan and other cronies of Dan's, and a deputy commissioner. Larne put an arm around Dell's shoulders.

"Whatever you said to him, Frank, it seemed to help."

"I hope so," Dell said. "Listen, Captain, I'm going to get back down to Homicide."

"By all means," said Larne. "Back to work, lad. Find the bastard who caused this heartache."

In the days immediately following the funeral and burial of Edie Malone, the three detectives on the case worked and reworked the old leads, as well as a few new ones. A deputy state's attorney, Ray Millard, was assigned to analyze and evaluate the evidence as they progressed. Disappointingly, there was little of a positive nature to analyze.

"It's too soft," Millard told them in their first meeting. He was a precise, intense young lawyer. "First, you've got the guy she worked for: older man, married, concealed the relationship when first questioned. Solid alibi for the hours just before, during, and after his son's basketball game which he attended on the night of the murder. Decent alibi for the rest of the night: a statement by his wife that he was at home. He *could* have slipped out of his suburban home when everyone was asleep, driven into the city, and committed the crime—but *why* would he have done that, and who's going to believe it?

"Second, you've got the good-guy ex-boyfriend. He's well set up with a new girl-friend, and the two of them are practically joined at the hip: live together, work together, play together. Again, he *could* have slipped out of their apartment around midnight when his fiancée was asleep, gone to the Malone woman's apartment, a relatively short distance away, and killed her. But again, *why*? Let's remember that *he* dumped *her*, not the other way around. Soft, very soft.

"Third, bad-guy ex-boyfriend. The hillbilly bouncer." Millard paused. "Incidentally, I understand that the night after you guys interviewed him, somebody jumped him outside the club and broke his nose, one cheekbone, and both hands. You guys heard anything about that?"

The detectives shrugged in unison, as if choreographed. "Doesn't surprise me," Kenmare said.

"Me either," Dell agreed. "Scumbags like that always have people who don't like them."

"Well, anyway," the young lawyer continued, "bad-guy boyfriend would be a beaut to get in court. I could try him in front of a jury of his *relatives* and probably get a death sentence—except for one thing: He's got a home-free alibi on his job. No way he could have been away from the club long enough to go do it without his absence being noticed. He's the bouncer; he's got to be visible all the time." Millard sat back and drummed his fingers. "Anything else cooking?"

Kenmare shook his head. "We're back canvassing the neighbors again, but nothing so far. We had one little piece of excitement day before yesterday when a little old retired lady in the victim's building said she'd heard that the building super had been fired from his last job for making lewd suggestions to female tenants. We checked it out and there was nothing to it. Turned out she was just ticked off at him for reporting her dog making a mess in the hallway a couple times."

"Too bad," Millard said. "The super would've made a good defendant. Had a key to her apartment, found the body, whole ball of wax. He alibied tight?"

"Very. Lives with his wife on two. They went to a movie, got home around eleven, went right to bed. He's got a good rep—except for the little old lady with the dog."

"Had to be somebody she knew," Millard said. "No forced entry, no lock picked. No rape, no robbery. This was a personal crime. She let the guy in." He tossed the file across the desk to Kenmare. "Find me that guy and we'll stick the needle in his arm."

The three detectives took off early and went to a small Loop bar, where they settled in a back booth. Dell could sense some tension but did not broach the subject. He knew Kenmare would get around to whatever it was.

"We've enjoyed having you work with us, Frank," the senior detective finally said. "We had our doubts about your assignment, but it's turned out OK."

"Yeah, we had our doubts," Garvan confirmed, "but it worked out fine."

"I tried not to get in the way," Dell said.

"Hey, you've been a lot of help," Garvan assured him. "Got me away from this nag for a while," he bobbed his chin at Kenmare.

"Listen to him," the older man said. "Wasn't for me, he'd be directing traffic at some school crossing."

"What's on your mind, boys?" Dell asked, deciding not to wait.

Kenmare sighed. "It's a bit delicate, Frank."

"I'm a big boy. Shoot."

They both leaned toward him to emphasize confidentiality. "That first night in the apartment, you commented that Dan Malone and his daughter hadn't been close for a while," Kenmare recalled.

Garvan nodded. "You said he didn't approve of her lifestyle."

"You said he didn't talk much about her after she quit college and went out on her own."

Dell's expression tightened and locked. "You're getting very close to stepping over the wrong line," he said evenly.

"I'm sorry you feel that way, Frank," said Kenmare. "It's a step that has to be taken." He sat back. "You know as well as I do that if he wasn't one of our own, he'd have been on the spot from day one. As soon as we decided there was no forced entry, no rape, no robbery, we would have included an estranged father in our investigation. But Garvan and me, we kept hoping that evidence would lead us to somebody else. Unfortunately, it hasn't."

"Look, Frank," Garvan said in a placating tone, "it doesn't have to be a complicated thing. It can be, like, informal."

"Of course," Kenmare agreed, his own voice also becoming appeasing. "Drop in on him. Have a drink. Engage him in casual conversation. And find out where he was during the critical hours, that's all."

"Sure," said Garvan, "that's all."

Dell grunted quietly. Like it would be a walk in the park to handle a thirty-two-year veteran cop like that. He took a long swallow of his drink. His eyes shifted from Kenmare to Garvan and back again, then looked down at the table, where the fingers of one hand drummed silently. He did not speak for what seemed like a very long time. Finally Kenmare broke the silence.

"It's either that way or it'll have to be us, Frank. But it's got to be done."

With a sigh that came from deep inside of him, Dell nodded. "All right."

The tension that permeated the booth should have dissipated with that, but it did not. Dell once again became, as he had been at the very beginning of the investigation, an outsider.

Dan Malone smiled when he opened the door and saw Dell.

"Ah, Frank. Come in, come in. Good to see you, partner. I've missed you."

"Missed you too, Dan."

They embraced briefly, and, Dell sensed, a little stiffly.

"I was just having a beer after supper," said Dan. "You want one?"

"Sure."

"Sit down there on the couch. I'll get you one." He turned off a network hockey game, picked up a plastic tray on which were the remains of a TV dinner, and went into the kitchen with it. In a moment, he returned with an open bottle of Budweiser. "So," he said, handing Dell the beer and sitting in his recliner, "how's it going?"

"It's not going, Dan. Not going anywhere," Dell replied quietly, almost dejectedly.

"Well, I figured as much. Else you'd have been in closer touch. Not getting anywhere on the case?"

"No, I've been meaning to drop by and talk to you about it, but I thought you probably still had family staying with you."

"My two sisters were here for a week," Dan said. "And there've been nieces and nephews running in and out like mice. Finally I had enough and ran them all off. Then my phone started ringing off the hook all day, so I finally unplugged that just to get some peace and quiet. I guess they all think I'm suicidal or something."

"Are you?" Dell asked.

Dan gave him a long look. "No. Any reason I should be?"

Dell shrugged. "Sometimes things like this are hard to get over. Some people want to do it quickly."

"That's not the case with me," the older man assured him. "I lost Edie a long time ago, Frank. I think I probably started losing her when she slept with her first man. Then every man after that, I lost her a little more. Until finally she was gone completely."

"Were there that many men?"

"You're working the case; you ought to know."

"We've only found three."

Malone grunted cynically. "You must not have gone back very far." He stared into space. "I used to follow her sometimes. She'd go into a bar and come out an hour later with a man. Night after night. Different bars, different men. It was like some kind of sickness with her."

They both fell silent and sat drinking for several minutes. Dell, who had always been so comfortable with his partner, felt peculiarly ill at ease, as if he had now become an outsider with Dan Malone as he had with the two homicide detectives. Finally he decided not to prolong the visit any more than necessary.

"How long have we known each other, Dan?" he asked.

"What's on your mind, Frank?" the older policeman asked knowingly. It had been he who taught Dell that reminiscing frequently led to other things.

"The night of Edie's murder."

"What about it?"

"I need to know where you were."

Malone nodded understandingly. "I wondered when they'd get around to it." He smiled a slight, cold smile. "Suppose I tell you I was right here at home, alone, all night. What then?"

"Tell me what you did all night."

"Watched the fights on television. Drank too much. Passed out here in my chair."

"Who was fighting in the main event?"

Malone shrugged. "Some Puerto Rican against some black guy, I think. I was sleepy by the time the main go came on; I don't remember their names."

"Neither do I," said Dell.

"What?" Dan Malone frowned.

"I don't remember their names either. But you weren't alone that night. That was the night I dropped over. We both drank too much. I fell asleep on the couch. Didn't wake up until after one o'clock. Then I put you to bed and went home. That was the night, wasn't it, Dan?"

The older man's frown faded and his face seemed to go slack. "Yes," he said quietly. "Yes, I do believe that was the night."

There was silence between them again. Neither of them seemed to know what to say next, and they could not look at each other. Malone stared into space, as he had done earlier; Dell stared at the television, as if it had not been turned off. Only after several minutes did Dell drink the rest of his beer and put the bottle down. He rose.

"I'll be going now. You won't be coming back to work, will you, Dan?"

Malone looked thoughtfully at him. "No," he replied. "I'm thinking of putting in for retirement. My sisters in Florida want me to move down there."

"Good idea. You'd probably enjoy yourself. Lots of retired cops in Florida." Dell walked to the door. "Goodnight, Dan."

"Goodnight, Frank."

Only when he got out into the night air did Dell realize how much he was sweating.

The next morning, Dell typed up a summary of Dan Malone's statement, along with his own corroboration of the alibi. After signing it, he handed the report to Kenmare. The lead homicide detective read it, then passed it to Garvan to read.

"You've thought this through, I guess," Kenmare said.

"Backwards and forward," Dell told him.

Garvan raised his eyebrows but said nothing as he handed the report back to Kenmare.

"I don't think the brass will buy this," Kenmare offered.

"What are they going to do?" Dell asked. "Suspend Dan *and* me? Open an internal investigation? On what evidence? And how would it look on the evening news?"

"The higher-ups might feel it was worth it," said Garvan.

"Worth it why?" pressed Dell. "What's the gain? The department's getting rid of Dan anyway; he'll be retiring."

"But you won't," Garvan pointed out.

"So? What have I done that the department would want to get rid of me?"

"Helped him get away with it, that's what," said Kenmare.

"*If* he did it," Dell challenged. "And we don't know that he did. All we know is that we can't find anybody else right now who *did* do it." He decided to throw down the gauntlet right then. "You guys going to let this report pass, or are you going to make an issue of it?"

"You didn't mention this alibi last night when we were talking," Kenmare accused.

"Maybe I had my days mixed up." Dell shrugged. "Maybe I thought it had been Monday night I had dropped in; maybe Dan had to remind me it was Tuesday."

"Maybe," Kenmare said. He looked inquiringly at his partner.

"Yeah, maybe," Garvan agreed.

"You're sure Malone's retiring?" Kenmare asked.

"Positive," Dell guaranteed.

Kenmare pulled open a desk drawer and filed the report. "See you around, Dell," he said.

"Yeah," said Garvan. "Take it easy, Dell."

Dell walked out of the squad room without looking back.

That night, when Dell came into the Three Corners Club and took his regular seat at the end of the bar, it was the owner, Tim Callan, who poured his drink and served him.

"I've missed you, Frankie," he said congenially. "How've you been?"

"I've seen better days," Dell allowed.

"Ah, haven't we all," Callan sympathized. He lowered his voice. "I'm really sorry about the young lady. Edie, was that her name?"

"Yeah, Edie." Dell felt the back of his neck go warm.

"I seen her picture in the paper and on the news. Took me a few looks to place her. Then I says to myself, why, that's the young lady Frankie used to bring in here. Always wanted the booth 'way in the back for privacy.'" Callan smiled artificially. "I remember that every time I loaned you the key to use the apartment upstairs I had to make you promise to be out by midnight so's I could get the poker game started. And you never let me down, Frank. Not once. 'Course, we go back a long ways, you and me." Now Callan's expression saddened, genuinely so. "I'm really sorry, Frank, that things didn't work out between you and Edie."

"Thank you, Tim. So am I." Dell's heart hurt when he said it.

"They still don't know who did it?"

Dell looked hard at him. "No."

They locked eyes for a long moment, two old friends, each of whom could read the other like scripture.

"What was the name of that brother-in-law of yours charged with receiving stolen property?" Dell finally asked.

"Nick Santore," said Callan. "Funny you should ask. His preliminary hearing's day after tomorrow."

"I'll talk to the assistant state's attorney," Dell said. "I'll tell him the guy's going to be a snitch for me, that I need him on the street. I'll get him to recommend probation."

"Ah, Frankie, you're a prince," Callan praised, clasping one of Dell's hands with both of his own. "I owe you, big time."

"No," Frank Dell said, "we're even, Timmy."

Both men knew it was so.

PETER ROBINSON
1950–

One of the best current writers of the British police procedural, Peter Robinson was born in Castleford, Yorkshire. He received his B.A. Honours Degree in English Literature at the University of Leeds. After moving to Canada, where he now resides, he earned his M.A. in English and Creative Writing at the University of Windsor, studying with Joyce Carol Oates. He finished his academic education with a Ph.D. in English from York University. He often returns to Yorkshire in England to update his information on the region and the police there. Although Robinson has taught at various Toronto colleges and has been Writer-in-Residence at the University of Windsor, he considers himself a full-time author dedicated to creating excellent mysteries featuring the Yorkshire police.

His first novel, *Gallows View* (1987), introduced Detective Chief Inspector Alan Banks, and was nominated for a best first novel award in Canada and for the John Creasy Award in the United Kingdom. *Past Reason Hated* (1991), the fifth Banks' book, won the Crime Writers of Canada's Arthur Ellis Award for Best Novel. The sixth book, *Wednesday's Child* (1992) was nominated for both the CWC Award and the Edgar Award from the Mystery Writers of America. His best known Inspector Banks novel, *In a Dry Season* (1999), was nominated for an Edgar, won the Anthony Award, and was named a *New York Times* Notable Book. It is both an outstanding puzzle mystery and a glimpse of Yorkshire history.

Robinson's Detective Chief Inspector Alan Banks is a charming, dry-witted, introspective policeman who is a master of the psychological puzzle, and often deals with cases that illustrate how strongly the past imposes itself on the present. To read Robinson is to realize how brutal human beings can be to each other: mentally, emotionally, and physically. "Missing in Action" first appeared in *Ellery Queen's Mystery Magazine*, November 2000, and won the Edgar Award for Best Short Story of 2000.

Recommended Robinson works: *Past Reason Hated, Wednesday's Child, In a Dry Season.*

Other recommended authors: Reginald Hill, Ian Rankin, Charles Todd.

Missing in Action

People go missing all the time in war, of course, but not usually nine-year-old boys. Besides, the war had hardly begun. It was only the twentieth of September, 1939, when Mary Critchley came hammering on my door at about three o'clock, interrupting my afternoon nap.

It was a Wednesday, and normally I would have been teaching the fifth-formers Shakespeare at Silverhill Grammar School (a thankless task if ever there was one), but the Ministry had just got around to constructing air-raid shelters there, so the school was closed for the week. We didn't even know if it was going to reopen, because the idea was to evacuate all the children to safer areas in the countryside. Now, I would be among the first to admit that a teacher's highest aspiration is a school without pupils, but in the meantime the government, in its eternal wisdom, put us redundant teachers to such complex, intellectual tasks as preparing ration cards for the Ministry of Food. (After all, *they* knew what was coming.)

All this was just a small part of the chaos that seemed to reign at that time. Not the chaos of war, the kind I remembered from the trenches at Ypres in 1917, but the chaos of government bureaucracies trying to organize the country for war.

Anyway, I was fortunate enough to become Special Constable, which is a rather grandiose title for a sort of part-time dogsbody, and that was why Mary Critchley came running to me. That and what little reputation I had for solving people's problems.

"Mr. Bashcombe! Mr. Bashcombe!" she cried. "It's our Johnny. He's gone missing. You must help."

My name is actually *Bascombe*, Frank Bascombe, but Mary Critchley has a slight speech impediment, so I forgave her the mispronunciation. Still, with half the city's children running wild in the streets and the other half standing on crowded station platforms clutching their Mickey Mouse gas masks in little cardboard boxes, ready to be herded into trains bound for such nearby country havens as Graythorpe, Kilsden, and Acksham, I thought perhaps she was over-reacting a tad, and I can't say I welcomed her arrival after only about twenty of my allotted forty winks.

"He's probably out playing with his mates," I told her.

"Not my Johnny," she said, wiping the tears from her eyes. "Not since . . . you know . . ."

I knew. Mr. Critchley, Ted to his friends, had been a Royal Navy man since well before the war. He had also been unfortunate enough to serve on the fleet carrier *Courageous*, which had been sunk by a German U-boat off the southwest coast of Ireland just three days ago. Over 500 men had been lost, including Ted Critchley. Of course, no body had been found, and probably never would be, so he was only officially "missing in action."

I also knew young Johnny Critchley, and thought him to be a serious boy, a bit too imaginative and innocent for his own good. (Well, many are at that age, aren't they, before the world grabs them by the balls and shakes some reality into them.) Johnny trusted everyone, even strangers.

"Johnny's not been in much of a mood for playing with his mates since we got the news about Ted's ship," Mary Critchley went on.

I could understand that well enough—young Johnny was an only child, and he always did worship his father—but I still didn't see what I could do about it. "Have you asked around?"

"What do you think I've been doing since he didn't come home at twelve o'clock like he was supposed to? I've asked everyone in the street. Last time he was seen he was down by the canal at about eleven o'clock. Maurice Richards saw him. What can I do, Mr. Bashcombe? First Ted, and now . . . now my Johnny!" She burst into tears.

After I had managed to calm her down, I sighed and told her I would look for Johnny myself. There certainly wasn't much hope of my getting the other twenty winks now.

It was a glorious day, so warm and sunny you would hardly believe there was a war on. The late-afternoon sunshine made even our narrow streets of cramped brick terrace houses look attractive. As the shadows lengthened, the light turned to molten gold. First, I scoured the local rec where the children played cricket and football, and the dogs ran wild. Some soldiers were busy digging trenches for air-raid shelters. Just the sight of those long, dark grooves in the earth gave me the shivers. Behind the trenches, barrage balloons pulled at their moorings on the breeze like playful porpoises, orange and pink in the sun. I asked the soldiers, but they hadn't seen Johnny. Nor had any of the other lads.

After the rec I headed for the derelict houses on Gallipoli Street. The landlord had let them go to rack and ruin two years ago, and they were quite uninhabitable, not even fit for billeting soldiers. They were also dangerous and should have been pulled down, but I think the old skinflint was hoping a bomb would hit them so he could claim insurance or compensation from the government. The doors and windows had been boarded up, but children are resourceful, and it wasn't difficult even for me to remove a couple of loose sheets of plywood and make my way inside. I wished I had my torch, but I had to make do with what little light slipped through the holes. Every time I moved, my feet stirred up clouds of dust, which did my poor lungs no good at all.

I thought Johnny might have fallen or got trapped in one of the houses. The staircases were rotten, and more than one lad had fallen through on his way up. The floors weren't much better, either, and one of the fourth-formers at Silverhill had needed more than fifteen stitches a couple of weeks ago when one of his legs went right through the rotten wood and the splinters gouged his flesh.

I searched as best I could in the poor light, and I called out Johnny's name, but no answer came. Before I left, I stood silently and listened for any traces of harsh breathing or whimpering.

Nothing.

After three hours of searching the neighbourhood, I'd had no luck at all. Blackout time was 7:45 P.M., so I still had about an hour and a half left, but if Johnny wasn't in any of the local children's usual haunts, I was at a loss as to where to look. I talked to the other boys I met here and there, but none of his friends had seen him since the family got the news of Ted's death. Little Johnny Critchley, it seemed, had vanished into thin air.

At half past six, I called on Maurice Richards, grateful for his offer of a cup of tea and the chance to rest my aching feet. Maurice and I went back a long time. We had both survived the first war, Maurice with the loss of an arm and me with permanent facial scarring and a wracking cough that comes and goes, thanks to the mustard gas leaking through my mask at the Third Battle of Ypres. We never talked about the war, but it was there, we both knew, an invisible bond tying us close together while at the same time excluding us from so much other, normal human intercourse. Not many had seen the things we had, and thank God for that.

Maurice lit up a Passing Cloud one-handed, then he poured the tea. The seven o'clock news came on the radio, some such rot about us vowing to keep fighting until we'd vanquished the foe. It was still very much a war of words at that time, and the more rhetorical the language sounded, the better the politicians thought they were doing. There had been a couple of minor air skirmishes, and the sinking of the *Courageous*, of course, but all the action was taking place in Poland, which seemed as remote as the moon to most people. Some clever buggers had already started calling it the "Bore War."

"Did you hear Tommy Handley last night, Frank?" Maurice asked.

I shook my head. There'd been a lot of hoopla about Tommy Handley's new radio program, "It's That Man Again," or "ITMA," as people called it. I was never a fan. Call me a snob, but when evening falls I'm far happier curling up with a good book or an interesting talk on the radio than listening to Tommy Handley.

"Talk about a laugh," said Maurice. "They had this one sketch about the Ministry of Aggravation and the Office of Twerps. I nearly died."

I smiled, "Not far from the truth," I said. There were now so many of these obscure ministries, boards, and departments involved in so many absurd pursuits—all for the common good, of course—that I had been thinking of writing a dystopian satire. I proposed to set it in the near future, which would merely be a thinly disguised version of the present. So far, all I had was a great idea for the title: I would reverse the last two numbers in the current year, so instead of 1939, I'd call it *1993*. (Well, I thought it was a good idea!) "Look, Maurice," I said, "it's about young Johnny Critchley. His mother tells me you were the last person to see him."

"Oh, aye," Maurice said. "She were round asking about him not long ago. Still not turned up?"

"No."

"Cause for concern, then."

"I'm beginning to think so. What was he doing when you saw him?"

"Just walking down by the canal, by old Woodruff's scrap yard."

"That's all?"

"Yes."

"Was he alone?"

Maurice nodded.

"Did he say anything?"

"No."

"You didn't say anything to him?"

"No cause to. He seemed preoccupied, just staring in the water, like, hands in his pockets. I've heard what happened to his dad. A lad has to do his grieving."

"Too true. Did you see anyone else? Anything suspicious?"

"No, nothing. Just a minute, though . . . "

"What?"

"Oh, it's probably nothing, but just after I saw Johnny, when I was crossing the bridge, I bumped into Colin Gormond, you know, that chap who's a bit . . . you know."

Colin Gormond. I knew him all right. And that wasn't good news; it wasn't good news at all.

Of all the policemen they could have sent, they had to send Detective bloody Sergeant Longbottom, a big, brutish-looking fellow with a pronounced limp and a Cro-Magnon brow. Longbottom was thick as two short planks. I doubt he could have found his own arse even if someone nailed a sign on it, or detect his way out of an Anderson shelter if it were in his own backyard. But that's the caliber of men this wretched war has left us with at home. Along with good ones like me, of course.

DS Longbottom wore a shiny brown suit and a Silverhill Grammar School tie. I wondered where he'd got it from; he probably stole it from some schoolboy he caught nicking sweets from the corner shop. He kept tugging at his collar with his pink sausage fingers as we talked in Mary Critchley's living room. His face was flushed with the heat, and sweat gathered on his thick eyebrows and trickled down the sides of his neck.

"So he's been missing since lunchtime, has he?" DS Longbottom repeated.

Mary Critchley nodded. "He went out at about half past ten, just for a walk, like. Said he'd be back at twelve. When it got to three . . . well, I went to see Mr. Bashcombe here."

DS Longbottom curled his lip at me and grunted. "Mr. Bascombe. *Special* Constable. I suppose you realize that gives you no real police powers, don't you?"

"As a matter of fact," I said, "I thought it made me your superior. After all, you're not a *special* sergeant, are you?"

He looked at me as if he wanted to hit me. Perhaps he would have done if Mary Critchley hadn't been in the room. "Enough of your lip. Just answer my questions."

"Yes, sir."

"You say you looked all over for this lad?"

"All his usual haunts."

"And you found no trace of him?"

"If I had, do you think we'd have sent for you?"

"I warned you. Cut the lip and answer the questions. This, what's his name, Maurice Richards, was he the last person to see the lad?"

"Johnny's his name. And yes is the answer, as far as we know." I paused. He'd have to know eventually, and if I didn't tell him, Maurice would. The longer we delayed, the worse it would be in the long run. "There was someone else in the area at the time. A man called Colin Gormond."

Mary Critchley gave a sharp gasp. DS Longbottom frowned, licked the tip of his pencil, and scribbled something in his notebook. "I'll have to have a word with him," he said. Then he turned to her. "Recognize the name, do you, ma'am?"

"I know Colin," I answered, perhaps a bit too quickly.

DS Longbottom stared at Mary Critchley, whose lower lip started quivering, then turned slowly back to me. "Tell me about him."

I sighed. Colin Gormond was an oddball. Some people said he was a bit slow, but I'd never seen any real evidence of that. He lived alone and he didn't have much to do with the locals; that was enough evidence against him for some people.

And then there were the children.

For some reason, Colin preferred the company of the local lads to that of the rest of us adults. To be quite honest, I can't say I blame him, but in a situation like this it's bound to look suspicious. Especially if the investigating officer is someone with the sensitivity and understanding of a DS Longbottom.

Colin would take them trainspotting on the hill overlooking the main line, for example, or he'd play cricket with them on the rec or hand out conkers when the season came. He sometimes bought them sweets and ice creams, even gave them books, marbles, and comics.

To my knowledge, Colin Gormand had never once put a foot out of line, never laid so much as a finger on any of the lads, either in anger or in friendship. There had, however, been one or two mutterings from some parents—most notably from Jack Blackwell, father of one of Johnny's pals, Nick—that it somehow *wasn't right*, that it was *unnatural* for a man who must be in his late thirties or early forties to spend so much time playing with young children. There must be something not quite right in his head, he must be up to *something*, Jack Blackwell hinted, and as usual when someone starts a vicious rumour, there is no shortage of willing believers. Such a reaction was only to be expected from someone, of course, but I knew it wouldn't go down well with DS Longbottom. I don't know why, but I felt a strange need *to protect* Colin.

"Colin's a local," I explained. "Lived around here for years. He plays with the lads a bit. Most of them like him. He seems a harmless sort of fellow."

"How old is he?"

I shrugged. "Hard to say. About forty, perhaps."

DS Longbottom raised a thick eyebrow. "About forty, and he plays with the kiddies, you say?"

"Sometimes. Like a schoolteacher, or a youth-club leader."

"Is he a schoolteacher?"

"No."

"Is he a youth-club leader?"

"No. Look, what I meant—"

"I know exactly what you meant, Mr. Bascombe. Now you just listen to what I mean. What we've got here is an older man who's known to hang around with young children, and he's been placed near the scene where a young child has gone missing. Now, don't you think that's just a wee bit suspicious?"

Mary Critchley let out a great wail and started crying again. DS Longbottom ignored her. Instead, he concentrated all his venom on me, the softie, the liberal, the defender of child molesters. "What do you have to say about *that*, Mr. Special Constable Bascombe?"

"Only that Colin was a friend to the children and that he had no reason to harm anyone."

"*Friend*," DS Longbottom sneered, struggling to his feet. "We can only be thankful you're not regular police, Mr. Bascombe," he said, nodding to himself in acknowledgment of his own wisdom. "That we can."

"So what are you going to do?" I asked.

DS Longbottom looked at his watch and frowned. Either he was trying to work out what it meant when the little hand and the big hand were in the positions they were in, or he was squinting because of poor eyesight. "I'll have a word with this here Colin Gormond. Other than that, there's not much more we can do tonight. First thing tomorrow morning, we'll drag the canal." He got to the door, turned, pointed to the windows, and said, "And don't forget to put up your blackout curtains, ma'am, or you'll have the ARP man to answer to."

Mary Critchley burst into floods of tears again.

Even the soft dawn light could do nothing for the canal. It oozed through the city like an open sewer, oil slicks shimmering like rainbows in the sun, brown water dotted with industrial scum and suds, bits of driftwood and paper wrappings floating along with them. On one side was Ezekiel Woodruff's scrap yard. Old Woodruff was a bit of an eccentric. He used to come around the streets with his horse and cart yelling, "Any old iron," but now the government had other uses for scrap metal—supposedly to be used in aircraft manufacture—poor old Woodruff didn't have any way to make his living anymore. He'd already sent old Nell the carthorse to the knacker's yard, where she was probably doing her bit for the war effort by helping to make the glue to stick the aircraft together. Old mangles and bits of broken furniture stuck up from the ruins of the scrap yard like shattered artillery after a battle.

On the other side, the bank rose steeply toward the backs of the houses on Canal Road, and the people who lived there seemed to regard it as their personal tip. Flies and wasps buzzed around old Hessian sacks and paper bags full of God knew what. A couple of buckled bicycle tires and a wheelless pram completed the picture.

I stood and watched as Longbottom supervised the dragging, a slow and laborious process that seemed to be sucking all manner of unwholesome objects to the surface—except Johnny Critchley's body.

I felt tense. At any moment I half expected the cry to come from one of the policemen in the boats that they had found him, half expected to see the small, pathetic bundle bob above the water's surface. I didn't think Colin Gormond had done anything to Johnny—nor Maurice, though DS Longbottom had seemed suspicious of him, too, but I did think that, given how upset he was, Johnny might just have jumped in. He never struck me as the suicidal type, but I have no idea whether suicide enters the minds of nine-year-olds. All I knew was that he *was* upset about his father, and he *was* last seen skulking by the canal.

So I stood around with DS Longbottom and the rest as the day grew warmer, and there was still no sign of Johnny. After about three hours, the police gave up and went for bacon and eggs at Betty's Cafe over on Chadwick Road. They didn't invite me, and I was grateful to be spared both the unpleasant food and company. I stood and stared into the greasy water a while longer, unsure whether it was a good sign or not that Johnny wasn't in the canal, then I decided to go and have a chat with Colin Gormond.

"What is it, Colin?" I asked him gently. "Come on. You can tell me,"

But Colin continued to stand with his back turned to me in the dark corner of his cramped living room, hands to his face, making eerie snuffling sounds, shaking his head. It was bright daylight outside, but the blackout curtains were still drawn tightly, and not a chink of light crept between their edges. I had already tried the light switch, but either Colin had removed the bulb or he didn't have one.

"Come on, Colin. This is silly. You know me. I'm Mr. Bascombe. I won't hurt you. Tell me what happened."

Finally, Colin turned silently and moved out of his corner with his funny, shuffling way of walking. Someone said he had a clubfoot, and someone else said he'd had a lot of operations on his feet when he was a young lad, but nobody knew for certain why he walked the way he did. When he sat down and lit a cigarette, the match light illuminated his large nose, shiny forehead, and watery blue eyes. He used the same match to light a candle on the table beside him, and then I saw them: the black eye, the bruise on his left cheek. DS Longbottom. The bastard.

"Did you say anything to him?" I asked, anxious that DS Longbottom might have beaten a confession out of Colin, without even thinking that Colin probably wouldn't still be at home if that were the case.

He shook his head mournfully. "Nothing, Mr. Bascombe. Honest. There was nothing I *could* tell him."

"Did you see Johnny Critchley yesterday, Colin?"

"Aye."

"Where?"

"Down by the canal."

"What was he doing?"

"Just standing there chucking stones in the water."

"Did you talk to him?"

Colin paused and turned away before answering "No."

I had a brief coughing spell, his cigarette smoke working on my gassed lungs. When it cleared up, I said, "Colin, there's something you're not telling me, isn't there? You'd better tell me. You know I won't hurt you, and I just might be the only person who can help you."

He looked at me, pale eyes imploring. "I only called out to him, from the bridge, like, didn't I?"

"What happened next?"

"Nothing. I swear it."

"Did he answer?"

"No. He just looked my way and shook his head. I could tell then that he didn't want to play. He seemed sad."

"He'd just heard his dad's been killed."

Colin's already watery eyes brimmed with tears. "Poor lad."

I nodded. For all I knew, Colin might have been thinking about *his* dad, too. Not many knew it, but Mr. Gormond senior had been killed in the same bloody war that left me with my bad lungs and scarred face. "What happened next, Colin?"

Colin shook his head and wiped his eyes with the back of his hand. "Nothing," he said. "It was such a lovely day, I just went on walking. I went to the park and watched the soldiers digging trenches, then I went for my cigarettes and came home to listen to the wireless."

"And after that?"

"I stayed in."

"All evening?"

"That's right. Sometimes I go down to the White Rose, but . . . "

"But what, Colin?"

"Well, Mr. Smedley, you know, the Air-Raid Precautions man?"

I nodded. "I know him."

"He said my blackout cloth wasn't good enough and he'd fine me if I didn't get some proper stuff by yesterday."

"I understand, Colin." Good-quality, thick, impenetrable blackout cloth had become both scarce and expensive, which was no doubt why Colin had been cheated in the first place.

"Anyway, what with that and the cigarettes . . . "

I reached into my pocket and slipped out a few bob for him. Colin looked away, ashamed, but I put it on the table and he didn't tell me to take it back. I knew how it must hurt his pride to accept charity, but I had no idea how much money he made, or how he made it. I'd never seen him beg, but I had a feeling he survived on odd jobs and lived very much from hand to mouth.

I stood up. "All right, Colin," I said. "Thanks very much." I paused at the door, uncertain how to say what had just entered my mind. Finally, I blundered ahead. "It might be better if you kept a low profile till they find him, Colin. You know what some of the people around here are like."

"What do you mean, Mr. Bascombe?"

"Just be careful, Colin, that's all I mean. Just be careful."

He nodded gormlessly, and I left.

As I was leaving Colin's house, I noticed Jack Blackwell standing on his doorstep, arms folded, a small crowd of locals around him, their shadows intersecting on the cobbled street. They kept glancing toward Colin's house, and when they saw me come out, they all shuffled off except Jack himself, who gave me a grim stare before going inside and slamming his door. I felt a shiver go up my spine, as if a goose had stepped on my grave, as my dear mother used to say, bless her soul, and when I got home I couldn't concentrate on my book one little bit.

By the following morning, when Johnny had been missing over thirty-six hours, the mood in the street had started to turn ugly. In my experience, when you get right down to it, there's no sorrier spectacle, nothing much worse or more dangerous, than the human mob mentality. After all, armies are nothing more than mobs, really, even when they are organized to a greater or lesser degree. I'd been at Ypres, as you know, and there wasn't a hell of a lot you could tell me about military organization. So when I heard the muttered words on doorsteps, saw the little knots of people here and there, Jack Blackwell flitting from door to door like a political canvasser, I had to do something, and I could hardly count on any help from DS Longbottom.

One thing I had learned both as a soldier and as a schoolteacher was that, if you had a chance, your best bet was to take out the ringleader. That meant Jack Blackwell. Jack was the nasty type, and he and I had had more than one run-in over his son Nick's bullying and poor performance in class. In my opinion, young Nick was the sort of walking dead loss who should probably have been drowned at birth, a waste of skin, sinew, tissue, and bone, and it wasn't hard to see where he got it from. Nick's older brother, Dave, was already doing a long stretch in the Scrubs for beating a night watchman senseless during a robbery, and even the army couldn't find an excuse to spring him and enlist his service in killing Germans. Mrs. Blackwell had been seen more than once walking with difficulty, with bruises on her cheek. The sooner Jack Blackwell got his call-up papers, the better things would be all around.

I intercepted Jack between the Deakins' and the Kellys' houses, and it was clear from his gruff "What do you want?" that he didn't want to talk to me. But I was adamant.

"Morning, Jack," I greeted him. "Lovely day for a walk, isn't it?"

"What's it to you?"

"Just being polite. What are you up to Jack? What's going on?"

"None of your business."

"Up to your old tricks? Spreading poison?"

"I don't know what you're talking about." He made to walk away, but I grabbed his arm. He glared at me but didn't do anything. Just as well. At my age, and with my lungs, I'd hardly last ten seconds in a fight. "Jack," I said, "don't you think you'd all be best off using your time to look for the poor lad?"

"Look for him! That's a laugh. You know as well as I do where that young lad is."

"Where? Where is he, Jack?"

"You know."

"No, I don't. Tell me."

"He's dead and buried, that's what."

"Where, Jack?"

"I don't know the exact spot. If he's not in the canal, then he's buried somewhere not far away."

"Maybe he is. But you don't *know* that. Not for certain. And even if you believe that, you don't know who put him there."

Jack wrenched his arm out of my weakening grip and sneered. "I've got a damn sight better idea than you have, Frank Bascombe. With all your *book* learning!" Then he turned and marched off.

Somehow, I got the feeling that I had just made things worse.

After my brief fracas with Jack Blackwell, I was at a loose end. I knew the police would still be looking for Johnny, asking questions, searching areas of waste ground, so there wasn't much I could do to help them. Feeling impotent, I went down to the canal, near Woodruff's scrap yard. Old Ezekiel Woodruff himself was poking around in the ruins of his business, so I decided to talk to him. I kept my distance, though, for even on a hot day such as this, Woodruff was wearing his greatcoat and black wool gloves with the fingers cut off. He wasn't known for his personal hygiene, so I made sure I didn't stand downwind of him. Not that there was much of a wind, but then it didn't take much.

"Morning, Ezekiel," I said. "I understand young Johnny Critchley was down around here yesterday."

"So they say," muttered Ezekiel.

"See him, did you?"

"I weren't here."

"So you didn't see him?"

"Police have already been asking questions."

"And what did you tell them?"

He pointed to the other side of the canal, the back of the housing estate. "I were over there," he said. "Sometimes people chuck out summat of value, even these days."

"But you did see Johnny?"

He paused, then said, "Aye."

"On this side of the canal?"

Woodruff nodded.

"What time was this?"

"I don't have a watch, but it weren't long after that daft bloke had gone by."

"Do you mean Colin Gormond?"

"Aye, that's the one."

So Johnny was still alone by the canal *after* Colin had passed by. DS Longbottom had probably known this, but he had beaten Colin anyway. One day I'd find a way to get even with him. The breeze shifted a little and I got a whiff of stale sweat and worse. "What was Johnny doing?"

"Doing? Nowt special. He were just walking."

"Walking? Where?"

Woodruff pointed. "That way. Towards the city center."

"Alone?"

"Aye."

"And nobody approached him?"

"Nope. Not while I were watching."

I didn't think there was anything further to be got from Ezekiel Woodruff, so I bade him good morning. I can't say the suspicion didn't enter my head that *he* might have had something to do with Johnny's disappearance, though I'd have been hard pushed to say exactly why or what. Odd though old Woodruff might be, there had never been any rumor or suspicion of his being overly interested in young boys, and I didn't want to jump to conclusions the way Jack Blackwell had. Still, I filed away my suspicions for later.

A fighter droned overhead. I watched it dip and spin through the blue air and wished I could be up there. I'd always regretted not being a pilot in the war. A barge full of soldiers drifted by, and I moved aside on the towpath to let the horse that was pulling it pass by. For my troubles I got a full blast of sweaty horseflesh and a pile of steaming manure at my feet. That had even Ezekiel Woodruff beat.

Aimlessly, I followed the direction Ezekiel had told me Johnny had walked in—toward the city center. As I walked, Jack Blackwell's scornful words about my inability to find Johnny echoed in my mind. *Book learning.* That was exactly the kind of cheap insult you would expect from a moron like Jack Blackwell, but it hurt nonetheless. No sense telling him I'd been buried in the mud under the bodies of my comrades for two days. No sense telling him about the young German soldier I'd surprised and bayonetted to death, twisting the blade until it snapped and broke off inside him. Jack Blackwell was too young to have seen action in the last war, but if there was any justice in the world, he'd damn well see it in *this* one.

The canal ran by the back of the train station, where I crossed the narrow bridge and walked through the crowds of evacuees out front to City Square. Mary Critchley's anguish reverberated in my mind, too: "*Mr. Bashcombe! Mr. Bashcombe!*" I heard her call.

Then, all of a sudden, as I looked at the black facade of the post office and the statue of the Black Prince in the center of City Square, it hit me. I thought I knew what had happened to Johnny Critchley, but first I had to go back to his street and ask just one important question.

It was late morning. The station smelled of damp soot and warm oil. Crowds of children thronged around trying to find out where they were supposed to go. They wore nametags and carried little cardboard boxes. Adults with clipboards, for the most part temporarily unemployed schoolteachers and local volunteers, directed them to the right queue, and their names were ticked off as they boarded the carriages.

Despite being neither an evacuated child nor a supervisor, I managed to buy a ticket and ended up sharing a compartment with a rather severe-looking woman in a brown uniform I didn't recognize, and a male civilian with a brush mustache and a lot of Brylcreem on his hair. They seemed to be in charge of several young children, also in the compartment, who couldn't sit still. I could hardly blame them. They were going to the alien countryside, to live with strangers, far away from their parents, for only God knew how long, and the idea scared them half to death.

The buttoned cushions were warm and the air in the carriage still and close, despite the open window. When we finally set off, the motion stirred up a bit of a breeze, which helped a little. On the wall opposite me was a poster of the Scarborough seafront, and I spent most of the journey remembering the carefree childhood holidays I had enjoyed there with my parents in the early years of the century: another world, another time. The rest of the trip, I glanced out of the window, beyond the scum-scabbed canal, and saw the urban industrial landscape drift by: back gardens, where some people had put in Anderson shelters, half covered with earth to grow vegetables on; the dark mass of the town hall clock tower behind the city center buildings, a factory yard, where several men were loading heavy crates onto a lorry, flushed and sweating in the heat.

Then we were in the countryside, where the smells of grass, hay, and manure displaced the reek of the city. I saw small, squat farms, drystone walls, sheep and cattle grazing. Soon, train tracks and canal diverged. We went under a long noisy tunnel, and the children whimpered. Later, I was surprised to see so many army convoys winding along the narrow roads, and the one big aerodrome we passed seemed buzzing with activity.

All in all, the journey took a little over two hours. Only about ten or eleven children were shepherded off at the small country station, and I followed as they were met and taken to the village hall, where the men and women who were to care for them waited. It was more civilized than some of the evacuation systems I'd heard about, which sounded more like the slave markets of old, where farmers waited on the platforms to pick out the strong lads, and local dignitaries whisked away the nicely dressed boys and girls.

I went up to the volunteer in charge, an attractive young countrywoman in a simple blue frock with a white lace collar and a belt around her slim waist, and asked her if she had any record of an evacuee called John, or Johnny, Critchley. She checked her records, then shook her head, as I knew she would. If I were right, Johnny wouldn't be here under his own name. I explained my problem to the woman, who told me her name was Phyllis Rigby. She had a yellow ribbon in her long wavy hair and smelled of fresh apples. "I don't see how anything like that could have happened," Phyllis said. "We've been very meticulous. But there again, things *have* been a little chaotic." She frowned in thought for a moment, then she delegated her present duties to another volunteer.

"Come on," she said, "I'll help you go from house to house. There weren't that many evacuees, you know. Far fewer than we expected."

I nodded. I'd heard how a lot of parents weren't bothering to evacuate their children. "They can't see anything happening yet," I said. "Just you wait. After the first air raid you'll have so many you won't have room for them all."

Phyllis smiled. "The poor things. It must be such an upheaval for them."

"Indeed."

I took deep, welcome breaths of country air as Phyllis and I set out from the village hall to visit the families listed on her clipboard. There were perhaps a couple of hundred houses, and less than fifty percent had received evacuees. Even so, we worked up quite a sweat calling at them all. Or I did, rather, as sweating didn't seem to be in Phyllis's nature. We chatted as we went, me telling her about my schoolteaching, and her telling me about her husband, Thomas, training as a fighter pilot in the RAF. After an hour or so with no luck, we stopped in at her cottage for a refreshing cup of tea, then we were off again.

At last, late in the afternoon, we struck gold.

Mr. and Mrs. Douglas, who were billeting Johnny Critchley, seemed a very pleasant couple, and they were sad to hear that they would not get to keep him with them for a while longer. I explained everything to them and assured them that they would get someone else as soon as we got the whole business sorted out.

"He's *not* here," Johnny said as we walked with Phyllis to the station. "I've looked everywhere, but I couldn't find him."

I shook my head. "Sorry, Johnny. You know your mum's got a speech impediment. That was why I had to go back and ask her exactly what she said to you before I came here. She said she told you your father was missing in action, which, the way it came out, sounded like missing in *Acksham*, didn't it? That's why you came here, isn't it, to look for your father?"

Young Johnny nodded, tears in his eyes. "I'm sorry," he said. "I couldn't understand why she didn't come and look for him. She must be really vexed with me."

I patted his shoulder. "I don't think so. More like she'll be glad to see you. How did you manage to sneak in with the real evacuees, by the way?"

Johnny wiped his eyes with his grubby sleeve. "At the station. There were so many people standing around, at first I didn't know . . . Then I saw a boy I knew from playing cricket on the rec."

"Oliver Bradley," I said. The boy whose name Johnny was registered under.

"Yes. He goes to Broad Hill."

I nodded. Though I had never heard of Oliver Bradley, I knew the school; it was just across the valley from us. "Go on."

"I asked him where he was going, and he said he was being sent to Acksham. It was perfect."

"But how did you get him to change places with you?"

"He didn't want to. Not at first."

"How did you persuade him?"

Johnny looked down at the road and scraped at some gravel with the scuffed tip of his shoe. "It cost me a complete set of 'Great Cricketers' cigarette cards. Ones my dad gave me before he went away."

I smiled. It would have to be something like that.

"And I made him promise not to tell anyone, just to go home and say there wasn't room for him and he'd have to try again in a few days. I just needed enough time to find Dad . . . you know."

"I know."

We arrived at the station, where Johnny sat on the bench and Phyllis and I chatted in the late afternoon sunlight, our shadows lengthening across the tracks. In addition to the birds singing in the trees and hedgerows. I could hear grasshoppers chirruping, a sound you rarely heard in the city. I had often thought how much I would like to live in the country, and perhaps when I retired from teaching a few years in the future I would be able to do so.

We didn't have long to wait for our train. I thanked Phyllis for all her help, told her I wished her husband well, and she waved to us as the old banger chugged out of the station.

It was past blackout when I finally walked into our street holding Johnny's hand. He was tired after his adventure and had spent most of the train journey with his head on my shoulder. Once or twice, from the depths of a dream, he had called his father's name.

I could sense that something was wrong as soon as I turned the corner. It was nothing specific, just a sudden chill at the back of my neck. Because of the blackout, I couldn't see anything clearly, but I got a strong impression of a knot of shifting shadows, just a little bit darker than the night itself, milling around outside Colin Gormond's house.

I quickened my step, and as I got nearer I heard a whisper pass through the crowd when they saw Johnny. Then the shadows began to disperse, slinking and sidling away, disappearing like smoke into the air. From somewhere, Mary Critchley lurched forward with a cry and took young Johnny in her arms. I let him go. I could hear her thanking me between sobs, but I couldn't stop walking.

The first thing I noticed when I approached Colin's house was that the window was broken and half the blackout curtain had been ripped away. Next, I saw that the door was slightly ajar. I was worried that Colin might be hurt, but out of courtesy I knocked and called out his name.

Nothing.

I pushed the door open and walked inside. It was pitch dark. I didn't have a torch with me, and I knew that Colin's light didn't work, but I remembered the matches and the candle on the table. I lit it and held it up before me as I walked forward.

I didn't have far to look. If I hadn't had the candle, I might have bumped right into him. First I saw his face, about level with mine. His froth-specked lips had turned blue, and a trickle of dried blood ran from his left nostril. The blackout cloth was knotted around his neck in a makeshift noose, attached to a hook screwed into the lintel over the kitchen door. As I stood back and examined the scene further, I saw that his downturned toes were about three inches from the floor, and there was no sign of an upset chair or stool.

Harmless Colin Gormond, friend to the local children. Dead.

I felt the anger well up in me, along with the guilt. It was my fault. I shouldn't have gone dashing off to Acksham like that in search of Johnny, or I should at least have taken Colin with me. I knew the danger he was in; I had talked to Jack Blackwell before I left. How could I have been so stupid, so careless as to leave Colin to his fate with only a warning he didn't understand?

Maybe Colin *had* managed to hang himself somehow, without standing on a stool, though I doubted it. But whether or not Jack Blackwell or the rest had actually laid a finger on him, they were all guilty of driving him to it in my book. Besides, if Jack or anyone else from the street *had* strung Colin up, there would be evidence—fibers, fingerprints, footprints, whatever—and even DS bloody Longbottom wouldn't be able to ignore that.

I stumbled outside and made my way toward the telephone box on the corner. Not a soul stirred now, but as I went I heard one door—Jack Blackwell's door—close softly this time, as if he thought that too much noise might wake the dead, and the dead might have a tale or two to tell.

APPENDIX A
Notable Annual Awards for Mystery and Detective Fiction

Agatha Awards. Mystery authors and fans who attend the annual Malice Domestic convention held in Bethesda, Maryland, vote for the best traditional mysteries of the previous year. Awards were first presented in 1989. Named for Agatha Christie, exemplary writer of classic mysteries.

Anthony Awards. Winners selected by attendees of Bouchercon World Mystery Convention, mystery fiction's largest fan and author convention, held annually in various cities since 1971. Awards were first presented in 1986. Categories include: Best Novel, Best First Novel, Best True Crime, Best Individual Short Story, Best Short Story Collection/Anthology, and Best Critical Work. Named for Anthony Boucher (William Anthony Parker White), mystery writer and critic. Boucher was the winner of the Edgar Award for Outstanding Mystery Criticism in 1946, the first year the Edgars were presented.

Dagger Awards. Given by the United Kingdom Crime Writers Association (CWA), formed in 1953. Gold and Silver Dagger awards are given for outstanding works in several categories. The most prestigious award is the **Diamond Dagger Award**, now known as the Cartier Diamond Dagger Award, for a writer's lifetime achievement. The Cartier company designed a diamond dagger, worth over £30,000, for display at the annual awards ceremony and presents the winner with a Diamond Dagger brooch or cufflinks. The CWA is the only major presenter of awards in the UK. The name comes from a type of short knife with a sharp point used for stabbing, a weapon used in some classical mystery stories. The CWA also presents the John Creasy Memorial Award in honor of its founder, mystery writer John Creasy.

Dilys Award. Awarded by the Independent Mystery Booksellers Association for the book that members vote was "the most fun to sell." The award was established in 1992 and is presented at the annual Left Coast Crime Convention. Named for Dilys Winn, founder of Murder Ink, the world's oldest mystery bookstore, located in Manhattan in New York City, and author of *Murder Ink* (1977) and *Murderess Ink: The Better Half of Mystery* (1979).

Edgar Awards.   The oldest and most prestigious of the mystery awards, presented by the Mystery Writers of America (MWA), formed in 1945. Four awards were presented in 1946 for works in the previous year. The number of award categories has expanded to numerous categories of detective and mystery fiction, including best novel, short story, nonfiction critical work or biography, young adult mystery, juvenile mystery, television episode and feature, film, and best play. A committee of MWA members judges each category. A ceramic bust of Edgar Allan Poe is presented to the winners and a scroll to the nominees. The MWA's highest honor is the **Edgar Grand Master Award,** presented to a writer who has made important lifetime contributions to the mystery field, producing significant and consistently high quality works. The first recipient of the Edgar Grand Master Award was Agatha Christie in 1955. Named for Edgar Allan Poe, considered the writer of the first mystery story.

Lambda Literary Awards for Mystery.   Annual awards by the Lambda Literary Foundation, a national non-profit organization dedicated to recognizing and promoting the best in gay and lesbian literature, and publishers of the *Lambda Book Report.* The "Lammy" Awards are selected by committees and are presented for a variety of literary categories, including awards for best gay men's mystery novel and best lesbian mystery novel. The awards are presented at an annual banquet. The first awards were made in 1989 for works published the previous year. Named for the sponsoring organization.

Macavity Awards.   Members of Mystery Readers International vote on awards in a variety of categories. The award was established in 1987. Presented at the annual Bouchercon convention. Named for Macavity, the elusive mystery cat in T. S. Eliot's *Old Possum's Books of Practical Cats* (1939).

Shamus Awards.   Given by Private Eye Writers of America (PWA) to honor excellent work in the Private Eye genre, defined as any mystery protagonist who is a paid investigator but not a police officer or government agent. The award for Lifetime Achievement is called the Eye. Winners are chosen by a committee of PWA members. Presented annually since 1982 and awarded at the annual Bouchercon convention. A joint St. Martin's Press/PWA Best First Novel contest is for unpublished works, with the winning manuscript to be considered for publication by the press. The Shamus Award takes its name from "shamus," a slang term for a police officer or more commonly for a private investigator.

Numerous other awards for mystery and detective fiction are presented by various groups and organizations in the United States as well as in other countries, including Australia, Canada, Denmark, Finland, Germany, Japan, the Netherlands, Sweden, and the United Kingdom. Most awards are presented annually for works published the previous year. Outstanding works are honored by being nominated as well as for receiving the awards.

APPENDIX B
Bibliography of Critical Essays and Commentaries

Auden, W. H. "Detective Story." *The Vintage Book of Classic Crime*. Michael Dibdin, ed. New York: Vintage Crime/Black Lizard, 1997. 215–216.

Ball, John. "Murder at Large." *The Mystery Story*. John Ball, ed. New York: Penguin Books, 1978. 1–26.

Chandler, Raymond. "The Simple Art of Murder." *The Simple Art of Murder*. New York: Vintage, 1988. 1–18.

Kaufman, Natalie Hevener and Carol McGinnis Kay. "Grafton's Place in the Development of the Detective Novel." *"G" is for Grafton*, revised edition. New York: Henry Holt and Company, 2000. 417–444.

Levine, Stuart and Susan Levine, eds. *Edgar Allan Poe: Thirty-Two Stories*. Indianapolis/Cambridge: Hackett Publishing Company, 2000. 131–158.

Maida, Patricia D. and Nicholas B. Spornick. "The Puzzle Game." *Murder She Wrote: A Study of Agatha Christie's Detective Fiction*. Bowling Green, Ohio: Bowling Green State University Popular Press, 1992. 83–109.

McBain, Ed. "The 87th Precinct." *The Great Detectives*. Otto Penzler, ed. New York: Penguin Books, 1979. 86–97.

Panek, LeRoy Lad. "The Police Novel." *An Introduction to the Detective Story*. Bowling Green, Ohio: Bowling Green State University Popular Press, 1987. 169–188.

Talburt, Nancy Ellen and Juana R. Young. "The Many Guises of the Contemporary Amateur Detective." 2003. (Published first in this anthology.)

CREDITS

INDEX OF AUTHORS AND TITLES